KU-528-209

DARBYSHIRE
ON
THE ENGLISH
LEGAL SYSTEM

WITHDRAWN

LIVERPOOL JMU LIBRARY

3 1111 01359 6620

DARBYSHIRE ON
THE ENGLISH
LEGAL SYSTEM

By

PENNY DARBYSHIRE PhD, MA
Reader in Law,
Kingston Law School,
Kingston University

TENTH EDITION

SWEET & MAXWELL

THOMSON REUTERS

First Edition 1971
Second Edition 1977
Third Edition 1982
Fourth Edition 1987
Reprinted 1990
Fifth Edition 1992
Sixth Edition 1996
Seventh Edition 2001
Reprinted 2003
Eighth Edition 2005
Ninth Edition 2008
Tenth Edition 2011

Published in 2011 by Sweet & Maxwell
100 Avenue Road, London NW3 3PF
part of Thomson Reuters (Professional) UK Limited
(Registered in England and Wales, Company No. 1679046. Registered Office and
address for service: Aldgate House, 33 Aldgate High Street, London EC3N 1DL)

For further information on our products and services,
visit *www.sweetandmaxwell.co.uk*

Typeset by Servis Filmsetting Ltd, Stockport, Cheshire
Printed in England by T.J. International, Padstow, Cornwall

No natural forests were destroyed to make this product, only farmed timber was
used and replanted

A CIP catalogue record for this book is available from the British Library

ISBN 978-0-414-04602-3

Thomson Reuters and the Thomson Reuters logo are trademarks of Thomson
Reuters. Sweet & Maxwell ® is a registered trademark of Thomson Reuters
(Professional) UK Limited.

Crown copyright material is reproduced with the permission of the controller of
HMSO and the Queen's Printer for Scotland.

All rights reserved. No part of this publication may be reproduced or transmitted
in any form or by any means, or stored in any retrieval system of any nature
without prior written permission, except for permitted fair dealing under the
Copyright, Designs and Patents Act 1988, or in accordance with the terms of a
licence issued by the Copyright Licensing Agency in respect of photocopying
and/or reprographic reproduction. Application for permission for other use of
copyright material including permission to reproduce extracts in other published
works shall be made to the publishers. Full acknowledgment of author, publisher
and source must be given.

© Thomson Reuters (Professional) UK Limited 2011

Preface

My aim is to explain the legal system of England and Wales to the reader who knows nothing about it. There is a lot more about the law and the legal system to learn and I hope you will enjoy your voyage of discovery as much as I still do.

Studying law requires an enormous amount of reading. Remember, however, that law exists in the real world, not just in books. Read about the courts here, then take yourself off to watch them. They are a free source of entertainment, Monday to Friday. You will learn a lot, especially if you visit a variety. While you are there, speak to a lawyer or a magistrate or a judge but read the relevant chapters of this book first so that your conversation is better informed. You can also watch tribunal proceedings, or ask to work-shadow a lawyer, or paralegal, or judge, or magistrate for a day or more.

Learning about the English common law and the legal system is exciting, because its long history and worldwide importance are awesome. It has been developing since before the Norman invasion of 1066. It changes continually so remember to keep up to date with the news. By the time you read this book, it will be out of date, like every law book.

Have fun!

Penny Darbyshire
Kingston, August 2011

Online Updates

A free online updating service is available in conjunction with this text. It can be accessed by going to the Sweet & Maxwell academic website at *www.sweetandmaxwell.co.uk*. This service will provide periodic updates from 2012.

Contents

PART I: Sources

1. Understanding the English Legal System

2. Sources of English Law

PART V: Laypeople in the Law

PART VI: Access to Justice

Table of Cases

Table of Statutes

xxxi

Table of Statutory Instruments

Table of Conventions

Note on Neutral Citation of Cases

Where a case has been given a neutral citation number, this has been used in the text. Where none is available, the case has been cited by reference to the court and date only – this applies to cases pre-dating 2001 and the judgments of the European Court of Justice and the European Court of Human Rights.

Part I: Sources

1. Understanding the English Legal System

1. What is law? The rule of law

Societies and their subcultures govern themselves by countless **1–001** sets of rules, written or unwritten. These include our own internalised moral code, rules of etiquette and expectations of civilised behaviour. We may adhere to the tenets of a religion and a particular church. We may belong to a private organisation, such as a political party or a sports club with its own constitution and membership rules but none of these codes, however complex, carries the force of law. The constitution of the California Parent Teachers' Association is lengthier and much more complex than the Appropriation Act 2011 but it is not law. It cannot be interpreted or enforced by a court. Courts generally refuse to enforce non-legal rules. For example, in *R. (on the application of Proud) v Buckingham Pubwatch Scheme* [2008] EWHC 2224, it was held that a public house is a private place so, under the Licensing Act 2003, licensees were entitled to make decisions as to whom to admit. The applicant had been banned by pubs in the Buckingham Pubwatch area. He was refused judicial review on the ground that, if the matter could not be dealt with by a private law action, which it could not, it did not mean that the matter was justiciable under traditional judicial review principles or the Human Rights Act. The ban unarguably fell into an area of life with which the courts do not interfere.

What, then, is special about legal rules? A rudimentary definition of law is a rule that is backed by a sanction for its breach, ultimately enforceable by a court, a tribunal or other public body with enforcement powers. There is considerable overlap between non-legal rules and the law. For instance, the basic rules of most major religions are astonishingly similar. They condemn murder, as do all legal systems, although what constitutes murder and how

3

it is punished differs from one legal system to another. In another overlap, dropping litter in the street would be condemned by most people as anti-social behaviour but it is also illegal and subject to a fine enforceable in a criminal court. Nevertheless, many forms of anti-social behaviour, such as spitting in a crowded street, might offend people as a breach of the rules of civilised behaviour but are not illegal. We must also distinguish between the immoral and the illegal. Adultery used to be illegal but morals changed and Parliament decided it should no longer be an offence. It is, however, a breach of many people's religions or moral codes. Sanctions for breach of the law take many forms, apart from the obvious example of sentences passed for breaches of the criminal law. When part of the Merchant Shipping Act 1988 was found by the European Court of Justice, in the *Factortame* cases, to be in breach of the Treaty of Rome, the operation of the offending sections of the Act had to be suspended and the UK government had to compensate Spanish fishermen who had been prevented from plying their trade in UK coastal waters. The UK was in breach of public international law, notably EU law. This story is told in Ch.3. If I breach my contract with you, you can ask a civil court to compensate you by awarding damages against me, or to enforce my obligations under the contract. If a government minister makes a new set of regulations, they can be quashed by the High Court if she failed to follow procedure prescribed in the enabling Act of Parliament which gave her the power to make the regulations, such as consulting affected parties.

Modern democracies claim to adhere to "the rule of law". This concept was emphasised and defined by the important constitutional lawyer, Dicey, in 1885 but he did not invent it. It can be traced back to Aristotle. The best modern definition and analysis is provided by Lord Tom Bingham, senior law lord 2000–2008, one of the greatest ever British judges. His book, *The Rule of Law*, was his parting gift to us just before his death in 2010. Every law student should read it and certainly every politician. What follows is a summary of Lord Bingham's thesis. Dicey's first meaning is very well known: no-one can be punished or made to suffer "in body or goods", except for a distinct breach of the law, established in a legal manner, before the ordinary courts. The roots of this are undoubtedly the famous cl.39 of Magna Carta 1215,

> "No free man shall be seized or imprisoned or stripped of his rights or possessions, or outlawed or exiled, or deprived of his standing in any other way, nor will we proceed with force against him, or send others to do so, except by the lawful judgment of his equals or by the law of the land."

Magna Carta was declared void by the Pope within 10 weeks but it was reissued in 1216, 1217 and 1225. In any event, these principles were not a novelty. The writ of habeas corpus was available before Magna Carta and used from the fifteenth century to challenge unlawful detention. Dicey's second meaning is also universally accepted in democracies: everyone, of whatever rank, is subject to the ordinary law of the land; no-one is above the law. As Dr Thomas Fuller famously said, in 1733, "Be you never so high, the law is above you". As Lord Bingham pointed out, after the English Bill of Rights 1689, "(n)o monarch could rely on divine authority to override the law" (p.24). Lord Bingham modified and expanded Dicey's definition, as follows:

1. "The law must be accessible and so far as possible intelligible, clear and predictable" (Bingham Ch.3). The common law assumes that everyone knows the law and ignorance of the law is no defence when we are accused or breaching it so this rule is an obvious requirement for fairness and we will return to it in Ch.2.
2. "Questions of legal right and liability should ordinarily be resolved by application of the law and not the exercise of discretion" (Bingham, Ch.4), meaning that governmental decisions should be based on stated criteria and amenable to legal challenge.
3. "The laws of the land should apply equally to all, save to the extent that objective differences justify differentiation" (Bingham, Ch.5). While modern democracies have generally grasped and applied some definition of equality, in terms of gender, ethnicity and sometimes age and sexuality and disability, Lord Bingham pointed out that the UK and the US and others seem reluctant to apply equal rights to non-citizens.
4. "Ministers and public officers at all levels must exercise the powers conferred on them in good faith, fairly, for the purpose for which the powers were conferred, without exceeding the limits of such powers and not unreasonably" (Bingham, Ch.6). There is an irrebuttable presumption that decisions will be made in accordance with the law, meaning a presumption that cannot be trumped. This requirement is applied by the High Court when testing the fairness and legality of government action in judicial review proceedings, discussed below. The rules of natural justice (fair trial), originally applied by the High Court in testing the legality of proceedings in the lower courts, have been extended by the High Court to government decision makers. The decision-maker must be unbiased and everyone liable to have an

adverse decision made against them must have a right to be heard.

5. "The law must afford adequate protection of fundamental human rights" (Bingham, Ch.7). This is a twentieth century addition which Dicey would not have recognised. We examine the European Convention on Human Rights in Ch.4.

6. "Means must be provided for resolving, without prohibitive cost or inordinate delay, bona fide civil disputes which the parties themselves are unable to resolve" (Bingham, Ch.8). This encompasses what has fashionably become known as "access to justice". There is no point in having a civil right if you cannot enforce it through the civil courts. Chapter 10, below, on civil procedure, has much to say about this. Chapter 6, below, on the civil courts discusses the controversy between judges and government about the cost of civil court fees. The phrase has also been used to denote access to legal advice and legal services, discussed in Ch.17. I have argued for many years, in previous editions of this book, that these services must, logically, be a requirement of the rule of law.

7. "Adjudicative procedures provided by the state should be fair" (Bingham, Ch.9). Lord Bingham draws attention to requirements going beyond the rules of natural justice. For instance, the European Court of Human Rights requires "equality of arms". He says "in retrospect most legal systems operating today will be judged to be defective in respects not yet recognised". There is no universal interpretation of this requirement. For instance, while judges in England and Wales have been careful to distance themselves from party politics from about the mid-twentieth century, the American judicial system is shot through with party politics from top to bottom. Judicial independence has become a multi-faceted concept and is examined in Ch.14, on judges, but its root is the Act of Settlement 1701.

8. "The rule of law requires compliance by the state with its obligations in international law as in national law" (Bingham, Ch.10). International law is examined, briefly, in Ch.2.

As Lord Bingham pointed out, the UN puts the rule of law at the heart of its mission. Interestingly, the World Bank deploys some of its staff exclusively on the rule of law, including judicial independence. They try to persuade borrowing countries of the need to respect the rule of law. The UN Declaration of Human Rights 1948 and the European Convention on Human Rights 1950, discussed in Ch.4, refer to the rule of law.

2. Distinguishing between different types of law

Substantive and procedural

1–002   While the former prescribes, proscribes and regulates areas of human activity, the latter sets down rules for the manner of enforcing substantive law. The Theft Acts and many leading cases define what conduct and mental elements constitute the offence of theft but the procedures for arresting the suspect, questioning, charging and trying him are contained in several quite different statutes (Acts of Parliament), cases and sets of procedural rules, and codes which are not law, but the breach of which may be taken account of by a court.

Private and public

1–003   The former governs relations between private citizens or bodies, the latter applies to public bodies which are publicly regulated and normally created by an Act of Parliament, including the departments of local and central government, and public services, such as the Highways Agency. The twentieth century, especially the period since 1981, saw the massive growth in a public law, the body of law regulating the conduct of public bodies. It covers such topics as regulating police behaviour and the judicial review by the High Court of the *legality* of decisions taken and rules and policies made by public bodies. The grounds of challenge have been expanded by the Human Rights Act 1998, as described in Ch.4. As will be seen in Ch.11, as the extent of government activity expanded in the twentieth century, so a system of tribunals grew up, to provide citizens with a mechanism to challenge the *merits* of decisions affecting them.

Domestic and international

1–004   Our domestic law is applicable in and enforceable by the courts of England and Wales and, sometimes, throughout the UK. International law, also described in Ch.2, is contained in conventions and treaties devised, signed and ratified by countries concerned to regulate activities in which they have a common interest or which take place across national boundaries, covering everything from air traffic to drug trafficking. Its interpretation and enforcement may be the task of an international court, recognised in or established by such a treaty. Frequently, detailed laws giving practical effect to treaty requirements are enacted into domestic law. The Misuse of Drugs Act 1971 provides domestic UK law in accordance with the requirements of the international conventions on narcotics. It is very important to understand that EU law and the law of the European Convention on Human Rights, are not foreign law. They are types of international law that have been incorporated into UK law, but in different ways, as explained in Chs 3 and 4.

Civil and criminal

1–005   Private civil law regulates relations between private persons or bodies and it is usually invoked only by those parties seeking to protect their private rights or interests. For instance, if I commit a tort against you by, say, negligently backing my muck spreader over your gatepost, the State, as such, has no interest in taking me to court to sue for damages on your behalf but you may sue me in a civil court. The State simply provides the courts to enable you to enforce your private rights, as required by Magna Carta. It is not going to step in if you do not act. Having said that, elements of the State, such as government agencies, have a vast range of statutory and common law powers to invoke the civil law against private individuals and, of course, a private party may take a civil court action against an element of the State, such as suing the police over a death in custody, but all of these activities between citizen and State are subject to the rules of public law as well.

By contrast, a criminal offence is a wrong against the State and punishable as such, in the criminal courts. Criminal law is a type of public law. The State has no interest in pursuing your civil claim for damages but if you are a victim of a crime, such as theft, the State may prosecute the offender, regardless of your views. The aim of taking a criminal case to court is to punish the wrongdoer, rather than to compensate, although judges and magistrates may attach a compensation order to any sentence they pass. In English law, victims of crime retain the right of private prosecution and so may prosecute the offender in the criminal courts, if the State chooses not to prosecute.

All of this is very confusing but the new law student will soon be able to recognise the difference. Suffice it to say that virtually all the foundation subjects studied in a law degree, such as tort, contract, land law, equity, most of public law and most EU law are elements of civil law. Most of criminal law is taught under the heading of "criminal law". A true story may help to distinguish. When I was a law student, I was cycling to college to sit the last of my finals when a car driver knocked me off my bike. The police arrived on the scene and took details of the accident and interviewed her and the witnesses. She was prosecuted in criminal proceedings in Kingston Magistrates' Court, pleaded guilty to the criminal offence of careless driving and was fined. My solicitor, acting on my behalf, threatened to sue her in civil proceedings in Kingston

County Court for damages for the losses I had suffered, as a result of her negligent driving, a tort. I needed the cost of a new bike, and damages for the pain and shock of my injuries. Luckily, the driver's motor insurance company, acting on her behalf, agreed to settle out of court for the sum we sought. This was typical. As we shall see in Ch.10, the vast majority of civil disputes are settled out of court, following negotiations between the parties or their representatives. What is also typical was my solicitor's tactic of waiting for the outcome of the criminal case before threatening a civil action against her. A civil case is much easier to prove than a criminal one. The civil *quantum*, standard, of proof is lower, so my solicitor knew that the driver's criminal conviction would make the civil case easy to prove. A crime must be proven beyond reasonable doubt, whereas civil liability need only be established on the balance of probabilities. To help matters, the police had given him their file of statements, taken as criminal evidence, to use as civil evidence.

Civil and criminal cases: getting the language right

Here is a list of the correct terminology used in most civil and criminal cases. Try to get it right.   **1–006**

CIVIL	CRIMINAL
The claimant	The prosecutor
sues	prosecutes
the defendant	the defendant
in the county court or High Court.	in the magistrates' court or Crown Court.
Most cases are settled without a trial, as no defence is entered.	Most cases are heard without a trial, as the defendant pleads guilty.
If a defence is entered, the case goes to trial and it is heard before a single judge, who determines fact and law. In exceptional cases, a jury decides.	If the defendant pleads not guilty the case goes to trial and is heard by a district judge (magistrates' court) or lay magistrates, who determine fact and law. In the Crown Court, the jury determines issues of fact (the verdict) and the judge rules on points of law.

If the judge finds the case proven, she enters judgment for the claimant.	If the magistrates or jury find the case proven, they bring in a verdict of guilty and convict the defendant.
She may make an order, such as an award of damages, against the defendant.	The magistrates or judge may pass sentence on the defendant e.g. a fine.
If the judge does not find the case proven, she enters judgment for the defendant.	If the magistrates or jury find the case is not proven, they acquit the defendant.

In either case, if the losing party appeals, she becomes "the appellant" and the other side "the respondent". If she seeks judicial review, she becomes "the applicant".

Common law and equity

1–007   These two used to be separate systems of law and legal remedies until the common law absorbed equity in 1873–75. If a claimant proves his case at common law, he has a right to a remedy but if seeking an equitable remedy, he has no right to it. The judge has a discretion and will examine the claimant's behaviour. Chapter 8 on history gives a full explanation. An example from a case where a plaintiff (claimant) sought specific performance of a contract is *Milward v Earl Thanet* (1801) 5 Ves 720n, where Lord Alvanley M.R. said "A party cannot call upon a Court of Equity for specific performance, unless he has shewn himself ready, desirous, prompt, and eager".

3. What is the English legal system?

1–008   The study of the English legal system applies to the powers, procedures and activities of the group of courts and statutory tribunals in England and Wales and the people who work in them and/or whose job it is to resolve legal problems. The State is the United Kingdom, comprising Great Britain (England, Wales and Scotland), plus Northern Ireland. The legal systems of Scotland and Northern Ireland are separate. They have distinct court structures, different procedures and sometimes apply different rules of substantive law, as explained in the next chapter. The Isle of Man and the Channel Islands are not part of the UK. They are self-governing Crown Dependencies. They are part of the group of islands known, *geographically*, as The British Isles.

We speak of the English legal *system* as if it were a coherent structure with the constituent parts working in a smooth, interrelated fashion but it is very important to bear in mind that no-one has custom-designed it. Think of it as a heap of *Lego* bricks, some of which are joined together, rather than a sophisticated construction of *Lego Technic*. It has been given to us in little boxes, over the last 11 centuries or more. Parts have been deconstructed and reconstructed from time to time. We fiddle with it. For instance, in the 1990s, Lord Woolf was asked to consider how to enhance access to justice by reforming civil procedure and in 1999–2001, Lord Justice Auld was asked to consider reforms to the practices, procedures and rules of evidence applied by the criminal courts but no-one ever examines the workings of the whole English court structure. We take it for granted that we need two levels of first instance court (trial court). We take it for granted that we need both a Court of Appeal and a Supreme Court because it has been that way beyond living memory. The general issues paper of the *Civil Justice Review*, 1986, raised the radical question of whether we really need both the county courts and the High Court dealing with civil cases and the Master of the Rolls asked this again, in 2005. It is true to say, however, that, considering nothing much had happened in the English legal system since the 1870s, we have scrutinised and reconfigured an enormous number of bricks in our *Lego* pile since 1985, largely thanks to the radical Conservative Lord Chancellor, Lord Mackay and his Labour successors, Lord Irvine and Lord Falconer. Ken Clarke, the Coalition Lord Chancellor is now busy deconstructing some of the structure built by Lord Irvine, in 1999.

Hallmarks of the English legal system

The common law
The English legal system is a "common law" system. This means   **1–009** that many of our primary legal principles have been made and developed by judges from case to case in what is called a system of precedent, where the lower courts are bound to follow principles established by the higher courts in previous cases. The term "common law" historically distinguished the law made by judges in the royal courts in Westminster and commonly applicable throughout the kingdom, from canon law (ecclesiastical law) and the local systems of customary law which predominated until 1066 and survived beyond. This is examined in Ch.8.

Judge-made law is at least as important to us as statute law made by Parliament. For instance, there is no statute telling us that murder is a crime and defining it for us. It is a common law crime. The required guilty act, of causing death, and the necessary degree of guilt, malice aforethought, have been prescribed and defined, over the centuries, by judges. Similarly, the law of negligence was the invention of a judge who wanted to find a remedy for a woman who had suffered gastro-enteritis when she drank from an opaque bottle of ginger beer, wherein lurked the decomposing remains of a stray snail. She was given the ginger beer and thus had no contract with the retailer or manufacturer. The judge, Lord Atkin, decided that, as a matter of principle, she should have a right to damages against the manufacturer, as they owed her a "duty of care". Thus, he invented what became the law of negligence.

Adversarial procedure

1–010   Another characteristic of the English legal system and all common law systems is that basic trial procedure is essentially adversarial. This means that the two parties to the case are left to their own devices to prepare and present their cases unaided by the court. Crass comparisons are made between this typical common law procedure and the type of "inquisitorial" procedure, with officials of the court involved in the fact finding process, which is said to be a hallmark of continental European legal systems. As we shall see, however, our trial system has not always been adversarial and inquisitorial elements are appearing at many points in the system. Also, it is wrong to label European procedural systems as inquisitorial. See further, Ch.9 on the adversarial process.

Jury trial and orality

1–011   Historically, certainly since 1215, jury trial was central to the English legal system in both criminal and civil cases, although its use in civil cases is now rare and it is confined to the most serious cases in the criminal courts. The need to argue cases before a jury has shaped our rules of evidence, procedure and substantive law and has meant, historically, that most arguments were presented to the court orally, by the parties, through oral examination and cross-examination of witnesses. Again, the emphasis on orality is rapidly disappearing, with the admission of more and more written statements and documentary evidence in hard copy and electronically retrievable form. Since 1995, in civil cases, lawyers now have to present the court with a skeleton argument so the advocate's art of oral story-telling has been replaced by a scene in a typical civil court room where all heads are face-down in "the bundle" of documents and the "skeleton", flicking through to make cross-references, incomprehensible to the casual observer. It has taken some fun out of court watching, because it is difficult to follow the story.

Lay magistrates

The bulk of criminal cases are heard in magistrates' courts, **1–012** mostly by lay justices. There are almost 30,000 of them and no other legal system makes such heavy use of laypeople as decision-makers. In exporting the common law, we exported the concept of magistrates but they tended to be professionals. When you add to them the thousands of lay arbitrators, tribunal panel members and jurors, you start to realise how many important decisions are taken by laypersons in the English legal system.

4. The mother of all common law systems

Just as England has been called "the mother of parliaments", **1–013** because so many others have been modelled on the UK Parliament, I have called the English legal system the mother of all common law legal systems, worldwide. English common law is the most widespread legal system in the world, governing 30 per cent of the world's population. Twenty-seven per cent of the world's 320 legal jurisdictions use common law, according to research by Prof Philip Wood, Allen and Overy, reported at (2009) 159 N.L.J. 245. We exported the common law and our legal system, along with the English language, into our old colonies and the Commonwealth. The common law daughters of the English legal system include the US, Canada, Australia, New Zealand and most of India and Pakistan but we maintain our direct link with the living common law of many Commonwealth countries, through the Judicial Committee of the Privy Council. This court sits in London and is the highest court of appeal for those jurisdictions. Since it is mainly composed of UK Supreme Court Justices, this provides for harmonious development of principle throughout all of these common law jurisdictions. Decisions of the Judicial Committee (JCPC) are persuasive and not binding precedents on the English courts but they are heavily influential, since everyone realises that when those senior judges metamorphose back into UKSC Justices, they are not likely to contradict legal principles which they carefully established when doing their job as privy councillors.

This common law cross-fertilisation is by no means confined to Commonwealth countries, however: see Cooke. Certain areas of the common law, such as tort and criminal law, have developed globally, with judges in the courts of one country sometimes persuaded by the reasoning of their brethren in another jurisdiction. You only have to flick through the pages of an English text on criminal law to see how other countries tackle some of the interpretive problems facing our criminal courts. Where no precedent exists, English judges may be persuaded by a precedent from America, Australia or Canada, and so on, such as the trial judge in a manslaughter judgment: *R. v Pagett* (1983) 76 Cr App Rep 279. At the same time, English common law is still alive throughout the US, even in forms which have been replaced in England. For instance, the actions constituting an attempted crime in California are determined by old English case law, replaced in England by the Criminal Attempts Act 1981. Californian property law uses concepts straight out of medieval English property law, abolished by the English in the Law of Property Act 1925. If you buy property or sign a contract in the US, you may be astonished by quaint concepts and ancient English terminology.

To mark the transformation of the law lords into the UK Supreme Court, the Canadian Chief Justice, Beverley McLachlin and South African Justice Kate O'Regan wrote an article, "Views from Canada and South Africa: We owe a great debt to the work of the judges", acknowledging the contribution of the law lords to the worldwide spread of common law: October 1, 2009, *Timesonline*. The law lords and now the UKSC play a prominent role in the development of international common law and human rights, evidenced by dozens of sources, not least in some of the 51 essays in *Tom Bingham and the Transformation of the Law*. For instance, Michael Kirby, former Justice of the Australian High Court said "Decisions have no binding force whatsoever. . .the greatest tribute to the House of Lords can be found in the fact that. . .they continue to be cited in so many fields." Similarly, Andenas and Fairgrieve, referring to his judgments on liberty and anti-terror, said "Lord Bingham persuades through his reasoning. . .his judgments are comparative law sources, as persuasive authority, all over the world". Zeno-Zencovich, in the same book, details the court's internationalism. Of 475 decisions in 2000–07, 250 centred on interpretation of or made use of transnational or international law, including 100 human rights and 50 EU law cases, plus a number citing American, Canadian and Commonwealth authorities. He said, "A comparativist finds in the House of Lords reports a *bonanza* for his classes and case-books". Andenas and Fairgrieve claimed Bingham to have been a pioneer in developing comparative law in modern court practice. They pointed to his willingness to use European human rights law to develop the common law.

5. The comparison with other European systems

1–014   Since, in our popular rhetoric and our legal analysis, we are always comparing ourselves with continental legal systems, notably the French, and since we, along with all other EU Member States, now have to absorb EU law into our domestic legal systems, we students of the English legal system need to understand something more about the world's most extensive "family" of laws, the "Romano–Germanic" family, as David and Brierley describe it, in *Major Legal Systems in the World Today*. Apart from Ireland, a common law country, the legal systems of all of our EU partners are, historically, members of that other major family.

Different roots. . .

Law applied in the Romano–Germanic family was developed by scholars in the European universities from the Renaissance of the twelfth and thirteenth centuries. There was a need for an autonomous law, independent of canon (Church) law, to replace inadequate and bitty customary law. This is called civil law, as distinct from canon law but here the phrase "civil law" has this different meaning from the phrase "civil law", meaning non-criminal law, described above. Renaissance scholars latched onto Roman law as a neat, pre-existing body of rules and set about refining it. Law was seen as a fairly abstract body of principles of justice, and its teaching was linked to the teaching of philosophy, theology and religion. It emerged from France and Italy but was taught in this way in Spain, Portugal, Scandinavia and even Oxford and Cambridge. The teaching of national law was not taken up until the seventeenth and eighteenth centuries. The flexibility and abstract nature of this civil law, refined and taught in Europe, can be contrasted with the rigidity of the common law rules developing in the Westminster courts in London. Eventually, Roman law was translated into the basis of national laws for practical application. This could not be done in England because the rules of common law were already too entrenched. From the thirteenth to the sixteenth centuries, the law as taught in European universities had considerable influence. Jurists, not governments, developed the law, so the countries of the Romano–Germanic family had jurists and legal practitioners who derived their concept of law, approach and reasoning from Roman law.

The study and refinement of Roman law naturally progressed to its codification. Codes were developed independently but the most influential of these was the Napoleonic Code of 1804. The French code was received in Belgium, the Netherlands, the Rhenish provinces, Luxembourg, Poland and Italy. Thanks to colonisation by the Spanish, Portuguese, French and Dutch, elements of Romano–Germanic civil law spread throughout South America, parts of North America (Louisiana and Quebec) and Africa. The French influence extends to Turkey, Egypt, Iran, Syria, Iraq, Japan,

1–015

Taiwan, Vietnam and Cambodia. Certain countries have a mixture of common law and civil law. Examples are Scotland, Israel, South Africa, Zimbabwe and Botswana. Because the French Napoleonic Code was absorbed into so many legal systems, this made France an even more fecund mother of legal systems than the English. Notice that Germany did not adopt the French code but devised one of its own, so some comparativists talk of a French family and a German family.

. . .And different branches

1–016   The same divisions of law can be found throughout the Romano–Germanic legal systems and some of them, such as "the law of obligations", are alien to the common lawyer.

Written constitutions

1–017   The UK is one of only three countries in the developed world without a written constitution. As a consequence, we lacked any clear notion of fundamental rights until very recently. There is almost no awareness amongst the public at large of what the UK constitution amounts to. There is no talk of fundamental constitutional rights, as is common in Germany and France, and as is drummed into each small child's memory in the US, because we do not think we have any. Indeed, we have only spoken in terms of human rights in the last few years, since the Human Rights Act 1998 came into force, in October 2000. In most other jurisdictions, the legality of the law of the land can be tested against a written constitution in a special constitutional court and struck down if it offends against some constitutional requirement. In the UK, we are used to the idea that the law of our land is untouchable. Parliament is supreme, sovereign, and, prior to 1973, only Parliament could undo what a previous parliament had done. Maybe it is this inability to conceptualise any law superior to that made by Parliament which partly explains why we reacted so badly to the effrontery of the rulings of the European Court of Justice (ECJ) in the *Factortame* cases, which resulted in the suspension of part of an Act of the UK Parliament (see Ch.3). Similarly, the Blair government reacted adversely in December 2004, when the law lords condemned the Anti-Terrorism, Crime and Security Act 2001 as contravening the European Convention on Human Rights (see Ch.4).

Public law and private law in Europe

1–018   Romano–Germanic legal systems all recognise the distinction between public and private law which, historically, English common law did not acknowledge. The French, for instance, have a separate set of courts, headed by the Conseil d'Etat, administering a separate body of public law developed by those courts to a sophisticated level by the first half of the twentieth century. French law has, in this respect, been highly influential over Belgian and Dutch law. Those countries also have courts which are modelled on the Conseil d'Etat. In the English legal system, however, the development of public law was stifled, until the enactment of the Crown Proceedings Act 1947, by the rule that the Crown could not be sued, and until 1981 by the difficulties in applying for judicial review. It is only since the 1960s that we have acknowledged the separate existence of a body of public law, worthy of being taught as an independent subject. We still do not have a separate set of public law courts, along French lines, but at least we now list most applications for judicial review to be heard in the Administrative Court, with a simplified procedure, which has allowed the rapid development of a coherent body of public law.

The concept of law

The very way in which law is conceived of in the legal systems **1–019** of the Romano–Germanic family is radically different from the way we approach it and it has developed in the common law countries, and this goes a very long way towards explaining why EU law and the judgments of the ECJ were so much easier, in the early days, for our European partners to assimilate than for us. This is how David and Brierley, in their classic analysis, explain *la différence*:

"In countries of the Romano-Germanic family, the legal rule is formulated, characterised and analysed in the same way. In this family, in which doctrinal writing is held in high esteem, the legal rule is not considered as merely a rule appropriate to the solution of a concrete case. It is fashionable to view with a certain disdain, and as casuistic, the opposite view which places the rule of law at the level of concrete cases only. Digests of decided cases, form books and legal dictionaries are certainly useful working instruments for practitioners, and they provide much of the raw material for jurists in their work. But these compilations do not enjoy the high prestige associated with legal scholarship. The function of the jurist is to draw from this disorganised mass first the rules and then the principles which will clarify and purge the subject of impure elements, and thus provide both the practice and the courts with a guide for the solution of particular cases in the future." (p.94)

In common law countries, just about the opposite is going on. The initial approach is one of pragmatism in individual cases, rather than abstract principle. The common law is developed, whether the judges are dealing with a judge-made law or interpreting a statute, on a case by case basis. The concern of the judge is to find the solution to the instant case. When a sufficient body of case law has developed, through the application and extension of judicial reasoning in the system of precedent, then it may be possible to elevate these judicial rulings to the level of principle. In other words, judicial reasoning in a common law country is said to be "bottom up" and in a civil law country it is "top down".

Because judicial reasoning is such an important source of law, we are heavily dependent on law reports. Academics certainly comment on judicial reasoning but scholars cannot be said, for the most part, to be the source of legal doctrine themselves. Indeed, there was a convention that judges did not cite living authors. The exception is that, where there is no precedent, the courts will resort to examining what are known as "books of authority"—early writings in the common law. It is now quite common for judges to refer to modern textbooks or articles.

Sources of law and the judicial approach

1–020   The primary source of law in the Romano–Germanic legal systems is codified law, the drafting and interpretation of which is influenced by, or is the task of, academic jurists. In common law countries, we depend on a mixture of judge-made law (common law) and statute, as interpreted by judges, whose reasoned opinions we must read in the law reports. If we take the French legal system as a contrasting example, we can see that the judge is not considered to be a source of law. Indeed, following the revolution, judges' powers were curtailed and they were prohibited from creating binding rules of precedent. Of course, this is constitutional theory but in reality, French judges have had to make law, to a certain extent, and some critics say that the notion that they do not make law is an academic myth. While even the judgments of the Cour de Cassation are not meant to form binding precedents, they are followed by the lower courts in most cases. Certainly French public law is almost entirely judge-made since it was developed after the Napoleonic era of codification. The French ambivalence is illustrated by the way law is taught. Textbooks emphasise codified law (legislation), with cases relegated to footnote illustrations, yet tutorials concentrate on case commentaries.

The nature of a French judgment is very different. Whereas some of our leading UKSC decisions contain the reasoned opinions of five to nine Justices, distinguishing and applying a long list of precedents and stretching through over 100 pages in the law reports, French judgments, even emanating from the Cour de Cassation, are very short. They are in the form of a syllogism: they set out the facts, the legal issue in context and the conclusion, without, usually, citing any previous case authority. Because judgments are so short, they are normally published accompanied by academic commentary.

Procedural differences

We most commonly see the English legal system contrasted with European systems in terms of procedure, notably criminal procedure. Broadly speaking, European systems were characterised by common lawyers as "inquisitorial", with the examining magistrate, then the court, taking a significant part in fact-finding and examining witnesses. This caricature was contrasted with the adversarial or accusatorial system, which the common law population likes to insist is so much fairer, with the judge acting as an unbiased umpire, permitting both sides to prepare and present their cases and examine witnesses, independent of court interference. Both the English and continental legal systems have recently departed from the purity of their respective models, however, especially with the procedural changes of the 1980s and 1990s. The Italian criminal process has recently become much more adversarial and in 2009, French President Sarkozy announced the abolition of investigating magistrates. 1–021

Bad Europeans

I have endeavoured to explain at some length the contrast between the English legal system and the Romano–Germanic systems of our EU partners for two reasons. First, we need to see where the English legal system sits, in worldwide terms, and secondly, we need to understand why EU law seems a bit more difficult for us to get used to than for our European counterparts. EU procedural law and its concept of law are derived directly from the French legal system, the mother or sister of all the other EU legal systems, apart from Ireland and Germany. 1–022

The French influence can be seen in the procedure of the Court of Justice of the European Union. French was the original working language of the court. Lawyers' oral submissions are strictly limited to 30 minutes' argument. Common lawyers, trained in the tradition of oral advocacy, had to be helped by the Court's staff to reduce their arguments into writing, in the early days. The roles of the advocate-general and judge-rapporteur are modelled on the French. They have no common law equivalent. The system of references for preliminary rulings bears a direct similarity to references of questions of law from the French inferior courts to the Cour de Cassation. Again, there is no common law equivalent. The early judgments of the European Court of Justice (ECJ) looked just like

French judgments, with very little reasoning and no precedents cited. This was one of the most difficult aspects of EU law for the common lawyer to comprehend but the Court of Justice has now changed. For the sake of consistency, it takes serious account of its own precedents and cites them in its judgments, and reported decisions contain much more reasoning than they formerly did, thus looking much more like common law judgments. The Court certainly accepts and applies broad principle in the same way that a court in a Romano–Germanic legal system would.

6. Who runs the English legal system?

1–023   The Lord Chancellor (Secretary of State for Justice) is the cabinet minister in charge of the Ministry of Justice. It is the successor of the Department for Constitutional Affairs, formerly the Lord Chancellor's Department. On its surprise creation in 2007, it also took many functions from the Home Office. It is responsible for corrections (prisons and so on), criminal justice, HM Courts and Tribunals Service, tribunals, judicial diversity, family justice, coroners' courts and legal aid. The Home Office is responsible for immigration and passports, the police, drugs policy, crime and counter-terrorism. HM Courts and Tribunals Service is an independent agency, formed in 2011, running the courts. The minister in charge of prosecutions is the Attorney General and prosecutors are described in Ch.12 on criminal procedure. The judiciary is independently run by the Lord Chief Justice, under the Constitutional Reform Act 2005, as described in Ch.14. The Ministry of Justice runs legal aid and legal services, described in Ch.17. Lawyers are regulated by a variety of bodies, overseen by the Legal Services Board, described in Ch.13.

7. Keeping up-to-date with the English legal system

1–024   Most of the law changes frequently and this subject changes most. Like all law books, this one, finished in 2011, will be out of date by the time you read it. Here are some tactics for keeping up-to-date.

- Never read out-of-date law books. They are as dangerous as last week's cream cakes.
- Show tutors/examiners that you have kept up to date by reading a quality newspaper, such as *The Times*, *The Financial*

Times, The Guardian or *The Independent. The Times* has the most legal content. It also contains brief law reports of recent cases, to help you keep up with all your legal studies. They are produced much more quickly than any other hard copy set of law reports. *The Guardian* contains useful analysis of social issues in the legal system, as does *The Independent.* You can also search old newspapers in various subscriber databases, which most libraries have, or on *LexisNexis* or *Westlaw.* By keeping abreast of the news, you can make the law more interesting for yourself by understanding how law is about real people, in the real world. Law is not just in books.

- Take yourself to court. The courts are a free source of daily entertainment, Mondays to Fridays. Justice in England and Wales is meant to be open to the public. Courts and tribunals are everywhere. Go and see how law operates in practice, in solving people's disputes and responding to their offences. In this way, you will learn a lot about procedure, the court structure, lawyers, magistrates and judges.
- Regularly browse the legal news journals, such as *The New Law Journal*, *Legal Action*, the Law Society's *Gazette* or *The Lawyer.*
- Listen to *Law in Action* on BBC Radio 4. Old programmes are on iPlayer.
- Visit relevant websites and check on "What's New?" and the press releases. The most useful departmental website is that of the Ministry of Justice.

USEFUL WEBSITES (CHECKED IN JUNE 2011)

Administrative Justice and Tribunals Council *http://www.justice.gov. uk/ajtc.*   **1–025**

Association of Women Barristers *http://www.womenbarristers.co.uk/.*
Association of Women Solicitors *http://www.womensolicitors.org.uk/.*
Attorney General *http://www.attorneygeneral.gov.uk/.*
Bar Council *http://www.barcouncil.org.uk/.*
British and Irish Legal Information Institute *http://www.bailii.org/.*
Central Office of Information, including government press releases *http://www.coi.gov.uk/.*
Centre for Effective Dispute Resolution (ADR) *http://www.cedr.com.*
Citizens Advice *http://www.citizensadvice.org.uk/.*
Civil Justice Council: see judiciary website
Criminal Cases Review Commission *http://www.ccrc.gov.uk/.*
Criminal Courts Review *http://www.criminal-courts-review.org.uk/.*
Crown Prosecution Service *http://www.cps.gov.uk/.*

Department for Constitutional Affairs, the predecessor of the Ministry of Justice, a very informative archive *http://webarchive. nationalarchives.gov.uk/20100512160448/http://www.dca.gov.uk/ index.htm.*

DirectGov government information *http://www.direct.gov.uk/en/ index.htm.*

European Court of Human Rights *http://www.echr.coe.int/echr/.*

European Union institutions and documents, including European Commission and Court of Justice of the EU *http://europa.eu/.*

European Commission Representation in the UK, for EU news, publications and information *http://ec.europa.eu/unitedkingdom/.*

Her Majesty's Courts and Tribunals Service *http://www.hmcourts-service.gov.uk/.*

Home Office: *http://www.homeoffice.gov.uk/.*

International Courts of Justice are best accessed via the United Nations website *http://www.un.org/.*

Intute Social Sciences, including law *http://www.intute.ac.uk/ socialsciences/.*

Judicial Appointments Commission *http://jac.judiciary.gov.uk/.*

Judicial Committee of the Privy Council *http://www.jcpc.gov.uk/.*

Judiciary *http://www.judiciary.gov.uk/.*

JUSTICE *http://www.justice.org.uk/.*

Justices' Clerks' Society *http://www.jc-society.com/.*

Law Commission *http://www.justice.gov.uk/lawcommission/index. htm.*

Lawlinks, links to legal internet resources *http://www.kent.ac.uk/ lawlinks/.*

Law Society, including the *Gazette http://www.lawsociety.org.uk/home. law.*

Legal Abbreviations *http://www.legalabbrevs.cardiff.ac.uk/.*

Legal Action Group, including items from *Legal Action http://www. lag.org.uk/.*

Legislation *http://www.legislation.gov.uk/.*

Liberty *http://www.liberty-human-rights.org.uk/.*

National Assembly for Wales *http://www.assemblywales.org/.*

UK National Statistics *http://www.statistics.gov.uk/.*

UK Parliament *http://www.parliament.uk/.*

UK Supreme Court *http://www.supremecourt.gov.uk/.*

US Supreme Court *http://www.supremecourtus.gov/.*

Welsh Assembly Government *http://wales.gov.uk/.*

BIBLIOGRAPHY AND FURTHER READING

1–026   M. Andenas and D. Fairgrieve (eds), *Tom Bingham and the Transformation of the Law* (2009).

T. Bingham, *The Rule of Law* (2010).

Rt Hon. Lord Cooke of Thorndon KBE, *Turning Points of the Common Law* (1997).

C. Dadamo and S. Farran, *The French Legal System* (1996).

R. David and J.E.C. Brierley, *Major Legal Systems in the World Today* (1985).

H.P. Glenn, *Legal Traditions of the World* (2007).

T. Honoré, *About Law: An Introduction* (1995).

Department of Constitutional Affairs, *A Guide to Government Business involving the Channel Islands and the Isle of Man*, (2002).

A really entertaining and wide ranging book, giving a brilliant introduction to English law in general, is G. Rivlin, *Understanding the Law* (latest edition).

The best comprehensive texts on ELS are S.H. Bailey, J.P.L. Ching and N.W. Taylor, *Smith, Bailey & Gunn, The Modern English Legal System* (2007) and M. Zander, *Cases and Materials on the English Legal System* (latest edition).

2. Sources of English Law

"The inevitable duty of the Courts is to make law and that is what all of us do every day." (Lord Cooke of Thorndon, cited by Lord Bingham, *The Business of Judging* (2000) p.34).

"We're a common law court. Of course we 'make' law as we go along." (US Supreme Court Justice Sandra Day O'Connor, quoted by J. Toobin, *The Nine* (2007) p.97).

The sources of English and Welsh law are statute law (Acts of the UK Parliament and statutory instruments), other delegated legislation including Welsh Acts, common law (case law), EU law, the European Convention on Human Rights, other international law, royal prerogative including orders in council, books of authority and custom. Mechanisms for making and reforming the law are discussed in Ch.5 on law reform.

2–001

1. Legislation

Acts of the UK Parliament

The most obvious source of codified law is an Act of the UK Parliament. In the unwritten UK constitution, "parliamentary sovereignty" is fundamental. It recognises that supreme power is vested in Parliament and that there is no limit to its law-making capacity. This is now tempered by membership of the Common Market since 1973 (now EU) and the further effect given to the European Convention on Human Rights by the Human Rights Act 1998, from 2000. Nevertheless, unless it conflicts with EU law, the Courts will always apply an Act of Parliament. They have no power to ignore it. Where statute law provides a remedy, the citizen is expected to resort to that, not to a common law remedy: *Marcic v Thames Water Utlities* [2003] UKHL 66. A person whose property

2–002

was flooded by overflowing sewers had an adequate statutory complaints procedure, without resorting to the tort of nuisance. In *R. v Goldstein, R. v Rimmington* [2005] UKHL 63, the law lords held that good practice and respect for primacy of statute over the common law required that people should be prosecuted for a statutory offence where possible. Therefore, prosecutions for common law offences such as public nuisance should be rare.

The courts' acceptance of parliamentary supremacy is derived from the seventeenth century conflict between the Stuart kings and Parliament. In that conflict, the courts took the side of Parliament and have since acknowledged Parliamentary sovereignty, whilst Parliament has readily allowed the independence of the judiciary. This was established in the Act of Settlement 1701 and is discussed in depth in Ch.14 on judges. The contrast with countries with a written constitution (most countries) is, however, very marked in that their Supreme Courts have the power to overrule legislation as being "unconstitutional". No such power exists in the UK. In *British Railways Board v Pickin* [1974] A.C. 765, an unsuccessful attempt was made to persuade the courts to intervene, on the grounds that the Board had obtained powers in a private Act of Parliament by misleading Parliament. The only role of the courts is to "interpret" statutory provisions to the circumstances of any given case. They must, where possible, interpret Acts so as to give effect to Convention rights and they are obliged to recognise EU law as supreme, if it conflicts with English law.

The Queen in Parliament

2–003   The UK Parliament is made up of three constituent elements: the monarch, the House of Lords and the House of Commons. An Act normally has approval of all three elements. Under certain conditions, it can be passed without the approval of the Lords, using the Parliament Acts 1911 and 1949. This has only been done a few times and occurred in 2004 with the Hunting Act. The monarch's place in Parliament is a formality. She attends the opening of a new Parliamentary session each autumn and after each General Election when a new government is elected. She reads the "Queen's speech" from the throne, which is the Government's statement of its legislative proposals for the coming Parliamentary session. It is written by the Prime Minister and does not reflect her personal views. All legislation must receive the Royal Assent before it becomes law. Assent has not been refused since the reign of Queen Anne in 1707 and will never be refused. Such is the strength of the constitutional convention that the monarchy does not interfere in politics.

Another unsuccessful attempt to overturn an Act was made in *R. (Jackson) v Att-Gen* [2005] EWCA Civ 126. In this case, pro-hunt supporters challenged the validity of the Hunting Act 2004, arguing that it was invalid because it was passed under the procedure laid down by the Parliament Act 1949 which was in itself invalid. The 2004 Act, banning foxhunting, was hotly controversial. The Government had used their powers under the 1949 Act to pass the Bill through the House of Commons only, without the consent of the House of Lords, who had rejected a previous version. The 1949 Act had amended the Parliament Act 1911, which permitted a Bill to be passed by the Commons alone, in certain circumstances, provided a two-year period had elapsed. The 1949 Act reduced that period to one year. Lord Woolf C.J. in the Court of Appeal (CA) remarked that it was very rare for the courts to entertain a challenge to an Act but the challenge was permissible because the 1911 Act was very unusual. The House of Lords, House of Commons and the King had used the machinery of legislation to make a fundamental change to the constitution. It was "perfectly appropriate" for the courts to consider the issue, since they were helping Parliament and the public by clarifying the legal position when such clarification was obviously necessary. The law lords agreed with the CA: while *Pickin* sought to investigate the internal workings of Parliament, this case questioned whether the Parliament Acts were indeed enacted law. The CA held that the UK's unwritten constitution *could* be amended by the legislature and it was clear that such an amendment was intended by the 1911 Act but that did not mean it was intended that the 1911 Act could not be amended by the 1949 Act. The decision was upheld on appeal to the law lords.

Procedure

An Act starts off as a Bill. Most are Public Government Bills. Their   **2–004** clauses will have been agreed by the "sponsoring" government department, usually after considering responses to consultation papers placed on the departmental website. Consultation papers were named "green papers", as they were green, in the days when they were only published in hard copy. The Bill will have been drafted by parliamentary counsel and often a "white paper" is published alongside it, explaining the government policy of the Act. At the time of writing, the Justice Minister is consulting on proposed changes to legal aid and civil justice, before publishing Bills containing the mechanism for his reforms.

Before the Bill becomes an Act, and the clauses become sections, it must undergo five stages in each House. It may start off in the Commons or Lords. Once the Bill with any amendments has been approved both by the Commons and, normally, the Lords, it needs only the Royal Assent to become an Act. It comes into immediate effect unless it contains its own starting date, or it has a provision which allows different parts to be brought into force at different times, by statutory instrument. For instance, parts of the Criminal Justice Act 2003 were still being brought into force in 2005 and some sections will probably never be implemented. The Human Rights Act 1998 did not come into force till 2000, to give the courts, public bodies and the public time to prepare. For a comprehensive explanation of Parliamentary procedure, Bills and Acts, in plain English, visit the UK Parliament website, especially "Making Laws", under "How Parliament Works". Even better, go and watch proceedings yourself, free. Alternatively, you can watch a choice of live proceedings or archived debates via the website. There is a very brief explanation of Welsh law on the National Assembly for Wales website.

The form of an Act of Parliament

2–005   Statutory language must be precise. Every Act must relate to existing legislation on the subject so clauses often amend old Acts or cross-refer to others. For example, the Tribunals, Courts and Enforcement Act 2007, Pt 2, changing the eligibility conditions for judicial appointments, alters the wording of dozens of statutory provisions, to which it cross-refers. This makes it difficult to read and understand. Further, although the modern aim is to draft the law in plain English, the endeavour to close loopholes also makes Acts complex. The reader can browse Acts on the Legislation website for evidence of this. In 1995, I watched an argument between a parliamentary draftsman and a tax lawyer, at a conference on legislation. The tax lawyer accused the draftsman of making the annual Finance Acts too complicated for ordinary people to understand. The draftsman retorted that if clients stopped paying tax lawyers like him large amounts of money to find loopholes, he could draft them in simpler language. Controversial or big Bills suffer many amendments, especially by the Government who introduced them. It is said that there is a tendency to introduce Bills in outline and fill in the details as they pass through Parliament. These factors combine to make statutes complicated and notoriously difficult for the lay person to understand. Although the earliest statutes had long titles and preambles, since the Short Titles Act 1896, Acts of Parliament have been given a short title and preambles are normally very short now. To try and make law more comprehensible, governments since 1998 publish explanatory notes alongside many new Acts. The Coroner Reform Bill 2006 contained a plain English translation alongside each clause. It spelled out in full the relevant sections of previous legislation, instead of just making a reference and forcing the reader to look up the old statute. In the autumn of 2006, it was reviewed by a panel of 15 members of the public who had had recent experience of using the court. The Plain English

Campaign called it a "great step forward". Luckily, on the new legislation website, we can read the amended versions of Acts.

Citation and publication

From 1963, every Act is given a Chapter number for the year in which it receives the Royal Assent. This abolishes the centuries-old system by which Acts were given a Chapter number for the session of the parliament in question designated by the regnal year of the monarch. Acts are now referred to by their short title and Chapter number: for example, The Gender Recognition Act 2004 (c.7). Acts are published by The National Archives. They make new legislation available for sale to the public as soon as it has been given the Royal Assent. It is available free online, including all public Acts from 1988 and some from 1801–1987.

2–006

Public Bills and Private Bills

A Public Bill affects the public at large, and applies throughout England and Wales. Most Bills are Public and sponsored by the Government. A Private Bill is legislation which affects a limited section of the population, either by reference to locality or by reference to a particular family or group of individuals. These are known respectively as Local and Personal Bills. A Private Member's Bill is a Public Bill introduced by a back-bench Member of Parliament, who has been successful in the ballot. A Hybrid Bill may cover work of national importance but in a local area. Examples are the Channel Tunnel Bills of the 1970s and 1980s.

2–007

Consolidation, codification and statute law revision

Consolidation is the process by which provisions in a number of Acts are brought together and re-enacted in one Act. It is not a method for changing the law but it does make the law easier to find. In order to ease the passage of such measures, they go through Parliament in a special procedure. For example, legislation concerning sentencing was consolidated in the Powers of the Criminal Courts (Sentencing) Act 2000. The Government's Discrimination Law Review published a consultation paper in June 2007 which identified nine pieces of discrimination legislation and concluded that we needed a single Equality Act. This was enacted in 2010. Codification is the term used for an Act which brings together all the existing legislation and case law and forms a complete restatement of the law. It can involve changes in the law and is thus one method of law reform. Lord Bingham C.J., as he then was, added his weight to academics' demand for a codification of the criminal law and Professor Spencer added a persuasive argument for codifying criminal procedure. The Government included plans for

2–008

a code in its 2001 White Paper, Criminal Justice: The Way Ahead, although the project now seems to have stalled.

The Law Commission, which was set up under the Law Commissions Act 1965, has the responsibility to keep under review all the law with a view to its systematic development and reform, including codification. The Commission also has overall responsibility for advising the repeal of obsolete and unnecessary enactments. Since 1993–94, a Special Public Bill Committee "fast-track" procedure has been used for legislation proposed by the Commission and other non-contentious Bills. This "Jellicoe procedure" employs a committee of specialists, such as judges and lawyers on the Arbitration Bill 1996, instead of a committee of the whole House. We return to all of this in Ch.5 on law reform.

Pre-legislative scrutiny

2–009　　Pre-legislative scrutiny has been favoured since Tony Blair came to power in 1997. Gordon Brown took this further by announcing the contents of the next autumn's Queen's speech in July 2007, in the Green Paper The Governance of Britain—The Government's Draft Legislative Programme (CM 7175). In May 2008, he published a Green Paper Preparing Britain for the Future—the Draft Legislative Programme 2008–09 (CM 7372), inviting responses. This followed his undertaking in the 2007 Paper to "modernize and open up the legislative process". Additionally, some departments published draft bills for consultation. The Coalition Government, formed in 2010, has continued this trend.

Post-legislative scrutiny

2–010　　A 2006 Law Commission consultation demonstrated support for extending and formalising post-legislative scrutiny. The aim is to "improve the accountability of governments for the legislation they pass and ultimately lead to better and more effective law", according to Sir Terence Etherton, the Commission's then chairman. The Commission estimated that there were 10,000 pages of domestic legislation and the same amount in European Directives each year.

Delegated legislation

2–011　　This is the name given to law made in documentary form by subordinate authorities acting under powers delegated by Parliament or the sovereign, acting under her prerogative. Parliament does not have time or expertise to fill in the details or technicalities of the law so most big Bills are mere frameworks. The big difference between Acts of the UK Parliament, primary legislation, and subordinate or delegated legislation is that the courts can quash the latter if it is outside the remit of delegated power (substantively ultra vires) or has not been made procedurally correctly (procedurally ultra vires). The CA confirmed that it was entitled to review subordinate legislation on the grounds of illegality, procedural impropriety or *Wednesbury* unreasonableness, even where it had been debated and approved by affirmative resolution of both Houses of Parliament: *R. (Javed) v SS for Home Department* [2001] EWCA Civ 789. Such legislation can take the following forms.

Statutory instruments

The most common form of delegated legislation is a statutory instrument, made under power given to a minister to make law for a specified purpose. As each SI is published, it is given a number for the year, for example, the Greenhouse Gas Emissions Trading Scheme (Amendment) Regulations (SI 2004/3390). Much more of our law is contained in SIs than Acts. Almost all EU law comes into English law via SIs, like the one just mentioned.

2–012

Byelaws

Parliament delegates to local authorities and other public bodies the power to make local laws or laws limited to their particular functions so local authorities can make byelaws, for their areas. For instance, there are often rules governing behaviour in parks or leisure centres. The authority has to obtain confirmation from the named central government minister before the byelaws take effect. The power to make byelaws also belongs to public bodies such as the Civil Aviation Authority. Byelaws can be quashed on judicial review by the senior courts if they are ultra vires, or their illegality can be used as a defence where someone is prosecuted for infringing them. This happened to Lindis Percy, a protester against US defence forces in the UK. She appealed to the Crown Court against her conviction for breach of byelaws by repeatedly entering a secure defence installation. The Crown Court upheld her appeal, holding the byelaws to be ultra vires the Military Lands Act 1892, the enabling Act: *SS for Defence v Percy* [1999] 1 All E.R. 732.

2–013

Welsh law

Wales gained considerable autonomy in making delegated legislation, from 1999. Under the Government of Wales Act 1998 and subsequent legislation, this includes areas of government such as agriculture, planning and the environment, health and social services, education and industry, housing and local government, sport and leisure and the Welsh language. In turn, the Assembly has delegated many of its powers to its First Minister, who leads the Welsh Assembly Government. Under the Government of Wales Act 2006,

2–014

the Welsh Assembly was given enhanced legislative power from 2011. The need to refer back to the UK Parliament was dispensed with. It should be remembered, however, that Welsh Acts, like Acts of the Scottish Parliament, are delegated legislation. They are thus reviewable by the UK Supreme Court. The validity of Scots law was tested for the first time in this way in *Martin v HM Advocate* [2010] UKSC 10.

Comment on delegated legislation

2–015   Since the early twentieth century, there has been increasing concern that Parliament, the legislature, has been delegating too much law-making power to the executive government. Lord Hewart C.J. complained of this creeping growth of executive power in *The New Despotism* in 1929. Acts are mere frameworks, giving substantial powers to Ministers to fill in the details through delegated powers. For instance, the Energy Act 2010 provides for carbon capture and storage and places duties on the relevant minister (Secretary of State) in relation to gas and electricity markets, empowering him to licence producers of electricity and provide a scheme of financial assistance, but it leaves it up to him to devise the schemes and the regulations.

Hewart was also concerned about the use of "Henry VIII" clauses in Acts which permit a minister to amend primary legislation, an Act, through a statutory instrument. For instance, the Legislative and Regulatory Reform Act 2006 permits any minister to amend *any* legislation to get rid of red tape. See Burns. In 2010, Lord Judge C.J. repeated his predecessor's concern, castigating the Government for introducing a new Bill with sweeping Henry VIII clauses. The Government backed down. Bodies like the Law Commission were listed in Sch.7 of the Public Bodies Bill, a Henry VIII clause that would have allowed them to be merged or abolished by secondary legislation. (There were *seven* Henry VIII clauses in the Bill.) All of this has serious implications for independence in the distribution of resources and the scrutiny of the government, which is what these bodies were created to do. In his Mansion House speech, in July 2010, Lord Judge told the Lord Chancellor, Ken Clarke, that Henry VIII clauses should be "confined to the dustbin of history", reminding us that in 1539 Henry persuaded Parliament to pass the Statute of Proclamations, giving his proclamations the same force as acts of the legislature. It was repealed on Henry's death. Lord Judge had tried to find out how many there were: 120 had been passed in the last session of Parliament alone. In December 2010, the LCJ then told the Constitution Committee in the House of Lords that schedules of the Bill could potentially be used to abolish the Judicial Appointments Commission, Criminal Cases Review Commission and so on, bodies whose independence from government was vital. The Government backed down, announcing that it would not abolish public bodies using a Henry VIII clause, after all.

2. Statutory interpretation

"Rules" for statutory interpretation

Disputes arise as to the meaning or application of primary or delegated legislation and the judges' task is to interpret it. The rest of us need to interpret statute law too: law lecturers and students; lawyers advising their clients; judges of the lower courts, for their own judgment-formation and sometimes for juries; magistrates' clerks (legal advisers) need to advise their bench and civil servants and local government officers need to know how to apply the law to us. Most importantly, as ordinary citizens, all of us are presumed to know the law so we need to understand the way our business and social lives are regulated and what are our rights (for instance, as an employee) and duties (for instance, to pay tax). Before considering the "rules" for interpretation, we should note that two experts on statutory interpretation, Cross and Bennion, insist that there are no such "rules". In Bennion's first edition of *Statutory Interpretation* (1984) he said "Instead there are a thousand and one interpretive criteria" (see Bennion's 1997 letter). Nevertheless, judges have developed a set of common law *principles* to help them interpret statutes that are sometimes known as the rules of statutory interpretation. Judges do not describe themselves as applying these "rules" but they do tend to apply them sequentially.

2–016

The first tactic judges use is to look for definitions of contentious words. The Interpretation Act 1978 is used. One of its better-known sections provides that "unless the contrary intention appears (a) words importing the masculine gender include the feminine (and vice versa) (b) words in the singular include the plural, and words in the plural include the singular". Most statutes contain definitions of the words they use, especially if they are novel, so the Crime and Disorder Act 1998, s.85 defines "action plan order" and "drug treatment and testing order". Sometimes words are left undefined, though, and it is for the courts to determine their application. The Protection from Harassment Act 1997 does not define harassment but the High Court decided it did not include the activities of Microsoft, intimidating a software counterfeiter by provoking police raids, conducting oppressive litigation and telephoning the claimants at night: *Tuppen v Microsoft* (*The Times*, November 15, 2000).

2–017   The first principle (**the literal rule**) of interpretation is that the judge should apply the words according to their "ordinary, plain and natural meaning". In *Clarke v Kato* [1998] 1 W.L.R. 1647 the law lords held that as a matter of ordinary language, a car park did not qualify as a road for the purposes of the Road Traffic Act 1988 so as to be an area in respect of which a motor insurance policy had to provide cover. In *Welsh v Stokes* [2007] EWCA Civ 796 the CA gave the word "normal" its "core" meaning of "conforming to type". The appellants lost their appeal against liability under the Animals Act 1971 s.2 (2) (b), making the keeper of an animal liable for damage unless due to characteristics not normally found in animals of the same species. It was *normal* for a horse to bolt in certain circumstances and in this case a safe horse had thrown its rider who had suffered a serious head injury. In *Boss Holdings v Grosvenor West End Properties* [2008] UKHL 5, the House of Lords applied a literal interpretation to the definition of a "house". It was originally "designed or adapted for living in" in the 1730s and so satisfied this definition in the Leasehold Reform Act 1967, even though it had become dilapidated.

In *R. (on the application of National Grid Gas Plc (formerly Transco Plc) v Environment Agency* [2007] UKHL 30, the HL applied a common sense and literal interpretation. The case concerned liability for the cost of removing harmful coal tar residues found beneath the gardens of 11 homes, deposited by private gas companies before gas was nationalised in 1948. The phrase "person . . .who has caused or knowingly permitted" pollution, in the Environmental Protection Act 1990, s.78F was not to be construed as including every person who became a successor in title to the polluters. "This is, in my opinion, a quite impossible construction to place on the uncomplicated and easily understandable statutory language. The emphasis in section 78F. . .is on the actual polluter, the person who '. . .caused or knowingly permitted. . .'" (per Lord Scott at para.20). The courts will always construe penal legislation restrictively, applying limited meaning to statutory language, as can be seen from *R. v Johnson, R. v Hind* [2005] EWCA Crim 971, cited in Ch.12 on criminal procedure.

Unfortunately, the courts sometimes find themselves bound by the literal words of an Act into an interpretation which they consider leads to a daft result. In *Horsman* [1998] Q.B. 531 Waller L.J. said:

> "however anomalous, if the words of the section are clear, there is no room for construing them in any other way. . .the question whether there should not be some amendment [by Parliament] should be looked at with some haste".

R. v Smith [2002] EWCA Crim 2907 was another case where the CA reluctantly felt itself bound by a literal interpretation of statute. Section 14(5) of the Criminal Appeal Act 1995 seemed to say that once the Criminal Cases Review Commission (CCRC), on whatever grounds, had made a reference to the court, the appellant might add any further grounds, including those expressly rejected by the CCRC. Their Lordships were "very surprised indeed" at this and respectfully suggested that Parliament should make an amendment.

Sometimes judges are frustrated that a legislative oversight can **2–018** produce a harsh result in unforeseen circumstances. A poignant example was *R. v Human Fertilisation and Embryology Authority Ex p. Blood* [1996] 3 W.L.R. 1176. Diane Blood and her husband had decided to have a baby. Before she got a chance to conceive, her husband died of meningitis. While he was still in a coma, a sample of sperm was removed and frozen and his widow wanted to use it to conceive. The Human Fertilisation and Embryology Act required a man's written consent for the storage or use of his sperm in the UK. Much as the judge and the public had "universal sympathy" (Stephen Brown J.) for the weeping Mrs Blood's "double bereavement", he could not surmount the clear requirement of the Act. Baroness Warnock, whose committee's finding led to the Act, blamed herself for not foreseeing such a case and Lord Winston, the famous fertility specialist, called the result "cruel and unnatural". The CA too felt "all the courts. . .can do is give effect to the clear language of the Act" (per Woolf M.R.). Happily, they allowed her appeal on a separate argument, a point of Community (EU) law. They ruled that she had the right to take the sperm for insemination elsewhere in the EU: [1997] 2 W.L.R. 807. She conceived in 1998 and had a second child in 2002.

Judges are more liberal in giving broad interpretations to words now than they used to be, if they feel they can produce a just result. The CA held that a generous interpretation should be put on "building", under the Cremation Act 1902, to permit Hindu open air funeral pyres. There was no reason not to give the word its natural and *relatively wide* meaning. They thought it should be possible to make a building in a private location with substantial openings: *R (Ghai) v Newcastle-upon-Tyne City Council* [2010] EWCA Civ 59. The outcome here was surely fairer than the outcome of the very narrow interpretation in the 1970 *Hobbs* case, below.

Sometimes a case can be spared a bad outcome which would result from a literal interpretation, because a second principle, which became known as **the golden rule**, is that the literal application need not be applied, if to do so would lead to absurdity or to inconsistency within the statute itself. An outstanding example of the golden rule occurred in *Re Sigsworth* [1935] Ch. 89, where a man was found to have murdered his mother. In the statute dealing with the distribution of the mother's estate it was laid down that the estate was to be distributed amongst "the issue" (children). The son was her only child. The judge held that the common law rule that a murderer cannot take any benefit from the estate of a person he had murdered prevailed over the apparently clear words of the statute.

A third principle is that if the so-called literal or golden rules fail to assist, the judge is entitled to consider **the mischief rule**. This rule, which was first settled in *Heydon's Case* (1584 3 Co. Rep. 79), allows the judge to consider: (1) what was the common law; (2) what was the defect or mischief in the common law; and (3) what remedy Parliament in the legislation has provided for the defect. Here, a judge is entitled to examine existing legislation and case law before coming to a decision, with the intention that the ruling will "suppress the mischief and advance the remedy." In *R. v Bournewood Community and Mental Health NHS Trust Ex p. L* [1999] 1 A.C. 458, the House of Lords held that the statutory predecessor to s.131(1) of the Mental Health Act 1983 was designed to cure the mischief caused by the assumption that compulsory powers had to be used unless the patient could express a positive desire for treatment.

2–019   The court is not easily persuaded to reject the plain words of the statute, though. Lord Scarman in *Stock v Frank Jones (Tipton) Ltd* [1978] 1 W.L.R. 231 explained that:

> "if the words used by Parliament are plain there is no room for the anomalies test, unless the consequences are so absurd that without going outside the statute, one can see that Parliament must have made a drafting mistake... but mere manifest absurdity is not enough; it must be an error (of commission or omission) which in its context defeats the intention of the Act".

An example was *Inco Europe v First Choice Distribution* [2000] 1 W.L.R. 586. The House of Lords said the courts must be able to correct obvious drafting errors. In suitable cases, the court can add, omit or substitute words. Before doing so, they must be abundantly sure of three matters:

(1) the intended purpose of the statute or provision in question;
(2) that by inadvertence, the draftsman and Parliament had failed to give effect to that purpose in the provision in question; and
(3) the substance of the provision that Parliament would have made, although not necessarily the precise words that it would have used, had the error in the Bill been noticed.

Drafting errors and omissions may occur because of the number of amendments made as a big Bill passes through Parliament. A famous example of this is s.16 of the Theft Act 1968, which became known as "a judicial nightmare" and remained uncorrected until the Theft Act 1978. Lord Goff closely examined *Hansard* and recounted its messy legislative history in *Preddy* [1996] A.C. 815 and commented:

> "hurried amendments to carefully structured comprehensive Bills are an accident-prone form of proceeding; and the new s.16. . .proved to be so incomprehensible as to be unworkable in practice".

Lord Denning used to say "we fill in the gaps" (in legislation). Sometimes the courts have to rewrite statute law in order to make sense of it. In *R. v Zafar* [2008] EWCA Crim 184, the Lord Chief Justice redrafted s. 57 of the Terrorism Act 2000 to require an *intention* to use an article for a terrorist purpose.

Other "rules" (aids to interpretation)

It is accepted practice that "(t)he policy and objects of the Act must **2–020** be determined by construing the Act as a whole": *Padfield v Minister of Agriculture, Food and Fisheries* [1968] 997. It follows that a judge must relate a word or phrase in a statute to its place in the context of the whole measure. Where specific words are followed by general words, the general words must be given effect in the light of the foregoing specific words. This is called the ejusdem generis rule. An example is *Hobbs v CG Robertson Ltd* [1970] 1 W.L.R. 980 where the CA had to construe the following phrase concerning the provision of goggles in the Construction (General Provision) Regulations 1961 "breaking, cutting, dressing or carving of stone, concrete, slag or similar materials" in circumstances where a workman injured an eye, through the splintering of brickwork from a chimney breast which he was required to remove. The Court applied the ejusdem generis rule in holding that brick was not "a similar material" to stone, concrete or slag; the provision of goggles was, therefore, not compulsory and the workman's claim failed. This narrow interpretation, producing such a harsh result, would not be the likely approach of modern judges. A connected rule is that where, in a statute, there is a list of specified matters, which is not followed by general words, then only the matters actually mentioned are caught by this provision of the Act. The Latin phrase for this is *expressio unius est exclusio alterius*. In *R. v Inhabitants of Sedgley* (1831) 2 B. and Ad. 65, a statutory provision for rating occupiers of "lands, houses, tithes and coal mines" was held not to apply to any other kind of mine and in *B v DPP* [1999] 3 W.L.R. 116, the CA applied the rule (without saying they were doing so) in interpreting the Sexual Offences Act 1956. The inclusion of a specific statutory defence in two sections demonstrated conclusively that Parliament did not intend that the defence should be available for other offences where a defence was not mentioned. The rule *noscitur a sociis* means that where two or more words follow each other in a statute, they must be taken as related for the purpose of interpretation. For example, in *Inland Revenue Commissioners v Frere* [1965] A.C. 402 the House of Lords held that in the phrase, "interest, annuities or other annual payments" the word "interest" meant annual interest.

Presumptions

2–021
(1) There is no change in the existing law beyond that expressly stated in the legislation.

(2) The Crown is not bound unless the Act specifically makes it so. The Windsors can only be prosecuted for speeding because the Road Traffic Acts spell out that they bind the Crown.

(3) Legislation is not intended to apply retrospectively, unless this is expressly stated to be the case. This is very rare. An example was the War Crimes Act 1991, designed to target Nazi war criminals.

(4) Any change in the law affecting the liberties of the subject must be expressly and specifically stated.

(5) Any liability for a criminal offence must be on the basis of fault, unless the words of the statute clearly intend otherwise.

(6) The legislation applies throughout the UK unless an exemption for Scotland or Northern Ireland is stated. Because Scotland, in particular, has its own legal and local government system, it is common for Parliament to legislate for Scotland separately and now much of this legislative power has been passed to the Scottish Parliament. As explained above, Welsh legislative power is enhanced from 2011.

(7) If the provisions of two Acts appear to be in conflict, the court will endeavour to reconcile them, since there is no presumption of implied repeal. If reconciliation is not possible, logic demands that the later provision be given effect. For instance, in *Padmore v Inland Revenue Commissioners (No.2)* [2001] S.T.C. 280, the Court had to resolve a conflict between two inconsistent tax provisions. The Chancery Division held that where the Act being construed is a consolidating Act, it is only permissible to take into account the earlier legislation if the later language is ambiguous, obscure or would lead to

an absurdity. Where there is a conflict between two sections in the same statute, the court must do its best to reconcile them and may read words into the statute, to give effect to plain legislative intent.

(8) Legislation must be construed so as not to conflict with EU law.

(9) Legislation must be construed so as to give effect to the European Convention on Human Rights *where possible*. (If not possible, then a senior court may make a declaration of incompatibility.)

(10) Parliament intends to give effect to international treaties to which the UK is a contracting party.

Intrinsic aids

The judge may be assisted by components of the statute. These **2–022** include the long title, marginal notes, headings, which may be prefixed to a part of the Act, and Schedules, which are part of the Act, although they do not affect words used in the body of the Act unless these are ambiguous. Punctuation is referred to in interpreting the meaning of a sentence in the same way as we use it as an essential guide to the sense of normal everyday English. In *R. v Montila* [2004] UKHL 50, the House of Lords ruled that headings and side notes could be used in interpretation but less weight should be attached to them than to parts of the Act that are open to debate in Parliament. Preambles may be used. EU legislation makes regular use of preambles. The famous "Eurobananas" Regulation of 1994, regulating standards of bananas, contains a preamble longer than the text. The Court of Justice of the EU examines preambles as a matter of course, in interpreting EU legislation.

Extrinsic aids

Judges refer to other statutes on the same subject and to general **2–023** knowledge. They decided that, as a general rule, they would refrain from consulting *Hansard,* the report of debates on a Bill through Parliament, and would only permit reference to preparatory documents to determine the mischief the Act sought to remedy. They set out guidelines in *Black-Clawson v Papierwerke* [1975] A.C. 591. The reason for this rule is that people should be entitled to know the law by taking an Act at face value. Furthermore the intentions of, say, the Lord Chancellor, in introducing the Legal Services Bill differed significantly from the "intention of Parliament", in passing the 2007 Act, after it had been hotly debated and repeatedly amended. Because of this rule, judges were unable, theoretically, to make use of Parliamentary debates, reports of committees or commissions, or what the government ministers involved had said about the measure, as evidence of Parliamentary intent. This rule, that no extrinsic aids would be used, ensured that Parliament had a complete obligation to express itself precisely when making new law.

Serious inroads into this rule, altering the judicial role in statutory interpretation, were made by the House of Lords in *Pepper v Hart* [1993] A.C. 593. In this case, the question arose whether, under the Finance Act 1976, Parliament had intended school teachers at private schools to be taxed on the full value of the "benefit in kind" of the private education offered to their own children. The House of Lords ruled, erroneously, that this had been Parliament's intention. Their Lordships' attention was later drawn to the statement of the minister who sponsored the Bill through Parliament. From this, it became clear that the true intention was that the teachers should only be taxed on the cost to their employers, which was minimal, so an Appellate Committee of seven law lords was reconvened and the case reargued, with reference to *Hansard*. Their Lordships held that Parliamentary materials should only be referred to where:

"(a) legislation is ambiguous or obscure or leads to an absurdity;
(b) the material relied on consists of one or more statements by a minister or other promoter of the Bill together if necessary with such other Parliamentary material as is necessary to understand such statements and their effect;
(c) the statements relied on are clear" (per Lord Browne-Wilkinson).

Despite their Lordships' warnings that this new activity was to be the exception, judges and counsel in cases since 1993 have made frequent use of the *Pepper v Hart* principle, even where there is little ambiguity in a statute, and case law has extended the rule to allow reference to preparatory material, such as Green Papers and White Papers, and reports of the Law Commission and Royal Commissions. Even back in the 1970s, the Master of the Rolls, Lord Denning, and the Lord Chancellor, Lord Hailsham, said they always consulted *Hansard*. Drawing attention to the dangers of all this, the editors of *Cross on Statutory Interpretation* (1995 edn) said it created more work for lawyers, in advising clients and preparing litigation. Resorting to all these extrinsic aids, they commented, was no substitute for the clearest possible drafting of the text of the statute. Dame Mary Arden, when chairman of the Law Commission, warned of the dangers of *Pepper v Hart*. In *R. v Secretary of State for the Environment, Transport and the Regions Ex p. Spath Holme Ltd* [2001] 2 A.C. 349, the law lords tried to put a stop to this. They deprecated the frequent citation of *Hansard* and said that the conditions laid down in *Pepper v Hart* should be strictly insisted upon. They were concerned with the cost of fruitless *Hansard* searches.

An example of the application of *Pepper v Hart* appears in *Mullen* **2–024** *(No.2)* [2000] Q.B. 520, where Auld L.J. resorted to parliamentary debates to interpret the Criminal Appeal Act 1995. The case appears in Ch.12 on criminal procedure. Looking at *Hansard*, he decided that the meaning of "unsafe" conviction in the amended form of the Criminal Appeal Act 1968 was meant to be the same as before the 1995 amendment. A very important example of the CA and the House of Lords referring to *Hansard* to help them in statutory interpretation was the case challenging the validity of the Hunting Act, *Jackson*, referred to above. Lord Woolf C.J., in the CA, said the 1911 Parliament Act, which allowed legislation to be passed through the House of Commons only, in certain circumstances, was passed to resolve a constitutional crisis. An examination of *Hansard* disclosed beyond doubt that both the Commons and the Lords fully appreciated the extent of the constitutional change to which they were agreeing.

In *Westminster City Council v National Asylum Support Service* [2002] UKHL 38, the law lords held that explanatory notes accompanying an Act could be used in interpretation, even if there were no ambiguity. They are more useful than other materials because they are updated as a Bill passes through Parliament and changes its wording and meaning. Judges seem to be much more ready, nowadays, to use other preparatory material, such as reports of reform bodies, to help them interpret the law. In both *Jackson* and *R. v G. & R.*, on recklessness, below, the law lords referred to a variety of background material. Different considerations apply in the case of a statute which incorporates an international convention. Here, exceptionally, the court *must* have regard to the full background so reference may be made to relevant material. For a discussion of the approach of the English courts in interpreting international law, including the *Pinochet* cases, see the very useful 2001 article by Qureshi.

The move towards a broader, contextual, "purposive" approach

From about the 1960s or 1970s, Cross and other commentators **2–025** argued that judges took a "contextual approach". (See Bell and Engle, *Cross on Statutory Interpretation*). In doing this, judges claim to be searching for "the will of Parliament" and sometimes they articulate this. For instance, in *R. v Chief Constable of the RUC Ex p. Begley* [1997] 1 W.L.R. 1475, Lord Browne-Wilkinson explained this limit on the law lords' role in developing the common law, as he saw it:

"It is true that the House has power to develop the law. But it is a limited power. And it can be exercised only in the gaps left by Parliament. It is impermissible for the House to develop the law in a direction which is contrary to the expressed will of Parliament."

Nevertheless, a legislature of over a thousand people cannot be said to have a single intention. Judges have to look for the true meaning of of what Parliament said, not what it meant: Lord Reid in *Black Clawson* [1975] A.C. 591, as cited by Bell, p.17. If the words of a statute fail to deal with a particular situation, there is no power in a court to fill the gap, despite Lord Denning's claim. Only Parliament may do so, with a new Act. Some judges get frustrated, though, because Parliament is too busy to amend faulty legislation. Eventually, the law lords became more bold, giving a purposive construction to legislation. In *Fothergill v Monarch Airlines Ltd* [1981] A.C. 251 Lord Diplock was explicitly critical of previous judges' "narrowly semantic approach to statutory construction, until the last decade or so". Judging from the wide application given to *Pepper v Hart*, many modern judges agree with this criticism. Taking a broad, purposive approach, they apparently relish the opportunity to consult extrinsic aids. On the other hand, they may decline to do so in the face of clear language. An example is the *Kato* case above. Here Lord Clyde rejected an invitation to include car parks in the definition of "road" to give a purposive construction, because it would strain the word "road" beyond what it meant in ordinary usage. Some commentators have made sweeping statements that judges now favour a broad purposive approach but this is not really true in many instances, as the above cases demonstrate and as can be seen from any trawl through recent *Times* law reports. The simple reason is that judges cannot use the purposive approach to avoid clear words. Lord Steyn said in *IRC v McGuckian* [1997] 1 W.L.R. 991:

"During the last 30 years there has been a shift away from the literalist approach to purposive methods of construction. When there is no obvious meaning of a statutory provision the modern emphasis is on a contextual approach designed to identify the purpose of a statute and to give effect to it."

He applied a purposive approach in *R. v A* [2001] UKHL 25 which I analyse in depth in Ch.4 on human rights. But Dame Mary Arden, quoting him, added that the courts could only apply a purposive approach where the purpose is sufficiently clear. One can identify some cases where judges clearly articulate that they are taking a purposive approach and they explain why. In one such case, judges were anxious to enforce safety on the railways and rejected the literal interpretation sought by Railtrack to excuse itself: *Railtrack Plc v Smallwood* [2001] EWHC Admin 78. Another excellent and explicit example of a purposive interpretation is *Callery v Gray (No.1)* [2001] EWCA Civ 1117 where the CA had to make sense of the Access to Justice Act's provisions as to costs in conditional fee agreement cases, discussed in Ch.10 on civil procedure. The *Jackson* case, above, provides another example of a broad, purposive approach, with the courts fully examining the political background and history of the Parliament Acts. Also, taking a practical view, Lord Woolf pointed out that a number of Acts had been passed according to the procedure the Parliament Acts had established. Unravelling all of them would not be easy.

Both the European Court of Human Rights and the Court of Justice of the EU take a broad purposive approach to interpretation, described as "teleological". English and Welsh judges are well aware of this and use it themselves in relevant cases. A purposive approach can lead to a different interpretation of words from a literal construction. In *Laroche v Spirit of Adventure* [2009] EWCA Civ 12, the CA held that a hot air balloon was an "aircraft" according to the Pocket Oxford Dictionary but the plain, ordinary meaning was not necessarily determinative. On a purposive construction of the Carriage by Air Acts (Application of Provisions) Order 1967, it was reasonable to suppose that Parliament intended such balloons to be included, as they were capable of being used for international transport.

The topics of interpreting EU law and the UK's obligations under the European Convention on Human Rights are dealt with in the next two chapters.

3. Critique of legislation

The attempt to make legislation more comprehensible has a long and somewhat fruitless history. The Statute Law Society was formed in 1968. Its main object was to procure technical improvements in the form and manner in which legislation is expressed and published so as to make it more intelligible. Its first report, in 1970, said procedures must be governed by the needs of the user. This was approved in 1975 by the Renton Committee. The Rippon Commission followed almost 20 years later and listed the following principles:

2–026

- Laws are made for the benefit of citizens.
- All citizens should be involved as fully and openly as possible in the way statute law is prepared.
- Statute law should be as certain and intelligible as possible for the benefit of citizens.
- Statute law should be rooted in the authority of Parliament and thoroughly exposed to democratic scrutiny.
- Ignorance of the law being no excuse, statute law had to be as accessible as possible.
- Although governments need to be able to secure the passage of their legislation, to get the law right and intelligible is as important as getting it passed quickly.

In a 1992 critique, *Making The Law*, the Hansard Commission recommended that for every Act of Parliament, the relevant government department and Parliamentary Counsel should prepare "notes on sections", an updated version of the "notes on clauses" prepared internally for a minister during the passage of a Bill. These should be published with the Act and used by the courts in interpreting it. At last, this has been done since 1998. Bills are being presented with fairly full "explanatory notes", written in clear and simple English. They do tend to be repetitive, however, and some explanations could be clearer.

In the meantime, tax lawyers, among others, were still frustrated by the complexity of Finance Acts. In 1996, the Inland Revenue admitted tax law could be simplified and a rewrite project was launched. The Capital Allowances Bill 2001 was subjected to a four-stage consultative process involving users of tax legislation. Also in 2001, the Lords and Commons set up a Joint Committee on Tax Simplification Bills.

Tax lawyers and taxpayers are not the only people who get frustrated by confusing legislation. The group which undoubtedly has the biggest struggle and suffers from the greatest volume of legislation, as well as some of the most ill-drafted, complex and often unworkable legislation, are magistrates' clerks (legal advisers). The Justices' Clerks' Society tries to answer interpretive questions and frequently identifies lacunae in the law. They have formulated the policy that where there is a lack of clarity, any doubt should be resolved in the defendant's favour.

2–027 Sometimes legislation proves to be completely unworkable and this has repeatedly occurred in the area of criminal procedure and sentencing, which has been the subject of far too much legislation, as discussed below. For instance, the Criminal Justice and Public Order Act 1994 purported to do away with committals from magistrates' courts to the Crown Court and to replace them with transfer proceedings. When Epsom Magistrates' Court tried to use the new transfer scheme in September 1995, the bench and clerk found it did not work. Eventually, the section was abandoned and a new scheme created in 1998. Academics and the Law Commission get very frustrated when they have warned that there are gaps in a Bill or defects and ministers just ignore or even ridicule them. This frustration is expressed by Ashworth in an editorial of the March 1996 *Criminal Law Review.*

In *R. v Chambers* [2008] EWCA Crim 2467, the CA realised that for seven years no-one had noticed that the law on confiscating smuggled tobacco had changed, so over 1,000 confiscation orders were flawed. The CA said this was symptomatic of a wider problem— that the law was inaccessible to everyone today, because most of it was secondary legislation; the volume of legislation had increased; legislation could not be found in a single place and there was no comprehensive statute law database.

This brings us back to Lord Bingham's first meaning of "the rule of law", that the law must be accessible, discussed in the previous chapter. In his third chapter, he examined what this required. He cited Sir Menzies Campbell, who, as leader of the Liberal Democrats in 2007, pointed out that there had been 382 Acts in the previous ten years, including 29 Criminal Justice Acts, and more than 3,000 new criminal offences had been created. He cited the well-known description of the Criminal Justice Act 2003 and other legislation on criminal procedure as "labyrinthine", which refers to two problems. There is layer upon layer of criminal justice legislation, often produced for the sake of a news sound bite depicting the minister as "tough on crime", with new Acts being passed before the previous one has been fully implemented. Secondly, the law's obscurity is exacerbated by parliamentary drafting where new Acts cross-refer back to old Acts and statutory instruments so one cannot make sense of an Act by reading it alone.

4. Case law

Remembering that the English legal system is a common law system, indeed the mother of all common law systems, the significance of case law, i.e. common law, in creating and refining our laws cannot be underestimated. The law produced by the courts can be just as important as the law produced by Parliament. For instance, in 1991, in *R. v R.,* the House of Lords abolished the rule protecting a husband from criminal responsibility for raping his wife. By case law, I mean the decisions of judges laying down legal principles derived from the circumstances of the particular

2–028

disputes coming before them. Describing the method of reasoning of common law judges, Lord Goff said,

> "We tend to avoid large, abstract, generalisations, preferring limited, temporary, formulations, the principles gradually emerging from concrete cases as they are decided. In other words, we tend to reason upwards from the facts of the cases before us, whereas our continental colleagues tend to reason downwards from abstract principles embodied in a code." ("The Future of the Common Law" (1997) 46 I.C.L.Q. 745 at 753, as cited by Bell (2008), at. p.13).

I referred to this contrast in Ch1. Common law judges reason from the bottom up. Judges in civil law countries, notably European jurisdictions, reason from the top (principles) down.

The meaning of precedent

2–029   The doctrine of judicial precedent is known as stare decisis (to stand by decisions). In a system of *binding* precedent, When a judge comes to try a case, she *must* always look back to see how previous judges in the senior courts have dealt with cases (precedents) involving similar facts in that branch of the law. She expects to discover relevant legal principles. She tries to apply those principles to reach a decision consistent with the precedents and if the facts of her case are slightly different, she may need to develop the principle a little further. The advantages and disadvantages of precedent are straightforward and set out in the 1966 practice statement, cited below.

The doctrine of precedent in operation

2–030   The system operates as a hierarchy.

The Court of Justice of the EU and the European Court of Human Rights

2–031   Decisions of the former are binding on all English and Welsh courts. Decisions of the latter must be "taken account of", following the Human Rights Act 1998 but the UKSC has now determined that they are *not* binding. Indeed, in some cases, a dialogue has arisen between the ECtHR in Strasbourg and the UK's top court. In *R. v Horncastle* [2009] UKSC 14, the UKSC declined to follow the ECtHR on Art.6 (fair trial), in a case on hearsay evidence, yet previously, it had said the HL was bound by the ECtHR in a case on control orders, *Home Secretary v AF* [2009] UKHL 14. There is a useful commentary by E. Craven & R. Pennington-Benton, in 2010. In the 2009 case, Lord Hoffmann felt that the ECtHR decision was wrong but that the UKHL had to submit, or be in breach of our Convention obligation. In the later case, however, the seven-panel UKSC expressed concern as to whether the ECtHR fully understood the domestic (English) procedure or took account of common law safeguards against an unfair trial. It recognised the possibility of a dialogue between the two courts and, in turn, the ECtHR adjourned the reference of its own previous decision to a grand chamber, pending the UKSC decision. The authors point out that judicial dialogue between the two courts has occurred before, on Art.8 and housing possession proceedings. In *Doherty v Birmingham CC* [2008] UKHL 37, the UKHL (law lords) declined to follow the ECtHR in *McCann v UK* (2008) 47 EHRR 40, Lord Hope commenting that the Strasbourg decision was "almost useless". In the past, the ECtHR has overturned its own previous decision, following "clarifications" of domestic law by the law lords: *Osman v UK* (2000) 29 EHRR 245, which is a testament to the powerful international influence of the UK's top court, discussed in the last chapter. We now await the ECtHR's decision in *Horncastle*.

The House of Lords Appellate Committee/UK Supreme Court

Decisions of the House of Lords and, from 2009, the UK Supreme Court, are binding on all the courts lower in the hierarchy. Until 1966, the law lords considered themselves bound by their own precedents but, by a formal Practice Statement, they announced that in future they would not regard themselves as necessarily bound by their own previous decisions. The Practice Statement (HL: Judicial Precedent) [1966] 1 W.L.R. 1234 is worth quoting at length, as it gives us a neat summary of the arguments for and against a rigid system of binding precedent.

2–032

"Their Lordships regard the use of precedent as an indispensable foundation upon which to decide what is the law and its application to individual cases. It provides at least some degree of certainty upon which individuals can rely in the conduct of their affairs, as well as a basis for orderly development of legal rules. Their Lordships nevertheless recognise that too rigid adherence to precedent may lead to injustice in a particular case and also unduly restrict the proper development of the law. They propose, therefore, to modify their present practice and, while treating former decisions of this House as normally binding, to depart from a previous decision when it appears right to do so. In this connection they will bear in mind the danger of disturbing retrospectively the basis on which contracts, settlements of property and fiscal arrangements have been entered into and also the especial need for certainty as to the criminal law. This announcement is not intended to affect the use of precedent elsewhere than in this House."

There have not been many instances of the law lords departing from a previous decision. In *Herrington v British Railways Board* [1972] A.C. 877 the Court revised a long-standing legal principle concerned with the duty of care owed to a child trespasser. Under the old law, child trespassers were unprotected and by 1972, the law lords considered this rule far too harsh. In *R. v Shivpuri* [1987] A.C. 1 the House departed from a decision given only one year earlier when reconsidering the law relating to criminal attempts. A very significant instance was *R. v G & R* [2003] UKHL 50 which reversed the effect of *R. v Caldwell* [1982] A.C. 341, which had redefined and broadened the meaning of "recklessness" in the Criminal Damage Act 1971 (and consequently criminal law in general) to include offenders who had not foreseen a risk. The House noted that *Caldwell* had been subject to forceful academic, judicial and practitioner criticism, as producing unfair results. They examined the Law Commission's Draft Criminal Code Bill and its working paper prior to the 1971 Act and decided Parliament had never intended to broaden the ambit of the criminal law in this way. In this case, the House clearly saw themselves as morally justified in departing from precedent in correcting its unfair effects. In *A. v Hoare* [2008] UKHL 6, on the urging of the CA, the law lords overruled *Stubbings v Webb* [1993] A.C. 498, to avoid the harshness of the limitation period and thus allow victims to sue in historic abuse and rape claims—another decision driven by morality. See, similarly *Horton v Sadler* [2006] UKHL 27. By way of contrast, in *Jindal Iron and Steel Co Ltd v Islamic Solidarity Shipping Co Jordan Inc* [2004] UKHL 49, the House declined to overturn a 1957 precedent, because it had stood for 50 years, had worked satisfactorily, had not produced unfair results and an enormous number of transactions had taken place assuming that it was the law. In the final case the law lords decided, in July 2009, before transforming into the UKSC, *R. (on the application of Purdy) v DPP* [2009] UKHL 45, they ruled that Art.8(1) of the European Convention on HR was engaged, when a terminally ill person sought assisted suicide, departing from their previous decision in *R. (on the application of Pretty) v DPP* [2002] 1 All E.R. and instead following the ECtHR in *Pretty v UK* (2346/02) [2002] 2 F.C.R. 97. These cases are discussed in Ch.4 on human rights.

The UKSC has followed the practice of the law lords, in departing from its previous decisions where it sees fit. In *Manchester CC v Pinnock* [2010] UKSC 45, the Court considered a number of ECtHR cases expressing the principle that in housing possession cases, the proportionality principle must apply and they departed from previous HL judgments. In *Spiller v Joseph* [2010] UKSC 53, they renamed the defence of "fair comment" in defamation actions to "honest comment" because it was too narrow and "society and its concerns" had changed because "millions now talk and thousands now comment in electronically transmitted words, about recent events. . ." (per Lord Walker).

The Court of Appeal

Unless they conflict with the Human Rights Act 1998, House of Lords decisions are binding on the CA, even if the Court is very unhappy with an unjust result: *A v Hoare* [2006] EWCA Civ 395, but below, I describe a 2006 case where the CA decided to follow the persuasive precedent of the Judicial Committee of the Privy Council (JCPC), rather than the binding precedent of the HL, because it knew the JCPC decision represented the views of contemporary law lords, sitting as the JCPC. The Civil Division of the CA binds all courts except the House of Lords. The CA binds itself for the future, according to the decision in *Young v Bristol Aeroplane Co* [1944] K.B. 718, although it may escape if: (i) a later decision of the House of Lords (or UKSC) applies; (ii) there are previous conflicting decisions of the CA; or (iii) the previous decision was made *per incuriam*, i.e. in error, because some relevant precedent or statutory provision was not considered by the Court. An example of such a decision, which the Divisional Court of the Queen's Bench Division considered was decided *per incuriam*, was *Thai Trading* [1998] Q.B. 781, on the legality of a contingency fee agreement entered into by a solicitor. The House of Lords authority of *Swain v Law Society* [1983] 1 A.C. 598 had not been cited. It was obviously binding on the CA and they decided wrongly, in ignorance of it, so *Thai Trading* is a *per incuriam* decision and not binding on any court. Note that the respondents in the case were unrepresented and without a lawyer to do the legal research, the binding precedent had been overlooked. With an increasing number of litigants in person, this problem is bound to occur, which is why judicial assistants were invented, in the 1990s, to do background research for judges in cases like this. Litigants in person (LIPs) are examined in Ch.10 on civil procedure. Later case law added another exception: (iv) the CA is not bound by an interlocutory decision of two CA judges. There appear to be more exceptions, according to Smith, Bailey and Gunn, the textbook mentioned at the end of Ch.1: (v) Where a CA decision conflicts with an earlier HL or UKSC decision, (vi) where a previous CA decision conflicts with international law and (vii) where the CA is the court of last resort, with no appeal available to the UKSC. Furthermore, (viii) the CA will not follow its previous decision which conflicts with the Human Rights Act 1998.

2–033

The Criminal Division of the CA does not consider itself always bound by its own decisions. Where the liberty of the subject is concerned, the court feels itself free to overrule a previous decision if it appears that the law was misunderstood or misapplied "and if a departure from authority is necessary in the interests of justice to an appellant": *R. v Spencer* [1985] 2 W.L.R. 197, affirmed in [1987] A.C. 128. An example occurred in *R. v Shoult* [1996] 2 Cr. App. R. (S.) 234. The Court declined to follow *R. v Cook* [1996] 1 Cr. App. R. 350, in considering an appeal against a prison sentence for a drink-driving conviction. This flexible approach has especially applied since October 2000, where the court has chosen to modify the law in accordance with the European Convention on Human Rights and can clearly be seen in the case law on the Criminal Appeal Act discussed in Ch.12 on criminal procedure. A court of five may overrule a bench of three.

The High Court

2–034 Decisions of a single judge in the HC are binding on the lower courts but not on other HC judges. If a HC judge is presented with a precedent from a previous HC case he will treat the precedent as "persuasive", and not as "binding". Decisions by a Divisional Court of the HC are binding on judges of the same Division sitting alone but not necessarily on future Divisional Courts: *R. v Greater Manchester Coroner Ex p. Tal* [1985] Q.B. 67. The Upper Tribunal and Administrative Court should follow one another's decisions, because of judicial comity and the common law method, despite the fact that HC judges do not normally bind one another: *R. (on the application of B) v Islington LBD* [2010] All E.R. (D) 97 August 2010.

The county court, the Crown Court and magistrates' courts

2–035 The decisions of these courts are seldom reported and not binding.

Binding and persuasive

2–036 Depending on the status of the court, a precedent may be binding or persuasive. Precedents which come from the JCPC or other common law jurisdictions are persuasive, and the adoption of concepts developed in other common law courts has influenced English common law, as described in Ch.1. Sometimes, the top court considers developments in other common law jurisdictions but decides not to adopt them into English law. This occurred in *Transco Plc v Stockport MBC* [2003] UKHL 61. The House restated the rule in *Rylands v Fletcher* (1868) L.R. 3 H.L. 330, rejecting a submission that it had been absorbed into the law of negligence, as held in the Australian High Court.

In a unique decision, *R. v James, R. v Karimi* [2006] EWCA Crim 14, the Court of Appeal decided to follow a JCPC decision instead of an earlier HL decision. The JCPC had decided in *R. v Holley* [2005] UKPC 23, an appeal from Jersey, that the House of Lords precedent on provocation in murder, *R. v Smith (Morgan)* [2000] 3 WLR 654 had been wrongly decided. The board of the JCPC consisted of nine of the 12 Lords of Appeal in Ordinary (law lords) and this fact and their lordships' comments indicated to the CA that they had decided to use the case as a vehicle to review *Morgan Smith* as it applied in English law, not just in the law of Jersey. The Lord Chief Justice said that if they followed *Morgan Smith*, the law lords would be sure to overrule them and the law would be reduced to a game of ping-pong.

Terminology

Where a judge finds that a precedent to which she is referred is not strictly relevant to the facts of the case before her, she is said to "distinguish" that case. As such, the case is not binding upon her. If, on the other hand, she holds that a precedent is relevant, and applies it, she is said to "follow" the reasoning of the judge in the earlier case. When an appeal court is considering a precedent, it may "approve" or "disapprove" of the principle of law it established. It can "overrule" the principle if the case was decided by a court junior in status. A decision is said to be "reversed" when a higher court, on appeal, comes to the opposite conclusion to the court whose order is the subject of the appeal.

2–037

Ratio decidendi and obiter dicta

The most important and binding element of a judgment is the legal principle which is the reason for the decision, the ratio decidendi. The remainder of the judgment, such as explanatory statements and other legal principles argued before the court, are called obiter dicta or things said by the way. The whole of a dissenting (disagreeing minority) judgment is obiter. It is the ratio of a decision which constitutes the binding precedent, or rationes if there is more than one reason. When a court is referred to a precedent, the first task is to decide what was the ratio of that case, and to what extent it is relevant to the principle to be applied in the present case. Whilst an obiter dictum is not binding, it can, if it comes from a highly respected judge, be very helpful in establishing the legal principles in a later case. Of course, most cases are decided in the lower courts, according to their facts. The judge assesses the strength of the evidence and makes findings of fact. These do not form part of the ratio.

Trying to extrapolate the ratio from multiple judgments with differing sets of reasoning is a miserable task, as the CA complained

2–038

in *Doherty v Birmingham CC* [2006] EWCA Civ 1739 when they had to make sense of six law lords' judgments. They referred to Lord Bingham's definition of the rule of law again: that the law should be accessible and intelligible. Since Doherty, there have been many judicial speeches and articles on this subject. Carnwath L.J., Arden L.J. and Neuberger M.R. are critical of multiple judgments and have been urging the UKSC to give single judgments. Most UKSC Justices are sympathetic with this. They claim they try to give simple judgments more often but cannot always achieve it. At the UKSC's first anniversary seminar, in September 2010, Baroness Hale was campaigning for single judgments. She presented a paper, "Judgment Writing in the Supreme Court", which can be found on the UKSC website. She said the Judicial Assistants had rated the *Jewish Schools* case as the lowest point in the first year, because of its nine judgments. She said that when they had been law lords, they rarely tried to devise jointly authored or "plurality" opinions, though *R. (Aweys) v Birmingham City Council* [2009] UKHL 36 was a joint effort between her and Lord Neuberger. In the UKSC, they could deliver judgments in whatever order they chose. A judicial assistant had examined the first 57 decided cases.

> "He found that in 20, there was a 'judgment of the court'; and in a further 11, there was either a single judgment (with which all the other Justices agreed), or a single majority judgment (with which all the Justices in the majority agreed), or an 'effectively' single or single majority judgment (because separate judgments were simply footnotes or observations). So 31, or more than half, came out as plurality or effectively plurality judgments."

She examined the well-known arguments for and against multiple judgments. For instance, Lord Reid felt that single judgments were undesirable because they were treated as if they were words in an Act of Parliament. He and Lord Bingham had criticised single JCPC judgments as inferior in quality for developing the law. Nevertheless, said Baroness Hale,

> "I suggest that we should have a flexible approach in which each Justice is free to write but a climate of collegiality and co-operation in plurality judgments is encouraged. At the very least, however many judgments there are, there should never be any doubt about what has been decided and why."

She said that if you had plurality judgments, you could still have certain sorts of concurring judgment. This approach to judgment-writing is common elsewhere in the world: the US, Canada and the ECtHR. This is not the same as prohibiting dissent, as in the US Supreme Court and the Court of Justice of the EU. Baroness Hale said it promotes "much more collegiality".

Law Reports

A system of binding precedent is dependent on the publication of **2–039** reported cases. Law reporting dates back to the thirteenth century. The earliest case summaries were collected in manuscript form in what became known as the *Year Books*. These were prepared by students or practitioners and circulated among the judges and leading barristers. With the invention of printing, the production of law reports between the sixteenth and nineteenth centuries became common practice. They are published under the reporters' names. They have been republished in a series called *The English Reports*, covering 1220–1865.

In 1870, the Incorporated Council of Law Reporting was established. It publishes the Official Law Reports (See Reeves). They are published some time after the judgment has been given, but are regarded as authentic because the judges have corrected them. Approved judgments handed down in the HC or CA can be copied immediately. Unapproved judgments are only given to the parties involved. HC and CA decisions are available online, via HM Courts & Tribunals Service website and UKSC decisions are available on the UKSC website. The *Weekly Law Reports* (W.L.R.) and *All England Law Reports* (All E.R.) are published commercially by firms of law publishers. They are in hard copy and online on subscriber databases. All decisions of the Crown Court, HC and above, whether or not reported elsewhere, are stored on *Westlaw* and *Lexis*. The best free source of full law reports is the British and Irish Legal Information Institute website. As well as these full reports, a number of law magazines carry summaries of recent case decisions, as do *The Times* and *Independent*. From 2001, all judgments of the senior courts are numbered and have numbered paragraphs, not pages. This neutral citation of judgments caters for those cited from electronic sources.

Citation of judgments

To try to control the multiple citation of precedents of different **2–040** value in reports of varying accuracy, the Lord Chief Justice has issued a number of Practice Directions. Approved reserved judgments of the CA and HC can be cited as soon as handed down. No more than ten authorities should be included in the bundle. If a case is reported in the official Law Reports, that one should be used. If not but it appears in the *Weekly Law Reports* or *All England Law Reports*, then they can be cited. If not reported in any of these, specialist private reports may be cited. Unreported cases may not be cited without permission. In the civil courts, county court judgments and those on applications may not normally be cited. Advocates are now required to state, in their skeleton argument, the proposition of law demonstrated by each authority they wish to cite and they must justify citation of more than one authority for each proposition. If advocates wish to cite foreign authorities they must justify doing so and certify that there was no English authority on the point. The CA is constantly reminding careless advocates of these requirements: *TW v A City Council* [2011] EWCA Civ 17.

Advocates have a common law duty to the court to achieve and maintain appropriate levels of competence and care: *Harley v McDonald* [2001] UKPC 18. They still have a duty to draw to the attention of the court authorities which support their *opponent's* case. Doubtless this attempt by the judges to limit citations stems from the uncontrolled growth in the number of precedents lawyers will incorporate in their arguments, as demonstrated by a small piece of statistical research by Zander. In 2000, he showed that the number of authorities referred to in judgments had almost doubled since Diamond's research in 1965, from an average of 8.9 to 15.6. The percentage of those authorities cited which were unreported had almost quadrupled and the percentage of overseas authorities cited had increased from 3.7 per cent to 7.5 per cent.

5. Prerogative power

2–041   As the monarch no longer has any power under our unwritten constitution, the residue of the monarch's power is exercised by the Prime Minister or another Government minister. The prerogative includes the power to conduct foreign relations, enter treaties, declare war and peace, confer honours, issue pardons, secretly vet jurors and a list of more uncertain activities. To help clarify prerogative powers, a House of Commons Committee published a list in 2003. Where a statute deals with an activity previously exercised by way of prerogative power, the courts will presume that the statute has eclipsed and replaced it. In 2004, Professor Jeffrey Jowell suggested that they should be codified. In 2006, The House of Lords Constitutional Affairs Committee examined the Government's use of prerogative power to declare war, prompted by our involvement in Iraq. They called for evidence on whether a statutory framework should be introduced and whether the Prime Minister should be required to explain the legal justification for war.

Orders in Council are laws made by the Prime Minister, within the Privy Council. In *R. (Bancoult) v SS for Foreign and Commonwealth*

Affairs (No.2), [2008] UKHL 61, the law lords held that an Order in Council was *primary* legislation, like an Act of Parliament, but did not share the characteristics of an Act of Parliament. Sovereignty of Parliament was founded on the unique authority of Parliament which derived from its representative character. An OC was an act of the executive and was thus reviewable by the courts. Roger Smith pointed out some concerns about OCs. They by-pass Parliamentary debate and thus the procedure for certification of compliance with the Human Rights Act: "Beyond satirical debate?" (2009) 159 N.L.J. 212 and see a JUSTICE pamphlet on *The Constitutional Role of the Privy Council and the Prerogative*. OCs are often used in controversial circumstances. Margaret Thatcher used one to ban union membership at the Government Communication Headquarters. An OC was also used to frustrate a court ruling and prevent the Chagos islanders returning home, which was unsuccessfully challenged in the *Bancoult* case, above.

6. Custom

English "common" law was derived from the different customary laws of the existing Anglo-Saxon tribal groups, and was developed into a common, nationally applicable law, after England became one nation, with one king and one government, hence the phrase "common law". Custom then continued to play a part over the medieval period. Customs were absorbed into the legal system, sometimes in the form of legislation and sometimes, particularly in the earliest period, by the judges giving decisions which were based on custom. The gradual result was that custom virtually disappeared as a creative source of law. Nowadays, exceptionally, custom may be recognised by a court if it can be convinced that a particular local custom applies. Custom may be pleaded as a defence. The rules for its acceptance are strict. Recognised custom does, however, play a very important part in the interpretation of international law, as explained below.

2–042

7. Books of authority

Certain books of antiquity can be regarded as a source of law. The following works, most of which were written by judges, are accepted as books of authority.

2–043

Blackstone, *Commentaries on the Laws of England* (1765): a survey of the principles of English law in the mid-eighteenth century, intended for students. It was meant as a commentary but was taken as a statement of the law by early American lawyers.

Bracton, *De Legibus et Consuetudinibus Angliae* (c.1250): mainly commentaries on the forms of action with case illustrations; a major study of the common law.

Coke, *Institutes of the Laws of England* (1628): an attempted exposition of the whole of English law.

Fitzherbert, *Nature Brevium* (c.1534): a commentary on the register of writs.

Foster, *Crown Cases* (1762): criminal law.

Glanvill, *De Legibus et Consuetudinibus Angliae* (c.1189): authoritative on the land law and the criminal law of the twelfth century.

Hale, *History of the Pleas of the Crown* (1736) (60 years after Hale's death): the first history of the criminal law.

Hawkins, *Pleas of the Crown* (1716): a survey of the criminal law and criminal procedure.

Littleton, *Of Tenures* (c.1480): a comprehensive study of land law.

Modern textbooks are not treated as works of authority although they are frequently referred to in court. Advocates are permitted to adopt a textbook writer's view as part of their argument. Judges will often quote from a textbook in the course of giving judgment. In *R. v Shivpuri* [1987] A.C. 1 the law lords paid tribute to an article in the *Cambridge Law Journal* by Professor Glanville Williams. This article had a considerable influence on the court in persuading it to reverse its previous ruling. Sometimes the judge will decide that a statement in a textbook on a particular point is incorrect. In *R. v Moloney* [1985] A.C. 905 the House of Lords held that the definition of "intent" in *Archbold*, the virtual bible of criminal court practice, was "unsatisfactory and potentially misleading". The reason why no textbooks since Blackstone's *Commentaries* have been accepted as works of authority seems to be that: (i) case reports have become fuller and much more easily accessible; and (ii) by that time the principles of the common law were fully established.

8. International law as a source of English law

2–044   There are two types, private and public international law. The former deals with such things as family law—what happens when there is a divorce between nationals of two different jurisdictions, who has care and control of the children and what happens if one kidnaps the children and takes them abroad. It also determines, for instance, what law should govern a dispute arising out of a car accident between nationals of two different states which takes place in a third. Private disputes between individuals or commercial organisations, such as those arbitrated in London, discussed in Ch.11 on alternatives to the civil courts, may also be governed by elements of international law. Public international law (PIL) governs relations between states and the entities of states and creations of states, such as the United Nations and the World Bank. Over the decades of the twentieth century and even before, we have created a number of fora to resolve international disputes. The War Crimes Tribunal for the former Yugoslavia, in the Hague, tried the former President Milosovic in 2005 and has just started trying Ratco Mladic, in 2011. Those who wish to keep up with war crime trials may do so via the links on the United Nations website. PIL regulates such matters as the carriage of goods by air and sea, use of illegal drugs and war crimes. As individuals become more mobile in their domestic, social and working lives and with globalisation of the market place, so UK governments sign up to more and more treaties obliging us to enact domestic legislation giving effect to them and so we see more international litigation in the English courts. In Ch.1, we saw that Lord Bingham regarded the rule of law as requiring compliance by states with their obligations under international law and Ch.10 of his book, *The Rule of Law*, is an informative plain-English analysis of the position of international law. Qureshi's very useful articles examine the attitude of the English courts to PIL issues. One fascinating aspect of PIL these explain is the recognition of custom in PIL. We bind ourselves to the explicit obligations of treaties but are also bound by the tacit rules of custom. Customary international law (CIL) is law which is a product of consensus amongst the community of nations. States regard it as binding in their dealing with other states. English courts have regarded CIL as part of the common law since *Triquet v Bath* (1764) 3 Burr. 1478. Qureshi quoted Lord Lloyd in the first *Pinochet* case [2000] 1 A.C. 61 on the effect of CIL in English law:

"The application of international law as part of the law of the land means that, subject to the overriding effect of statute law, rights and duties flowing from the rules of [customary international law] will be recognised and given effect by the English courts without the need for any specific act adopting those rules into English law."

In applying and interpreting international conventions, the courts will apply a purposive construction, as the House of Lords did in *Sidhu v British Airways Plc* [1997] A.C. 430. This case also determined that domestic common law cannot override a convention to which the UK is a contracting party. In this case, the parties sought to sue for damages at common law but the Lords held that their remedies were limited to those available for international carriage by air according to the Warsaw Convention. It provided a comprehensive code with a uniform international interpretation which could be applied in the courts of contracting parties, exclusive of any reference to domestic law. Remember this case the next time your luggage goes missing or gets damaged when you fly. The European Convention on Human Rights and EU law are such important elements of international law in the UK that they merit separate chapters of this book.

BIBLIOGRAPHY & FURTHER READING

2–045   Dame Mary Arden, "Modernising Legislation" [1998] P.L. 65.

J. Barnes, "The continuing debate about "plain language" legislation: a law reform conundrum" (2006) Stat. L.R. 83.

R. Buxton, "How the common law gets made: Hedley Byrne and other cautionary tales" (2009) 125 L.Q.R. 60–78, *Westlaw*.

C. Banner and T. Boutle, "Challenging the Commons" (2004) 154 N.L.J 1466.

J. Bell "Sources of Law", in A. Burrows (ed.), *English Private Law* (2008).

J. Bell and G. Engle, *Cross on Statutory Interpretation* (1995).

F.A.R. Bennion, letter, (1997) 147 N.L.J. 684.

F.A.R. Bennion, "A Naked Usurpation" (1999) 149 N.L.J. 421.

Rt Hon. Lord Bingham of Cornhill C.J., "A Criminal Code: Must We Wait Forever?" [1998] Crim. L.R. 694.

T. Bingham, *The Business of Judging* (2000).

S. Burns, "Tipping the Balance" (2006) 156 N.L.J. 787.

E. Craven and R. Pennington-Benton, "When Strasbourg speaks" 160 (2010) N.L.J. 377.

Editorial on post-legislative scrutiny, *Statute Law Review*, April 2008, p.1.

J.D. Heydon, "Limits to the Powers of Ultimate Appellate Courts" (2006) 122 L.Q.R. 399–425 (on precedent).

C. Jenkins, "Helping the Reader of Bills and Acts" (1999) 149 N.L.J. 798.

Lord Judge C.J., speech at the Mansion House dinner for HM judges, on the tyranny of Henry VIII clauses, July 13, 2010.

Professor Jowell was appearing on BBC Radio 4 in the *Unreliable Evidence* series.

C. Manchester and D. Salter, *Exploring the Law* (latest edition).

K.M. Qureshi, "International Law and the English Courts" (2001) 151 N.L.J. 787.

K. Qureshi QC, "International Rescue" (2009) 159 N.L.J. 223 and 255, on the increased use of public international law in the ELS.

P. Reeves, "Law Reporting from the 13th to the 21st Century" (2000) 164 *Justice of the Peace* 1023.

J. Rozenberg, "Bin Henry VIII clauses Ken Clarke told", *Guardian*, July 15, 2010.

J. R. Spencer, "The Case for a Code of Criminal Procedure" [2000] Crim. L.R. 519.

M. Zander, "What precedents and other source materials do the courts use?" (2000) 150 N.L.J. 1790.

M. Zander, *The Law Making Process* (latest edition).

Articles on the Diane Blood case in *The Times*, October 18, 1996 and other news media in 2001.

British and Irish Legal Information Institute.
Parliament.
Welsh Assembly Government.
Scottish Parliament.
The Statute Law Review.

3. EU Law: Its Impact on English Law and the English Courts

"DETERMINED to lay the foundations of an ever closer union among the peoples of Europe". (The first aim of the preamble of the Treaty of Rome 1957).

"The Treaty is like an incoming tide. It flows into the estuaries and up the rivers. It cannot be held back". (Lord Denning M.R. in *HP Bulmer v J Bollinger SA* (1974, CA)).

"The rise of the City firms of solicitors (and parallel firms in other cities) has made Britain the legal capital of Europe". (Robert Stevens, 1994).

1. EU law is part of UK law

Membership of the European Union, formerly Common Market, **3–001** has dramatically curtailed the sovereignty of Parliament in the UK constitution, in certain contexts. It is simply unrealistic to consider the English legal system or English sources of law in isolation from the EU, as the ambit of EU power is extended, so the bulk of substantive law accelerates in growth, and it is no longer appropriate to consider EU law as a single subject. Apart from the Treaties and Regulations, which are directly applicable in all Member States without further ado (and made binding in UK law by the European Communities Act 1972, s.2), most statute law comes into the UK "by the back door", through the medium of delegated legislation, but it is scrutinised in Parliament by committees in both Houses. The UK Parliament website provides details.

The interpretive and other judgments of the Court of Justice of the European Union are also a source of EU law and they and the

EU Treaties and secondary legislation have to be interpreted by the English and Welsh courts. All our magistrates, judges and other adjudicators must treat questions as to the meaning or effect of the Treaties and EU instruments as questions of law to be determined in accordance with principles laid down by the Court of Justice. On any such question, they must take judicial notice of the Treaties, the *Official Journal* and decisions or opinions of the Court of Justice or General Court. This is laid down in the European Communities Act 1972, s.3, as amended. This means that all Court of Justice rulings are binding precedents to be applied in the English and Welsh courts. Here, I provide a simple and very basic guide to the institutions of the EU and the sources of EU law. I return to EU law in the UK below. Until December 1, 2009, EU law was officially known as "Community law". The website explains "Community law has therefore become European Union law, which also includes all the provisions previously adopted under the Treaty on European Union as applicable before the Treaty of Lisbon". In this chapter, the term Community law is used in case law and instruments created before December 2009.

London is one of the major legal centres in the world. Historically a centre for international trade, insurance, litigation and arbitration, it now hosts large American and international law firms, established here as a springboard into Europe. Indeed, firms from 40 different countries have offices in London. UK lawyers are the most mobile in Europe, the most likely to establish practice in the other Member States, a right established under an EC Directive. The sooner the law student grasps the importance of EU law as part of UK law, the better. It is not some foreign law imposed on us by Brussels, as some English news media portray it.

2. The Treaties

3–002   The Common Market was created by the signing of the Treaty of Rome in 1957. The primary aims of its first six members were economic, to set up a common market, but as the Treaty states, its signatories were "determined to lay the foundations of an ever closer union among the peoples of Europe . . .by. . .pooling their resources to preserve and strengthen peace and liberty". The Treaty of Rome, EC Treaty, now consolidated with the amending Reform Treaty (Treaty of Lisbon 2007) became known as the Treaty on the Functioning of the EU, on December 1, 2009. The TFEU remains an essential source of EU law, as well as the EU's constitution. Incorporation of the Treaty of Rome and the other EU Treaties into

English law was brought about by the European Communities Act 1972. The other major instruments are the Single European Act of 1986, which created the single European market, effective by the end of 1992; the Treaty on EU (TEU, Maastricht Treaty), ratified in 1993, which extended the scope of EU competence and provided for economic and monetary union and Union citizenship; the Treaty of Amsterdam, signed in 1997 and in force in 1999 and the Treaty of Nice, in force in 2003, which expanded the Union from 15 Member States to 25. The European Union used to consist of three pillars: the European Community, the central law making and law enforcing unit, and the two outside pillars, Justice and Home Affairs and Foreign and Social Policy. This structure has now gone, thanks to the Lisbon Treaty. The Nice Treaty resulted from the Inter Governmental Conference of 2000. It provided for enlargement, and for alterations to the Council and Commission, increasing the Assembly (Parliament).

In October 1991, the European Economic Area was created, including States subjected to EU law on the internal market and competition but not represented in the institutions. Ten of those States joined the Union after the Treaty of Nice came into effect. Bulgaria and Romania joined in 2007. After a failed attempt to introduce an EU constitution, The Treaty of Lisbon was signed in 2007 and, after ratification by all Member States, came into force in 2009. The detail of the Treaty is on the Europa website but its headlines are:

"**A more democratic and transparent Europe**, with a strength-ened role for the European Parliament and national parliaments, more opportunities for citizens to have their voices heard and a clearer sense of who does what at European and national level. . .

A more efficient Europe, with simplified working methods and voting rules, streamlined and modern institutions for a EU of 27 members and an improved ability to act in areas of major priority for today's Union. . .

A Europe of rights and values, freedom, solidarity and secu-rity, promoting the Union's values, introducing the Charter of Fundamental Rights into European primary law, providing for new solidarity mechanisms and ensuring better protection of European citizens. . .

Europe as an actor on the global stage will be achieved by bringing together Europe's external policy tools, both when developing and deciding new policies. The Treaty of Lisbon gives Europe a clear voice in relations with its partners world-wide. It harnesses Europe's economic, humanitarian, political and diplomatic strengths to promote European interests and values worldwide, while respecting the particular interests of the Member States in Foreign Affairs." (from "The Treaty at a Glance").

A more serious description is the information note on the Treaty of Lisbon published on the website by the General Secretariat of the Council of the EU. There is more information on all the treaties on the Europa website.

> There are 27 Member States. The six founder members of the Common Market in 1957 were France, Germany, Italy, Belgium, Luxembourg and The Netherlands. The UK joined in 1973. By 2002, the Union consisted of 15 counties after the accession of Denmark, Greece, Spain, Ireland, Austria, Portugal, Finland and Sweden. In 2004, the EU was joined by 10 more states: Estonia, Lithuania, Latvia, Poland, Hungary, the Czech Republic, Slovakia, Slovenia, Malta and Cyprus. Romania and Bulgaria joined in 2007.

3. Institutions

3–003   There are now seven basic EU institutions. We are concerned with the Parliament, the Council, the European Council, the Commission and the Court of Justice. Details of the Court of Auditors, European Central Bank and other EU bodies are all on the Europa website.

The European Parliament (Arts 223–234 TFEU)

3–004   The 736 MEPs are directly elected by their Member States. They are not delegates, mandated by national interests; they are representatives. It is essential to grasp that, unlike conventional Parliaments on the Westminster model, this is not the legislature of the EU, although its powers were enhanced by the 1986 Single European Act, the Treaty on European Union 1992 and the Treaty of Lisbon. This has gone some way to remedy the institutional imbalance in the EU and the "democratic deficit" complained of by critics, that the unelected Council is the primary legislature. The Treaties of Amsterdam and Nice extended its powers of co-decision. Parliament now has a legislative role on several levels, advisory and consultative, a right to participate in conciliation and co-operation procedures and a right of co-decision in certain defined areas. The importance of the Treaty of Lisbon was to enhance Parliament's power in over 40 fields so that co-decision has now become the normal method of law-making. It has a supervisory role over the Commission, which must report to it, submit proposals when requested, and answer questions.

Parliament's dissatisfaction with the Commission, through a motion of censure, led to all the Commissioners resigning in 1999. Acting with the Council, under Art.314 TFEU, "it shall establish the Union's annual budget". It may set up set up a committee of inquiry to investigate maladministration or breaches of EU law. The Parliament has been influential over the other institutions in recognising and adopting the European Convention on Human Rights. The European Ombudsman investigates allegations of maladministration and reports to Parliament.

The Council (the Council of the European Union) (Arts 237–243 TFEU)

This body is really the legislature of the Union, though Parliament has gained much more legislative power since 2009. It is composed of one minister from each Member State. These delegates change according to the nature of the subject under discussion. For instance, on agricultural policy, states will send their agriculture ministers. On economic issues, finance ministers will attend. There are ten configurations of the Council. These are chaired by a President and the Presidency is held by each Member State on a six-month rota. The exception is the Foreign Affairs Council, which, since 2009, is chaired by a new High Representative of the Union for Foreign Affairs and Security Policy. This is currently the UK Commissioner, Baroness Ashton. The Council's job is to ensure the Treaty objectives are attained. The website summarises its role as follows.

3–005

- It adopts legislative acts (Regulations, Directives, etc.), in many cases in 'co-decision' with the European Parliament;
- It helps co-ordinate Member States' policies, for example, in the economic field;
- It develops the common foreign and security policy, on the basis of strategic guidelines set by the European Council;
- It concludes international agreements on behalf of the Union;
- It adopts the Union's budget, together with the European Parliament."

It has the final say on most EU secondary legislation but, in most cases, can only act on a proposal from the Commission. Following the implementation of the TEU, it has shared decision-making with the Parliament in some respects, indeed *most* respects, since 2009. Since the Treaty of Lisbon, it can act on a proposal signed by a million citizens. Voting strength is specified by the Treaties in accordance with the population size of each Member State. The UK is one of the four most powerful states. Not only is the Council criticised for being unelected (the democratic deficit) but it used to lack transparency. This was the only legislature outside North Korea and Cuba to sit in secret—a cause for concern for British MEPs for some years. In September 2005, the leaders of all British political groups in Brussels made an unprecedented joint declaration calling for it to sit in public. At long last, thanks to the Lisbon Treaty, the Council now sits in public when voting on legislative proposals or conducting a general debate and this is broadcast live on the internet. Discussions on foreign affairs are not public. Since it is not a permanent body, much of the Council's day to day work, initially sifting and scrutinising Commission proposals, is delegated to COREPER, the committee of permanent representatives of the Member States. It, in turn, delegates its workload to working groups. Again, COREPER lacks accountability and transparency.

EU legislative competence does not normally extend to criminal law and procedure but in *Commission v Council* (C-440/05) [2007] E.C.R. I-9097, the Court of Justice decided that it is permissible to require Member States to impose criminal penalties when the EU legislature considers it necessary to combat serious environmental offences. The UK media reacted typically on the day following the initial 2005 decision. *The Times* announced "a dramatic transfer of power from national capitals to Brussels", in an article entitled "Europe wins the power to jail British citizens" and condemned it in a leader entitled "LEGAL TRESPASS". The UK has criminalised pollution for many years so the results of the case are unremarkable in the context of environmental law. What alarmed commentators, however, was that the judgment could be interpreted to apply far beyond environmental law, as confirmed in a communication adopted by the Commission at the end of November 2005. At first glance, this seems to conflict with the principle of subsidiarity (leaving States to legislate for themselves as much as possible). The Home Office dismissed the press reaction as "nonsense".

"The provisions in question have already been agreed within the framework of the European Union, which requires Member States to implement the provisions through their national legislation. This position will remain unchanged, although in future the provisions will be adopted under EU law rather than intergovernmentally under the police and judicial co-operation part of the EU Treaty."

The European Council (Arts 235–236 TFEU)

When the Council is composed of heads of state or government **3–006** it is known, confusingly, as the European Council. It became an EU institution under the Treaty of Lisbon, on December 1, 2009. It has a President, whose renewable term is 2.5 years and it meets at least twice a year, with the Commission President. It can invite the President of the Parliament to be heard. The High Representative takes part in its work. It does not legislate. It develops Union policy and priorities, in effect setting the EU agenda.

The Commission (Arts 244–250 TFEU)

This is the EU executive and employs a civil service of over **3–007** 24,000. There is no separation of powers in the EU and it also has legislative power delegated to it by the Council. There is one Commissioner from each of the 27 Member States but each must act independently of state control. They are appointed for five years (currently 2010–14), renewable. Each has a portfolio for a particular Union activity and heads a Directorate-General. For example, the UK Commissioner, Catherine Ashton, is in an exceptionally powerful position, as the High Representative. The 2010–14 Commission is headed by its President, José Manuel Barroso, the Portuguese Commissioner. It is clear from the Lisbon Treaty that he is first among equals. The Commission's functions are as follows:

The motor

It takes the initiative on making new law and policy, making **3–008** proposals of the Commission. The Council may request the Commission to undertake studies and submit appropriate proposals. Nevertheless, this power of initiative makes the Commission very powerful in setting the agenda of the Council and Parliament. It consults widely. It draws up the budget for approval by the Parliament and Council and supervises how money is spent.

The watchdog

The Commission enforces the Member States' Treaty obligations **3–009** and may take an errant Member State to the Court of Justice, under Art.258 TFEU, should persuasion fail. An example is the Court's decision against Italy in 2002 that it was in breach of the Treaty and Directive 89/48 in failing to provide foreign lawyers with the infrastructure and freedom to provide their services in Italy: *Commission v Italy* (C-145/99) [2002] E.C.R. 1-2235. Another example was the 2003 Court of Justice ruling that Italy was in breach of its treaty obligations in insisting that British chocolate should be called "chocolate substitute" because it contained vegetable fat other than cocoa butter: *Commission v Italy* (C-14/00) [2003] E.C.R. 1-513. The

Commission can impose big fines and penalties on those in breach of EU competition law, or those who ignore decisions taken against them. Accordingly, it has extensive investigatory powers. For instance, because Germany failed to comply with rulings on water purity and protection of birds, it imposed a daily fine of £350,000 while the infringement continued.

The executive

3–010   Policies formed by the Council need detailed implementation by the Commission. Much of this is done by legislation, which requires a final decision by the Council. The Commission has its own decision-making powers and enforces competition policy.

Negotiator

3–011   In relation to the EU's external policies, the Commission acts as a negotiator, leaving agreements to be concluded by the Council, after consulting the Parliament, where this is required by the Treaty.

> What does the European Union do? It makes law and policy on: trade and enterprise, customs, consumer affairs, economic and monetary union, agriculture, fisheries, competition, freedom of movement of workers, freedom to establish business, education and training, energy, the environment, food safety, employment and social affairs, sex equality, public health, regional policy, transport, tax. It also makes policy and encourages co-operation on justice and home affairs, including human rights, foreign policy and security, external trade and humanitarian aid. See the Europa website for the full list.

The Court of Justice of the European Union (Arts 251–281)

3–012   Along with The General Court (formerly Court of First Instance) and the Civil Service Tribunal, this, the Court of Justice, is now part of the Court of Justice of the European Union.

> Do not confuse the Court of Justice with the European Court of Human Rights (ECtHR), described in Ch.4. The Court of Justice sits in Luxembourg and interprets EU law for the 27 Member States of the EU. The ECtHR is **not** an institution of the EU, It interprets and enforces the European Convention on Human Rights 1950 for the 47 contracting states that have ratified the Convention. It sits in Strasbourg.

Composition

The Court of Justice consists of 27 judges: one for each Member **3–013**
State. They are assisted by eight advocates general (AGs). It is an
AG's task to assist the Court by making a detailed analysis of all
the relevant issues of fact and law in a case before the Court and
submitting a report of this, together with recommendations, to
the Court. Thus, they can express their personal opinions, which
the judges cannot, and they can examine any related question
not brought forward by the parties. Article 253 TFEU stipulates
that both judges and AGs "shall be chosen from persons whose
independence is beyond doubt and who possess the qualifications
required for appointment to the highest judicial offices in their
respective countries or who are jurisconsults of recognised competence" (such as academic lawyers). Each judge and AG is appointed
for a renewable term of six years.

Procedure

The Court's workload has increased since 1970 when 79 cases **3–014**
were lodged, to 631 lodged in 2010 (mostly references for preliminary rulings: 385), with 636 being set down before the General
Court. This is the highest number ever. There were 799 cases pending before the Court of Justice, as of December 31, 2010, yet it only
completed 522 and the General Court only completed 527. The
General Court was created to help with this workload but, still, it
has proved necessary to devise another coping mechanism. This
has been the tendency to hear cases before a chamber of three or
five judges, reserving the Grand Chamber of 13 judges for the more
important cases (14 per cent in 2010). In his 2010 *Annual Report*
the Court's President reports "a very significant improvement in
efficiency as regards the duration of proceedings". It is currently
taking an average of 16.1 months to deal with references for preliminary rulings, which is apparently the speediest the court has ever
been. Case throughput has accelerated thanks to the adoption of an
expedited procedure for urgent preliminary references and a simplified procedure, without a hearing, and giving some judgments
without an AG's opinion. The UK has been a constant critic of the
Court's slowness and, despite the President's optimism, a 2011
committee of the House of Lords (in the UK Parliament) reported
that the Court was in "crisis" and urgently needed to appoint more
advocates-general. As of May 2011, there are still only eight.

The case for each party is submitted in written pleadings. The
President allocates one of the judges to act as a judge-rapporteur to
each case. She prepares a public report after the written procedure,
ready for the short oral hearing. It contains a summary of the facts
and legal argument. She prepares a private report to the judges,

containing her view of whether the case should be assigned to a chamber.

Meanwhile, an AG may also have been assigned to the case. This is now only done in about half of all cases. They are not assigned to cases brought by or against their native Member State. The AG prepares an opinion which is delivered orally, at the end of the oral hearing. It contains a full analysis of relevant EU law, which may give a more complete and accurate account than that produced in argument by the parties, since the lawyers appearing in the case may appear before the Court of Justice only once in their legal careers. The AG also gives his opinion as to how the Court should decide the case. It is true that the Court follows this opinion in most cases and it is thus a good indicator as to how the Court is likely to decide, as well as providing an essential explanation of the reasoning behind the Court's decision, after the event, but this opinion should never be referred to as a "ruling", as it is sometimes misreported by the British news media. After this, the AG drops out of the picture and the judges deliberate in secret, without interpreters, in a common language (traditionally, French). After deliberations, the judge-rapporteur will draft and refine the decision. There is no charge to use either court and legal aid is available to persons of "insufficient means", under their national rules.

Function

3–015   The Court is the supreme authority on all matters of EU law. In its practices and procedure, it draws on continental models, notably French procedure, but in substantive law, it borrows principles from all Member States. The TFEU is a framework, generally speaking, with few of its provisions spelled out in detail. This gives the Court latitude as a court of interpretation, in effect creating EU law and jurisprudence. Its boldness used to be matter of controversy but since we were and are watching the emergence of a whole new legal system and body of law, it is hardly surprising that the Court's decisions contain sweeping statements of principle, especially given that the Treaty of Rome was silent, even on such fundamentals as the relationship between EU law and national law (see, for instance *Costa v ENEL* (6/64) [1964] E.C.R. 1141, discussed below).

When developing new legal principles, the Court's first reference points are the objectives of the EU and the Articles of the TFEU. Over the years, it has built up a body of reported decisions. Like our UKSC, the Court is not bound by its own previous decisions but usually follows them. The judgment is a single one but without much indication of the reasoning behind it (especially in the older cases). This is where the submission of the AG comes in useful, as an explanation.

Jurisdiction

The Court of Justice's work consists mainly, but not exclusively, **3–016**
of the following list.

1. References for preliminary rulings on the interpretation of EU law from Member States' courts (Art.267 TFEU).
2. Actions brought by the Commission or a Member State against Member States for failure to fulfil obligations under EU law (Art.258 TFEU).
3. Judicial review actions for annulment of legislative or other acts of the Council, Commission or Bank, other than recommendations or opinions (Art.263 TFEU). The Lisbon treaty widened the scope for judicial review. For instance, the Committee of the Regions may challenge measures on the basis that they violate the subsidiarity principle.
4. Actions for failure to act, in infringement of the Treaties, against the Council, European Council, Commission or Parliament (Art.265 TFEU).
5. Disputes between Member States under the Treaties (Art.273 TFEU).
6. Determining the procedural legality of acts of the European Council (Art.269 TFEU).
7. Staff disputes (Art.270 TFEU).
8. Appeals on points of law from The General Court (Art.256 TFEU).
9. Actions for damages (Art.268 TFEU).

The Court of Justice of the EU does not have jurisdiction over common foreign and security policy (Art.275 TFEU), or police and law enforcement operations within Member States, or their internal security (Art.267 TFEU). Point 1 above is most important for our purposes, as this is the mechanism through which EU law is developed and interpreted in its domestic context, in English case law. Any case may be referred to the Court of Justice from any English or Welsh court or tribunal, under Art.267 TFEU (formerly Art.234 EC), where there is an item of EU law to be interpreted. The Court of Justice gives its interpretation and then remits the case to the domestic court, leaving them to apply that interpretation and then decide the case accordingly. UK courts made 29 applications in 2010 and have made 505 since 1974. Germany has made 1,802 since 1964.

General Court (Art.225)

The Single European Act (1986) provided for the establishment **3–017**
of a Court of First Instance, now called the General Court and it

began its work in 1989. Its 27 judges usually hear cases in chambers of three or five, any of whom, apart from the President, may be called upon (unusually) to act as Advocate General. Its jurisdiction was quite limited. In 1992, however, the TEU provided that the Council could transfer any area of the Court's jurisdiction to the CFI, except for preliminary rulings. A lot of work was transferred in 1993, to relieve pressure on the European Court of Justice, as the upper court was then called. By 1996, the CFI was hearing as many cases as the Court of Justice. From 2005, cases involving the EU's staff moved into the EU Civil Service Tribunal. The Nice Treaty also enabled certain Art.267 references to be transferred to the CFI *but it is very important to note that this was never done.* The General Court's current jurisdiction is listed on the Europa website and detailed in its annual report. Following the Treaty of Lisbon, Art.256 TFEU, it has jurisdiction to determine first instance actions under Arts 263, 265, 268, 270 and 272.

Article 267 TFEU Preliminary Rulings (Formerly Art.234 EC)

3–018   "The Court of Justice of the European Union has jurisdiction to give preliminary rulings on the interpretation of European Union law and on the validity of acts of the institutions, bodies, offices or agencies of the Union." (Information note on references from national courts for a preliminary ruling (2009/C 297/01)). Any court or tribunal of any Member State may make a reference. The Court's ruling on the point is then sent back to the national court to be applied in the pending case, which will have been suspended in the meantime. All national courts have a duty to apply and enforce EU law but this ability to refer when they are uncertain is designed to prevent divergent interpretation throughout the EU. These references are a significant volume of the Court's workload, as can be seen from the statistics above, and they have proven to be the essential vehicle for the Court to develop its principles and precedent. The wording of Art.267 TFEU is very important:

"The Court of Justice of the European Union shall have jurisdiction to give preliminary rulings concerning:

(a) the interpretation of this Treaty;
(b) the validity and interpretation of acts of the institutions, bodies, offices or agencies of the Union;

Where such a question is raised before any court or tribunal of a Member State, that court or tribunal may, if it considers that a decision on the question is necessary to enable it to give judgment, request the Court to give a ruling thereon.

Where any such question is raised in a case pending before a court or tribunal of a Member State against whose decisions there is no judicial remedy under national law, that court or tribunal shall bring the matter before the Court.

If such a question is raised in a case pending before a court or tribunal of a Member State with regard to a person in custody, the Court of Justice of the European Union shall act with the minimum of delay."

Paragraph (b) includes all Art.288 TFEU legislative acts, and also includes most non-binding recommendations and opinions. The Court cannot rule on facts or questions of national law so cannot rule that a national provision is incompatible with EU law but has said it will provide the national court with all necessary criteria to enable it to answer such a question. It will not rule on how law is to be applied by the domestic court but will offer guidance. It has interpreted international treaties entered into by the EU but cannot rule on the validity of the EU Treaties. From 2008, an urgent reference may be made in matters concerning police and judicial co-operation in criminal matters, visas, asylum and immigration and free movement of persons.

National Courts or Tribunals that may refer

Where the law (as opposed to a private contract) imposes an arbitrator to resolve disputes, then a question can be referred to the Court of Justice. It does not matter if the court is at the lowest level. In *McCall v Poulton and MIB* [2008] All E.R. (D) 212, the CA upheld a county court decision to refer a question on the obligations of the JMIB to compensate victims of uninsured drivers. Even a body exercising functions preliminary to its judicial function may refer. In *Pretore di Salo v Persons Unknown* (14/86) [1987] E.C.R. 2545, an Italian public prosecutor, who would later act as examining magistrate, was allowed to refer. In *El-Yassini v Secretary of State for the Home Dept* (C-416/96) [1999] All E.R. (EC) 193, the Court permitted a reference from an Immigration Adjudicator, because he was determining disputes according to statutory powers. In *Dorsch Consult* (C-54/96) [1997] E.C.R. 1-4961 the Court held

3–019

"The Court takes into account a number of factors, such as whether the body is established by law, whether it is permanent, whether its jurisdiction is compulsory, whether its procedure is *inter partes*, whether it applies rules of law and whether it is independent".

The discretion to refer

3–020   The Court has emphasised that it will not answer hypothetical questions or act on references from disputes contrived simply to test EU law. It is essential for the national court to explain why it considers a ruling to be necessary and define the factual and legislative context of the question. The timing of a reference is left to the national court, though the Court of Justice has issued guidance on its website. A national court or tribunal cannot be prevented from making a reference by a national law that it is bound to follow the decision of a higher court on the same question of EU law. In other words, our Court of Appeal (CA) could still make a reference, if they considered it necessary, despite the existence of a House of Lords or UKSC precedent on the same question of EU law. The Court emphasised in the *Rheinmuhlen-Dusseldorf* case (166/73) [1974] E.C.R. 33 that, as the object of Art.267 is to ensure that the law is the same in all Member States, domestic law cannot limit the lower court's power to make a reference if it considers the superior court's ruling could lead it to give judgment contrary to EU law.

"Necessary"

3–021   Before exercising its discretion to refer, the national court must consider a reference necessary. The Court defined this in *CILFIT v Italian Ministry of Health* (283/81) [1982] E.C.R. 3415. There is no need to refer if:

1. the question of EU law is irrelevant; or
2. the provision has already been interpreted by the Court, even though the questions at issue are not strictly identical; or
3. the correct application is so obvious as to leave no scope for reasonable doubt.

This matter must be assessed in the light of the specific characteristics of EU law, the particular difficulties to which its interpretation gives rise and the risk of divergences of judicial decisions within the Community.

"Necessary" in English Law

3–022   In *Bulmer v Bollinger (No.2)* [1974] Ch. 401 Lord Denning M.R. set out guidelines for English courts, other than the House of Lords, for deciding when it was necessary to make a reference. They were influential in a number of cases but did not meet with uncritical approval. Bingham J. warned that the Court of Justice was in a better position to determine questions of EU law because, for instance, of their expertise, their unique grasp of all the authentic language texts of that law and their familiarity with a purposive construction of EU law. Once he became Master of the Rolls, he set out this important dictum in *R. v International Stock Exchange Ex p. Else* [1993] Q.B. 534:

> "if the facts have been found and the Community law issue is critical to the court's final decision, the appropriate course is ordinarily to refer the issue to the Court of Justice unless the national court can with complete confidence resolve the issue itself. In considering whether it can with complete confidence resolve the issue itself the national court must be fully mindful of the differences between national and Community legislation, of the pitfalls which face a national court venturing into what may be an unfamiliar field, of the need for uniform interpretation throughout the Community and of the great advantages enjoyed by the Court of Justice in construing Community instruments. If the national court has any real doubt, it should ordinarily refer."

Commenting on this case, Weatherill and Beaumont, in *EU Law*, praised Lord Bingham for doing a great service in creating a presumption that national courts and tribunals should make a reference if they are not completely confident as to how the issues can be resolved.

> "This is a *communautaire* approach consistent with the spirit of judicial co-operation that is needed if the Article 234 system is to do its job of ensuring uniform interpretation of EU law throughout the Community" (3rd edn, 1999).

It is, nevertheless, a rebuttable presumption, so the English law reports have many examples of the courts declining to refer. An example is *R. v Ministry of Agriculture, Fisheries and Food Ex p. Portman Agrochemicals Ltd* [1994] 3 C.M.L.R. 18. Brooke J., in declining to refer, took account of the guidelines in previous case law but was influenced by the fact that neither of the parties wished for the case to be referred and that, given the usual 18-month delay to be expected in receiving the Court's interpretation, the answer would be redundant by the time they would receive it. Some judges have warned that English courts should exercise great caution in relying on the doctrine of "acte clair" in declining to make a reference. The Court accepts that national courts will apply this doctrine, borrowed from French law, when the interpretation of a provision is clear and free from doubt (see below). It is possible, in the English legal system, for an appeal to be made against a lower court's decision to refer. Such an appeal was successfully made in *Ex p. Else* (above), the CA holding that it was not necessary to refer.

The obligation to refer

3–023   Two questions arise here. Firstly, when is a court "a court or tribunal of a Member State against whose decisions there is no judicial remedy under national law"? There are two theories, abstract and concrete. Under the former, only the UKSC would be obliged to refer. Under the more practical concrete theory, any court from whom there is no appeal or from which appeal has been refused should be obliged to refer. The rulings of the Court of Justice seem to support the latter: *Costa v ENEL* (6/64) [1964] E.C.R. 585 (obiter). This seems to be fairer to the parties, especially where they have been refused permission to appeal and it seems more likely to achieve the harmonisation of law Art.267 is aiming at. The matter has been resolved by the ECJ itself in *Lyckeskog* (C-99/00 [2003] 1 W.L.R. 9). The Court of Justice held that courts which could be challenged did not fall into the category of court under an obligation to refer. Some critics were disturbed by this result in terms of access to justice because it presupposes the parties have the time and money to litigate right through to the last possible court before being able to obtain a reference.

The second question relates to the circumstances in which the obligation to refer arises. Although the wording of this paragraph looks mandatory, as if courts like the UKSC must refer every point of EU law to the Court of Justice, the Court has ruled, in the *Costa v ENEL* case (see below) that this is not necessary where the question raised is materially identical to a question which has already been the subject of a preliminary ruling in an earlier case. In *CILFIT* (above) the Court spelled out what they considered to be the discretion available to courts of last resort, as above, despite the wording of Art.267. They said that courts of last resort have the same discretion as others, to decide whether a reference is necessary, and that there is no obligation to refer if the criteria laid down are satisfied.

Satisfying the conditions for the application of the third *CILFIT* criterion will not, however, be easy, as the Court laid down the condition that the national court must be convinced that the matter is equally obvious to the courts of the other Member States and to the Court of Justice and they reminded courts that, in satisfying themselves of this criterion, they should bear in mind the plurilingual nature of that law and the Court's use of purposive and contextual construction. While many English judges would not shy away from a purposive and contextual approach, I am at a loss to see how the UKSC has the facilities to delve into the domestic law reports of the other 26 Member States to see how a point has been variously interpreted by other national courts, in their many national languages.

There are examples of the law lords refusing to refer a case to the Court, mainly relying on the first *CILFIT* exception, that the EU law point was irrelevant, including a case in which they refused to follow the *Von Colson* principle: *Finnegan v Clowney Youth Training Programme Ltd* [1990] 2 A.C. 407. In the very important case of *Three Rivers DC v Bank of England (No.3)* [2003] 2 A.C. 1, the law lords declined to refer. Another example occurred in *Abbey National Plc v OFT* [2009] UKSC 6. Of course the danger of not referring lies in the risk that different Member States will resolve the same issue in different ways. The information note on the website (2009/C 297/01), tells us when it is appropriate to make a reference but it really states the existing principles, as set out by case law. It is cross-referred to in the civil, criminal and specialist practice directions applicable in English and Welsh courts and tribunals (HMCTS website).

4. Sources of EU law

The sources of EU law are as follows.   3–024

1. The Treaties.
2. EU secondary legislation (regulations, directives and decisions).
3. International agreements entered into by EU institutions on the Community's behalf, using their powers under the Treaty.
4. Decisions of the Court of Justice and General Court, including general principles, developed over the years.

Article 10(5) of the EC Treaty obliged all Member States to "take all appropriate measures, whether general or particular, to ensure fulfilment" of all these obligations. This obligation, reworded, is now in Art.4(3) of the Treaty on European Union.

Secondary Legislation (Legislative Acts) Art.288 TFEU

The law-making powers of the EU institutions are laid down in   3–025
Art.288 TFEU:

"To exercise the Union's competences, the institutions shall adopt regulations, directives, decisions, recommendations and opinions.

A regulation shall have general application. It shall be binding in its entirety and directly applicable in all Member States.

A directive shall be binding, as to the result to be achieved, upon each Member State to which it is addressed, but shall leave to the national authorities the choice of form and methods.

A decision shall be binding in its entirety. A decision which specifies those to whom it is addressed shall be binding only on them.

Recommendations and opinions shall have no binding force."

These are all called "acts". Distinguish between binding and non-binding acts. Only the first three are binding.

Regulations are generally applicable and designed to apply to all situations in the abstract. Since they are binding in their entirety and directly applicable in all Member States, they may give rise to rights and obligations for states and individuals without further enactment.

Directives are binding as to the result to be achieved, upon each Member State to which they are addressed. The State thus fills in the details by enacting domestic law in accordance with the principles it is directed to put into law.

Decisions are individual acts, addressed to a specified person or persons or States. They have the force of law and, therefore, have effect without further expansion.

Acts which do not conform with procedural safeguards may be annulled. Recommendations and opinions have no binding force in law, although they are of persuasive authority.

5. Direct applicability and direct effect

3–026   To understand the application of EU law, it is necessary to have a basic grasp of the distinction between the principles of direct applicability and direct effect. It is also necessary to understand the distinction between horizontal and vertical direct effect, that is, between provisions directly effective between individuals, giving rise to rights or obligations enforceable between individuals and provisions giving rise to rights of individuals against the Member States. When the European Communities Act 1972 took the UK into the EU, or Common Market, as it then was, EU law became directly applicable, in international law terms, as if it were domestic law. The terminology becomes confusing, however, because provisions of international law which are found to be capable of application by national courts at the suit of individuals are also termed directly applicable. To spare confusion, therefore, all British writers on EU law have adopted the term "directly effective" to express this second meaning, that is, to denote provisions of EU law which give rise to rights or obligations which individuals may enforce before the national courts.

Whether a particular provision of EU law gives rise to directly effective, individually enforceable rights or obligations is a matter of construction, depending on its language and purpose. Since principles of construction vary from State to State, the same provision may not be construed as directly effective everywhere. For lawyers in the English legal system, whether a provision is directly effective is crucially important because, thanks to the concept of primacy of EU law, a directly effective provision must be given priority over any conflicting principle of domestic law. The Treaty specifies, in Art.288 TFEU, that regulations are directly applicable, but it has been left to the Court of Justice to set out, in a group of leading cases, which and when other EU provisions can have direct effect.

Treaty Articles

The issues of whether and when a Treaty Article could have direct effect was first considered in *Van Gend en Loos* (26/62) [1963] E.C.R. 3. The question arose as to whether former Art.12 EC, which prohibited States introducing new import duties, could confer enforceable rights on nationals of Member States. The Court held that it could because the text of the Article set out a clear and unconditional duty not to act. The prohibition was, thus, perfectly suited by its nature to produce direct effects in the legal relations between Member States and their citizens. The Court clearly thought it desirable that individuals should be allowed to protect their rights in this way, without having to rely on the European Commission or another Member State to take action against an offending Member State.

3–027

This case involved a flouted prohibition but Court of Justice case law soon extended direct effect to positive Treaty obligations, holding that an Article imposing upon a Member State a duty to act would become directly effective once a time-limit for compliance had expired. The Court of Justice has found a large number of Treaty provisions to be directly effective, in relation to free movement of goods and persons, competition law and discrimination on the grounds of gender or nationality. The Court applies the following criteria to test whether a provision is amenable to direct effect. It must be:

- clear and precise, especially with regard to scope and application;
- unconditional; and
- leave no room for the exercise of implementation by Member States or EU institutions.

The Court has, however, applied these conditions fairly liberally, with results as generous as possible to the individual seeking to rely on the Article. Although the *Van Gend* case involved vertical direct effect, that is, a citizen enforcing rights against a State, later case law, notably *Defrenne v SABENA* (43/75) [1981] 1 All E.R. 122, demonstrated that Treaty Articles could also have horizontal direct effect, that is, could be relied on between individuals, such as private employer and employee. A good example of the invocation of *vertically* directly effective Treaty Articles is the *Factortame* case, discussed below.

Regulations

3–028   Regulations are, as stated above, designed to be directly applicable and, thus, directly effective. It is important to understand that this means both vertically and horizontally.

Directives

3–029   Directives are instructions to Member States to enact laws to achieve a certain end result, so it was originally assumed they could not be directly effective. Nevertheless, in *Grad v Finanzamt Traunstein* (9/70) [1970] E.C.R. 825 the Court held that no such limitation applied. Here, a German haulier was allowed to rely on a directive and decision on VAT which the German government had ignored. The direct effect of directives was confirmed in *Van Duyn v Home Office* (41/74) [1975] Ch. 358. The Court held that Mrs Van Duyn, a Scientologist, was allowed to rely on a directive to challenge the UK's refusal to allow her to enter the UK. The conditions for effectiveness are the same as those applied to test Treaty provisions: clarity, precision, being unconditional and leaving no room for discretion in implementation. Once a time-limit for implementation has expired, the obligation to implement it becomes absolute but a directive cannot be directly effective before that time-limit has expired: *Ratti* (148/78) [1979] E.C.R. 1629. Directives have to be interpreted and applied by our courts and tribunals in the same way as UK statutes do. Unlike statutes, however, we are given lengthy preambles to help us interpret them. If you take a look at any EU directive, you will see what I mean. Directives provide effective rights, in practice. In 2007, The Royal Cornwall Hospital Trust tried sacking 36 people of over 65 on the day before the UK age discrimination regulations came into force and had to reinstate them when the Trust learned it was bound by the directive on age discrimination, even before it became part of national law.

Horizontal or vertical direct effect?

3–030   One of the most difficult issues before the Court has been the issue of whether directives can be declared effective horizontally, that is, to enforce rights and obligations between private parties.

All the case law above relates to the enforcement of private rights against a State, giving *vertical* direct effect. This is unproblematic, since the Court is merely enforcing rights and obligations against a State which it has failed to implement in its domestic law. The Court is not so keen to hold private parties bound by a directive which a State has neglected to implement, when the default is clearly the State's.

The leading case is *Marshall v Southampton & South West Hampshire Area Health Authority (Teaching)* (152/84) [1986] Q.B. 401 but, as we shall see, subsequent case law, in particular the *Marleasing* case and *Foster v British Gas*, left the law in a position which is far from clear. The decision in the *Marshall* case is clear enough. Mrs Marshall was an employee of the Area Health Authority and she challenged their compulsory retirement age of 65 for men and 60 for women as discriminatory and in breach of the EC Equal Treatment Directive 76/207. Different retirement ages were permissible in domestic English law, under the Sex Discrimination Act 1975. On a reference from the Court of Appeal, the Court held that the different retirement ages did indeed breach the directive and that Mrs Marshall could, in the circumstances, rely on the directive against the State (here represented by the Area Health Authority) regardless of whether they were acting in their capacity as a public authority or her employer. The issue of horizontal and vertical effect of directives had been fully argued before the Court and they determined that: "a directive may not of itself impose obligations on an individual and that a provision of a directive may not be relied upon as such against such an individual." This looks like a very straightforward refusal to permit directives to have direct effect but problems remain.

- Here, Mrs Marshall could rely on the directive against her employers because they were a part of the State so how is "State" to be defined? The wider the definition, the more individuals will be allowed to rely on directives as directly effective.
- Is the time now ripe for directives to be given horizontal direct effect?
- Has the Court of Justice permitted individuals to avoid the harshness of this ruling against horizontal effect by requiring domestic courts to apply directives indirectly, as a matter of interpretation (the *Von Colson* principle)?

What is the State?

In *Marshall* then, a Health Authority was regarded as an arm **3–031** of the State, as was the Royal Ulster Constabulary in *Johnston v*

RUC (222/84) [1987] Q.B. 129, but what of other publicly funded organisations such as universities or publicly run corporations? The House of Lords sought a preliminary ruling from the Court on the status of the British Gas Corporation and in their response, in *Foster v British Gas* (C-188/89) [1991] 1 Q.B. 405, the Court took the opportunity to provide a definition, although it is not definitive. The Court ruled that a directive may be relied on as having direct effect against "a body, whatever its legal form, which has been made responsible, pursuant to a measure adopted by the State, for providing a public service under the control of the State and has for that purpose special powers beyond those which result from the normal rules applicable in relation between individuals."

The court ruled that:

1. It was up to them, the Court of Justice, to rule which categories of body might be held bound by a directly effective directive.
2. It was up to the domestic court to decide whether a particular body fell within that category.

On the first of these points, it is still unclear which bodies will be classed as part of the State. On the second point, the refinement of the concept of State is laid open to differences of interpretation by Member States' domestic courts. The UK's definition of a state body was addressed in *Doughty v Rolls Royce* [1992] 1 C.M.L.R. 1045. Here, the CA ruled that Rolls Royce did not qualify as part of the State, within the *Foster* definition because they did not provide a public service, nor possess any special powers, despite being wholly owned by the State. The issue as to what is an emanation of the State was addressed again by the ECJ in *Kampelmann v Landschaftsverband Westfalen-Lippe* (C-253/96) [1997] E.C.R. I-6907 and seems to have been expanded. The Court defined it by repeating the exact words they had used in Marshall but then added "or other bodies which irrespective of their legal form, have been given responsibility, by the public authorities and under their supervision, for providing a public service". See Tayleur. This was confirmed in *Rieser* (C-157/02) [2004] E.C.R. I-1477. A private company undertaking a public duty fell within *Marshall*.

Should horizontal direct effect be extended to directives?

3–032   In three cases in 1993 and 1994, AGs separately argued that the Court should reverse its decision in *Marshall* and give horizontal direct effect to directives. In *Faccini Dori v Recreb Srl* (C-91/92) [1995] All E.R. (EC) 1, an Italian student sought to rely on a 1985 directive, unimplemented by Italy, to cancel a contract she had entered into with a private company and now regretted. A number of reasons had been put forward by the AGs in these cases and by academic commentators for an extension of the concept. For instance, the Court is prepared to give horizontal direct effect to Treaty Articles, despite the fact that, like directives, they are addressed to Member States. Secondly, the emergence of the single market in 1993 necessitated enforcing equality of the conditions of competition and the prohibition on discrimination. Thirdly, the TEU had amended the EC Treaty to require publication of directives in the *Official Journal* (so private persons had less excuse not to know their responsibilities under a directive). A full Court of 13 judges nevertheless declined to adopt this reasoning and extend the concept of horizontal direct effect. They reiterated that the distinguishing basis of vertical direct effect was that the State should be barred from taking advantage of its own failure to comply with EU law, confirmed in *Pfeiffer* (C-397/01) [2004] E.C.R. I-8835.

Decisions

The *Grad* case, discussed above, confirmed that decisions could **3–033** be directly effective, provided they met all the required criteria. This does not pose any of the moral problems of horizontal direct effect of directives, since decisions are, in any event, only binding on the addressee. Where the addressees of a decision are Member States, an individual cannot rely on it in legal proceedings in contract against another individual: *Carp* (C-80/06, June 7, 2007).

International Agreements

As to whether international agreements to which the EU or a **3–034** Member State is party can be given direct effect, the case law is inconsistent.

6. The Von Colson principle and Marleasing: indirect effect

Where individuals seeking to rely on a directive cannot show **3–035** that their opponent is a branch of the State, all may not be lost, because of a principle developed in *Von Colson and Kamann* (C-14/83) [1984] E.C.R. 1891. Miss Von Colson was claiming that the German prison service had rejected her job application in breach of the Equal Treatment Directive 76/207 and German law provided inadequate compensation. At the same time, another claimant, Miss Hartz, was making the same claim against a private company.

Thus, the issue of horizontal/vertical direct effect and the public/ private distinction was openly raised. The Court avoided opening up these distinctions by ingenious reliance on Art.5 EC. Article 5 required States to "take all appropriate measures" to ensure fulfilment of their EU obligations. This obligation falls on all parts of a State, said the Court, including its courts. Thus, the courts in a Member State must interpret national law in a manner which achieves the results referred to in Art.189 EC (now Art.288 TFEU), that is, the objectives of a directive. The German courts were thus obliged to interpret German law in such a way as to enforce the Equal Treatment Directive. The Court added an important qualification to this obligation: "it is for the national court to interpret and apply the legislation adopted for the implementation of the directive in conformity with the requirements of EU law, in so far as it is given discretion to do so under national law." These qualifying words were moderated in *Marleasing* (below) to "as far as possible". The significance of this case is that it provides horizontal effect in an indirect way. Even though EU law is not applied directly, it may still be applied indirectly through the medium of domestic interpretation.

The principle was extended in a significant way by the case of *Marleasing SA v La Comercial Internacional de Alimentacion SA* (C-106/89) [1990] E.C.R. I-4035. The Court held that a national court was required to interpret its domestic legislation, whether it is legislation adopted prior to or subsequent to the directive, as far as possible within the light of the wording and purpose of a directive, in order to achieve the result envisaged by it. Some argue this case is a large step towards accepting the horizontal direct effect of directives. The end result of such interpretation certainly appears to be the same, as far as the individual litigants are concerned. This principle has been applied many times over. One example was *Oceano Grupo Editorial v Rocio Murciano Quintero* (C-240/98) [2000] E.C.R. I-4941. Oceano sought to rely on Spanish law to bring an action in a Barcelona court. Part of the Unfair Contract Terms Directive, which only became enforceable in Spanish law after their claim arose, would have deprived the Barcelona court of jurisdiction. The Court reaffirmed that a national court is obliged, when it applies national law provisions, predating or postdating a directive, to interpret those provisions, so far as possible, in the light of the wording of the directive, even if this meant ruling that it did not have jurisdiction to entertain the claim.

The Court has qualified the principle. It declined to apply the principle to extend criminal liability: *Pretore di Salo v Persons Unknown* (14/86) [1987] E.C.R. 2545. It is unclear to what extent national courts are required to depart from national law in order to achieve the result sought by a directive. To achieve such a result may involve the national court departing significantly from the wording of national law. For instance, in the *Von Colson* case, the national law clearly limited the compensation payable to the two women to a nominal amount, whereas the Court held that the directive required the amount to be effective. It does seem, however, that the national court is not required to override the clear wording and intent of national law in order to make it comply with a directive which cannot be construed as directly effective.

7. Damages from a tardy State: the Francovich principle

Another remedy is available for a citizen who has suffered as a **3–036** result of the non-implementation of a directive but where the conditions for direct effect are not satisfied. In another case giving a bold interpretation to former Art.5, the Court held that, in certain conditions, the aggrieved citizen may have a remedy against the State in damages. In *Francovich v Italy* (C-6/90) [1991] E.C.R. I-5357, the applicants were employees of businesses which became insolvent, leaving substantial arrears of unpaid salary. They brought proceedings in the Italian courts against Italy, for the recovery of compensation provided by Directive 80/987, which Italy had not implemented. The directive should have guaranteed payment of unpaid remuneration in the case of insolvency by the employer. The applicants could not rely on the concept of direct effect, because the directive's terms were insufficiently precise. Happily for the applicants, the Court held that they were entitled to compensation from the State. Inherent in the Treaty, they said, was the principle that a Member State should be liable for damage to individuals caused by infringements of EU law for which it was responsible. Their interpretation rested, in particular, on Art.5, which placed a duty on Member States to take all appropriate measures to ensure the fulfilment of Treaty obligations. The Court argued that to disallow damages against the State in these circumstances would weaken the protection of individual rights. The Court laid down three conditions for an individual claiming damages against a Member State for failing to implement or incorrectly implementing a directive:

1. The result laid down by the directive involves the attribution of rights attached to individuals.
2. The content of those rights must be capable of being identified from the provisions of the directive.

3. There must be a causal link between the failure by the Member State to fulfil its obligations and the damage suffered by the individuals.

The Court has left it up to each Member State to determine the competent courts and procedures for actions for damages against the State. The procedures must be not less favourable than those relating to similar claims under domestic law and must not make it difficult or practically impossible to obtain damages from the State. In *Becker v Finanzamt Munster-Innestadt* (8/81) [1982] E.C.R. 53, the Court held that provisions of directives could be invoked insofar as they define rights which individuals are able to assert against the State. Only a person with a direct interest could invoke a directive but this might include a third party: in *Verholen* (C-87–89/90) [1991] E.C.R. I-3757, a husband could bring a claim where his wife was discriminated against in a social security benefit, as it disadvantaged him.

Damages from a state whose legislature flouts EU law

3–037   In *Factortame (No.4)*, properly known as the joined cases *Brasserie du Pecheur SA v Federal Republic of Germany and R. v Secretary of State for Transport Ex p. Factortame Ltd (No.4)* (C-46/93 and C-48/93) [1996] E.C.R. I-1029, the Court extended the *Francovich* principle to permit a claim of damages against a State whose national *legislature* had passed a law which was in serious breach of EU law. In the first case, French beer manufacturers were claiming damages against Germany for passing beer purity laws that effectively excluded the import of their beer. In the second case, the UK Parliament had passed the Merchant Shipping Act 1988, which effectively excluded foreign fishing vessels, notably Spanish, from their right to fish in British coastal waters, by laying down registration conditions of residence, nationality and domicile of vessel owners. Spanish fishermen complained that the Act offended against Art.52 EC (now Art.49 TFEU), which guaranteed freedom of establishment. In prior cases, the Court had already ruled the domestic legislation to be in breach of EU law. What was now at issue was whether the aggrieved parties could claim damages against the respective states in the national courts. The *Factortame* case had been referred by the Queen's Bench Divisional Court for a preliminary ruling. The Court of Justice decided the following, (paraphrased).

1. The *Francovich* principle applied to all state authorities, including the legislature.
2. The conditions of a damages claim were

a. that the rule of breached was intended to confer rights on the individuals who had suffered loss or injury;
b. that the breach was sufficiently serious;
c. that there was a causal link between the breach and the damage sustained by the individuals.

3. The State must make reparation, in accordance with its national law on liability but the conditions laid down must not be less favourable than for a domestic claim and must not make it excessively difficult to make a claim. (In the context of English law, it was virtually impossible for the Spanish fishing vessel owners to claim damages in the English courts, because we had no substantive or procedural law enabling a claim for damages against Parliament.)
4. Such a claim could not be made conditional on establishing a degree of fault going beyond that of a sufficiently serious breach of EU law.
5. Reparation must be commensurate with the damage sustained and this might include exemplary damages. It was left to the domestic legal system to set the criteria.
6. Damages could not be limited to those sustained after a judgment finding such an infringement of EU law.

The upshot of these cases was that the onus was on the UK to find some procedure, in the English courts, for making a claim against the State for a breach of EU law by Parliament. We were obliged to devise some substantive cause of action in damages. In 1997, the Spanish brought their claim through the Queen's Bench Divisional Court and were awarded damages. This was upheld by the CA then the House of Lords so the Secretary of State for Transport lost in all three courts. The law lords found that the Government, in introducing this legislation, had deliberately discriminated on grounds of nationality in the face of a clear and fundamental provision of the EC Treaty, Art.7 (now Art.18 TFEU). This was done in good faith and to protect British fishing communities rather than to harm the Spanish but inevitably it took away or seriously affected their rights to fish. There was a fundamental breach of Treaty obligations. It was a sufficiently serious breach to entitle Factortame and 96 others to compensation in damages: *R. v SS for Transport Ex p. Factortame Ltd and others (No.5)* [2000] 1 A.C. 524.

Factortame (No.4) was swiftly followed by a case which clarified how bad the breach of EU law had to be before damages could be claimed. In *R. v HM Treasury Ex p. British Telecommunications Plc* (C-392/93) [1996] Q.B. 615, the Court of Justice repeated the rule that damages could be claimed by individuals who had suffered loss as a consequence of a State's enacting a directive incorrectly (this much was not new) but here the breach of EU law was not sufficiently serious to merit damages. The UK had acted in good faith and simply made a mistake in its enactment into UK law of the relevant directive. The wording of the directive was ambiguous and several other Member States had also misinterpreted it so there was no manifest and grave breach of EU law, as required by *Factortame (No.4)*. In 2003, the same cause of action was extended to a supreme court, in *Köbler v Republik Osterreich* (C-224/01) [2004] Q.B. 848. *Factortame* was applied and damages were awarded in the UK courts in *Byrne* [2008] EWCA Civ 574, in relation to restrictions on claiming compensation of victims of untraced drivers, and *Thin Cap* [2009] EWHC 2908 (Ch), about faulty tax rules.

8. Direct effect of EU law in the UK

3–038   The European Communities Act 1972 gave legal effect to EU law in the UK. Pay close attention to the wording of s.2(1):

> "All such rights, powers, liabilities, obligations and restrictions from time to time created or arising by or under the Treaties, and all such remedies and procedures from time to time provided for by or under the Treaties, as in accordance with the Treaties are without further enactment to be given legal effect or used in the United Kingdom shall be recognised and available in law, and be enforced, allowed and followed accordingly; and the expression 'enforceable Community right' and similar expressions shall be read as referring to one to which this subsection applies."

In *Factortame (No.1)* [1990] 2 A.C. 85, the House of Lords interpreted "enforceable Community right" to mean directly effective legal right. This section gives effect to all directly effective EU law, whether made prior to or after the passing of the Act.

Section 3 binds all our courts to interpret matters of EU law in accordance with the rulings of the Court and requires our courts to take judicial notice of EU legislation and the opinions of the Court of Justice. Our courts have had no problem in applying directly effective provisions. They seem to have been reluctant in some cases, however, to apply the *Von Colson* principle. In *Duke v Reliance Systems Ltd* [1988] A.C. 618, Duke complained that she had been forced to retire at 60, despite the fact that her male colleagues were permitted to work until 65. Equal Treatment Directive 76/207 was not enacted into domestic law until the Sex Discrimination Act 1986. Duke could not rely on the directive as directly effective because her employer was a private company. She argued that the English courts should construe the unamended Sex Discrimination Act 1975 in a manner consistent with the Equal Treatment Directive, treating her enforced retirement as unlawful dismissal. The House of Lords considered the case of *Von Colson* but opined that it did not provide a power to interfere with the method or result of the interpretation of national legislation by national courts. They noted that the Equal Treatment Directive post-dated the Sex Discrimination Act 1975 and thought it would be unfair on Reliance to "distort" the construction of the Act to accommodate it. Nevertheless, the House *was* prepared to make a distinction when construing national legislation that has been passed in order to implement a directive. In *Pickstone v Freemans Plc* [1989] A.C. 66 the House adopted a purposive construction in interpreting an amendment to the Equal Pay Act 1970, in order to make it consistent with the UK's obligations under the Equal Pay Directive. The same purposive approach was taken in *Litster v Forth Dry Dock & Engineering Co Ltd* [1990] 1 A.C. 564. In this case, Lord Templeman said he thought the *Von Colson* principle imposed a duty on the UK courts to give a purposive construction to UK legislation which had been passed to give effect to directives. In *Webb v EMO Air Cargo (UK) Ltd* [1993] 1 W.L.R. 49, Lord Keith said it was the duty of the UK court to construe domestic legislation in accordance with the Court of Justice's interpretation of a relevant EU directive "if that can be done without distorting the meaning of the domestic legislation". He noted that, according to the European Court of Justice, this obligation on the domestic courts only arises where domestic law is open to an interpretation consistent with a directive. The House ruled that the applicant had not suffered discrimination under English law. They nevertheless asked the Court of Justice to construe the relevant directive and the application of the principle of equal treatment to the circumstances of the case. The Court of Justice sent back its interpretation, flatly disagreeing with the House and ruling that the case disclosed discrimination. The House applied the Court's ruling in 1995. The report provides an interesting example of how the House had to construe an English statute in accordance with EU law in a way which seemed to run contrary to the instincts of domestic courts at all levels, at that time. (The Employment Appeal Tribunal and CA had reached the same conclusion.)

9. Supremacy of EU law in the UK

Curiously, the founding Treaty of the Common Market (European Community, EU), the Treaty of Rome 1957, did not prescribe the   3–039

89

supremacy of EU law over national law. It was left to the embryonic European Court of Justice in developing its limbs, to describe the conception of its supremacy in *Costa v ENEL* (6/64) [1964] E.C.R. 1141. This principle is as oft-cited and as jurisprudentially significant as Lord Atkin's famous neighbour principle, which developed the English law of negligence. In addition, the words below are so constitutionally significant, they should be learned and absorbed by every UK citizen.

> "By creating a Community of unlimited duration, having its own institutions, its own personality, its own legal capacity and capacity of representation on the international plane and, more particularly, real powers stemming from a limitation of sovereignty or a transfer of powers from the States to the Community, the Member States have limited their sovereignty rights, albeit within limited fields, and have thus created a body of law which binds both their nationals and themselves.
>
> The integration into the laws of each Member State of provisions which derive from the Community, and more generally the terms and the spirit of the Treaty, make it impossible for the States, as a corollary, to accord precedence to a unilateral and subsequent measure over a legal system accepted by them on a basis of reciprocity."

By 1970, the Court had asserted the supremacy of EU law, even over Member States' constitutions (the *Internationale Handelsgesellschaft* case). By 1977, in *Simmenthal* (35/76) [1976] E.C.R. 1871, the Court had explained that this meant that every domestic court, however lowly, was under a duty to disapply national law in favour of EU law, where there was a clear conflict. Furthermore, in the *Brasserie du Pecheur/Factortame (No.4)* case, the Court added that national courts must be capable of protecting claimed EU law rights in the face of clear contrary provisions in national law, pending the Court of Justice's final ruling on the precise nature of those rights.

The effects of EU sovereignty within the UK

3–040   In the European Communities Act 1972, the UK Parliament effectively gave away its legislative sovereignty in matters within the EU's sphere of activity, recognising the principle of supremacy of directly effective Community (EU) law. The crucial words of s.2(4) are both retrospective and prospective: ". . . any enactment passed or to be passed. . .shall be construed and have effect subject to the foregoing provisions of this section". This means that, where domestic law conflicts with directly effective EU law, the latter must be applied and the only way of altering this position is to repeal this subsection. The House of Lords, in *Factortame (No.1)* recognised that this was the effect of this subsection, when they disapplied part of the Merchant Shipping Act 1988, the clear words of which flew in the face of established EU law rights, including freedom of establishment and non-discrimination.

In this case, as explained above, Spanish owners of fishing vessels sought to register as British so that they would have access to the British fishing quota under the common fisheries policy. The 1988 Act attempted to limit registration to British managed vessels. Factortame and others sought a judicial review in the HC of the legality of the Act. The HC referred the question of Community (EU) law to the Court of Justice but, meanwhile, the procedural question of how to grant interim relief found its way up to the House of Lords. The House declined to grant an interim injunction against the Crown, as an injunction could not, in English law, bind the Crown. Furthermore, the applicants' EU law rights were "necessarily uncertain" until determined by the Court of Justice and appeared to run directly contrary to Parliament's sovereign will. They sought a preliminary ruling from the Court of Justice. The Court answered by saying that where the sole obstacle preventing a national court from granting interim relief based on EU law is a rule of national law, that rule must be set aside. Not surprisingly, when the Court ruled on the substantive question, they upheld Factortame's complaint that part of the Merchant Shipping Act ran contrary to Community (EU) law.

A comment on *Factortame (No.4)*

The UK media reacted especially badly to the *Factorame (No.4)*   **3–041** ruling, affronted at the thought of having to pay damages to the Spanish for stopping them coming and raiding "our" fish stocks. What is so ridiculous is that the UK politicians and journalists reacted as if the ruling were a surprise. When the UK Parliament passed this piece of protectionist legislation in 1988, the Thatcher government was warned formally by the Commission, in 1989, acting under their former Art.169 powers (now Art.258 TFEU), that the UK was were in breach of the EC Treaty so it should have been obvious that the ultimate punch line would be that the UK would have to pay damages to the Spanish. The UK reacted with the same indignant horror to *Factortame (No.1)*, in 1990, which effectively ruled that a part of the Merchant Shipping Act would have to be suspended, as if we were shocked at this assault on the legislative sovereignty of Parliament. Apparently many UK citizens had not noticed, or worked out, that we had given part of this away, on joining the common market, as it then was, in January 1973. As if to rub salt into the wound made by *Factortame (No.4)*, in March 1996, the

BSE beef crisis broke out within days of the judgment. We reached the hypocritical position of arguing that the Court's powers should be curbed, by the 1996 Intergovernmental Conference (the renegotiation of Maastricht); yet at the same time lodging a claim before the Court against the Commission for losses caused by the export ban on British beef.

10. General principles of law

3–042   The Court of Justice has built up and interpreted a body of general principles. They must be applied in interpreting EU law, including elements of domestic law. These principles, developed by the Court just as the English courts have developed the common law, should be distinguished from the fundamental principles of the Treaty (e.g. free movement of goods and persons; non-discrimination). In part, the general principles are derived from fundamental rights in individual Member States. The Court looks for principles common to Member States' constitutions and is guided by international treaties to which Member States are signatories, the most obvious and important being the European Convention on Human Rights. The rights include, for example:

- proportionality: administrative authorities must not use means more than appropriate and necessary to achieve their ends;
- legal certainty: includes the principle of legitimate expectation (same as English law) and the principle of non-retroactivity;
- natural justice: the right to a fair hearing (same as English law), the duty to give reasons, due process;
- the right to protection against self-incrimination (same as English law);
- equality;
- subsidiarity: the EU can only act if its objectives cannot be achieved by the Member States.

11. The EU and the European Convention on Human Rights and the Charter of Fundamental Rights of the European Union (2010/C 83/02)

3–043   All the Member States are signatories of the Convention so one would think the obvious way for the Court to guarantee rights would be for the EU to be a signatory of the Convention. An early attempt to do this was initially declared invalid by the Court. The 1996 Intergovernmental Conference failed to have accession incorporated into the Treaty of Amsterdam. The Court of Justice nevertheless continues to apply the Convention rights within its jurisdiction, as part of its general principles. In the meantime, since the Lisbon Treaty provided for the EU to accede to the Convention, it is, in 2011, part way through the process of doing so.

Also, the Charter was signed at the end of 2000. It was declaratory. It was given binding legal effect, on a level with the Treaties, by the Treaty of Lisbon, in December 2009. It puts social and economic rights on the same footing as civil and political rights. Examples of the rights are listed below.

1. Dignity (e.g. right to life, prohibition on torture).
2. Freedoms (e.g. liberty and security, respect for private and family life, right to marry, freedom of thought, religion, expression; right to education).
3. Equality (e.g. non-discrimination, cultural, linguistic and religious diversity; rights for children, the disabled and the elderly).
4. Solidarity (e.g. workers' rights to information and consultation; social security, health care, environmental and consumer protection).
5. Citizenship rights (e.g. voting, good administration, access to documents, the Parliament and the Ombudsman and diplomatic and consular protection).
6. Justice (e.g. effective remedy and fair trial, presumption of innocence and fair trial).

The full text can be seen on the Eur-Lex section of the Europa website. As can be seen, there is an overlap with the European Convention on Human Rights, described in the next chapter, which is NOT a treaty of the EU. The Charter preamble explains that it *includes* the Convention rights, subject to the principle of subsidiarity. The UK and Poland think they secured a sort of opt-out, in Protocol 30 to the Treaties, restricting the interpretation of the Charter by the Court of Justice and national courts, in those two countries.

12. Harmonisation of laws: the Corpus Juris project and the creation of a European Area of Justice

3–044

> In 2005, Europol, the EU police co-ordinating agency, claimed there were 4,000 criminal gangs operating in Europe. According to the International Monetary Fund, the profits of organised crime account for 2.5 per cent of the world's gross domestic product.

Corpus juris would be a common law of Europe in certain fields if it were ever achieved, but it would take decades to achieve and would be technically and politically extremely difficult. The phrase seems to be little used in the EU nowadays, probably because it is so provocative. Below, two examples are mentioned, contract law and the small claims procedure.

Most importantly, the Commission has always pressed for a greater measure of control over criminal investigation and prosecution within Member States, to combat organised crime. The aim is to protect the financial interest of the EU (protecting the budget; tax evasion). It is directed at crimes such as fraud, market rigging, abuse of office, misappropriation of funds, disclosure of secrets derived from office-holding, money laundering and receiving and conspiracy. This is now extended to protect citizens and so includes such matters as child pornography and terrorism. Consequences may include an EU police force, customs service and courts and ultimately a legal service. Europol, the European Police Force, was set up in 1992 and is based in The Hague. In 2010, previous bodies designed to harmonise justice were placed under the supervision of the European Commission's Directorate General for Justice. There are four directorates, Civil Justice, Criminal Justice, Fundamental Rights and Union Citizenship and, since January 2011, the Directorate for Equality. The Directorate's mission is set out on its pages of the Europa website. It is quite comprehensive and includes aims to:

"   • Promote and enforce the Charter of Fundamental Rights of the European Union: such as personal data protection, the rights of the child, the rights laid down in Chapter VI of the Charter, like the right to an effective remedy and to a fair trial, as well as the rights of persons belonging to minorities.
   • Develop the European area of justice, based on mutual recognition of judicial decisions, mutual trust between justice

authorities achieved through common rules and by building on the legal traditions of the EU Member States.

• Develop a coherent criminal policy for the EU based on mutual recognition of judicial decisions, approximating substantive and procedural criminal law, enhancing mutual trust between criminal justice authorities, and strengthening Eurojust and combating fraud against the financial interests of the Union by means of criminal law."

As an example of its activity, in May 2011, Justice Commissioner Viviane Reding proposed a directive on minimum standards for victims in the EU. In 2002, the Council established Eurojust, to enhance the development of Europe-wide co-operation in criminal justice cases. As its website explains, "Eurojust is composed of 27 National Members, one from each EU Member State. These are senior and experienced judges, prosecutors, or police officers of equivalent competence, who together form the College of Eurojust." A European arrest warrant came into effect, as a result of a decision in 2002. It replaces extradition proceedings between Member States with a system of surrender between judicial authorities. In 2004, the Commission adopted a proposal for a Council framework decision on certain procedural rights in criminal proceedings throughout the EU. All of these developments rest on the principle of mutual recognition where criminal justice systems operate differently, as they all do because, in practice, the interpretation of what constitutes a fair trial differs fairly radically throughout Europe. There have been examples of English courts refusing extradition to France, on the ground that the suspect would not get a fair trial, and a similar refusal by a French court to extradite to Spain, on the ground that the suspect might be tortured. The problem with some of these proposed new rights, as Alegre points out, is their vagueness, so a right to legal advice does not even extend to a right to have a lawyer present during questioning. For further discussion see Alegre and for detail, see the Commission website. If a Fundamental Rights Agency were established, it could monitor whether these rights were applied in practice. To a large extent, though, some of this discussion is now redundant, because of the future accession to the European Convention on Human Rights, as explained above, and its incorporation in the Charter of fundamental Rights. Stephen Jakobi, who for many years ran Fair Trials Abroad, a group of lawyers who endeavour to help those detained and tried abroad, was all too familiar with the shortcomings of other legal systems. He warned, in 2002, that efficiently administered justice systems would be forced to recognise decisions made by under-funded and ill-managed courts. JUSTICE wants the UK

Government to take a lead on harmonisation. The Director, Roger Smith, said the UK "has a generally creditable record in the defence of suspects and defendants. Our citizens have much to gain from all countries in the EU attaining the same standards", at (2006) 156 N.L.J. 206.

Small claims

3–045 As well as some harmonisation of criminal procedure, harmonisation of civil procedure is also being attempted. A new cross-border procedure for claims under 2,000 Euros was agreed by justice ministers in 2006.

European Code of Contract Law

3–046 This has been under development since 1982. It is not easy because of the significant differences between the common law in Ireland and the UK, and the civil law applicable in most Member States, such as in the concept of consideration and the question of whether caveat emptor, "buyer beware" applies. It cannot become a common European code, however, because the EU treaties do not give the Commission the power to impose such a thing and it would offend freedom of contract. Many commercial parties, worldwide, chose English law as their contract law. A consultation on European contract law was commenced in 2010. Opponents say commercial contractors will choose the contract law of other common law countries, if English law is changed. The Bar of England and Wales are deeply opposed to this plan. The Bar chairman said, in *Counsel*, March 2011, "This is a naked attempt to draw work away from London and to diminish the commercial importance of English contract law".

BIBLIOGRAPHY

3–047 S. Alegre, "EU fair trial rights—added value or no value?" (2004) 154 N.L.J. 758.

A. Arnull, "The Law Lords and the European Union: swimming with the incoming tide" E.L. Rev. (2010) 35(1) 57–87. This looks at their performance in 1973–2009.

S. Jakobi, "Tattered Justice", *Counsel*, April 2002, p.18.

S. Nash and M. Furse, "Human Rights Law Update" (1999) 149 N.L.J. 891.

N. Padfield, "The Spread of EU Criminal Law", *Archbold News*, August 2006.

R. Smith, "Fundamentally right" (on the EUCFR) (2005) 155 N.L.J. 229.

R. Stevens, "On being nicer to James and the children" (1994) 144 N.L.J. 1620.

T. Tayleur, "Emanations of the State" (2000) 150 N.L.J. 1292.

FURTHER READING AND SOURCES FOR UPDATING THIS CHAPTER

Updates of this book, from spring 2012 and 2013, on the Sweet & **3–048**
  Maxwell website.
Europa, Official portal to the EU. Start here because it links to all
  the others: *http://europa.eu.int/.*
European Charter of Fundamental Rights: *www.eucharter.org.*
European Commission: *http://europa.eu.int/comm/index_en.htm.*
European Commission in the UK: *http://www.cec.org.uk/.*
Court of Justice of the EU: *http://curia.europa.eu/.* See annual reports
  and press releases.
Eurojust: *http://www.eurojust.europa.eu/.*
Portal to European Union Law, Eur-Lex: *http://eur-lex.europa.eu/.*
The UK Parliament: *www.parliament.uk.*

REFER TO THE LATEST EDITIONS OF THE FOLLOWING

A. Arnull, *The European Union and its Court of Justice.* **3–049**
Cambridge Yearbook of European Legal Studies (annually).
C. Barnard and O. Odudu (eds), *The Outer Limits of European Union
  Law.*
D. Chalmers et al., *European Union Law: Cases and Materials.*
P. Craig and G. De Burca, *EU Law, Text Cases and Materials.*
N. Foster, *Blackstone's EU Treaties and Legislation* (new edition
  annually).
V. Mitsilegas, *EU Criminal Law.*
A. O'Neill et al., *EU Law for UK Lawyers.*
S. Weatherill, *Cases and Materials on EU Law.*

4. The European Convention on Human Rights and English Law

> "He regarded the European Convention as 'a gift from victory' in the Second World War, a product of victory over the principles and governance of wicked men, led by Adolf Hitler" (Attorney General Lord Goldsmith QC, obituary for Lord Scarman, law lord 1977–1986, *Counsel*, February 2005).

In Ch.1 we saw that Lord Bingham considered the rule of law as requiring adequate protection of fundamental human rights.

1. Incorporation into UK law

The European Convention on Human Rights 1950 (the Convention) was drafted by British lawyers, notably Sir David Maxwell-Fyfe, who had been a prosecutor at the Nuremburg trials. It followed the Universal Declaration of Human Rights by two years and grew out of disgust with fascism and an anxiety to protect basic freedoms. It is a Treaty of the Council of Europe, which was formed in London in 1949 from a 1946 idea of Winston Churchill that we needed a "United States of Europe" to make all of Europe "free and happy" and peaceful, after World War II. (See Council of Europe website.) The UK, led by a Labour government, was the first state to ratify. Many Convention rights reflect the common law and the 1689 Bill of Rights. I emphasise these points so that the reader understands that the Convention rights are not foreign ideas inflicted on the British by "Europe", the impression given by some politicians and elements of the UK media. The Human Rights Act 1998 and the Convention are often criticised in the UK and there is confusion over the ambit of the Convention and EU law. In 2007, Frances Lawrence, widow of a murdered head teacher, expressed concern that his murderer,

4–001

Learco Chindamo would not be deported at the end of his sentence because of the Human Rights Act but the decision was based on EU law, not the HRA. As it happens, the EU embarked on accession to the European Convention on Human Rights in 2010 but it must be understood that the Convention is *not* an EU treaty and it was created independently, years before the Common Market.

From 1966, individuals were permitted to bring claims to the European Court of Human Rights (ECtHR) against the UK. By 1998, 99 cases had been taken to the Strasbourg court, more than any country except Italy, and the UK had been found to be in violation of the Convention 52 times. It was a frequent defendant before the ECtHR, partly because the UK lacks a written constitution or modern Bill of Rights. Prior to 2000, however, the individual could not assert their Convention rights through the domestic (UK) courts. Judges of the UK were powerless to apply it. The courts, in any event, took a fairly conservative approach. Lord Bingham C.J. urged incorporation of the Convention into UK law and in the Court of Appeal (CA) he and his fellow judges expressed dissatisfaction with their powerlessness to allow appeals in a case which raised Convention issues: *R. v Morrisey* [1997] 2 Cr. App. R. 426. In the meantime, the Conservative governments of the early 1990s had set their face against incorporation. They had grown hostile to the ECtHR, especially because of decisions such as the damages award against the UK in favour of the families of IRA members assassinated by the UK Government in the Death on the Rock case. Minister Michael Heseltine called this decision "ludicrous" and called for an alteration to the powers of the ECtHR. The Government were dilatory in enforcing the judgments of the ECtHR that they did not like, as Bindman explained.

In 1996, the Labour opposition issued a consultation paper on their plans to incorporate Convention rights. The Lords had a two-day debate, in which the Conservative Mackay L.C. expressed the view that UK citizens were adequately protected by the common law. Enacting a Bill of Rights would, he feared, give the courts wide discretion over matters which were properly the preserve of Parliament. The generalised wording of the Convention would leave too much scope for judicial interpretation and litigation. (As we shall see in this chapter, the same point has been revived in arguments about the Human Rights Act, in 2009–11.) Lord Irvine, Shadow Lord Chancellor in 1996, opened the case for the Opposition, pointing out that the UK was virtually alone amongst the major nations of Western Europe in failing to give its citizens the means to assert Convention rights in their courts (see Hudson). Once in Government, in 1997, New Labour swiftly published a White Paper, *Rights Brought Home*. In the Tom Sergeant Memorial Lecture in 1997, the newly appointed Lord Chancellor Irvine said:

"The Human Rights Bill. . .will be a constitutional change of major significance, protecting the individual citizen against erosion of liberties. . .It will promote a culture where positive rights and liberties become the focus and concern of legislators, administrators and judges alike".

The Bill would, he said, require judges to produce a decision on the morality of conduct, not simply its compliance with the bare letter of the law. He thought the traditional common law approach to the protection of liberties, described as a negative right (the right to do anything not prohibited by law), offered little protection against creeping erosion of individual liberties by a legislature.

The Human Rights Act 1998

The Human Rights Act 1998 (HRA 1998) gave *further effect* to the Convention rights in UK and thus English law from 2000 and made them enforceable in UK courts and tribunals. Section 1 and Sch.1 of the HRA do *not* incorporate the Convention rights but restated the Conventions and Protocols as part of UK law with the exception of Art.13. Article 13 would have given a remedy for violation in any court or tribunal. The Government did not want to give them sweeping, new, inappropriate powers. People have to seek monetary remedies in the higher courts, on appeal or in judicial review proceedings. The relationship between the Convention and the HRA 1998 is explored in *Al-Skeini* [2007] UKHL 26. The objective of the HRA was to create rights that are co-extensive with Convention rights, except where expressly excluded by the 1998 Act. The Convention could apply to state acts in an area outside its jurisdiction, over which it exercised "effective control". The geographical extent of the HRA is co-extensive with the Convention.

4–002

Very importantly, s.2 of the HRA provides that when a court or tribunal is determining a question in connection with a Convention right it "must take into account" judgments, decisions or declarations of the ECtHR, and opinions or decisions of the Commission or the Committee of Ministers. This does *not* mean that the Court's decisions are binding, as explained in Ch.2 and emphasised by the UKSC in *Horncastle* (2009). This is in distinct contrast with the binding decisions of the Court of Justice of the EU, as provided by the European Communities Act 1972. Section 3 of the HRA 1998 says "(s)o far as possible, primary legislation and subordinate legislation must be read and given effect in a way which is compatible with the Convention rights".

Notice that this applies to all of us in interpreting legislation, not just the courts, but the obligation is qualified. Section 6 makes it unlawful for any public authority, including any court or tribunal, to act in a way incompatible with a Convention right. The lack of clarity in the meaning of "public authority" has been criticised. Any party to any legal proceedings can rely on a Convention right. This means, for example, that it can be used to apply for a stay (stop) of proceedings, or as a defence, or a ground of appeal, or to found an application for judicial review. If a court or tribunal is satisfied of a violation, they may award anything appropriate within their jurisdiction. Damages or compensation may only be awarded by those courts or tribunals empowered to do so (s.8).

Where courts cannot interpret a piece of legislation as compatible, then some senior courts may make a *declaration of incompatibility*, under s.4(2), meaning the High Court, Court of Appeal, UKSC, Judicial Committee of the Privy Council and the Courts Martial-Appeal Court. A lesser court or tribunal must apply the incompatible law and the case will have to be taken on appeal until one of these courts is reached. This may take two levels of appeal. For instance, the Employment Appeal Tribunal does not have this power. The declaration of incompatibility does not affect validity of the law and is not binding on the parties (s.4). In any case where a court is considering making a declaration of incompatibility, the Crown (meaning the Government) is entitled to notice and to be joined as a party to the proceedings (s.5). Section 11 provides for a fast-track legislative procedure designed to remove the incompatibility, so a minister can use a statutory instrument to amend offending primary legislation and, as explained in Ch.2, this "Henry VIII" section of the Act is controversial. People can still apply to the ECtHR in Strasbourg but they will have to show that they have exhausted all domestic remedies.

4–003   When a new Bill is published, s.19 obliges the sponsoring minister to make a written statement that it is compatible, or decline to make a statement but indicate that the Government wishes to proceed. A Joint Parliamentary Committee on Human Rights,

> "undertakes inquiries on human rights issues and reports its findings and recommendations to the House. It scrutinises all Government Bills and picks out those with significant human rights implications for further examination." (Parliament website).

Like the ECJ, the ECtHR takes a highly purposive approach to legislative interpretation. Examining relevant case authorities since the Act came into force in 2000, we can see that our own judges have, to an extent, taken this approach themselves. It was obvious in 1998 that there would be an impact on precedent and judicial interpretation of statute and this has proven to be the case. In order to enforce a Convention right, the CA may consider itself not to be bound by previous binding precedents which are incompatible with Convention rights. This was explained in the 1997 White Paper. Examples appear in Ch.12 on criminal procedure. A number of extra judges were created to deal with what the Government predicted would be a heavy workload generated by the HRA 1998. A statistical analysis by the Department of Constitutional Affairs showed that its first-year impact was not as significant as predicted. Many far-fetched claims have failed and any court observer can find some amusement in these, like the claim mentioned in Ch.1 that a pub ban constitutes a breach of human rights. In *R. (on the application of M and Leon La Rose) v Commissioner of Police of the Metropolis* [2001] EWHC Admin 553, the High Court warned lawyers that the Convention should not be invoked when the deprivation of rights was merely theoretical or illusory.

2. The Convention Rights

These are appended to the HRA 1998 as Sch.1, where they are **4–004** spelled out in full. Briefly, they are, by Article:

2. Right to life.
3. Prohibition of torture.
4. Prohibition of slavery and forced labour.
5. Right to liberty and security.
6. Right to a fair trial.
7. No punishment without law.
8. Right to respect for private and family life.
9. Freedom of thought, conscience and religion.
10. Freedom of expression.
11. Freedom of assembly and association.
12. Right to marry.
13. Right to an effective remedy—not incorporated into English law (see above).
14. Prohibition of discrimination.
16. Restrictions on political activity of aliens.
17. Prohibition of abuse of rights.
18. Limitation on use of restrictions on rights.

Some rights are absolute, such as 3. Some admit exceptions, such as 2, and most are subject to restrictions to ensure respect for other rights and freedoms.

3. The European Court of Human Rights

4–005 | Do not confuse the ECtHR with the court of Justice of the EU, described in Ch.3. The latter sits in Luxembourg and interprets EU law for the 27 Member States of the EU. The ECtHR is *not* an institution of the EU. It interprets and enforces the Convention for the 47 countries that have ratified it. It sits in Strasbourg.

The fulltime Court was opened in 1998. It composition is described in Ch.6 on civil courts. Procedure is described on its website. Each application is assigned to a section and a rapporteur. Three judges filter applications, with most decision-making done on the papers. Admissible cases go to panels of seven judges. The President of a chamber may invite other interested parties and other member states to join in the proceedings. Initially, or at any time in proceedings, a case may be referred to a Grand Chamber of 17 judges "where a case raises a serious question of interpretation of the Convention or where there is a risk of departing from exist-ing case-law". Chambers decide by a majority vote. Any judge in the panel is entitled to append to the judgment a separate opinion, concurring or dissenting. Within three months of the judgment, any party may request that the case be referred to the Grand Chamber if it raises a serious question of interpretation or applica-tion or a serious issue of general importance. Following a finding of a breach of the Convention, the State is legally obliged to make reparation. Where the domestic law affords only partial repara-tion, Art.41 provides that the Court can award an applicant "just satisfaction".

One practical drawback is the Court's backlog. The Interlaken Conference on Reform of the European Court of Human Rights, February 2010, devised an action plan. See (very poor) website for January 2011 response. From June 2010, the ECtHR can strike out cases where the applicant has not suffered a "significant disadvan-tage". Judges are now elected for nine years maximum and may not seek re-election. By 2011, the UK Government is very concerned that the Court's backlog has grown year on year and is now 140,000.

The Committee of Ministers is the decision-making organ of the Council of Europe and is composed of the foreign Ministers of the contracting States. It supervises the execution of the Court's judg-ments and can check that a State has taken steps to amend offend-ing legislation. The Court may, at the request of the Committee of Ministers, give advisory opinions on legal questions concerning the interpretation of the Convention and Protocols. A.T.H. Smith explained the principles upon which the ECtHR has acted.

1. A generous approach is taken when determining what comes within the scope of the rights.
2. There are four requirements before conditions can be imposed on a right:

    - interference must be lawful;
    - it must serve a legitimate purpose;
    - it must be necessary in a democratic society;
    - it must not be discriminatory.

3. The Convention is a "living instrument", which means that the older a decision, the less value it may have as a guide to construction.

The Court has held that the Convention, not the domestic court, determines whether proceedings are civil or criminal. In *R. (on the application of McCann) v Manchester Crown Court* [2002] UKHL 39, the law lords held that proceedings for anti-social behaviour orders under Crime and Disorder Act 1998, s.1, were civil proceedings and did not involve a criminal charge under Art.6 of the Convention. In *Georgiou v UK* (40042/98) [2001] S.T.C. 80 the ECtHR held that penalty assessments for VAT were criminal matters.

4. Examples of the Convention's application in English law

It should be understood that cases against *any* State before the ECtHR are of equal value to the English and Welsh courts in assisting them to apply the Convention. Below, I list just a few cases, most of which involved the UK as a respondent, as well as some in our courts. This is only a sample, not a comprehensive list, so the reader can start to understand the impact of Convention law on English law.   **4–006**

Article 2 right to Life

As Lord Bingham pointed out, in *The Rule of Law*, while English law has long outlawed murder, manslaughter, infanticide and so on, the ECtHR has gone further and interpreted Art.2 as imposing on states a positive obligation to establish legal frameworks to protect life.   **4–007**

Coroners' juries and inquests into deaths in custody

In *R. (Middleton) v West Somerset Coroner* [2004] UKHL 10, the House of Lords held that the State's procedural obligation to   **4–008** investigate a death which might have violated the right to life because it was a death in custody, required an inquest jury to draw conclusions on the central factual issues of the case. The word "how" in the Coroners Act 1988 and the Coroners' Rules should be interpreted as meaning not simply "by what means" but also "in what circumstances" the person died. Where a death in custody occurs, the State has a duty to ensure a reasonably prompt, effective investigation before an independent body with an opportunity for the relatives of the deceased to participate: *R. v SS for the Home Dept Ex p. Amin* [2003] UKHL 51. In this case, where the victim had been killed by his cellmate in Feltham Young Offender Institution, there had been an investigation into the death by the Prison Service, the police and the Commission for Racial Equality but the Minister had refused the family's request for an independent public inquiry. It was held that the Minister had not met minimum standards set down by the ECtHR in other cases involving deaths in custody in the UK. One of these was *Edwards v UK* (39647/98) 15 B.H.R.C. 189, in which the ECtHR had held that there had been a violation of Arts 2 and 13. The applicants complained that the authorities had failed to protect the life of their son who was stamped on and kicked to death whilst sharing a cell at Colchester police station. These decisions have caused changes in detention practices and in the conduct of inquiries and inquests, following deaths in custody. The coronial system has been restructured, as explained in Ch.6 on civil courts. These cases also engage Art.8, by requiring that the family be involved and informed.

Armed forces

4–009   The HRA does not apply to armed forces on foreign soil and there is no automatic right to an investigation into the death of a serviceman abroad: *R. (on the application of Smith) v SS of Defence* [2010] UKSC 29.

Witnesses

4–010   Articles 2 and 8 were breached where the police failed to protect a prosecution witness, who was shot dead days before he was due to give evidence: *Van Colle v Chief Constable of Herts* [2007] EWCA Civ 325.

The right to die

4–011   In *Pretty v UK* (2346/02) [2002] 2 F.L.R. 45, the dying Diane Pretty took her case to the ECtHR in Strasbourg, after the law lords refused to rule that the Director of Public Prosecutions (DPP) should be told by the courts to grant her husband immunity from prosecution in assisting her planned suicide. Her application was unanimously declared inadmissible. Article 2, right to life, did not extend to a right to die. Article 8 (private and family life) *was* engaged because under it, notions of the quality of life took on significance but there was no violation of Art.8, because, in regulating behaviour for the protection of public morals, the state's "margin of appreciation" was particularly in evidence (in other words, the state had a lot of discretion) so the Suicide Act, criminalising assisting a suicide, did not amount to a disproportionate interference with the applicant's right. Mrs Pretty died a few days later. In *R. (on the application of Purdy) v DPP* [2009] UKHL 45, the circumstances were almost identical. Mrs Purdy wanted clear guidelines as to whether her husband would be likely to be prosecuted if he assisted her suicide. The law lords accepted the ECtHR ruling on Art.8 and ruled that the DPP was obliged to publish his policy identifying the facts and circumstances he would take into account in deciding whether to prosecute someone for assisting the suicide of a terminally ill person.

Death penalty

In *Al-Saadoon and Mufdhi v UK* (61498/08), (2009) 49 E.H.R.R.,   **4–012** the British transferred the applicants to Iraqi courts, regardless of the ECtHR and the fact that they risked the death penalty, which breached Art.2, and they made no attempt to negotiate with the Iraqi courts to prevent the risk of the death penalty.

Article 3 Prohibition of torture and inhuman or degrading treatment or punishment

Prohibition of reliance on evidence derived from torture

In *A (FC) v SS for the Home Department* [2005] UKHL 71 the law   **4–013** lords ruled that evidence obtained by torture was inadmissible in English courts. Although their Lordships relied on Art.3 of the Convention, their primary authorities were the common law and international law. (Torture was prohibited by statute in England in 1640. The Bill of Rights 1689 prohibited cruel and unusual punishments.) Examining the ancient sources of common law on repugnance to torture, Lord Bingham concluded that it was a constitutional principle, not just a rule of evidence. Lord Bingham's judgment is a great education on ancient common law sources, modern relevant precedents and international law on the point. The ECtHR has held that, as the Convention is a "living instrument", it must be interpreted according to modern conditions so higher standards may apply, over time.

The State's duty to protect children

4–014   The UK breached the article in failing to protect children against serious long-term neglect and abuse: *Z v UK* (29392/95) [2001] F.L.R. 612.

Minimum standards of treatment in custody

4–015   The blanket ban on prisoners' voting was a disproportionate interference in rights: *Hirst v UK (No.2)* (74025/01) (2006) 42 E.H.R.R. 41. The UK Labour government considered this decision repugnant so ignored it. In *Green v UK* [2010] ECHR 60041/08, the Strasbourg court reiterated that the UK must remove the ban. This issue is now proving extremely controversial and we will come back to this point, below, in the last section. Breaches of Art.3 were also found in failure to protect a prisoner who committed suicide, in *Keenan v UK* (27229/95) (2001) E.H.R.R. 38; detaining a disabled prisoner in cells without suitable facilities, in *Price v UK* (33394/96) (2002) E.H.R.R. 53 and failing to monitor the condition of an asthmatic heroin addict who died in prison, in *McGlinchey v UK* (50390/99) (2003) 37 E.H.R.R. 41.

Article 4 Prohibition of slavery and forced labour

4–016   English law already prohibited these. There are exceptions, such as compulsory military service, in other contracting states, and forced work in prisons.

Article 5 Liberty and Security

4–017   See also Ch.12 on criminal procedure. In *The Rule of Law*, Lord Bingham acknowledged that the Article had enabled the courts to go further in protecting liberty than the common law, Magna Carta, habeas corpus and other English remedies.

Detention without a judicial review of its lawfulness

4–018   In *Hussain v UK, Singh v UK* (1996) 22 E.H.R.R. 1, breaches were found when juveniles were sentenced indeterminately "at Her Majesty's pleasure". They were unable to have the lawfulness of their continued detention reviewed by a court. The lack of adversarial proceedings before the Parole Board prevented it from being a court or court-like body.

In *Stafford v UK* (46295/99) (2002) 35 E.H.R.R. 32 the Home Secretary decided to keep S in prison longer than recommended by the Parole Board. The fact that a politician rather than a judge kept S in prison went against the "spirit of the Convention" as too arbitrary. This was one of a series of cases diminishing the power of the Home Secretary over sentencing. Home Secretary David Blunkett expressed disappointment but no other country in the

Council of Europe allowed a Government minister to determine sentence length for individuals. See also many other decisions condemning proceedings before the Parole Board, such as *Waite v UK* (53236/99) (2003) 36 E.H.R.R. 54 and the House of Lords in *R. v Parole Board Ex p. West* [2005] UKHL 1. In *Reid v UK* (50272/99) (2003) 37 E.H.R.R. 9, breaches of Art.5(4) were found in placing the burden of proof on R to establish that his continued detention in a mental hospital did not satisfy conditions of lawfulness and in the long delay in determining his appeal: application 1994, appeal to the HL, 1998.

Detention of asylum seekers

The House of Lords held, in *R. (Saadi) v SS for the Home Dept* [2002] UKHL 41, that detaining asylum seekers while their claims were determined was not a breach of Art.5. **4–019**

Indefinite internment—The Belmarsh Case

December 2004 saw an unusual panel of nine law lords taking **4–020** a radical decision on a very controversial piece of legislation in a case which Lord Hoffmann said was one of the most important in recent years: *A (FC) v SS for the Home Dept* [2004] UKHL 56. The appellants challenged the lawfulness of their indefinite detention under the Anti-Terrorism, Crime and Security Act 2001, an Act which enabled the internment without trial of foreign nationals whom the Home Secretary suspected were terrorists, which had been passed swiftly after the terrorist destruction of the New York World Trade Centre on September 11, 2001. There were no similar powers over British citizens. The Act had always been opposed by civil libertarians. The Government had derogated from (opted out of) its obligations under Art.5, as provided for by the Convention where there is "a public emergency threatening the life of the nation". No other European country had done this in the wake of "9/11". Seven law lords ruled that indefinite detention without trial was unlawful because it was a disproportionate interference with liberty (Art.5) and equality (Art.14). Lord Hoffmann went further, claiming the nation was not under threat, as required for derogation. Like seven of his fellow law lords, he saw the Act as offensive to fundamental constitutional principles:

> "The real threat to the life of the nation, in the sense of a people living in accordance with its traditional laws and political values, comes not from terrorism but from laws such as these. That is the true measure of what terrorism may achieve. It is for Parliament to decide whether to give the terrorists such a victory."

Baroness Hale said "We have always taken it for granted that we cannot be locked up in this country without trial or explanation". Lord Hope said it was impossible to overstate the importance of liberty in a democracy. Lord Scott said "Indefinite imprisonment, on grounds not disclosed, is the stuff of nightmares, associated with. . .Soviet Russia in the Stalinist era." They were not persuaded by the Attorney General's argument, on behalf of the Government, that the Act did not offend against Art.5 because it allowed for review by the Special Immigration Appeals Commission, which could hear the evidence against the accused (too sensitive to be admitted in a court) and overrule the Home Secretary. Nor were they at all impressed by the Attorney's argument that they, the judges, were an unelected and undemocratic body who should not second guess ministers. This had been a favourite argument of Home Secretary Blunkett in his repeated attacks on the judges. Their Lordships made a ruling that the 2001 Act was incompatible with the Convention.

In the ensuing days, the Government were faced with what much of the media portrayed as a constitutional crisis. The new Home Secretary declined to release the suspects but announced he would await a decision by Parliament on the legislation, due for its annual renewal in spring 2005. This caused some of the special Government-appointed advocates for the detainees to threaten to resign and caused some backbench MPs to threaten trouble. In March 2005, Parliament passed the Prevention of Terrorism Act to replace the offending 2001 Act but it was ferociously debated. Opponents of the Bill, including all civil liberties groups, did not cite the Convention so much as ancient liberties fundamental to the British constitution, such as habeas corpus, laid down in Magna Carta. The 2005 Act again derogates from the requirements of the Convention. It allows British and foreign terrorist suspects to be placed under a control order (meaning house arrest), by the Home Secretary. Although this will be reviewed by a judge, it did not satisfy critics that it amounts to detention without trial. They asked why we are the only country in Europe which considers it necessary to do this. Other countries' laws permit the admission of evidence obtained by surveillance, such as telephone tapping so such suspects could be tried for say, incitement or conspiracy to commit terrorist offences. The conditions of detention under a control order are much more draconian than those of house arrest under the old apartheid regime in South Africa. Control orders under the 2005 Act provoked more challenges in the courts. See, for example, under Art.6, below.

Defaulters in the magistrates' Court

Magistrates who jailed fine defaulters or council tax defaulters **4–021**
breached Arts 5 and 6: *Beet v UK* (47676/99) (2005) 41 E.H.R.R. 23.
Legal aid had not been available in these cases before 1997.

Article 6 Fair Trial

Lord Steyn said in *R. v DPP Ex p Kebilene* [2000] 2 A.C. 326 "when **4–022**
article 6 of the Convention becomes part of our law, it will be the
prism through which other aspects of our criminal law may have
to be re-examined". The biggest cluster of cases and legislative
changes generated by the Human Rights Act have been those on
criminal procedure, mostly Art.6. Some are dealt with here and
the rest in Ch.10 on criminal procedure. Nevertheless, the most
dramatic impact of Art.6 was that it necessitated wholesale constitutional reform to the office of Lord Chancellor and the position of
the law lords, explained below, in s.8.

Courts martial—appearance of bias

The ECtHR repeatedly found against the UK in relation to courts **4–023**
martial proceedings. Systems of military adjudication which had
been in place for over 600 years have had to be altered. Since a
defendant's commanding officer and other officers participated in
proceedings, they were insufficiently independent. In response to
Findlay v UK (22107/93) (1997) 24 E.H.R.R. 221, the Armed Forces
Act 1996 was passed but it was inadequate to remedy the defect.
The Armed Forces Discipline Act 2000 was an attempt to make the
system compliant with the Convention but in 2002 the system had
to be suspended and investigated further. At the time of the *Findlay*
case, there were 50 others outstanding, which are costing millions
of pounds to settle. See discussion of courts martial by Wade.

Delay

The ECtHR has frequently found a breach of Art.6 in cases where **4–024**
it takes a long time to bring proceedings to a conclusion. They
delivered 248 judgments against Italy in the first eight months of
2000. The Art.6 requirement that justice be reasonably swift applies
to civil as well as criminal proceedings: see for example *Eastaway
v UK* (74976/01) (2005) 40 E.H.R.R. 17 and *King v UK* (13881/02)
(2005) 41 E.H.R.R. 2.

Legal aid—equality of arms

In *McVicar v UK* (46311/99) (2002) 35 E.H.R.R. 22, Linford Christie **4–025**
sued the applicant journalist for defamation in alleging that he used
performance-enhancing drugs. The ECtHR held that the unavail-
ability of legal aid did not violate Arts 6 or 10, as a well-educated

journalist was capable of forming a cogent argument. Defamation law was not so complex as to require representation. The same issue arose in an application made by the two defendants in the famous "McLibel case", the longest trial in English legal history, lasting 313 days in 1994–96. The saga was finally resolved in *Steel and Morris v UK* (6841/01) [2005] 41 E.H.R.R. 22. The ECtHR held that there had been a breach of Art.6 here, because the applicants were denied legal aid, in defending themselves against a defamation action by McDonalds, after distributing leaflets attacking the fast food chain. The Court said the Convention was intended to guarantee practical and effective rights. That was particularly so of the right of access to courts, in view of the prominent place of the right to fair trial in a democratic society. It was central to the concept of a fair trial, civil or criminal, that a litigant was not denied the opportunity to present his or her case effectively before the court and that he or she was able to enjoy equality of arms with the opposing side. The question whether legal aid was necessary was to be determined on the facts. It depended on what was at stake for the applicant, the complexity of law and procedure and the capacity of the applicants to represent themselves. The applicants argued they were severely hampered by lack of resources, such as note-taking and photocopying, not just legal advice. The facts were complex, involving 40,000 pages of documentary evidence. Nor was the law straightforward. Extensive legal and procedural issues had to be resolved even before the trial started. Although the applicants were articulate and they had some help from pro bono (free) lawyers, they mainly acted alone. The trial length was a testament to their lack of skill and experience. They had been deprived of the opportunity to present their case effectively and there was inequality of arms. See also Art.10. In *Ezeh and Connors v UK* (39665/98) (2002) 35 E.H.R.R. 28, the ECtHR found a breach of Art.6(3) where prisoners were denied legal aid or advice before a disciplinary hearing which could have resulted in detention for an extra 42 days.

Separation of powers and judicial independence: judges must determine sentences, not ministers

4–026   In *R. (on the application of Anderson) v SS for the Home Dept* [2002] UKHL 46, the law lords held that the Home Secretary's power to determine the length of a life sentence was incompatible with Art.6. He was not independent of the executive. Complete functional separation of the judiciary from the executive was "fundamental", since the rule of law depended on it. Home Secretary Blunkett promised that the Government would establish a clear set of principles to fix minimum tariffs and a new judicial authority would consider tariffs for current lifers. Similarly, see *Easterbrook v UK* (48015/99)

(2003) 37 E.H.R.R. 40. In *Whitfield v UK* (2005) 41 E.H.R.R. 44, the applicant complained of unfairness in prison disciplinary proceedings. The applicants were denied legal aid and the opportunity to consult a lawyer and there was a lack of judicial independence. The Prison Governor, answerable to the Home Office, had drafted the charges, investigated, prosecuted and tried the case, determining the applicants' guilt and innocence and sentences.

Terror suspects

In *SS for the Home Dept v AF* [2009] UKHL 28, the law lords ruled 4–027
that the appellant's rights had been violated, as he had been the subject of a control order (house arrest plus), as a terror suspect, pursuant to the Terrorism Act 2005, s.2, for three years and his detention had been based on "general assertions". Trial procedure could never be considered fair if a party was kept in ignorance of the case against him, applying *A v UK* (3455/05). Where the interests of national security were concerned, in combating terrorism, it might be acceptable not to disclose the source of the evidence. The law lords had already ruled that the 18 hour curfew in control orders breached the Convention. These cases received intense publicity. See media reports of June 11, 2009. There were repeated calls for control orders to be banned.

Teachers

R. (on the application of G) v X School [2010] EWCA Civ: profession- 4–028
als who faced disciplinary proceedings should have a right to legal representation. Here a school applied for a teacher to be subjected to a lifetime ban on working with children.

Article 7 No punishment without law

In *The Rule of Law*, Lord Bingham remarked that this was a simple 4–029
rule which a child could understand and it had featured in most legal systems since Roman times. As explained in Ch.2 of this book, in English law, it is a presumption of statutory interpretation.

Article 8 Right to respect for private and family Life

This is qualified, like Arts 9, 10 and 11, by a community excep- 4–030
tion. Rights can be restricted in the interests of the community at large. Lord Bingham explained that the protections afforded by English common law have been patchy. Although Coke famously said in his *Institutes*, 1628, one of the ancient common law books of authority, listed in Ch.2, that "a man's house is his castle", a 2007 pamphlet by the Centre for Policy Studies found 266 ways that the State was empowered to enter one's home. Lord Bingham added that this was a considerable understatement. One very important

omission of the common law is that it has never protected privacy. For instance, there is no tort of invasion of privacy.

Gays in the Armed Forces

4–031   Military investigations into the sexuality of gay members of the armed forces and their subsequent dismissal were grave breaches: *Lustig-Prean and Becket v UK (No.1)* (2000) 29 E.H.R.R. 548.

Transsexuals' rights

4–032   In gender reassignment cases, where applicants born as males sought to be re-registered as females, the ECtHR held that the Government was under no positive duty to amend its system of birth registration: *Sheffield and Horsham v UK* (23390/94) [1998] 2 F.L.R. 928 but in *Goodwin v UK* (28957/95) 35 E.H.R.R. 18, a Grand Chamber of the Court took a different approach. Where G had undergone gender re-assignment surgery, it was a breach of Art.8 for the State not to recognise a change of legal gender. Since the surgery was provided by the State, this was illogical. The very essence of the Convention was respect for human dignity and freedom. It was unsatisfactory for post-operative transsexuals to live in an intermediate zone. Since 1986, the Court had emphasised the importance of keeping the need for appropriate legal measures under review, having regard to scientific and societal developments. There had also been a breach of Arts 8 and 12, in denying the applicants a right to marry someone the opposite of their new sex. The State could not bar a right to marry. See also Art.12, below.

Gross indecency in private

4–033   A conviction for gross indecency, when it took place *in private* constituted an unnecessary interference with the right to respect for private life. Following a search of his premises, police had seized photos and videos of the applicant and other consenting men engaging in oral sex and mutual masturbation. The acts took place in the applicant's home and did not involve physical harm: *ADT v UK* (35765/97) [2000] 2 F.L.R. 697. The opposite and surprising result was reached in *Laskey, Jaggard and Brown v UK* (1997) 24 E.H.R.R. 29. Another consenting group of homosexuals, in private, engaged in sado-masochistic maltreatment of the genitals with nettles and staples, ritualistic beating and branding. They had been convicted under the Offences Against the Person Act 1861, which, it was agreed, was an interference in their right to respect for private life but the arrest was carried out "in accordance with the law" and pursued a legitimate aim of "protection of health or morals". The only issue before the Court was whether the interference was "necessary in a democratic society". The Court observed that there was a significant degree of injury and wounding and the State authorities were entitled to consider the potential harm to health.

Prison correspondence

A policy that prisoners must be absent when privileged legal **4–034** correspondence held in their cells was examined by prison officers was unlawful. The House of Lords reached this conclusion by applying the common law but it was supported by the Art.8(1) right to respect for correspondence: *R. v SS for the Home Dept Ex p. Daly* [2001] UKHL 26. This case is very important as the House ruled that the courts must apply a proportionality test in judicial review cases, including Human Rights cases, as proportionality is now a principle of English law.

Artificial insemination

In *Dickson v UK* (44362/04) (2006) 46 E.H.R.R. 41, the UK policy **4–035** of requiring exceptional circumstances to be demonstrated before a life prisoner could have access to artificial insemination was a violation.

Deaths in custody

The series of cases involving deaths in custody, described above, **4–036** showed that Art.8 was engaged, requiring families to be fully informed and involved, in any inquest or inquiry.

Prison visitors

The law lords, in *Wainwright v Home Office* [2003] UKHL 53 took **4–037** a restrictive approach to the issue of privacy rights. Prison visitors had been strip searched in 1997 because the authorities suspected that their relative, the prisoner, had been dealing in drugs in prison. This was a very important case, as the House held that there was no general tort of invasion of privacy at common law and Art.8 did not guarantee a right to privacy, as such. Lord Hoffmann said there was nothing in the jurisprudence of the ECtHR which suggested the adoption of some high-level right of privacy.

Supermodel in rehab

The House did not depart from this principle in *Campbell v MGN* **4–038** [2004] UKHL 22. This case arose from the *Daily Mirror*'s disclosure that, despite her denials, supermodel Naomi Campbell was secretly attending meetings of Narcotics Anonymous. The House was split 3:2 on the result, because they differed on how to apply the law to the facts but they agreed on the law and the correct approach. "Put crudely," said Baroness Hale, "it is a prima donna celebrity against a celebrity-exploiting tabloid newspaper". Where

Art.8 was engaged, the court had to carry out a carefully focused and penetrating balancing exercise to reconcile the restrictions that the Art.8 and Art.10 rights imposed on one another, applying the principle of proportionality. In media cases where both articles were engaged, it was necessary to conduct a parallel analysis, looking at the comparative importance of the rights being claimed in the individual case and at the justifications for interfering with or restricting each right, and applying the proportionality test to each. The majority held that, on the facts, the *Mirror* had gone too far in the details they had published.

Celebs again

4–039   In the long running saga of litigation arising out of *Hello!* magazine's use of surreptitious photos of the wedding of Michael Douglas and Catherine Zeta-Jones, *OK!* magazine was one of the parties, as they had bought exclusive photographic rights from the Douglases. In *Douglas v Hello!* [2005] EWCA Civ 595, the CA accepted that Art.8 privacy rights had to be enforced via "the cause of action formerly described as breach of confidence." It was no longer necessary for the information to have been imparted in circumstances "importing a duty of confidence." See also *Murray v Express Newspapers* [2008] EWCA Civ 446: J.K. Rowling's son's privacy was breached. A child had a reasonable expectation that he would not be targeted in order to obtain photographs. As I write, in 2011, the news media are obsessed with stories of celebrities obtaining High Court "superinjunctions", not only stopping publication of their affairs but also preventing anyone naming them as the applicant. Journalists object that the courts have gone too far in protecting privacy. The judges were criticised in Parliament but Lord Chief Justice Judge said they were only enforcing the law passed by Parliament. In the meantime, the situation dissolved into farce as people mischievously exposed applicants' identities on Twitter and in foreign newspapers. Lord Neuberger M.R. and others established a committee to discuss how to resolve the row.

Embryos

4–040   *Evans v UK* (6339/05) [2007] All E.R. (D) 109 went to the Grand Chamber of 17 judges. Miss Evans lost her sad fight to preserve embryos belonging to her and her ex-boyfriend. The court held that in such sensitive moral and ethical issues, the state had a wide margin of appreciation. Evans had known as a matter of law that her boyfriend could withdraw consent to the use of the embryos. Also, embryos did not have an independent right to life under Art.2.

Fingerprints

Storing suspects' DNA samples and fingerprints, when they have not been convicted, was disproportionate interference with Art.8 rights: *S and Marper v UK* (30562/04 and 30566/04) (2009) 48 E.H.R.R. 50. This case provoked a political controversy which is still live in 2011.

4–041

Stop and search

Gillan and Quinton v UK (4158/05) (2010) 50 E.H.R.R. 45: police stop and search powers under the Terrorism Act 2000 violated Art.8. The interference with the right of respect to private life was different from an airport search, as anyone could be stopped, any time. There was no requirement that the stop and search be necessary, only "expedient". The officer's decision to stop was based on hunch or intuition. This was remedied by a remedial order on March 17, 2011. "Police will only be able to stop and search people without reasonable suspicion where it's considered necessary to prevent terrorism." (Home Office website press release).

4–042

Prosecution criteria

In *R. (on the application of Purdy) v DPP* [2009] UKHL 45, as above, the law lords ruled that the DPP was obliged to publish his policy identifying the facts and circumstances he would take into account in deciding whether to prosecute someone for assisting the suicide of a terminally ill person.

4–043

Housing possession

LB of Hounslow v Powell [2011] UKSC 8 confirmed that in housing repossession cases, an independent tribunal must consider proportionality before evicting. See also *Manchester CC v Pinnock* [2010] UKSC 45. The UKSC considered a number of ECtHR cases expressing the above principle and departed from previous HL judgments. This case was mentioned in Ch.2, in the section on precedent.

4–044

Sex offenders

In *R. (on the application of F) v SS for the Home Department* [2010] UKSC 17 the Court held that sex offenders had a right to some form of review of the requirement to be on the register. Placing them on a register for life, with duties of notification, was a disproportionate invasion of privacy. Provisions to review exist in other jurisdictions. Some politicians and news media reacted as if "review" meant "release". This is silly. Dangerous mass-murderers such as the Yorkshire Ripper and Rosemary West have a right to have their prison sentences reviewed but that does not mean they are about to be released.

4–045

Article 9 Freedom of thought, conscience and religion

4–046   Lord Bingham summarises the Convention's position as:

> "you may believe what you like provided you keep your beliefs to yourself or share them with like-minded people, but when you put your beliefs into practice in a way that impinges on others, limits may be imposed, if prescribed by law, necessary in a democratic society and directed to one of the specified purposes." (*The Rule of Law*, pp.76–77)

Islamic dress

4–047   The ECtHR held there to be no breach of Art.9 in a ban placed on Islamic headscarves by the University of Istanbul. Turkey's Constitutional Court guaranteed democratic values, including the freedom of religion but restrictions could be placed on this freedom if necessary, to defend other values and principles, including secularism and equality: *Sahin v Turkey* (44774/98) [2004] E.L.R. 420. In *R. (on the application of Begum) v Denbigh High School Governors* [2006] UKHL 15, a girl insisted on attending school wearing a jilbab. The law lords dismissed her appeal. There was evidence that her family had chosen a school outside their catchment area. There was no evidence of any real difficulty in her attending one of the three schools in her catchment area that permitted the wearing of the jilbab. The shalwar kameeze was worn by B for her first two years, without objection. On the facts, there was no interference with B's right to manifest her belief in practice or observance.

Corporal punishment

4–048   Although the statutory ban on corporal punishment in UK schools was capable of interfering with Art.9 rights, Parliament was entitled to take the view that the ban was necessary in a democratic society to protect children: *R. (on the application of Williamson) v SS for Education and Employment* [2005] UKHL 15.

Articles 10 Freedom of expression and 11 freedom of assembly and association

4–049   At common law, people could say or write what they liked, unless it breached a law, for instance in constituting the torts of libel or slander. Journalists have always felt that the law of defamation, enforced by these torts, unduly hampered their free speech. Lord Bingham said Art.11 went far beyond the common law, which provided no positive right of assembly or association but relied on the absence of prohibitions.

Government spook spilling the beans

In *R. v Shayler* [2002] UKHL 11, the Official Secrets Act was **4–050** challenged. Lord Bingham said the ban on disclosures was not absolute. A former member of the MI5 could have made disclosures to others—the staff counsellor, a higher ranking former civil servant, or the Attorney General, police or DPP if unlawfulness were alleged. If misbehaviour or maladministration were alleged, concern could have been expressed to Government ministers, or two Parliamentary committees, or one of three other security commissioners.

S argued all of these mechanisms were ineffective in practice. Lord Bingham accepted that possibility. In that case, the MI5 officer could seek authorisation to disclose to a wider audience, then whoever might be called on to grant authorisation should not treat the decision as a routine or mechanical process. They should bear in mind the importance attached to the right of freedom of expression and the need for any restriction to be "necessary, responsive to a pressing social need and proportionate". If a refusal to allow disclosure were unjustified, the officer could seek judicial review. The House relied on changes to the nature of judicial review since the HRA came into force. John Wadham, for Liberty, welcomed the decision as "a real step forward".

The tension between freedom of expression and protection from defamation

In *Steel and Morris v UK*, the successful appeal by the McLibel **4–051** two, discussed above, the ECtHR said the central issue on an Art.10 application was whether the interference with freedom of speech was necessary in a democratic society. In a democratic society even small and informal campaign groups, like London Greenpeace, to which the pair belonged, had to be able to carry on their activities effectively. The fact that the burden of proof was on them, the defendants, to prove the truth of their allegations was *not* incompatible with Art.10, though.

Public demonstrations

In *R. (on the application of Laporte) v Chief Constable of Gloucestershire* **4–052** [2006] UKHL 55, Lord Bingham said that while Art 10 and 11 rights were not absolute, they were fundamental in a democratic society. Coaches full of demonstrators had been intercepted and turned away from Fairford RAF base, after having given the required notice of their plans.

Article 12 Right to marry

Transsexuals

4–053   In *Bellinger v Bellinger* [2003] UKHL 21 the House of Lords ruled that a transsexual could not be legally recognised in her new gender so her marriage was void under the Matrimonial Causes Act 1973. The House was bound by this UK statute but it declared UK law to be incompatible with the Convention, Arts 8 and 12. The Government promised a Bill to give transsexuals legal recognition. This was done via the Gender Recognition Act 2004.

Article 13 Effective remedy

4–054   In a number of the cases above, such as those arising out of deaths in custody, the ECtHR also held there was a breach of this article, because the inquests held were an ineffective remedy.

Article 14 Prohibition against discrimination in enjoying Convention rights

4–055   As can be seen, this is not a free-standing prohibition on discrimination. For a detailed example on homosexual rights, see *Ghaidan v Godin-Mendoza* [2001] EWCA Civ 1533 and [2004] UKHL 30, analysed below in s.6.

Widowers

4–056   Bereaved fathers were equally entitled to the "widowed mother's allowance", conceded the UK, in *Cornwell v UK* (36578/97) (2000) 29 E.H.R.R. CD30. In the long term, the Government dealt with this problem by introducing the Welfare Reform and Pensions Act 1999.

Later protocols

4–057   These were added to the Convention. The First Protocol, Art.1, protects property so even though land may be compulsorily purchased for certain public purposes, the owner must be compensated. This is in line with English law. Article 2 provides a right to education, including parents' rights to ensure teaching in conformity with their religious and philosophical convictions and the UK had provided this for years.

5. The approach of English courts to Convention rights and interpretation of domestic law

Does the Convention allow judges to make law?

Prior to the implementation of the HRA 1998 in October 2000, the Government sought to stop fears that the courts would be swamped with claims by pointing out that the Convention had been in force in Scotland since May 1999 and 98 per cent of challenges had failed. There was a great deal of speculation in the Parliamentary debates on the Bill and in law journals as to how the courts might or should approach the Convention. Emmerson is reported as predicting "a major shift of power from Parliament to judges. They will, in effect, be able to rewrite sections of Acts by reading into them words that are not there and by massaging away any potential conflicts with the Constitution." (*The Times*, November 26, 1998). Nevertheless, in 1999, the House of Lords was swift to point out, in *Kebilene*, that the Convention gave way to Parliamentary sovereignty. In the words of Lord Steyn:

> "It is crystal clear that the carefully and subtly drafted Human Rights Act 1998 preserves the principle of Parliamentary sovereignty. In a case of incompatibility, which cannot be avoided by interpretation under section 3 (1), the courts may not disapply legislation. The court may merely issue a declaration of incompatibility which then gives rise to a power to take remedial action: see section 10."

As for common law remedies, Irvine L.C. said in Parliament:

> "In my view, the courts may not act as legislators and grant new remedies for infringement of Convention rights unless the common law itself enables them to develop new rights and remedies. I believe that the true view is that the courts will be able to develop the common law by relying on the existing domestic principles of trespass, nuisance, copyright, confidence and the like, to fashion a common law right to privacy."

A clear exposition of the approach of the courts in the years immediately following the importation of Convention rights in 2000 was set out by Kavanagh in 2004. She made the following observations, paraphrased:

4–058

1. Section 3 does not require any ambiguity before it comes into operation: *R. v Lambert* [2001 UKHL 37.
2. It is only a rule of interpretation, not legislation, according to many judges.
3. Section 3 does require judicial law-making but it is much more limited in scope and effect than law-making by the legislature.
4. The way judges interpret s.3 and the word "possible" will affect their interpretive approach.
5. The interpretive issues posed by the Convention cannot be resolved linguistically. For instance, there is no point in using a dictionary to determine whether the right to life in Art.2 includes a right to death.
6. If judges merely declared the law, all they could do in some cases was to say that the HRA is indeterminate on the matter.
7. Broad evaluative terms in the Convention necessitate the judges engaging in moral reasoning.
8. Interpretation combines applying and making the law.
9. Where there is no previous case law on the point, judges are required to make the law.
10. Judges are also under a duty to arrive at a just decision in the instant case.
11. HRA case law shows that even where judges are engaged in innovative decision-making, they are still concerned to preserve continuity, authority and stability to the greatest possible degree.
12. When judges make law under s.3, they do so by interpretive reasoning.
13. Legislators, on the other hand, are entitled to create new frameworks or radically alter existing ones.
14. Much judicial law-making is by way of filling in the gaps in legislation and they will read in words in order to make legislation Convention compliant but they cannot rewrite a whole statute.
15. The fact that judicial law-making is incremental places limits on the ability or willingness of the judges to reform the law, as in *Bellinger v Bellinger*, above, where Lord Nicholls said the recognition of gender assignment for the purposes of marriage is part of a wider problem which should be considered as a whole so it was preferable to leave this to Parliament.
16. Judges are trained to resolve legal issues and are ill-equipped to make decisions about general policy.
17. A "possible" meaning of legislation is not necessarily its ordinary meaning, nor is it unlimited.

18. Where there is an outright contradiction between the words of a statute and Convention rights, then judges cannot "read or give effect" to those terms. Lord Steyn, in *R. v A*, below, pointed out that Parliament rejected the New Zealand legislative model whereby judges find a "reasonable interpretation."

An Example from 2001

R. v A [2001] UKHL 25 was a landmark precedent because **4–059** it demonstrated how the House was prepared to interpret and apply their own duty under s.3 of the HRA. The House had to construe s.41 of the Youth Justice and Criminal Evidence Act 1999, restricting evidence and questioning about the victim's sexual history, and determine whether it conflicted with the Convention. A man accused of rape wanted to bring evidence of his previous sexual relationship with the complainant, to support his defence that she had consented. The trial judge had ruled this out because of the 1999 Act but considered that his ruling breached Art.6. The law lords applied their interpretive duty under s.3 of the HRA and gave proper regard to the protection of the complainant but effectively "read into" the statute protection for the accused under Art.6. They told the trial judge he could proceed with the case in the light of their ruling—in other words, telling him to make a bold interpretation and allow this evidence in for the sake of protecting the accused under Art.6. I will analyse Lord Steyn's interpretive methods sequentially, with my explanations italicised.

1. *He plunged straight into a purposive construction of the 1999 Act*: in the criminal courts, outmoded beliefs about women and sexual matters lingered on. *Referring to approaches in another common law country, in Canadian jurisprudence*: they had been referred to as discredited twin myths "that unchaste women were more likely to consent to intercourse and in any event, were less worthy of belief".
2. *Statement of moral principle*: "such generalised, stereotyped and unfounded prejudices ought to have no place in our legal system". It resulted in an absurdly low conviction rate in rape cases.
3. *Interpretation of purpose of the 1999 Act*: The Sexual Offences (Amendment) Act 1976 did not achieve its object so "(t)here was a serious mischief to be corrected".
4. *Statement of the problem before the House*: the blanket exclusion of prior sexual history between the complainant and the accused posed an acute problem of proportionality.

5. *Applying what he called "common sense"*: a prior relationship between accused and accuser might be relevant to the issue of consent in rape.
6. *His interpretation of the court's duty under the HRA 1998*: when a question arose as to whether, in a criminal statute, Parliament had adopted a legislative scheme which made an excessive inroad into the right to a fair trial, the court was qualified to make its own judgment and had to do so.
7. *Application of ECtHR jurisprudence*: it was well established that the guarantee of a fair trial under Art.6 was absolute. A conviction obtained in breach could not stand. The only balancing permitted was in respect of what the concept of a fair trial entailed. Applying proportionality, in determining whether a limitation was arbitrary or excessive, a court should ask itself whether:

   a. the legislative objective was sufficiently important to justify limiting a fundamental right;
   b. the measures designed to meet that objective were rationally connected to it, and
   c. the means used to impair the right or freedom were no more than necessary to accomplish the objective.

8. Two processes of interpretation had to be distinguished. Ordinary (traditional, English) methods of purposive and contextual interpretation might yield ways of minimising the "exorbitant breadth" of the section, i.e. the blanket ban on questioning a woman about her sexual history. The second was the interpretative obligation of HRA, s.3(1) (so far as possible, primary legislation had to be given effect in a way compatible with the Convention).
9. *He applied the first method, looked at the wording of the section and relevant domestic cases on evidence prior to the 1998 Act and concluded this could not solve the problem.*
10. *Interpreting s.3 of the 1998 Act*: he cited *Kebilene*. The HRA s.3 obligation went far beyond the rule which enabled the courts to take the Convention into account in resolving any ambiguity in a legislative provision. Parliament specifically rejected the legislative model requiring a reasonable interpretation. It placed on a court a duty to strive to find a possible interpretation compatible with Convention rights. It was much more radical than the ordinary method of interpretation which permitted a departure from language of an Act to avoid absurd consequences. In accordance with the will of Parliament, in enacting the HRA, it would sometimes be necessary to adopt an interpretation which linguistically might

appear strained. The techniques to be used would not only involve the reading down of express language in a statute but also the implication of provisions.

11. *Interpreting s.4 of the HRA 1998*: a declaration of incompatibility was a measure of last resort.

12. *Conclusion, inferring Parliamentary intent*: the legislature, if alerted to the problem, would not have wished to deny the accused the right to put forward a full defence by advancing probative material. It was possible to read into s.41 of the 1999 Act the implied provision that any evidence or questioning required to ensure a fair trial under Art.6 should not be inadmissible.

13. *Implications for future trials*: sometimes logically relevant evidence of sexual experience might be admitted but where the line was to be drawn was up to the trial judge.

An example from 2004, reading words into a statute

The same bold approach, demonstrating that the courts are prepared to read words into a statute, effecting quite substantial rewriting, was adopted by the CA and then the House of Lords in *Ghaidan v Godin-Mendoza* [2001] EWCA Civ 1533 and [2004] UKHL 30. Here, M, the homosexual partner of the deceased tenant of a flat, appealed from a decision that he could not be awarded a statutory tenancy under the Rent Act 1977. He could not qualify as a "spouse" under the Act and thus did not enjoy the benefit granted to an unmarried heterosexual partner in the same position. The Court held that, in cases involving Art.14, four questions must be asked:

1. Do the facts fall within the ambit of one or more of the substantive rights under the Convention?
2. If so, was there different treatment as respects that right between a complainant and other persons put forward for comparison?
3. Were the chosen comparators in an analogous situation to the complainant's situation?
4. If so, did the difference have an objective and reasonable justification? Did it pursue a legitimate aim and bear a reasonable relationship of proportionality to the aim sought to be achieved?

Deference to Parliament has a minor role to play, said the Court of Appeal, where issues of constitutional importance, such as discrimination, arise. Discrimination on grounds of sexual orientation was now impermissible, on the same level as any others under

4–060

Art.14. Section 3 of the HRA required that words should be read into the Rent Act. The words defining "spouse" as "his or her wife or husband" should be read to mean "as if they were his or her wife or husband". In the House of Lords, it was held that s.3, wide statutory interpretation, was the core remedy provided by the HRA and the s.4 declaration of incompatibility should only be a last resort. As long as it did not go against the grain of the legislative measure, *there was no limit to the words that could be read in or out of a legislative measure* (my emphasis).

The Impact of the Convention on the Judicial Approach in Judicial Review Cases

4–061   Notice that the new approach that the courts are required to take, of evaluating "proportionality" of the State's actions, replaces the test of "reasonableness" in judicial review cases. This was made clear by the House of Lords in *Daly* [2001] UKHL 26. The High Court's traditional power to review the legality of executive action and decisions of the lower courts was developed and refined by the courts in the twentieth century. The courts had traditionally declined to examine the merits of a decision, provided it had been taken procedurally correctly and provided the decision-maker had taken account of all relevant factors and decided rationally. This was known as the *Wednesbury* test of irrationality or unreasonableness, based on the test laid down in *Associated Provincial Picture Houses v Wednesbury Corporation* [1948] 1 K.B. 223. In *Kingsley v UK* (35605/97) (2002) 35 E.H.R.R. 10, the ECtHR held that this was inadequate. The nature of judicial review proceedings which restricted the court to examining the quality of the decision-making process rather than the merits of the decision meant that an applicant alleging bias had not had a fair hearing. Here, the CA had held that the Gaming Board of GB had taken a biased decision but had no power to remit the decision to the Board. The reviewing court should not confine itself to examining the quality of the decision-making process and not the merits. The reviewing court must ask itself whether:

1. the objective is sufficiently important to justify limiting a fundamental right;
2. the measures designed to meet the objective are rationally connected to it; and
3. the means used are no more than necessary to accomplish the objective.

In *Kay v UK* (37341/06) [2011] H.L.R. 2, the ECtHR welcomed the UKSC's statements in *Kay* and elsewhere that expanded conventional judicial review grounds beyond *Wednesbury* reasonableness to proportionality.

Other Points on Interpretation

Pepper v Hart was applied in *Wilson v SS for Trade and Industry* **4–062** [2003] UKHL 40: when the court was required to evaluate legislation under the HRA, it was entitled to look at ministerial statements to determine the policy behind an Act. In *McKerr, Re* [2004] UKHL 12, the House held that it was now settled that the HRA was not retrospective.

6. Who can bring an action and against whom can actions be brought?

The person deprived of their right can bring an action, usually in **4–063** the High Court, for judicial review, but other groups would like to join in on public interest test cases. The Civil Procedure Rules were amended to enable "any person" to apply to file evidence or make representations at the judicial review hearing. The UKSC welcomes multiple interveners regularly. There were five in the 2009 *Jewish Schools* case. It was accepted by the House of Lords in *R. (Rusbridger) v Att Gen* [2003] UKHL 38 that the courts were prepared to grant a declaration, to clarify the law, where no wrong had been alleged.

As for the persons against whom an action can be taken, the 1998 Act does not explain "public bodies" but it includes central and local government departments, non-departmental public bodies and the courts and tribunals. Section 6(3)(b) of the Act provides that it shall be unlawful for a private person exercising a public function to act in a way incompatible with a Convention right. There have been many academic articles on whether the Act provides rights against private bodies. This debate is fuelled by the ambiguous HRA. On the one hand, s.3 requires primary and subordinate legislation to be read as far as possible in a way which is compatible with Convention rights but this instruction is not limited to public authorities or just the courts. Under s.2, courts and tribunals must take into account ECtHR jurisprudence. The Government could have specifically excluded private parties from the scope of the Act, as other jurisdictions have done, but did not. On the other hand, ss.6 and 7 only allow challenges to actions of public authorities, generally, with the exception of any person exercising "functions of a public nature". We are not helped by the statements made by the Lord Chancellor who sponsored the Bill through the House of Lords.

Dawn Oliver pointed out that, by 2004, the case law was very confusing. "Public functions", mentioned in some cases did not equate to "functions of a public nature". It was unclear whether liability arose when a private contractor was working for a public authority, gardening or cleaning. These, she suggested, are "functions of a private nature". The contractors enjoy Convention rights which have to be balanced against the recipients' rights. Putting them under HRA duties might have negative implications for many charitable or not-for-profit organisations, providing services for the disabled, the elderly and the homeless. She was diametrically opposed to the suggestion in the seventh report of the Joint Parliamentary Committee on Human Rights (2003–04) that a broader approach should be taken by the courts. Many academics have expressed opinions on the broader issue of whether Convention rights apply "horizontally" between private parties. These can be found in textbooks and articles on public law.

In *YL v Birmingham City Council* [2007] UKHL 27, two of five law lords decided that a private care home was not conducting public functions for the purposes of the HRA. See comment by Parkhill and Murray. They pointed to "a sharp difference of opinion" between the law lords. The jurisprudence of the ECtHR was referred to in interpreting s.6(3)(b). The section emphasises the function, not the body. The judges were agreed that whether there was a statutory basis for its operations or powers to support its operations was a relevant consideration. The issue of whether it applied to particular functions would have to be decided on a case by case basis. The writers were lawyers for Birmingham City Council and commented that this result left uncertainty and was unsatisfactory for the public sector. In *London and Quadrant Housing Trust v R. (on the application of Weaver)* [2009] EWCA Civ 587, the CA held that although the Trust was a private body, a number of its activities, taken together meant that it was carrying out public acts and had to comply with the HRA, though they reiterated that liability had to be decided on a case by case basis.

7. The dramatic effect of Art.6: repositioning the judiciary in the UK constitution

4–064   The most radical consequence of the importation of the Convention into UK law was constitutional reform to the role of Lord Chancellor (L.C.), the top court and the rest of the judiciary, effected by the Constitutional Reform Act 2005. The Act originated in a 2003 announcement by the Labour Government that they intended to make sweeping constitutional reforms. They proposed to abolish the 1,400 year old office of Lord Chancellor, convert the law lords into a Supreme Court, reform the system of judicial appointments and consider abolishing Queen's Counsel. Affected parties were shocked, because these were presented as decisions, as a *fait accompli*, without consultation or forewarning. The architect of previous constitutional reforms including the HRA itself, Irvine L.C., had dismissed suggestions for these further reforms so he had to go. On the same day as the reforms were announced, Cabinet was reshuffled and Lord Falconer replaced him, his Department being renamed the Department of Constitutional Affairs.

For those of us who had watched politics very closely, on the other hand, the announcements were an acceptance of the inevitable. It had become apparent that the tripartite role of L.C., holding significant power in all three organs of government, was untenable, under the Convention. A series of cases had made it clear that Art.6 (fair trial) was breached if a member of the executive (government) sat as a judge and the L.C. was both head of the judiciary and an important Cabinet minister. Then two outspoken law lords, Bingham and Steyn, repeatedly said in well-publicised speeches and in writing, that the L.C.'s position was an unacceptable breach of the separation of powers, under the Convention, and that the law lords should move out of Parliament and into a Supreme Court. The last straw came in spring 2003, when the Council of Europe then made it crystal clear that the L.C.'s role was a flagrant breach of Art.6.

The first crucial Art.6 case, as Lord Bingham saw it, was *Findlay v UK*, described above, in relation to courts martial. Then, applying the same reasoning, requiring judicial independence, the role of a Scottish temporary sheriff was successfully challenged before the Judicial Committee of the Privy Council, in *Starrs v Ruxton* (2000) J.C. 208. The dual role of the Bailiff of Guernsey, as legislator and judge, was then successfully challenged before the ECtHR in *McGonnell v UK* (28488/95) 30 E.H.R.R. 289. The Bailiff's role was directly paralleled by the Lord Chancellor. The ECtHR reaffirmed the same principle in *Kleyn v Netherlands* (39343/98) (2004) 38 E.H.R.R. 14, in May 2003. *McGonnell* was cited extensively in the Scottish Court of Session judgment in *Davidson v Scottish Ministers (No.2)* [2004] UKHL 34. The issue here was the legality of a Scottish decision of a panel of judges which included a member of the House of Lords who had been directly involved in the passage of the legislation central to the decision. The decision was overturned. At the same time, the separation of powers argument had moved to the forefront of Convention challenges to English institutions, such as the Parole Board cases, discussed above.

Again advocating a Supreme Court in May 2002, the Senior Law Lord, Lord Bingham, set out his reasons and the various alternative models for a new court. I examine these in Ch.6 on the civil courts. Also speaking in 2002, another law lord, Johan Steyn, was much more strident. Most of his attack was directed at the L.C.'s position, although his speech was entitled "The Case for a Supreme Court." Lord Steyn, a South African, took a comparative view, examining the functional separation of powers, or lack of it, in the UK, in the context of the rest of the democratic world:

> "nowhere outside Britain, even in democracies with the weakest forms of separation of powers, is the independence of the judiciary potentially compromised in the eyes of citizens by relegating the status of the highest court to the position of a subordinate part of the legislature. And nowhere outside Britain is the independence of the judiciary potentially compromised in the eyes of citizens by permitting a serving politician to sit as a judge, let alone in the highest court which fulfils constitutional functions."

He examined in some depth the concept of separation of powers and the reasons for it, dismissing British defences of the status quo. His brilliant exposition is well worth reading and explains elegantly and in detail why the Government were forced to attempt to unravel some of those powers, in the Constitutional Reform Act 2005.

> "Justice Brandeis said that the separation of powers serves, not to promote efficiency but to prevent the exercise of arbitrary power. . .For protection, citizens must look to the courts. Tensions between these ideals arise from time to time. The executive and the judiciary are not on the same side. The stability of democratic institutions ultimately depends on public confidence."

4–065 Within a year of these two powerful law lords expressing disquiet, so did the Parliamentary Assembly of the Council of Europe. They published a report called *Office of the Lord Chancellor in the constitutional system of the United Kingdom* (Doc. 9798, a report to their Committee on Legal Affairs and Human Rights), in April 2003 saying,

> "Whilst the office of Lord Chancellor may be venerable and as yet remain unchallenged before the European Court of Human Rights, continuation of the current system creates real problems of lack of transparency and thus of lack of respect for the rule of law".

In the previous month, the author of this report, Erik Jurgens, Rapporteur to that committee, had appeared before the newly formed House of Commons Committee on the Lord Chancellor's Department. He was polite enough not to use the word hypocrisy and recognised that the ancient British constitution was venerated, but his evidence shows exasperation at the British failure to understand the requirements.of the separation of powers, when he was trying to promote it throughout Europe.

> "Every day in my Council of Europe work I am in confrontation with new democracies from central and Eastern Europe, who I tell they should not do certain things, and they say, 'What about the British? They have these appointed Members of Parliament in the upper House. They have a Lord Chancellor'. . .If you say he is a link between the Cabinet and the judges I think you are saying something very dangerous. . .I do not think judges should say anything to the Cabinet except in public and I do not think the Cabinet should say anything to the judges except in public because transparency is just about the most important point."

Countries who had been on the other side in World War II had made great efforts to develop new constitutions in compliance with the Convention. It was time to review the old, unchanged constitutions. Mr Jurgens' evidence was broadcast on the media. On hearing his words, I realised the Lord Chancellor's role would have to be dismantled. Only three years earlier, New Labour had "brought Convention rights home" in the HRA 1998. They could hardly be seen to be ignoring its very guardian, the Council of Europe. Ironically, the minister who introduced the 1998 Act was Irvine L.C. himself . As he was not persuaded of the need to give away his powers, Prime Minister Blair had no alternative but to replace him. I examine the consequences for the law lords in Ch.6 on the civil courts and the consequences for the L.C. in Ch.14 on judges.

8. Evaluations of the Human Rights Act

As can be seen from this chapter, the Act has had an impact on **4–066** a broad spectrum of English law, enhancing and extending rights for diverse groups from terror suspects to teachers. More examples can be seen in later chapters, such as 6, 10 and 14. The HRA came into force in 2000. Lord Irvine, in a November 2002 speech, said the courts had not dissolved into chaos; there was not a politicised judiciary or the inauguration of the rule of lawyers. We had developed a domestic "margin of appreciation". The Convention had reinvigorated the common law and "legal reasoning applied here carries weight in Strasbourg—as we hoped it would when drafting the Bill."

The civil liberties group, Liberty, has welcomed decisions such as *A (FC) v SS for the Home* [2004] UKHL 56, the Belmarsh case on terrorist suspects. Lord Woolf C.J., in a 2002 speech, said that if people rejected the 1998 Act's values, then they were rejecting the standards of Western society. Speaking at the ECtHR in January 2003, he said the Convention had had a "remarkably smooth transition into English law". English lawyers and judges felt "instinctively at home with Strasbourg jurisprudence". Sir John Laws said that the Convention embodies "values which no democratic politician could honestly contest". The Human Rights Lawyers Association, in a pamphlet celebrating ten years of the 1998 Act, 2000–10, said it had enabled the courts to balance the competing rights of different groups. People were spared the expense and delay of taking a case to the Strasbourg courts. It had strengthened rights without weakening Parliament by allowing judges to read legislation compatibly with the HRA. Decisions of the senior courts on human rights had been cited in Canada, India, New Zealand, South Africa and Australia. They gave further specific examples of groups who had benefited from the Act.

On the other hand, politicians, according to Nicol, do not and did not share these positive views. Parliamentary debates on such controversial areas as terrorism and asylum, during 2000–03 demonstrated that "the more 'fundamental' the rights at stake, the fiercer the desire of politicians to preserve their right to have the final say" and this became worse in the years after he wrote this. Nevertheless, the Joint Committee on Human Rights has been very proactive in drawing parliamentarians' attention to human rights issues. It decided to scrutinise all Bills.

In 2001, the UN Human Rights Committee called for the UK to establish a body to monitor human rights. The Equality and Human Rights Commission at last started work during a Labour administration, in 2008. It has a duty to promote and monitor human rights and enforce and promote equality. In 2007–08, both Prime Minister Gordon Brown and Justice Secretary Jack Straw expressed support for a UK Bill of Rights.

4–067 In opposition, in 2007–09, the Conservatives kept saying they would repeal the Human Rights Act and replace it with a Bill of Rights. DPP Kier Starmer QC, an internationally renowned human rights expert, heavily criticised those who attacked the HRA 1998: CPS Annual Lecture, October 21, 2009. He referred to, "those who. . .propose to replace the Human Rights Act. . .with other human rights which they consider to be more appropriately geared to 'British' society. . . the United Kingdom played a major role in the design and drafting of the European Convention. . . The idea that these human rights should somehow stop in the English Channel is odd and, frankly, impossible to defend."

Immediately before the 2010 election, the Conservative plans on human rights were unclear. Their spokesperson said on Radio 4, "I don't know. I haven't drafted the Bill yet". Conservative lawyers had established a HR Commission in 2007 and it had been divided. Ken Clarke, a Conservative, who is now the Minister of Justice, had said in 2006 that to replace the HRA with a HR Bill was "xenophobic and legal nonsense". In the meantime, David Cameron wrongly said in 2010 that the HRA had enabled a prisoner to have hard core porn, and that the police were not allowed to put criminals' faces on wanted posters. He was corrected by the police in 2007, after making the same speech to the Police Federation but seemed to have forgotten. See R. Smith, "Executive decision" (2010) 160 N.L.J. 296. The Labour Ministry of Justice launched a Green Paper Bill of Rights in March 2009. It included rights such as health care and rights for crime victims. It listed citizens' responsibilities too. In the JSB Annual Lecture, March 2009, retiring law lord, Lord Hoffmann, expressed strong views about the role of the ECtHR. He said the Strasbourg Court had been unable to resist the temptation to aggrandise its jurisdiction and impose uniform rules on member states. David Pannick QC said there were two answers to this. (1) The ECtHR took account of contracting states' margin of appreciation, and (2) The UK courts were not bound by ECtHR decisions. Under s.2 of the HRA, courts only had to take into account its judgments: see D. Pannick, "The European rights court has its uses—to keep us on our toes", *The Times*, May 7, 2009. In 2010, the Conservative party formed a Coalition government with the Liberal Democrats who would never allow the HRA to be repealed so the Conservative threat became academic; but J. Cooper and C. Warburton listed the reasons why the UK could not repeal the HRA:

- It would not benefit anyone.
- Following the Lisbon Treaty, EU member states were obliged to comply with the EU Charter of Fundamental Rights, which built on the Convention.
- The common law had a long tradition of protecting basic rights. Human rights thinking was highly influential before the HRA.

In March 2010, the UK Parliamentary Joint Committee on HR published a report, *Enhancing Parliament's role in relation to human rights judgments.* They said the UK's compliance record was generally good but there were lengthy delays, up to five years, in implementation in some cases. The UK should be "leading by example". The Coalition Government responded in July 2010, in Cm. 7892. They recognised that the UK is obliged to implement ECtHR judgments under Art.46 of the Convention. Compliance is overseen by the Committee of Ministers of the Council of Europe. Since 2000, there had been 26 declarations of incompatibility in the UK courts. Despite the pre-election Conservative rhetoric, they said:

"The Government remains committed to the European Convention on Human Rights. . .[but]. . .wants to look afresh at how human rights are protected in the United Kingdom to see if things can be done better and in a way that properly reflects our traditions. . .a Commission will be created to investigate the creation of a Bill of Rights that incorporates and builds on all our obligations. . .ensures that these rights continue to be enshrined in British law, and protects and extends British liberties. The Government will also seek to promote a better understanding of the true scope of these obligations and liberties" (p.5).

They said the Government had a good track-record on implementation and there was only one outstanding matter. There were not many repeat cases and only one per cent of judgments were against the UK in 2009 but the UK was slow to pay "just satisfaction" damages. Zander said the UK is in the top ten slowest countries to implement leading cases.

In November 2010, a new row broke out. Prime Minister David Cameron said the ECtHR ruling in *Green*, above, on prisoners' voting made him feel "physically ill". In February 2011, the Commons, in debate, rejected the *Green* ruling. Apparently, it is common in the other contracting states to find rulings of the ECtHR repugnant. Some MPs were also offended by the UKSC ruling that people should have the right to appeal for removal of their names from the Sex Offenders' Register. Theresa May said "It is time to assert that it is Parliament that makes our laws, not the courts, and that the rights of the public come before the rights of criminals and above all that we have a legal framework that brings sanity to cases such as these". On March 18, 2011, David Cameron announced the creation of (another) Human Rights Commission, despite the fact that his previous one had disintegrated (MoJ news release). Roger Smith, in the N.L.J., reported that the controversy was inflamed by *Bringing Rights Back Home* by M. Pinto-Duschinsky for the

Conservative "think tank", The Policy Exchange. He argued that the UK is not obliged to follow judgments of the ECtHR.

The UK has only failed to obey one ruling, in the "death on the rock" case, explained above, when the Conservatives refused to compensate the families of IRA members assassinated by the UK. On March 15, 2011, the Attorney General, Conservative Dominic Grieve, was interviewed by J. Rozenberg on Radio 4, in *Law in Action*. He said there was no chance that we would be departing from our commitment under the European Convention on HR. Indeed, we are taking over the chair of the Council of Europe in autumn 2011. There is a desire in the UK to reform the way the Court operates, during that period. He said there is a 140,000 case backlog before the ECtHR; last year it was 120,000. Some of the judges are "not very well focussed" on their work. "The court appears to be far too willing to try to micro-manage Convention rights in individual states." This exact concern is shared by the other 46 contracting states. In April 2011, they signed a declaration intended to curb the court (see Ford and Gibb). Ken Clarke said it should stop acting as if it were an appeal court from our own Supreme Court. Nevertheless, it seems that Prime Minister Cameron's Attorney General and Justice Minister have by now explained to him that the very idea of repealing the HRA and derogating from the Convention is repugnant to most UK common lawyers who understand the simple point that I made at the beginning of this chapter: the Convention was drafted by British lawyers and much of it was modelled on the common law.

BIBLIOGRAPHY

The Rt Hon. Lady Justice Arden DBE, "Building a Better Society",   **4–068**
    speech, October 21, 2008; "Is the Convention ours?" speech,
    January 29, 2010, Judiciary website.

G. Bindman, "Contempt of the European Court", *New Statesman*,
    November 15, 1996.

Rt Hon. Lord Bingham of Cornhill C.J., "A New Supreme Court
    for the United Kingdom", May 1, 2003, The Constitution Unit,
    University College, London, *http://www.ucl.ac.uk/constitution-
    unit*, and see his 2001 speech "The Evolving Constitution", Law
    Society, October 4, 2001.

J. Cooper and C. Warburton, "HRA 1998: irreversible?" (2010) 160
    N.L.J. 1605.

H. Fenwick, G. Phillipson and R. Masterman (eds), *Judicial Reasoning
    under the UK Human Rights Act* (2007).

R. Ford and F. Gibb, "Human rights court will be reined in over
    deportation" *The Times*, April 28, 2011.

S. Fredman, "Judging Democracy: The Role of the Judiciary under the HRA 1998" (2000) 53 C.L.P. 98.

Lord Hoffmann, "The Universality of Human Rights", speech, April 1, 2009.

R. Hudson, (1996) 146 N.L.J. 1029.

Human Rights Lawyers Association, "Ten years of the Human Rights Act: Providing Protection, Participation and Accountability", 2010.

A. Kavanagh, "The Elusive Divide between Interpretation and Legislation under the Human Rights Act 1998" (2004) 24 (2) *Oxford Journal of Legal Studies* 259.

Lord Irvine, "The Human Rights Act Two Years On: An Analysis", speech delivered on November 1, 2002, reproduced at [2003] P.L. 308.

R. Masterman, "A Supreme Court for the United Kingdom: two steps forward, but one step back for judicial independence" [2004] P.L. 48; *Democracy Through Law* (2004).

Lord Neuberger M.R., "Protecting human rights in an age of insecurity" (discussion of the judiciary's role), speech, February 7, 2011, judiciary website.

D. Nicol, "The Human Rights Act and the politicians" (2004) 24 *Legal Studies* 451.

D. Oliver, "Functions of a Public Nature under the Human Rights Act" [2004] P.L. 329.

A. O'Neill, "Judicial Politics and the Judicial Committee: the Devolution Jurisprudence of the Privy Council" (2001) 64 M.L.R 603.

L. Parkhill and C. Murray "A difference of opinion", (2007) 157 N.L.J. 1378–1379.

J. Raine and C. Walker, *The Impact on the Courts and the Administration of Justice of the Human Rights Act 1998*, LCD Research Report 9/2002, archived on the Department of Constitutional Affairs website.

A.T.H. Smith, "The Human Rights Act and the Criminal Lawyer: The Constitutional Context" [1999] Crim. L.R. 251 and see other articles in the same issue.

K. Starmer and others, articles in *The Times*, October 2, 2001, reviewing the Act's first year.

Lord Johan Steyn, "The Case for a Supreme Court" (2002) 118 L.Q.R. 392.

The Joint Committee on Human Rights 2010 report and government response are on the Parliament website.

A.L. Young, *Parliamentary Sovereignty and the Human Rights Act* (2008).

A. Wade, "Forces need final push to match civil justice", *The Times*, January 25, 2005.

J. Wadham and R. Taylor, "The Human Rights Act two years on" (2002) 152 N.L.J. 1485.

Supplements to *The Times*, September 26, 2000 and October 2, 2001.

R. White, *The English Legal System in Action* (1999).

Lord Woolf, "Human Rights: Have the Public Benefited?" speech, October 15, 2002.

M. Zander, "Could do better" (on how well the UK responds to human rights judgments) (2010) 160 N.L.J. 1249.

FURTHER READING AND SOURCES FOR UPDATING THIS CHAPTER

Updates from spring 2012 and 2013 on the Sweet & Maxwell **4–069** website.

Council of Europe: *www.coe.int.*

European Court of Human Rights: *www.echr.coe.int* See Annual Reports, press releases and judgments.

European Human Rights Law Review.

Human Rights Lawyers Association *www.hrla.org.uk.*

Judges' speeches on the judiciary website and the UKSC website.

JUSTICE *www.justice.org.uk.*

Parliament website, notably the reports of the Joint Select Committee on Human Rights.

Public Law journal, also on *Westlaw.*

Regular updates on human rights in *Legal Action* and the *New Law Journal* (N.L.J. is also on *Lexis*).

5. Law Reform and the Changing Legal System

"Everyone nowadays regards law reform as 'a good thing'. It was not always so. It was a proud boast of Lord Bathurst the 18th century Lord Chancellor, that when he left office, he had left English law exactly as he had found it." (Carnwath L.J., former Chairman of the Law Commission, 2002.)

1. The inevitability of change

How much easier the lawyer's life must have been in those days. All areas of law are characterised by change. New governments want to make their mark and a government with a powerful majority will succeed in having most of the Bills implementing their policies passed by Parliament. Parliament is choking with the sheer volume of legislation it is expected to scrutinise. To the 15,000 annual pages of domestic legislation we can barely digest, we have to add 5,000 of European regulations, over which the UK Parliament has no control, and directives, most of which are enacted through statutory instruments. The higher courts develop and change the common law. There are more judges and more cases than ever before. The more complex the society, the more complex the law and the disputes that arise. 5–001

2. Methods of law reform

Parliament

Most Acts result from Government Bills, sponsored by the relevant Minister. Education legislation, for example, will be introduced by the Secretary of State for Education and will have 5–002 been prepared by that department. Only a very few private Members of Parliament succeed each year in getting a Public Act on to the Statute Book. Parliamentary time is so valuable that the Government demands almost all of it. Pressure groups like JUSTICE, Liberty, the Statute Law Reform Society and the Legal Action Group, as well as the Bar Council, the Law Society and specialised interest groups campaign for changes in the law and legal system and lobby for Bills to be introduced, dropped, drafted or amended. Some, like the CBI, are very powerful organisations with wide national support but sometimes small pressure groups lobby successfully for change. Bills may be introduced, or delegated legislation passed, following the report of a Royal Commission or advisory committee, or another ad hoc review body, such as those described below. Parliament is so busy that it can take a long time to close a legal loophole. The Domestic Violence, Crime and Victims Act 2004, s.5 closed the gap in the law of murder which allowed parents or carers to get away with murdering children and the vulnerable, where two or more carers both denied the offence and there were no witnesses to the harm. This problem was well known even before it was discussed by the Royal Commission on Criminal Justice Report 1993.

The judiciary

5–003 Judges can effect dramatic changes in the law through statutory interpretation and reinterpretation of the common law. In 1991, the law lords abolished the rule that a husband could not be guilty of raping his wife: *R. v R* [1991] 3 W.L.R. 767. We saw in Ch.2 that the law lords, now UKSC, will readily change the common law to keep up with social change, as they have done recently in recognising pre-marital contracts and broadening the defence to defamation. The higher courts have been forced to change their approach to statutory interpretation and become much more proactive, by the Human Rights Act 1998 and by our membership of the EU, as can be seen from the previous two chapters. As demonstrated in Ch.4, by reading words into statutes, the law lords have extended people's Convention rights.

Judges sometimes draw attention to anomalies and call for change, as can be seen in Ch.2. An example occurred in *R. v Kai-Whitewind* [2005] EWCA Crim 1092, where the Court of Appeal (CA) highlighted defects in the law on infanticide and complained that it was unsatisfactory and outdated. Also, senior judges make public speeches calling for law reform. Senior judges sometimes spoke in law reform debates in the House of Lords, before the Constitutional Reform Act 2005 removed them. As well as contributing to, or even provoking, the debates on constitutional reform, from 2003, they turned out in force in the debate on the Human Rights Bill. Judges also have the Judges' Council as a vehicle for discussing proposed changes in law and policy. For example, in 2011, they condemned the Minister of Justice's plans to cut legal aid.

The Law Commission—a story of frustration and wasted taxpayers' money

This is an independent body established by the Law Commissions Act 1965 with a duty under s.3(1):

> "to take and keep under review all the law with which they are. . .concerned with a view to its systematic development and reform, including in particular the codification of such law, the elimination of anomalies, the repeal of obsolete and unnecessary enactments, the reduction of the number of separate enactments and generally the simplification and modernisation of the law".

It does this through codification of the law, consolidation of statutes and statute law revision. The commissioners are five lawyers (practitioners and academics) seconded for a five-year period. The chairperson is always a HC or CA judge. Despite criticism, there are no laypeople. They have a Chief Executive, about 20 members of the Government Legal Service, two Parliamentary Counsel who draft Bills for them and a number of research assistants (highly qualified law graduates), a librarian and administrative staff.

They conduct many projects simultaneously. They research an area of law which has been criticised by judges, lawyers, government departments or the public, to identify defects, then publish proposals in a consultation paper. Once responses have been considered, they publish a report, usually with a draft Bill appended. Uncontentious law reform measures can be speeded through Parliament in the "Jellicoe" procedure, which allows the use of a Special Public Bill Committee, without using parliamentary time allocated to normal Bills. The procedure was used for the Public International Law Act 1994 which implemented three Law Commission reports. Their projects and reports appear on their website.

They have repealed over 5,000 redundant Acts since 1965. For instance, in 2008 a Statute Law (Repeals) Bill was introduced to repeal 260 Acts and part-repeal 68 Acts, covering such activities as raising tolls for turnpikes and financing workhouses. The oldest statute affected was passed in 1695. Codification is inevitably a long-term plan, since in each case the objective is a single self-contained code, which will be "the statement of all the relevant law in a logical and coherent form".

5–004

The annual report and now law reform reports show which of their recommendations have been implemented. Until the 1990s, they were especially frustrated in their lack of progress in persuading governments to allocate parliamentary time to Bills designed to enact their Draft Criminal Code, which they published in 1989. In the 1990s, successive chairmen of the Commission complained bitterly at the backlog of their reports ignored by governments. The 1994 Annual Report complained of "serious unease among many people" that the work of the Commission was being neglected. The chairman, then Sir Henry Brooke, said there were 36 reports "stuck in the log-jam".

5–005 The Jellicoe procedure for speeding Bills through Parliament was introduced in 1994 and Hudson commented "(h)ow it can have taken until now to devise such an obvious procedure beggars belief" ((1994) 144 N.L.J. 1668). Disappointingly, the next chairman, Dame Mary Arden, commented in 1998 "the procedure has not worked quite as had been hoped as it makes very heavy demands on the time of members of the committee and of ministers and their officials". In the 1996 Annual Report, in an open letter to the Lord Chancellor, she accused the Government of wasting taxpayers' money by delaying implementation of law reforms. One of the reports ignored was on conspiracy to defraud, noting defects in the law. In *Preddy* [1996] A.C. 815, the House of Lords ruled that mortgage fraud was not covered by the law of theft. Eleven prosecutions had to be dropped and many others were not brought. At last, the Fraud Act 2006 placed most common law fraud and conspiracy to defraud on a statutory footing. Most of the Bill was drafted by the Law Commission to accompany its 2002 paper on fraud.

Another scandal relates to the state of offences against the person, embodied in the decrepit, inappropriate, contradictory and archaically-worded Offences Against the Person Act 1861, upon which the Commission reported in 1993. Commissioner Stephen Silber QC complained of inaction in 1996. He illustrated it with the example of stalking. Had their proposals been implemented, there would have been none of the uncertainty that arose in the courts as to whether it was a criminal offence. In 2005, 80,000 cases per year were being prosecuted under this anachronistic Act. By 2007, the Chairman, then Sir Terence Etherton, was still complaining in the Annual Report that "A continual concern of the Commission since its inception has been the rate and speed of implementation of the Commission's recommendations".

In March 2003, the Department of Constitutional Affairs (DCA) published the *Quinquennial Review of the Law Commission*. John Halliday, its author, recommended strengthening its relationships with government. The aim should be to maximise public benefits derived from law reform. Performance would be at its best, he said, when:

- the projects selected were those most likely to result in public benefits through successful law reform;
- government committed itself in advance to act on the outcomes;
- projects were managed to the highest standards, with regular reviews to ensure timeliness;
- links between the Commission and its stakeholders (mainly Government departments) were strong;
- the Commission's internal systems and systems for managing the relationship with Government were strong; and
- the Commission and the DCA had the necessary vision, commitment, skills and resources.

He made a number of recommendations to improve the work and organisation of the Commission and its links with government and the public. Most of these had been implemented by 2005. In 2007, the Chairman reported improved publicity, "we are raising our profile in Westminster and Whitehall, and sending more clearly our message to those who need to hear it" but the second bullet point is a precondition for success and this has not yet been achieved. In 2008, the Minister of Justice made a welcome announcement. He expressed the Government's intention to put a stop to the Law Commission's perpetual frustration.

"For 40 years the Law Commission has played a vital role. . .but I intend to strengthen its role by placing a statutory duty on the Lord Chancellor to report annually to Parliament on the government's intentions regarding outstanding Law Commission recommendations."

The chairman welcomed this as the most important structural change between the Commission, Parliament and the executive since the Commission's creation. This led to the Law Commission Act 2009 which now requires an annual report to be laid before Parliament on implementation of the Commission's proposals. The first report was published in January 2011. On 15 issues, the government is still considering its position. Five matters have been dismissed by Government (Ministry of Justice News release January 24, 2011). Also, resulting from the 2009 Act, in 2010, a protocol was laid before Parliament on the relationship between the Commission and the Lord Chancellor (Minister of Justice). Government departments will undertake to take forward relevant law reform; keep the

Commission up to date on policy developments that may impact on its proposals and provide an interim response within six months of LC proposals and a full response within a year. In its turn, the Law Commission will consult ministers about potential law reform projects in their areas; support all its final reports with an impact assessment and take full account of the minister's views in deciding whether and how to continue with a project at agreed review points. Thus, by 2011, it looks as if the Government has at long last understood that it is a pointless waste of public money to establish a body of experts to painstakingly plan and consult on law reform and then just ignore it.

Advisory committees

5–006   Standing committees of experts and interested parties are statutorily appointed to keep specific areas of law and policy under review and to provide information and recommendations. They range through such diverse topics as disabled persons, pets, nutrition, drugs, gene therapy, protection of the sea, pesticides, nuclear safety, herbal medicines, construction and advertising.

Royal Commissions

5–007   These are appointed ad hoc, to conduct major reviews of the law or legal system. The recommendations of the Royal Commission on Criminal Procedure (1980) led to the passing of the Police and Criminal Evidence Act 1984 (PACE). In 1991 the Royal Commission on Criminal Justice was established, at the height of public concern over famous miscarriages of justice. It reported in 1993 and some of its recommendations have been followed, such as those on appeals, in the Criminal Appeal Act 1995. Others have been ignored, such as those on the right to silence. Royal Commissions are very expensive and since the mid-1990s governments have preferred to appoint individuals to recommend legal system reform, such as those listed below.

Other bodies and individuals

5–008   On legal system reform, the Lord Chancellor (Minister of Justice) is advised by several standing and many ad hoc committees, such as the Legal Services Commission, the Administrative Justice and Tribunals Council and the Youth Justice Board. At the time of writing, the future of many of these remains uncertain, as the Coalition Government plans to abolish several, if it can persuade Parliament to do so in the Public Bodies Bill, known as "the bonfire of the quangos". There are rule committees on family, civil and criminal procedure rules. The Justice Minister also appoints non-statutory working parties. The Research Secretariat of the Ministry of Justice sets a research agenda, funding projects often executed by academics. In the last decade, two judges and a retired judge were appointed to report on reforming the work and organisation of the civil courts (Lord Woolf), the criminal courts (Auld L.J.) and tribunals (Sir Andrew Leggatt). This book contains countless examples of specially commissioned reports, especially the last chapter.

(Green) Consultation Papers and (White) Policy Papers

All government departments may publish Green Papers setting out their proposals for legislative change. These are open invitations for comment by the interested public at large. Once gathered in, these responses help to modify final legislative proposals, which are set out in a White Paper.   **5–009**

Statute law revision

Dame Mary Arden, who chaired the Law Commission, provided an interesting account of this. The Renton Committee on the Preparation of Legislation, in 1995, made detailed recommendations on the drafting of statutes, parliamentary procedure and statutory interpretation. In 1992 the Hansard Commission reported on the legislative process. Dame Mary said badly drafted legislation encouraged litigation and was, therefore, expensive; unclear legislation transferred the power to determine the law from an elected legislature to the courts and it was a fundamental civil liberty that people should be able to know and understand the laws that govern them. She told the story of the Tax Law Rewrite. In 1995, the Inland Revenue published two documents listing criticisms of the 6,000 pages of tax legislation, including: **5–010**

- Complicated syntax, long sentences and archaic or ambiguous language.
- The principles underlying the rules were not apparent. This forced the courts to interpret strictly according to wording.
- Too much detail, covering every conceivable situation.
- Many sections could not be understood in isolation.
- Some rules were wide and, therefore, uncertain.
- It was difficult to find all the rules.
- Definitions were inconsistent and spread throughout different statutes.
- There was an imbalance between primary and secondary legislation.
- There was a lack of consultation and openness in drafting statutes.

The Inland Revenue decided to organise a project, a five-year plain English rewrite, consulting representative bodies and taxpayers and employing 40 lawyers. A special joint committee of the Lords and Commons would scrutinise Bills.

Consolidation and codification

5–011   Consolidating statutes endeavour to simplify the law by replacing multiple statutes (Acts) with a single Act. The Consolidation of Enactments (Procedure) Act 1949 permits the Lord Chancellor to pilot consolidating Bills. Thus, for example, the whole of the legislation concerned with tribunals and inquiries was brought together and updated in the Tribunals and Inquiries Act 1992. The consolidating procedure is not possible where the Bill involves changes of substance in the law, known as "codification". A codifying measure brings together the existing statute and case law, in an attempt to produce a full statement as it relates to that branch of law. The main examples of successful codification date from the end of the nineteenth century when the following four statutes were passed: the Bills of Exchange Act 1882, the Partnership Act 1890, the Sale of Goods Act 1893 and the Marine Insurance Act 1906. The Bills of Exchange Act 1882 involved the consideration of 17 statutes and 2,500 decided cases. These were compressed to make a statute 100 sections long. After these Acts were passed, there was no more codifying legislation until the Theft Act 1968.

The difference between consolidation and codification is classically illustrated by the example of the Powers of Criminal Courts (Sentencing) Act 2000, designed to pull together all the legislative strands of sentencing, which was such a struggle in application for judges and an even greater struggle for justices' clerks and other magistrates' legal advisers. The problem was and is, however, that this neat fabric was already unravelling, with a new statute in 2001, and has been further unwound annually, by later statutes. Doubtless, the Government will never resist the temptation to pick away at sentencing and criminal procedure, as it does every year, usually in more than one statute. What the Law Commission, Lord Chief Justices and academics are clamouring for is a proper criminal code, which would include all substantive criminal statute law, criminal procedure and sentencing, like the California Penal Code and that of every other US state. Then, anyone could buy or download the latest version every year. When the Government is tempted to pick away at procedure, it will have to weave its amendments into the existing cloth of such a code, instead of unravelling it, and confusing everybody by adding a new statute.

The Law Commission, frustrated at inaction on a criminal code, pointed out on its website in 2001 that we are almost the only country in the world without one. Lord Bingham C.J. told this pathetic history of English criminal law in exasperated tones, "The plea for such a code cannot, I fear, startle by its novelty":

- 1818, both houses petitioned the Prince Regent to establish a Law Commission to consolidate statute law.
- 1831, Commission established to inquire into codifying criminal law.
- 1835–1845, it produced eight reports, culminating in a Criminal Law Code Bill, ultimately dropped.
- 1879, Royal Commission recommended code containing 550 clauses.
- 1844–1882, Lord Brougham and others made eight parliamentary attempts to enact a code.
- 1965, Law Commission established.
- Criminal Code Team established, including Professor Sir John Smith "the outstanding criminal lawyer of our time" (Bingham).
- Code published 1985, revised and expanded 1989.

He concluded:

"even the most breathless admirer of the common law must regard it as a reproach that after 700 years of judicial decision-making our highest tribunal should have been called upon time and again in recent years to consider the mental ingredients of murder, the oldest and most serious of crimes" (at p.695).

Spencer added a plea for a code of criminal procedure, because in this context English inaction looks even more pathetic in the face of a 1995 Scottish code:

". . . the sources are at present in a shocking mess, as a result of which the law is not readily accessible to those who have reason to discover it. . . dispersed among. . .some 150 statutes. . . even the modern ones are mainly messy and unsystematic and hard for the user to find his way around: a succession of Criminal Justice Acts, each a disparate jumble of new rules, or of new amendments to old ones" (at p.520).

Almost all the law of evidence was uncodified and our haphazard way of creating rules resulted in "all sorts of astonishing contradictions". He, the Law Commission and others were, doubtless, pleasantly surprised by the government announcement, in their White Papers in 2001 and 2002, that they intended to start work on a criminal code. Quickly taking advantage of government interest in codification, the Law Commission started updating its 1989 Draft Criminal Code. It employed two outside experts to help and it circulated draft sections to interested parties by email, such as practising and academic lawyers' groups. On the website, they reported their progress. In 2009, however, they abandoned the project because of "complexity of the common law, the increasing pace of legislation, layers of legislation on a topic being placed on another with bewildering speed and influence of European legislation": Ian Dennis, editorial [2009] Crim. L.R. 1. He also said piecemeal codification of the criminal law, such as the common law on self-defence was "a pointless exercise": [2008] Crim. L.R. 507. Lawyers already know the law and it will not help non-lawyers to work out what they can reasonably do to fend off a burglar or assailant.

In 2005 the bold step was finally taken of reducing all the rules of criminal procedure to one set. They have now been set out in one place, on a dedicated website, but are still a hopeless mish-mash. The Criminal Procedure Rule Committee now has the awful task of organising them into some sensible form and rewriting them in plain English. They re-issued them in 2010. Disappointingly, however, the Government established a committee to work on the codification of primary legislation on criminal procedure but recently withdrew funding for the project, to Spencer's frustration (2007).

BIBLIOGRAPHY AND UPDATING SOURCES

5–012   Updates of this book from spring 2012 and 2013, on the Sweet & Maxwell website.

Dame Mary Arden, "Modernising Legislation" [1998] P.L. 65.

Rt Hon. Lord Bingham of Cornhill C.J., "A Criminal Code: Must We Wait for Ever?" [1998] Crim. L.R. 694.

Interview with Sir Henry Brooke, *The Magistrate*, February 1994.

Carnwath L.J., "The art of the possible" *Counsel*, February 2002, p.20.

S.M. Cretney, "The Law Commission: True Dawns and False Dawns" (1996) 59 M.L.R. 631 (historical).

Judiciary of England and Wales website, especially judges' speeches.

Law Commission website: *www.justice.gov.uk/lawcommission*.

Lord Neuberger M.R., "Law reform—where will it all end?" speech, December 2, 2010, judiciary website.

J.R. Spencer, "The Case for a Code of Criminal Procedure" [2000] Crim. L.R. 519.

J.R. Spencer, editorial [2007] Crim. L.R. 331.

Sir Roger Toulson, "Law reform in the twenty-first century" (2006) 26 (3) *Legal Studies* 321–328.

Part II: Institutions

THE COURT STRUCTURE

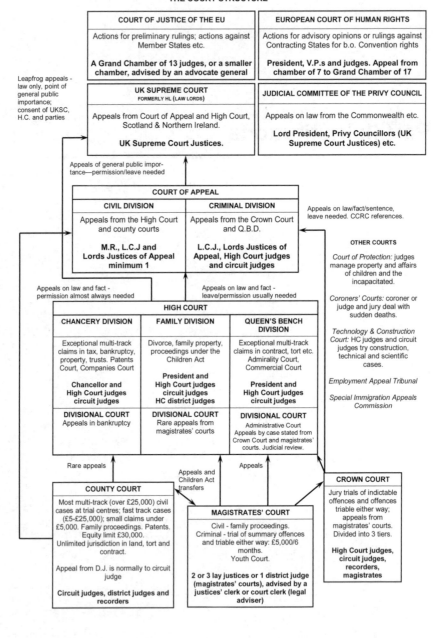

COURT OF JUSTICE OF THE EU

Actions for preliminary rulings; actions against Member States etc.

A Grand Chamber of 13 judges, or a smaller chamber, advised by an advocate general

EUROPEAN COURT OF HUMAN RIGHTS

Actions for advisory opinions or rulings against Contracting States for b.o. Convention rights

President, V.P.s and judges. Appeal from chamber of 7 to Grand Chamber of 17

Leapfrog appeals - law only, point of general public importance; consent of UKSC, H.C. and parties

UK SUPREME COURT
FORMERLY HL (LAW LORDS)

Appeals from Court of Appeal and High Court, Scotland & Northern Ireland.

UK Supreme Court Justices.

JUDICIAL COMMITTEE OF THE PRIVY COUNCIL

Appeals on law from the Commonwealth etc.

Lord President, Privy Councillors (UK Supreme Court Justices) etc.

Appeals of general public impor- tance—permission/leave needed

COURT OF APPEAL

CIVIL DIVISION

Appeals from the High Court and county courts

M.R., L.C.J and Lords Justices of Appeal minimum 1

CRIMINAL DIVISION

Appeals from the Crown Court and Q.B.D.

L.C.J., Lords Justices of Appeal, High Court judges and circuit judges

Appeals on law/fact/sentence, leave needed. CCRC references.

OTHER COURTS

Court of Protection: judges manage property and affairs of children and the incapacitated.

Coroners' Courts: coroner or judge and jury deal with sudden deaths.

Technology & Construction Court: HC judges and circuit judges try construction, technical and scientific cases.

Employment Appeal Tribunal

Special Immigration Appeals Commission

Appeals on law and fact - permission almost always needed

Appeals on law and fact - leave/permission usually needed

HIGH COURT

CHANCERY DIVISION

Exceptional multi-track claims in tax, bankruptcy, property, trusts. Patents Court, Companies Court

Chancellor and High Court judges circuit judges

FAMILY DIVISION

Divorce, family property, proceedings under the Children Act

President and High Court judges circuit judges HC district judges

QUEEN'S BENCH DIVISION

Exceptional multi-track claims in contract, tort etc. Admirality Court, Commercial Court

President and High Court judges circuit judges

DIVISIONAL COURT
Appeals in bankruptcy

DIVISIONAL COURT
Rare appeals from magistrates' courts

DIVISIONAL COURT
Administrative Court Appeals by case stated from Crown Court and magistrates' courts. Judicial review.

Rare appeals

Appeals and Children Act transfers

Appeals

COUNTY COURT

Most multi-track (over £25,000) civil cases at trial centres; fast track cases (£5-£25,000); small claims under £5,000. Family proceedings. Patents. Equity limit £30,000.
Unlimited jurisdiction in land, tort and contract.

Appeal from D.J. is normally to circuit judge

Circuit judges, district judges and recorders

MAGISTRATES' COURT

Civil - family proceedings. Criminal - trial of summary offences and triable either way: £5,000/6 months.
Youth Court.

2 or 3 lay justices or 1 district judge (magistrates' courts), advised by a justices' clerk or court clerk (legal adviser)

CROWN COURT

Jury trials of indictable offences and offences triable either way; appeals from magistrates' courts. Divided into 3 tiers.

High Court judges, circuit judges, recorders, magistrates

6. Civil Courts

"**I don't give a fuck whether we're peers or not**" (Senior Law Lord, Lord Bingham, on being asked by Boris Johnson MP whether he would not miss being in "the best club in London" if the law lords moved out of Parliament and into a new Supreme Court, *The Spectator*, May 2002).

"**Inadequate information technology; stressed administrative staff; too few books for the judiciary; rushed listing; and judges required to wander down to waiting rooms to collect their next case because there is no one else to do it for them. . .The public areas of some civil courts are run down and squalid.**" (Hazel Genn, *Judging Civil Justice*, The Hamlyn Lectures 2008).

"**To no-one will we sell, to no-one deny or delay right or justice**". (From Magna Carta 1215, cl.40).

The work of the civil courts was reformed in the 1990s. Following **6–001** the Civil Justice Review 1988, the Lord Chancellor was given powers under the Courts and Legal Services Act 1990 to reorganise the business of the High Court and the county courts. The Review recommended a shift of work down to the county courts, as the High Court was clogged up with trivial cases. The Woolf Report, *Access to Justice*, 1996, recommended an overhaul of civil procedure, implemented by the Civil Procedure Rules (CPR) 1998. From 2005–09, the development at the pinnacle of the three UK court structures was the creation of a UK Supreme Court. A picture of court business is drawn in the annual *Judicial and Court Statistics*, on the website of the Ministry of Justice, the responsible government department. The latest at the time of writing, April 2011, are the 2009 statistics. Courts are administered by Her Majesty's Courts and Tribunals Service, an independent government agency, created in its present form in April 2011.

1. Magistrates' courts

6–002   Trial courts, where cases start off, are called "courts of original jurisdiction" or "courts of first instance". There are 330 magistrates' courts in England and Wales in 2011 but 93 are about to close. From around 1200, a number of knights were appointed in each county to keep the peace. By a series of statutes in 1327–1377, they became known as justices of the peace, the predecessors of modern JPs, also known as magistrates. Cases are heard by two or three lay magistrates or a professional district judge (magistrates' courts). Most cases are criminal but their civil work is important. Under the Children Act 1989, their domestic courts were renamed "family proceedings courts", where specially trained magistrates can make and enforce financial provisions following a family breakdown and can make orders protecting adults and children. Unlike the county courts and High Court, they cannot grant divorces. Under the 1989 Act, they share jurisdiction in children cases with the High Court and county courts and those cases are allocated according to complexity. They can make a range of orders relating to children, including care, supervision, adoption, contact and residence.

Other civil work includes Council Tax, VAT enforcement and the imposition of anti-social behaviour orders. In 2005, the magistrates lost their liquor licensing work to local authorities. This was a logical change. Magistrates used to carry out all local government functions until the Local Government Act 1888 created local councils. Licensing was a relic of this administrative work.

2. County courts

6–003   Since their establishment by the County Courts Act 1846, they have provided a local and relatively inexpensive alternative to the High Court for civil business. They do not follow county boundaries. Their name is historical. There are around 216 in 2011 but 49 are about to close. Circuit judges specialise in the more complex work. District judges' jurisdiction to assess damages is now unlimited, unless otherwise directed. They preside over the small claims court, where the limit is £5,000. They handle most pre-trial case management and hear 80 per cent of contested county court trials. Circuit judges generally hear matters where over £25,000 is claimed. Recorders are lawyers who sit part time, doing similar work. Deputy district judges are lawyers sitting part-time. All judges sit alone, although circuit judges and recorders may sit with a jury of eight, in categories of case described in the chapter on the jury. The Lord Chancellor nominates, or "tickets", a number of judges to sit in proceedings under the Children Act. Specialist circuit judges are nominated to sit in the the mercantile, chancery, and technology and construction courts. Designated Civil Judges manage civil judges in their area and Designated Family Judges manage family work at care centres.

Under the Courts and Legal Services Act 1990, s.3, the county court was given almost all the powers of the High Court, with some restrictions. They try the bulk of civil cases, such as tort, contract, property, insolvency and bankruptcy, with the High Court reserved for a few special cases. In 2009, over 1,800,000 cases were started, nine per cent fewer than 2008. Over 1,200,000 of these were money claims, 98,000 were social landlord repossessions, 94,000 were mortgage repossession claims and 76,000 were insolvency petitions. Most cases are resolved without a trial. There were 20,000 trials and 47,000 small claims hearings. Some county courts have the jurisdiction to hear "equity" cases, about trusts, and contested probate up to the value of £30,000. Under the Civil Procedure Rules 1998, cases are divided into small claims, fast track and multi-track and the county courts hear all small claims, most fast track and most multi-track claims. Almost all divorces are granted by the county courts. They share jurisdiction under the Children Act with the magistrates' courts and the High Court. Public law care cases involve parties other than just the parents, such as the local authority, and are heard at special county courts called care centres. Family hearing centres hear private family proceedings, where only the parents and children are involved. County Courts include five specialist mercantile courts (the provincial equivalent of the Commercial Court) and a patents county court, all of which have specialist circuit judges. Big city county courts have been renamed Civil Justice Centres, as they offer ADR as well as litigation facilities.

3. The High Court of Justice

The High Court of Justice (HC) and the Court of Appeal (CA) **6–004** were brought into being as the Supreme Court of Judicature under the Judicature Acts 1873–1875. At that time, the HC consisted of five Divisions representing the old separate courts it replaced, the Queen's Bench, Chancery, Probate, Divorce and Admiralty (PDA), Exchequer, and Common Pleas. The last two were merged in the Queen's Bench Division (QBD) in 1880 and the remaining three continued unaltered from then until the 1970 redistributed of the PDA functions created the Family Division. The Constitutional Reform Act 2005 renamed the HC and CA as the Senior Courts of England and Wales.

The HC sits at the Royal Courts of Justice in the Strand and, for the convenience of litigants and their lawyers, there are a number of district registries and trial centres in the larger cities in England and Wales. There are 108 High Court judges, 18 in Chancery, 18 in Family and 72 in the QBD. Trials may be conducted by deputy HC judges (lawyers sitting part-time) and circuit judges authorised ("ticketed") to hear HC cases. All HC judges generally sit alone, with the exception of certain judicial review cases and commercial arbitrations. Jury trial is permitted in the QBD in five torts and at the discretion of the judge but is very rare in other cases. The most common and well-publicised jury trials are defamation actions.

The Queen's Bench Division

6–005 This, the great common law court, takes its name from the fact that the early royal judges sat on "the bench", "*en banc*", at Westminster. It absorbed the whole common law jurisdiction, when the High Court was reformed. The present jurisdiction of the Division is thus both civil and criminal, original and appellate and the QBD is much larger than the other two Divisions.

In its general civil jurisdiction, most cases are contract or tort. There is a right to jury trial in fraud, libel, slander, malicious prosecution and false imprisonment. It is headed by a President. Cases are managed, pre-trial, by Masters of the HC in London (in a part of the Royal Courts of Justice called "the Bear Garden") and by district judges outside London. The QBD contains the Commercial Court and the Admiralty Court. In the latter, one judge and registrars hear cases relating to ships, such as collisions and damage to cargo. Most HC cases are disposed of in London but some are heard in specialist district registries. A "commercial list" was established in the High Court in 1895. The 15 judges who sit in the Commercial Court hear cases normally involving over £1 million, on contracts relating to shipping, commerce, insurance, banking, international credit and questions arising from arbitrations. A specialist Administrative Court was added in 2000. Most QBD judges spend half their time sitting on circuit hearing serious Crown Court cases or civil cases heard outside London. The QBD administers the Technology and Construction Court (TCC) which hears such things as technical construction disputes, computer and sale of goods litigation, torts relating to the occupation of land and questions arising from arbitrations in building and engineering disputes. Specialist QBD judges also sit in the Employment Appeal Tribunal. Five full-time TCC circuit judges sit in London, supervised by two HC judges. Over 40 circuit judges and recorders are nominated, "ticketed" to hear TCC cases in 11 provincial centres. In a *Times* article, its then head, Jackson J., reminded us that the construction industry accounted for about 10 per cent of GDP and the IT industry was also a significant part of our economy (Law supplement, June 14, 2005). Its judicial strength was enhanced in 2005, following concern that too few cases were being brought in the TCC and too many before the Commercial Court, because people perceived that they would get a superior service from its HC judges. This seems to have worked as TCC proceedings have increased.

The Divisional Court of the Queen's Bench Division

In its appellate jurisdiction, the QBD, like the other two Divisions, 6–006 has what is rather confusingly called a Divisional Court. This is, in most instances, an appeal court. In the QBD its jurisdiction includes such matters as follows:

- appeals on a point of law by way of case stated from magistrates' courts and the Crown Court;
- judicial review—the supervisory jurisdiction of the HC over the lower courts and tribunals and, most importantly, over governmental and other public bodies. Specialist judges of the Administrative Court hear applications for judicial review. For instance, challenging the closure of a hospital, or a refusal to grant asylum, or a decision to evict gypsies from public land. The Administrative Court also sits in four regional centres;
- applications for habeas corpus (challenging the legality of detention); and
- appeals and applications on planning matters.

There are currently 37 High Court judges nominated ("ticketed") to hear these cases, including family and chancery judges. Some matters are determined by a single judge, such as applications for leave to apply for judicial review (on paper or in person) and others must be heard by at least two judges, usually a HC judge and a Lord Justice of Appeal. Judicial Review work was expected to expand significantly from 2000, when the Human Rights Act 1998 made the European Convention on Human Rights enforceable in the English Courts. There was a 60 per cent increase in the caseload of the Administrative Court in 2004–08, not because of human rights claims but because of asylum and immigration claims, which formed two thirds of its workload. 90 per cent are found to have no merit in law. The Lord Chief Justice complained in 2008 that this was placing a strain on the QBD judges. There was a 27 per cent increase in judicial review applications in 2009. Of the 9,000, 6,660 were on asylum and immigration. By contrast, only 18,600 proceedings started in the QBD general list in 2009, compared with over

112,000 in 1996, because of the shift of work down to the county court. Reconsideration applications in asylum and judicial review were transferred to the new Upper Tribunal in February 2010 so this will have relieved the heavy burden on the Administrative Court.

The Chancery Division

6–007   This is the direct descendant of the Lord Chancellor's equity jurisdiction, and the pre-1873 Court of Chancery. It also has statutory responsibility for such matters as the winding-up of companies and revenue cases. Its 18 specialist judges are headed by the Chancellor. Interlocutory matters are heard by HC Masters in London and district judges outside. Its jurisdiction can be summarised as:

- disputed intellectual property, copyright or patents;
- the execution or declaration of trusts;
- the redemption and foreclosure of mortgages;
- conveyancing and land law matters;
- partnership actions and other business and industrial disputes;
- the administration of the estates of deceased persons (contested probate);
- revenue issues, i.e. taxation cases;
- insolvency;
- professional negligence claims against solicitors, accountants surveyors and others.

It contains two specialist courts: the Patents Court, dealing with patents and registered designs, and the Companies Court, which deals mainly with company insolvency. It sits at the Royal Courts of Justice and eight provincial HC centres. Most of the substantial work in the provinces is handled by circuit judges "ticketed" for HC Chancery work. The Divisional Court of the Chancery Division heard tax appeals from the Commissioners of Taxes and from the county courts in bankruptcy cases. Some of these tax appeals are shifting into the Tax and Chancery Chamber of the Upper Tribunal. Because of its intellectual property and copyright jurisdiction, the litigants we are most likely to hear of in Chancery are involved in the music industry, such as the Spice Girls, Bruce Springstein and George Michael.

The Family Division

6–008   This Division shares family jurisdiction with the magistrates' court and the county court. Cases may be transferred. Its 19 High Court judges and 29 HC district judges are headed by a President.

HC judges sit in the Royal Courts of Justice and some hear cases while travelling on circuit. District judges sit in the Principal Registry of the Family Division, in Holborn. Most cases outside London are heard by authorised ("ticketed") circuit judges. The main work is:

- complex defended divorce cases, either in London or district registries with divorce jurisdiction;
- complex applications relating to children, under the Children Act, for instance applications for care orders, adoptions, wardship, residence and contact orders, where the contest is acrimonious or complex or one or more parties lives abroad. Only this court may deal with wardship applications, in which the court orders a child to be made a ward of court and subject to its control; and
- the grant of probate or letters of administration to authorise the disposal of a decreased person's estate where the matter is uncontested. This work is done at the Principal Registry and 11 District Probate Registries.

The Divisional Court of the Family Division used to hear appeals from decisions of magistrates but these now go to the county court, since 2009. There were 31 appeals in 2009, mostly under the Children Act.

A unified family court has been debated since the 1960s and was recommended by the Finer Committee in 1974. It has been mooted ever since and the recommendation was repeated in the Family Justice Review 2011 but proceedings remain divided between the three courts, which causes immense confusion and stress to some parties and delay, inefficiency and consequent expense. Repeated claims by politicians and judges that we are on the verge of a family court are an exaggeration and lack insight into this chaos.

4. The Court of Appeal (Civil Division)

The Court of Appeal (CA) was created by the Judicature Acts **6–009** 1873–1875 and now forms part of the senior courts, as explained above. It was intended that the CA should be the final appeal court, but a change of plan led to the Appellate Jurisdiction Act 1876, under which the House of Lords in its judicial capacity was retained as the highest appeal court (until 2009).

Thirty-seven Lords Justices sit in the CA. The Master of the Rolls heads the Civil Division. The President of the Family Division and the Chancellor and HC judges sit occasionally. It hears appeals on fact and law from the HC and the county courts. Until recently, the Court was composed of three Lords Justices but, after the Access to Justice Act 1999, s.54, the Court may be composed of one or more judges, depending on the importance and complexity of the case. The rationale behind this was "proportionality and efficiency", explained in the 1998 Government White Paper *Modernising Justice*. In a case of great importance (see *Ward v James (No.2)* [1966] 1 Q.B. 273) a "full court" of five judges is convened. It sits in the Royal Courts of Justice in the Strand but sat in Cardiff for the first time in 1999. There were about 1,200 appeals in 2009, the same as previously, though there has been a big decrease on interlocutory appeals and applications for appeal since 2005.

5. The House of Lords Appellate Committee transforms into the Supreme Court

6–010   From the Appellate Jurisdiction Act 1876 until July 2009, the Appellate Committee of the House of Lords was the final court of appeal in civil matters from all courts in the UK and in all criminal cases except those from Scotland. There were 12 Lords of Appeal in Ordinary, known colloquially as the "law lords". Other senior judges could sit, such as the Master of the Rolls, the Lord Chief Justice, foreign appeal judges and peers who had held high judicial office. They were called Lords of Appeal and sometimes law lords. By constitutional convention, members of the House of Lords who were not judges did not take part. Normally, five judges heard an appeal. If a case was exceptionally important, such as the 2004 *Belmarsh* case, discussed in Ch.4, or the first Hunting Act case, discussed in Ch.2, seven or nine law lords could sit. The cases were heard in two Lords committee rooms in the Palace of Westminster. The appeals always raised a point of law of general public importance, the sole ground for obtaining leave. Leave was very rarely granted by the court below so applications were made to the Appeal Committee. After reaching their judgments, "opinions", The Court gave notice of their decision to the House of Lords itself, in the chamber.

The Constitutional Reform Act 2005 replaced the Appellate Committee with a UK Supreme Court from October 2009. Chapter 4 on human rights explains the background to the Act and the arguments about a UKSC. This Act resulted from the Government announcement in 2003 that it was determined to reform the constitution, by abolishing the Lord Chancellor (they did not achieve this but reformed his role), reforming judicial appointments and transforming the law lords into a Supreme Court.

The problem with the law lords, apart from their inclusion of the Lord Chancellor, discussed in Ch.14 on judges, was their place in the legislature and consequent perceived danger that they could be involved in debates on Bills which they might later have to interpret and apply in court. Further, despite the constitutional convention that law lords should not take part in political debates in the House of Lords chamber, some law lords had done so, albeit very rarely. Both in reality and in appearances, the law lords breached the separation of judicial and legislative power required by the European Convention on Human Rights, Art.6. In 2003, the Government was persuaded by the reform campaigners, law lords Bingham and Steyn. Lord Steyn invoked the words of the famous constitutionalist Walter Bagehot, that the "the Supreme Court of the English people. . .ought not to be hidden beneath the robes of a legislative assembly". He was alarmed at the confusion of functions in the eyes of the public and foreign observers, reminding us that when the law lords delivered their judgments in the first *Pinochet* case, in the Lords' chamber, foreign television viewers thought Lady Thatcher was part of the dissenting minority, opposing the extradition of General Pinochet in 1998. He reminded us of the requirements for judicial independence under Art.6, the UN, the Council of Europe's Charter of the Statute for Judges and the Universal Charter of the Judge.

Although it had been mooted, as recently as the 1960s, that the law lords should be abolished, leaving the CA as the final appellate body, that argument was rarely heard by 2000. Stevens pointed out, in various of his works, cited in Ch.14, that the 1873 Judicature Act abolished appeals to the House of Lords and set up "the Imperial Court of Appeals", sitting in the Strand. It was only a group of Tory mavericks that led it back to the House of Lords, three years later, for the purpose of "dignity", said Stevens. In the comment examined below, Baroness Hale also examined the option of abolishing the top court.

The reasons for questioning the future of the law lords were, said Lord Bingham in 2002, the recent reforms of the House of Lords as a parliamentary chamber, the Human Rights Act and the new role of the Privy Council in devolution issues. The last development raised the issue of whether the law lords and the Judicial Committee of the Privy Council (JCPC) should be merged. He examined the four different models for a Supreme Court, as he saw them: **6–011**

1. Amalgamating the law lords and JCPC as a UK Supreme Court.
2. A new constitutional court, operating *alongside* courts in the three UK jurisdictions (Northern Ireland, Scotland and England and Wales).

3. A court modelled on the European Court of Justice, giving authoritative rulings on points of law referred to it by other courts, as opposed to appeals.
4. Simply severing the law lords from the legislature, re-housing and renaming them but with their powers unchanged and with the JCPC continuing alongside.

He preferred the fourth option. The following year, in June 2003, under pressure from the Council of Europe, as described above in Ch.4, the Government announced their intention to form a Supreme Court. In the consultation paper, *Constitutional Reform: a Supreme Court for the United Kingdom,* they relied heavily on Lord Bingham's ideas. Below, I paraphrase and summarise the main questions it raised and the responses. Notice that the Government did not ask *whether* there should be a Supreme Court. "The Government *will* legislate to abolish the jurisdiction of the House of Lords" (my emphasis) but they said they had no intention of creating a US style supreme court, with the power to strike down legislation:

"Parliament is supreme in our constitution and must remain so. Nor, in the absence of a codified, clearly delineated body of constitutional law, do we see a role for a Constitutional Court" (Department of Constitutional Affairs Press Release 296/03).

The 2003 consultation paper asked the following questions:

1. *Should the UKSC's jurisdiction include the devolution cases dealt with by the JCPC (explained below)?* 86 per cent of respondents were in favour.
2. *Do you agree that its members should remain at 12, with access to a supplementary panel?* 74 per cent agreed.
3. *Should retired Supreme Court members be appointed to the House of Lords (i.e. the upper House of Parliament)?* 68 per cent agreed.
4. *Should the court sit in panels, as the law lords did, or should every member sit on every case (as in the US Supreme Court)?*
   69 per cent of respondents thought the Court should sit in panels. Several respondents cited Lord Bingham's concern that if all members of the court decided all cases, the appointing authority might try and influence decision-making when filling vacancies.
5. *Should the Court decide for itself which appeals it hears?* 64 per cent felt the procedure should remain unchanged.

Six law lords considered the proposals unnecessary and harmful. They believed the law lords' presence in Parliament to be beneficial to the law lords, the house and litigants. The cost would outweigh any benefit. One of the new ones, in 2004, was the outspoken Brenda Hale, for whom the planned UKSC was not radical enough (see below). By 2008, some law lords had retired and been replaced so only two opposed a new Court. All were agreed that a Supreme Court should enjoy an independent budget.

There were formidable critics. New Zealander, former Lord of Appeal, Lord Cooke considered that in the British constitution, mixing powers "works in a way envied outside Britain". Law reform debates in the chamber had benefited from the contribution of serving and former law lords. Lord Bingham's own maiden speech, urging incorporation of the European Convention, cited in Ch.4, was a perfect model. The suggestion that the law lords violated the European Convention was, Cooke thought, "a figment in the imagination of a controversialist". Retired Lord of Appeal, Lord Lloyd referred to the proposed reforms as "constitutional vandalism". The most outspoken critic was Lord Woolf C.J. He delayed retirement to stay and "fight for the independence of the judiciary". In the 2004 Squire Centenary Lecture, he remarked that the proposed court would be a "poor relation" of the world's other supreme courts, because of its more limited role:

> "We will be exchanging a first class Final Court of Appeal for a second class Supreme Court. . .Separating the House of Lords in its legislative capacity from its activities as the Final Court of Appeal could act as a catalyst causing the new court to be more proactive than its predecessor. This could lead to tensions. Although the law lords involvement in the legislative chamber is limited, the very fact that they are members of the legislature does provide them with an insight and understanding of the workings of Parliament." (Judiciary website.)

Lord Falconer L.C. responded in the House of Lords, when introducing the Constitutional Reform Bill for its second reading:

> "The Law Lords are appointed to the final Court of Appeal, not the legislature. They are judges. We. . .believe in the supremacy of Parliament. Ultimately, laws must be made by Parliament. The judges, in accordance with law, must construe and interpret those laws. However, unlike systems such as that in the United States of America, we do not want policy issues such as capital punishment, abortion or racial discrimination to be decided by judges. . .That most certainly does not make our system any

worse or better than that in the United States of America; it is simply different. . .It will not make our new Supreme Court in any sense second rate." (*Hansard*, March 7, 2004).

6–012   The Bill was almost defeated but the Government rescued it by promising that it could be scrutinised by a Parliamentary select committee. It was delayed. The committee made 400 amendments. Lord Woolf, placated by the Government's promise of £45 million to fund the new building, decided to support the Bill. By Christmas 2004, it was clear there would be a separate supreme court and the only outstanding issue was to find a prestigious building.

Some academics and others had advocated a supreme court for years. To them, the reforms were too hasty and ill-thought-through. Their writings (the best collection being in *Legal Studies*, as cited in the bibliography) show frustration that the proposals did not go far enough. They either wanted a US style constitutional court or considered that the UKSC would be one in disguise. Robert Stevens (in that volume) was cynical, considering the Government's reasoning to be *Alice in Wonderland* "if we say often enough that our judges are apolitical they will be." The consultation paper emphasised the supremacy of Parliament, yet the reality was that the Human Rights Act and the European Communities Act had required the law lords to apply a fundamental law and act as a type of constitutional court.

Baroness Hale (Brenda Hale), former academic, the first ever woman Lord of Appeal, carefully examined the ramifications of abolishing the top court altogether, an option ignored by most other commentators. The main argument for retaining the new court's jurisdiction over ordinary civil cases was uniformity of approach (in England and Wales, Scotland and Northern Ireland) but she was cynical. The opportunity for error-correction in such cases only arose rarely and randomly, dependent on whether one of the parties wanted to appeal. The argument for retaining a final appellate court rested on the deficiencies of the Court of Appeal, which worked under a great deal of pressure and was heavily dependent on the quality of the arguments prepared before it.

She asked, "If we are to have all the upheaval this will entail, is it not worth contemplating doing something a little more radical?" She argued that a supreme court was there to bridge the gap between law and society and to protect democracy. It could be confined to cases of constitutional importance, on human rights, devolution, Europe, international treaties and perhaps adding in those ordinary cases where a serious inconsistency had arisen between the UK's jurisdictions. Such a transformation would raise an argument for fundamental change in composition. It was commonplace for members of other supreme courts to come from much wider professional backgrounds than the law lords. As a consequence, the style of judgments might change: to an informed and intelligent non-lawyer, the judgments of the European Court of Human Rights were much easier to read and understand than those of the law lords.

Professor John Bell, writing in the same collection, complained **6–013** that there had been no attempt at strategic thinking in the consultation papers, "It is constitutional reform by way of incremental change". Comparing ours with continental supreme courts, he raised these questions, which I paraphrase:

1. Why have a *single* Supreme Court? European courts have specialist panels and some jurisdictions have separate courts to apply and interpret administrative law. Do we need a larger range of expertise? Is there a case for a specialist reporting judge, as on the continent?
2. How should it act as the authoritative interpreter of the law? The principal role of other supreme courts is to quash, rather than re-decide, wrongly decided cases. The suggestion of a referral for a preliminary ruling on a point of law (like the Court of Justice of the EU) was dismissed in the consultation paper without discussion but this might be a more efficient way of securing decisions on significant points of law. If the court was to be limited to difficult or important points of law, should these not be paid for by public funding?
3. Was it to be a constitutional court? Under the devolution legislation, abstract review of legislation is permitted. On the other hand, the European Convention is pervasive. It might be difficult to separate out constitutional cases.
4. Should it give advisory opinions? Some European supreme courts do. The concept was not alien to our courts, as they could give declaratory rulings.
5. How did it relate institutionally to law reform? The Swedish Supreme Court could make suggestions for law reform, technically scrutinise Bills and comment on proposed reforms. The annual reports of French supreme courts make suggestions for law reform.
6. What would be its place within the judiciary? European supreme courts use younger judges as judicial assistants, helping them to learn judicial technique.

Many more opinions were expressed on the composition of the new UK Supreme Court and selection of judges. I come back to this issue in Ch.14 on judges. The Bill was ultimately passed as the Constitutional Reform Act 2005, after months of Parliamentary scrutiny, debate and amendment. Part 3 provided for a UK Supreme Court, and transferred to it the judicial functions of the Appellate Committee of the House of Lords and the devolution jurisdiction of the Judicial Committee of the Privy Council (JCPC). It opened in October 2009. It consists of 12 judges appointed by her Majesty, under letters patent. The number can be increased by Order in Council. It has a President and Deputy. The others are called Justices of the Supreme Court. They are not lords but given the courtesy title "Lord" or "Lady". The law lords were the first Justices. Selection and appointment is detailed in Pt 3 of the Act, and discussed here in Ch.14. The bench should generally consist of an uneven number of judges and a minimum of three. Supplementary acting judges may be appointed, drawn from the CA or equivalent in Scotland and Northern Ireland and from a panel consisting effectively of the same people who could have sat as Lords of Appeal. For instance, Lord Judge C.J. and Lord Neuberger M.R. have already sat with them. The Court may appoint and hear from a special adviser. The Court's rules are made by the President, with a view to securing that the Court is "accessible fair and efficient" and they must be "both simple and simply expressed". They were drafted after consultation. The Lord Chancellor appoints a Chief Executive, in consultation with the President, and the President appoints other staff. The Lord Chancellor is responsible for providing an appropriate buildings and resources. The selected building is Middlesex Guildhall, across Parliament Square from the Palace of Westminster. It was very contentious, since the law lords wanted a dedicated new building, not a converted Crown Court. It has annoyed building historians and conservationists, since they consider its interiors to have been one of the most important examples of gothic revivalist architecture. (See *The Guildhall Testimonial*, 2006, by the pressure group *Save Britiain's Heritage.*)

The Act lays down the rules as to precedent. An appeal from one jurisdiction in the UK will not be binding on the courts of another UK jurisdiction so a Scottish appeal would not be binding on England and Wales. In devolution proceedings, however, all cases are binding throughout the UK, except on the Court itself. The statute is silent on the details of procedure and, indeed, on the court's power to select cases it wishes to hear, so the Justices are free to devise their own practice. The transformation into the UKSC made the law lords think about their procedures. For example, at the time of writing, 2011, I have noted the following points, gleaned from my personal observations, discussions with UKSC Justices and the many articles listed in the bibliography below.

- They are now more inclined to sit as a panel of seven or nine, though this is the continuation of a law lords' trend. This can be seen from case reports on their website.
- They are endeavouring to give more unified judgments, though this does not always work. There is a debate raging about unified judgments, with Carnwath and Neuberger L.JJ. and Lady Hale campaigning for more, and Arden L.J. campaigning for them to be more user-friendly. See judges' speeches on the Judiciary website, notably Neuberger M.R., 2009. He favours US Supreme Court style judgments. This is further discussed in Ch.2, in the section on case law.
- They are more ready to hear interveners, giving them a maximum of 15 minutes' argument.
- One aim is that the UKSC should be much more accessible to the public. They welcome visitors and have a website that is much more informative than that of the law lords, with details of upcoming cases and excellent press releases summarising their judgments (though the website still shows room for improvement). The court attracts many visitors, though there is astonishingly little media interest, given that they can make use of the continuous TV feed.
- All Justices may now comment on applications for leave to appeal, though these are still determined in secret by three Justices, as they were in the law lords. They complain that there is still no public list of *reasoned* decisions on permission to appeal and parties' written submissions are not made public.
- Proper conference rooms now enable them to do a tiny bit of pre-deliberation before case hearings.
- A blog commentary has been established by lawyers. Human rights cases still dominate the lists.

There was a well-publicised clash of opinions in autumn 2009 on the nature of the UKSC. Lord Neuberger M.R. said it might become a constitutional court, with power to overrule legislation. Lord Phillips, its first President, and Lord Bingham, previous Senior Law Lord were adamant that it would not. The argument is summed up by Lord Neuberger M.R. in a speech on December 3, 2009, "Is the House of Lords losing part of itself?"

"In the light of this climate, I have expressed the concern that one unintended consequence of the Supreme Court's creation might be the eventual emergence of a constitutional court; that it would in time consider that it had, like other Supreme Courts, had the power to review the legality of law, to declare Acts of Parliament unconstitutional. Might we see a UK Supreme Court at some time in the future have its own *Marbury v Madison* moment, with a future Supreme Court President declaring like US Chief Justice Marshall, that a particular law was 'repugnant to the constitution' and therefore no law at all. Let me be clear I am not saying that this will or that it should happen. I am saying it may happen. Many eminent people, Lord Phillips and Lord Bingham among them, say that it won't, and they may well be right. . . Section 40(5) of the Constitutional Reform Act 2005 could imply a power to review the constitutionality of statutes. It provides that the Supreme Court 'has power to determine any question necessary to be determined for the purposes of doing justice in an appeal to it under any enactment.' What if the question is whether an Act of Parliament is contrary to a fundamental right, a constitutional right? It might, I suppose, be argued that this provides more than the US Constitution does as a guide as to whether constitutional judicial review lies within the ambit of the Supreme Court" (paras 23–24).

The UKSC has been criticised in 2010–11 over its human rights decisions, as discussed in Ch.4. The transformation of the law lords into a UKSC has provoked a large amount of academic commentary. For a synopsis of this material and empirical research on the way the top court works, including interviews with and observations of the Justices, see Ch.15 of Darbyshire, *Sitting in Judgment: The Working Lives of Judges* (2011).

6. The Court of Justice of the EU

6–014   This is described in the chapter on EU law. It consists of one judge per Member State of the EU. Each must be qualified to hold the highest judicial office in their own country, appointed for a six-year term by their governments. They are assisted by eight advocates-general who prepare reasoned conclusions on the cases heard. Judges sit in odd number chambers with the most important cases being heard by a Grand Chamber. The ECJ's job is to ensure that EU law is interpreted and applied consistently in each member state. The Court is not bound by judicial precedent and has a flexible approach to the interpretation of the Treaties.

7. The European Court of Human Rights

6–015   This is described in Ch.4 on human rights. Remember it is totally separate from the EU. It was set up in Strasbourg by the Council of

Europe Member States in 1959 to deal with alleged violations of the 1950 European Convention on Human Rights. It is composed of a President, Vice President and judges elected by the Parliamentary Assembly of the Council of Europe and nominated by the member states of the Council, for a six-year period. Judges are allocated to one of the court's four sections, which are geographically and gender balanced. The Court sits in Chambers of seven judges or, in exceptional cases, as a Grand Chamber of 17. The Committee of Ministers of the Council supervises the execution of the Court's judgments. Since 2000, UK litigants must exhaust all their remedies through the UK courts before petitioning the ECtHR.

8. The Judicial Committee of the Privy Council

The JCPC was established in 1833, by the Judicial Committee Act. **6–016** It is composed of Privy Councillors who have held or now hold high judicial office, mostly the UKSC Justices. It sat in Downing Street but moved to the Supreme Court building in 2009. Its primary job is as the ultimate appeal court from some UK overseas territories (such as the Cayman Islands) and Crown dependencies (Jersey, Guernsey and the Isle of Man) and from some Commonwealth states. In 2003, New Zealand withdrew from the JCPC's jurisdiction and created its own supreme court, having debated it for 100 years. The Committee hears appeals from certain ecclesiastical and obscure domestic courts and tribunals in England and Wales, such as the Disciplinary Committee of the Royal College of Veterinary Surgeons. It acquired jurisdiction over devolution issues in 1998 but lost that jurisdiction to the UKSC in 2009. Each case must be heard by a board of not more than five and not less than three members of the Committee, although one group of exceptional cases in 2004, on the constitutionality of the Jamaican death penalty, was decided by a board of nine. It usually consists of five UKSC Justices, assisted (very rarely now) by a senior judge from the country concerned. Its civil work is varied. Recently it has included cases on commercial arbitration, banking, employment, revenue, land disputes, juries and matrimonial matters.

Its criminal jurisdiction is controversial. Since the 1990s, its liberal-minded judges, hostile to the death penalty, have provoked the impatience of the governments of independent Caribbean countries who send appeals to it in death penalty cases. It frequently allows appeals against conviction (e.g. *Boodram v State of Trinidad and Tobago* [2001] UKPC 20), or against the imposition of the death penalty. In one decision, *Lewis* [2001] 2 A.C. 50, it ruled that hundreds of death row prisoners in the Caribbean should be given a stay of execution. Similarly, in *Reyes v The Queen* [2002] UKPC 11 and two other murder appeals in 2002, the JCPC ruled that the imposition of the mandatory death penalty was uncon-stitutional in seven Caribbean countries. Its automatic imposition for some crimes was held by the JCPC to be inhuman or degrad-ing treatment, offending against international standards of human rights. A similar decision was reached on the unconstitutionality of the death penalty of Jamaica, by a nine judge Judicial Committee, in *Watson v The Queen* [2004] UKPC 34. In two cases decided on the same day, however, their Lordships felt constrained by the word-ing of the constitutions of Barbados and Trinidad and Tobago. "The language and purpose of [the relevant constitutional provisions] are so clear that whatever may be their Lordships' views about the morality or efficacy of the death penalty, they are bound as a court of law to give effect to it", said Lord Hoffmann, in giving the major-ity judgment in *Boyce and Joseph v The Queen* [2004] UKPC 32.

These death penalty cases are argued by the pro bono (mean-ing working without charge) units of large London law firms and English human rights barristers. They have had a very high success rate since the mid-1990s. Consequently, governments and some judges in Caribbean countries see the JCPC as a group of unduly liberal judges who undermine their efforts to tackle high murder and violence rates and drug trafficking on their islands. They have long debated whether to abolish the JCPC's jurisdiction and replace it with a regional court of appeal. In 1970, at the Sixth Heads of Government Conference in Jamaica, the home delega-tion proposed the establishment of a Caribbean Supreme Court. In 2001, an agreement was signed to establish it and a building was set aside in Trinidad. It was obvious that as a consequence of its forma-tion, many people then waiting on death would be executed. In a 2005 ruling of great constitutional significance, *Independent Jamaica Council for Human Rights v Marshall–Burnett* [2005] UKPC 3, how-ever, the JCPC ruled that three Acts of the Jamaican Parliament, designed to give effect to the agreement to establishment of the Caribbean Court of Justice were not enacted in accordance with the procedure laid down in Jamaica's constitution and were thus void. Lord Bingham started the judgment by giving an assurance that the judges had no interest of their own in the outcome of the case. They merely existed in that capacity to serve the wishes of the people of Jamaica. If and when the people of Jamaica decided that they no longer did so, they were fully entitled to end the role of the JCPC. In *Bowe v The Queen* [2006] UKPC10, the court abolished the death penalty in the Bahamas. Keir Starmer, the human rights QC (since appointed DPP), said this was the culmination of a 10-year litigation strategy to abolish the death penalty in the English-speaking Caribbean. In 2001, however, the Caribbean Court of Justice was established and it is taking over appeals from some Caribbean countries. See its website for details.

There is a problem with trivial JCPC cases wasting the time of **6–017** the UKSC Justices, especially when many of them would like to sit more often in panels of seven or nine in the UKSC. Recently, they heard a case arising out of a truck crash and another that resulted from a long-term feud by rival busnessmen. Cases cannot be excluded where leave has been granted by the local court or where, astonishingly, appeal lies as of right. Imposing a requirement that they obtain leave, or leave from the JCPC, would require legislation in all those countries sending such appeals to the JCPC. JCPC work used to occupy almost as many sitting days as law lords work but is rapidly diminishing. It heard 105 cases in 2006 but only 47 in 2009. Procedure changed in 2009, replacing oral leave hearings with paper applications. Hearings are shorter than in the UKSC. Advocates must justify hearings lasting more than one day, rather than the two days normally permitted for UKSC hearings. To save their time, judges changed practice to sit more often in benches of three, from 2009, to make up for using nine Justices more frequently in the UKSC, though it has backtracked a bit as Commonwealth countries have objected.

9. Other civil courts

Ecclesiastical courts

They exercise control over the Church of England clergy. In **6–018** each diocese there is a consistory court, or equivalent, the judge (Chancellor) of which is a barrister or a judge appointed by the bishop. Appeal lies to the Arches Court of Canterbury or the Chancery Court of York, and further appeal lies to the JCPC.

Court of Protection

Under the Mental Capacity Act 2005, the Court of Protection is **6–019** a superior court of record, with a President, VP and specialised circuit and district judges, sitting in London and six provincial centres.

The coroner's court

The Coroner's Court is used to inquire (by an inquest) into unex- **6–020** plained deaths. Its proceedings are inquisitorial, unlike those of a court. The coroner may, and sometimes must, call a jury of seven to

11, to return a verdict as to the cause of death. The coroner must be legally or medically qualified. In 2003, the Government published a fundamental review of the coronial system and in 2004 started a programme of reform, taking account of case law on coroners' proceedings that had arisen under the Convention, described in Ch.4 on human rights. The Review recommended:

- all coroners should be legally qualified;
- inquests should be held into deaths in custody, traumatic workplace deaths, public transport crashes and certain deaths of children;
- exceptionally complex or contentious inquests should be conducted by a circuit judge or High Court judge;
- the outcome should be a factual account of the cause and circumstances of death and an analysis of whether there were systemic failings;
- coroners should report findings swiftly to any relevant body;
- families should have a right to meet the investigator and be kept informed;
- juries should be used in most cases where Art.2 of the Convention is engaged, such as deaths in custody.

By January 2005, the new system for these penetrating, inquiry-like inquests was in use. In 2007–08 a high profile inquest into the deaths of Princess Diana and Dodi Al-Fayed was conducted by Scott Baker L.J. and a jury and in 2010–11, Hallett L.J. presided over the "London 7/7 bombings" inquest.

The Employment Appeal Tribunal

6–021   This was established by the Employment Protection Act 1975 to hear appeals from decisions of Industrial Tribunals (now employment tribunals), in particular those relating to unfair dismissal, equal pay and redundancy. The composition of the court for a hearing is one High Court judge, or a "ticketed" circuit judge, sitting with two lay people who have specialised employment knowledge. It sits at the level of the High Court. This means its decisions are not subject to judicial review and appeals on points of law go direct to the Court of Appeal.

10. Court management

6–022   The system of court management was fundamentally restructured in 2005, under the Courts Act 2003, following the recommendations of the 2001 *Review of the Criminal Courts of England and*

Wales (the Auld Review). The Lord Chancellor (Secretary of State for Justice) and his department, the Ministry of Justice, created in 2007, run the courts, court staff and buildings. Under the Courts Act 2003, he is under "a duty to ensure that there is an efficient and effective system to support" the running of the courts. A unified courts agency, Her Majesty's Courts Service (now HM Courts and Tribunals Service), was established in 2005, to administer the day-to-day running of the courts. This replaces the Court Service and the local magistrates' courts committees, committees of magistrates who were responsible for running their courts. In 2004–05, the Lord Chancellor established local courts boards under s.4 of the Courts Act. In 2011, there are 21. Under s.5, they have the function of scrutinising, reviewing and making recommendations about the way the Lord Chancellor is running the local Crown Court, county courts and magistrates' courts. The Lord Chancellor issues them with guidance as to how they should carry out their functions and must give due consideration to their recommendations. Each courts board consists of seven people—one judge, two magistrates, two people with knowledge and experience of how the courts operate in their area (such as lawyers, or victim support) and two people representative of the area.

Note the quotation from Magna Carta that heads this chapter. Judges, the Civil Justice Council and lawyers are highly critical of the government's reluctance to spend money and make the civil courts self-funding. They consider that the courts should be run as a public service. Some consider that civil justice is treated as a poor relation, so that when money is spent on information technology or other improvements it is directed to the criminal courts. In a 1997 speech objecting to fee increases, Sir Richard Scott V.C. said the idea the civil courts should be self-financing was "indefensible from a constitutional point of view". They are frustrated that their IT provision still does not begin to equate with that recommended by Lord Woolf in his 1996 review of civil procedure, *Access to Justice*. In 2003, the Master of the Rolls, head of civil justice, warned that without enough funding for new technology, the civil justice system was in danger of seizing up. In 2002, Lord Woolf C.J. accused the Government of "flawed thinking". The self-funding policy was "self-evidently nonsense". No other country in the world had such a policy and its effects were "pernicious and dangerous". In 2003, Mance L.J. said the Government must face the fact that civil justice would never pay for itself. He said that in other Commonwealth countries, New Zealand and Australia, fee income paid for less than half the cost of civil and family courts. High fees put people off bringing their cases to court and would mean that commercial cases would subsidise family cases.

In a November 2004 speech, Brooke L.J. said he had spent 19 years promoting IT in the courts. He complained of "chronic underfunding". Things were getting worse, with an inadequate IT infrastructure and very poor pay in the court service, leading to a high turnover of staff. In the sixth Woolf survey carried out by the Law Society in 2003, solicitors complained of administrative problems, with 40 per cent declaring that inefficient administration of court offices had impacted on their clients' ability to pursue claims. A third had had clients who had been discouraged from proceeding because of cost, especially in the High Court. Court fees were increased again in 2005, and again recently. In 2007, on the BBC news, Judge Paul Collins, of the Central London Civil Justice Centre (county court) said "We are operating on the margins of effectiveness, and with further cuts looming we run the risk of bringing about a real collapse in the service".

6–023   The Lord Chief Justice published his first ever *Review of the Administration of the Courts* in 2008. He complained that the courts suffered from a serious shortage of judges, a high turnover of under-paid staff, unreliable statistical information and continuing IT problems. Very controversially, civil court fees were ramped up very dramatically in 2008. The cost of taking child care proceedings rose from £150 to £5,225 so local authority applications to protect children at risk reduced by 25 per cent. By 2009, there was a £90 million shortfall in collection of fees. The maintenance backlog in courts amounted to £200 million. In an interview on *Law in Action*, BBC Radio 4, in October 2009, Lord Judge C.J. said a civil justice system was "A cardinal requirement of a civilised society". He complained that although the civil courts sometimes made 115 per cent profit, it was not permissible to plough the money back into the system.

There have been decades of complaint that London's commercial courts: the Commercial Court, the Admiralty Court and the Technology and Construction Court have inadequate facilities and this risked losing commercial court business from London to foreign destinations. The Lord Chancellor's Department, predecessor to the Ministry of Justice, published a consultation in 2002. Until 2011, the commercial court sat in office blocks around the Royal Courts of Justice and in St. Dunstan's house, nearby, described by one judge as "a public disgrace", because of its cramped courtrooms and lack of waiting and consultation facilities. The London business community share the judges' frustration. Lawyers are well aware that the civil courts' IT systems are extremely poor, compared with those of large London law firms. The Commercial Court is important in attracting foreigners in to use London's legal services, which feed the Treasury with at least £850 million a year in taxes. In around 70 per cent of Commercial Court cases, one litigant is foreign. In around 50 per cent both sides are foreign so the fear of losing work to foreign jurisdictions is a real one. Lord Phillips M.R., then head of the civil courts, said in 2005 that the number of trials had recently dropped by one third and this was a reflection on better commercial court facilities in Amsterdam, Dublin and elsewhere. At last, a site in Fetter Lane is under development. The new Rolls Building will house the Commercial Court, the Chancery Division and the High Court section of the TCC, from October 2011. It is claimed it will be the world's biggest business court.

> An example of the Commercial Court's work: the BBCI bank collapsed in 1991, losing clients £9 billion. The BCCI liquidators launched a landmark legal action against the Bank of England, alleging misfeasance in its failure to supervise BCCI. The trial opened in January 2004 and the first witness was called in June 2005, by which time trial costs were estimated to be £70 million (source: *The Times*, June 14, 2005).

At the lower levels of the court structure, judges complain that court closures reduce public access to justice. By concentrating courts in a few larger centres, it is increasingly difficult and expensive for parties, witnesses, lawyers and other court users to get to the few remaining courts. Since one of the advantages of lay justices used to be their familiarity with their locality, this problem has an added dimension in the context of the widespread closure of magistrates' courts since the 1980s. In 2002, John Killah, writing in *The Times*, complained that 110 local courts had closed in the previous 10 years, to save money. He pointed out that it was already difficult enough to get witnesses to turn up to court, without making it worse. Kingston people, after a vigorous campaign, managed to fend off plans to close their magistrates' court, which has sat in Kingston since 1230 but in 2011, the Minister of Justice is again determined to close it. Courts of all types have been closing and been replaced with modern combined court centres. This is because the old buildings lack adequate facilities, such as access for the disabled and consultation rooms. The problem is that some of the grand old courthouses are listed buildings, where even the interiors are listed and cannot be altered. The tendency has been to close these and let them rot, rather than attempt to adapt them. They are of no use to developers, because of their listed status. This is of concern to those interested in our architectural heritage, as well as lawyers, magistrates and judges. SAVE Britain's Heritage reported on the problem in 2004, in *Silence in Court, the future of the UK's historic law courts*. Eight hundred courts had closed since

1945. Despite protests, the Lord Chancellor announced, in 2005, the closure of the historic Bow Street Magistrates' Court (1879) and its famous police station next door, home of the first police service, the Bow Street Runners. Oscar Wilde, Reggie Kray and Dr Crippen all appeared before the court.

6–024   At the time of writing, 2011, matters have taken a dramatic turn for the worse for those who emphasise the important of localised justice. Following consultation, the Ministry announced on December 14, 2010, the closure of 49 county courts 93 magistrates' courts. They claim they will save £41 million and may make £38 million from the sale of assets. The Ministry said:

> "Her Majesty's Courts Service currently operates out of 530 courts, many of which do not meet the needs of modern communities. Their number and location does not reflect recent changes in population, workload or transport and communication links over the many years since they were originally opened. . .Some courts lack appropriate facilities for victims and witnesses such as separate waiting areas, do not have secure facilities for prisoners, or are not accessible to disabled court users, limiting the type of case that can be heard."

The Ministry said that magistrates' courts sit for 64 per cent of their available time and county courts sit on average for 130 days per year. Senior Presiding Judge, Goldring L.J., drew attention to a series of "significant errors" in the proposal. For instance, Abergavenny MC was listed for closure, because it was said not to have been used since 1999, yet it was refurbished and re-opened in 2010. He said that poor public transport meant many court users would not be able to get to court before 10.00. For further reading on the impact of closing 93 magistrates' courts, see the Magistrates' Association *National Response to Consultation on Court Closures*, October 2010, and news media in 2010–11.

New courts vary in design and there have been ample examples of design defects which have delayed court openings or irritated judges, court users and court staff, such as in South Wales in 2004–05. For instance, some courts have jury boxes facing public galleries. Bizarrely, the Court Standards Design Guide was only published as recently as 2004. The new guide follows a key recommendation of the Auld Review 2001. All new Crown Courts, county courts and magistrates' courts will now have a standard layout. The guide will ensure better access for all users, including the disabled and parents with young children. It recommends separate waiting areas for witnesses and defendants. Court designers and architects will be expected to incorporate IT such as video links, video conferencing, email, in-court intranet and public display screens in their designs. Details of the progress, or lack of it, of the modernisation programme for the civil courts can be found on the Her Majesty's Courts & Tribunals Service website, in its Annual Reports. For a picture of the dismal current state of the impoverished courts see recent empirical research reported in Ch.17 of Darbyshire, *Sitting in Judgment* (2011), cited above.

11. Open justice?

As Lord Neuberger pointed out in a 2011 speech, the principle of openness is central to English justice and the concept of the rule of law and goes back to "time immemorial", i.e. before July 6, 1189. There has been increasing pressure in recent years for the courts, especially family courts, to be more open and approachable. In a democracy, government, including the judiciary, derives its authority from the people. Members of the public should, therefore, have a right to attend court. After all, justice is administered on their behalf and paid for by the taxpayer. Public scrutiny is an incentive for judges and other court professionals to behave politely, fairly and competently. It should encourage consistency in the conduct of proceedings and in the decisions made, such as sentencing. Openness and approachability should encourage civil litigants to take their cases to court, thus enhancing access to justice. In criminal cases, if the apprehension, conviction and sentencing of offenders is to have any generally deterrent effect then criminal cases must be reported, locally and nationally.

6–025

Further, most international judicial instruments emphasise that the right to a public trial is the right of a litigant. Of course, a civil litigant may not want publicity, hence the popularity of arbitration and other forms of alternative dispute resolution, described in Ch.11. Nevertheless, as far as court proceedings are concerned, Art.6(1) of the European Convention on Human Rights (right to a fair trial) provides:

"In the determination of his civil rights and obligations or of any criminal charge against him, everyone is entitled to a fair and public hearing within a reasonable time by an independent and impartial tribunal established by law. Judgment shall be pronounced publicly but the press and public may be excluded from all or part of the trial in the interests of morals, public order or national security in a democratic society, where the interests of juveniles or the protection of the private life of the parties so require, or to the extent strictly necessary in the opinion of the court in special circumstances where publicity would prejudice the interests of justice."

Lord Phillips C.J. said that it was a basic principle of the administration of justice that court proceedings should take place in public, with freedom to report, and he explained the exceptions: *Times Newspapers Ltd, Re* [2007] EWCA Crim 1925.

Some proceedings are closed to the public. Where a defendant is refused bail by magistrates and applies to the Crown Court, he appears before a judge in chambers. Reporting restrictions are regularly imposed, under the Contempt of Court Act 1981, in some other Crown Court proceedings. The youth court, in the magistrates' court, is closed to ordinary members of the public, to protect the young defendant. Proceedings may be reported but the youngster will not be named, unless the judge or justices make an exception to permit this.

6–026   The procedure in all civil courts is now regulated by the Civil Procedure Rules 1998 (CPR). The general rule for hearings in court is set out in CPR 39.2: This states that "(1) The general rule is that a hearing is to be in public". Under (3), a hearing, or any part of it, may be in private if publicity would defeat its object, or it involves national security, or confidential information or it is necessary to protect a patient or child, or for various other reasons, or where the court considers it necessary, "in the interests of justice". The Rules direct the civil judge to Art.6 of the Convention. In *Al Rawi v Security Service* [2010] EWCA Civ 428, the CA held that was not open to a court to use a closed procedure to examine the defendant's evidence in the course of an ordinary civil trial. In this case, former Guantanamo Bay inmates, including Moazzam Begg and Binyam Mohamed were suing the Government in tort, claiming it had been complicit in their torture. Lord Neuberger M.R. relied on the common law, not Art.6. It was a fair trial (natural justice) requirement for a party and their lawyer to see and hear all the evidence and argument in open court. In principle, a litigant should know the reasons why he has won or lost his case and this should enable to judiciary to provide sufficient reasons. Trials should be conducted in public and judgment delivered in public. A party was entitled to know the elements of his opponent's case in advance and of the documents in his control. These rules were so "embedded in the common law" that no judge should override them in an ordinary civil claim without parliamentary authority. Also, the CPR provided no authority for a closed material procedure and it was precluded by the overriding objective. See further Gibb and Wellington. It was upheld by the Supreme Court: [2011] UKSC 34.

Bearing in mind that small claims and most other proceedings are heard by district judges in the county court, in the judge's own room ("chambers"), these all took place behind closed doors until 1999. They have now had to be opened up to the public, because this is required by Art.6 and by the CPR. I suggest that the present position is far from satisfactory, however. Most civil district judges have key coded security doors on their chambers so a member of the public is likely to be deterred from asking if they could watch proceedings, even if they were aware that they are open to the public.

One of the greatest anomalies related to family proceedings, the closed nature of which became very contentious, since 2000. While these were open in the magistrates' court, identical cases in the county courts and High Court were closed to the public and unreported. This is a reversal of the position in the early twentieth century, when the newspapers would print salacious details exposed in divorce cases. Hewson explained that the judges of the time thought such cases ought to be open, as a matter of principle. In *McPherson v McPherson* [1936] A.C. 177, the Privy Council said that a divorce pronounced in private was voidable, because the judge had denied the public their right to be present. Lord Blansbourgh said "publicity is the authentic hallmark of judicial, as distinct from administrative procedure". In *Ambard v Att Gen for Trinidad and Tobago* [1936] A.C. 322, Lord Atkin remarked "Justice is not a cloistered virtue". The history of publicity in family cases and the inconsistent position in different courts are described at length in the judgments in *Allan v Clibbery* [2002] EWCA Civ 45. The judges recognised in this and other cases that the courts have to effect a balancing exercise between the right to respect for family life and privacy in Art.8 of the European Convention on Human Rights and the right to freedom of expression in Art.10. They remarked that it is widely recognised in European jurisprudence that the balance in children cases is in favour of confidentiality, see *B v UK, P v UK* (36337/97) [2001] 2 F.L.R. 261. In *Allan v Clibbery*, Allan, described as a prominent businessman, lost his appeal against his former mistress being permitted to disclose to the *Daily Mail* and Hong Kong media the details of their private lives that came to light in the property dispute that arose after their relationship broke down. It had become apparent at the hearing that she was one of several mistresses and the appellant claimed to have paid her to be at his disposal, for sex. In *Blunkett v Quinn* [2004] EWHC 2816 (Fam), Ryder J. decided to deliver in open court his judgment in a case involving the then Home Secretary, David Blunkett and his ex-lover and her child. He said he did this in order to correct false information already in the public domain, in the publicity surrounding the case.

In 2004–05, many fathers' groups, such as the aggressive *Fathers 4 Justice*, represented by Spiderman, Batman and other demonstrators, argued that more family proceedings should be open to the public. They were aggrieved at what they saw as the courts' failure to enforce contact orders allowing them to see their children where a mother disobeys court orders. They considered that publicity would expose the unreasonableness, as they saw it, of disobedient mothers and ineffectual judges. Some judges also argued for greater publicity, for different reasons. For example, Thorpe L.J. was quoted by Gibb, in January 2005, as considering that it would be "healthy" to remove privacy. Exposing the system to public scrutiny would reveal the family justice system to be in good condition. He reminded us that in Scotland, family proceedings have always been in public. "Campaigners say that the judges have a vested interest in maintaining privacy because it enables them to carry on making these 'wicked' decisions in private". In 2005, the House of Commons Constitutional Affairs Select Committee published a report, *Family Justice: the Operation of the Family Courts*. They concluded that a greater degree of transparency was required in family courts. They suggested the press and public should be allowed into the courts subject to the judge's discretion to exclude them. In *Harb v His Majesty King Fahd Bin Abdul Aziz* [2005] EWCA Civ 632, the CA overturned a ruling by the former President of the Family Division that a case against King Fahd by his former wife should be heard in secret.

6–027   In 2007, David Pannick regretted that the Ministry of Justice, having consulted on making family courts more open, backtracked, in its paper called "Openness in Family Courts—A New Approach" (CP 10/07). He pointed to the anomalies in the law at that time. This sentiment was shared by Palin. She summarised the contradictory state of the law. In 2008, Jack Straw, then Justice Secretary, published the response to the consultation on opening up family proceedings. He announced that accredited media would be able to visit all family courts, removing inconsistencies. The courts are able to restrict access, for the welfare of children or safety of parties. A pilot project was then started to:

> "place anonymised judgments online, give parties involved a copy of the judgment and look at the practicalities of retaining judgments so that children involved in proceedings can access them when they are older".

A new consultation was launched, called *Family Justice In View*. It proposed to allow parties to disclose information about their case to advisors (including MPs) while a case was still in progress and to allow "more information to be made accessible to the public about the way the family courts work and how decisions are made" (MoJ website, December 16, 2008). On January 21, 2010, the MoJ announced that parts of the Children, Schools & Families Bill were aimed at encouraging media attendance at family courts. Research showed that rule changes in April 2009, permitting journalists to report anonymised proceedings had had some impact—25 per cent of court staff said journalists had attended at their court. The Bill would permit broader reporting of family proceedings but included an indefinite ban on identifying the parties. A pilot scheme operated at three courts, publishing results of family cases on the internet. The Bill became an Act in 2010. In the meantime, there was an enormous amount of comment (see bibliography). Geoffrey Robertson QC, said on the Radio 4 *Today* programme, on June 30, 2009, that although the courts were opened to journalists from that April, no-one went into family courts because they "could not report anything" but it had encouraged people to settle their disputes because they did not want their affairs exposed to the public.

The courts are a source of free, public entertainment and education. Until the late twentieth century, public galleries were routinely populated by local onlookers. Now that TV is more fun, courts are rarely visited, with exceptions such as the Old Bailey and certain cases in the Royal Courts of Justice. In the 1980s, the Bar Council campaigned to televise court proceedings. They gave up. In 1994, Sir Thomas Bingham M.R. spoke in favour, while an experiment was being conducted in Scotland. In 2004, Falconer L.C. launched a consultation paper and at the same time, an experiment started in recording the proceedings of the CA (Civil Division). Footage was not broadcast but used for evaluation. With the exception of the UKSC, it has been illegal since 1925 to take photographs or record proceedings in court, or even to make drawings. Court artists, whose depictions appear in the news media, have to leave the courtroom and sketch from memory. Mohammed Zahir, who used his mobile phone to take pictures of defendants in the dock of Birmingham Crown Court, was jailed for nine months in 2004.

In the USA, all 50 states permit cameras in some courts and 39 allow them into trial courts. *Court TV* broadcasts high profile trials. Some are broadcast internationally, such as the Rodney King beatings trials and the O.J. Simpson trial in the 1990s but Lord Chancellor Falconer remarked, in November 2004, "We don't want our courts turning into US-style media circuses. . .Justice should be seen to be done but our priority must be that justice is done." Judge L.J., then Deputy Chief Justice (and now L.C.J.), took part in a seminar debating broadcasting the courts in 2005. He said he was deeply committed to open justice but was worried that witnesses would be deterred and for that reason, he distinguished televising the courts from televising Parliament. Also in 2005, the DCA announced the results of its consultation on broadcasting the courts. Opinion was divided but there was a very strong view that witnesses, victims and jurors should not be filmed. No further conclusions or plans were announced. The second murder trial of Sion Jenkins at the Old Bailey in July 2005 saw a new form of instant court reporting. Sky News broadcast an almost instantaneous transcript of Rafferty J.'s summing up. Under a protocol agreed by the Lord Chancellor and broadcasters they may, with the judge's permission, make news from the live feed from the court stenographer's transcript. Interestingly, the Constitutional Reform Act 2005 exempts the UKSC from the ban on photography. They make available a broadcast feed of all proceedings, for anyone who wants to make use of it and two TV documentaries on the UKSC were broadcast in 2011. Jack Straw, the Labour Justice Minister was opposed to televising but his successor, Ken Clarke, is in favour. In the 2011 Judicial Studies Board lecture, Lord Neuberger M.R. advocated televising civil hearings. Since the 1980s, courts have been holding open days to try and help the public to understand the courts. The initiative started in the magistrates' courts and has spread to the Crown Court and combined court centres. Visitors can explore the courtrooms and prison vans and participate in mock sentencing exercises. I am strongly in favour of this and of televising the courts because research has shown that members of the public are shockingly ignorant of their justice system and this should be a cause of concern since their taxes pay for a system that purports to be administering justice on their behalf.

BIBLIOGRAPHY

6–028 Speeches by Lords Bingham and Steyn are referenced in Ch.4.

Department for Constitutional Affairs, *Constitutional Reform: a Supreme Court for the United Kingdom*, CP 11/03, July 2003 and responses, archived on the Department of Constitutional Affairs website, along with Lord Falconer's press release 296/03.

The articles on the UKSC remain especially valuable. Those by Professor Robert Stevens, Baroness Hale, Sir Thomas Legg and Professor John Bell all appear in a special issue of *Legal Studies*, on the proposed Supreme Court, Vol.24, March 2004.

J. Battle, "Filming courts: time to lift the ban" *The Times*, October 3, 2006.

R. Cranston, *How Law Works* (2006).

P. Darbyshire, *Sitting in Judgment: The Working Lives of Judges* (2011).

B. Dickson, "The processing of appeals in the House of Lords" (2007) 123 L.Q.R. 571.

H. Genn, *Judging Civil Justice*, The Hamlyn Lectures 2008 (2009).

F. Gibb and J. Killah, "Magistrates will be packaged off to vast justice factories in large urban centres", *The Times*, July 2, 2002.

J. Jaconelli, *Open Justice* (2002).

A. Le Sueur, *Building the UK's new supreme court: national and comparative perspectives*, 2004.

Lord Mance, "Constitutional Reforms, the Supreme Court and the Law Lords", (2006) 25 *Civil Justice Quarterly* 155–165.

Lord Neuberger M.R., "Insolvency, internationalism and Supreme Court judgments", November 11, 2009, from para.20; "Open Justice Unbound?", JSB annual lecture 2011, March 16, 2011, judiciary website.

J. Rozenberg, "Britain's new Supreme Court" *The Times Literary Supplement*, September 2, 2009.

H. Schleiff, "Cameras in courts" (2004) 154 N.L.J. 1745.

Sir Richard Scott's 1997 speech is quoted at (1997) 147 N.L.J. 750.

K. Wellington, "Case closed!" (on *Al Rawi*) (2010) 160 N.L.J. 939. See also widespread news coverage such as F. Gibb, "Judges reject secret evidence strategy in torture claim case", *The Times*, May 5, 2010.

Lord Windlesham, "The Constitutional Reform Act 2005: The Politics of Constitutional Reform Part 2" [2006] *Public Law* 35–57.

Lord Woolf C.J., Squire Centenary Lecture, March 4, 2004, Cambridge, "The Rule of Law and a Change in the Constitution", Judiciary website.

On open family courts: F. Gibb, "Fathers winning battle to have custody hearings in public." *The Times*, January 10, 2005; B. Henson, "Why have secrecy in the family courts?" (2003) 153 N.L.J. 369; G. Morris, (2008) 158 N.L.J. 750; F. Gibb, *The Times*, April 27, 2009; *The Times* leading article, "In Open Court", April 27, 2009; E. Floyd (2009) 159 N.L.J. 451; R. Newitt (2009) 159 N.L.J. 843; T. Roberts & S. J. Boon (2010) 160 N.L.J. 126; S. Palin, "The Slur of Secrecy" (2007) 157 N.L.J. 1224; E. Harris (2007) 157 N.L.J. 1225; D. Pannick, "Family courts should be led out of the dark ages" *The Times*, July 17, 2007 and many other news and law journal articles.

FURTHER READING AND SOURCES FOR UPDATING THIS CHAPTER

Updates of this book from spring 2012 and 2013 on the Sweet & Maxwell website. **6–029**

Architectural heritage, including campaigns against the destruction of old courts: *www.savebritainsheritage.org*.

Department of Constitutional Affairs website, archived (the pred-
ecessor of the MoJ for documents to mid-2007).
Her Majesty's Courts and Tribunals Service website, especially
annual reports of various courts.
Family Justice Council: *www.family-justice-council.org.uk.*
Court of Justice of the EU website.
European Court of Human Rights website.
Judicial Committee of the Privy Council: *http://www.jcpc.gov.uk/.*
Judges' speeches are on the Judiciary website.
Magistrates' Association website.
Ministry of Justice website, including annual *Judicial and Court
Statistics.*
UKSC Blog *www.ukscblog.com.*
UKSC website.

7. Criminal Courts

"The very idea of a Magistrates' Court is that it should administer summary justice locally." Lord Judge C.J., speech, November 2008.

There are two criminal trial courts (courts of original jurisdiction, or "courts of first instance") in England and Wales and all criminal cases are heard in one of these two, the magistrates' court or the Crown Court. Auld L.J., in his *Review of the Criminal Courts of England and Wales* recommended a unified criminal court divided into three tiers, or failing this, a unified courts administration. The first was rejected but this last recommendation was carried out and HM Courts Service was created in 2005 and merged with the Tribunals Service in 2011. Part 7 of the Courts Act 2003 defines criminal courts (s.68). The Act is one of the outcomes of the Auld Review. In the previous chapter, the sections on court management and open justice also apply to the criminal courts. Criminal procedure is examined in Ch.12.

7–001

1. Magistrates' courts

As explained in the previous chapter, in 2011, there are over 300 magistrates' courts, although their numbers have diminished because of court closures and bench amalgamations since the 1980s and many more are about to close. Over 95 per cent of defendants to criminal charges are proceeded against at the magistrates' court (1.79 million in 2009, including 156,000 in the youth court, according to the *Judicial and Court Statistics*). It should be obvious from this statistic that magistrates' courts do not deal with trivia, although many members of the public and even lawyers and judges underestimate their importance. Proceedings in the magistrates' court are known as summary proceedings. Trials are

7–002

called summary trials and there were 180,000 in 2009. Most cases are heard by lay magistrates and the fact that they hear the bulk of criminal cases makes the English legal system unique in this respect, worldwide. Until 1949 these courts were known as police courts and many are situated close to police stations. This is unfortunate since it conveys the impression that the court sits at the convenience of the police to distribute punishment in accordance with police evidence. As the police inevitably figure prominently in the magistrates' court, it is not surprising that the public has tended to think of it as the police court (see Darbyshire, "Concern", 1997). Happily, there are not so many uniformed police officers in today's courts as there were prior to 1985. The Prosecution of Offences Act 1985 replaced police prosecutors with Crown Prosecutors and the 1990s saw private security officers replacing police court security officers.

For most people who appear in a criminal court, as a defendant, witness or victim, the court involved will be the magistrates' court. The least serious category of offence is the summary offence. Almost all summary offences must be heard in the magistrates' court. They are all statutorily defined. They include the vast bulk of traffic offences, the most trivial of which many people wrongly assume not to be normal criminal offences. Even a parking offence is a criminal offence, in English law. We do not have a third species of law, "violations", as they do in the US. Common assault is a summary offence, as are many regulatory offences, prosecuted by government departments. The category of offences of medium seriousness is called "triable either way" and most are tried in the magistrates' court. Here, the defendant may elect trial in the magistrates' court or in the Crown Court, unless the magistrates insist on a Crown Court trial. Most defendants in the "either way" category opt for summary trial in the magistrates' court.

Magistrates' jurisdiction is statutory. They can send an offender to prison for up to six months, or a maximum of 12 for more than one offence and/or impose a fine of up to £5,000. This was fixed by the Powers of the Criminal Courts (Sentencing) Act 2000 but if the Criminal Justice Act 2003, s.154 ever comes into force, magistrates' sentencing powers will double to one year's imprisonment. At the time of writing, 2011, this seems unlikely. If, after conviction, the bench feels their powers of sentence are inadequate, they may send the offender to the Crown Court for sentencing. A district judge (magistrates' court) sitting alone generally has the same powers as a bench of two or three lay justices. At the hearing of any case, the bench is assisted by the justices' clerk or, more usually, a court clerk (sometimes called legal adviser). The former and many of the latter are legally qualified. The magistrates' clerk may advise the magistrates on the law. Magistrates and their clerks are discussed more fully in Ch.15.

Throughout the nineteenth and twentieth centuries, more and more work has been shifted down onto the shoulders of the magistrates, by reclassifying offences as summary only or by shifting them out of the indictable category into the "triable either way" category. The result is that magistrates deal with over 95 per cent of all criminal cases and 95 per cent of all sentencing. It is a big mistake, therefore, to think of this court as dealing with trivia. Of course, if magistrates' sentencing powers are ever increased, under the 2003 Act, even more work will shift out of the Crown Court and into the magistrates' court. For discussion see Darbyshire ("Neglect", 1997).

In 2009, virtual courts were being piloted, as discussed in Ch.12 on criminal procedure.

The community justice centre

In December 2004, a pilot project commenced, establishing a   7–003
Community Justice Centre in North Liverpool. The aim in establishing it was to engage the local community in finding solutions to anti-social behaviour, social exclusion and crime. It was modelled on the Red Hook Project in New York. The court started with the jurisdiction of the magistrates' court and its remit may be expanded. It is meant to act as an outreach centre for the local community, using the court building for community activities. It is accompanied by a programme of community consultation and engagement. One of its themes is restorative justice. The first judge was a local circuit judge who was formerly a district judge (magistrates' court). He monitors the progress of the sentences he passes. For more details of the Red Hook project and other models, see Brimacombe and see the Centre's website for more details of its work. This idea was copied in 10 new centres, including London, Nottingham, Wales, Yorkshire and the South West. Local people help to select the judges.

Domestic violence courts

In 2011, there are over 140.   7–004

"The specialist domestic violence court programme promotes a combined approach to tackling domestic violence by the police, the Crown Prosecution Service (CPS), magistrates, courts and probation together with specialist support services for victims." (MoJ, March 19, 2010.)

Mental health courts

7–005   They were piloted at two magistrates' courts in 2009, to identify defendants with mental health issues. The process evaluation was published in September 2010 and found the court "strengthened collaboration between health and criminal justice agencies enabling needs to be addressed at an early stage" (MoJ).

Drugs Courts

7–006   These commenced with two experimental courts and have expanded. Offenders convicted of low level crime can be sent there for sentencing. The sentencing judge reviews their progress every six weeks (they are drug tested twice weekly). They might get a hug and a bagel from the judge. See Tendler. *The Dedicated Drug Courts Pilot Evaluation Process Study* was published in January 2011 (MoJ research 1/11). They found the courts were perceived as useful, in providing goals and enhancing offenders' self-esteem, making offenders accountable and facilitating agency partnerships. Continuity of the bench (magistrates or DJs) was a key element. Though the courts were helpful, rather disappointingly, staff and offenders thought courts' ability to reduce reoffending was limited.

2. The Youth Court

7–007   In the UK, the age of criminal responsibility is 10. Ten to 17-year-olds are almost all tried in the Youth Court, which is a special court within the magistrates' court. This is a very important court, since the peak age of offending in England and Wales is around 17–18 (source: *Annual Criminal Statistics*), although the majority of young offenders are diverted from the criminal process by the official cautioning scheme, put on a statutory basis by the Crime and Disorder Act 1998. The bench comprises specially trained lay magistrates (lay justices), who usually sit in mixed gender threesomes, or a district judge (magistrates' court). The predecessor of the court, the juvenile court, was formed in 1908, by the Juvenile Offences Act. It was thought desirable to keep adult defendants separate from juveniles. Ideally, the Act's progenitors would have liked to have seen a separate system of courts for young offenders. Separate courts have never been developed, except in large cities like London, Nottingham, Birmingham and elsewhere, where the caseload warranted it. Instead, it became the habit at smaller courts to convene the juvenile court on a separate day from the adult court. Eventually, this was whittled down to an hour's gap between adult and juvenile courts but this was abandoned. This is a great pity. It seems to have been forgotten that the original aim was to protect children from contact with adult criminals. Recently, the Magistrates' Association expressed disquiet that juveniles were being put into the adult list. The 1908 Court originally dealt with the "deprived" as well as the "depraved". In other words, in addition to criminal cases, it heard civil applications by the local authority, to take the child into care for its own welfare. This work was given away to the family proceedings court when the youth court was created by the Children Act 1989 so it now has a purely criminal jurisdiction. Importantly, the public are excluded from the youth court and procedure is more informal than that of the adult court. The youth court has a variety of powers. For example, as well as fining the child and/or parent, it can impose a supervision order, which is like a probation order for children, or order detention and training for up to two years, so magistrates are more powerful in this court than in the adult court.

Only those youngsters who commit very serious crimes or those tried with an adult may be sent up for trial in the Crown Court (explained in Ch.12 on criminal procedure). This means something like murder or rape, or serious assault. Jamie Bulger's killers, Thompson and Venables, were tried in the Crown Court. Auld L.J. recommended, in his *Review of the Criminal Courts*, that serious crimes should be heard in a youth court composed of a judge and two youth panel magistrates. In the Courts Act 2003, all judges were given the jurisdiction to sit in the magistrates' court but there are no current plans to carry out Auld L.J.'s suggestion and remove children from the Crown Court altogether. In 2009, the juvenile court/youth court celebrated its centenary, prompting articles in *The Magistrate* and *The JP* (on *Westlaw*) and other legal publications.

3. The Crown Court

The Courts Act 1971, which abolished assizes and quarter sessions, replaced them with one unified Crown Court. England and Wales are divided into six circuits based in London, Bristol, Birmingham, Manchester, Cardiff and Leeds. There are 77 Crown Court Centres of three types. *First tier* centres are visited by High Court judges for serious Crown Court work and HC civil business. *Second tier* centres are visited by HC judges for Crown Court criminal business only. *Third tier* centres are not normally visited by a High Court judge. Circuit judges and recorders (part-time judges) sit at all three. At least two presiding High Court judges are appointed to each circuit and help to organise judicial deployment in the Crown Court. Indictable offences are recognised at common law or by statute and are the most serious type of offence. "Triable

7–008

either way" offences, of medium seriousness, can also be tried at the Crown Court. By Practice Direction, the Lord Chief Justice directs that Crown Court business should be classified into three.

Class 1: The most serious offences are generally tried by a HC judge, unless released by the presiding judge to an authorised ("ticketed") circuit judge. They include treason and murder.

Class 2: These are generally also tried by a HC judge and include manslaughter and rape.

Class 3: These include all other offences and are normally tried by a circuit judge or authorised recorder. They include kidnapping, burglary, grevious bodily harm and robbery.

The Crown Court also hears appeals against conviction and/or sentence from those convicted in the magistrates' court. Appeals are usually heard by a circuit judge and two magistrates. The Crown Court also sentences defendants who have been committed for sentencing by magistrates, after having been summarily convicted of an either-way offence. In 2009, 94,300 cases were disposed of by the Crown Court and 38,700 were committed there for sentence. The most famous Crown Court Centre is the Central Criminal Court, known as the "Old Bailey" in the City of London. It has a fascinating and gruesome history over several centuries and is a world famous tourist attraction. It deals with the most serious offences from London and the south of England. About 95 per cent of its workload is heard at other Crown Court Centres, such as Kingston, so it is left with only the most serious cases of murder, fraud, terrorism, rape and so on.

As part of a modernisation programme the Crown Court has been linked to prison service video conferencing facilities so that prisoners can "appear" from secure conditions in preliminary hearings without having to be transported to court. Prisoner transport is notoriously expensive and the cause of frustrating delays. The same new technology allows vulnerable witnesses to give evidence from outside the courtroom. Another part of the programme is the installation of XHIBIT which allows all trial participants to track the progress of a case through modern technology, using the internet and texting to mobile phones and pagers. Witnesses and police officers will not need to wait around in court but will be able to come when needed. During the 1990s the courts endeavoured to make themselves more user-friendly, to court users and visitors. A Courts Charter was published and is available from the HMCTS website. Details of how courts have provided better facilities for users are listed in the press releases on the MoJ website. Examples include: training staff in sign language; sending staff into solicitors' offices to learn how the court could improve its service; providing consulting rooms and dedicated Witness Support suites with separate entrances. HMCTS Annual Report gives updates on the modernisation programme. Nevertheless, a National Audit Office Report on Crown Court Administration, in March 2009, painted a depressing picture of poor facilities, uncoordinated information and waste of public money.

4. The Divisional Court of the Queen's Bench Division

This court hears prosecution and defence appeals "by way of **7–009** case stated" on points of law from the magistrates' courts and the Crown Court, excluding appeals relating to trial on indictment, which go to the Court of Appeal. It conducts judicial reviews of the legality of proceedings in magistrates' courts. In doing this it is exercising the High Court's prerogative power to review the legality of proceedings in inferior tribunals. These are discussed more fully in Ch.6.

5. The Court of Appeal (Criminal Division)

The CA (Criminal Division) (CACD) was established by the **7–010** Criminal Appeal Act 1966 to replace the Court of Criminal Appeal. Its jurisdiction is contained in the Criminal Appeal Act 1968, as amended by the Criminal Appeal Act 1995 and the Criminal Justice Act 2003. Its work is fully described in Ch.12. It usually sits only in the Royal Courts of Justice in the Strand but in 1999, Lord Bingham C.J. took it to sit in Liverpool and Bristol, and it sat at Snaresbrook in 2002. The Court is made up of the Lord Chief Justice, the Vice-President of the Criminal Division, Lords Justices of Appeal, the judges of the Queen's Bench Division and a number of circuit judges specially nominated by the Lord Chief Justice. It normally sits as a bench of three: one Lord Justice of Appeal and two High Court judges, or one Lord Justice of Appeal, one High Court judge and a circuit judge. The jurisdiction of the CACD is:

1. to hear appeals against conviction on indictment with the leave of the CA or if the trial judge certifies that the case is fit for appeal (Criminal Appeal Act 1995, s.1);

2. to hear appeals against sentence pronounced by the Crown Court provided that the sentence is not one fixed by law and provided that the court grants leave. An application for leave may be determined by a single judge, but if leave is refused, the appellant can require a full court, i.e. two or more judges to determine the matter;

3. to hear appeals referred to it by the Criminal Cases Review Commission, under the Criminal Appeal Act 1995;

4. to hear appeals against a verdict of "not guilty by reason of insanity" or against findings of fitness and unfitness to plead;

5. to hear an appeal by the prosecution against an acquittal on a point of law at the trial in the Crown Court. This provision involves an application by the Attorney General for the opinion of the Court on the point of law and is known as an "Attorney General's Reference". The result cannot affect the acquittal and the defendant is not named in the appeal;

6. to hear an appeal by the prosecutor, again as an "Attorney General's Reference" against a lenient sentence. In this case the Court will set out sentencing guidelines for the future but may also increase the actual sentence imposed; and

7. to hear prosecution appeals against judge's rulings, under the Criminal Justice Act 2003, as described in Ch.12.

The CACD publishes an annual review, providing statistical details of its caseload. See HMCTS website. It has a big case load and the judges who sit in it are under enormous pressure to deal with long lists of appeals very swiftly. According to the *Judicial and Court Statistics*, in 2009, it heard 1,240 renewed (oral) applications for leave to appeal, 430 appeals against conviction and 1,887 sentencing appeals. It is normal for a bench of three judges to deal with a mixed list of sentencing appeals and applications for leave to appeal all morning (eight cases or more) and a substantive appeal in the afternoon. High Court judges normally sit in the court for a maximum shift of three weeks at a time, as the pressure of work is so great, usually requiring the judges to work long hours into the night and at weekends, reading papers and writing judgements. Bear that in mind the next time you read the law report of a criminal appeal.

6. The UK Supreme Court

7–011   This, and its predecessor, the Appellate Committee of the House of Lords, are described in Ch.6. It hears appeals from the CACD and those that have leapfrogged from the High Court. Either prosecutor or defendant may appeal, provided the CA certifies that a point of law of general public importance is involved and that either court feels that the point should be considered by the UKSC and grants leave. The UKSC, in disposing of the appeal, may exercise any of the powers of the CA, or remit the case to it (Criminal Appeal Act 1968, as amended).

7. The Court of Justice of the EU and the European Court of Human Rights

These are described in Chs 3 and 4.   7–012

8. The Special Immigration Appeals Commission

Although this is classed as a tribunal, it is a superior court of   7–013
record and is both an appellate administrative tribunal and has a criminal jurisdiction. It was established by the Special Immigration Appeals Commission Act 1997 to hear such cases as appeals from deportation orders but it achieved notoriety as the last route of appeal for foreign nationals detained on the grounds of being terrorist suspects, under the Anti-Terrorism, Crime and Security Act 2001, the Act which fell foul of the European Convention on Human Rights in the 2004 House of Lords case *A (FC) v SS for the Home Dept* (The *Belmarsh* case) described in Ch.4. Suspects who appeared before it and risked being detained in prison indefinitely were represented by special advocates, appointed by the Government.

9. Justice for All 2002

This White Paper set out the Labour Government's response   7–014
to the Auld recommendations and the comments thereon and explained the Government's plans for criminal justice, much of which they then put into effect, especially via the Courts Act 2003 and the Criminal Justice Act 2003. One of the Government's promises was to "integrate the management of the courts within a single courts administration and allow the Crown Court judges to conduct trials in magistrates' courts" (Executive Summary, 0.12). Under the heading "Joining up the CJS" they resolved, "we must bring the component parts of the CJS together to form a coherent

whole". This required joining up criminal justice agencies and "linking up the targets, delivery objectives, strategic plans, IT systems and the daily work of every individual in each criminal justice agency". Auld L.J. had recommended Criminal Justice Boards, in the hope of making the management of criminal justice much more coherent. Virtually all of this had been put into operation by 2005, as explained here, and in Chs 6 and 10.

BIBLIOGRAPHY

7–015   H. Brimacombe, "Bringing justice closer to the community", *Legal Action*, December 2004, p.10.

P. Darbyshire, "An Essay on the Importance and Neglect of the Magistracy" [1997] Crim. L.R. 627.

P. Darbyshire, "For the New Lord Chancellor—Some Causes of Concern About Magistrates" [1997] Crim. L.R. 861.

P. Darbyshire, *Sitting in Judgment: The Working Lives of Judges* (2011), Chs 8, 9, 14 and 17.

Justice for All, July 2002.

Lord Judge C.J., "The Criminal Justice System in England and Wales—Time for Change?" speech, November 5, 2008.

S. Tendler, "Sentenced to a hug and a bagel", *The Times*, March 15, 2007.

FURTHER READING AND SOURCES FOR UPDATING THIS CHAPTER

7–016   Updates of this book from spring 2012 and 2013 on the Sweet & Maxwell website.

Auld L.J., *Review of the Criminal Courts of England and Wales* (2001).

Annual Reports of HMCTS and the annual review of the CACD on HMCTS website.

Ministry of Justice website, especially news releases, consulation papers, research and the annual *Judicial and Court Statistics*.

Sources as listed at the end of Ch.6.

8. History

1. Continuity

The UK's system of government, and the legal institutions which form part of it, are only explicable in terms of their long history. Whereas most continental legal systems rely heavily on legal principles derived from Roman law, adopted during the Rennaissance (see Ch.1), the English legal system has remained comparatively uninfluenced by this source. The reason for this is the unbroken historical development of the system in England, where at no time was it felt necessary to look outside the principles of common law or equity for assistance. Inevitably, through the ecclesiastical courts in particular, some Roman law influence can be traced but in general terms this is very limited. Indeed, the reason why England resisted the "invasion" of Roman law, was that a unified common law system was already growing in strength prior to the Norman Conquest.

8–001

2. Early history

Anglo-Saxon laws

The earliest English laws of which there is documentary evidence date from the Anglo-Saxon period. These are not strictly English laws; more accurately they relate to a particular tribal area such as Kent, Wessex or Mercia. They were based on the customs of the local settlers.

8–002

The Norman Conquest (1066)

The Anglo-Saxon divisions were just giving way to a national entity when the Norman invasion of England occurred. The result of the Battle of Hastings in 1066 led to William the Conqueror ascending the English throne, determined on a process of centralisation.

8–003

193

William's tactics were to impose strong national government and this he did by causing his Norman followers to become the major land-owners throughout the country. The system used was "subin-feudation" under which all land belonged to the monarch and was by him granted to his followers on certain conditions. In turn they could grant their land to their tenants. Subject to conditions, those tenants could make similar grants and so on, down the ladder. This method created the complete feudal system under which tenants owed duties to their lord, whilst he owed duties to his lord and so on up to the monarch, as the supreme point of the feudal pyramid. Nevertheless, the system never became as firmly entrenched in this country as it did, for instance, in France.

Feudal courts

8–004   A characteristic benefit to the feudal lord was the right to hold his own court. This provided financial benefits and effective power over the locality. So far as the ordinary individual was concerned this local manor court was the one which affected him most. Bearing in mind that the concept of central legal and governmental authority was still comparatively new, it took a long time before the royal courts were able to exercise control over these local courts. Although the passage of centuries saw the transfer of real power from local to national courts, these feudal courts remained in many instances until the property legislation of 1925. Until then, there was a feudal court relic, a tenure of property called "copyhold", which involved the registration of the transaction in the local court roll so that the person held the land by "copy" of the court roll.

Royal Courts

8–005   Following the Norman Conquest, monarchs soon realised that besides the need for strong national government there was also a need for a national law and order system. To this end the closest advisers of the monarch—the *"curia regis"*, or "King's council"—encouraged the establishment of three separate royal courts which sat at Westminster. These were:

- the Court of Exchequer which was mainly concerned with cases affecting the royal revenue, but which also had a limited civil jurisdiction;
- the Court of King's Bench which, taking its name from the original concept of the monarch sitting with his judges "en banc"—on the bench—at Westminster, dealt with civil and criminal cases in which the King had an interest; and
- the Court of Common Pleas, which was established to hear civil cases brought by one individual against another.

In the Court of Exchequer sat judges called Barons, with a presiding judge known as the Chief Baron. This Court appears to be the oldest, emerging in recognisable form in the early thirteenth century, having developed out of the financial organisation responsible for the royal revenues. The Court of King's Bench had its own Chief Justice and judges, and was closely linked with the monarch and the Great Council. This was due to the understanding that this court followed the King's person. The Court of Common Pleas had a Chief Justice and dedicated judges and left records from the early thirteenth century. All three courts were required by the monarch, said Stow in his survey of London in 1224, to make their base in Westminster Hall and there arose continuing conflicts between them over jurisdiction. The importance of getting more and more work was largely brought about by the fact that the judges were paid out of the court fees. At any rate these three royal courts, later added to by the introduction of a Court of Chancery, survived five centuries before being reconstructed into the present High Court of Justice in the Judicature Acts 1873–1875. The ultimate merger of Exchequer and Common Pleas into the Queen's Bench Division came about in 1880.

3. The common law

Origin

As a centralised system of law and order developed, so customary laws gave way to national law, which became known as the common law. It was called "common" because it was common to the whole country, as opposed to the local customs. Since inevitably the different customs at times conflicted, the judges' decisions, absorbing certain customs and rejecting others, came to be of predominant importance. They were creating "the law of the realm". The common law was thus derived entirely from case law.

8–006

Development

The Norman Kings, in attempting to weld the country together, made use of royal commissioners to travel the country to deal with governmental matters. The production of the *Domesday Book*, in 1087, as a property and financial survey, is the best known example. The extension of these activities to the judicial field seems to have arisen not long after the Conquest. The king appointed judges as royal commissioners, charged with certain royal powers, to travel the country to deal with civil and criminal cases. This system of "itinerant justices in Eyre" dates from not

8–007

long after the Conquest; but the assize system, as later developed, really dates from the reign of Henry II (1154–89). It only ended with the Courts Act 1971 BUT High Court judges of all three HC divisions still travel the six circuits, endeavouring to demand high standards of the advocates who appear before them and ensuring that undesirable localised practices do not get established. It was an important part of the work of these judges to formulate the principles of the common law, by meeting together formally and informally to resolve problems which had arisen in the cases coming before them. As these judges were linked with the courts in Westminster Hall, this helped to develop national laws. Nevertheless, the common law never completely supplanted local custom. As we saw in Ch.2 on sources, custom remains a source of law today.

Forms of action and the meaning of common law

8–008   In addition to settling national legal principles, the courts began to establish formal procedural rules. Actions were commenced by the issue of a royal writ. The claim had to be set out in an accepted fashion. This was called a form of action. Eventually, the system became rigid. The judges ruled that unless a claimant could fit their claim into an appropriate "form of action" it was not one known to the law. The court officials responsible for issuing writs tried initially to satisfy the demands of claimants by drawing up new forms of action, but the judges frowned on this and the practice was stopped by the Provisions of Oxford 1258. So great was the resulting dissatisfaction that 30 years later, by the Statute of Westminster 1285, this strict approach was slightly relaxed, so that the officials could issue a new writ, where the new situation was closely related to that covered by an existing writ. These new writs became known as writs *"in consimili casu"*. The effect which the writ system had on the development of the legal system is seen below in the section on equity. The common law is still being developed today, via the system of precedent, case law, as explained in Ch.2. Thanks to Parliamentary sovereignty, legislation supplements it, codifies it and replaces it. There are several different meanings attaching to the term.

- In the historical sense, explained above, common law refers to the national law, as opposed to local law or custom. It is the law "common" to England and Wales.
- The law made by the judges, in contrast to legislation.
- The law not historically derived from the courts of equity.
- A "common law country" or "common law jurisdiction" is one that originally applied English law.

4. Equity

Origin

The difficulty of bringing cases in the common law courts, thanks   8–009
to the rigidity of the writ system, led to increasing dissatisfaction.
Litigants petitioned the monarch. He handed these petitions on to
the Lord Chancellor, who, as Keeper of the King's Conscience and
an ecclesiastic, seemed to be a suitable person. He set up his own
Court of Chancery where he, or his representative, would sit to
determine these petitions. He would be guided by equity, or fairness. The legal principles which successive Lord Chancellors made
came to be known collectively as equity. The system became well
established in the fifteenth century. Because of the rapid increase
in judicial work, it was soon found necessary to have a lawyer as
Lord Chancellor. The discretion vested in early Lord Chancellors
gradually gave way to a system of precedent, but it was a long time
before the common law joke died, about equity being as long as the
Chancellor's foot (meaning the outcome depended on the mood of
the LC). Both common law and equity came to operate as parallel
systems, with each set of courts regarding itself as bound by its own
judicial precedents.

Development

Equity soon found itself establishing a jurisdiction over matters   8–010
where the common law had failed, and continued to fail, to recognise legal rights and duties. Equity was always a "gloss" on the
common law; it always presumed the existence of the common law
and simply supplemented it where necessary.

New rights

The whole of the law of trusts owed its existence to the willing-   8–011
ness of equity to recognise and enforce the obligation of a trustee to
a beneficiary. Equity accepted the use of the mortgage as a method
of borrowing money against the security of real property, when the
common law took a literal view of the obligation undertaken by
the borrower. It introduced the "equity of redemption" to enable a
borrower to retain the property which was the security for the loan,
even where there was default under the strict terms of the mortgage deed.

New remedies

At common law, the only remedy for breach of contract was   8–012
damages, a money payment as compensation for the loss suffered. Equity realised that in some cases damages was not an adequate remedy, and therefore proceeded to introduce the equitable

remedies of injunction and specific performance. An injunction is used to prevent a party from acting in breach of their legal obligations; a decree of specific performance is used to order a party to carry out their side of a contract. A party to a contract cannot just decide to break it and pay damages. Other equitable remedies are the declaratory order or judgment; the right to have a deed corrected by the process known as rectification and the right to rescind (withdraw from) a contract. The willingness of equity to intervene where fraud was proven and its preparedness to deal with detailed accounts in the law of trusts and the administration of estates, also gained it wide jurisdiction. The appointment of a receiver is an equitable solution to the problem of the management of certain financial matters.

New procedures

8–013   In contrast to the rigidity of common law remedies, equity favoured a flexibility of approach. Consequently it was prepared, by a "subpoena", to order witnesses to attend, to have them examined and cross-examined orally, to require relevant documents to be produced, known as discovery of documents, to insist on relevant questions being answered, by the use of interrogatories, and to have the case heard in English, where the common law for centuries used Latin. In the event of a failure to comply with an order, equity was prepared to impose immediate sanctions for this contempt of court.

A classification sometimes employed is to define the jurisdiction of equity as exclusive, concurrent and auxiliary. In the exclusive jurisdiction sense, equity recognised actions, as in trusts and mortgages, where the common law would provide no remedy; in the concurrent jurisdiction sense equity would add to the remedies provided by the common law, as by the introduction of the injunction and the decree of specific performance; in the auxiliary jurisdiction sense equity employed a more flexible procedure than the common law.

Maxims

8–014   Among the most famous principles are:

He who comes to equity must come with clean hands;
Equity will not suffer a wrong to be without remedy;
Delay defeats equity; and
Equity looks to the intent rather than to the form.

The maxims emphasise that equity, based in fairness and natural justice, attempted to maintain this approach throughout its later history. Judges retained their personal discretion so that equitable remedies were not, and are not, obtainable as of right. It is very important to understand that, whereas the litigant has a right to a remedy, at common law, once she has proven her case, this is not so with equity. All equitable remedies are still discretionary.

Relationship between common law and equity

Early relations between the two systems were comparatively strained. The common lawyers regarded equity as an interloper, lacking the firmly-based principles with which they were familiar. They were unable to see that equity was invaluable in remedying deficiencies in the common law and in encouraging the latter to develop its substantive law and procedure. As the Court of Chancery built up its jurisdiction and the two systems could be seen to be operating on a parallel basis, the question arose as to what was to happen in the unusual instance when there was a conflict. This problem was solved by James I, in the *Earl of Oxford's* case (1615), by a ruling that where there was such a conflict, the rules of equity were to prevail. The later history of equity was dogged in the eighteenth and nineteenth centuries by the courts of Chancery becoming overburdened with work, with increasing reliance being placed on judicial precedent and consequent delays. Dickens' attack in his novel, *Bleak House*, on the delays and costs in the system, seems to have to been thoroughly justified, with some examples of cases awaiting judgment dragging on for scores of years until both parties were dead. In the 1850s, Parliament endeavoured to ease the position, by the Common Law Procedure Acts 1852–1854 and the Chancery (Amendment) Act 1858 but the dual systems continued, sometimes to the substantial detriment of litigants, until 1873–1875.

8–015

5. Nineteenth-century developments

The Supreme Court of Judicature Acts 1873–1875

This legislation reorganised the existing court structures completely and formally brought together the common law courts and the courts of Chancery. In the Supreme Court of Judicature set up by the Acts, the three original royal courts became three divisions of the new High Court of Justice. The Court of Chancery which administered equity became the fourth division, i.e. the Chancery Division of the High Court, and a fifth division, dealing with those matters not within common law or equity, became the Probate, Divorce and Admiralty Division. By Order in Council in 1880, the three royal courts were merged to form the Queen's Bench Division, thus leaving the three Divisions of the High Court—Chancery, Queen's

8–016

Bench, and Probate, Divorce and Admiralty—which remained unchanged for 90 years. The Acts placed on a statutory basis the old rule that where common law and equity conflict, equity shall prevail. It gave power to all the courts to administer the principles of common law and equity and to grant the remedies of both, as circumstances in a case demanded. Consequently, the old conflict no longer arises, although common law and equity principles still exist.

By bringing the two systems together administratively, and allowing the High Court judge to exercise the principles, procedures and remedies of common law and equity in a single case, it seemed that the two systems had merged. That this was somewhat superficial is borne out by the exclusive jurisdictions left to the Queen's Bench and Chancery Divisions. The work formerly done by the Court of Chancery is exactly that dealt with in the Chancery Division. A Chancery case and its procedure remains something quite unlike a common law case. The whole of the legislation has now been consolidated in the Supreme Court Act 1981, now renamed Senior Courts Act.

Probate, Divorce and Admiralty jurisdiction

8–017   These three important legal topics fell neither within the common law nor equity jurisdictions, since probate (which is concerned with wills) and divorce were, for centuries, treated as ecclesiastical matters, and there was a separate Admiralty Court inevitably influenced by international shipping practices. Probate and divorce were transferred from the ecclesiastical courts to the ordinary civil courts in 1857 by the setting up of a Court of Probate and a separate Divorce Court. The ancient High Court of Admiralty gradually lost its widest jurisdiction to the common law courts, but retained powers over collisions at sea, salvage and prize cases. All other aspects of the law merchant, that is the law affecting traders had, over the centuries, been transferred to the common law courts.

Appeal courts

8–018   As described in Ch.6, the Judicature Acts, in creating a Court of Appeal alongside the new High Court of Justice, had intended that this Court with its specially designated Lords Justices of Appeal should be the final appellate court for civil matters. Political considerations intervened, however, and the proposal to remove judicial functions from the House of Lords was shelved. The Appellate Jurisdiction Act 1876 provided for the retention of the House of Lords as the final appeal court in civil cases and for the creation of special judges, Lords of Appeal in Ordinary, as life peers to staff the court.

6. Twentieth-century developments

Criminal courts

In 1907, the Criminal Appeal Act established the Court of Criminal Appeal to provide for the first time a general right of appeal for persons convicted and sentenced in indictable criminal cases. A further appeal in matters of general public importance lay to the House of Lords. The Court of Criminal Appeal became the Court of Appeal (Criminal Division) by the Criminal Appeal Act 1966. The role of the Queen's Bench Divisional Court in ruling on points of law arising by way of case stated in summary criminal cases was amended by the Administration of Justice Act 1960. This Act enabled an appeal in a case of general public importance to go to the House of Lords (now UKSC) if the Divisional Court granted a certificate and leave was obtained from the top court. The court structure for trying indictable criminal cases was substantially changed by the Courts Act 1971 which abolished the historically derived Court of Quarter Sessions and Assizes and replaced them with a single Crown Court.

8–019

Civil courts

The Administration of Justice Act 1970 created a Family Division of the High Court and amended the jurisdiction of the Queen's Bench and Chancery divisions, redistributing the functions of the former Probate Divorce and Admiralty Division. One novel change in appeal provisions was the introduction by the Administration of Justice Act 1969 of a possible "leapfrog" appeal from the High Court to the House of Lords (now UKSC), bypassing the Court of Appeal. The procedure was, however, made subject to stringent conditions which in practice limit its use. The Courts and Legal Services Act 1990 gave concurrent jurisdiction in civil matters to the High Court and the county court, with the exception of judicial review, an exercise of prerogative power vested in the High Court. Twenty-first century developments are dealt with in the other chapters.

8–020

FURTHER READING

J. H. Baker, *An Introduction to English Legal History* (4th edn, 2002).

8–021

Part III: Procedures

9. The Adversarial Process

"Anglo-American culture has long been beset with a pervasive myth about the conduct of criminal justice in European States. Continental criminal procedure is thought to be unjust and oppressive. It is called "inquisitorial", a term that has lost its neutral meaning and is now largely an epithet harkening back to the witchcraft trials and heresy persecutions of distant centuries. Among English speaking peoples the belief is widespread (and quite mistaken) that in Continental procedure the accused is presumed guilty until he proves himself innocent."
(J.H. Langbein, *Comparative Criminal Procedure: Germany* (1977), p.1.)

A contrast used to be drawn between the English legal system as **9–001** "adversarial" and continental European systems, mostly daughters of the French legal system as "inquisitorial", as is explained in Ch.1. That comparison is crude and somewhat inaccurate. Nevertheless, our type of procedure is accurately described as adversarial. Historians like Langbein attribute it to the rise of lawyers, in the eighteenth century.

1. Elements of the adversarial (accusatorial) system

The judge as umpire

It has often been said that the essence of the role of the English **9–002** judge, or magistrate, is as an unbiased umpire whose job it is to listen to evidence presented by both sides, without interfering in the trial process. This was often contrasted with the role of the *juge d'instruction*, the French first instance judge who performed an inquisitorial role in some criminal cases, directing investigations, cross-examining the defendant and compiling a dossier of evidence for the trial court. There is no comparable English equivalent. The court takes a much greater role in gathering evidence and is involved at an earlier stage in the process. Similarly, the role of the German judge is to take an active part in the assembling of evidence and the questioning of witnesses, before and at trial. Nevertheless, the European Convention on Human Rights, binding on continental systems and ours, provides that a fair civil or criminal trial, required by Art.6, must be adversarial. The European Court of Human Rights has ruled that the "equality of arms" principle requires equal access to information (with strict exceptions), adequate notification of the case that the defendant has to answer, equal opportunities to present evidence and challenge other evidence, and free legal representation and interpretation where necessary to achieve this. See, for instance, *Rowe and Davis v UK* (2000) 30 E.H.R.R. 1, a criminal case, and *McVicar v UK* (2002) 35 E.H.R.R. 22, a civil case described in Ch.4 on human rights.

It has been said that the English judge's role, as a non-interfering umpire, is a reflection of the English sense of fair play: each side has an equal opportunity to win the litigation "game" (in civil cases) by convincing the judge of the merits of their argument, collecting supporting evidence and citing favourable case authorities. The judge does not interfere in the presentation of evidence by examining and cross-examining witnesses. This is left to the parties or their advocates. The role of the judge was set down clearly by Lord Denning M.R. in *Jones v National Coal Board* [1957] 2 Q.B. 55 and can be summarised thus. The judge should:

1. listen to all the evidence, only interfering to clarify neglected or obscure points;
2. see that advocates behave and stick to the rules;
3. exclude irrelevancies and discourage repetition;
4. make sure he understands the advocates' points; and
5. at the end, make up his mind where the truth lies.

If the judge interferes unduly in the advocates' speeches or adduction of evidence, it may constitute a ground of appeal. As Jackson explained, his research, with Sean Doran, demonstrated that the presence of a jury encourages the judge to be especially passive. Very few civil trials are determined by a jury but juries determine the verdict in almost all Crown Court criminal trials.

The parties control the evidence

9–003   Prior to the 1990s the parties generally brought whatever evidence they saw fit to prove their case. The court would seldom limit it. The parties would decide which and how many witnesses to call. The court has power to call witnesses but seldom does so. Parties were able to "keep their cards close to their chest" pre-trial, which was sometimes likened, mixing metaphors, to "trial by ambush". This, plus the complexity of English procedural rules, plus the rigid adduction of evidence by examination and cross-examination, meant that unrepresented parties were at a disadvantage and it was sometimes the case that the best lawyer or richest party won. All of this is explained in graphic detail by Lightman J., in the 2003 lecture cited in Ch.10 on civil procedure.

The stronger case wins

It is the court's job to determine the relative strength of the parties' cases, according to the law, on the evidence presented, not to determine where the truth lies. Having said that, the Court of Appeal has sometimes said in recent cases that its job is to do justice, as can be seen in Ch.12 on criminal procedure. It is up to the person bringing the case (claimant in a civil case, or prosecutor in a criminal case) to prove it (called the *burden* of proof), to the satisfaction of the court, according to the required *standard* or *quantum* of proof. In civil cases, the standard is proof "on the balance of probabilities", meaning the claimant must show his version of events is more likely than not to be correct. In criminal cases, there is a massive power imbalance between the prosecutor (the State, normally the Crown Prosecution Service) and the defendant. This is one reason why the standard is much higher. The prosecutor must satisfy the magistrates or jury of the accused's guilt "beyond reasonable doubt", giving the benefit of any doubt to the defendant. Historically, the burden of proof in the English adversarial system meant that the defendant was entitled to see the (civil) claimant's or (criminal) prosecutor's case in full before starting to defend himself.

9–004

The principle of orality

This is often seen as a relic of jury trial but was elevated to the level of principle. Most cases were argued by word of mouth, from start to finish. Witnesses were (and in criminal cases most still are) publicly examined by their own side and cross-examined by the opposition. Evidence, such as exhibits and documentation, was, and is, brought out in open court and acknowledged orally. Reported speech, such as the transcription of a suspect's interrogation, is brought in evidence and often re-enacted in court before the jury. All of the evidence has to be summarised, acknowledged or adduced in open court and must be clearly audible. The oral trial proceedings are routinely tape-recorded in all courts, civil and

9–005

criminal, except the magistrates' court, which is not a "court of record". Rock argued that the principle of orality did not apply in magistrates' courts.

2. Criticism of the adversarial system

9–006   Lightman J.'s 2003 criticisms of the adversarial nature of English civil procedure are typical.

1. Success turns very much on the performance on the day. If a party or witness underperforms or counsel lets him down, there is no chance of a replay.
2. Performance at trial turns on investment in the litigation "money talks loud and clear". Cases are won or lost by the quality of representation.
3. The limitation on the role of the judge means his search for truth is confined to the evidence placed before him by the parties.
4. The adversarial system is expensive and time-consuming. He attacked the silk system—the high fees paid to QCs, as can be seen from the quotations in Ch.13 on lawyers.
5. The deficiencies of the adversary system are aggravated by the case law system: "judges are increasingly. . .bombarded. . .with torrents of authorities. The judges make too little efforts to keep their judgments as brief as the reasoning requires."

Added to this is the problem that it is left to the parties to select witnesses. This means that there may be a witness who could give damming evidence against both sides, so the court does not get to know of their existence, or testimony, or a crucial witness is not called because of a lack of defence resources in a criminal case, resulting in a wrongful conviction, as can be seen in the chapter on criminal procedure.

The plight of the unrepresented in criminal cases has been well documented in socio-legal research (Dell (1971); Carlen (1976); Darbyshire (1984)). Lay people find it very difficult to present their "story" to the court by means of examining witnesses. To add to this problem, they are often very nervous and in unfamiliar surroundings. Where a defendant is unrepresented, mostly in the magistrates' court, he is wholly dependent on the goodwill and expertise of the bench or, more realistically, the clerk, to help him put his case and examine witnesses and explain what is being asked of him, for example, choice of venue in a triable-either-way offence. Some clerks are much more prepared and skilled to help than others. The same problem occurs in a civil case where one or both sides is a litigant in person. The increasing numbers of litigants in person have created difficulties for judges, in our adversarial process, as explained in Ch.10 on civil procedure.

The Royal Commission on Criminal Justice 1991–1993 (RCCJ), was concerned that the English criminal trial, allowing the accused to keep his defence secret until having seen the whole of the prosecution case, permitted him to "ambush" the prosecution with an unpredictable defence. As Jackson explains, the English adversarial criminal trial has concentrated on the opposing interests of prosecution and defence, with victims and witnesses given too little independent protection. (See Rock's research and other research to which he refers.) From the 1990s, victims' involvement in the criminal process has been enhanced, as explained in Ch.12 on criminal procedure.

3. Erosion of the adversarial process

The last quarter of the twentieth century saw an erosion of this archetype at work in the English legal system: **9–007**

- In criminal cases, there has been increased use of statutory powers to admit uncontentious witness evidence via a statement, instead of calling the witness to court. In civil cases, case managing judges will readily use their powers to curtail the number of witnesses, or ask for their evidence to be given in writing and each witness's evidence in chief is submitted in a written statement, with very limited opportunities to add to this orally.
- The RCCJ considered whether the court should have an investigative role before and during the criminal trial. They examined continental trial systems. They did not recommend this but that:
  "Wherever practicable in complex cases judges should take on responsibility for managing the progress of a case, securing its passage through the various stages of pre-trial discussion to preparatory hearing and trial and making sure that the parties have fulfilled their obligations both to each other and to the court." (p.10, recommendation 254).
  The 1995 Practice Direction on Plea and Directions Hearings in the Crown Court went some way towards this aim and, as explained in Ch.12 on criminal procedure, judges' trial management powers in criminal cases have been emphasised

and significantly enhanced by the Criminal Procedure Rules 2005, now 2010.

- The Heilbron–Hodge Committee (1993) and Lord Woolf (1996) recommended an interventionist role for the civil trial judge, and active case management is now the hallmark of civil procedure, with the judge controlling the speed and length of the civil case, limiting the evidence presented. For an excellent and entertaining analysis of the implications of this change in the judicial role see Lightman J. at (1999) 149 N.L.J. 1819.

- The interim report of the Civil Justice Review (1986) prompted the courts to require, by Practice Directions, that the parties exchanged witness statements, forcing them to lay some of their cards on the table. Openness was massively enhanced by the requirement for skeleton arguments and document bundles to be exchanged pre-trial and presented to the court.

- Since the 1990s, skeleton arguments, bundles and use of witness statements have made a significant shift from oral case argument to arguments on paper with the judges and opposition reading them, pre-trial. No longer can a student observe court proceedings and expect to be entertained to a full story unfolding in the courtroom. Oral argument has been limited in the US since 1849 but until the 1990s, advocates in England and Wales dictated the length of trials by simply giving an estimate to the court. The CA first introduced a requirement for skeleton arguments in 1989. See the comparative account by Leggatt L.J. and the horror of the American, Martinau, at the primitive nature of unreformed, oral civil appeals in the 1980s.

- In civil cases, since the Civil Procedure Rules 1998 have been in force, parties have been encouraged to share a single expert. Nevertheless, in a criminal case, a jury or magistrates will routinely find themselves having to decide between two experts (for example, on psychiatric or forensic evidence).

- Jolowicz considered that most judges wanted to do substantive justice in the case (get to the truth), not just procedural justice, and that the Woolf reforms would help them to realise that objective, which is to be welcomed ((1996) C.J.Q. 198).

- Small claims in the county court have always been an exception to the adversarial stereotype. Research by Applebey (1978) showed some registrars (now called district judges) employed an inquisitorial technique. Many of those who appear are unrepresented and, therefore, the progress of the case depends on the district judge's being somewhat interventionist. This was explored and confirmed by Baldwin's research. These research findings are cited in Ch.10 on civil procedure. The *Civil Justice Review* (1998) recommended that judges adopt a more standardised inquisitorial role in small claims.

- In family cases relating to children's care, control and/or residence, judges sometimes say they take an inquisitorial role. The cases are multi-party and multi-issue. The child is both the object of the dispute and a party. They may have both a guardian and a legal representative. The judge must focus on the best interests of the child and sometimes comes up with a solution no-one has argued for. See research by Darbyshire, 2011.

BIBLIOGRAPHY AND FURTHER READING

Applebey, Baldwin, The Civil Justice Review, Heilbron and Woolf **9–008** are cited in Ch.10 on civil procedure.

P. Carlen, *Magistrates' Justice* (1976).

M. Damaska, "Evidentiary Barriers to Conviction and Two Models of Criminal Procedure" (1973) 121 *University of Pennsylvania Law Review* 507.

P. Darbyshire, *The Magistrates' Clerk* (1984).

P. Darbyshire, *Sitting in Judgment: the Working Lives of Judges* (2011).

S. Dell, *Silent in Court* (1971).

J.H. Langbein, *The Origins of the Adversary Criminal Trial* (2003).

Leggatt L.J., "The Future of the Oral Tradition in the Court of Appeal" (1995) 14 C.J.Q. 1. (*Westlaw*).

Sir Gavin Lightman's 2003 lecture at Sheffield University is reproduced as Lightman L.J., "The Civil Justice System and Legal Profession—The Challenges Ahead" (2003) 22 C.J.Q. 235.

J. Jackson, "The Adversary Trial and Trial by Judge Alone", in M. McConville and G. Wilson, *The Handbook of The Criminal Justice Process* (2002).

R. Martineau, *Appellate Justice in England and the United States: A Comparative Analysis* (1990).

P. Rock, *The Social World of an English Crown Court* (1993) and see the material he cites therein.

The Royal Commission on Criminal Procedure 1993 is cited in Ch.12 on criminal procedure.

M. Zander, *Cases and Materials on the English Legal System* (latest edition), Ch.4.

10. Civil Procedure

"English institutions have tended to reflect the traditions and values of upper class England. English civil procedure has always reflected the values and traditions of the English sport of cricket most markedly in the adversary system of justice, and not only in the sense that both are slow and boring. In summary, each side prepares its team for the contest. One side in turn goes into bat (i.e. address the court and call its witnesses) and faces the bowling of the other side (i.e. the cross-examination of its witnesses); then the other side takes its turn at the wicket, calling its witnesses. Each side then has the opportunity in final speeches to make its case and unmake that of its opponent. Throughout, an independent third party umpire, selected on grounds of his relative expertise and experience, watches, listens, and enforces the rules, and at the end of the game gives his decision to the winner. . .The adversary system has a number of disturbing features for those who are more interested in the achievement of justice than in the playing of the game." (Lightman J., of the High Court, Chancery Division, in the Edward Bramley Memorial Lecture, University of Sheffield, April 4, 2003.)

In the last chapter, we saw what is meant by adversarial procedure in the English legal system. This chapter explains civil procedure, normally activated when one private citizen or enterprise seeks to bring another to court for a civil wrong against them, such as a breach of contract, or a tort. In Ch.1 we saw that it is up to the claimant to bring a civil case, not the State, and the State has no interest in the outcome of the case, unless it happens to be one of the litigants. It just provides the courts to enable resolution of a private dispute. At the end of this chapter we examine a procedure that can be used in civil or criminal cases, called judicial review, where an aggrieved person may challenge the procedural legality or decision **10–001** of a lower court, or public body. On the general subject of access to civil justice, this chapter must be read in conjunction with Ch.11, on alternative dispute resolution (ADR) and Ch.17 on legal services, because to enforce the civil law and civil rights, people need access to user-friendly dispute resolution for which they can afford to pay, or obtain alternative funding.

Before we examine the formal rules for taking a civil action through the courts, we have to bear in mind that the vast majority of people who could obtain a civil law remedy to their problem do not take it to court or even to any alternative forum, such as those described in the next chapter. They resolve them between themselves or, even if they see a solicitor, solicitors negotiate settlements on behalf of most of their rational clients because, as a CA judge remarked in my research on the judiciary, "You'd never do it yourself, would you?", meaning, take a case to court, knowing how much it costs to litigate. Even in that tiny proportion of cases where civil proceedings are issued, almost all settle pre-trial. All this, and the fact that most people do not even get round to seeing a solicitor was well known before its confirmation by Genn's research, reported in her book, *Paths to Justice*. This has led Michael Zander to conclude that most people simply cannot be bothered to go to court, however much you simplify procedure and make the courts more accessible:

> "When a dispute occurs, most people are prepared to complain and many are prepared to go so far as to take advice, but on the whole, for a great variety of understandable reasons, they show little interest in using any of the forms of civil justice. I believe that this is not to be regarded as necessarily a bad thing, there is probably very little that can be done to change the situation." (2000, p.38).

1. Civil procedure after "the Woolf reforms"

10–002   There was a time when there was a premium on ambush and taking your opponent by surprise: litigation was a sport and the outcome turned very much on who you could afford to instruct as your advocate and champion." (Lightman J., 1999.)

Thankfully, after centuries of complaint that English civil litigation was an embarrassment, conducted as a lawyers' Dickensian game and was slow, expensive and complex, the Civil Procedure Rules 1998 (CPR) were passed, in the hope that one simplified set of rules for the High Court and county courts, written in plain English and introducing judicial case management, would rid us of some of these problems. The Rules were drafted according to the recommendations of Lord Woolf, in his famous 1996 report, *Access to Justice*. The CPR and over 50 Practice Directions replaced two separate sets of rules for the High Court and county court, in April 1999. They embodied a radically different approach to civil procedure from what had gone before. The Rules and Practice Directions are continually updated and can all be downloaded from their own web pages, run by the Ministry of Justice. The background to this "new scenario", called the Woolf reforms, is explained below, in s.5, along with an evaluation of how the reforms are working in practice, after the description of civil procedure. One of the major problems with the old system is that an adversarial system, where the parties are left to battle it out, uncontrolled by the court, is inherently unfair, where the parties are not equally matched in terms of resources, information or wealth, such as where a patient who suffered negligent surgery sues a health authority or a consumer sues a large company, or an employee sues an employer.

Paving the way to the reforms, s.1 of the Civil Procedure Act 1997 provided for one set of practice rules for the Court of Appeal (CA), High Court (HC) and county courts, "with a view to securing that the civil justice system is accessible, fair and efficient". Section 2 provided for a Civil Court Rule Committee to include people "with experience in and knowledge of" consumer affairs and lay advice. Section 6 established a Civil Justice Council comprising the Master of the Rolls (which, in 1999, was Lord Woolf himself), judges, lawyers, consumer/lay advisors and litigant representatives, to keep the civil justice system under review (including alternative dispute resolution (ADR) and tribunals), advise the Lord Chancellor and suggest research.

2. The Civil Procedure Rules 1998 (CPR)

The Overriding Objective

The overriding objective is set out in r.1.1:   **10–003**

"The rules enable the court to deal with a case justly—

   a. ensuring the parties are on an equal footing;
   b. saving expense;
   c. dealing with the case in a way which is proportionate:

        to the amount of money involved;
        to the importance of the case;
        to the complexity of the issues;
        to the financial position of parties;

    d. ensuring that it is dealt with expeditiously and fairly; and

    e. allotting to it an appropriate share of the court's resources."

The court must apply the overriding objective in interpreting the rules and exercising their powers. It is not waffly sentiment. It has repeatedly been applied by the Court of Appeal. The CA has held that there is no need to refer to Art.6 of the European Convention on Human Rights (fair trial) because of the court's obligation in the Rules to deal with cases justly: *Daniels v Walker* [2000] 1 W.L.R. 1382.

> "To the outsider these objectives of a civilised legal system would appear self-evident, and the surprise lies, not in their statement in the CPR, but in the need to state them and their absence prior to implementation of the reforms" (Lightman J., 2003.)

Pre-action protocols

10–004   These are statements of best practice in negotiation, encouraging exchange of information and putting the parties into a position to settle fairly, as explained in the Practice Direction on Protocols. Fairness in negotiation is very important because only a small fraction (under 20 per cent) of civil disputes are ever brought to court (Genn, 1999; Zander, 2000). If one party behaves obstructively, they can be penalised in costs, if the action later comes to court. Protocols have been issued for personal injury litigation and clinical disputes, construction and engineering, professional negligence, defamation, disease and illness, housing disrepair, judicial review and other topics of litigation. A Practice Direction on "Pre-action behaviour" came into force in 2009, taking a more robust stance on encouraging reasonable pre-action negotiation. It tries to help parties to settle so that proceedings do not have to be issued. It encourages early exchange of information and alternative dispute resolution. The parties MUST, for example, exchange information in reasonable time, disclose relevant documents, consider minimising the cost of experts, and attempt ADR, though they cannot be forced to do so. The Court MUST take account of compliance with this PD and pre-action protocols when making directions.

Starting proceedings (Pt 7)

10–005   The claimant (formerly plaintiff) or court issues and serves the claim on the defendant. This must include particulars of the claim (statement of case) or they must be served within four months. They may include points of law, witness lists and documents and must include statements of truth and value, and specify the remedy sought. By 2005, money claims could be issued and defended online and a number of other documents could be emailed to some courts. One of the Her Majesty's Courts Service (HMCS) "promises" made in May 2007 was lower fees for claims issued online. All forms are meant to be in plain English on what is now HMCTS website. The claimant then has four months to serve the claim form on the defendant.

The defendant must, within 14 days, admit the claim or file a defence (statement of case) or acknowledge the claim. If he files a defence, the case is automatically transferred to his home court. If not, the claimant may request a *default judgment* (Pt 12). This means asking the court to grant his claim because the defendant has not entered a defence. Most cases end at this point. Over three quarters of county court claims are "default actions" where the claimant, usually a company, is collecting a debt from a customer and, in the absence of a defence, judgment is automatically issued, without the involvement of a judge. Most are bulk claims issued at the centralised Claims Production Centre in Northampton, by claimants such as banks, credit/store card issuers, mail order catalogues and utilities. Most are then enforced by warrants issued at the County Court Bulk Centre. The defendant may issue a claim against a co-defendant or third party or make a counterclaim (Pt 20). The claimant may reply to this and defend. The parties may write direct to others requesting further information (Pt 18).

Procedural judges and allocation

Judges manage cases. This means masters in the Royal Courts **10–006** of Justice and district judges in the county court and High Court district registries, outside London. Unusually, Commercial Court judges manage their own cases. Hearings may be by telephone. Defended claims are allocated to one of three tracks, as follows, once the defendant has completed the pre-trial checklist. The judge may transfer a case to another court.

Small claims

For most actions under £5,000, with specified exceptions. Claims over £5,000 may be allocated to the small claims track, by consent. The small claims limit is likely to be raised by legislation in 2011. See below.

Fast track

For most cases £5–£25,000, which can be tried in a day. Oral expert evidence is limited to two fields and one expert per field.

Multi-track
Claims over £25,000 or over one day's trial. These will normally be transferred to county court trial centres.

Claims with no monetary value
Such as applications for injunctions, are allocated where the judge considers they will be dealt with most justly.

Discretionary factors
The procedural judge must have regard to:

- the nature of the remedy sought;
- the complexity of facts, law and evidence;
- the number of parties;
- the value of the counterclaim;
- oral evidence;
- the importance of the claim to non-parties;
- the parties' views;
- the circumstances of the parties.

The Woolf Report 1996 suggested the following cases for the multi-track:

- those of public importance;
- test cases: an example was successful negligence litigation by ex-miners, suffering from respiratory diseases, against British coal, which encouraged many others to claim compensation, in 1998;
- clinical disputes (formerly medical negligence);
- cases with the right to jury trial.

The court's duty to manage cases (r.1.4)

10–007   This duty had already been introduced, as a matter of good practice (rather than law), from 1994 in Practice Directions. It then included timetabling, the requirement for skeleton arguments and limitation of oral argument. The duty now includes:

- encouraging parties to co-operate;
- identifying issues at an early stage;
- deciding promptly which issues can be disposed of summarily;
- deciding the order of issues;
- encouraging ADR;
- helping parties settle;
- fixing timetables;

- considering cost benefit;
- grouping issues;
- dealing with a case in the absence of one or more parties;
- making use of IT; and
- directing the trial process quickly and efficiently.

Sanctions for failure to comply with case management

These include striking out (meaning dismissing the case), cost **10–008** penalties and debarring part of a case or evidence. Trials will only be postponed as a last resort. Sanctions should be designed to prevent rather than punish non-compliance with rules and timetables. The CA suggested there are more flexible ways of controlling claimants' default and delay rather than a draconian strike-out: *Biguzzi* [1999] 1 W.L.R. 1926.

Interim Orders

The parties may apply for the interim orders listed below but the **10–009** 1998 Rules permit the court to act on its own initiative. There is an obligation to apply early.

- Pre-action remedies if urgent.
- Applications without notice (formerly called ex parte).
- Extensions or shortening of time.
- Requiring attendance.
- Separating or consolidating issues or excluding issues.
- Deciding the order of issues.
- Staying (pausing) all or part of the case, hoping for settlement.
- Interim injunctions/declarations.
- Freezing injunctions (formerly called *Mareva* injunctions), which can also be made against a third party and search orders (formerly *Anton Piller* orders) may only be ordered by a HC or authorised judge. The effect of these orders is draconian. The former freezes a party's financial assets, such as bank accounts.
- Pre-action disclosure of evidence (formerly discovery) or inspection, including against non-parties.
- Interim payments and offers to settle.
- A summary assessment of costs.

Other points

Summary judgment
10–010

May be initiated by the claimant, defendant or court, where the claim or defence "has no real prospect of success". The court may enter judgment, dismiss the case, strike out a claim, or make a conditional order.

District judges

Have unlimited jurisdiction to assess damages, unless otherwise directed. They should not deal with complex cases. There is a Practice Direction on case allocation to judges.

A group litigation order (Pt 19)

May be made to allow for case management in multi-party actions. An example of group litigation is *Deep Vein Thrombosis and Air Travel Group Litigation* [2005] UKHL 72.

RTA claims:

A streamlined procedure was introduced in 2010 for road traffic accident personal injury claims of £1,000–£10,000, with fixed fees and stages. Apparently there were 30,0000 fraudulent claims in 2010, including fake, staged accidents.

Basic procedure in defended cases

Small claims procedure (Pt 27)

10–011   The claimant completes the simple claim form, online, or from a county court office. H.H. Judge Madge, who had a wealth of experience in handling small claims as a district judge, reported (2004) that "litigants in person", people conducting their own cases, had little difficulty in preparing them. Once a claim has been allocated to this track, standard procedural directions, such as requiring the exchange of documents, will be issued. Hearings are meant to be in public (European Convention on Human Rights, Art. 6, fair trial) but will normally be held in the district judges' chambers. The public very rarely observe these proceedings and are probably unaware that they are open. Costs are low and fixed so, however much the litigant spends on her side of the case, she cannot expect to recoup extravagant expenses. Keeping the costs down is meant to enhance access to justice by encouraging people to enforce their rights by using the small claims procedure. The rules require the parties to help the court in furthering the overriding objective. It is rare for evidence to be taken on oath.

The district judge may adopt any procedure she considers fair, including hearing lay representatives. Baldwin's research indicated differences in procedure from one judge to another. Judges may follow traditional adversarial procedure, with speeches and examination of witnesses in the traditional trial order, or a more inquisitorial approach. H.H. Judge Madge observed "An interventionist approach . . . is effective in eliciting evidence from litigants in person. It is seen by unrepresented parties as a 'helping hand' . . . By discussing the facts of the case, judges find what common ground does exist between the parties . . .". He felt the key judicial skills were maintaining a balance between informality and fairness, and ensuring a level playing field. Judges give formal judgments, applying the law, and state their reasons orally.

The first small claims courts were developed outside the court system, in London and Manchester, in 1971, to deal with small consumer complaints, for which county court procedure was too elaborate and expensive. Although they were thus a type of privately accessible ADR (alternative dispute resolution), they proved so popular that they were absorbed into the county court system in 1973. It is important for costs to be low and fixed so that litigants will know in advance the cost of bringing an action. Procedure has always been simple, with district judges permitted great leeway to assist the parties so that people can represent themselves. The vast majority of litigants are unrepresented and so what was meant to provide cheap DIY justice seems to have succeeded. For this reason, legal aid is seldom granted.

Prior to the reforms, in 1997, Baldwin found that at least three **10–012** quarters of small claims litigants were contented with the way their cases had been handled, whereas, of those involved in formal, county court open court trials, 40 per cent considered them inappropriate and disproportionately expensive for this kind of dispute. Baldwin found small claims tended to be used by professional people or businesses and had not provided the poor with an avenue for redress. He continued to research the effects of increasing the small claims limit to £5,000 and litigants' levels of satisfaction with small claims. In 2002, he advised against raising the small claims limit again as there was some evidence that, in larger claims, litigants needed more advice and benefited from representation.

H.H. Judge Madge presented a snapshot of the types of case he had heard in the first six months of 2002: 44 per cent were business debts, 22 per cent landlord and tenant disputes, 16 per cent road traffic claims and 10 per cent complaints about services, such as work by builders or plumbers. Forty-two per cent were for less than £1,000. Half the litigants were individuals and the other half were companies or firms. Fewer than one in five were represented. The time between issuing the claim and final hearing was less than six months, in 70 per cent of cases. Permission to appeal was sought in only six per cent of cases but not granted.

Fast track procedure (Pt 28)

The intention is for the court to maintain "proportionality", **10–013** which means limiting the costs recoverable from the unsuccessful party. For instance, where counsel is briefed, the court cannot normally order costs for a solicitor to accompany her. The aim is to increase access to justice by removing uncertainty. The fast track aims to help the parties to obtain justice speedily. The court directs the timetable and fixes the trial date no more than 30 weeks ahead. The intention is to provide little scope for either party to create extra work to gain a tactical advantage. Lord Woolf said it was important for the court to protect the weaker party against oppressive or unreasonable behaviour by a powerful party. Standard directions include disclosure and the exchange of witness statements and expert evidence. Parties are encouraged to use a single expert, or a court-appointed expert. The standard timetable is nine months from the issue of proceedings to trial. An indexed, paginated bundle must be produced to the court three to seven days pre-trial and may include an agreed case summary. The judge pre-reads the bundle. The costs regime is currently under consideration, in 2011, as part of the Jackson reforms, explained below.

Multi-track procedure (Pt 29)

10–014   This varies. Simple cases are treated like fast track ones. Complex ones may have several directions hearings:

1. a case management conference attended by lawyers familiar with the case;
2. a pre-trial review of the statement of issues;
3. other directions hearings.

Practice Directions make more detailed requirements for different types of multi-track case. They may require the submission and exchange of skeleton arguments and document bundles pre-trial.

Disclosure (formerly known as discovery) (Pt 31)

10–015   Lord Woolf thought one of two major generators of unnecessary cost was uncontrolled discovery so standard disclosure requires only documents on which a party relies and documents which:

- adversely affect his case;
- adversely affect another party's case;
- support another party's case;
- are required by a Practice Direction.

In *Digicel v Cable & Wireless* [2008] EWHC 2522, Morgan J. accepted that a reasonable search did not require that no stone was left unturned. Unfortunately, parties usually disclose all documents of any relevance and the CA has strongly criticised solicitors for not changing practice.

The court's power to control evidence (Pts 32 and 33)

The court has power to control the issues, the nature of the evi- **10–016** dence and its delivery: whether it is prepared to hear oral, hearsay, or written evidence, and so on.

Expert witnesses (Pt 35)

The 1990s saw the massive growth in the use of expert witnesses **10–017** and they used to act as "hired guns", giving evidence for the party who paid them. Lord Woolf was of the strong opinion that this had made litigation costly and unduly adversarial. He denounced the development of the "large litigation support industry. . .This goes against all principles of proportionality and access to justice." (1996). The assumption is now that one expert will do, in small claims and fast track cases (re-emphasised from 2009). The expert's overriding duty is to help the court and no party may call an expert or use a report without permission. The court has a duty to restrict expert evidence and can make a costs order against an expert who has caused significant expense: *Phillips v Symes* [2004] EWHC 2330. Problems remain with experts and the rules were tightened in 2009. See below.

Offers to settle (Pt 36)

This procedure encourages the parties to settle by financial incen- **10–018** tive. Under the old rules, the defendant could make a payment into court and force the plaintiff to take a gamble: take the money or proceed to trial and risk paying both sides' costs since the time of the payment in, which could be a Pyrrhic victory for a winning plaintiff. This happened to Albert Reynolds, former Irish Prime Minister, in 1996 when he won a libel action against the *Sunday Times* but had to pay over £1 million in costs. The intention of Pt 36 is that allowing the claimant to make an offer to settle, as well as the defendant, alters the balance of power. Where the offer is the same as or better than that ordered by the judge, the offeror is rewarded by having the judge order that the other side will pay both sides' costs since the date of expiry of the offer, including interest. Payments used to be made into court, to back the offer, but this is no longer necessary, since 2007. Incidentally, the trial judge knows nothing of the offer, otherwise the gamble would not work. For more detail, see *Gibbon v Manchester CC* [2010] EWCA Civ 726. See now, Legal Aid, Sentencing and Punishment of Offenders Bill/Act 2011.

Basic trial procedure

The reforms were intended to cut the length of trial. Suitable cases **10–019** may be disposed of without a hearing (r.1.4(2)). The statutory right to jury trial is unaffected in deceit, libel, slander, malicious prosecution and false imprisonment cases. Generally, hearings must be in open court, as discussed in Ch.6, on the civil courts. There are exceptions where hearings may be in private (formerly known as "in camera", "in chambers"), such as mortgage possession cases and proceedings involving children. In fast and multi-track trials procedure is as follows:

1. The claimant/claimant's advocate makes her opening speech.
2. Traditionally, the claimant's first witness was examined by the claimant or advocate and then cross-examined by the defendant or her advocate but pre-trial witness statements, including expert reports, count as evidence-in-chief in the trial so the witnesses are only cross-examined, to save time. Supplementary questions may be asked only for "good reason". If there is a single joint expert, whose evidence is agreed, it may not be necessary to call him to appear in court. Witnesses may appear via video link.
3. This is repeated for each subsequent claimant witness.
4. At the end of the claimant's case, the defendant may submit to the court that there is "no case to answer", where he considers the claimant's case has no real prospect of success. If the court agrees, it will uphold that submission. Appeal lies to the CA from a circuit judge's finding of "no case".
5. The defendant or defence advocate makes his opening speech.
6. Each defence witness is (examined and) cross-examined, in turn, as above. Expert's reports are dealt with as above.
7. Closing speeches are made by the claimant, or her advocate, and defendant, or advocate.
8. Unless a jury is present, the judge decides whether the claimant has proven the case to her satisfaction. The quantum of proof in a civil case is "proof on the balance of probabilities", which is a much lower quantum or standard of proof than in a criminal case, which has to be proven "beyond reasonable doubt", explained in the previous chapter.
9. The judge delivers judgment, or, if a jury is present, she sums up the evidence to them and they deliver their verdict, again applying the civil standard of proof. The judge makes an order. The CA has said that the judge has a duty to give reasons, which is a function of due process. Parties should know why they have won or lost; the losing party will know whether there is a ground of appeal; giving reasons concentrates the mind so the decision is more likely to be soundly based on the evidence: *Flannery v Halifax Estate Agencies Ltd* [2000] 1 W.L.R. 177.

10. The judge hears arguments on costs then makes an order as to costs.
11. The judge then hears any application for permission to appeal.
12. The whole trial will have been recorded so that a transcript may be requested if one of the parties is considering an appeal or if they need it for any other reason.

Costs (Pt 44)

Under the pre-1999 regime, in most cases costs would "follow" **10–020** the event so the outcome would amount to "winner takes all". Under the 1998 rules, the judge must assess costs in accordance with which party won different issues and the judge's view as to how reasonably the parties behaved. The court may make a wasted costs order against a representative if she has acted improperly, unreasonably or negligently and her conduct has caused unnecessary costs to the other party. Throughout the proceedings, costs must be kept down to a proportionate level. In *Lownds v Home Office* [2002] EWCA Civ 365, the CA held that, when assessing costs, the court should firstly consider whether the total sum claimed was proportionate and then conduct an item-by-item assessment. If the sum claimed was proportionate, all that was required was that each item should have been reasonably incurred for a reasonable amount but if the sum claimed was disproportionate, the court would have to be satisfied that the work in relation to each item was necessary and that the amount incurred was reasonable. Courts have been granting costs capping orders for years, limiting the amount of costs a party can recover. It is good practice for a lawyer to estimate costs for his client: *Garbutt v Edwards* [2005] EWCA Civ 1206. It is incumbent on everyone to take all the steps to reduce costs: *Pastouna v Black* [2005] EWCA Civ 1389, reiterating their duty under CPR 1.1 and 1.3. Brooke L.J. castigated solicitors and counsel for coming to London from Liverpool at taxpayers' expense, when the brief hearing could have been conducted by video conference. He reminded them that the VCF facility was explained on the CA's website. As is discussed below, costs in many cases have been wildly disproportionate so the Jackson Review was established and reforms are in progress at the time of writing, 2011.

General points

Judicial behaviour

Judicial bias is a ground of appeal because it breaches judicial **10–021** independence. Bias is examined in more depth in Ch.14 on judges. If a judge interferes too much in the presentation of the case, he risks breaching the common rules of "natural justice", or fairness and, consequently, Art.6 of the European Convention (fair trial). The CA had to consider what level of intervention is tolerable in a judge, in *Alpha Lettings Ltd v Neptune Research and Development Inc* [2003] EWCA Civ 704. The trial judge had shown irritability with the defendant's witnesses and counsel and made numerous interventions. The CA judges remarked that part of the trial had been "depressing to hear on the tape" and "depressing to read on the transcript". They rejected the defendant's argument, however, because the judge had not at any time prevented the witnesses from giving evidence, nor had he prevented the advocates from eliciting that evidence. He had occasionally expressed surprise at certain answers but had never betrayed a refusal to be persuaded of any factual proposition. They approved the words of Sir Thomas Bingham M.R. in *Arab Monetary Fund v Hashim (No.7)* [1993] 1 W.L.R. 1014:

> "In some jurisdictions the forensic tradition is that judges sit mute, listening to the advocates without interruption, asking no question, voicing no opinion, until they break their silence to give judgment. That is a perfectly respectable tradition but it is not ours . . . The English tradition sanctions and even encourages a measure of disclosure by the judge of his current thinking . . . An expression of scepticism is not suggestive of bias unless the judge conveys an unwillingness to be persuaded of a factual proposition whatever the evidence may be".

Advocate to the court

10–022 Formerly known as an amicus curiae, one may be appointed by the Attorney General, at the court's request, where there is a danger of an important and difficult point of law being decided without the court hearing relevant argument. The Advocate represents no-one and will not normally lead evidence, cross-examine witnesses or investigate the facts. An advocate to the court is sometimes instructed by the Treasury Solicitor where the court wants to hear specialist argument by a neutral lawyer. This often happens in chancery cases about pensions where the appellant is unrepresented, e.g. *SS for Work and Pensions v Morina* [2007] EWCA Civ 749.

Technical errors should not be regarded as incurable: *Law v St Margaret's Insurances Ltd* [2001] EWCA Civ 30. The courts will not be rigid where an injustice would be caused or the right to fair trial would be violated: *Goode v Martin* [2001] EWCA Civ 1899.

Advocates have a common law duty not to mislead the court: *Vernon v Bosley (No.1)* [1997] 1 All E.R. 577 and a duty to keep up-to-date with recent law reports: *Copeland v Smith* [2000] 1 W.L.R. 1371.

Authorities produced by the judge: As explained in the previous chapter, in the adversarial procedure, the parties are expected to bring all relevant evidence, authorities and legal argument to the court. The court has no duty to research the law for itself but, where a judge does find a case that she considers relevant, she should give the parties the opportunity to address her on it: *Silva v Albion Hotel (Freshwater) Ltd* [2002] EWCA Civ 1784.

3. Appeals from the High Court and county courts from 2000

In *Access to Justice*, 1996 (the Woolf Report), Lord Woolf said: **10–023**

"Appeals serve two purposes: the private purpose, which is to do justice in particular cases by correcting wrong decisions, and the public purpose, which is to ensure public confidence in the administration of justice by making such corrections and to clarify and develop the law and to set precedents." (p.153.)

The Government explained the rationale behind the new civil appeals regime, Pat 52 of the CPR 1998, in its 1998 White Paper, *Modernising Justice*. The resulting procedure is contained in the Access to Justice Act 1999, in the CPR 1998 and in various Practice Directions. The whole regime was explained by the CA (Civil Division) in *Tanfern Ltd v Cameron-Macdonald* [2000] 1 W.L.R. 1311. The Government explained that they planned to achieve their objectives of proportionality and efficiency (the same as in the rest of civil procedure) by diverting from the CA those cases which, by their nature, did not require the attention of the most senior judges in the country and by making various changes to the working methods of the Court, "which will enable it to deploy its resources more efficiently and effectively".

The guiding principles are now as follows.

- Permission to appeal will only be given where the court considers that an appeal would have a real prospect of success.
- In normal circumstances, more than one appeal cannot be justified.
- There should be no automatic right to appeal. Permission, previously called leave, is required in virtually all appeals to the CA.

Jurisdiction

10–024 The Government decided routes of appeal should be as follows.

- In fast track cases heard by a district judge, appeal lies to a circuit judge, with permission. Grounds are not restricted. Appeal lies to a circuit judge and there is a guarantee of an oral hearing, which is a review, not a rehearing.
- In fast track cases heard by a circuit judge, appeal lies to a HC judge.
- In multi-track cases, appeals against final orders lie to the CA, regardless of the original judge.
- In multi-track cases, appeals against a procedural decision of a district judge will be to a circuit judge; decisions by a master or circuit judge lie to a HC judge and from procedural decisions of a HC judge lie to the CA.
- Exceptional cases involving important points of principle or which affect a number of litigants may go straight to the CA.

Composition

10–025 Changes to the composition, procedures, working methods and management of the CA (Civil Division) are designed to help it operate more efficiently. Under the Access to Justice Act 1999, the CA can now consist of as few as two judges, or even one, according to the importance and complexity of the case. If there are two judges and they cannot agree, the case may have to be re-argued before a new court of three. This has occurred and is unfortunate and expensive for the litigant so judges rarely, if ever, sit in pairs.

Procedure (set down in Practice Directions)

10–026 Trial judges should routinely ask parties if they want permission to appeal but if in any doubt whether the appeal would have a real prospect of success or involves a general point of principle, should decline permission and let the litigant seek it from the CA. Permission can be granted if, though there is no real prospect of success, there is a public interest issue. On a point of law, permission should not be granted unless the judge thinks there is a real prospect of the CA coming to a different conclusion on a point of law which will materially affect the outcome of the case. A point of law includes an appeal on the ground that there was no evidence to support the finding. On an appeal on a question of fact, the CA will rarely interfere with a decision based on the judge's evaluation of oral evidence but permission is more appropriate where a party challenges the judge's inference from primary facts or where the judge has not benefited from seeing witnesses. Where there is a lot of evidence, the judge should give reasons for refusing permission.

The CA has been attempting to cut down delays and the length of hearings since about 1994. The judges work at a very fast rate, as I discovered in empirical observational research reported in 2011. They have vast amounts of papers to read, in preparing for appeals. They normally sit in court four days a week, so have to fit in judgment-writing and all this reading into their one reading day, plus evenings and weekends. They do not have the time to read irrelevant material or to deal with skeleton arguments or document bundles which come in late. (I sometimes saw bundles delivered at 10.15 for a 10.30 hearing.) Exasperated with practitioners who do not seem to understand this, they amended the appeal Practice Direction (PD52) in 2004. The CA explained these changes in *Scribes West Ltd v Relsa Anstalt (No.1)* [2004] EWCA Civ 835. They complained bitterly of a "proliferation of bundles . . . (and) widespread ignorance of provisions . . . which were designed to assist the court but did not succeed in their object." (per Brooke L.J.) The Direction requires the exclusion of all extraneous documents, with a costs penalty for unnecessary copying or incomplete bundles. The appellant must file a skeleton argument 14 days in advance and the respondent a week in advance, or the court may refuse to hear an argument. The Direction is strict but its purpose is to support the CA's determination to streamline its work and prevent this being defeated by inefficient lawyers. Nevertheless, the problem has continued and the CA has had to make repeated warnings about massive bundles and repetitive, lengthy skeletons. In *Midgulf International v Groupe Chimique Tunisien* [2010] EWCA Civ 66, there were 15 level arch files of bundles, five containing 100 authorities, and a 132 page skeleton.

Grounds

The appeal court will only allow an appeal where the lower court **10–027** was wrong (in substance) or where it was unjust because of a serious procedural or other irregularity. Under the new procedure, the decision of the lower court attracts a much greater significance so this makes it all the more important for decisions to be recorded accurately.

Admitting fresh evidence

The leading case is *Ladd v Marshall* [1954] 1 W.L.R. 1489, which **10–028** requires that the evidence could not have been obtained with reasonable diligence at the trial; it would probably have an important influence on the result and it must be apparently credible. In *Riyad Bank v Ahli United Bank (UK) Plc* [2005] EWCA Civ 1419, the court reiterated and clarified the test: to what extent would the evidence affect points on which permission to appeal has been given or to

229

LIVERPOOL JOHN MOORES UNIVERSITY
LEARNING SERVICES

what extent would the evidence support a new ground? The court should be especially cautious about admitting further evidence of questions and answers after a trial, where that witness had been examined at trial.

Approach and powers

10–029   Every appeal is limited to a review of the decision of the lower court, unless Practice Direction provides otherwise, or the court considered that in the circumstances of an individual appeal, it would be in the interests of justice to hold a rehearing. The general rule is that an appeal court has all the powers of the lower court. It also has the power to affirm, set aside or vary any order or judgment of the lower court, to refer any claim or issue for determination by the lower court, to order a new trial or hearing and to make a costs order. The CA is very reluctant to overturn a trial judge's findings of fact, because, unlike them, she has seen the witnesses or their statements. They are even more reluctant to overturn a jury's decision. As we can see from the quotation from *R. v McIlkenny*, in the Criminal Division, discussed in Ch.12 on criminal procedure, this is mainly because judges accord juries a special constitutional position, which they are reluctant to usurp, as a matter of principle. Also, as juries do not give reasons, that makes it all the more difficult to draft an appeal or reconsider their findings of fact.

The last word and binding House of Lords precedent on the conditions in which the CA will overturn a civil jury's decision is *Grobbelaar v News Group Newspapers* [2001] EWCA Civ 33. The CA overturned an £85,000 damages award to a former Liverpool goalkeeper for a defamation action in which the jury were persuaded that he had been falsely accused of match fixing, despite strong video and audio-taped evidence (repeatedly shown on TV) of his taking bribes (he was handed an envelope) and boasting of a previous conspiracy. Simon Brown L.J. warned, in the CA: "the court must inevitably be reluctant to find a jury's verdict perverse and anxious not to usurp their function" but he was satisfied that the CA had the jurisdiction to entertain an appeal on the ground of perversity, if the verdict, on all the evidence, was not properly and reasonably open to the jury. A lengthy and detailed examination of the facts led the court "inexorably to the view that Mr Grobbelaar's story is, quite simply, incredible. All logic, common sense and reason compel one to that conclusion." Mr Grobbelaar appealed to the House of Lords. They allowed his appeal because they *could* find a rational explanation for the jury's verdict, on an examination of the facts, but they agreed with Simon Brown's reasoning on appellate courts' reluctance to overturn a jury verdict: [2002] UKHL 40. Lord Bingham set out the position of an appellate court in examining a civil jury verdict:

"The oracular utterance of the jury contains no reasoning, no elaboration. But it is not immune from review. The jury is a judicial decision-maker of a very special kind, but it is a judicial decision-maker nonetheless. While speculation about the jury's reasoning and train of thought is impermissible, the drawing of inevitable or proper inferences from the jury's decision is not, and is indeed inherent in the process of review. . .it is a very serious thing to stigmatise as perverse the unanimous finding of jurors who have solemnly sworn to return a true verdict according to the evidence. A jury may, of course, from time to time act in a wholly irrational way, but that is not a conclusion to be reached lightly or if any alternative explanation not involving perversity presents itself" (para.7).

The House nevertheless reduced the damages to a nominal £1, or "derisory damages" as Lord Millett called them, Lord Bingham explaining that the appellant "acted in a way in which no decent or honest footballer would act".

In exceptional cases, the CA has power to re-open an appeal already determined. This was done on grounds of alleged bias, in *Taylor v Lawrence* [2001] EWCA Civ 119. Lord Woolf C.J. said it had implicit powers to do that which was necessary to achieve the dual objectives of an appellate court, articulated above. This could be done only where the CA was satisfied that leave to appeal would not be given by the House of Lords. This is a very important decision of a five-judge court, headed by the Lord Chief Justice and Master of the Rolls.

Second appeals

The CA in *Tanfern* said Parliament had made it clear in the Access **10–030** to Justice Act 1999 that second appeals would now be a rarity. The decision of the first appeal court should be given primacy, unless the CA itself considered that the appeal would raise an important point of principle or practice, or that there was some other compelling reason for it to hear a second appeal. Only the CA can grant permission for a second appeal from the county court or HC: *Clark v Perks* [2001] EWCA Civ 1228. In *Uphill v BRB (Residuary) Ltd* [2005] EWCA Civ 60, the CA gave guidance on permission to appeal for a second time.

4. The background to the Woolf reforms

The problems of English civil procedure have been the subject **10–031** of scrutiny for centuries. Prior to the *Civil Justice Review* 1988, there had been 63 reports since 1900. With tedious and frustrating repetition, they all identified the same core problems so that the opening words of Ch.2 of Lord Woolf's interim report, 1995, gave commentators a frisson of *déjà vu*: "The process is too expensive, too slow and too complex." His Lordship said these problems militated against the provision of an accessible system of civil courts which is necessary for people to enforce their rights. Indeed, the very title of the Woolf report, *Access to Justice*, seemed like an ironic cliché, after years of concern over the lack of it.

The Civil Justice Review was remarkable for the breadth and depth of its scrutiny of the system, its radical approach and its success rate, in that many of its recommendations were soon translated into law, in the Courts and Legal Services Act 1990 and subsequent delegated legislation. It recommended merging the jurisdiction of the county court and HC and enabling the Lord Chancellor to make rules allowing for flexible distribution of the caseload between them. This was done, as was the shifting down into the county court of most cases, leaving the HC for procedurally or evidentially complex cases and judicial review. Yet, despite the fact that its reforms were potentially the most radical since the Judicature Acts of 1873–1875, they did not satisfy critics. The two sides of the legal profession swiftly produced a 1993 report (Heilbron–Hodge) on the continuing problems of civil justice and their proposals for dealing with them so the Lord Chancellor commissioned Lord Woolf to carry out yet another scrutiny. In the meantime, the Heads of Division (Master of the Rolls, Lord Chief Justice and Vice-Chancellor) took matters into their own hands by issuing radical Practice Directions for the conduct of litigation in the HC. Described below are some of reviews and reforms which preceded and, indeed, pre-empted the Woolf reforms.

The Heilbron–Hodge Report 1993

10–032   The report, published by the Bar Council and Law Society, entitled "Civil Justice on Trial—The Case for Change" started with the working premise that:

> "It is axiomatic that in any free and democratic society all citizens should be equal before the law. This means that all litigants, rich and poor, however large or however small is the subject matter of their litigation, should have access to a fair and impartial system of disputes resolution." (para.1.3.)

They complained that:

- "An air of Dickensian antiquity pervades the civil process";
- "Procedures are unnecessarily technical, inflexible,

rule-ridden, formalistic and often incomprehensible to the ordinary litigant for whom they are ultimately designed";
- lawyers and judges were reluctant to change;
- progress of actions lay with the parties and their lawyers rather than the courts, causing avoidable delay;
- fear of costs of litigation deterred people from using the courts;
- most people wanted their dispute resolved rather than their "day in court".

The principles underlying their recommendations were:

- litigation should encourage the early settlement of disputes;
- litigants should have imposed upon them sensible time-frames;
- judges should adopt a more interventionist role to ensure that issues were limited, delays reduced and court time was not wasted;
- since court time was costly, a balance should be struck between the written and oral word and what could be achieved out of court rather than in court;
- justice should, where possible, be brought to the people;
- a widespread introduction of technology was urgently required;
- facilities for the litigant urgently need improving;
- additional resources should be found to improve the system.

Here are some of their main recommendations. Some reforms were effected by the 1994/95 Practice Directions. My comments are bracketed:

1. Merger of QBD and Chancery (not accepted; reconsidered and rejected in 2005).
2. HC listing should be computerised (done).
3. Common procedural rules for the HC and county court (done by the CPR 1998).
4. Judicial review cases to be heard on circuit (Welsh cases can be heard in Wales, since devolution, and there are now additional centres).
5. Revival of an ethos of public service amongst court staff and assistance to litigants (courts are now awarded a Charter Mark if they demonstrate how well they serve the public).
6. Plain English court documents (done).
7. A more interventionist approach by judges at trial and on appeal (already existed in small claims; now done with LIPs

and generally required by the court's duty to manage cases under the CPR).

8. Limits on discovery of documents; provision of skeleton arguments and bundles to the court and opposing parties (done since the 1994–95 Practice Directions were issued).

9. Judicial intervention at trial to avoid time wasting (now required by the CPR).

10. Promotion of alternative dispute resolution (ADR) (now included in the CPR).

The 1994/95 Practice Directions

10–033　The Heilbron–Hodge Report doubtless prompted these Practice Directions and the 1994 establishment of Lord Woolf's scrutiny. Directions were issued for all three HC divisions. They emphasised the importance of reducing cost and delay and threatened that "failure by practitioners to conduct cases economically will be visited by appropriate orders for costs". The court was encouraged to limit documents, oral submissions, examination of witnesses, the issues on which it wished to be addressed, and reading aloud from documents and authorities. Witness statements would generally stand as evidence-in-chief. Bundled documents and skeleton arguments were to be lodged in court pre-trial. Opening speeches were to be succinct and, where appropriate, lawyers had to verify that they had considered the possibility of ADR with their client. These directions had a significant impact on the shape of the civil trial. The parties and the judge now read most of the arguments and documentation in advance of trial, thus departing radically from the oral tradition characteristic of the common law, adversarial procedure. The Directions also encouraged the judge to control the nature and content of the cases presented, again signifying a departure from the traditional judge's role as a non-interfering umpire, allowing the parties to dictate the shape and pace of the case. See the discussion in Ch.9.

The Interim Woolf Report 1995

10–034　This repeated many of the recommendations of its predecessors, the Civil Justice Review and the Heilbron–Hodge Report. Amongst Lord Woolf's main recommendations were these:

1. An effective system of case management by the court, instead of allowing the parties to flout rules and run the cases.

2. An expanded small claims jurisdiction of £3,000 (introduced, in 1996, then expanded to £5,000) and a fast track for cases up to £10,000.

3. Judicial, tailored case management for cases over £10,000.

4. Encouragement of early settlement, assisted by enabling either party to make an offer to settle, replacing the system of payment into court.
5. The creation of a new Head of Civil Justice.
6. A single set of High Court/county court rules.
7. Court appointment of single, neutral expert witnesses.
8. Promotion of the use of IT for case management by judges; use of video and telephone conferencing.

Almost all of this was repeated in the final report, *Access to Justice*, in 1996, then translated into the law, in the 1997 Act and 1998 CPR and directions, as set out above. There were some amendments, as can be seen. For example, on point 7 above, the court does not appoint experts but normally requires the parties to agree on a single joint expert. As can be seen below, point 8 of Woolf's plan has not been fulfilled. Progress on IT in the civil courts is worse than dismal.

5. Reactions to the Woolf report

Zander (1995) was highly critical. He said the overwhelming **10–035** majority of cases settled, so did not need management; "we have virtually no information about either delays or costs" and Woolf had not commissioned research on his proposals; they had been trying to reform the system in the US for 20 years without success; English judges had no familiarity with case management; many studies showed pre-trial hearings designed to make trials shorter made them longer and added to cost; US research showed litigants were interested in an unbiased, careful hearing, not informal hearings. In 1996, he added that he feared increasing judicial discretionary powers of case management would create inconsistent decisions, making the process arbitrary and unpredictable: "My own view is that training can do little to deal with the problem because inconsistency stems from legitimate differences in philosophy as to how a judge should go about the business of judging". He also said lawyers would be unable to stick to time-limits. Case management was a common theme throughout Canada, the US and Australia. In 1997 he cited a study of 10,000 US cases by the Rand Corporation which found that some US judges considered case management to be an attack on judicial independence and believed it emphasised speed and efficiency at the expense of justice. The study also found case management added to costs because lawyers spent an extra 20 hours responding to court directions, even in cases which would have settled anyway. Costs would become front-loaded. Lord Woolf responded that Zander's criticisms were "strident . . . misleading and inaccurate" (1997). Zander defended himself many times (2000) but his warning on "front-loading" of costs came back to haunt Woolf and everyone else involved in civil litigation, as we shall see.

6. Evaluating the Woolf reforms: research, surveys and comments

Research and surveys

10–036   There is very little research and a lot of opinion surveys and comment. The first national consumer satisfaction survey of court users, in 2001, found 79 per cent satisfied with the overall level of service. A survey of heads of legal departments of UK companies by Eversheds, lawyers, found 54 per cent of respondents considered civil litigation improved in 1999–2000; 52 per cent found litigation quicker but only 22 per cent considered it cheaper; 43 per cent were settling cases earlier. Clients no longer sought aggressive, uncompromising lawyers and 41 per cent had used ADR. Only 24 per cent thought litigants were getting better justice, though, and 44 per cent said they were not. Costs had risen according to 19 per cent of respondents.

A 2000 MORI survey of 180 firms found that 76 per cent said there had been faster settlements and less litigation, although most respondents thought the outcome would have been the same under the old system. The early-settlement offer, bringing heavy penalties to those refusing to settle, had had the biggest impact on litigation, according to 66 per cent. Mediation had increased (see Ch.11). The Civil Justice Audit comprising of this and a CEDR survey of 30 judges found: 80 per cent of lawyers were satisfied with the Rules; 36 per cent believed litigation had decreased; 47 per cent reported settling cases faster; 60 per cent thought judges should initiate settlement discussion; 58 per cent thought cases should be stayed for mediation and 78 per cent of in-house lawyers thought mediation should be required before a business dispute went to court ((2000) 150 N.L.J. 531). A Wragge survey of in-house commercial lawyers found: 81 per cent thought courts did not have enough resources; 89 per cent liked the changes and found litigation quicker; 41 per cent found costs cut; and 80 per cent found alternative dispute resolution (ADR) had proved popular (*The Times*, May 2, 2000). A 2001 Law Society survey of 130 solicitors showed they were concerned that the assessment of costs was arbitrary and unpredictable, often causing them to make a loss over litigation. They thought judges were unwilling to apply sanctions and lacked consistency. New procedures making more work at the beginning of litigation ("front loading") were not cheaper for clients and led to more work, as Zander, above, had warned. Most respondents considered the use of joint experts inappropriate in multi-track cases.

In 2002, the Lord Chancellor's Department published an evaluation of the reforms, confirming their "broad success". The use of pre-action protocols and offers to settle had diverted cases from litigation. About eight per cent settled at the court door and 70 per cent settled earlier. Time from claim issue to trial had dropped from 639 days in 1997, to 498 in 2000–01. There had been a levelling off in the use of ADR: "Civil Justice Reform Evaluation—Further Findings". A 2002 Court Service survey of court users showed 20 per cent of lawyers found procedures difficult to understand but 45 per cent thought the reforms had simplified procedures. In 2002, Lord Phillips M.R. said case management had reduced the average length of time for a case to come to trial from 600 days to 520 days and for claims over £5,000 from 750 to 450 days. Nevertheless, there was a lot of anecdotal evidence to the effect that the Woolf Reforms had increased the cost of litigation in relation to cases that go the whole way.

A 2002 report, *More civil justice?* by Goriely and others reported the results of the first detailed piece of research. They examined the impact on pre-action behaviour. They concluded that the Woolf reforms had enhanced access to justice. Early disclosure had led to more settlements at the pre-action stage and they were based on better information. Most practitioners regarded the reforms as a success, citing clearer structure and greater certainty in the fast track. They praised the invention of claimants' Pt 36 offers and considered that pre-action protocols enabled informed settlement. They complained of a lack of sanctions for breach, however. Expert evidence continued to be problematic, although the instruction of agreed experts had almost eradicated the concept of an expert owned by one side. Many felt that the courts were inefficient in listing. Problems caused by lack of IT were well known. In Department of Constitutional Affairs Research Report 09/2005 *The Management of Civil Cases: the courts and the post-Woolf landscape*, the researchers concluded that the litigation culture had changed for the better, noting the drop in civil cases since 1997, from 2.2 million to 1.5 million in 2003. Costs per case had increased and were front-loaded. In January 2010, the Ministry of Justice published *Monetary Claims in the County Courts (1996–2003)*, research summary 1/10, which found that in most of 2010 cases, the rules were followed, questionnaires were completed on time and guidelines on trial scheduling were followed.

Comments

10–037   Robert Turner, Senior Master (case manager) in the HC, welcomed the new rules ((2000) 150 N.L.J. 49). The adversarial approach had been replaced by co-operation. Settlements were achieved earlier, procedures were defining the real issues between the parties, and solicitors would find the quicker disposal rate allowed them to do more work. In the short term, however, the new rules had not succeeded in attacking cost, delay and complexity because the new system was costly at the commencement of the action ("front loaded"); the new procedures with pre-action protocols, allocation and listing questionnaires and case management conferences were more complex. Another master, John Leslie commented on "a new spirit of co-operation abroad". He found around 50 per cent of cases stayed (suspended) for a settlement attempt did settle. He too complained of a lack of IT, though (*Counsel*, 2000). Zander, in 2000, described the Woolf reforms in a more tempered way than before, praising some elements, but he reiterated his criticism of front-loading of costs, in the manner of "I told you so".

Suzanne Burn, an experienced civil litigator, wrote a very useful article in 2003, summarising many evaluations of Woolf and adding comments from her experiences. There had been very limited research into the impact of the reforms. Lightman J. (2003) drew the following conclusions, from his 32 years at the Bar and nine as a HC judge:

1. Although the pre-action protocols had front-loaded costs they had substantially reduced the number of claims.
2. Summary orders for costs had led to parties "feeling the pain" earlier and so they were more cautious. Unnecessary cases were avoided.
3. Full case management powers enabled the court to ensure delay was minimised.
4. The limitation on expert witnesses had removed a drain on resources and court time.
5. Small claims provided a public service of inestimable value.

Nevertheless, in 2007, Sir Anthony Clarke M.R. told the American Bar Association that he was unhappy with the continuing "evils of delay, inefficiency and costs". In her Hamlyn lectures 2008, published as *Judging Civil Justice* (2009) Professor Dame Hazel Genn was heavily critical of the poverty of resources in the civil courts and the passion for ADR:

"We are witnessing the decline of civil justice—the downgrading of the importance of civil justice, the degradation of court facilities, and the diversion of civil cases to private dispute resolution, accompanied by the anti-litigation/anti-adjudication rhetoric that interprets these developments as socially positive. . .The anti-law story suggests that society is in the grip of a litigation explosion or compensation culture. . .the civil justice system has few friends in government, since it is through civil cases that the government is directly challenged."

The first anniversary of the CPR's operation, in 2009, saw the publication of many opinions. Jackson, below, had already published his critical preliminary report. Lord Woolf acknowledged that one of his aims, cost reduction, had not been achieved. This was partly not of his making. The government had replaced most legal aid with CFAs. The related insurance premiums had increased costs. Court costs had soared. "This has been a very retrograde step". "I was relying on the client controlling the costs. They have not exercised sufficient control." He would have liked to have introduced a docketing system, with each case always being managed by just one judge. Zander, Woolf's constant critic, said most of his fears had been justified. He again pointed to the front-loading of costs. The trouble was, this applied to all cases, not just the tiny minority that went to trial but also the other 90 per cent, that would have settled anyway. He felt delay had remained the same. Goriely's 2002 research showed that while the post-claim stage had got quicker, the pre-issue stage was slower. District Judge Robert Hill, a member of the CPR Committee considered the fast track "Hugely successful. . . I have tried many fast-track cases. None has ever gone over the one-day allowed". He felt the most successful change effected by the CPR was in expert evidence. Experts used to be "hired guns". Now, the rules emphasised their duty to the court and all fair experts welcomed this, causing huge savings. "I can think of many cases, typically modest building disputes, where a single joint expert's report has been the key to unlocking the case".

The total volume of litigation

This has fallen since 1999 but this is the continuation of a previous **10–038** trend. The rate of settlement pre-trial has increased. One of Woolf's aims was to encourage early, fair settlements by placing the parties on an equal footing. Whether settlements are for fair amounts of damages is almost impossible to quantify. Qureshi pointed out that Woolf considered that individuals had a constitutional right to an accessible and effective system of civil litigation, via the courts, yet, in 1998–2002, there had been a 500 per cent reduction of proceedings commenced in the Queen's Bench Division. My reaction to this would be to point out that parties may be resorting to ADR and Qureshi acknowledges that this may be one reason. I would comment that we can never measure this, because ADR is unquantifiable. It is mostly unregulated and operated as a multitude of private enterprises, whose statistics are not made public. If ADR is increasing then I suggest that this can be seen as a success of the Woolf reforms, not a failure, since Woolf wanted to encourage ADR. The case law reinforces this by costs. I would add that the mischief of the Courts and Legal Services Act 1990 was to shift the civil case load onto the county courts, reserving the HC for complex or unusual cases and the 1998 Rules continue this aspiration, so if the QBD has lost work that too is a success. One needs to take account of the total civil case load. Examining county court business as well, we can see that its case load has diminished too, from about 2,245,000 in 1998, to 1,879,000 in 2009. That this is a continuation of a previous trend is disclosed by the statistics, as in 1990 there were over 3,311,000 claims.

Making the process simpler?

10–039　It is arguable whether this has been achieved. While the Rules and forms are simple and in plain English, Burn pointed out that there were over 500 forms and the Rules and Practice Directions were (and are) longer than the old rules. Amendments are frequent. In 2009, Thompson, general editor of *The Civil Court Practice*, said the 391 pages of the old *The County Court Practice* were replaced with 2,301 pages, "a 550% increase!" He said "The aims of simplification and unification of procedures were admirable but they have not been achieved".

Has there been a culture change among lawyers?

10–040　Woolf hoped for a significant shift from adversarialism, the battle approach. Burn considered that lawyers were now more careful about sending deliberately aggressive letters to the opposition and "tactical" applications were less frequent but the "costs war" on conditional fees (see below) indicated adversarialism. Zander (2009) acknowledged that there had been a diminution in the adversary culture. Allen (2009), a director of the Centre for Effective Dispute resolution, described the massive shift in lawyers' behaviour:

> "When I train mediators in. . .Ireland, Scotland, Pakistan, India and South Africa, it always jolts me that, except in England and Wales, it is still largely true that not to ambush is negligent. Trials can still start with undisclosed documents, witness statements and expert reports. . .Suddenly hundreds if not thousands of applications for particulars or further discovery vanished from

the chambers' lists of masters and district judges, and the Bear Garden was translated to its current status as a haven of peace".

There are some exceptions, though. Litigation taking 12 years over the collapse of the BCCI bank in 1991 scandalised the business world and led to criticism that the reforms were not working as intended. The BCCI bank was set up in Pakistan in 1972. Many British Asians deposited money. It became a money laundry for drug smugglers and defrauded its clients. Deloitte, the liquidators, decided to litigate against the Bank of England for letting BCCI go on for so long. The BoE refused repeated offers to settle. The case was hopeless as Deloitte could not prove negligence or misfeasance and they dropped the case after 12 years. There were several pre-trial hearings and a case went up to the House of Lords as to whether the claim should proceed. In court, the lawyers' opening statements took 86 days and 119 days. The parties spent 256 days in court. The bank sought £73.5 million in costs, plus £8 million in interest. The Commercial Court judge, Tomlinson J., said he had warned Lord Woolf C.J. that the case was a farce, and it could "damage the reputation of our legal system". He criticised Gordon Pollock QC, Deloitte's barrister, for "sustained rudeness". Lord Woolf himself had criticised the length of HC cases, saying that judges had failed to stop them spiralling out of control: Chong.

Pre-action protocols as a culture change

In personal injury cases, over 85 per cent settle at the protocol **10–041** stage. Burn said concerns had been expressed in all surveys that these front-loaded costs. This is because the pre-action protocols require a lot of work from solicitors *before* a claim is issued, in investigating their client's case and disclosing information to the other side. (Affirmed by judges interviewed in Darbyshire, 2011.) Another complaint was that the courts rarely penalise parties for non-compliance with a protocol.

Case management

Burn concluded that "There seems to be no consensus about **10–042** the value of judicial case management". Plotnikoff and Woolfson found that judges were comfortable in the role of case manager but some practitioners, said Burn, complained that judges did not read the case papers in advance. Case management conferences varied considerably from court to court. Burn remarked that:

"the one great advantage of CPR case management over the old-style laissez-faire approach is that cases no longer drift—there is always a return date to ensure judges keep an eye on progress

241

... Many practitioners, sadly, are their own worst enemies if they wish to minimize judicial 'interference'."

She remarked on failure to complete forms correctly and disproportionate costs estimates and "a casual attitude to case management". From spending several weeks in 2002–03, looking over the shoulders of eight district judges, I can verify this. They frequently showed me that papers sent in to them by solicitors were a "dog's breakfast". They routinely referred cases back to solicitors for forms to be correctly completed. See also D.J. John.

Sanctions and cost penalties

10–043   Burn said that relatively few cases were struck out under the Rules for non-compliance with court directions and orders. She concluded that dealing with cases "justly", rather than by the rule book was working well.

7. Problems remaining in 2011 and the Jackson Review of Costs

Disproportionate costs, the "costs war" and the "chilling effect" of CFAs

10–044   Conditional fee agreements (CFAs) were Irvine L.C.'s alternative solution for claimants who could not afford to litigate, after he withdrew legal aid from some of them, following the Access to Justice Act 1999, explained in Ch.17 on legal services. A CFA means a "no win no fee" contract between a private client and a solicitor. Until 2011, the client took out insurance against losing, as he would then be liable to pay the winner's costs. He agreed to pay a success fee to the solicitor, a percentage of the costs, if he won. This has to be repaid by the loser of the case. The success fee enables the solicitor to build up funds to finance the cases he loses. Under the pre-2001 law, the clients did not mind what level of success fee they agreed to, because they knew they would pay nothing at all, whether they won or lost. A problem arose because litigants who lost cases, often insurance companies, felt solicitors were profiteering by charging unreasonable percentages as success fees and satellite litigation, arguing about these amounts, bedevilled the civil courts after 2000. In *Callery v Gray* [2002] UKHL 28, the House of Lords felt that regulating civil litigation was the CA's business. Defendant insurers continued to bring technical challenges to CFAs and the CA ran out of patience. They awarded costs against the defendants and said such litigants should "stop all this nonsense". The Civil Justice

Council commissioned research, in 2003, on how to calculate the reasonableness of a success fee and the Master of the Rolls decided to mediate a settlement between the two sides in the costs war. In the 2002 Annual Report of the Civil Justice Council, he complained that costs were the "Achilles heel" of the (Woolf) reforms. CFAs were under new regulations after 2005.

This did not stop the problem. In 2004, 13 media organisations complained that high fees in CFAs were severely damaging press freedom in privacy and libel cases. They were forced to settle even weak claims. Claimants' lawyers were encouraging defamation suits and charging disproportionate fees. Naomi Campbell took a case against the *Daily Mirror* to the House of Lords under a "no win no fee" contract (described in Ch.4 on Human Rights). Alastair Brett, of News International complained of "a revolting state of affairs with some lawyers displaying a greed unparalleled in any other profession". The total costs were over £1 million, including a success fee of over £250,000 and the law lords ordered MGN to pay her costs in the CA and HL, yet she had been awarded just £3,500 in damages at first instance. MGN lost their argument that such a success fee inhibited freedom of expression and was thus a breach of Art.10 of the European Convention on HR but they *won* on this point in the European Court of Human Rights, in *MGN v UK* (39401/04) in 2011. The court held that the recovery of success fees was disproportionate.

In the meantime, there were many examples of disproportionate costs, usually caused by success fees. In 2007, Peter Bassano, conductor of the Oxford University Sinfonietta, was ordered to pay £185,000 costs after a case over an unpaid builder's bill of £16,000. In *Baigent v Random House Group* [2007] EWCA Civ 247, a case about *The Da Vinci Code*, the costs were over £3 million. *Douglas v Hello!* [2007] UKHL 21, the fight about the wedding photos of Catherine Zeta-Jones and Michael Douglas, ended in the House of Lords, after six years, having incurred estimated costs of £8 million. In *Peakman v Linbrooke Services Ltd* [2008] EWCA 1239, three CA judges criticised the case. The dispute was about £2,232 small claim but the lawyers' fees were over £100,000. The DJ had allocated it to the multi-track because of a spurious counterclaim. The judge should have taken control and struck out the counterclaim much earlier so the claim could have reverted to the small claims track. Finally, there came the straw that broke the camel's back. One ridiculous case prompted the Jackson Review of Costs from 2009 and costs reform in 2011. This was *Multiplex Constructions UK Ltd v Cleveland Bridge UK Ltd* [2008] EWHC 2220 (TCC), in a four-year dispute about the construction of Wembley Stadium. It absorbed £22 million in costs, including £1 million on photocopying. Multiplex claimed

£25 million in damages but Jackson J. ordered only £6.1 million, observing that each party had thrown away golden opportunities to settle. He considered the costs outrageous and complained bitterly and publicly. As a consequence, he was tasked by the judiciary with conducting a fundamental review of costs in civil litigation.

Do we have a compensation culture?

10–045   Teachers, businesses, insurers, local authorities and public bodies, notably the NHS, complained from the 1990s that they were suffering from a compensation culture, fuelled by potential claimants' ability to obtain CFAs from solicitors and claims handling companies. Claimants' lawyers retorted that the compensation culture was a myth. Prior to the 1990s, citizens of England and Wales were, allegedly, very reluctant to litigate compared with Americans and Germans, who the English considered to be overly litigious. When organising the civil justice system and access to legal services, the Government needs to balance the competing interests of access to justice and combating social exclusion on the one hand and greed and profiteering on the other. In 2003, The Law Society and the Federation of Small Businesses sought action from the Lord Chancellor to curb the growth of "ambulance chasers" (claims-handlers), blamed for increasing insurance liability premiums by encouraging employees to sue for accidents in the workplace under "no win no fee" arrangements. They called for a regulatory body to monitor these companies, with the power to discipline those found guilty of acting unethically.

By 2003, the Chief Medical Officer expressed alarm at clinical negligence litigation, costing the NHS double what it had in 1998. He proposed an NHS run fast track redress scheme. Since healthcare for Wales is run separately, Wales already had a scheme for mediating even very large clinical disputes. This is discussed further in Ch.11.

The Better Regulation Task Force published *Better Routes to Redress* in 2004, commissioned by the Government. Their report concluded that there was no compensation culture but the perception that there *was* caused a fear of litigation. They gave examples of the amounts paid out by public bodies. One highway authority spent £2 million of its £22 million budget settling claims. The news media were fond of reporting outlandish claims but neglected to report their outcome—that they often got nowhere. They acknowledged that the emergence of the "no win no fee" contract and claims management companies had encouraged more claims but some claims were well founded and made public authorities and others better at managing risk. On the negative side, the "have a go" culture drained public resources, made organisations cautious, contributed to higher insurance premiums and clogged up the system for meritorious claimants. They recommended:

- better regulation of claims companies;
- consumer advice;
- restrictions on advertising in hospitals and surgeries;
- raising the small claims limit in personal injuries;
- examining the overlap between ombudsmen;
- more encouragement of mediation;
- researching the possibility of contingency fees;
- promoting NHS rehabilitation and risk management.

Falconer L.C. announced in 2005 that he was disappointed that claims farmers had not regulated themselves. He warned that a regulator would be imposed. In a speech on May 26, 2005 Tony Blair said:

"Public bodies, in fear of litigation, act in highly risk-averse and peculiar ways. We have had a local authority removing hanging baskets for fear that they might fall on someone's head, even though no such accident has occurred in the 18 years that they have been hanging there."

In *The Report of an Enquiry into the Compensation Bill and the Compensation Culture* (2005), an all-party group of MPs told the Law Society to tighten control over solicitors who link with claims farmers, including "some very dodgy and ruthless people". The Government introduced a Compensation Bill, now Compensation Act 2006. Part One is about the law of negligence and seeks to address misperceptions that encourage a disproportionate fear of litigation and thus risk-averse behaviour (such as schools declining to organise field-trips for children, fearing they would be sued for any accident). The Act makes clear that when considering a claim in negligence, a court is able to consider the wider social value of the activity in the context of which the injury or damage occurred. Part Two provides for the regulation of claims management services. A regulator is responsible for ensuring that they abide by clear rules and a code of practice. They are required to give consumers clear advice about the validity of their claim and options for funding the costs. Between 2007 and 2011, the Ministry of Justice closed 200 rogue firms.

Most judges have been robust in stifling a compensation culture. **10–046** In *Cole v Davies-Gilbert* [2007] EWCA Civ 396, the CA dismissed Mrs Cole's claim against the British legion for £150,000. She broke her leg falling into a hole left by a maypole on a village green. Scott

Baker L.J. said if they upheld the claim "There would be no fetes, no maypole dancing and no activities that have come to be a part of the English village green." In February 2009, the MoJ launched a consultation on "Controlling costs in defamation proceedings", proposing to cap costs, limit hourly rates and emphasise proportionality. This does not seem to have solved the problem. Another government-commissioned report was produced by Lord Young, in 2010, *Common Sense, Common Safety*. He also suggested referral fees should be scrapped, like Jackson L.J. in point 3 below, and agreed that success fees should not be recoverable. He said the opportunity to reform clinical negligence claims had been missed. In 2009–10, the NHSLA paid out £279 million in damages and £163.7 million in costs, 75 per cent of which went to pay claimants' solicitors.

The Jackson Review of Costs

10–047   Now promoted to be Jackson L.J., he did a lot of comparative research, finding out how other countries solved the problem of high litigation costs. The Law Society opposed his interim suggestion of increasing the small claims limit, because thousands of litigants would have to pay for their own lawyers, or represent themselves, burdening the courts. The Association of Personal Injury Lawyers said the small claims limit for personal injuries should stay at £1,000 because fixed costs were inappropriate for personal injuries. They advantaged well-resourced defendants. On the other hand, the Consumers Association said 85 per cent of small claims litigants liked the rules as they were, with the parties paying their own costs. The small claims procedure was doing well without lawyers. Raising the PI small claims limit would upset lawyers but *would* increase access to justice. Jackson's *Review of Civil Litigation Costs: Final Report* 2009 made the following recommendations. The quotations are from the press release on the judiciary website and many may be implemented if the Legal Aid, Sentencing and Punishment of Offenders Bill 2011 is passed.

1. He re-emphasised proportionality. He suggested abandoning the test in *Lownds*, explained above, because "Disproportionate costs do not become proportionate simply because they were 'necessary'".
2. Most controversially, he suggested success fees and "after the event" insurance premiums should cease to be recoverable by the winner from the loser in "no win no fee" cases. . ."as these are the greatest contributors to disproportionate costs", and while these are congenial for lawyers, the costs have to be borne by taxpayers, council tax payers, insurance premium payers and uninsured defendants.

Incidentally, a Ministry of Justice consultation paper suggested that success fees in defamation cases should be no more than 10 per cent. Jackson recommended that lawyers' success fees, now a maximum of 100 per cent, should be limited to 25 per cent. No other jurisdiction allows success fees to be recoverable. He found that in no win no fee cases, costs are no less than 158–200 per cent of damages awarded. In other cases, costs are 47–55 per cent. While his recommendations were still being debated, in 2011, his disgust was echoed by the European Court of Human Rights, who ruled in the Naomi Campbell case, as explained above, that success fees breached the Convention.

3. "To offset the effects. . .general damages awards for personal injuries and other civil wrongs should be increased by 10 per cent".

4. "Referral fees should be scrapped—these are fees paid by lawyers to organisations that 'sell' damages claims but offer no real value to the process."

5. There should be "Qualified 'one way costs shifting'—claimants will only make a small contribution to defendant's costs if a claim is unsuccessful. . .removing the need for after the event insurance".

6. There should be fixed costs for fast track cases—"a high public interest", to make litigation proportionate and certain. Very importantly, Lord Woolf wanted this in 1996 but it was not implemented in the CPR.

7. "Establishing a Costs Council to review fixed costs and lawyers' hourly rates annually".

8. "Allowing lawyers to enter into Contingency Fee Agreements, where lawyers are only paid if a claim is successful, normally receiving a percentage of actual damages won" but clients must be independently advised. K. Underwood welcomed this. He spent a lot of time working for US law firms and said that commercial clients loved them and it was common to get a higher fee for a speedy settlement, with the lawyers doing *less* work—"deeply counterintuitive to UK lawyers". As explained in Ch.17, the English have always considered these American inventions (contingency fees) to be the work of the Devil though they have long been permitted in Scotland. Moorhead (2010) critically analysed the idea that they caused a claims explosion in the US and might cause one here. These are permitted in the Bill, as "damages based agreements".

9. There should be promotion of "before the event" legal insurance, encouraging people to take out legal expenses insurance e.g. as part of household insurance.

10. There should be a serious campaign to promote ADR but it should not be compulsory. (The Centre for Effective Dispute Resolution think he should have gone further. See their website.)
11. Costs management should be included in continuing professional development training for lawyers and judges.
12. He was concerned about the huge cost of clinical negligence to the National Health Service. After his report, in 2010, Penningtons Solicitors LLP reported a 12.2 per cent rise in these claims in 2009. Damages payments made were £769.2 million, with a further £13.3 billion potential liabilities. Clinicians continue to refuse to apologise, despite the fact that research showed this lessened the chance of being sued.
13. He recommended "concurrent evidence" of experts, known as "hot tubbing", in Australia and Canada. The judge controls the proceeding and she and the lawyers can question the experts and they can challenge one another's evidence.

Jackson L.J. will oversee the implementation of his recommendations. Some will need legislation and in 2010, the Minister of Justice, Ken Clarke, consulted on them then announced in 2011 that the Government had adopted almost all Jackson's suggestions and was introducing legislation to implement them, despite the fact that some attracted more criticism than support. As for the point on referral fees, these are currently under consideration by the Legal Services Board. Businesses who find themselves defending expensive actions welcomed the proposals. The Association of Personal Injury Lawyers are critical. They think the Government has been panicked into thinking there is a compensation culture. At the same time, the Minister launched a consultation, *Solving disputes in the county courts: creating a simpler, quicker and more proportionate system.* This re-emphasises proportionality and proposes raising small claims to £15,000. The HC would be limited to cases over £100,000 and housing equity cases over £300,000. The simple, speedy online system for road accidents would be expanded to personal injury. There would be fixed costs in some types of case up to £100,000 and a requirement that all small claims should have attempted mediation.

Litigants in person, McKenzie friends, lay representatives, litigation friends and vexatious litigants

10–048   I include this section under "problems", not because there is an inherent problem with people representing themselves but because they undoubtedly slow case progress and if the Minister of Justice's proposals to cut legal aid radically, outlined in Ch.17, are accepted in 2011, there will soon be very many more of them in the civil and family courts. On February 24, 2011, the Judges Council reported its concern over proposals to cut legal aid. They forecast a "huge increase" in litigants in person (people representing themselves (LIPs)) and said the legal aid cost savings would be offset by additional costs imposed on the court system (Hirsch, 2011).

Every civil judge, including those of the CA, frequently has LIPs appearing before them. That they dominate civil and family judges' work is clear from my observational research published in 2011. If the case is factually and/or legally complex, say in the Technology and Construction Court, and there are litigants in person on both sides, then the judge has really got her work cut out. Much judicial time and energy is spent in helping them to argue their cases. Outside the courtroom, much of the time and resources of court staff and volunteers is devoted to helping them. The treatment of this group is a yardstick by which to measure whether government (in this case, New Labour, from 1997) achieved its professed aim of enhancing access to justice by reforming civil procedure and redirecting funds spent on legal services. Moorhead (2003) remarked that the case law on LIPs and their helpers reflected three competing values: access to justice, court efficiency and the interests of regulated legal service providers. People representing themselves are at an inherent disadvantage in our adversarial system, which requires each party to bring all relevant argument and information to the court and requires the adduction of evidence through examination and cross-examination, as explained in Ch.9. Very few lay people can cope with this and they become dependent on the court to help them through the process. There is an almost unrestricted right to represent oneself and in small claims, the procedure is meant to be simple enough for people to argue their case without legal help. Generally, public funding for representation (legal aid) will not be granted. In 1997, Applebey remarked on the "explosion" of LIPs but, by now, numbers have risen even more dramatically. There are several reasons for this:

1. The 1980s and 90s saw legal aid decline to the extent that even those on state benefits were above the financial limit for eligibility (see Ch.17).
2. The small claims limit had increased from £100 in 1973 to £5,000 (it may now increase again, in 2011).
3. Lawyers are very expensive in the UK. Often people go to court to recover money, or defend themselves over money claims, or appear because they have been made bankrupt and they can ill afford the court fees, let alone legal representation.

4. There are many appellants who, although they were represented in the lower court, have had their public funding (legal aid) withdrawn after losing their case or cannot afford a lawyer at this stage.
5. Some LIPs choose to represent themselves, even though they could afford a lawyer. The 1998 Rules are drafted in plain English, available to the public on the internet.

The 1990s saw England's longest ever trial, which became known as "the McLibel Trial". Two people defended themselves against McDonalds, in a defamation action (described in Ch.4). Trials such as this, where the presence of unrepresented parties massively slowed litigation and expended much judicial time, caused the Judges' Council to establish a working party, chaired by Otton L.J. They reported in 1995 on the sharp rise of LIPs in the Royal Courts of Justice (RCJ). These were occupying a disproportionate amount of time, resources and staff. LIPs could be "seriously disadvantaged", compared with those who were represented. Some had no case; others could not cope with the complexity of proceedings. They lacked objectivity and advocacy skills. The Otton report recommended strengthening the resources of the Citizens' Advice Bureau in the RCJ and encouraging court staff to recommend that LIPs should seek their legal advice. At the same time, HC judges were given a pool of judicial assistants on whom they could call for legal assistance, where one or both parties were incapable of researching the law.

Lord Woolf, reporting in 1996, considered that courts should be more pro-active in helping LIPs with information and advice, provided via people, leaflets (in English and other languages), kiosks and IT. Judges should be interventionist, in helping LIPs to understand procedure, present their case and test the evidence. They should treat them with respect and not give priority to lawyers. Much of what Woolf and Otton recommended has been achieved. The Rules are simplified, in plain English; Latin has been eliminated; the courts have developed user guides, simplified forms and leaflets in many languages. Legal advice and other support is provided in the RCJ but remains patchy elsewhere, however.

10–049   The Citizens' Advice Bureau (CAB) in the RCJ was described by Mummery L.J. in a 2004 *Times* interview, as "a kind of legal casualty department". It employs solicitors and 250 volunteer legal advisers, from almost 60 city firms of solicitors. It helped 11,000 people and deals with 14,000 inquiries per year, which gives an idea of the scale of support needed by LIPs. In some cases, the CAB can arrange free representation from the Bar Pro Bono Unit. Mummery L.J. drew attention to recent important precedents in which the CAB had acted. He remarked on how much CA judges appreciated the help of the CAB. The CAB has been supplemented, since 2001, by the Personal Support Unit (PSU) in the RCJ. By 2011, its 200 volunteers support 6,000 people per year: LIPs, witnesses, victims and family members, with advice on court procedure, and they accompany people in court to provide emotional support but not legal advice. They also operate at the Principal Registry of the Family Division, Manchester and Cardiff Civil Justice Centres and Wandsworth County Court. The PSU remarked in their 2003 report that LIPs can behave in an unrestrained manner, are often obsessional and usually stressed. Frequently, their behaviour causes stress in court staff and judges. The report contained quotations from judges praising the work of the PSU for improving court efficiency and enhancing access to justice. See further Burke.

The Department of Constitutional Affairs published Research Report 2005/2, *Litigants in person—Unrepresented litigants in first instance proceedings*, by Moorhead and Sefton. It explored quantitative and qualitative data on unrepresented litigants in four courts in first instance civil and family cases, excluding small claims. It provided a detailed picture of the prevalence and nature of unrepresented litigants and the impact of non-representation on them, the courts and their opponents. The main findings were:

1. LIPs were common, usually as defendants. Obsessive or difficult litigants were a very small minority but posed considerable problems for judges and court staff.
2. A large part of the reason for non-representation was non-participation. Some LIPs were partially represented. Significant numbers had some advice but this help was ad hoc.
3. In a small proportion of cases, one party was an LIP throughout. Cases where both were LIPs were rare. Some LIPs were vulnerable.
4. The issues at stake were significant for the LIPs. There was a range of reasons for non-representation, including the lack of free or affordable representation.
5. There was little evidence of an explosion of LIPs though the position was unclear in family courts.
6. Cases with LIPs could involve more court-based activity than those without.
7. Most participation took place in the court office not the courtroom.
8. LIPs participated at a lower intensity than represented parties but made more mistakes. They struggled with substantive law and procedure.

9. There was modest evidence that their cases took longer, though they were less likely to settle.
10. Some courts were better at helping LIPs than others. They were not confident in directing LIPs to alternative help.
11. Judges responded to the challenge of handling LIPs with varying degrees of intervention. Court staff recognised LIPs' needs but were unsure of what help was permissible because of a "no advice" rule.
12. Court staff and judges perceived that improvements could be made.

Naturally, judges have to be very patient and sensitive in handling LIPs and they must take care to ensure that their rights to a fair trial are upheld, according to the common law rules of natural justice and Art.6 of the European Convention. Recognising the problems of LIPs, the law provides them with some rights to help in court:

1. A "litigation friend" may represent a child or mental patient, under Pt 21 of the CPR.
2. A "McKenzie Friend" may accompany the LIP in court, to support and take notes but has no right to speak.
3. A lay representative is permitted to represent an LIP in a small claim, under s.27 of the Courts and Legal Services Act 1990 but the LIP must be present. The court has a general discretion to hear anyone.
4. A lawyer with appropriate rights of audience may represent the individual without charging (pro bono).

In *O (Children), Re* [2005] EWCA Civ 759, the CA was quite tolerant. It held that in family cases there was a very strong presumption permitting representation by a McKenzie friend. Article 6 of the Convention (fair trial) was engaged. LIPs were entitled to be treated courteously. They were often nervous, anxious or upset. A McKenzie friend, unless they are a lawyer with rights of audience, or appearing in a small claim, has no right to speak but the court has discretion to permit them to do so. Judges and staff in the Royal Courts of Justice (HC and CA) are well aware that there is a growing industry of people who are prepared to act as lay representatives and charge money for it. It is not unusual for the courts to allow them to argue a case for an LIP. There are competing values and uneven results here, as Moorhead observed. On the one hand, the judges sympathise with LIPs who cannot obtain publicly funded services and they permit such representatives as a means of enhancing access to justice. On the other hand, they have to protect the legal profession's rights of audience. Practically, some courts have observed in their judgments how useful a lay representative can be (*Izzo v Philip Ross & Co Ltd* [2002] B.P.I.R. 310) but in other cases, incompetent McKenzie friends can be a nuisance. Moorhead described the cases of *Paragon Finance Plc v Noueiri* [2001] EWCA Civ 1402. In this group of cases, the McKenzie friend was an experienced LIP. He submitted futile appeals and told the LIP he would win £250,000 and that he wanted 20 per cent of that. The CA was satisfied that he was practising advocacy in the RCJ as an unqualified person and that he must be stopped, in the public interest. He was incompetent, took hopeless points and advanced futile arguments. The CA made an order banning him acting on anyone else's behalf in the RCJ, except with a judge's permission, and they gave general guidance on McKenzie friends, now revised in 2010. Kennedy, a non-practising solicitor who works for a charity training McKenzie friends, praises them. She says they are made "welcome with open arms" in magistrates' courts, where any kind of intervention helps to speed up cases and produce a more just outcome. In the county court, they were welcomed by all but one DJ.

For some LIPs, their litigation becomes a fulltime pursuit. I spent **10–050** many research days, shadowing judges in the RCJ in 2004 and was told by judges' clerks and judges of litigants who virtually "live" in the Royal Courts of Justice. When LIPs become obsessive, attempting to persecute one or more parties or making multiple hopeless applications, they may be classed as "vexatious litigants" and can be banned from initiating proceedings. In the cases of *Bhamjee v Forsdick* [2003] EWCA Civ 1113 and *R. (Mahajan) v Central London County Court* [2004] EWCA Civ 946, the CA set out guidelines as to the court's duties and power when faced with such pests. The first LIP, as can be seen from the case law, had acted against a number of defendants, and was attempting to sue five barristers. The second LIP was involved in numerous claims in the county court, HC and CA. In a third case, *HM Att Gen v Chitolie* [2004] EWHC 1943 (Admin), Mr. Chitolie was found to be a vexatious litigant after involvement in 18 civil actions. These cases were followed, in October 2004, by a new Rule (3.11) setting out the courts' powers to make a civil restraint order (CRO) against a vexatious litigant. For some, vexatious litigation is a disease, known elsewhere in Europe as De Clerambault's syndrome. Naturally, vexatious litigants often try to sue their lawyers, the judges and the courts. In the period 1997–2003, the Lord Chancellor's Department (now Ministry of Justice) spent £3 million defending itself from such actions. Lord Clarke M.R. said in a 2006 speech that vexatious litigants denied access to justice because they wasted precious time that should be used on genuine litigants. See fascinating article by Mahendra. Among other examples he mentions *AG v Benton* [2004] EWHC

1952 (Admin). He had issued 32 separate proceedings in 25 months. He was suffering from a fixed delusional syndrome.

Unregulated experts

10–051   Lord Woolf called the uncontrolled use of experts one of the biggest generators of costs under the pre-1999 regime. Wealthy litigants would line up an array of them to try and defeat the opposition. All that is now gone. The outstanding problem is the unregulated "industry" of experts. Anyone can claim to be an expert. The two bodies representing experts have failed to agree on how to regulate them. Worse, the system is open to fraud, as demonstrated by the conviction of Barian Baluchi, in 2005. An ex-taxi driver, he had gained registration by the General Medical Council in 1998 by stealing the identity of a Madrid psychiatrist. He bought a PhD from a "distance learning" college and gave evidence on over 2,000 asylum seekers, 1,000 of whom were allowed to stay in the UK. His name appeared in the 2002 Expert Witness Directory, endorsed by the Law Society. In 2004, the Legal Services Commission proposed that experts regularly providing forensic services should be quality-assured and hired on fixed fees. In 2005, a new Practice Direction was issued, (No.35) The Civil Justice Council launched a new protocol, attached to it, on the instruction of experts in civil cases. It reminds them that they do not serve the exclusive interests of those who retain them; they should not act as mediators and they should not take it upon themselves to advocate one party's case. See, however, Levy. In 2009, the rules on experts were strengthened. There is a requirement for proportionality in putting questions to experts; their statements of truth are revised and the rules requiring single joint experts tightened, to prevent "forum shopping" produced by inconsistent application of the rules by judges. In *Jones v Kaney* [2011] UKSC 13, the UKSC abolished expert witnesses' immunity from being sued for breach of contract or negligence. The decision was predicted to mark the end of the amateur expert.

Court fees

10–052   As described in Ch.6 on civil courts, there is a continuing argument between the Civil Justice Council and the judges, and the Government. The latter is determined to make the civil courts pay for themselves but the judges think increases in court fees deny people access to justice. They, and lawyers, think the courts should be viewed as a public service, as they are in other countries. Civil court fees rose by up to 150 per cent in January 2005. In December 2004, the Association of Personal Injury Lawyers said that, in the previous 24 years court fees had risen by up to 4,150 per cent.

Commercial lawyers are concerned at competition from foreign courts. Adrian Jack pointed out that a high value five day case in the High Court would cost £6,100 in the UK but only £2,300 in Germany.

The failure to enforce judgments

If people cannot get their damages payments from defendants **10–053** after winning their case, there is no point in their having gone to court in the first place and no access to justice. They will have expended extra money in court fees and will be even worse off. In 2003, Baldwin published research examining civil claims ending in a "default judgment". This means, as described above, where the defendant fails to enter a defence so the claimant gets judgment in his favour automatically. He found that only a small proportion of claimants received full payment within the time ordered by the court. He and Cunnington argued, in 2004, that where the courts' enforcement mechanisms are ineffective, there is a breach of the claimant's human rights, under both Art.6 of the Convention (fair trial) and Art.1 of Protocol 1 (right to respect for possessions). They alluded to an enforcement review, then in progress, which was established by the government in 1998. They considered that it was being conducted in an "information vacuum", as little was known about which type of defendant paid up or which was the most effective type of enforcement. They found that "Very many defendants were highly elusive". Only 13.3 per cent of HC claimants surveyed had received full payment and some had had to go to considerable lengths to get it. The more money was at stake, the less likely claimants were to be paid. The futility of the court process led to feelings of "bitterness, frustration, cynicism, anger, disenchantment and powerlessness". Some ensured that recalcitrant defendants were bankrupted or blacklisted for credit, by being entered on the register of county court judgments. They concluded that "it is unlikely that any workable and fair system of enforcement will be capable of producing more than moderate rates of payment". The courts, they argued, could not be expected to assume responsibility for debt recovery that fell on lenders and "Since the interests of creditors and debtors are often quite irreconcilable, no system of enforcement could be devised that would achieve even a satisfactory balance between them".

IT

The Woolf reforms were launched without the supporting IT **10–054** systems in place that Lord Woolf had envisaged. In 1998, the Lord Chancellor admitted that the courts would not be ready to cope with the reforms because they lacked the technology, but the Court Service published a consultation paper, in 2001, *Modernising the Civil Courts*. Much of it was about IT: the "virtual court" issue of claims and enforcement procedures online or from a digital TV; "Court on Call", enabling procedures to be handled by telephone; and "gateway partnerships" between advice agencies and court staff, enabling the client to access the court and advice at the same time. This was never achieved. They planned centralised information and advice via the Internet, call centres and advice kiosks, allowing them to reduce the county courts to a network of hearing centres. They would share more courts with magistrates. This sharing plan has been achieved in some cases but makes matters very confusing for the public. In 2000, video conferencing commenced, from Cardiff and Leeds to the CA, for civil applications for permission to appeal. People could give evidence or make submissions via video link. Moving on from these pilots to all county courts has been astonishingly slow or non-existent in some cases. Some of the above remains a very distant aspiration.

This has caused frustration to judges, problems for the court staff and annoyance to court users who could not email large documents into the commercial court, or even email most courts (*Court of Appeal (Civil Division) Review of the Year* 2004). Only in 2005 was progress commencing on the sort of electronic communication between parties and courts that was envisaged by Lord Woolf. Even now, the civil courts are having to take second place far behind the LINK communication and case management system currently being installed in the criminal courts and criminal justice agencies so no end is in sight. The Lord Chief Justice and the Master of the Rolls never miss an opportunity to complain, in annual reviews and speeches. In his *Annual Review of the Administration of Justice* 2008, the Lord Chief Justice listed all the IT deficiencies caused by "the continued lack of funding for a modern case-management system such as that promised almost ten years ago when the reforms to civil procedure and the new Civil Procedure Rules were introduced, following Lord Woolf's *Access to Justice* Report in 1996". District Judge David Oldham (2009) said electronic filing and document management had been abandoned, except for the Commercial Court. Meanwhile, solicitors swamp courts with email, fax and hard copies of all documents. He said proposals for e-filing for courts had been shelved so courts work with paper files. These get lost regularly and there were fewer staff to manage the files and keep them up to date. He encouraged parties to email a case summary and draft directions to the court, provided they copy-in their opponents.

8. *Judicial review*

Historically, a person aggrieved with an error of law or the **10–055** procedure of a lower court could petition the monarch to refer the proceedings for examination in the High Court. The HC now exercises this residuary monarchical prerogative, in judicial review proceedings. The procedure is available in civil and criminal cases. Procedure is determined by CPR Pt 54 and a Practice Direction. The claim is made in the Administrative Court, in the QBD, or the Administrative Court for Wales in Cardiff. The question of permission is normally considered without a hearing. At the substantive hearing, the judge examines the legality and procedural correctness of the decision of the lower court or tribunal and whether the body has exceeded its powers (acted ultra vires). The court may impose a quashing order on a defective decision (formerly certiorari), or make a mandatory order that a public body carry out its duty (formerly mandamus) or order an injunction, preventing an illegality. An applicant may ask the Administrative Court to declare what the law is, where it is uncertain. The judge has no concern with substituting a new finding of fact. Guidance was given by Lord Steyn in *R. v SS for the Home Dept Ex p. Daly* [2001] UKHL 26. He emphasised the difference between proportionality, under the European Convention on Human Rights and traditional grounds for review, despite the overlap. He said:

> "the doctrine of proportionality may require the reviewing court to assess the balance which the decision maker has struck, not merely whether it is in the range of rational or reasonable decisions. . .The proportionality test may go further than the traditional grounds of review in as much as it may require attention to be directed to the relative weight accorded to interests and considerations."

Since the 1960s and especially since the procedure was made easier in 1981, there has been an enormous growth in judicial review cases and most of them have been challenges to the legality of public bodies' decisions, mostly local or central government. Challenges have been made to a broad list of such decisions: planning, hospital closure, policing tactics, benefits which apply differently to men and women, decisions relating to the National Lottery and so on. It was thought that this court would be very busy with challenges under the Human Rights Act and this has occurred to a certain extent, although the courts were not swamped, as it was predicted they would be.

9. Family procedure

10–056   Family procedure is the subject of a special set of rules, not covered by this book. The Courts Act 2003, Pt 7, provides for a Family Procedure Rule Committee and allows the President of the Family Division to issue Practice Directions, with the concurrence of the Lord Chancellor, which bind magistrates' courts and the county courts as well as the High Court. Thorpe L.J., Deputy Head of Family Justice, complained in *Allan v Clibbery* [2002] EWCA Civ 45:

> "In recent years the family justice system has seemed something of a Cinderella. In reality the reforms as to access and reporting introduced in the wake of civil justice reforms have not been replicated in the family justice system . . . That state of affairs only heightens the case for the resumption of the rolling programme for the reform of family law and practice".

From 2011, the Family Procedure Rules 2010 apply. They are very similar to the CPR, with an overriding objective, early identification of issues, effective management by the court and an emphasis on mediation. Law magazines and journals in 2011 provide ample explanations.

BIBLIOGRAPHY

10–057 G. Applebey, "The Growth of Litigants in Person in English Civil Proceedings" (1997) 16 C.J.Q. 127.

T. Allen, "A few home truths" (2009) 159 N.L.J. 489, responding to Zander's 2009 article.

J. Baldwin, "Monitoring the Rise of the Small Claims Limit: Litigants' Experiences of Different Forms of Adjudication" LCD Research Series 1/97, DCA archived website; *Small Claims in the County Court in England and Wales: The Bargain Basement of Civil Justice* (1997); "Small Claims Hearings: The 'Interventionist' Role Played by District Judges" (1998) 17 C.J.Q. 20 "Increasing the Small Claims Limit" (1998) 148 N.L.J. 274; "Lay and judicial perspectives on the expansion of the small claims regime" LCD Research Series 8/02; "Evaluating the Effectiveness of Enforcement Procedures in Undefended Claims in the Civil Courts" DCA Research Study 3/03 (2003).

J. Baldwin and R. Cunnington, "The Crisis in Enforcement of Civil Judgments in England and Wales" (2004) 23 C.J.Q. 305.

J. Burke, "A helping hand" *Counsel*, March 2011, p.30.

S. Burn, "The Woolf Reforms in Retrospect", *Legal Action*, July 2003, p.8.

L. Chong, "Deloitte's 12-year case puts Woolf reforms in question", *The Times,* April 13, 2006.

Civil Justice Review: Report of the Review Body on Civil Justice, Cm.394 (1988).

Sir Anthony Clarke M.R., "Vexatious litigants & access to justice: past, present, future", speech, June 2006; "A UK Perspective on EU Civil Justice—Impact on Domestic Dispute Resolution," speech, October 25, 2007.

Editorial "Civil Litigation: A Public Service for the Enforcement of Civil Rights" (2007) *Civil Justice Quarterly* Vol.26, 1–9.

P. Darbyshire, *Sitting in Judgment: The Working Lives of Judges* (2011).

General Council of the Bar and Law Society, "Civil Justice on Trial—The Case for Change" (The Heilbron–Hodge Report).

H. Genn, *Paths to Justice* (1999); *Judging Civil Justice,* The Hamlyn Lectures 2008 (2009).

F. Gibb, "How pruning dispute grew into an £80,000 legal bill", *The Times,* May 4, 2007.

T. Goriely, R. Moorhead and P. Abrams, *More Civil Justice? The impact of the Woolf reforms on pre-action behaviour,* Civil Justice Council and Law Society (2002).

R. Gosling, "Survey of Litigants' Experiences and Satisfaction with the Small Claims Process" DCA research report 9/2006.

District Judge Robert Hill, "10 years on—a personal view" Association of HMDJs *Law Bulletin,* Winter 2008/9 20 (1), p.6.

A. Hirsch, "Legal aid cuts will cost more in long run, say judges", *www.guardian.co.uk,* February 24, 2011.

A. Jack, "Court fees: the new stealth tax?" (2004) 154 N.L.J. 909.

District Judge Terence John, "The District Judge as scrutineer" (2006) 156 N.L.J. 569.

J. Kennedy, "McKenzie Friends Re-United" (2011) 161 N.L.J. 416.

D. Kitchiner, "The Compensation Bill, clause 1—an undesirable deterrent?" (2005) 155 N.L.J. 1793.

J. Levy in "Will they ever learn?" (2006) 156 N.L.J. 1671.

Lightman J., "The case for judicial intervention" (1999) 149 N.L.J. 1819 (an excellent brief account of how civil litigation used to be, prior to the Woolf Reforms).

Sir Gavin Lightman's 2003 speech is reproduced as Lightman J., "The Civil Justice System and Legal Profession—The Challenges Ahead" (2003) 22 C.J.Q. 235.

N. Madge, "Small Claims in the County Court" (2004) 23 C.J.Q. 201.

B. Mahendra, "A law unto themselves" (2008) 158 N.L.J. 1278.

Ministry of Justice, "Solving disputes in the county courts: creating a simpler, quicker and more proportionate system—a consultation on reforming civil justice in England and Wales", Cm.8045 Consultation Paper CP6/2011 (March, 2011).

R. Moorhead, "Access or Aggravation? Litigants in Person, McKenzie Friends and Lay Representation" (2003) 22 C.J.Q. 133; "An American Future? Contingency Fees, Claims

Explosions and Evidence from Employment Tribunals" (2010) 75 (3) M.L.R. 752.

D. Oldham, "Online justice" (2009) 159 N.L.J. 615 and (2009) 159 N.L.J. 1223.

J. Plotnikoff and R. Woolfson "Judges' Case Management Perspectives: the Views of Opinion Formers and Case Managers" LCD Research Series 3/02, DCA archived website.

P. Thompson QC, "Woolf's litigants" (2009) 159 N.L.J. 293 (on 10 years of Woolf).

District Judge Monty Trent, "The old days" (2010) 160 N.L.J. 476 (a short, very evocative description of litigation, pre-Woolf).

K. Underwood, "Contingency Matters" 160 (2010) N.L.J. 387 (in praise of American contingency fees).

S. Vogenauer and C. Hodges, *Civil Justice Systems in Europe* (2009) on EU systems and the prospects for harmonisation.

Summary of Lord Woolf's final report *Access to Justice*, 1996, in the Law Society's *Gazette*, August 2, 1996.

Lord Woolf "Cutting costs and delays: why we are doing well but can do better" *The Times*, June 11, 2009.

K. Williams, "State of fear; Britain's 'compensation culture' reviewed" (2005) 25 (3) *Legal Studies* 499.

M. Zander on the Woolf report: (1995) 145 N.L.J. 154; (1996) 146 N.L.J. 1590; (1997) 147 N.L.J. 353 and 539; Woolf on Zander (1997) 147 N.L.J. 751; Zander defends himself: (1997) 147 N.L.J. 768 and *Civil Justice Quarterly*. See responses to Zander and other critics by Greenslade at (1996) 146 N.L.J. 1147. Zander had the last word in *The State of Justice* (2000), Ch.2. See also his tenth anniversary article "Zander on Woolf" (2009) 159 N.L.J. 367.

A.A.S. Zuckerman and R. Cranston (eds), *Reform of Civil Procedure— Essays on Access to Justice* (1995).

FURTHER READING AND SOURCES FOR UPDATING THIS CHAPTER

10–058 Updates to this book from spring 2012 and 2013 on the Sweet & Maxwell website.

Civil Procedure Rules Homepage: *http://www.justice.gov.uk/guid-ance/courts-and-tribunals/courts/procedure-rules/civil/index.htm*.

Civil Justice Council website.

Civil Justice Quarterly for updates, commentary, research and academic analysis (*Westlaw*).

Her Majesty's Courts & Tribunals Service website.
Judges' speeches, Judiciary website.
Ministry of Justice.
Legal Action; *New Law Journal*; *Guardian: www.guardian.co.uk* (free) and *The Times*.

NB The reader is urged to follow the progress of the Legal Aid, Sentencing and Punishment of Offenders Bill/Act 2011 and consequent legislation.

TRIBUNAL STRUCTURE FROM 2010

UK UPPER TRIBUNAL

Senior President (LJ) and Deputy (HC judge)

Immigration & Asylum Chamber	Lands Chamber	Administrative Appeals Chamber	Tax & Chancery Chamber
Immigration and asylum appeals	Jurisdiction formerly exercised by the Lands Tribunal (land appeals)	Appeals from the chambers below, on points of law; judicial review of criminal injuries comp; appeals from Traffic Commissioners; appeals from the General Regulatory Chamber.	Appeals from Tax & Duties Chamber; charity appeals; pension regulation; financial services.
President, Vice President (HC judges), other HC judges, circuit judges, UT immigration judges	President, Vice President, (HC judges), other HC judges, circuit judges, UT judges	President, VP, HC judges, circuit judges, UT judges	President, VP, HC and circuit chancery judges, Upper Tribunal judges, non-legal members

Appeals on point of law or judicial review

FIRST TIER TRIBUNAL

Immigration & Asylum Chamber	War Pensions & Armed Forces Compensation Chamber	Social Entitlement Chamber	Health, Education & Social Care Chamber	General Regulatory Chamber	Tax & Duties Chamber
Immigration and asylum	War pensions and armed forces compensation	Asylum support; social security and child support; criminal injuries compensation; housing benefit; council tax benefit, etc.	Care standards; mental health review; special educational needs and disability; family health services appeals.	Charities; consumer credit appeals; estate agents; transport; gambling; claims management services; information appeals; immigration services.	Tax, VAT and duties.
President, Deputies (circuit judges), First Tier immigration judges, non-legal members	President, Deputies (circuit judges), First Tier tribunal judges, members of armed forces	President, Deputies, First Tier tribunal judges	President, Deputies, lay members, doctors, psychiatrists, etc.	President, etc.	President, non-legal members, etc.

Employment Appeal Tribunal

Employment Appeals
President (High Court judge), HC and circuit judges, employment judges, non-legal members

Employment Tribunals

Unfair dismissal; redundancy; discrimination, etc.
Employment judges and non-legal members

Employment is not part of the new structure.

Most first instance appeals will be heard in the First Tier Tribunal. The Upper Tribunal is a Superior Court of Record, like the High Court. Appeals from the UT on important points of law lie to the Court of Appeal. Non-legal members sit in some UT and some FTT cases (in accordance with the tribunals they replaced). Court of Appeal judges may sit in the UT.

11. Alternatives to the Civil Courts: Institutions and Procedures

"Having spent years in court reading the papers for cases only to be told at the last minute that the parties have come to terms, I am persuaded that alternative dispute resolution is something that people ought to try first." (Lord Browne-Wilkinson, former law lord turned mediator, quoted in *The Times*, March 16, 2005.)

"It avoids the trauma of court proceedings. . .Any sensible person who finds himself party to a dispute will wish to resolve it, if possible, by negotiation. Over 90% of actions that are commenced in England end in a negotiated settlement before trial. One reason for this is the cost of litigating under the adversarial process." (Lord Phillips C.J., "Alternative Dispute Resolution: An English Viewpoint", speech, March 29, 2008.)

"The only reason the strong and the rich will negotiate, arbitrate or mediate with their weaker and poorer opponents is the knowledge that ultimately there is the authority and power of the justice system standing behind the arbitration and mediation systems. Furthermore, unless there is a healthy justice system, with judges developing the law to keep pace with the ever accelerating changes in social, commercial, communicative, technological, scientific and political trends, neither citizens nor lawyers will know what the law is." (Lord Neuberger M.R., "Swindlers (including the Master of the Rolls) not Wanted: Bentham and Justice Reform", Bentham lecture 2011, March 2, 2011).

This chapter deals with alternative hearings for civil disputes, **11–001** outside the court system. There is a big difference between them, however. With tribunals, Parliament has decided that certain disputes will not go to court but to an alternative forum. The litigant has no choice. With arbitration and Alternative Dispute Resolution (ADR), on the other hand, it is generally the litigants who have chosen to use a private alternative because they have the sense to realise what all judges know: it is an incomparably cheaper, simpler and more civilised means of resolving a civil disagreement.

1. Tribunals

11–002 | The Special Commissioners of Income Tax celebrated their 200th birthday in 2005. Income tax, intended as a temporary measure, was introduced by Pitt the Younger to raise funds to fight the Napoleonic wars. (Source: *Counsel*, February 2005.)

Function

11–003 Outside the court system, over 130 types of specialist civil dispute are determined by statutory tribunals, which deal with over 500,000 cases per year. This constituted 130 separate adjudicatory systems. Very importantly, in 2010–11, many of them have been restructured and streamlined together into a single First Tier Tribunal, with appeals routed to an Upper Tribunal, as depicted in the diagram above. They were sometimes referred to as "administrative tribunals", because almost all of them hear appeals by the citizen against an administrative decision or, like the Civil Aviation Authority, they take the initial decision.

As the State grew throughout the twentieth century so it created statutory schemes of administration to confer benefits or regulate people's activities in more and more ways. Those statutes created individual systems of tribunals to adjudicate in disputes arising out of those schemes, between citizen and State. The variety of disputes can be seen from the diagram and there are many more outside the new structure, like the Plant Varieties and Seeds Tribunal. Some of them deal with disputes between private citizens. Employment Tribunals, which happen to be outside the new structure, hear employees' claims against employers relating to unfair dismissal, redundancy and discrimination. These are more like court-substitutes and there is no logical reason why the county court should not have been given this jurisdiction.

Characteristics

Creation

All tribunals are creatures of separate statutes but the Tribunals, **11–004** Courts and Enforcement Act 2007 prescribed the new unified structure that absorbed many tribunals. They were decided by the Franks Committee (1957) to be "machinery for adjudication", in other words, court-like bodies, not part of the administrative set-up. The Franks Report said they should be run according to the principles of "openness, fairness and impartiality". Some appellate bodies are superior courts of record, on a level with the High Court, such as the Upper Tribunal, the Employment Appeal Tribunal and the controversial Special Immigration Appeals Commission, the court that hears appeals from terrorist suspects facing deportation from the UK.

Composition

Some are composed of a lawyer alone and some have a lawyer **11–005** chair (some are now renamed "tribunal judge") and two laypeople. Characteristics can change, as has been the case with those dealing with immigration and asylum and social security. Where laypeople are used, they are normally representative of certain groups, such as employers and employees in the employment tribunals; or they provide expertise, such as doctors and psychiatrists in the mental health review section of the First Tier Tribunal, or accountants in the Tax and Duties Chamber of the First Tier Tribunal. Indeed, like lay magistrates and jurors, this is another significant way in which the ELS makes use of non-lawyers as adjudicators. In his 2010 *Review of the Administration of the Courts*, Lord Judge C.J. acknowledged the importance of this group.

> "After the magistracy, the next largest group of judiciary is the tribunals' judiciary, of whom there are around 7,000. These are a mixture of salaried and fee-paid judiciary, many of whom are legally qualified but who also include a wide variety of other specialists, from doctors and other medical professionals to chartered surveyors and those with experience of life in the armed forces".

Appointments used to be made by the relevant government department but the Judicial Appointments Commission is taking over the selection process for most, following the Constitutional Reform Act 2005. The Judicial College provides training. Some HC judges sit in the Upper Tribunal, as indicated on the diagram and described below, and all Chancery Division judges are members of its Tax and Chancery Chamber.

Procedure

11–006   The Administrative Justice & Tribunals Council published model procedural rules. When tribunals were reformed under the new structure, the intention was that they would have uniform procedure rules but as can be seen from HM Courts and Tribunals website, this did not come to fruition and the different chambers have specialist rules. From 2008, early dispute resolution for many tribunal cases was being piloted. Case loads vary enormously. Some hear over 300,000 cases per year. The Sea Fish Licence Tribunal and the Antarctic Act Tribunal usually hear none.

Organisation

11–007   The Ministry of Justice administers the mainstream ones. They were run by separate government departments but the Tribunals Service, an agency created in 2006, took over responsibility for the major tribunals, as listed on its website. In 2011, this merged with HM Courts Service, into HM Courts and Tribunals Service. Some Tribunals sit nationwide, such as those dealing with tax, employment, benefits, and so on, and some sit in a central location. From 2008, multi-jurisdictional hearing centres were being created in some towns and cities. Some tribunals have never been constituted. No Mines and Quarries Tribunal has ever been convened, since provision was made for it in 1954.

Appeal and judicial review

11–008   From most tribunals, there is no appeal on fact, except from those with an appellate level. For instance, appeal lies from employment tribunals to the Employment Appeal Tribunal. The Court of Appeal (CA) held, in *P v SS of the Home Dept* [2004] EWCA Civ 1640 that an appellate tribunal should not determine the facts afresh. They should accept the facts found by the lower tribunal unless it was shown that the evidence did not support the findings made, or the findings were clearly wrong. Appeal on a point of law lies, with permission, to the Upper Tribunal, as indicated in the diagram, or, for tribunals outside the new structure, to the High Court or CA, under various statutes. The UT deals with some judicial review cases that have recently been transferred from the Administrative Court, such as mental health, immigration and asylum and tax. It is not constrained in its approach to its functions in the way that an appellate court usually felt itself constrained on appeal. Contrary to the *P v SS* case above, it has been held that the Upper Tribunal comes to is own decision on the evidence and it can receive further evidence: *Pensions Regulator v Michel van de Wiele NV* [2011] All E.R. (D) 138. In terms of precedent, The Upper Tribunal and Administrative Court should follow one another's decisions, because of judicial comity and the common law method, despite the fact that HC judges do not normally bind one another: *R. (on the application of B) v Islington LBD* [2010] All E.R. (D). Decisions of the Upper Tribunal (if not judicial reviews themselves) are amenable to judicial review by the HC: *R. (on the application of Cart) v The Upper Tribunal* [2010] EWCA Civ 859. Losers may seek permission from the UT or CA to appeal to the CA, where either considers it would raise some important point of principle or practice. If a tribunal acts outside its powers (ultra vires) procedurally or by taking an unreasonable decision, an aggrieved party can apply for judicial review, in the UT or, in some instances, HC.

The Administrative Justice & Tribunals Council

This supervisory body was created by the Tribunals, Courts and **11–009** Enforcement Act 2007, s.44, to replace the Council on Tribunals. Its purpose is to:

> "help make administrative justice and tribunals increasingly accessible, fair and effective by:
> playing a pivotal role in the development of coherent principles and good practice, promoting understanding, learning and continuous improvement [and] ensuring that the needs of users are central" (website).

It consists of 10 to 15 part-time lay members and its function is to keep the administrative justice system (defined in Sch.7 of the Act), tribunals and inquiries under review and report on them to the Lord Chancellor and Scottish and Welsh ministers. It can make special reports and conduct reviews of issues referred to it by the Lord Chancellor. It makes recommendations to the LC and disseminates research results. Its predecessor Council was recommended by the Franks Committee. In 2010, the Ministry of Justice announced its intention to abolish this independent watchdog, along with many others, in "the bonfire of the quangos". If Parliament agrees to permit its abolition, in the Public Bodies Bill 2011, this is a huge loss as the Council is very active and acts as an independent scrutineer of government and of tribunals, as can be seen from its website and newsletter, safeguarding the interests of tribunal users and researching tribunal work and promulgating reform. For example, in a report called *Time for Action*, 2011, it criticised delays in benefit appeals as causing homelessness.

Advantages and disadvantages

The early tribunal systems were established by Labour and Liberal **11–010** governments to keep disputes out of the courts and the grasp of

Conservative or conservative judges who they distrusted. Now, new tribunals are frequently created. An example is the Gender Recognition Panel, created by the Gender Recognition Act 2004.

H.W.R. Wade, in his authoritative text *Administrative Law*, claimed they were cheap, speedier and more accessible than the courts. Harlow, 2001, challenged this. More specifically, benefits were said to be: low cost—there are no court fees and people can supposedly manage without lawyers; informal procedure and tribunal members can assist the parties; jurisdiction is limited so members become specialists, compared with a district or circuit judge, who is a "Jack-of-all-trades" and they involve laypeople as adjudicators. They are not bound by precedent but those tribunals with an appeal level, such as employment and immigration, have developed their own specialist sets of law reports, which effectively act as precedents.

Critics of tribunals point to their informality, lack of visibility, lack of precedent and consequent unpredictability as endangering a fair hearing. Worse, legal aid had only been made available for applicants to four tribunals until 2000, so in all but a handful of cases, people have to pay for a lawyer or represent themselves. It is still not available before most tribunals. This is unfair in those tribunals which have become very like courts, because of the frequent use of private lawyers by those who can afford them, and because they have developed their own case law, such as Employment Tribunals. Research (e.g. Genn and Genn, 1989) showed that being represented at a tribunal enhanced the appellant's chances of success. Conversely, employers now see tribunals as biased against them. A 2005 CBI survey showed that employers lacked confidence in the system, often settling weak or vexatious claims to avoid using it. A survey of 40 employers showed that all firms sampled with under 50 staff settled every claim, despite advice that they could win half. Of the employers surveyed, 45 per cent believed the system was ineffective and 50 per cent reported a rise in vexatious claims in the previous 12 months.

The Citizens' Advice Bureaux complained, in 1995, that tribunals were neither expeditious nor free from technicality, as proponents claimed. The Human Rights Act 1998 prompted Irvine L.C. to authorise the Legal Services Commission to extend publicly funded legal representation to more tribunals. In 2000, it was extended to hearings before the immigration adjudicators and Immigration Appellate Authority (now Immigration and Asylum Chamber of the First Tier Tribunal) and in 2001, he announced an extension to proceedings on VAT and income tax and any other tribunal dealing with criminal-type penalties, in order to comply with the European Convention on Human Rights. See Harlow, cited below.

Ironically, some tribunals have become so court-like that they **11–011** have lost any advantage, especially after civil court procedure was radically simplified by the Woolf Reforms of 1998–99, so ADR is now offered as an alternative. For instance, from 2001, parties can opt out of the overcrowded employment tribunals and into an ACAS arbitration scheme for simple unfair dismissal claims. Formal pleadings, jurisdictional arguments, complex legal issues and cross-examination are banned and lawyers have no special status. This was copied with an early dispute resolution process in other types of tribunal. In response to some of these concerns, the employment tribunal rules were changed in 2001, with the insertion of the overriding objective, the extension of case management powers, and power to penalise an advocate with a costs order, all ideas borrowed from the Woolf reforms to civil procedure.

It was often pointed out that tribunals were administered and clerked by the department whose decision was being appealed against so they appeared to lack independence. This is why the independent Tribunals Service was created.

Many condemned as cost-saving measures the reorganisation of social security tribunals in the Social Security Act 1998. Oral hearings were reduced, despite government statistics which showed the applicant's chances of success were greater with an oral hearing. Three-person tribunals were cut down, meaning the elimination of laypeople (see Adler). Many more criticisms were made in 2000–01.

The Leggatt Review of Tribunals—background to the new tribunals structure

Tribunals developed piecemeal. Numbers increased significantly **11–012** in the twentieth century. Their growth was questioned by the Committee on Ministers' Powers (1932) and the Franks Committee on Administrative Tribunals and Enquiries (1957) and they were under review in 2000–01 by the Review of Tribunals (Leggatt Committee). The Franks Report, having concluded that tribunals were judicial bodies, recommended judicial safeguards of openness, fairness and impartiality. Consequently, the Tribunals and Inquiries Act 1958 Act provided for procedural rules, reasoned decisions, appeals on points of law to the High Court, lawyers in the chair and the establishment of the Council on Tribunals.

The Leggatt Review was prompted by what Lord Irvine called, at its launch, the "haphazard growth of tribunals, complex routes of appeal and the need for mechanisms to ensure coherent development of the law". The Review body proposed a series of benchmarks against which the achievement of fairness should be tested: independence from departments; accessible and supportive systems; suitable jurisdiction; simple procedures; effective and suitable decision-making process; proportionate remedies; speed; authority, expertise and cost effectiveness. They invited comments on these and I summarise the most important ones below.

Adler and Bradley (in Partington, 2001) identified problems in the old system, such as lack of appeal provision, poor resources and the incapacity of the Council on Tribunals to stop sporadic tribunal development and effectively review the system. They examined proposals for reform and described two models of unified tribunal systems. Robson had proposed to the Franks Committee (1957) an Administrative Appeal Tribunal, which could generate a set of general principles, enabling the system to be more simple and coherent. Similarly, the Whyatt Report (1961) proposed a general tribunal, modelled on a Swedish one, to deal with complaints where there was no specialist tribunal. The JUSTICE–All Souls Report (1988) had, however, rejected an administrative appeal tribunal, because of the sheer volume of work. Adler and Bradley examined the Australian Administrative Review Tribunal, two-tiered, with the first comprising a number of specialist review tribunals and the second being a panel to review first tier decisions raising substantial questions of law or mixed fact and law. They also examined the Quebec system. They proposed a Unified Appeal Tribunal (UAT) with ten specialist divisions. There would be a right of appeal from all government discretionary decisions. Procedure and training would be standardised. The UAT would be able to commission research. Appeals on law would go from the upper tier to the courts. Existing tribunals would be brought into this unified structure:

"Those who consider our proposal as altogether too ambitious and too radical might stop briefly to consider what the state of the ordinary courts would be like if there were as many specialised courts as there are tribunals and if, every time Parliament created some new private law rights or new regulatory offences, a new civil or criminal court were to be created."

Harlow (in Partington, 2001) examined the implications of the Convention and Community law, recognising that the Franks Report requirements of "openness, fairness and impartiality" and reasoned decisions, differed little from Art.6(1) of the Convention. She noted the lack of legal aid but remarked that the ECtHR had not been generous in its attitude to legal aid. She considered English administrative justice to possess an advantage over the continental model of specialist administrative courts. French administrative court procedures had been found to be in breach of the Convention on a number of occasions, with the adjudicators held to be insufficiently independent of the executive. An Independent Tribunal

Service would strengthen the independence of the system and make it less vulnerable to challenge.

Leggatt Report recommendations

Sir Andrew Leggatt's *Report of the Review of Tribunals, Tribunals* **11–013**
for Users One System, One Service was published in 2001. It concentrated on 70 "statutory bodies which provide a specialised machinery for the adjudication of cases that would otherwise be decided by the civil courts".

Tribunals or courts?

Leggatt suggested three criteria for giving disputes to tribunals **11–014**
instead of courts:

- Users should, with help, be able to prepare and present their own cases (most tribunals did not satisfy this aim).
- Where expertise, or accessibility to users, is a major issue in the resolution of disputes.
- Where a tribunal can be effective in dealing with the mixture of fact and law.

Tribunals should do things diferently from courts but be equally independent.

Identifiable problems in 2001

"The most striking feature of tribunals is their isolation. . .nar- **11–015**
rowness of outlook. . .duplication of effort. Each tribunal invents its own IT. . .internal processes, and. . .standards. There is under-investment in training. . . The bigger tribunals have good accommodation. . .; the smaller ones are scratching around for. . .venues. . . Most. . .IT is primitive and is years behind the systems we found in Australia. Most tribunals find it difficult to retain suitable staff." (para.1.18.)

The relationship with sponsoring departments

"There [is]. . .an uneasy relationship. . .the chairmen and mem- **11–016**
bers feel that they cannot be seen as independent. . .paradoxically, many tribunals do not enter into the appropriate dialogue which would enable departments to learn from adverse tribunal decisions and thereby to improve their primary decision-making." (para.1.19.)

The relationship with users

There were unacceptable delays, because of inefficient **11–017**
document-handling, poor listing and too many adjournments.

Communications with users were sometimes terse and impersonal and they were frequently "left in the dark" (para.1.22).

Procedures

11–018   "In some tribunals, proceedings are informal. In others, they are at least as formal as those of the courts. . .approaches sometimes differ within the same tribunal. . .the biggest challenge. . .is to enable users. . .to come to the tribunal without undue apprehension, and to leave feeling that they have been given a fair opportunity to put their case." (paras.1.24–1.25.)

A more independent system

11–019   Most consultation respondents thought tribunals were not perceived to be independent from government departments. Although Leggatt examined the separate system of administrative courts in the major European systems, he concluded that this would be wholly disproportionate to the identified problems. On the European Convention, he concluded that Art.6(1) (fair trial) did not apply to some tribunals but the "equality of arms" principle had implications for Mental Health Review Tribunals and immigration tribunals. He interpreted the Convention case law as requiring "institutional and structural impartiality", like courts. That should guide the operation of tribunals in the future (para.2.25). He reproduced some telling quotations from the tribunal users' survey to illustrate the perception of partiality: "obviously it is on their [the Government department's] side, they are paying for everybody, aren't they?" (para.2.16). There must therefore be a clear separation between ministers whose decisions are tested by tribunals and the minister who appoints and supports them. Tribunals should be formed into a coherent system to sit alongside the ordinary courts, with administrative support provided by the Lord Chancellor (para.2.27).

A more coherent system

11–020   There should be a single system. This would enable the citizen to submit an appeal in the knowledge that it would be allocated to the correct tribunal. It would provide a clearer and simpler system for developing the law. The Tribunals Service should be an executive agency. The Woolf reforms to civil justice should be quickly adapted for tribunals, to ensure that procedures were speedy, proportionate and cheap. On land, property and housing, there were confusing overlaps between courts and tribunals as well as between tribunals (Ch.3).

A more user-friendly system

Users should be given information on how to start, prepare **11–021** and present a case by themselves, compliant with the European Convention on HR. Decision-makers should provide information on what the appellant's statutory entitlement was, what had been decided, the reasons, and whether there was a right of appeal. Legal aid should be provided for representation in more tribunals but on a case-by-case basis (Ch.4).

Structure and powers

The Tribunals System should be divided by subject-matter into divi- **11–022** sions, one of which should deal with disputes between citizens and the rest disputes between citizen and state. There should be a single route of appeal to an appellate division. Generally, there should be a right of appeal on law from first-tier to second-tier and from second-tier to the CA. Appeal should remain to the CA from expert tribunals which deal with exceptionally complex cases (paras 6.1–6.15).

Precedent

"First tier tribunals should continue to consider each case on **11–023** its merits. . .Their decisions should not set binding precedents" (para.6.19) but a system of designating binding cases should be adopted throughout the appellate division.

Judicial review

Second tier tribunals should be statutorily excluded from judicial **11–024** review (JR) and JR from first-tier tribunals should be precluded unless all rights of appeal had been exhausted. The aim of the new appellate Division would be to develop a coherent approach to precedent and the law. The Senior President and other Presidents would be High Court judges so it would be inappropriate to subject them to JR by another equal status judge.

Presidents

The Tribunals System should be headed by a Senior President, **11–025** who should be a HC judge. Some of the Division Presidents should be HC judges. They should co-ordinate consistency in decision-making and uniformity of practice and procedure and should hear the most difficult, novel or complex cases (Chs 6 and 7).

A Tribunals Board

The system should be directed by a Board, consisting of the **11–026** Presidents and others, which would oversee the appointment of members, co-ordinate training, investigate complaints and recommend changes in procedural rules.

The conduct of tribunals

11–027   Tribunal members should take an "enabling" approach, "giving the parties confidence in their ability to participate" (para.7.5). Recruitment and training should emphasise the need for inter-personal skills to help users to overcome communication difficulties. All should be subject to performance appraisal. A Judicial Appointments Commissioner should supervise appointment of the lawyers and another the non-lawyers. The Council on Tribunals should monitor the development of the new system. Their duty should be championing of users' causes. Their reports should be published widely and the Government should reply formally. They should comment on draft legislation and be made responsible for upholding administrative justice and keeping it under review, for monitoring developments in administrative law and for recommending improvements to the Lord Chancellor. They should be able to commission research (Ch.7).

Active case management

11–028   The recommendations here have similar aims to case management under the Civil Procedure Rules 1998 (Ch.8).

Relationship with departments

11–029   Government departments should introduce internal review procedures to establish that their side of the case is correct in fact and law and that contesting the appeal was the only realistic action and a justifiable use of public funds. Departments should adopt a central capacity for scrutinising tribunal decisions and disseminating lessons learned. Tribunals should be able to identify systemic problems and suggest remedies (Ch.9).

Leggatt outcomes and the Tribunals, Courts & Enforcement Act 2007

11–030   In 2003, The LC announced the launch of the Tribunals Service and a policy to increase tribunal accessibility, raise service standards, and improve administration. In 2004, a white paper was issued by the Department of Constitutional Affairs, *Transforming Public Services: Complaints, Redress and Tribunals*. The summary claimed that the programme of reform:

> "goes further than just looking at tribunals—it sets out proposals to improve the whole...dispute resolution process ... This means helping to improve standards of decision making across government and. . .promoting quicker and more effective means of dispute resolution, so that fewer cases come before tribunals. . . the new [Service] will be more than just a federation of existing

tribunals. . .Its mission will be to help prevent and resolve disputes, using any appropriate method".

Notice the language here and the breadth of vision. Government recognised the need to prevent disputes arising in the first place and that the whole handling system for citizens' complaints about government needed restructuring. It is also a formal acknowledgement of the irony I pointed out above, that tribunals, originally established as informal, cheap and quick alternatives to the courts, had themselves become so elaborate and complex that ADR was needed to avoid a tribunal hearing. The White Paper's main points were as follows, with the outcomes bracketed.

1. The creation of a Senior President of Tribunals. (TCE Act s.2. Carnwath L.J.'s appointment was announced by 2005. He has a similar role in the tribunal judiciary as the Lord Chief Justice with the mainstream judiciary—training, guidance, welfare and so on. The L.C.J. can delegate supervision of complaints and discipline).
2. A unified and cohesive system of deployment for those sitting in first-tier tribunals and another for those sitting in appellate tribunals (TCE Act ss.4–8).
3. The renaming of legal members of tribunals as "Tribunal Judge" and "Tribunal Appellate Judge" respectively. This is being done progressively. In December 2007, full-time chairmen of employment tribunals became "employment judges".
4. Simplifying the arrangements whereby panel members can sit in more than one jurisdiction while safeguarding necessary expertise (Outcome as in 2).
5. Further improving arrangements for training and appraisal. (Training is fairly integrated with that of the mainstream judiciary. See annual reports and other documentation on the Judicial College section of the Judiciary website).
6. Structural changes include a statutory tribunals rule committee (rules are made under TCE Act s.22); a more coherent structure of appeals and reviews (TCE Act s.2 provides for a First Tier Tribunal and Upper Tribunal, as recommended by Leggatt. The Upper Tribunal is a superior court of record, equivalent to the Administrative Court in the HC and divided into three chambers. It may be and indeed has been granted a (limited) judicial review jurisdiction, under the 2007 Act, exercised by HC judges only. The first tier is divided into Chambers with Presidents, as in the diagram. Appeals are as described above. There should be a new and enhanced role

for the Council on Tribunals, which will in time evolve into an Administrative Justice Council (as explained above, the AJTC was created by the TCE Act s.44 but is under threat in 2011).

All of this took until 2010 to achieve. The Judicial Appointments Commission, created in 2006, has taken over the recruitment process for tribunal members, as recommended by Leggatt. In addition to the chambers depicted in the diagram, a new Land Property and Housing Chamber is planned for the First Tier, because the Lands Chamber of the Upper Tribunal currently has no appellate jurisdiction. For the remainder of the reform programme, the reader should consult the HMCTS website, especially the annual reports on tribunals.

Academic and research papers

11–031   There is far too little research in this country on the working of tribunals, compared with that in other jurisdictions (see Cane, 2009). Since its creation, the AJTC has been proactive in commissioning research and disseminating results to those who need to learn lessons. This is usually very specific. For instance, in March 2011, they published a report on the experiences of patients appealing against detention to the First Tier Tribunal (Mental Health). They identified complaints about defects in representation, distress caused by delay and lack of communication, concern about limits to case-presentation and lack of information about appeal rights.

> "The report makes recommendations for improvement aimed at. . .hospital managers and staff, the Tribunals Service, the tribunal judiciary, mental health clinicians and other health care professionals, the CQC [Care Quality Commission], the Legal Services Commission and the Law Society." (Press release, March 30, 2011).

In conclusion, almost all of Leggatt's recommendations have been accepted, with very little alteration. There has been a fundamental streamlining of the hotch-potch of tribunals, or at least the main ones. This is to be welcomed and copies the sensible model laid down in other countries many decades ago. Nevertheless, dozens of tribunals still lie outside this new structure, notably the busy employment appeal tribunals; legal aid is still not available for representation in the vast majority of hearings and abolishing the AJTC would be a truly retrograde step, taking us back to 1956, before we invented the Council on Tribunals.

2. Arbitration

Arbitration started as the nineteenth century merchants' alterna- **11–032** tive to the expense and delay of the High Court. It is classified by some as a form of ADR but, as it is more formal and results in a legally binding decision, most specialist ADR writers exclude it. It means the reference of a dispute to a third party or parties to decide according to law but outside the confines of normal courtrooms or procedure. The parties pay privately for the arbitration. It may arise in one of three ways.

1. By reference from a court. A judge of the Commercial Court may refer a suitable case to arbitration or herself act as arbitrator. Commercial Court judges have always been extremely keen on arbitration and if they can cut out part of one of their complex cases and send it to arbitration, they will do. The Lands Chamber of the Upper Tribunal (formerly lands tribunal) has a statutory power to act as arbitrator by consent.
2. By agreement after a dispute has arisen. For instance, if a contract has broken down, the parties might agree to refer their dispute to an arbitrator.
3. By contract. Contracting parties may agree that, in the event of a dispute arising under the contract, they will refer it to an arbitrator to be appointed by, say, the Chartered Institute of Arbitrators, or the Bar Council, or the International Chamber of Commerce. Such clauses are common in commercial contracts and insurance. Examine your own household or vehicle insurance policy if you want to see an example of an arbitration clause to which you are, unwittingly, a party.

Where a business contracts with a consumer, they must fully explain any arbitration clause. It will automatically be deemed unfair where disputes are for less than £5,000, under the Unfair Arbitration Agreements (Specified Amounts) Order 1999 and the Unfair Terms in Consumer Contracts Regulations 1999: *Mylcrist Builders v Buck* [2008] EWHC 2172 (TCC). It is unfair if it creates a significant imbalance in parties' rights and obligations, detrimental to the consumer.

Arbitrations are usually conducted by one or three people. An arbitrator may be a specialist lawyer or, more likely, a technical expert in the subject in dispute. Some are doubly qualified. The Chartered Institute of Arbitrators (CIA) has over 12,000 members, mostly non-lawyers. It provides training leading to qualification.

Arbitrations are governed by the Arbitration Act 1996. Section 1(a) states that the object of arbitration is "the fair resolution of disputes by an impartial tribunal without unnecessary delay or expense". Section 1(b) continues that "the parties should be free to agree how their disputes are resolved, subject only to such safeguards as are necessary in the public interest". Section 33 imposes a general duty on an arbitrator to act fairly. The arbitrator has both the right and the duty to devise and adopt suitable procedures to minimise delay and expense. Section 34 gives her absolute power over procedure. An arbitration agreement may incorporate specific rules of arbitration but if it does not, the default provisions of the Act apply. An arbitration will normally follow essentially the same stages as civil litigation: exchanging documents, factual and expert evidence and then a hearing, but frequently issues are dealt with by written submissions and then a telephone hearing. Often, there is not a general duty of disclosure, as in the courts, but only an obligation to identify the documents relied on by the party. Most arbitral rules permit the arbitrator to act inquisitorially and the Act provides that the arbitration is not bound by the strict rules of evidence. Unlike civil litigation, where the court is bound to decide according to the law, the arbitrator may decide the dispute in accordance with "such other considerations as are agreed by (the parties) or determined by the tribunal" (s.46). This means that an equity clause may be agreed, requiring the arbitrator to decide according to equity and good conscience.

11–033 Once parties have voluntarily and validly submitted to arbitration, the courts will not normally entertain one party if they try and ignore this agreement and make a court claim. The court will normally order a stay or stop of proceedings, under s.9. There is a major exception to this in relation to EU courts, however. In *Allianz SpA v West Tankers Inc* (C-185/07) [2009] 3 W.L.R. 696, the ECJ ruled that a court in one EU Member State had no power to rule that a party should drop a case in another EU state on the ground that the parties had agreed to refer any dispute to arbitration. While some lawyers feared this would allow people to avoid arbitrating in London and persuade others to arbitrate in countries where there is power to award anti-suit injunctions, such as New York or Singapore, thus robbing England of work, others disagreed. Peter Clough, head of disputes at Osborne Clarke, said London still has its appeal "founded on its respected framework for arbitration, legal expertise and English law being the law of choice in many commercial sectors". See Friel and Jones and see further Qureshi (2009).

The arbitrator gives a reasoned decision which is enforceable in court. There are three grounds on which an award may be challenged in court: jurisdiction, serious irregularity or a point of law. The question must be one of general public importance and the decision of the arbitrators should be at least open to serious doubt: *CMA v Beteiligungs-Kommanditgesellschaft* [2002] EWCA Civ 1878. The Act has been subject to considerable interpretation in case law. The courts can act as an appointing authority of last resort, where the parties cannot agree on an arbitrator. They can compel the production of evidence and enforce an arbitration award. Because many foreign arbitrations are conducted in London, difficult issues of private international law can arise. In *Lesotho Highlands Development Authority v Impregilo SpA* [2005] UKHL 43, the House of Lords reminded us that the philosophy and ethos of the Arbitration Act 1996 was to alter the relationship between arbitration and the courts. Lord Steyn said "A major purpose of the new Act was to reduce drastically the extent of intervention of courts in the arbitral process". He looked at the debate on the Bill and a departmental advisory committee report and concluded that we were subject to international criticism that our courts interfered too much.

Most disputes in shipping or aviation are referred to arbitration, as are those of multinational corporations. They are common in oil, gas, banking, commodities, insurance and securities and international trade. Arbitrations are very big, lucrative business to London's lawyers and are a product of London's prominence as an international commercial centre. Many cross-border disputes arose through the construction of the channel tunnel, for instance a £1 billion claim by Eurotunnel against Trans Manche Link, but they were often resolved by arbitration conducted through the International Chamber of Commerce in Paris. Other international arbitration bodies include the London Court of International Arbitration, the London Maritime Arbitrators Association and centres in New York, Geneva, Stockholm and Hong Kong. It is estimated that Paris has the most international arbitrations but, since the nature of arbitration is private, there are no statistics.

In the UK, a number of specialist schemes exist, such as **11–034** Professional Arbitration on Court Terms, run by the Law Society and Royal Institute of Chartered Surveyors as an alternative to courts determining lease renewal terms and commercial rents, and the Personal Insurance Arbitration Scheme, one of over 80 small claims schemes administered by the CIA, to provide arbitration under domestic insurance contracts such as holiday or car insurance. Under this scheme, the insurer is bound by the arbitrator's award but if the insured does not like it, he can have a second bite of the cherry by making a claim in the courts. Some barristers are trained as arbitrators and offer their services on a commercial basis. In 1999, the CIA launched the London Arbitration Scheme, with an attempt to keep the cost proportionate (20 per cent) to the subject of dispute. An example, run by The London Borough of Hackney was launched in 2004, an independent service aimed at curbing costly no-win, no-fee claims. It saves about £1 million per year. Tenants are offered £500 to pay for their legal costs and the arbitrator makes a decision within eight weeks. Litigating housing cases through the courts had cost £7,500 per case and could take two years. Other councils swiftly copied.

Arbitration became popular because it had the advantages of being quick, arranged at a date to suit the parties, cheaper than court proceedings and private. Obviously, this is desirable where time is of the essence, (e.g. a dispute about liability for damage to a perishable cargo) or the parties do not want their commercial secrets exposed in the courtroom. Sampson (1997), however, argued that, because of lawyer-domination, arbitration has become "a mirror image of litigation", with complex parallel procedures to civil litigation. He quoted Sir Thomas Bingham M.R.:

> "the arbitration process, by mimicking the processes of the courts and becoming over-legalistic and overlawyered has betrayed its birthright by allowing itself to become as slow, as expensive and almost as formal as the court proceedings from which it was intended to offer escape".

The 1996 Act was meant to reverse this process, by enabling arbitrators to force the pace of arbitration. The advantages offered by civil litigation in the courts are: if one party believes the other's case has no substance, she can ask for summary judgment; further parties can be added if necessary; the arbitrator has no power to consolidate arbitrations in a multi-party action.

Is arbitration moving out of London?

11–035   The very nature of arbitration is a private proceeding so there are no official statistics, nationally or internationally. Claims that London used to be the "arbitration capital of the world", or that "arbitration is moving out of London" to foreign competitors are common but extremely difficult to substantiate. Nevertheless, in 2003, the then Lord Mayor of London, barrister Gavyn Arthur, staged a conference in London, to ask why arbitrations were going to Paris. Smulian reported on this and observed that London's advantages are its financial and commercial power, its position in international time zones, the respect accorded to English law and its use in foreign contracts, which are also written in English. I would add that London is, historically, an international insurance and maritime law centre and is now used by international law firms, especially US firms, as a springboard into Europe. The disadvantages of arbitrating in London, as opposed to foreign jurisdictions are, according to practitioners cited by Smulian, expense, caused by labour intensive emphasis on document disclosure and examination of witnesses; longer hearings than those conducted by European civil lawyers; the cultural arrogance of English lawyers, convinced, like Americans, that their legal systems and methods are innately superior; and the use of barristers and retired judges as arbitrators, who attempt to replicate court procedure. I would caution, however, that it is very difficult to demonstrate that arbitration is shifting out of the UK since parties may simply be resorting to ADR, another type of unquantifiable, private procedure.

3. Alternative dispute resolution

This was reinvented in the US in the 1970s and became the fash- **11–036**
ionable development in England and Wales since 1990. Many British lawyers, notably the Lord Chancellors Mackay (Conservative) then Irvine (Labour) took a very active interest in this US import, as a means of avoiding the public and private expense and the private pain of litigation. ADR can be defined as any method of resolving a legal problem without resorting to the legal process. Experts consider that any subject can be referred to ADR but advisability depends on the parties' attitudes.

Types of ADR

ACAS The Advisory, Conciliation and Arbitration Service was established in 1974 to trouble-shoot employment disputes and keep potential complaints out of employment tribunals.

Adjudication A quick dispute resolution process designed for the construction industry, to make sure work is not unduly delayed. It was created by the Housing Grants, Construction and Regeneration Act 1996. There is a statutory right to adjudication at any time and decisions are enforceable in the courts.

Conciliation The conciliator takes a more interventionist role than a mediator, in bringing the two parties together and suggesting solutions to help achieve a settlement. Mediation and conciliation have been used in China for centuries. The United Nations Commission on International Trade Law provides a set of model rules.

Early neutral evaluation A neutral professional, often a lawyer or judge, hears a summary of each party's case and gives a non-binding assessment of the merits, which can be used as a basis for settlement or negotiation. Since a 1996 Practice Statement, the Commercial Court judges can offer this to parties appearing before them.

Expert determination An independent expert is appointed to reach a binding decision. It is not caught by the Arbitration Act and thus not elaborate and has no right of appeal. An example is the use of a surveyor at a rent review.

Formalised settlement conference Described at (1995) 145 N.L.J. 383.

Mediation A mediator helps both sides to come to an agreement which they can accept. It can be evaluative, where the mediator assesses the legal strength of a case, or facilitative, where the mediator concentrates on assisting the parties to define the issues. If an agreement is reached it can be written down and forms a legally binding contract, unless the parties state otherwise. If not, traditional civil litigation is still open, so proponents consider it a "no lose" option for a lawyer. Usually, the mediator acts as a go-between, negotiating with each party in their separate private rooms.

Med-arb This is a combination of mediation and arbitration, where the parties agree to mediate but if no settlement is reached, the dispute is referred to arbitration. The mediator may turn into an arbitrator.

Mini Trial The hiring of an independent person to give a non-binding decision on the issue. Hiring retired judges to do this is common in the US. The *Judge Judy* television programme is a somewhat crude example.

Neutral fact finding This is a non-binding procedure used for complex technical issues. A neutral expert is appointed to investigate the facts and evaluate the merits of the dispute. It can form the basis of settlement or negotiation.

Online dispute resolution There are a number of websites offering this, usually used for low-value disputes.

ADR is not suitable for every claim. For instance, where the parties refuse to speak to one another, or where, as in most civil cases, the defendant is silent and judgment is ordered in default to the claimant. It is not suitable where there is little room for compromise, such as in housing possession proceedings. If a case turns on a point of law and both parties want the law clarified or one wants to change the law, then ADR will be unsuitable. Similarly, where only a court order will suffice, such as a court-sanctioned settlement in family law or an injunction to stop an illegal act, then only a court order will do. It is ideal where the parties must continue in a relationship, such as neighbours or businesses. Also, it can save years of nit-picking argument, generating thousands of pounds of costs, in multi-party commercial disputes.

Examples of ADR

Family mediation

This began with the *Report of the Committee on One-Parent* **11–038** *Families* (1974) (The Finer Report), which referred to conciliation. Mediation became much more fashionable in the 1990s. Hundreds of lawyers trained as mediators. Barristers' chambers started offering mediation direct to the public. Under the Family Law Act 1996, attending a mediation information meeting was made compulsory for the legally aided, in certain circumstances. A family judge can order mediation but there are no sanctions for failing to attend. In 1997–99, 14 pilot schemes were launched and over 7,500 people attended information meetings but monitoring showed disappointing results. Although 90 per cent of attendees found the meetings useful, only seven per cent went on to mediation. Most attended alone, yet many of the options described required the commitment of both spouses. In 2004, a report by the Newcastle Centre for Family Studies reached similar findings. Public funding (legal aid) is available for mediation. Funded sessions rose from 400 in 1997 to 1,400 in 2003. There is a UK college of family mediators. Under the Law Society's Family Law Protocol 2002, unless inappropriate, solicitors were required to explain mediation and collaboration to clients. It is not appropriate where violence has been alleged or where drug or alcohol abuse is involved.

The problem with the 1996 Act was its hopeless lop-sidedness. Frequently, the other party is not legally aided. They are paying for their own representation and, as the law stood until 2011, could not be compelled to co-operate so the Minister of Justice announced that anyone wishing to contest the terms of a divorce must attend a mediation awareness session. The MoJ said:

> "National Audit Office figures on legally-aided mediation show that the average time for a mediated case to be completed is 110 days, compared to 435 days for court cases on similar issues. Mediation is also often cheaper than going to court—data from Legal Aid cases show the average cost per client of mediation is £535 compared to £2,823 for cases going to court."(News release, February 23, 2011.)

Resolution family lawyers said this had been done in haste so there will not be enough mediators. People will resort to rogue mediators. Also, all people have to do is tell the court they tried and failed to contact a mediator.

In the meantime, family resolution pilots were commenced in three locations, to try to keep child contact disputes out of court. A Green Paper was published in 2004, proposing to put this type of ADR on a statutory footing, giving judges power to direct parents to in-court conciliation and mediation, although it would not be compulsory, as research had shown compulsion would breed resentment. The Family Mediation Council (meaning Resolution, the Law Society and others) recommended compulsory mediation assessment meetings for all parents who want to go to court over children's contact and residence and parents arguing about money. The former was proposed in the MoJ 2010 Green Paper *Support for All—the Families and Relationships Green Paper*. In-court conciliation schemes conducted by family judges have been used for years. Trinder and Kellett, in a 2007 research report for the Ministry of Justice drew mixed conclusions on the success of "The longer-term outcomes of in-court conciliation". By 2005, more than 250 family lawyers had been trained in "collaborative law", a no-court divorce scheme that originated in the US. Parties get a signed guarantee that lawyers will not let things escalate or insist on going to court. The family lawyers' group, Resolution, said the use of collaborative law in divorce had increased by 87 per cent in 2006–07. Under the Family Procedure Rules 2010 Pre-Action Protocol for Mediation Information and Assessment, in force in April 2011, parties applying for some family court orders are required to attend an information meeting. There are many comments in the 2011 N.L.J. and specialist journals, such *as Family Law*, in 2011.

Commercial Court

11–039   Commercial Court judges are very keen on ADR. They established a working party to examine the scope for applying pressure on litigants to use ADR. Coleman J. enforced a mediation clause in a commercial contract in *Cable & Wireless Plc v IBM UK Ltd* [2002] EWHC 2059.

NHS

11–040   After reports by the National Audit Office that clinical disputes could cost £4.4 billion per year, the NHS set up a pilot project to help resolve claims quickly. An example of a large group mediation was that involving the parents of children whose organs were wrongly retained, after death, at the Alder Hey Children's Hospital. After the mediation, in 2003, each set of parents received a sum of money, an apology and a pledge to erect a plaque to commemorate the children. £100,000 was donated to charity. In 2005, a Speedy Resolution Scheme for some publicly funded clinical disputes involving Welsh

NHS trusts was piloted. The Trusts set out an accident plan in each case, to prevent future accidents, as well as offering an apology and explanation, where appropriate. The NHS Redress Act 2006 introduced a scheme for claims up to £20,000 in England. It encourages staff to report mistakes. Patients have a right to an investigation, explanation, apology or remedial care, if compensation is inappropriate. An example of how ADR can save cost occurred when the NHS and a number of claimant firms entered into an ADR protocol to manage over 200 claims over a suspended urogynaecologist. Had they been litigated, it would have taken 12.5 years to obtain 400 expert reports, costing £500,000; the claims would have cost £126,000 to issue; other costs would have been about £2.5 million. See Locke but see also Ch.10 on the cost of litigation when clinicians refuse to apologise.

Court settlement process

This has been launched in the Technology and Construction **11–041** Court. Judges who have received extra training in dispute resolution techniques may use a CSP at the request of the parties where it is felt such a procedure could achieve an amicable settlement.

Judicial Mediation in Employment Tribunals

A 2010 MoJ evaluation report on a pilot study found an experiment was "an expensive process to administer and was not offset by the estimated benefits". It was well-received and they considered charging employers for it but they recommended not extending it.

Government contractual disputes

The Government announced, in 2001, that it would be using **11–042** ADR in its disputes. Evaluating this shift in policy, the Department of Constitutional Affairs reported that, in the financial year up to March 2003, ADR had been used or attempted in 617 government disputes. It was successful in 89 per cent of cases, saving £6 million. Departments now include ADR clauses in their standard procurement contracts and all relevant literature and new schemes promote ADR, such as in the tribunal restructuring, described above.

EU cross-border disputes

The EU Directive on mediation in civil and commercial matters **11–043** was implemented in 2011. Member states should encourage mediator training and a code of conduct; provide judicial powers to invite parties to mediate; ensure mediated settlements are enforceable like court judgments; ensure confidentiality and suspend limitation periods during mediation.

Legal aid for ADR

11–044   Legal aid is discussed in Ch.17. It is available for early neutral evaluation, mediation and arbitration. In 2005, the Government announced a restructuring of aid to promote the resolution of disputes out of court, as described in that chapter. It also launched a National Mediation Helpline, to put callers in touch with an accredited independent mediator. For claims up to £50,000, costs are fixed and low. Aided clients are able to claim reasonable costs. To discourage unnecessary litigation, in clinical negligence cases and actions against the police, most applicants are now expected to pursue any available complaints system before they make a claim. This gives the public body the opportunity to respond: explaining or apologising. These changes followed a 2004 Legal Services Commission consultation paper "A new focus for civil legal aid—encouraging early resolution; discouraging unnecessary litigation". Minister of Justice Ken Clarke is determined to shift most civil disputes, especially family disputes, into ADR and his radical plans for legal aid, in 2010–11, are geared to encourage it.

Will the courts enforce ADR?

11–045   In *Frank Cowl v Plymouth City Council* [2001] EWCA Civ 1935, Lord Woolf C.J. said:

> "insufficient attention is paid to the paramount importance of avoiding litigation whenever this is possible . . . both sides must by now be acutely aware of the contribution alternative dispute resolution can make to resolving disputes in a manner which both meets the needs of the parties and the public and saves expense and stress" (para.1).

This case involved a judicial review of the closure of a care home, with residents complaining that there had been insufficient consultation and a violation of their Convention rights, under Arts 2, 3 and 8. Under pressure from the CA, the parties agreed to an ADR process. Lord Woolf said courts should take a pro-active approach to ADR. Parties should be asked why a complaints procedure had not been used. The courts should not permit judicial review proceedings, except for good reason, where a significant part of the issues could be resolved outside the litigation process. Lord Woolf asked the legal aid providers to co-operate in this approach and they have done so, expecting applicants for public funding (legal aid) to give details of alternatives to litigation. The issue is whether a private paying client would go to court rather than seeking to pursue alternatives, taking into account the likely effectiveness of alternatives, the attitude of the opponent and all other circumstances.

The CA held, in *Dunnett v Railtrack* [2002] EWCA Civ 303 that a party to litigation who turned down ADR, when it was suggested by the court, might suffer uncomfortable consequences in costs. Brooke L.J. reminded the parties that they had a duty to further the overriding objective of the Civil Procedure Rules. There have been a number of cases since then where this precedent has been applied and successful parties have had their costs refused or reduced. The Commercial Court gave a strong endorsement to ADR six months later in *Cable & Wireless Plc v IBM UK Ltd* (above). Colman J. held that a contractual term providing for mandatory ADR should not generally be held void for uncertainty. For the courts to decline to enforce contractual references to ADR on the grounds of intrinsic uncertainty would be to fly in the face of public policy. Even where there was an unqualified reference to ADR, a sufficiently certain and definable minimum duty of participation should not be hard to find. Further, an ADR clause was analogous to an arbitration agreement ancillary to the main contract and enforceable by a stay (pause) of proceedings or by an injunction. He remarked that the making of an ADR order in the Commercial Court had become commonplace, even where one or both parties objected. This case was applied by Blackburne J. in *Shirayama Shokusan Co Ltd v Danovo Ltd* [2003] EWHC 2006. He decided he had the power to order ADR in the face of repeated refusals by the claimants to accept the defendants' offers to mediate. He was persuaded by the defendants that the parties had a shared interest in mediating as they were likely to continue in a long-term relationship.

The courts backtracked, however, on their view that unwilling parties could be forced into ADR, in a very important CA ruling. In *Halsey v Milton Keynes General NHS Trust* [2004] EWCA Civ 576, the CA heard arguments from four (extra) interested parties, the Law Society, the Civil Mediation Centre, the ADR Group and the Centre for Effective Dispute Resolution. The court produced a definitive set of guidelines on two points: the court's powers to order ADR and whether a party who refuses to participate in ADR should be penalised in costs:

"It is one thing to encourage the parties to agree to mediation, even to encourage them in the strongest terms. It is another to order them to do so. . .It seems to us likely that compulsion of ADR would be regarded as an unacceptable constraint on the right of access to the court and, therefore, a violation of article 6. . .the court's role is to encourage, not to compel. The form of encouragement may be robust. . .mediation and other ADR processes do not offer a panacea, and can have disadvantages as well as advantages. . . " (para.9).

The question whether a party has acted unreasonably in refusing ADR must be determined having regard to all the circumstances of the particular case: (a) the nature of the dispute; (b) the merits of the case; (c) the extent to which other settlement methods have been attempted; (d) whether the costs of the ADR would be disproportionately high; (e) whether any delay in setting up and attending the ADR would have been prejudicial; and (f) whether the ADR had a reasonable prospect of success. These factors should not be regarded as an exhaustive check-list. This precedent was applied in *Reed Executive Plc v Reed Business Information Ltd* [2004] EWCA Civ 887, *McMillan Williams v Range* [2004] EWCA Civ 294 and *Burchell v Bullard* [2005] EWCA Civ 358. See discussion by Sautter, 2005. In *Hickman v Blake Lapthorn* [2006] EWHC, the costs were £435,000 and the award was £130,000 ("What happened to proportionality?" we ask). Had the defendants accepted the claimant's offer to settle for £150,000, they would have saved £205,000 in costs. They refused to mediate because, although their solicitor agreed to it, their barrister did not. Jack J. thought this was reasonable, however, observing that the parties should not be forced to settle. Criticising the case, Prince pointed out that the barrister was *not* being forced to settle but simply asked to attend a mediation. She noted the reluctance to order mediation, as part of case management, since *Halsey*. Sir Gavin Lightman was highly critical of *Halsey* in a June 2007 speech. In a May 2008 speech, the Master of the Rolls acknowledged that *Halsey* might have been over-cautious. Compulsory ADR did not appear to breach Art.6 of the European Convention on Human Rights and indeed was referred to in the EC Directive on Mediation. Compulsory ADR had been introduced in a number of US jurisdictions, demonstrating that compulsion did not breach fair trial rights in common law or European jurisdictions. *Halsey*, he said, "may be open to review". The statement suggesting that compelling ADR was unlawful was, in any event, obiter and should not stop district judges requiring parties to mediate. He pointed to powers of compulsion available in the Civil Procedure Rules. That was not to say, however, that the courts should penalise parties for refusing to take part in mediation, unless the refusal was unreasonable. This does not affect the enforceability of a contractual ADR clause. It was accepted by the CA in *Sunrock v SAS* [2007] EWCA Civ 882 that damages could be awarded for breach, where a party refused ADR. Shipman examines the conflict between compulsory mediation and the individuals rights under Arts 5 and 6 of the European Convention on HR. Examining the case law of the ECtHR, she concludes that while there appears to be little potential for conflict in the use of penalties such as imprisonment for contempt for refusal to comply with a mediation order, the automatic use of draconian penalties would be likely to violate the applicant's Convention rights. Below, we return to the issue of whether ADR ought to be compulsory.

The slow growth of ADR

The slow development of ADR in the last 21 years shows that **11–046** judges and the courts were much faster to learn about it and promote it than practising lawyers and the quotations from the case law above express judges' frustration with lawyers. By 1989, ADR was highly developed in the US. By 1992, the Law Society announced it was a priority in their continuing education scheme and it was favoured in the 1993 Heilbron–Hodge report on civil litigation, discussed in the previous chapter, and the Woolf Report 1996 and was promoted by Mackay L.C. in all his speeches and his Green and White Papers on legal aid in 1995 and 1996. Nevertheless, although it was much discussed in law journals from 1989 and, from 1990, firms started offering it commercially, many lawyers had still not heard of it by 1997. Also, lawyers were hostile to it, (Shapiro, 1997 and Genn, 1998). The very biggest commercial solicitors' firms were the first lawyers to catch on to ADR, with a 1997 survey of the 200 top property law firms showing that 70 per cent regarded mediation as effective. In a 1999 survey of the top 500 companies in the North West, 52 per cent of respondents said their solicitors had not discussed with them the possibility of resolving a dispute through mediation (Goriely and Williams, 1997). The same year, concerned at the lack of uptake of ADR, the Lord Chancellor's Department (now Ministry of Justice) published a discussion paper to try and ascertain why. Respondents said it was not easy to find out about different ADR services. There was no central register. Levels of awareness of ADR were low but 51 per cent of respondents had found benefits of ADR in time, cost or convenience. Benefits cited were: preserving or rebuilding relationships between disputants, privacy, flexibility, informality, stress reduction, the enabling of a win-win scenario, innovative solutions, greater client participation and the ownership of the process. Most thought that government should do more to promote ADR but that it should not be obligatory. The Civil Justice Council responded, warning that Art.6 of the Convention meant that access to the courts could not be excluded. They urged "a major educational push" to attract a wider public to the benefits of ADR and they gave an account of the Canadian Disputes Resolution Fund.

At last, by the late 1990s a critical core of big law firms had been attracted to mediation, the most popular form of ADR, in non-family cases. S.J. Berwin offered ADR to their clients from 1997. A breakthrough came in 1998, when a case funded by the Law Society and ADR group successfully challenged the Legal Aid Board's refusal to fund non-family mediation. Nevertheless, the biggest boost to ADR, especially mediation, is bound to come from its promotion by r.1 of the CPR, as explained above. A 2000 MORI survey of 180 law firms showed that, since the rules had come into force the previous year, 54 per cent said they were more likely to have been involved in mediation.

ADR trainers found that most people wishing to be trained as mediators were lawyers but they had to drop the adversarial habit of aggressive confrontation (*Gazette*, 1997). As late as May 2008, the Master of the Rolls said:

> "[e]ven now. . .far too many people know far too little about mediation. I think we can all agree that this has to change. ADR. . .must become an integral part of our litigation culture."

Since lawyers were slow to use ADR, it was left to the judges to devise schemes for it. In 1993, the Commercial Court announced in a Practice Note that the judges would encourage ADR in suitable cases and from 1996 permitted a judge to stay (suspend) a case to enable the parties to try ADR. From 1995, High Court Practice Directions required the parties' solicitors to certify whether they had considered resolving the dispute by ADR and discussed this with their client. From 1996, the London Patents County Court offered litigants the alternatives of expert arbitration or fast-track mediation. A mediation scheme was offered, virtually cost-free, at Central London County Court from 1996. Genn evaluated it after two years. She found that in only about five per cent of cases both parties accepted mediation. The joint demand for mediation was lowest where both parties were legally represented. Interviews with solicitors revealed widespread ignorance of mediation, apprehension about showing weakness and litigant resistance to compromise. Of those who mediated, 62 per cent settled and the settlement rate was highest where neither party was legally represented. Average settlement amounts were £2,000 lower than non-mediated settlements. Solicitors felt mediation had saved time but there was a common view that failure to settle at mediation increased costs. Some of the most successful mediators were barristers. From 1997, legal aid was available for the Central London scheme and another court-linked mediation scheme was commenced in Bristol. Following the Woolf Report 1996, the Civil Procedure Rules 1998, r.1, placed a duty on the court, as part of its active case management, to encourage the parties to use ADR, if the court considered it appropriate. The CA set up an ADR scheme, whereby invitations to participate in the scheme were sent out in almost all final appeals.

Acceptance of voluntary, court-annexed schemes was initially disappointing. From November 1998 to March 1999, parties in 250 CA cases were offered mediation but both sides agreed to mediate in only 12.

The courts were keen to establish more court-based mediation schemes and many county courts renamed themselves "Civil Justice Centres" to reflect the fact that they offer ADR as well as litigation. A 2004 evaluation of a small claims mediation scheme at Exeter showed that a high proportion of small claims referred to mediation settled. Parties generally found mediation useful. They thought the proceeding was more informal and the mediator a better listener than a judge. It was more likely to be successful between business parties than those in personal relationships or emotionally-charged disputes, with 90 per cent saying they thought they would use mediation again. A major advantage was that, even if the case failed, parties benefited from hearing the other side and receiving directions from the judge.

Following its mediation experiment, the Central London County Court was renamed Central London Civil Justice Centre. In 2004–07, it started a new scheme of automatic referral, copied from Ontario. Under this, about 20 random cases per week were automatically referred to mediation. This applied to personal injury, trade, or housing debts above the small claims limit. If one or both of the parties objected to mediation, they had to give reasons. A district judge decided whether the case should be referred to mediation, or proceed through court. If a party still declined to mediate, for reasons unsatisfactory to the judge, they risked being liable to pay costs. If mediation was unsuccessful, or only partially successful, they were free to continue with court proceedings. Manchester County Court (now Civil Justice Centre) introduced a free mediation adviser in 2004. From 2007, all county court mediation is organised through the National Mediation Helpline. The Lord Chancellor said in 2007,

> "We are providing a simpler and quicker service in the county courts through dealing with all but the most complex small claims through mediation. During a one year pilot here in Manchester, 86% of the mediations conducted were settled on the day, not one of which required any follow up".

The London scheme was researched by Hazel Genn in 1998 and 2007.

Another report by Genn (2002) reviewed the Commercial Court's **11–047** ADR scheme and the voluntary Court of Appeal ADR scheme, in 1996–2000. She concluded that voluntary take-up of ADR remained "at a modest level" and, outside commercial practice, "the profession remains very cautious about the use of ADR". In 2002, Lord Woolf C.J. said he felt we had not gone "nearly far enough" with ADR. The fact that it was not compulsory was delaying things.

Statistics from private ADR firms showed show a big rise in mediation by 2004. The Centre for Effective Dispute Resolution statistics demonstrated a significant increase in mediation after the Civil Procedure Rules came into force in 1999. There was then a slight decline until 2002, when the case of *Dunnett v Railtrack* (above) showed that the courts were prepared to penalise even winning parties in costs if they refused to mediate. Their 2004 statistics diclosed an overall increase of 35 per cent in mediation in 2003, and eight per cent in 2004. Most mediations lasted just one day with 75 per cent of cases settling on the day or shortly after. CEDR perform regular audits. The 2007 audit claimed that the market had grown 33 per cent in the previous two years.

A 2003 article by Lewis gave an interesting insight into why solicitors in big law firms used ADR. One observed that clients were now thinking about it as a first option and there was much more awareness of it. Another attributed the growth of ADR to the civil procedure pre-action protocols in his field, construction and engineering, which require the parties to state why they do not consider ADR appropriate in their case.

Turning to public and welfare law, by way of contrast, social welfare lawyers remained remarkably resistant to ADR. In 2002, Carr addressed this. She said they were concerned at the imbalance of power between their clients and the opposite party, whether a private employer or the State. Mediation could disguise the fundamental causes of social welfare problems and some, such as racial harassment or domestic violence, were not amenable to mediation. Such lawyers feared that the States's real purpose of advocating ADR in social welfare cases was a cost cutting exercise. Challenging their views, she argued that courts do not necessarily deliver justice, nor do legal rights of themselves solve the problems of social exclusion. She said the role of community mediation had been critical in an increased appreciation of what ADR could offer to address social exclusion. Tensions between neighbours in areas of social exclusion could easily escalate. There was further potential for mediation in landlord-tenant disputes.

11–048   In a 2004 conference organised by the Public Law Project, Maurice Kay L.J. said ADR had the greatest potential in housing, community care and education cases where there was an ongoing relationship between the claimant and a public body. The Administrative Court was trying to promote use of ADR. While lawyers acting for the socially disadvantaged in public law judicial review cases had been wary of ADR, experienced mediators pointed out the advantages. ADR could increase parties' sense of ownership of the case and the solution, in contrast with the limited remedies available in judicial review that did not address the real grievance. The grievance could be addressed directly. This reduced acrimony and promoted a continuing working relationship. It got away from the idea of winners and losers and focussed on practical solutions. Even if mediation did not succeed, it could focus issues for the court. Public interest lawyers were concerned that there was a tension between Government's desire to save costs on judicial review and the difficulty of finding competent and experienced mediators. Lord Woolf on his retirement as Lord Chief Justice took up a retirement post with the CEDR. He has trained as a mediator and arbitrator. Since writing his report on civil justice, *Access to Justice*, 1996 (The Woolf Report), he has been a very strong advocate of ADR. Judges remained frustrated at the low use of ADR. In his 2008 *Annual Review of the Administration of the Courts* Lord Phillips C.J. reported that:

"The numbers of those seeking the assistance of the HMCS sponsored National Mediation Helpline remains disappointingly low despite the efforts of HMCS staff to raise awareness of this service. The HMCS Small Claims Mediation Service has settled over 2,500 small claims since March 2007".

In 2011, it remains extremely difficult to collect statistics on ADR because by its nature it is private, yet annual stats are published on court business. The CEDR website remains a good source for statistics, research and discussion, but its annual audit can only give part of the ADR picture. Allen and Mackie (2010) reported on the CEDR mediation audit in May 2010. There were about 6,000 mainstream, non-family mediations compared with over two million court claims. While mediation is used regularly in, for instance, commercial and property disputes, the largest single areas of litigation are personal injury and clinical negligence. They still consider that the rate of mediation is disappointing. The NHS litigation authority is keen to mediate but claimant solicitors are not. The degree of ADR orders varies "wildly" around the country. They say judges should be trained about ADR. There is still a "palpable lack of information about and experience of mediation among practitioners". In 2009, law firm Nabarro LLP and others reported that local authorities were wasting public money; 97 per cent did not refer judicial reviews to mediation before court proceedings. Sir Rupert Jackson, in his review of litigation costs, discussed in Ch.10, considered ADR under-used. He said all litigation lawyers and judges, the public and small businesses should be informed about the benefits of ADR. The President of HM Association of District Judges called for all DJs to be trained in mediation: N.L.J. news, April 2010 and was supported in a speech by Lord Neuberger. Given their obligation under the CPR 1998, it is alarming that DJ training in ADR has only become routine from 2011.

On the other hand, Foggo and Ahmed were more optimistic, pointing out that the top 20 law firms promote their litigation practices as "dispute resolution". They felt the pro-ADR culture change Jackson L.J. called for had already happened for commercial litigators. Khawar Qureshi QC, chairman of The CityUK's Legal Services and Dispute Resolution Group, said 2010 research by his organisation showed ADR had been a major growth area in 2008–10, with over 34,000 disputes resolved through arbitration and mediation in 2009. He reiterated that London is in a pre-eminent position for international business disputes. Research by the School of International Arbitration, QMUL, in October 2010, *Choices in International Arbitration*, found London was the preferred seat of arbitration for 203 corporate counsel surveyed: N.L.J. news, October 15, 2010.

Should ADR be compulsory?

11–049   In her 2008 Hamlyn lectures (2009), Genn argues very forcefully that the anti-litigation pressure, especially from judges, has already gone too far.

"I want to focus on the decline of civil justice. . .the diversion of civil cases to private dispute resolution, accompanied by an anti-litigation/anti-adjudication rhetoric that interprets these developments as socially positive (p.4). . . The anti-law story suggests that society is in the grip of a litigation explosion or compensation culture. (p.32). . . The outcome of mediation is not about *just* settlement, it is *just about settlement*" (117).

She argued that civil justice reviews around the world had been conducted in the absence of research or principled discussion. They were all about efficiency, reducing civil case loads and diverting cases into alternatives, to save money. While evaluation of court-annexed mediation schemes showed high levels of satisfaction among those who volunteered, there was little demand from the parties. She said her 2007 research, *Twisting Arms*, had shown that people did not like being pressured to settle. Brunsdon-Tully argued that the advantages of ADR—consensuality, informality, cost and speed, are lost when ADR is coerced. Sir Rupert Jackson in his review of civil costs, discussed in Ch.10, was not in favour of compulsory ADR.

On the other hand, in two interesting articles, mediator Paul Randolph asked why litigation is so often preferred to mediation and whether mediation should be compulsory.

"Mandatory ADR is accepted globally, from the US, through Scandinavia and China, to Australia and New Zealand. Furthermore, there is no constitutional bar in the UK to mandatory mediation. . .Protracted litigation can be one of the most destructive elements in society: it destroys businesses, breaks up marriages and damages health. . .It cannot offer the degree of vindication that parties crave, nor the measure of public humiliation of the opponent they seek."

See now the 2011 consultation *Solving Disputes in the County Courts* referred to in the previous chapter.

BIBLIOGRAPHY & FURTHER READING

Tribunals

Adler (1999) 6 *Journal of Social Security Law* 99 and *Legal Action*, **11–050** September 1997.

P. Cane, *Administrative Tribunals and Adjudication* (2009).

Carnwath L.J., Senior President of Tribunals, "Tribunal justice—a new start", speech, November 20, 2008.

M. Harris and M. Partington (eds), *Administrative Justice in the 21st Century* (1999).

H. Genn and Y. Genn, *The Effectiveness of Representation at Tribunals* (1989).

H. Genn, B. Lever and L. Gray, *Tribunals for Diverse Users*, DCA Research Report 1/2006.

G. Richardson and H. Genn, "Tribunals in Transition—Resolution or Adjudication" (2007) *Public Law* 116–141.

M. Partington (ed.), *The Leggatt Review of Tribunals: Academic Seminar Papers* (University of Bristol, 2001).

M. Partington, N. Kirton-Darling and F. McClenaghan, *Empirical Research on Tribunals—An Annotated Review of Research Published between 1992 and 2007*, 2007, on the AJTC website.

Further reading and updating

Administrative Justice and Tribunals Council website if this body **11–051** still exists by the time you read this book.

HM Courts and Tribunals Service.

Ministry of Justice, especially consultation paper, *Transforming Tribunals*, November 2007, including list of research and academic work.

Review of Tribunals (2000), LCD Consultation Paper, and final report *Tribunals for Users One System, One Service* by Sir Andew Leggatt, 2001, *www.tribunals-review.org.uk.*
Tribunals journal, on *Westlaw.*

On Arbitration

11–052 There are many books on arbitration and dedicated journals such as *Arbitration*, on Westlaw.

Chartered Institute of Arbitrators *http://www.arbitrators.org.*

S. Friel and C. Jones, "London Waiting" (2009) N.L.J. 247.

T. Sampson, "Arbitration Act 1996—a fresh start?" (1997) 147 N.L.J. 261.

M. Smulian, "City feels the heat", Law Society's *Gazette*, June 19, 2003.

On ADR

11–053 T. Allen and K. Mackie "Higher resolution" (2010) 160 N.L.J. 1143.

V Bondy, "Who Needs ADR?" (article on the 2004 Public Law Project conference on ADR in judicial review cases), *Legal Action*, September 2004, p.6.

M. Brunsdon-Tully, "There is an A in ADR but does anyone know what it means any more?" (2009) 28 C.J.Q. 218–237.

H. Carr, "Alternative routes to justice", *Legal Action*, March 2002, p.1.

Sir Anthony Clarke M.R., *The Future of Civil Mediation*, speech, May 12, 2008.

G. Foggo and M. Ahmed, in "What's the alternative" (2010) 160 N.L.J. 1194.

H. Genn, "The Central London County Court Pilot Mediation Scheme Evaluation Report", LCD Research Report 5/98 (1998) and "Court-Based ADR Initiatives for Non-Family Civil Disputes: the Commercial Court and the CA", LCD Research Report 1/02 (2002); *Twisting Arms: Court Referred and Court Linked Mediation Under Judicial Pressure* , Ministry of Justice Research Series 1/07 (2007); *Judging Civil Justice* The Hamlyn Lectures 2008 (2009).

T. Goriely and T. Williams, "Resolving Civil Disputes: Choosing Between Out-of-Court Schemes and Litigation—A Review of the Literature", LCD Research Report 3/97 (1997).

M. Harris and M. Partington (eds), *Administrative Justice in the 21st Century* (1999).

Lord Judge C.J., at the Civil Mediation Council Conference, May 18, 2009.

J. Lewis, "Meet the Middleman", Law Society's *Gazette*, May 9, 2003.

Lightman J., *Mediation: An Approximation to Justice*, speech, July 31, 2007.

Lord Mackay of Clashfern, *The Administration of Justice* (1994), Ch.4.

J. Michaelson, "The A–Z of ADR" (2003) 153 N.L.J. 101, 146, 181, 232.

Nabarro LLP, 39 Essex Street and ADR Group, *The Effective Use of Mediation by Local Authorities in Judicial Review* (2009).

Lord Neuberger M.R., "Has mediation had its day?", speech, November 11, 2010, judiciary website.

S. Prince "Negotiating mediation" (2006) 156 N.L.J. 262.

K. Qureshi, N.L.J. news, September 24, 2010; "Money walks?" (2010) 160 N.L.J. 1361; "Absolute power" (2009) 149 N.L.J. 1393.

P. Randolph, "Compulsory mediation?" (2010) 160 N.L.J. 499 and "The mediation conundrum" (2011) 161 N.L.J. 207.

E. Sautter, "*Halsey*—mediation one year on" (2005) I55 N.L.J. 730.

S. Shipman, "Compulsory mediation: the elephant in the room" (2011) 30(2) C.J.Q. 163–191.

L. Trinder and J. Kellett, *The longer-term outcomes of in-court conciliation*, Ministry of Justice Research Report 15/07 (2007).

M. Zander, *The State of Justice* (2000), pp.35–38.

Further reading and updating

Arbitration journal. **11–054**

Centre for Effective Dispute Resolution website.

Articles on specialist ADR are in specialist journals so articles on family mediation are in *Family Law* and similar journals; articles on construction dispute resolution are in construction law journals and so on.

GENERAL SOURCES FOR FURTHER READING AND UPDATING THIS CHAPTER

Updates on this book from spring 2010 and 2013 on the Sweet & **11–055** Maxwell website.

Limited items from the Law Society's *Gazette* and *Legal Action*.

Civil Justice Quarterly.

Public Law (on *Westlaw*).

The *New Law Journal* (on *LexisNexis*).

Law journals: search *Lexis* and *Westlaw*.

Judges' speeches on the Judiciary website.

Ministry of Justice research reports on its website.

12. Criminal Procedure

"Having a Criminal Justice Bill before Parliament is like having a skip outside your house overnight. People take your rejected junk and other people stuff their junk into it." (Cambridge Professor John Spencer, 1996, quoting a contributor to the Justices' Clerks' Society Conference that year.)

"The criminal justice system and public confidence in it are readily susceptible to damage by disjointed, sporadic and precipitate change." (Auld L.J., *Review of the Criminal Courts of England and Wales* (2001)).

"[W]e are supposed to be considering summary justice but this example could more properly be described as a horror story. It involves a simple case of driving whilst over the legal limit. When it eventually came to trial, an application was made to stay the case on the basis that to pursue it was an abuse of process. Why? Because of the lapse of time. The driver had been stopped in August 2000 and the trial was due to be heard in October 2004...There had been no fewer than 44 court hearings over the intervening 4 years and the case had been bogged down by procedural requests for evidence, for disclosure, for scientific evidence, for material about the operation of the particular intoximeter. The list was endless." (Leveson L.J., Senior Presiding Judge, speech, December 12, 2007.)

"The criminal justice system included the old Assizes. On my Circuit, the High Court judge would travel from Aylesbury to Bedford then to Northampton, Leicester, with a possible stop off in Oakham, then on to Lincoln, finally back to Nottingham, delivering the jails. We no longer have Assizes, nor, and this is an important consideration, a system in which every case was

concluded—that is from the very start to a verdict—in a day or less." (Lord Judge C.J., speech, November 5, 2008.)

1. Sources and principles

12–001   Since the 1980s, criminal procedure and the criminal courts seem to be under continual and fundamental review and consequent restructuring. Much of this has been well thought through and long overdue. Added to this though and for the sake of a sound bite demonstrating he was tough on crime, each Labour Home Secretary could not resist making a list of statutory alterations every year in the 1990s. There were 29 Criminal Justice Acts and 3,000 new criminal offences in 1997–2007. Then the Minister of Justice made constant changes too. As explained in Chs 6 and 7, the Coalition Justice Minister, Ken Clarke, is busy closing dozens of local courts in 2011. He is also altering the sentencing structure and, as we will see in Ch.17, dismantling the legal aid system. The former DPP, Ken Macdonald, said, in 2009, that government departments were so keen on gimmicky changes that they would telephone him asking for "this month's idea". The result is a complex mish-mash of statutes amended by sets of other statutes and rules, which is a nightmare to apply for judges, magistrates' clerks and practising lawyers. Apart from the uncertainty of knowing which sections of new statutes are in force, there is often a problem that one statutory provision has barely been implemented before another supersedes it. Magistrates' clerks (legal advisers) work at the chalk face, their courts dealing with the bulk of criminal cases. They are the first to discover that a new bit of "junk" does not fit in to the rest, as they struggle to make sense of the latest whim of a Minister, in an endeavour to explain the law to their lay justices. Circuit judges in the Crown Court, determined to assert their independence, simply ignore many of the changes that they disapprove of, provided that they can get away with it without being appealed.

Procedure has been scrutinised by the Royal Commission on Criminal Procedure 1981, which resulted in the Police and Criminal Evidence Act 1984 (PACE) and the creation of the Crown Prosecution Service; then the Royal Commission on Criminal Justice 1993 (Runciman Commission), which resulted in the Criminal Justice and Public Order Act 1994, the Criminal Appeal Act 1995 and the Criminal Procedure and Investigations Act 1996, and then the Narey Report 1997 (*Review of Delay in the Criminal Justice System*), which resulted in the Crime and Disorder Act 1998. There has been a long list of White Papers, especially on young offenders. These resulted in a wholly new youth justice scheme and Board, set up by the 1998 Act and now closed in 2011 by Ken Clarke. In 2000, the Human Rights Act (HRA) 1998 came into effect and it has affected this area of law more than any other, especially through Arts 5 and 6, via the case law of the ECtHR and our own courts. Many statutory changes have had to be made, to render our procedure compatible with the Convention. Auld L.J. was asked to conduct another review, reporting in 2001. His *Review of the Criminal Courts in England and Wales* made sweeping proposals on criminal procedure and the rules of evidence. It provoked debate. The Government's responses were set out in the White Paper, *Justice for All* (2002). Many of his proposals were accepted, such as restructuring court management, widening jury participation, streamlining criminal procedure rules and making changes to disclosure and evidence. They have been enacted in the Courts Act 2003 and the Criminal Justice Act 2003 (CJA 2003). By 2011, some parts of these Acts have been brought into force but some will probably not be implemented. Added to these major Acts, there has been a battery of statutes on specific aspects of procedure. To spare us from confusion, Spencer called for a unified Code of Criminal Procedure and this was reiterated by Auld L.J. The first unified set of Criminal Procedure Rules was published in 2005 but the plan to codify statutes seems to have been abandoned, because the law is being changed too quickly to cope, as explained in Ch.5 on law reform.

The common law

The oldest source of fundamental general principles of criminal **12–002** procedure is English common law and the unwritten UK constitution. Principles are articulated in various instruments ranging from Magna Carta 1215 to books of ancient authority, such as the works of Hale and Coke, statute law and case law. Since British lawyers drafted the European Convention on Human Rights, they not surprisingly modelled much of it on ancient common law principles. The use of the writ of habeas corpus to challenge unlawful imprisonment dates back in England to the fifteenth century (Baker) and it is clearly the basis of Art.5. Lord Bingham said "It has been widely recognized as the most effective remedy against executive lawlessness that the world has ever seen" (*The Rule of Law*, p.14). Coke and other writers discussed the rules of natural justice at length and by the twentieth century they were articulated in clear rules of fair trial, now repeated in Art.6. The ancient English rule against torture clearly forms the basis of Art.3. Because the UK constitution is unwritten, the ancient principles of the English legal system, such as these and the rule of law tend to be treated by governments as mere rhetorical devices rather than practical constraints on law-makers and law enforcers so it is left to the judiciary to apply these principles to restrain politicians' natural tendency to grab and centralise power. In recent years, many significant human rights challenges have been brought before the law lords and now the UKSC and they have often found solutions in these ancient common law rules, rather than resorting to the Convention.

I have included an extract from Toulson L.J.'s judgment in this case below, because it shows how some judges prefer to decide cases by emphasising common law rights and remedies, where these are satisfactory, rather than the Convention. In this example, *TTM (By his litigation friend TM) v LB of Hackney* [2011] EWCA 4, the Court of Appeal found that detaining someone in breach of the requirements of the Mental Health Act 1983 was unlawful detention at common law.

> "Magna Carta 1297 provides:
> 'No freeman shall be taken or imprisoned, or be disseised of his freehold, or liberties, or free customs, or be outlawed, or exiled, or any other wise destroyed; nor will we not pass upon him, nor condemn him, but by lawful judgment of his peers, or by the law of the land.'
> The right to freedom enshrined in Magna Carta is a fundamental constitutional right. From ancient times two writs were fashioned for its enforcement—the writ of *habeas corpus* for obtaining release and the writ of trespass to the person for obtaining compensation where the right has been infringed. Trespass to the person can take different forms, one being false imprisonment. This action will lie where there is intentional deprivation of a person's liberty without lawful justification. Particular features of the cause of action are that the interference with the claimant's liberty must be a direct consequence of the defendant's act and that, if so, it is actionable per se: Clerk and Lindsell on Torts (2010) 20th ed, para 15-01." (per Toulson L.J., at paras 32–33, taken from *Bailii.org*)

He said the common law had developed the writ of trespass to the person so the unlawful detention was actionable for damages, as it was under Art.5 of the Convention, below.

The rule of law: state agents must be able to point to a legal basis for their action. No-one is above the law, derived from common law principles, well-established before Magna Carta cl.39 (above) encapsulated them, as explained by Lord Bingham in *The Rule of Law*. Modern writers have traced the concept back to authorities such as Aristotle.

The presumption of innocence: the burden of proving guilt is on the prosecutor. It should not be up to the defendant to prove his innocence. Critics are concerned that an increasing number of evidential burdens are on the defendant. See Ashworth (2006). The fairness of such "reverse burdens" was considered in *Sheldrake v DPP* [2004] UKHL 43. An evidential burden is not a burden of proof. It is a burden of raising an issue on the evidence for the consideration of the tribunal of fact. It is then for the prosecutor to prove beyond reasonable doubt that it does not avail the defendant. In *Grayson and Barnham v UK* (ECtHR, September 23, 2008) the Court decided the reverse burden in the Drug Trafficking Act 1994 did not breach Art.6. Drug traffickers were imprisoned and the judge imposed a £1.2 million confiscation order. They objected to the burden of proof upon them to show, on the balance of probabilities, that their realisable assets were less than the benefit. The Court applied *Phillips v UK* [2001] Crim. L.R. 817: the presumption of innocence is part of the right to a fair trial that applies throughout criminal proceedings but it is not absolute and presumptions of fact or law are not prohibited so long as they remain within limits. Here, such matters were in the applicants' particular knowledge and not difficult to prove. Professor Andrew Ashworth later commented that it is high time the European Court of HR spelled out exactly what content it is intended to give to the presumption of innocence: [2009] Crim. L.R. 200 at 202.

The right to speedy trial is prescribed in Magna Carta and now **12–003** reflected in Art.5. On English law, see Ashworth and Redmayne, Ch.8.

The quantum or degree of proof: guilt must be proven beyond reasonable doubt. This is a much higher burden on the prosecutor than the claimant's burden in a civil case, proof on the balance of probabilities. It dates back to the seventeenth century and is applied throughout the common law world. See Shapiro for its fascinating history.

The double jeopardy rule: a person cannot be tried twice on the same facts. CJA 2003 made an exception to this. See Hamer for discussion.

Procedure is adversarial: as explained in Ch.1 and Ch.9 on the adversarial process, the court is an unbiased umpire. In common law jurisdictions, in contrast with continental jurisdictions (historically), the court takes no part in directing the gathering of evidence, or shaping the case, in court. We have seen how France and Italy are currently moving more towards an adversarial procedure.

12–004 *The rules of natural justice: nemo judex in causa sua* (the judge must be impartial) and *audi alteram partem* (hear the other side) are reflected in Art.6 and were written into Magna Carta 1215, though applied before.

The right to confront accusing witnesses, by oral cross-examination, in public, was compared favourably by Blackstone (1769) with the Continental inquisitorial procedure, where depositions were taken in private and thus subject to the danger of "mendacity, falsehood and partiality", cited by Dennis, 2010. He says it is a rule ancillary to the presumption of innocence, reflecting the political relationship arising from the state's obligation to prove its case (p.261).

The rule against torture: its 500 year history is explored by the law lords in *A v SS for the Home Dept (No.2)* [2005] UKHL 71, which Kier Starmer QC called the leading judgment in the world on torture (quoted at 155 N.L.J. 1911). It is one hallmark of the difference between the English legal system and European civil law (Roman law) systems. See Langbein. The common law set its face against torture in the fifteenth century but it did not disappear until Star Chamber was abolished in 1640 (Bingham, p.16). Incidentally, the UK, like the US, is not without spectacular hypocrisy in modern armed conflict, outside their territorial jurisdictions. Armed forces and other state agents seem to forget the rule against torture when it comes to extracting information from detainees perceived to be enemy combatants. We examined the rule in Ch.4 on human rights.

Cruel and unusual punishments were prohibited by the Bill of Rights 1689.

The right to legal advice and representation is explained in Ch.17. This is not an ancient right. It was only in 1836 that defence counsel were given the right to address the jury. In 2009, the Recorder of London said there is no right to a McKenzie friend in a criminal trial.

The right to jury trial: Magna Carta 1215 is not the source; it is the Bill of Rights 1689. In indictable offences, I have argued that it is difficult to conceptualise this as a right: see Ch.16 on the jury.

The right of silence

12–005   This is not an ancient right. The defendant only became a competent witness in his own defence in 1898. During the twentieth century it became common to talk in terms of a right of silence. Until the Criminal Justice and Public Order Act 1994, the defendant had a virtually unqualified three stage right to silence, on the street, in the police station and at trial. In court, this extended to the right not to be asked questions. In other words, the accused could, and can, choose to stay in the dock and not answer questions. The judge could comment on a defendant's exercise of the right but not adversely. The right was considered by the Criminal Law Revision Committee, in 1972, the Royal Commission on Criminal Procedure, 1981, and the Royal Commission on Criminal Justice, 1993, and it has long been a subject of controversy.

Proponents hail it as a major safeguard of the English legal system that the defendant cannot be expected to convict himself out of his own mouth. It leaves the burden of proof entirely on the prosecution. Opponents criticise it as a rule protecting the guilty. They believe it encourages the police to intimidate suspects into confessing and some have said that it is sentimental to argue that the accused should not be allowed to convict himself.

In 1987, the Conservative Home Secretary set up a working party to examine the effects of abolishing the right to silence but this was quietly disbanded at the peak of public concern over wrongful convictions, such the successful appeals of the Guildford Four and, in 1991, the Birmingham Six. The 1991–93 Royal Commission on Criminal Justice considered the value and operation of the right. The majority recommended that adverse inferences should *not* be drawn from silence at the police station. Only when the prosecution's case had been fully disclosed should the defendant be required to offer an answer to the charges made against him, at the risk of adverse comment at trial on any new defence he then disclosed, or any departure from a previously disclosed defence (in other words, in the event of an "ambush defence").

The Criminal Justice and Public Order Act 1994 went much fur- **12–006** ther than this and, critics would say, effectively vitiates both stages of the right to silence. Sections 34–39 allow the court to draw "such inferences as appear proper" from the accused's failure to mention, under police questioning, any fact which he could have been expected to mention, or failure, under questioning, to account for any objects, marks or substances, or failure, under questioning, to account for his presence at a particular place, or failure to give evidence or answer questions at trial.

The provisions on silence in the 1994 Act were a heavily criticised area of a provocative statute. In operation, they have caused a lot of appeals and been the subject of critical comment. It is said that the sections offer no protection to the mentally disordered suspect and that the re-drafted police caution is so lengthy and complex that it is only fully understood by a minority of suspects. The CA swiftly ruled that the trial judge was required to remind the jury of certain rules still protecting the defendant, for instance, that the burden of proof lay on the prosecution and that the defendant was entitled to remain silent. They ruled that an inference drawn from silence could not on its own prove guilt, that the jury had to be satisfied that the prosecution had established a case to answer before drawing any inferences from silence and, finally, that if the jury concluded that his silence could only sensibly be attributed to the defendant's having no answer or none that would stand up to cross-examination, they *could* then draw an adverse inference. Beyond this, the silence rules have become impossibly complex. The Judicial Studies Board (now Judicial College) issued specimen jury directions for the use of trial judges. The rules are explained to judges in the Crown Court Bench book, on the judiciary website. The explanation occupies many pages and the suggested jury directions are far too lengthy for a juror to remember, when delivered orally.

Those who considered these sections a breach of Art.6 of the Convention were disappointed by the case of *Murray v UK* (1996) 22 E.H.R.R. 29, in which the ECtHR ruled, in respect of a similar Northern Irish provision, that there was no such thing as an absolute right of silence and it was only a matter of common sense to permit the drawing of adverse inferences where a defendant said nothing in the face of overwhelming evidence. The ECtHR, nevertheless, considered legal advice crucial to a defendant who exercised his right to silence so the Youth Justice and Criminal Evidence Act 1999 disapplied s.34 in cases where the suspect has not been allowed the opportunity to consult a solicitor prior to questioning. *Condron v UK* [2001] 31 E.H.R.R. 1 was the first case in which the ECtHR pronounced on the validity of s.34. The applicants had stood trial in 1995 on drugs charges. On the advice of their solicitor, they did not respond to questioning as they were suffering from withdrawal symptoms. The Court found a violation of Art.6(1) because the judge had left the jury at liberty to draw an adverse inference, even if they had been satisfied that the applicants remained silent for good reason on the advice of their solicitor. Jennings et al. drew the following conclusions from this and the mass of other case law that this legislation had generated:

- Legal advice is fundamentally important, especially where there is a possibility of adverse inferences.
- There may be other good reasons for remaining silent, apart from legal advice.
- A trial was not rendered unfair where adverse inferences were drawn from silence if the only reason was a professed policy of not speaking to the police.
- Adverse inferences may properly be drawn from silence where the situation clearly calls for an explanation.

The CA has continually struggled to interpret the section, among the mass of appeals coming before it. With each new nuance of interpretation, the specimen trial judge's direction to juries has had to be rewritten. *Betts and Hall* [2001] 2 Cr. App. R. 16 resulted in a rewrite but it was considered to be too favourable to the accused. It was rewritten again, as a result of *Beckles* [2004] EWCA 2766. The jury are now asked to consider whether the defendant *genuinely and reasonably* relied on the advice to remain silent. Apparently, suffering post-traumatic stress disorder, having been tortured and being at risk of self-harm does not let D off the adverse inference. Trial judges must weigh the public interest in having D's account against the risk to D's well-being: *R v Tabbakh* [2009] EWCA Crim 464 and [2010] Crim. L.R. 79.

The constant stream of appeals arises because the sections are **12–007** so difficult to apply, in practice, that judges quite often mistakenly permit the jury to draw an adverse inference in cases where they should not. As early as 1999, this led Birch to argue that on a cost-benefit analysis, s.34 should be repealed because it is "too expensive". It consumes too much judicial time at trial and on appeal. If the law is wrongly applied, it may result in the quashing of an otherwise respectable conviction. On the other hand, some appeals have demonstrated that its application has persuaded some juries to attach considerable, misplaced significance to silence. Despite Birch's article, nothing has been done to rid the courts of these confusing statutory provisions. In most relevant cases, there is a "partial failure" by the accused: he answers some questions under interrogation and not others. This makes it so difficult for the judge to work out how to instruct the jury that many judges avoid commenting altogether, for fear that any conviction will be quashed on appeal if they make a mistake. Waller L.J. said in *Bresa* [2005] EWCA Crim 1414:

> "It is a matter of some anxiety that, even in the simplest and most straightforward of cases, where a direction is to be given under section 34 it seems to require a direction of such length and detail that it seems to promote the adverse inference question to a height it does not merit".

I would simply add this: magistrates and juries will surely draw what inferences they see fit from the silence of the accused, regardless of what the law or the judge invites them to infer. Section 34 is *so* problematic that the CA has called it a "minefield" and warned that it should be used sparingly, because the mischief at which it was directed was the "ambush defence", following a "no comment" interview. Legal advisers are faced with a very complex and risky decision in advising their clients whether to remain silent under interrogation. Examining empirical research on the rate of use of silence before and after the 1994 Act, Sanders and Young conclude that although the number of suspects exercising their right appears to have declined, the rates at which admissions are made and convictions secured have not been affected (Ch.5). This pointless erosion of the right to silence in England and Wales is a sorry story of unprincipled legislation leading to hundreds of appeals, causing continuing confusion among judges, lawyers and suspects.

The privilege against self-incrimination

12–008   The right of the accused not to testify at his trial was argued by Ashworth and Redmayne (Ch.5) to be the most fundamental application of the privilege against self-incrimination. This English common law privilege was recognised by the ECtHR as part of the fair trial requirement of Art.6 in *Funke v France* (1003) 16 E.H.R.R. 297. In *Saunders v UK* (1997) 23 E.H.R.R. 313, the Court held that English statute law breached the privilege by requiring a fraud suspect to answer questions and produce documents. His refusal could be punished as a contempt of court and evidence gleaned could be used at his trial. Sanders and Young comment that such modern statutes are a reflection of extreme crime control and a drift away from due process. As a result of this case, the Youth Justice and Criminal Evidence Act 1999, s.59 and Sch.3 amended most such legislation to prevent evidence obtained in this way from being used at trial. This included statutes on companies, banking, insolvency, building societies, financial services, insurance and the like, all of which permit individuals to be required to answer questions. In *O'Halloran v UK* (15809/02) and *Francis v UK* (25624/02) [2008] 46 E.H.R.R. 21 the ECtHR ruled that there was no violation in the requirement to disclose driver details when cars were caught on speed cameras. Car owners were aware of the regulatory regime imposed on them because car use could cause serious injury. People who drive cars could be taken to have accepted certain responsibilities. They adopted the reasoning of Lord Bingham in *Brown v Stott* [2001] 2 W.L.R. 817.

European Convention on Human Rights, Arts 5 and 6

12–009   The HRA 1998 restated the Convention rights as part of English law, as explained in Ch.4 on human rights. Articles 5 and 6 have become the secondary yardstick against which all statute and case law must now be measured, in addition to the common law.

Right to a fair trial (Art.6)

1. In the determination of his civil rights and obligations and **12–010** of any criminal charge against him, everyone is entitled to a fair and public hearing within a reasonable time by an independent and impartial tribunal established by law. Judgment shall be pronounced publicly but the press and public may be excluded from all or part of the trial in the interests of morals, public order or national security in a democratic society, where the interests of juveniles or the private life of the parties so require, or to the extent strictly necessary in the opinion of the court in special circumstances where publicity would prejudice the interests of justice.
2. Everyone charged with a criminal offence shall be presumed innocent until proved guilty according to the law.
3. Everyone charged with a criminal offence has the following minimum rights:

   a. to be informed promptly, in a language which he understands and in detail, of the nature and cause of the accusation against him;
   b. to have adequate time and facilities for the preparation of his defence;
   c. to defend himself in person or through legal assistance of his own choosing or, if he has not sufficient means to pay for legal assistance, to be given it free if the interests of justice so require;
   d. to examine or have examined witnesses against him and to obtain the attendance and examination of witnesses on his behalf under the same conditions as witnesses against him;
   e. to have the free assistance of an interpreter if he cannot understand or speak the language used in court.

Right to liberty and security (Art.5, paraphrased)

1. Everyone has the right to liberty and security of person. **12–011** No-one shall be deprived of his liberty save in the following cases and in accordance with a procedure prescribed by law:

   - lawful detention after conviction;
   - lawful arrest or detention for non-compliance with a court order or to secure fulfilment of a legal obligation;
   - lawful arrest or detention, effected to bring someone before a competent legal authority on reasonable suspicion of having committed an offence or when it is

reasonably considered necessary to prevent his committing an offence or fleeing after having done so;

- detention of a minor by lawful order for the purpose of educational supervision or lawful detention to bring him before a competent legal authority;
- lawful detention to prevent spread of infectious diseases, of persons of unsound mind, alcoholics or drug addicts or vagrants;
- lawful arrest or detention to prevent unauthorised entry into the country, or for extradition or deportation.

2. Everyone who is arrested shall be informed promptly, in a language which he understands, of the reasons for his arrest and of any charge against him.

3. Everyone arrested . . . shall be brought before a judge or other authorised officer to exercise judicial power and shall be entitled to trial within a reasonable time or to release pending trial. Release may be conditioned by guarantees to appear for trial.

4. Everyone who is deprived of his liberty by arrest or detention shall be entitled to take proceedings by which the lawfulness of his detention shall be decided speedily by a court and his release ordered if the detention is not lawful.

5. Everyone who has been the victim of arrest or detention in contravention of the provisions of this Article shall have an enforceable right to compensation.

The Criminal Procedure Rules 2010

12–012 Auld L.J. (2001) agreed with Spencer (2000), about developing a code. What was needed, he said, was a concise and simply expressed statement of the current statutory and common law procedural rules. It should be laid in a manner so that it could be readily amended, without recourse to statute so when his idea was put into practice, the plan was to revise the rules twice a year "to help introduce certainty", as the Ministry of Justice (MoJ) website claimed. They are drafted by a Criminal Procedure Rule Committee which includes the Lord Chief Justice and, originally, Auld L.J. himself. Their central task was to reduce into 78 parts, in simple English, the chaos that was (and is) English criminal procedure. The principle aim was not just to consolidate but to make the law more accessible to ordinary people. The current aim is to review the rules to check that they are accessible, fair and efficient and to rewrite them so they are "simple and simply expressed", as required by the CJA 2003. This Code replaces 50 sets of rules. The first set were issued in 2005 and replaced in 2010. The writing of the Rules will be completed in 2015. Accompanying them is a Consolidated Criminal

Practice Direction, replacing dozens of Directions. It is not law. The Rules introduce a novel overriding objective and detailed regulations about case management, imposing duties even on defence lawyers and aiming to bring about "a culture change", according to Lord Woolf C.J. and Falconer L.C., on their introduction.

The Overriding Objective
Rule 1.1

"The overriding objective of this new code is that criminal cases **12–013** be dealt with justly."

[This includes (1.2)]

"(a) acquitting the innocent and convicting the guilty;
(b) dealing with the prosecution and the defence fairly;
(c) recognising the rights of a defendant, particularly under Article 6 of the European Convention on Human Rights;
(d) respecting the interests of witnesses, victims and jurors and keeping them informed of the progress of the case;
(e) dealing with the case efficiently and expeditiously;
(f) ensuring that appropriate information is available to the court when bail and sentence are considered; and
(g) dealing with the case in ways that take into account—

(i) the gravity of the offence alleged,
(ii) the complexity of what is in issue,
(iii) the severity of the consequences for the defendant and others affected, and
(iv) the needs of other cases".

Critique
The use of an overriding objective was undoubtedly prompted **12–014** by the overriding objective of the Civil Procedure Rules 1998. That one was uncontroversial and has been a successful waymark for civil trial judges and the appeal courts but this one is more problematic. Consider:

1. Under (a), is convicting the guilty meant to be as important as acquitting the innocent? The rhetoric of the English legal system has traditionally asserted that convicting the innocent is a much graver fault than acquitting the guilty. Ancient writers have made repeated claims that we are prepared to acquit some guilty people in the endeavour to protect the accused's due process rights and minimise the risk of

convicting an innocent. Blackstone (1769) set the ratio of risk as 1:10, but other writers have set it as 1:20 or as high as 1:100, in Bentham's case. Given the power of Blackstone's rhetoric over our thinking in the English legal system, we mostly seem to have settled for his 1:10 ratio. Auld L.J. gave considerable thought to the principles underlying the criminal justice system, in his Review, Ch.1. The Lord Chief Justice, when introducing the new Rules, emphasised the presumption of innocence and it is, of course, guaranteed by Art.6 of the Convention but some were surprised that it was not articulated in the Overriding Objective.

2. The last subsection seems to import the civil procedural concept of proportionality but is that appropriate in criminal cases? Does it mean trivial cases should be accorded less time and attention? That may suit the system and recognise how most cases are speeded through the magistrates' court following a guilty plea but does it recognise the seriousness to the accused of even a minor conviction of, say, theft?

3. Every case participant is under a duty to further the overriding objective, copying the same duty in civil proceedings, but is this appropriate in criminal proceedings? Whereas the law assumes civil litigants to be on an equal footing, the defence in a criminal case can never be on an equal footing with the prosecutor where, as in most cases, the prosecutor is the Crown, representing the full might of the State, with all the resources of the police and prosecuting authorities, so there is an inherent imbalance, which English law has traditionally recognised by giving many protective rules to the defendant. At common law, while the prosecutor's duty is to the court, the defence lawyer's duty is to his client. Is (g) compatible with this and, if not, is this satisfied by (c)?

Active case management under Pt 3

12–015   Criminal courts are placed under a duty to further the overriding objective by actively managing the case and the degree to which this is detailed is a novelty in the criminal process. This includes (paraphrased):

1. early identification of issues;
2. early identification of the needs of witnesses;
3. achieving certainty as to who is to do what, by timetabling;
4. monitoring progress and compliance with directions;
5. ensuring evidence is presented in the shortest and clearest way;
6. discouraging delay and avoiding unnecessary hearings;

7. encouraging co-operation;
8. making use of technology.

Case progression

Rule 3.4 requires a court officer, a "case progression officer", to **12–016** "progress the case", monitor compliance with directions and keep the court informed. Under r.3.5 the court may nominate a judge, magistrate or legal adviser to manage a case. Directions can be made by the court without a hearing. Communication can be made by telephone or email. A magistrates' court may give directions as to how the case is to proceed in the Crown Court. Under r.3.10, in order to manage a trial, the court may require a party to give information on which witnesses he intends to call, what arrangements need to be made for their giving of evidence, what points of law will be raised and what timetable he proposes.

Penalties

Very controversially, in r.3.5 the court is given powers to "specify **12–017** the consequences of failing to comply with a direction", including financial penalties for causing delay. Defence lawyers feared they would suffer losses from their already meagre remuneration. When this was proposed, some judges were disturbed at the prospect of being expected to fine lawyers. Rule 3.9 permits the court to require a certificate of readiness from the parties. A day in a busy court would demonstrate to an observer that it is frequently the police or prosecution that is ill-prepared. Defence solicitors in magistrates' courts are routinely delayed by their disorganised clients' failure to turn up to appointments to take instructions. What will be the penalty there? Delays are frequently caused by prison vans being late to court or court technology failing, or, in London, by reports not being ready because the probation service is overworked and underfunded. What then? Amending rules in force in 2008 spell out that if directions are not complied with, the court may cancel or adjourn a hearing, and so on. If someone behaves unreasonably or improperly then evidence may not be admitted or adverse inferences may be drawn, and so on.

Results

Despite these misgivings, judges, the Attorney General and the **12–018** Ministry expressed enthusiasm over the results of the pilots of the Effective Trial Management Programme, which commenced in 2003. By 2004, it was reported that at one Crown Court alone, 700 witnesses had been spared attendance and ineffective trials had been cut to 12.8 per cent. At the same time, prosecutors piloted a witness care scheme called "no witness no justice" and this had enhanced attendance so that eight out of ten witnesses now appeared when expected.

All of this is part of a longer term efficiency drive. It was reported in 2008 that ineffective Crown Court trials had been reduced from 23 per cent in 2002 to 12 per cent in 2007. This is very deceptive though. Trials were ineffective in 13 per cent of cases in 2009, according to the *Judicial and Court Statistics*, but 42 per cent of trials were cracked. An ineffective trial is usually caused by prosecution or defence not being ready but a cracked trial is caused by the defendant pleading guilty at the last minute, or the prosecution offering no evidence. Either way, court time and judge time has been wasted and witnesses have turned up needlessly. The former is a bigger waste of resources because the trial has to be rescheduled. Lord Judge C.J. said, in his February 2010 Review of the Administration of Justice, "I am troubled that the Rules are honoured more in the breach than in compliance. This needs to change."

Case collapse

12–019   As part of the same drastic efficiency drive, the rules permit the penalising of any third party with a wasted costs order if, through "serious misconduct" they caused a trial to collapse. (Courts Act 2003, s.93). This can be applied, for instance, to a newspaper that prejudicially reports a trial so it has to be abandoned, or to someone who intimidates a witness or tells a juror prejudicial information about the accused.

Background

12–020   The background to case management, apart from the Auld Review, is a 2002 Audit Commission Report, *Route to Justice*. It identified reforms necessary to make the criminal process more efficient, including the co-ordination of agencies, better information management and more logical incentives. Ministers told the media that a culture change was needed and there should be no advantage for lawyers "in stretching things out for long enough so that their client's case might slip through the cracks."

"Inefficiency hampers legal system"
Sir,
Recently I attended a Crown Court in London to represent the Crown in a criminal case. The defendant, a man with a history of mental illness, had been convicted of serious offences and remanded in custody for the preparation of a pre-sentence report (by the Probation Service) and a psychiatric report (by the prison medical team), both to be considered prior to sentencing.

In the event, neither report had been completed. The Probation Service is apparently understaffed and experiencing difficulties in obtaining appointments to see prisoners. The prison medical team has had funding withdrawn, as a result of which it cannot provide reports for the court.

The case was not heard for an hour after it had been listed. The company that has recently been awarded the contract for delivering prisoners to court was late in delivering the defendant; it then transpired that there were no dock officers available to provide security during the hearing. When the matter finally proceeded, nothing could be done save to remand the defendant back into custody while further attempts were made to secure reports upon his condition . . .

Those charged with the political responsibility for criminal justice would do well to address the chronic shortages in funding and human resources at the most fundamental levels, before turning their minds to the ever-increasing barrage of legislation to which we are subjected.

Yours faithfully,
MARK SIMEON JONES.
(Letter to *The Times*, February 21, 2005.)

Evaluative comments
Denyer (2008) said:

12–021

"The search for sanctions remains elusive. The situation will only improve as the culture changes and all lawyer participants regard it as their professional duty to comply, so far possible, with time limits set out in Rules and with pre-trial orders. Stringent costs regimes will almost certainly not do".

He says that, in reality, prosecution failures rarely lead to sanction because the state has an interest in ensuring that those charged with serious crime are tried and convicted and do not escape because of prosecutors' mistakes. On the other hand, non-compliance by the defence cannot be allowed to jeopardise the defendant's fair trial. Judges who try serious fraud say management techniques have worked (Julian, 2008) but these specialist judges keep a very tight rein over the advocates and insist that they prepare very carefully for such trials, at lengthy preparatory hearings.

2. Agencies involved in the criminal justice system

Government and independent agencies

12–022   The Ministry of Justice was created in 2007, headed by the Lord Chancellor (Justice Secretary). It took over responsibility for criminal procedure from the Home Office. The Courts Act 2003, Pt 1 sets out his duty to ensure that there is an efficient and effective support system for court business. He is responsible for the courts, the administration of justice, judges' numbers, pay and resources, legal services and the regulation of the legal profession. The Courts Boards are independent and were described in the chapters on the courts. The Sentencing Council (formerly Sentencing Guidelines Council) is independent and resulted from Auld's recommendations. The Youth Justice Board is a non-departmental body, established by the 1998 Act, though they may have been abolished by the time you read this book, by the Public Bodies Bill, going through Parliament in 2011, known as "the bonfire of the quangos". They advise the Justice Secretary on and monitor performance in the youth justice system. They are empowered to commission research. The Act created Youth Offending Teams in each local authority. "YOTs" comprise representatives of the police, Probation Service, social services, health, education, drugs and alcohol misuse and housing officers. The local YOT manager is responsible for co-ordinating the work of youth justice services.

The prosecutors

12–023   The Attorney General is a politician—a Government minister in charge of the prosecution policy and process in England and Wales and is answerable to Parliament for prosecution decisions, via AG's questions, in the Commons, and to the select committees. He is appointed by the Prime Minister and so may change when the Government changes. When New Labour were in power, 1997–2010, all their AGs were drawn from the House of Lords but prior to that they were normally MPs and the present AG, Dominic Grieve, is an MP. He heads the Law Officers' Department. His deputy is the Solicitor General. The most serious offences, such as those under the Official Secrets Act, may only be prosecuted by the AG but it is rare for him to appear in court. There are over 500 offences which require consent to prosecution. He may stop any prosecution with a *nolle prosequi*. He issues prosecution guidelines (see website). He refers prosecution appeals on points of law and unduly lenient sentences to the CA, as described below. The Attorney is responsible for the Treasury Solicitor's Department, the Crown Prosecution Service (CPS) and its Inspectorate and the Serious Fraud Office. His full list of jobs is so long it seems to be a recipe for conflicts of interest. I have not listed them all here. He has civil jobs too. He is meant to act in the public interest but this raises the question of whether the public interest is determined objectively or in his political capacity. The AG has wide *executive* and *quasi-judicial* powers and, as an MP, is a member of the *legislature*. He is the legal adviser to the Cabinet and House of Commons. This obvious breach of the separation of powers and consequent conflicts of interest led to public concern in 2007, especially sparked by Lord Goldsmith's activities. The AG attends Cabinet meetings to give advice but is not a Cabinet member and it is a constitutional convention that Cabinet do not interfere in his decisions. But, quite apart from years of criticism over lack of clarity on Goldsmith's advice to Prime Minister Tony Blair on the legality of the Iraq war, he was also attacked for not prosecuting BAE systems. This was alleged to be a political decision. Slapper complained that the office of the AG was a "conspicuous anachronism" (and see discussion in other media in 2007). In 2007, the HL Constitutional Affairs Select Committee examined the role of the AG. The Labour government promised reform, in 2008, in the Draft Constitutional Renewal Bill. Jack Straw explained to Parliament that it would make major reforms to the office and:

> "make the arrangements more transparent and to enhance public confidence. . .recasting the relationship between the Attorney. . .and the prosecuting authorities. . .[The AG] will cease to have any power to give directions to prosecutors in individual cases, save in certain exceptional cases which give rise to issues of national security. The Attorney. . .will have to report to Parliament on any exercise of that power. . . A protocol will set out how the Attorney. . . and the prosecuting authorities are to exercise their functions in relation to each other. . . We do not propose changing the. . .role as chief legal adviser to the government, or his or her attendance at Cabinet." (March 25, 2008.)

The proposed legislation would have introduced a new requirement for the Attorney to report to Parliament annually. It would have removed his power to give directions to the DPP or the Director of the Serious Fraud Office, except to safeguard national security. It would have transferred the requirement to obtain the consent of the Attorney for a prosecution to specified prosecutors in most cases and would have abolished the Attorney's power to stop a trial on indictment. Two further independent commentaries were published, a report of the Justice parliamentary select committee, in

June 2008, and a joint parliamentary committee report on the draft Bill, in July 2008, but the process stalled. The clauses were dropped from the Bill, without explanation, then the Bill was dropped. All that seems to remain in 2011, is a 2009 Protocol (not a law) on the Attorney's website, setting out the relationship between the Attorney and the Director of the prosecuting authorities for which he is responsible. It says:

> "4 a)2. It is a constitutional principle that when taking a decision whether to consent to a prosecution, the Attorney General acts independently of government, applying well established prosecution principles of evidential sufficiency and public interest."

It confirms that the AG may direct that a prosecution is not started or continued on the grounds of national security but if he does so, he must report to Parliament. It sets out guidelines for the involvement of the AG in "sensitive" cases and deals with the possibility of the AG consulting ministers when deciding what is in the public interest. It deals with the close liaison on policy development that is obviously necessary, between the AG and DPP and Director of the SFO.

12–024   The Director of Public Prosecutions (DPP) is in charge of the Crown Prosecution Service (CPS) and some prosecutions require his consent. His appointment is non-political. The protocol says the Attorney is responsible for safeguarding the DPP's and other prosecutors' independence. Prosecution policy must be agreed with the AG. The DPP issues a Code of Crown Prosecutors which applies to the CPS and the SFO. The DPP and the SFO Director report annually and the reports are laid before Parliament by the AG. The AG may issue guidance to prosecutors. 2009 saw the appointment of a new DPP, Keir Starmer QC, replacing Ken Macdonald QC. The appointment of this internationally eminent human rights lawyer was very heartening, as was the appointment of his predecessor, a defence lawyer. There is no danger of a lawyer with such a background becoming "prosecution-minded". For instance, Sir Ken opposed the government's plans for 42 day detention for terrorist suspects, loudly protesting that it was unnecessary. In his first press conference, Kier Starmer said he said he wanted a transparent prosecution service, firm and fair, renowned for high quality casework and high ethical standards.

The CPS is a national prosecution service, created by the Prosecution of Offences Act 1985 and it now undertakes most prosecutions, including those formerly taken by HM Revenue and Customs. Many others are initiated by those government departments (central or local) and government agencies with statutory powers of prosecution. For instance, offences such as using false documents to try to obtain a national insurance card are prosecuted by the Department of Work and Pensions. Private citizens retain their right to prosecute, unlike in Scotland.

The Crown Prosecution Service

The CPS is responsible for advising the police on potential pros- **12–025** ecutions, reviewing cases submitted by the police and preparing and prosecuting them in court. Ever since the CPS was created, there have been sporadic allegations that it is underfunded and that Crown Prosecutors are consequently overworked and too many cases are dropped or lost through lack of preparation. A 2000 survey of the CPS exposed their lack of moral. Another example occurred in 2010. A CPS Inspectorate report said that in the London CPS area, which handles almost one fifth of prosecutions in England and Wales, failings allowed lots of defendants to go free, through poor case preparation, with 15.4 per cent of cases being dropped before trial. Using in-house lawyers instead of independent advocates in the Crown Court led to a shortfall of lawyers in the magistrates' court so there had been a 290 per cent increase in the estimated spending on independent lawyers in magistrates' courts. Acquittals in contested cases were rising: 37.6 per cent in magistrates' courts and 48.6 per cent in the Crown Court. The CPS was bombarded with initiatives and prosecutors were struggling with caseloads, just "firefighting". Hammersmith had seven chief prosecutors in a year. In one borough, employees averaged 26 days sickness per year. See Gibb, 2010.

A 2001 report by Denman found extensive racism within the CPS and the DPP acknowledged the service was "institutionally racist" and announced a review of CPS case decisions for racism and sexism. The CPS established a Diversity Monitoring Project and an independent report *Race for Justice* was published in 2003. The researchers examined 13,000 files for evidence race or gender discrimination and discovered various inconsistencies. Prosecutors were more likely to oppose bail for black and Asian men. It recommended the use of specialist prosecutors for racist and religious crimes. For more detail, see the CPS website and Sanders, Young and Burton.

The Crime and Disorder Act 1998, s.53 provides that a member of the CPS staff who is not a Crown Prosecutor may prosecute guilty pleas in the magistrates' court and The Criminal Justice and Immigration Act 2008 permits designated CPS case workers to conduct summary trials and conduct contested bail applications in serious cases. DPP Ken Macdonald initiated a policy of expanding in-house prosecutions by barristers employed by the CPS and by paralegals in the magistrates' courts. See Gibb, 2008. This has been condemned by the Law Society and the The Bar Council. An internal CPS survey revealed that only half the 400 paralegals felt that they had had enough training for this. A third felt under pressure to do court work well beyond their abilities. There are two concerns:

1. The quality of prosecutions in magistrates' courts leaves a lot to be desired. Having observed cases in magistrates' courts over many years, it appears that some CPS case workers are poor advocates. Also, the expansion of non-lawyers appearing before lay justices, who are also non-lawyers, is worrying. The quality of performance by some independent barristers, often briefed with little notice, is even worse.
2. Some lawyers and judges are alarmed at the diminution in independent barristers available to prosecute. Incidentally, there is still a gross imbalance in remuneration between prosecutors and legally-aided defence lawyers so that it is not uncommon to see a junior (barrister) prosecutor against a silk and a junior defending. We return to this point in Ch.17.

The CPS has a highly-informative, user-friendly website which explains everything about prosecution decisions in the news and prosecution in general. The Code for Crown Prosecutors is written in simple terms, in 12 languages.

Others

Victims

12–026   Like the AG, The DPP is empowered to stop a prosecution. Victims can ask for judicial review of a decision to discontinue a prosecution: *R. (on the application of Joseph) v DPP* [2000] Crim. L.R. 489 but the courts are loath to interfere. The DPP is not obliged to follow the victim's wishes but there were repeated complaints by victims that they were not kept informed. The Code emphasises that the CPS does not act for victims but prosecutors should take account of their wishes in deciding whether it is in the public interest to prosecute and should abide by the Victims' Code. The Consolidated Criminal Practice Direction provides for the victim to make a personal statement and sets out good practice. It should be taken into account by the court in passing sentence, along with any supporting evidence. Victims can track the progress of their case online at many courts. The Domestic Violence, Crime and Victims Act 2004, s.32 requires the minister to produce a *Code of Practice for Victims of Crime* (CPS website) and appoint a Commissioner for Victims and Witnesses, who has a duty to promote their interests.

(Her web pages and press releases are on the Ministry of Justice website). He appointed a Victims' Advisory Panel in 2006. All criminal justice agencies have a duty to keep victims informed and victims who consider they have been mistreated may complain to the Parliamentary Commissioner for Administration (Ombudsman). An independent charity, Victim Support, provides advice and support and volunteers often accompany people to court. From 2010, there is a new National Victims Service. Vulnerable victims are given dedicated support but Hall (2010) challenged the rhetoric claiming that victims are at the heart of the CJ system.

Prosecution witnesses

There has traditionally been a ban on prosecutors interviewing witnesses prior to their court appearance and English law has generally frowned on the US practice of coaching witnesses. This means the CPS has no means of testing the reliability of witnesses and there is a risk that the case will collapse if a prosecution witness proves to be lying or unconvincing in the witness box, or if, as I observed in my research on judges, an expensively protected witness blurts out information on the defendant's criminal record, thus prejudicing a fair trial (see Darbyshire, 2011, Ch.9). As a result of the 2002 Damilola Taylor murder case, the AG proposed that prosecutors should interview all witnesses (not just the vulnerable) face to face, instead of relying on signed witness statements. Until the 1970s, the DPP used to be able to test the reliability of prosecution witnesses by requesting an old style full committal in the magistrates' court. This meant that the whole of the prosecution case would be presented to the examining magistrates and prosecution witnesses would be examined and cross-examined in exactly the same way as they would be when the trial later occurred in the Crown Court. **12–027**

Roberts and Saunders (2008) assessed the benefits of pre-trial interviewing, which are manifold: sifting out weak cases; improved witness care, keeping them better informed and making their experience less traumatic/alienating; more effective witness liaison, encouraging court attendance and making better-informed decisions on special measures; saving resources where the interview led to no charge, or discontinuance; generating additional information to inform trial strategy, reviewing the prosecutor's arguments, examination and presentation of other evidence; the possibility of inducing a guilty plea; educating the police on CPS work and interviewing, and generally raising the public profile of the CPS. Given the dangers of expensive cases collapsing through unbriefed or unreliable witnesses, I suggest that these reforms are years overdue and an obvious solution to needless waste of public money.

It has become popular to hire private training companies to prepare prosecution witnesses and this has resulted in defence appeals. The CA set out in *R. v Momodou* [2005] EWCA Crim 177 what is permitted for prosecution and defence: witness coaching is prohibited and always has been in English law. There should be no discussion of the proceedings. It is permissible to engage in witness familiarisation so that witnesses understand the layout of the courtroom and likely sequence of events. It is solicitors' and advocates' professional duty to inform the trial judge if any familiarisation process had taken place, using outside agencies.

12–028   Where children give evidence in criminal proceedings alleging violence or sex offences, they are interviewed in advance of the trial, on film, by specialists. This recording of the initial statement is played to the court. They then "appear" at trial by live video link and can be examined and cross-examined. There is a presumption, under the Youth Justice and Criminal Evidence Act 1999 that they will give evidence in this way. Special measures to protect other vulnerable witnesses were enacted in the Special Measures Directions etc Rules 2002. Measures include the ability to give evidence via live TV links, video recordings, or screens around the witness box. Trials may be conducted without wigs and gowns, and without people in the public gallery. Pilot projects commenced in 2002, to examine the possibility of allowing intermediaries to assist witnesses with communication difficulties, and the use of video recorded pre-trial cross-examination, and these measures are now in place. All measures to protect witnesses are a response to the concern that many prosecutions failed because witnesses failed to turn up to court or failed to perform as expected in the witness box. More than 30,000 cases were abandoned in 2001, as witnesses and victims refused or failed to give evidence: see Langdon-Down. A Home Office Report, *Narrowing the Justice Gap*, in 2002, made the same point. Of 5.17 million recorded crimes, only 1.02 million were punished, less than 20 per cent. Despite reforms, a joint report by the NSPCC and Witness Support, in 2004, found that young witnesses suffered almost a year's delay before their cases came to court and this exacerbated their fear and trauma. Half the respondents could not understand some of the questioning or found it confusing and one third still found the experience upsetting, despite the video link: *In their Own Words*. See also a 2003 Audit Commission report, *Victims and Witnesses* (2003). The CJA 2003, s.116 goes even further, allowing the admission of statements from witnesses who are too frightened to testify. In 2010, Ellison and Wheatcroft published results of a pilot study exploring the impact of written guidance on the accuracy of answers by mock witnesses under mock cross examination. They concluded that witness familiarisation allowed witnesses "to maintain greater control over their own testimony" (p.836), bearing in mind it is the advocate's aim to take control over the witness, but they observed, rather alarmingly, that "most adult witnesses. . .enter the witness box with the barest pre-trial preparation" (p.824).

Of course, when prosecution witnesses are heavily protected, defence lawyers will allege that the accused has suffered an unfair trial, in breach of Art.6 of the Convention. In a 2005 murder trial, two young victims, Charlene Ellis and Letitia Shakespeare, had been killed in cross-fire in a gangland revenge attack and it proved extremely difficult to persuade witnesses to come forward. Prosecution witnesses were given false names and various protective devices in court. The DPP said it was the only way the case could be brought to trial. The House of Lords held that the trial was unfair: *Davis (Iain)* [2008] UKHL 36. The Criminal Evidence (Witness Anonymity) Act 2008 was swiftly enacted, replacing common law powers to protect witnesses with a statutory regime of measures to protect identity. See comment by Ashworth at [2008] Crim. L.R. 915 and see editorial comment at [2008] Crim. L.R. 749, to the effect that the Act would *not* have classed the *Davis* trial as fair. There is a growing problem of witness intimidation but trials must be fair. Four test cases came before a five-judge Court of Appeal. See reports on *R v Mayers* and joined cases and comment by D. Ormerod at [2009] Crim. L.R. 272. The Court said the Act sought to preserve the delicate balance between the Art.6 rights of D and the witness's Art.2 (life), 3 (security) and 8 (privacy) rights. See now Coroners and Justice Act 2009, Pt 3, which replaces the 2008 Act, almost identically. The DPP and the AG issued guidance on anonymous witness applications.

In *R. (D) v Camberwell Green Youth Court* [2005] UKHL 4, it was held that the taking of evidence from a child witness by a video link did not breach Art.6. It was not a breach of the principle of equality of arms that the child defendants were not accorded the same facility.

Defence witnesses

Hungerford-Welch argued that prosecution interviews of defence **12–029** witnesses, permitted by the CJA 2003, from May 2010, provides insufficient safeguards for the accused. The provision was enacted to stop ambush defences and help "rebalance the justice system". He said it dilutes the burden of proof.

3. Stages of the criminal process

12–030   This book does not deal with police powers.

Bail

12–031   Police detainees may be released with no further action or officially cautioned if they admit their offence. These groups are normally released unconditionally but conditional cautions may now
be administered. Most people are tried in the magistrates' court and
not remanded at all, in custody or on bail. Most offenders who are
arrested by the police are bailed by them for a court appearance at
the next available court sitting of the magistrates' court. The police
may grant bail at the police station and the CJA 2003 enables "street
bail" from the scene of the arrest. Bail may include conditions, such
as a curfew, or specified residence, or exclusion from the environs
of the victim's home, or surrendering of a passport, and a surety
(money guarantee) may be required. Bail may be renewed by the
clerk or magistrates, if the defendant is not dealt with at the first
court appearance. The offender has a right to bail under the Bail
Act 1976, which reversed the common law presumption against
bail so, if the police oppose bail and the offender contests this, a bail
hearing will take place at the magistrates' court. Indeed, the court
(magistrates' or Crown Court) must consider whether bail should
be granted at each appearance. Where a court or constable grants or
refuses bail or imposes conditions, they must give written reasons
to the defendant (Bail Act s.5). The defendant accused or convicted
of an imprisonable offence need not be granted bail if the court is
satisfied that there are substantial grounds for believing that the
defendant, if released on bail, would fail to surrender to custody, or
commit an offence, or interfere with witnesses.

The defendant need not be granted bail if the offence is indictable or triable either way and he was already on bail for another
offence, or if the court is satisfied he should be kept in custody for
his own protection or (child) welfare, or he is serving a custodial
sentence, or if there has not been time to obtain sufficient information to decided on bail, or if he has been arrested whilst on bail,
or he is being remanded for a report and it would be impractical
to make inquiries without keeping him in custody. The CJA 2003
introduced a presumption against bail for an offender who had previously failed to surrender to custody ("jumped bail"). There is also
a presumption against bail for certain class A drug users. Where
the defendant is accused of a non-imprisonable offence, acceptable
reasons for refusing bail are more limited.

Those convicted of or charged with manslaughter, murder,
attempted murder, rape or attempted rape lost their right to bail

under the Criminal Justice and Public Order Act 1994 but since the Crime and Disorder Act 1998 came into force, they may be granted bail in exceptional circumstances. This amendment was made by the 1998 Act, in order to satisfy the requirements of Art.5 of the Convention (liberty and security of the person). The Article provides that no one shall be deprived of his liberty save in specified cases, in accordance with a procedure prescribed by law. Article 5(3) limits pre-trial detention because a person shall be released pending trial unless the State can show "relevant and sufficient" reasons to justify continued detention, which requires the exercise of judicial discretion. This 1994 Act, abolishing bail for certain offenders, was in breach of the Convention, which the UK Government accepted in *Caballero v UK* (2000) 30 E.H.R.R. 63.

The impact of Art.5 on bail has been the subject of a number **12–032** of ECtHR and domestic cases. In *R. v Havering Magistrates' Court Ex p. DPP* [2001] W.L.R. 805 the applicant argued that Art.5 had been breached at his hearing for breach of bail conditions, when the magistrates heard hearsay evidence. The Court held that if the process conformed with Art.5, it did not have to conform to Art.6 as well and the ECtHR case law simply underlined that the defendant could not be deprived of his liberty without a fair opportunity to answer the basis on which the order was sought.

The defendant may renew his application for bail, if the magistrates refuse it, or appeal to a judge in chambers. Under the Bail Amendment Act 1993, the prosecution may appeal against a grant of bail by magistrates, to a judge in the Crown Court. Sanders, Young and Burton (Ch.9) consider that the research demonstrates a lack of adversarialism in bail proceedings. Ashworth and Redmayne (Ch.8) consider that domestic law should be re-examined, after testing it against Strasbourg jurisprudence. See now Legal Aid, Sentencing and Punishment of Offenders Bill 2011, Sch.10.

The decision to charge

The CJA 2003 gave the CPS a new power to charge suspects, in **12–033** all but the most trivial of offences. This was justified on the basis that the police, not being lawyers, made mistakes as to charge. This follows a recommendation in the Auld Review 2001. This change was criticised, however, on the ground that it put CPS prosecutors into police stations, when the very reason for creating the CPS was to provide prosecutors who were independent from the police. It is important to understand, however, that unlike some of their Continental European counterparts, our prosecutors do not have the power to direct police investigations. This charging scheme was introduced in 2004 after pilot schemes resulted in a 40 per cent increase in early guilty pleas and a decrease of up to 90 per cent in discontinued, ineffective or changed cases. The Code for Crown Prosecutors sets out a "Threshold test" for charging. The Crown Prosecutor decides whether there is a reasonable suspicion and whether there is a realistic prospect of conviction. Under the CJA 2003, the police Custody Officer was given power to bail a person, without charge, to enable the DPP to decide whether to charge.

The decision to prosecute

12–034   There is no obligation on a Crown Prosecutor to prosecute all offences. Common law countries have opportunity systems not legality systems, such as that in Germany. This is classically expressed in Lord Shawcross's 1951 statement in the House of Commons, repeated in the *Code for Crown Prosecutors*:

> "It never has been the rule in this country—I hope it never will be—that criminal offences must automatically be the subject of prosecution."

For instance, most young offenders (10–17) are cautioned for the offences they admit. The practice of official cautioning for juveniles was developed and administered in different ways by various police forces during the course of the twentieth century and only placed on a statutory basis and thus regularised into a scheme of reprimands and final warnings, in the Crime and Disorder Act 1998. The scheme and guidance on its operation are very detailed and prescriptive, clearly designed to minimise the police discretion that had resulted in such a degree of variation. This has now been extended to adults, following a recommendation in the Auld Review. They may be given a simple or conditional caution by the police, following a decision by a Crown Prosecutor that it is in the public interest to divert the offender from prosecution. The CJA 2003 permits the CPS to issue a conditional caution, where there is sufficient evidence to charge a suspect with an offence which he or she admits, and the suspect agrees. If the suspect fails to comply with the conditions, he may be prosecuted for the offence. A restorative justice process has been developed, on a limited basis. Offenders and victims agree on what reparations the offender should make to the victim or the wider community, instead of being prosecuted.

In deciding whether to prosecute, CPS prosecutors review the file of evidence they receive from the police and apply the Code for Crown Prosecutors, which requires a two-stage test, the evidential stage and the public interest stage. The prosecutor must first decide on the sufficiency of the evidence to provide a realistic prospect of conviction and then, only if that test is satisfied, ask whether it is in the public interest to go ahead with the prosecution.

The evidential stage

The Crown Prosecutor must be satisfied that there is enough evi- **12–035** dence to provide a realistic prospect of conviction, meaning a court is more likely than not to convict. They need to be satisfied that the evidence is legally admissible and reliable, taking account of the witnesses. The 2010 Code instructs that they must "swiftly" drop cases that do not satisfy this test and cannot be strengthened.

The public interest stage

Once the evidential test is satisfied, prosecutors must take **12–036** account of public interest factors for and against prosecution but there is a presumption in favour of prosecution. The more serious the offence, the more likely it is to be prosecuted. Factors in favour include use of a weapon, premeditation, vulnerable victim, racism and so on. Factors against include likelihood of a minor penalty, the defendant having made reparation, and so on. The prosecutor must keep the decision under constant review.

Review and concern about fixed penalty notices and cautions

A decision not to prosecute is not ordinarily judicially review- **12–037** able. In *R. v DPP Ex p. Kebilene* [1999] 4 All E.R. 801, the law lords confirmed that, "absent mala fides or an exceptional circumstance, the decision of the Director (to consent to a prosecution) is not amenable to judicial review" (per Lord Steyn). A decision to prosecute can be challenged before the trial judge as an abuse of process, or form a ground of appeal, he said. By 2004 it seemed that the Administrative Court was weary of wasting time dismissing fruitless applications for judicial review of decisions to prosecute. The Senior Presiding Judge, Thomas L.J., warned that legal aid should not be granted for such applications, save in exceptional circumstances: *R. (Pepushi) v CPS* [2004] EWHC 798 (Admin). The ECtHR has held, in a group of cases heard against the UK in 2001, that in certain exceptional instances, where parties might reasonably expect a prosecution, that the DPP must give reasons for not prosecuting: *McKerr v UK* (2002) 34 E.H.R.R. 20.

In 2009, the Home Secretary, Lord Chancellor and AG launched a review of out-of-court disposals, such as cautions and on-the-spot fines (fixed penalty notices issued on the street by the police), doubtless prompted by the horrific BBC1 *Panorama* programme, *Assault on Justice*, in November 2009, on people committing hideous crimes such as violent burglary and "getting off" with a caution. The DPP also condemned the over-use of cautions and called for a review. See Gibb, November 2009. Her article mentions 40,000 on-the-spot cautions per year for assault, including a 15-year-old boy for rape and a man who smashed a beer glass into a pub landlady's face.

BBC Radio 4's *Law in Action* carried an interview with the outgoing DPP, Ken Macdonald, saying the same thing.

The *Panorama* programme included Mr Guest. He obtained a judicial review of the decision not to prosecute: *R. (on the application of Guest) v DPP* [2009] EWHC 594. He was asleep in bed when attacked at home. Goldring J. held, "it is wholly artificial to distinguish between the decision not to prosecute and the decision to administer a conditional caution", para.41. The decision was "fundamentally flawed". Both prosecution tests had been satisfied. The DPP's guidelines on cautioning did not permit cautioning for actual bodily harm. The victim had not been involved in the decision to caution, in breach of the guidelines. Indeed, it was clear he did not agree (he had written letters indicating this). He said, per curiam, that criminal litigation was not a game and:

> "By a decision to offer a conditional caution. . .the court is effectively bypassed. It means that someone who is guilty of committing a criminal offence is not prosecuted, does not appear before the court and is not sentenced by the court. The effect on the victim and the damage to the criminal justice system is self-evident if such a decision is taken without proper regard to the relevant guidance. . .decisions were taken without regard to the Code for Crown Prosecutors, the Director's guidance on Conditional Cautioning and the Secretary of State's Code of Practice. It seems to me astonishing. . .that the Crown Prosecution Service could seriously contemplate not prosecuting someone who, it was alleged, deliberately went to a person's house at night [and] attacked him inside that house with some ferocity. . ." (paras 56 and 57).

The decision not to prosecute and the decision to caution were quashed. The court distinguished *Jones v Whalley* [2006] UKHL 41 where the law lords said a private prosecution following a formal caution for the very same offence arising from the same facts was an abuse of process.

12–038   In *R. v Gore; R. v Maher* [2009] EWCA 1424, G was issued with a fixed penalty notice for a drunken altercation and M was issued with a FPN for a public order offence. Later, having reviewed the CCTV footage, both were charged with inflicting GBH. The Home Secretary's guidelines permit charging in these circumstances. The CA held it was abundantly clear that the Criminal Justice and Police Act 2001 only precluded prosecution for the same offence as that in the FPN. Again, *Jones v Whalley* was distinguished. Lawyers, judges and the public remain concerned about the increased use of FPNs and cautions. As Leveson L.J. said, in a November 2010 speech, "just to take penalty notices for disorder and cautions, were over 450,000 cases truly appropriate? Further, when we consider issues such as transparency and open justice the picture becomes a little more blurred. In issuing an out of court disposal the police are essentially acting as prosecutor and judge, outside the environment of an open court."

In 2001, HM Inspectorate of Constabulary and HMCPS Inspectorate published a joint study, *Exercising Discretion: The Gateway to Justice.* They called for a national strategy in using out-of-court disposals, because:

"In 2009, 38 per cent of the 1.29 million offences 'solved' by police were dealt with outside of the court system. We found that the use of out-of-court disposals has evolved in a piecemeal and largely uncontrolled way. . . public support ebbs away when they are used for persistent offenders. . . We found wide variations in practice across police force areas in the proportion and types of offences handled out of court." (Summary.)

Getting the case into court

Following the issue of a written charge by the police or prosecu- **12–039** tor, the defendant is issued with a requisition to appear in court, under s.29 of the CJA 2003, or a summons (Criminal Procedure Rules 2010, Pt 7).

The prosecutor's duty

In *Randall v R.* [2002] UKPC 19, the Privy Council set out clear **12–040** guidelines for fair trial, including a reiteration of the rule that the duty of prosecuting counsel was not to obtain a conviction at all costs but to act as a minister for justice and the jury's attention must not be distracted from its central task of deciding on guilt, to the required standard.

Pre-trial disclosure of evidence

By now, the rules governing the disclosure of evidence are **12–041** very complex. They are contained in the Criminal Procedure and Investigations Act 1996, as amended by the CJA 2003, The Criminal Procedure Rules Pts 22, the European Convention, Arts 5 and 6, considerable recent ECtHR and English case law applying the Convention to the Act, the AG's *Guidelines on Disclosure* and appended Commentary, along with *Disclosure: A Protocol for the Control and Management of Unused Material in the Crown Court* (2006).

Controversially, the 1996 Act introduced a requirement for pre-trial disclosure by the accused, with defaulters risking the court's drawing an adverse inference. It was condemned as a breach of the presumption of innocence and an unacceptable derogation from the right of silence. The Conservative Government of the day were concerned by the findings of the Runciman Commission 1993 (pp.91–97), that the defence were gaining an unfair advantage over the prosecution by disclosure requirements which had become unduly onerous in the wake of serious miscarriages of justice, such as the Birmingham Six and Judith Ward's case. Defence lawyers could delay trial and put obstacles in the way of a prosecution by requiring the disclosure of more and more evidence, yet the accused was still in the position of being able to ambush them with a surprise defence, at trial.

The Act was immediately attacked as unfair on the defence and a potential breach of the Convention. Defence lawyers made repeated challenges to it and there were widespread allegations of prosecution non-disclosure and an increasing number of prosecutions stopped by judges. One of the worst was a £5 million trial in 2000, alleging police corruption and drug smuggling, in which the judge said the CPS disclosure certificate had "all the intellectual content of a fax sheet cover". Corker commented that eight years after its introduction, the disclosure regime was a failure. Prosecutors, starved of resources and wary of becoming the scapegoat for wrongful convictions, chose to permit the defence access to all non-sensitive material. Judges, keen to secure fair trials, were reluctant to penalise defendants for not providing statements (Corker, *Archbold News*, 2004).

The CJA 2003, Pt 5 completely reorganised the disclosure procedure, following recommendations by Auld L.J. in his 2001 Review. It introduced a single objective test, requiring the prosecutor to disclose prosecution material that has not previously been disclosed and which might reasonably be considered capable of undermining the case for the prosecution against the accused, or of assisting the case for the accused. It places a continuing duty on the prosecutor to disclose material that meets the new test. The prosecutor is specifically required to review the material on receipt of the defence statement and to make further disclosure, if required.

12–042 The 2003 Act also amended the defence disclosure requirements, requiring the accused to provide a more detailed defence statement, setting out the nature of his defence, including any particular defences on which he intends to rely and indicating any points of law he wishes to take, including any points as to the admissibility of evidence or abuse of process. This is because the 1996 Act had not persuaded defendants to be forthcoming. Defence statements usually amounted to a couple of useless lines and judges were reluctant to penalise defence non-disclosure. Lord Judge C.J., in his

2008 speech, explained how one particular case, on the "7/7 bomb-ers" prompted the change.

"A stark example arose in the case tried by Fulford J of the 21st July bombers, that is the bombs in London which detonated but, by absolute sheer good fortune, did not explode. The judge was sure that some of the defendants had 'tried to mould their defences to the scientific evidence. . .rather than providing information that would enable useful tests to be undertaken at the outset'. . . As a result of his observations the law has been amended".

An updated defence statement may be required, to assist the man-agement of the trial, requiring the accused to serve details of his witness and experts, giving the police a new power to interview defence witnesses prior to trial. The judge has the discretion to dis-close the defence statement to the jury. If the defence fails to comply with the statute, the court or any other party can make such com-ments as appear appropriate and the court or jury can "draw such inferences as appear proper", in other words, adverse inferences (1996 Act, s.11, as substituted by the CJA 2003). In the leading case of *Rowe and Davis v UK* (29901/95) (2000) 30 E.H.R.R.1, the ECtHR said:

"The right to an adversarial trial means, in a criminal case, that both prosecution and defence must be given the opportunity to have knowledge of and comment on the observations filed and the evidence adduced by the other party. . .In addition, Article 6(1) requires, as indeed does English law. . .that the prosecution authorities should disclose to the defence all material evidence in their possession for or against the accused."

The Court warned, however, that "entitlement to disclosure of rel-evant evidence is not an absolute right". There are three competing interests that might lead to the withholding of evidence—national security, protection of witnesses and preserving secrecy in police investigations. This was applied when the case came back to the CA in *R. v Davis, Johnson and Rowe* (2001) 1 Cr. App. R. 8. Problems have arisen in relation to claims of public interest immunity (PII) by the prosecution, where they seek the judge's permission to withhold evidence from the defence on the grounds of its sensitivity, such as the national interest or, more usually, that they sought to protect the identity of a police informer. Where this application is made there is a pre-trial hearing by the judge and special counsel may be appointed to represent the interests of the accused. In *R. v H, R. v C* [2004] UKHL 3 the law lords held that appointing special counsel in an ordinary criminal trial, in a PII hearing, should be a course of last resort.

- If D could not be tried fairly, he should not be tried at all.
- Save in exceptional circumstances, the judge was not a factual decision-maker.
- Appointment of special counsel raised ethical issues.

The ECtHR held that the disclosure-judge system, using a different judge from the trial judge to determine public interest, was compatible with Art.6: *McKeown v UK* (C-6684/05), January 11, 2011. The 2006 protocol on disclosure of unused material, issued by the CA, demonstrated exasperation with lawyers for ignoring legal requirements. In the introduction they complained:

"Disclosure is one of the most important—as well as the most abused—of the procedures relating to criminal trials."

Lawyers' applications and judges' decisions had been based on misconceptions or a general laxity of approach. This was costly and had obstructed justice.

"In the past, the prosecution and the court have too often been faced with a defence statement that is little more than an assertion that the Defendant is not guilty. . .There must be a complete change in the culture. The defence must serve the defence case statement by the due date. Judges should then examine the defence case to ensure that it complies."

I would simply comment that demanding a culture change will not necessarily achieve it, given the underfunding of the CPS and the poor remuneration of defence solicitors, the caseloads they suffer and an ingrained culture of cynicism of and disregard for the disclosure regime. Research on disclosure was published by Quirk (2006), demonstrating that the protocol was "unlikely to succeed". Identifying prosecution material that needs to be disclosed needs time and effort. Neither police nor prosecution have sufficient personnel. Police officers are "ill-equipped by purpose, training and occupational culture". They find the job "onerous, time consuming and unpopular". Naturally, as non-lawyers, the police officers she interviewed had little understanding of what was required of them and some were prepared to admit that they were reluctant to give the defence exculpatory evidence. Many of the defence lawyers she interviewed and one third of Crown prosecutors were concerned that important material was omitted from the schedules. In 2011, the Ministry of Justice is yet again reviewing the prosecution's duty of disclosure "in cases which generate large volumes of investigative material, where a disproportionate part of the disclosure cost burden lies" (Ch.6 of their legal aid reform consultation, 2010).

The plea

In common law countries, once the accused has pleaded guilty, **12–043** this relieves the prosecutor from proving the case against the accused by bringing evidence and examining witnesses at trial. There is no trial. The guilty plea procedure was considered and approved by the European Commission on HR on at least two occasions. In *DPP v Revitt* [2006] EWHC, the Lord Chief Justice said the correct analysis was as follows. Where a defendant made an unequivocal plea of guilty which the court accepted, the defendant was thereupon "proved guilty according to law" with the meaning of Art.6(2). The presumption of innocence ceased to apply and he could be sentenced on the basis that he had been proven guilty. Where a plea was equivocal, it had to be treated as a plea of not guilty. Where he was unrepresented, it was the duty of the court to make sure the nature of the offence was made clear to him before a plea of guilty was accepted.

Plea bargaining and sentencing discounts

At any time prior to or during a criminal trial, it is very common **12–044** for a defendant to change his plea from "not guilty" to "guilty" on one or more counts. This results in what has become known as a "cracked trial". This wastes court time and public resources and, in relation to trial on indictment, was one of the concerns of the Royal Commission on Criminal Justice, 1993. It usually results from plea negotiations between prosecution and defence, which may be initiated by either, commonly known as "plea bargaining", though Ministers and judges deny that this phenomenon exists in England and Wales. This means the defendant agrees to plead guilty in exchange for a concession by the prosecutor, such as a reduced charge (charge-bargaining) or a concession that the facts of the crime were not so serious as originally alleged (fact-bargaining). The defendant may also plead guilty in the hope of a reduced sentence. The CA has long sanctioned a system of a 25–30 per cent "sentence discount", rewarding the defendant for pleading guilty but the case of *Turner* [1972] W.L.R. 1093 prohibited the trial judge becoming involved in a plea bargain to assure the defendant of a specific sentence discount. This prevented the development of a full-blown system of legally enforceable plea bargains, conducted in special hearings, before a judge, which exists in most of the US. There is an interesting US/English comparison and a critique of the *AG's Plea Negotiation Framework for Fraud Cases.* Vamos (2009). It is important to understand that plea bargaining in the UK cannot work in the fully entrenched way it does in the US because prosecutors do not have the same powers. For instance, they cannot recommend a sentencing range, unlike their US counterparts.

The Royal Commission said nothing about such pre-trial negotiations involving the judge but, in order to try and obviate the occurrence of cracked trials, recommended a "sentencing canvass", offering the defendant a graduated system of sentencing discounts: the earlier the plea, the greater the discount. Whilst acknowledging the danger that this might induce innocent people to plead guilty, the Commission, heavily influenced by the Bar Council's Seabrook Report (1992), concluded that this risk would not be increased by "clearer articulation of the long accepted principle" of sentencing discounts. Section 48 of the Criminal Justice and Public Order Act 1994 and later legislation gave statutory recognition to the system of informal sentencing discounts and, indeed, made it mandatory, by requiring the sentencing judge to take into account the timing and circumstances of a guilty plea and, if the punishment is accordingly reduced, to state so in open court.

According to *Turner*, advocates were not meant to pressurise clients into pleading guilty and judges were not meant to offer specific discounts but cases decided by the CA exposed the frequency of breaches of these rules by judges and counsel doing secret pre-trial deals in chambers. One such case was *R. v Dossetter* [1999] 2 Cr. App. R. (S) 248, where the CA reminded advocates that plea bargaining "forms no part of English criminal jurisprudence". Another was *Nazham and Nazham* [2004] EWCA Crim 491. Here counsel had seen the judge in his chambers and the judge had remarked "this has got plea written all over it and bags of credit". The CA declined to quash the convictions because they found the defendants' freedom of choice had not been inhibited but observed that the judge should not have made his remarks. They observed that, since there were, by then, sentencing guidelines for guilty pleas, there was no reason why a judge should not give an indication of sentencing parameters in open court.

12–045   In cases from the late 1990s, the courts moved towards enforcing promises held out to defendants. In *R. v Ricky Jackson* (2000) *Westlaw* WL 1741439 the judge had promised a sentence discount so the CA felt obliged to enforce it, despite the defendant's "appalling" driving record. This was swiftly followed by the *Attorney General's Guidelines on the Acceptance of Pleas* (2000), in which the Attorney reminded prosecutors that justice should be transparent. It was the duty of the advocate to remind the judge of the CA's decisions and disassociate himself from sentence discussions. This reflects concern over the number of Crown Court judges who flouted *Turner*.

The Bar has long advocated the formalisation of the system of plea bargaining, by offering these graduated sentencing discounts and they spelled out this "sentencing canvass" in their 1992 Seabrook Report, mentioned above. My view is diametrically opposed. I do not want to see the English legal system going down this US route. I set out a long list of reasons, in 2000. Not least of my objections are these.

1. Every piece of research into defendants discloses a subset who plead guilty while maintaining innocence, often induced to do so by the temptation of a lighter sentence. C. Yarnley, in a letter to *The Times*, June 14, 2010, said "A great many defendants can be described as of limited intellect and strength of character. The temptation to yield to the offer 'plead now and you can go home and we promise you lenient sentencing' could be overwhelming."
2. Rewarding someone for pleading guilty is morally repugnant and hypocritical, since it punishes those who exercise their right to trial.
3. Before the 1994 Act, magistrates, who do 95 per cent of sentencing, managed without discounts so I cannot see why they should be expected to give them now.
4. Scottish judges traditionally considered sentencing discounts immoral and inappropriate and spoke out against them.
5. Research by Henham found that the application of the discount was erratic in both the Crown Court and in magistrates' courts.

In his 2001 Review, Auld L.J. reiterated the Royal Commission's call for a formalised system of graduated sentencing discounts for guilty pleas, coupled with a system of advanced indication of sentence. The Government responded, in *Justice for All* (2002) that it intended to introduce a clearer tariff of sentence discounts. This is not incorporated in the CJA 2003. Section 144 requires the sentencing court to take account of the timing and circumstances of the guilty plea. Where the accused has been given an indication of sentence by magistrates, as explained below, no court may impose a custodial sentence, but apart from this, a sentence indication is *not* binding on a court and will not provide grounds of appeal.

In accordance with Auld L.J.'s recommendations, the newly created Sentencing Guidelines Council (now Sentencing Council) published guidance on its website, on a graduated discount structure for guilty pleas, to be applied by all courts from January 2005 (s.172, CJA 2003). The main elements are as follows.

1. The court considers remorse and any other mitigating factors and calculates the appropriate sentence. It also takes into consideration any other admitted offences (TICs).
2. The court discounts the sentence in accordance with a sliding scale: a maximum of one third for a plea at the first reasonable opportunity (in the police station); a maximum of one quarter discount after the trial date is set or a one tenth discount if the accused changes his plea to guilty at the court door or at trial.
3. Of course there is no discount if the accused is found guilty after trial.
4. The sliding scale applies even if the accused is caught red handed.

In *R. v Goodyear (Practice Note)* [2005] EWCA Crim 888, a five judge CA laid down guidelines on what judges should now do in the light of this "different culture". Re-emphasising the principle that the defendant's plea must be made voluntarily and free from any improper pressure, they said a defendant *could* seek an advance indication of sentence. The judge should confine himself to indicating the maximum sentence for a plea of guilty at that point and could only act at the request of the defendant, not on his own initiative or that of the defence lawyer. The judge could refuse an indication but, once given, it was binding on him or any other judge who became responsible for the case. The judge should never be invited to give an indication on the basis of a plea bargain. He should not be asked to indicate levels of sentence dependent on different pleas. The defence advocate was personally responsible for ensuring that his client fully appreciated that he should not plead guilty unless he was guilty, and that any indication remained subject to the AG's right to appeal against an unduly lenient sentence. Any agreed basis of plea should be reduced into writing before an indication was sought. If there were no agreement, there should be a hearing on the disputed facts, in front of the judge (called a *Newton* hearing). Any sentence indication should normally be given at a case management hearing and should be in open court and recorded. It would be wise to see how these new arrangements settled in at the Crown Court before copying the procedure in the magistrates' court.

Although the guidelines warn Crown Court judges against taking part in any apparent plea bargain, these graduated sentencing discounts are designed to encourage early guilty pleas and will encourage bargaining between prosecution and defence. Those of us who oppose plea bargaining have irretrievably lost the battle. In support of the system, sentencing discounts at least have the virtue of transparency—to offenders, judges, magistrates, victims and the public—on the Sentencing Council website. The scheme is highly unlikely, however, to produce consistency in sentencing, because sentencers will differ, as research shows they have done, in deciding on the starting point: the appropriate full, undiscounted sentence. The CA has warned judges that while a guideline is only a guideline, it is incumbent on the sentencing judge to explain why he is not following it, if he chooses not to do so: *R. v Bowering* [2005] EWCA Crim 3215; *R. v Gisbourne* [2005] EWCA Crim 2491.

In the summer of 2006, a case where a man had raped a small **12–046** baby but was given the automatic one third sentence discount, despite being caught in the act, caused a public outcry and the *Sun* newspaper waged a campaign against judges (described in the chapter on judges). The AG referred the case to the CA as unduly lenient. The CA said that the trial judge had been correct in applying the one third discount: *Att Gen's Reference (Nos 14 and 15 of 2006) (Tanya French and Alan Robert Webster)* [2006] EWCA Crim 1335. Following consultation, the Sentencing Guidelines Council (as it then was) amended the guidelines. They emphasise that reductions are recommendations not maximums and where the evidence is overwhelming (D caught red handed) only a 20 per cent discount need be given. The paper asked, for example, whether the discount should be disposed of for people who are caught red handed, where the prosecution case is so overwhelming that they have no grounds for pleading not guilty.

Justice Minister Ken Clarke caused a public outcry and calls for his sacking in May 2011 by repeating a proposal for a 50 per cent discount for defendants (he referred to rapists) who plead guilty and suggesting that some rapes were not "proper rapes". He had said in his 2010 legal aid consultation paper, referred to in Ch.17, below:

"[W]e have already asked the Sentencing Council to consider how sentence discounts might form part of a package of measures to encourage those who acknowledge their guilt to do so at the earliest opportunity. The earlier the guilty plea, the less trauma likely to be suffered by victims and witnesses at the prospect of giving evidence in court; and the lower the costs to the courts and other agencies".

The proposal was withdrawn in June 2011 but his legal aid consultation paper 2010, discussed in Ch.17, proposes a restructuring of advocates fees to encourage early guilty pleas and in his 2010 Administration of Justice Review, Lord Judge C.J. said "the criminal justice system must do all it can to encourage those who are guilty to plead at the earliest opportunity".

Extreme bargaining

12–047   Prosecutors have up their sleeves an even bigger incentive to offer defendants to help them than the astonishing 30 per cent discount routinely offered for a guilty plea. At common law, the prosecutor has always had power to grant immunity to someone against whom there is sufficient evidence to prosecute. This occurs where a prosecution witness offers to "turn Queen's evidence" and give evidence on behalf of the Crown, the prosecution, against a co-accused, in exchange for total or partial immunity from prosecution. English law gives enormous discretion to the police and to prosecutors, as described above. In 2006, the ELS took an alarming leap by introducing formalised US style plea bargaining. As a result of its *Fraud Review—Final Report*, the Government announced plans to introduce statutory binding pre-trial bargains. Witness immunity or short sentences may be offered to minor defendants in exchange for evidence against key defendants. This was supported by the Financial Services Authority, because of concern over the high level of city fraud but Lake warned that English law came unstuck previously, with the use of the "supergrass" system in Northern Ireland, by making similar offers in order to obtain evidence against alleged terrorists. Hundreds of convictions were overturned because the system was perceived to be open to abuse. Unsurprisingly, appellants pointed out that their convictions were obtained by relying on witnesses who had gained from massive incentives to give evidence against them. Nevertheless, by 2008, the Attorney General was consulting on a framework for plea negotiation in fraud. This smacked of desperation. The consultation paper overtly acknowledged concern about the cost of running fraud trials, the collapse of many expensive jury trials, as described in Ch.16 on the jury, and the low guilty plea rate compared with other common law countries. Lord Judge C.J. described the outcome in his 2010 *Review of the Administration of Justice*:

> "In May 2009, an amendment to the *Consolidated Criminal Practice Direction* was handed down. This governs the conduct of cases in which the prosecution and defence have sought to follow the Attorney General's *Guidelines on Plea Discussions in Cases of Serious or Complex Fraud*. These enable the prosecution and defence to discuss acceptable pleas before charges are brought, and to make joint submissions as to the appropriate sentencing

authorities and applicable sentencing ranges. The practice direction followed liaison with the Attorney General's Office as to the content of the Attorney General's guidelines. . ."

Also, the Serious Organised Crime and Police Act 2005, ss.71–75 introduced a type of statutory formalised extreme plea bargaining. Prosecutors can give contractual immunity from prosecution, undertakings about the use of evidence and offer reduced sentences in exchange for assistance with investigations. In *R. v P; R. v Blackburn* [2007] EWCA Crim 2290 the CA gave guidelines on applying ss.71–75. In 2009, Corker and others noted that "there is no desire to utilise ss. 71 or 72 in preference to the common law regime" but Grazia and Hyland, in 2011, a former US prosecutor and a CPS prosecutor strongly advocated greater use of ss.73 and 74 and explained a detailed US blueprint of "golden rules" developed by US prosecutors. They argued these should be copied by the UK in using the evidence of such "assisting offenders", as they are called, to safeguard against the "disastrous" collapse of the Northern Irish supergrass system. They support the system as a prosecuting tool, citing cases such as the defendant who enjoyed immunity in exchange for testimony against gang members who had killed 11-year-old Rhys Jones in Liverpool in 2007, and *R. v Bevans* [2009] EWCA Crim 2554, a gangland murderer who received a five year discount from a life sentence, for inculcating a corrupt police officer. Of course, they pointed out that it must be born in mind that if a witness is at risk, "co-operation triggers a life-long obligation to provide protection".

In *R. v D* [2010] EWCA Crim 1485 [2010] Crim. L.R. 725, after being sentenced for importing drugs and given a 20 per cent sentence discount, D entered into an agreement under the SOC and Police Act 2005, to provide details of 32 other drug traffickers. He did not agree to give evidence and did not provide full admissions of all his criminal activities. He applied to the Crown Court for his sentence to be reviewed. The judge considered a *further* 25 per cent discount was appropriate but D considered this insufficient. He thought he was due the "normal" discount of 50–66 per cent. The CA said that, as a matter of principle, any discount must be based on the value to the administration of justice, not on whether D had carried out his agreement, which was "much less comprehensive than it might have been". The risk to D from his former gangland colleagues was less than it would have been had he given evidence, as in *Blackburn* (2008). The judge should go back to the original starting point: the sentence that reflected his criminality.

It has been common practice to offer common law immunity or **12–048** sentence discounts to those who have given evidence against other offenders and the courts have upheld their part of the bargain by giving astonishingly generous discounts, typified by *R. v A* [2006] EWCA Crim 1803 where the CA said the courts were prepared to assist the authorities by giving discounts up to *two thirds*, depending on the quality of the material. These deals will continue, in addition to those under the statutory scheme.

In a recent case though, the train hurtling down the track into US-style plea deals was derailed. In *R. v Innospec Ltd* [2010] Crim. L.R. 665, the sentencing judge was Thomas L.J. An Anglo-American company pleaded guilty to corruption. The British subsidiary entered into a plea agreement with the Serious Fraud office to pay a confiscation order of $6.7 million and a civil recovery order of $6 million and the US company entered into a plea agreement with federal prosecutors, to pay $14 million in fines. Thomas L.J. determined that there was a problem with the plea agreement. Under the law of England and Wales, the prosecutor (SFO) could not enter into an agreement as to penalty. Sentencing submissions could not include a specific sentence or agreed range and that was made clear by the Consolidated Criminal Practice Direction and AG's guidelines on plea discussions in serious or complex fraud. The Practice Direction reflected the *constitutional principle* that, save in matters such as motoring offences, the imposition of a sentence was a matter for the judiciary. For transparency, a court must rigorously examine the basis of plea in open court to see whether it reflected the public interest. Judges who specialise in trying serious fraud were agreed that there was a place for plea bargaining in England and Wales. They were reluctant to develop a fully fledged US system but R.F. Julian comments that our pre-trial management system would accommodate it.

Cases heard in the magistrates' court

12–049   The Criminal Law Act 1977 divided offences into three categories: offences triable only on indictment in the Crown Court; offences triable only summarily in the magistrates' court; and between those two, offences triable either way. The Criminal Justice Act 1988 added a fourth category, summary offences triable on indictment. As I pointed out in 1997, in "An Essay on the Importance and Neglect of the Magistracy", in the twentieth century Parliament repeatedly downgraded indictable offences to triable either way, and triable either way offences to summary offences, thus shifting criminal business down onto the shoulders of the magistrates. Also, when new offences are created they tend to be summary or triable either way, thus guaranteeing that all of the first category and most of the second will be heard by magistrates. They now deal with over 95 per cent of criminal business from start to finish.

It should be obvious from that statistic that magistrates' work is not all trivial, although many people imagine this to be the case, including, unfortunately, many judges and lawyers.

The most obvious summary offences are almost all Road Traffic Act offences; drunk and disorderly behaviour; assaults such as common assault; minor criminal damage cases and cases prosecuted by government departments or agencies. Procedure in the magistrates' court is called summary procedure. Any case is now commenced by a written charge issued by the prosecutor and a requisition/summons requiring them to appear in the magistrates' court (CJA 2003, Pt 4). The Road Traffic Act allows defendants to motoring offences to plead guilty by post, avoiding a court appearance. Duty solicitors, private practitioners now funded by the Criminal Defence Service, are meant to be available, at each magistrates' court.

Speeding cases through the magistrates' court—the guilty plea

When the accused appears before the court, he is asked if he **12–050** pleads guilty or not guilty. The vast majority of offenders plead guilty. In 2009, there were 1.79 million defendants but only 180,000 trials following a not guilty plea (*Judicial and Court Statistics*). If he pleads guilty, he may be convicted and sentenced immediately, unless the magistrates require more information on the defendant, in which case they will adjourn for the preparation of a medical or psychiatric report, or a pre-sentence report, prepared by a probation officer or social worker.

The 1997 Narey Report on delay recommended various measures to speed criminal cases through the courts, responding to a concern that an "adjournment culture" pervaded most magistrates' courts. Sections of the Crime and Disorder Act 1998 are designed as time-saving measures. Under s.43, time-limits may be set. Section 46 provides that where a person is bailed (by the police) to appear before a magistrates' court, his appearance should be set for the next available court sitting so someone arrested on a Thursday night should appear before the court on Friday morning. If they plead guilty, they should normally be sentenced there and then. By 2008, the Ministry of Justice were operating a "simple, speedy, summary justice" scheme, claiming that the time from charge to conclusion of a case in the MC was 45 days, down from 62 days in March 2007 but their own researchers questioned this claim, at academic conferences. Nevertheless, Lord Judge C.J. claimed the initiative to be a success, relying on the official statistic, and explained:

"The very idea of a Magistrates' Court is that it should administer summary justice locally. The system was becoming bogged down in far too much process, and a tendency for relatively minor cases to be treated as if they were the trial of the century. Magistrates appointed to apply robust common sense were finding that because of interminable adjournments patience was a more valuable qualification for office than robustness." (Speech, November 2008).

An experiment with virtual courts commenced in 2009. Once a person is charged with an offence at a police station, they appear on a video link to a magistrates' court within two hours. The legal framework is the Police and Justice Act 2006. The government says that defendants are able to opt for real court hearings but Keogh, 2009, objected that research showed that they often did not know their rights. Under the same scheme in immigration and asylum cases, the British Refugee Council found that over 87 per cent of detainees did not know that they could request to appear in person. Keogh said 50 per cent of police station detainees are not represented. The pilot evaluation report was published in December 2010. The decision to expand this system was criticised, in the *New Law Journal* and other legal news journals, since they cost more.

"The findings indicate that the pilot was successful in reducing the average time from charge to first hearing, failure to appear rates and prisoner transportation and police cell costs. However, these savings were exceeded by costs of the pilot, particularly those associated with the technology used." (Ministry of Justice.)

The number of adjournments and hearings was more than the comparator; it was harder for prosecution and defence to communicate; the 15 minute time slots were perceived by magistrates and district judges to cause hasty justice; some magistrates and judges thought it was more difficult to impose authority remotely and so the defendant did not take it seriously and the representation rate was lower.

The not guilty plea and summary trial

12–051   If they plead not guilty, the defendant's first appearance may take the form of an early administrative hearing, under the Crime and Disorder Act 1998 s.50, at which their eligibility for criminal legal aid may be determined. Such hearings may be conducted by a single magistrate or a justices' clerk, or a legal adviser (court clerk) acting under delegated powers, including a lot of judicial trial management powers which are likely to be exercised at a later hearing called a pre-trial review. For instance, at an EAH or pre-trial review, a clerk may renew bail on conditions previously imposed. I have expressed concern about giving these judicial powers to clerks (see Ch.15 on magistrates). The Courts Act 2003, s.45, places on a statutory basis pre-trial case management hearings which have been held since the 1970s, as a matter of practice. If a plea of not guilty is entered, the prosecutor will outline the case against the accused, then call witnesses to substantiate that accusation. They may be cross-examined by the defence. Any witness may now give evidence by live video link from anywhere in the UK, provided that the court considers it to be in the best interests of efficient and effective administration of justice: Criminal Procedure Rules, Pt 29. The Met welcomed this way of permitting the police to give evidence.

No case to answer

As the onus of proving guilt is on the prosecution, it follows that **12–052** at the conclusion of the prosecution case, the defence may submit to the magistrates that there is "no case to answer". This submission means, simply, that the evidence produced by the prosecution does not prove that the defendant has committed the offence with which he is charged. It is up to the prosecution to establish guilt, not for the defendant to convict himself out of his own mouth. If the magistrates uphold that submission, the case is dismissed. If not, the case for the defence is then presented. The defendant may choose to enter the witness box, give evidence and be cross-examined; defence witnesses will be called; the prosecutor may cross-examine them and the magistrates will decide whether or not the evidence is sufficient for them to convict. If so, they may sentence the defendant. If they are considering custody or one of the alternatives, they will adjourn for a pre-sentence report. If they decide to acquit, the case is dismissed.

Legal advice/magistrates' powers

Magistrates can call for the assistance of their court clerk (legal **12–053** adviser) if the case raises issues of law or mixed fact and law and they can ask her advice on sentencing. This is explained in the chapter on magistrates. The maximum penalty open to the magistrates, unless a specific statute provides otherwise, is six months' imprisonment, and/or a £5,000 fine. If a defendant is convicted of two or more offences at the same hearing the magistrates have power to send him to prison for 12 months. If magistrates discover they have made a mistake, they may re-open a case to vary a sentence. They may send a convicted defendant to the Crown Court for sentencing, if they feel their powers are inadequate. Had the CJA 2003, s.282 come into force, it would have doubled the magistrates' maximum sentencing power to one year's custody for a single offence. Magistrates who were the subject of research by

Herbert were opposed to this change. Many felt they were already being asked to handle cases at the extreme of their ability. It has not been brought into force by 2011.

Young offenders 10–17

12–054   Most young offenders are tried in the youth court, which is a separate part of the magistrates' court. The courtroom is informal, normally with all participants on the same level and the accused sitting next to his appropriate adult and addressed by his first name. Magistrates' and judges are trained to "engage" with the young person and will speak directly to him. They must sit as a mixed-gender bench, although a district judge will sit alone. When Juvenile Courts were introduced in 1908, the intention was that they would be housed in a separate building, but this has not been achieved, other than in big cities (see Ch.7). The public are excluded and press-reporting restrictions may be imposed. Ball et al. cite research demonstrating that young offenders and their families can be confused as to court personnel, and observed that good practice requires the chairman to explain their functions.

Offences triable either way—mode of trial, "case allocation"

12–055   Where an adult accused is charged with an "either way" offence, a decision must be taken whether to allocate it to summary trial in the magistrates' court or trial on indictment in the Crown Court. Under the Magistrates' Courts Act 1980, the magistrates can send the case up to the Crown Court if they consider it too serious or complex for them but in most instances, they are content to accept jurisdiction. In this event, the accused is then given the choice as to mode of trial. The CJA 2003, Sch.3 introduced provisions to make magistrates' and the accused's decision-making on mode of trial better informed, following the recommendations of Auld L.J. Before deciding on mode of trial, the magistrates should be told of the accused's previous convictions. They must give prosecution and defence a chance to air their views and take account of the allocation guidelines issued by the Sentencing Council. If the court decides the case is suitable for summary trial, they must explain so, in ordinary language, to the accused and tell him he can choose a Crown Court trial but that, if the charge is of a certain violent or sexual offence, they can still commit him to the Crown Court for sentence if, having tried the case, they think their sentencing powers are too low.

The accused can then request an indication of the sentence he might get if he were to plead guilty in the magistrates' court, but the court is not obliged to provide this. If they do, they must allow the accused an opportunity to reconsider his plea, which he will have entered in the plea before venue procedure. If the accused does not change his plea, the CJA 2003 makes it clear that any sentence indication is not binding on a later court.

The vast majority of defendants who have an option choose to have the case tried by magistrates and the amendments to the allocation procedure were designed to provide more information to the magistrates and the accused, in the hope of persuading magistrates to keep more cases in their court and persuading even more defendants to choose summary trial in the magistrates' court. In Ch.16 on juries, the story is told of attempts to remove the accused's choice as to mode of trial. The Conservative government of the early 1990s was concerned to prevent trivial cases where the accused ends up pleading guilty going up to the Crown Court and wasting precious resources. Instead of abolishing the accused's right to choose jury trial, they introduced the plea before venue procedure, below. The Labour administration of Tony Blair tried to deal with the same problem, as told in Ch.16 on the jury, and now history is repeating itself. The Minister of Justice said, in his 2010 legal aid consultation (paraphrased):

"Too many criminal cases that could adequately be dealt with in the magistrates' court are going to the Crown Court. Increasing numbers of those cases go on to plead guilty, often at a late stage in the proceedings. This is inefficient and ineffective for the criminal justice system as a whole and does not represent best value in legal aid expenditure (Chapter 6).

In 2006–09, the number of cases received for trial in the Crown Court increased by 26% and the number of guilty pleas rose by 35%. Most were either way cases. 73% of either way cases at the Crown Court pleaded guilty, costing £1,700 average, or just over £3,200 for a cracked trial, compared with £295 at the magistrates' court. 60% of sentenced either way cases were within magistrates' eligibility limits. The number of defendants proceeded with at the magistrates' courts fell by 13%." (The paper is summarised and discussed in Ch.17.)

Lord Judge C.J. voiced the very same concern in his February 2010 Review of the Administration of Justice. In a November 2010 speech, Leveson L.J. said:

"Excluding the costs of legal aid for the accused, it may not be unrealistic to say that the average cost of trials in the Crown Court is nine times that of trials in the magistrates court. With legal costs, it will obviously be higher."

The plea before venue procedure

12–056   Section 49 of the Criminal Procedure and Investigations Act 1996 requires the magistrates, before determining mode of trial in triable either way cases, to ascertain the accused's plea. Where he indicates a not guilty plea, they must proceed to deal with the case summarily. Where the accused pleads not guilty, as explained above, they may choose to send the case up to the Crown Court or, where they decline to do so, they must still give the defendant the option of summary trial or trial on indictment at the Crown Court. In other words, if the defendant expresses an intention to plead guilty, he loses the right to opt for the Crown Court. The magistrates must hear the case but retain the right to send it up to the Crown Court for sentence, where they feel their own sentencing powers are too low. There is of course, nothing to prevent the accused from indicating a not guilty plea at this stage, then changing his plea to guilty at the Crown Court. In such cases, the section fails to achieve its desired objective, hence the introduction of the graduated sentencing discount to induce early guilty pleas, described above, and hence the 2010–11 concern of the Justice Minister, quoted above.

Sending young offenders to the Crown Court

12–057   Young offenders will only be sent to the Crown Court for trial if certain conditions are satisfied under Sch.3 of the CJA 2003, or other statutes. Thomas endeavoured to explain the complex rules applicable from 2005. He comments "It might be possible to devise a more convoluted scheme than this, but only with great difficulty."

1. A defendant under 18 must be sent to the Crown Court if he is charged with murder or manslaughter, or has committed certain firearms offences.
2. He must be sent if charged jointly with an adult or if called as a witness and so on.
3. If none of these conditions is satisfied but the offence is one to which s.91 of the Powers of the Criminal Courts (Sentencing) Act 2000 applies, the court must follow the plea before venue procedure. If he pleads not guilty and the court considers that, if convicted, it ought to be possible to sentence him to detention under s.91, or if the offence is a specified offence and he may be given a sentence to protect the public or an extended sentence, then he should be sent to the Crown Court. In all other cases he must be tried summarily.
4. If he has pleaded guilty and been convicted in the magistrates' court, he may be sent to the Crown Court for sentencing under certain circumstances and if the court feels the Crown Court has the power to sentence to detention. This

power does not apply to a young person who has been found guilty after trial.
5. He should be sent to the Crown Court if he has committed a "specified offence" and the court considers he qualifies for a sentence of detention for public protection or an extended sentence of detention.

When magistrates tried to apply the criteria, derived from old and new statutes, their legal advisers realised that the statutes gave them clashing obligations. In an appeal to the Divisional Court, Rose L.J., by now running out of patience with the avalanche of new legislation on criminal procedure that he had been obliged to interpret since 1997, was sympathetic:

"The provisions are not merely labyrinthine, they are manifestly inconsistent with each other. The most inviting course for the court. . .is to hold up their hands and say 'the Holy Grail of rational interpretation is impossible to find'".

Indictable offences at the Crown Court: Section 51 of the Crime and Disorder Act 1998

After previous failed statutory attempts, this section removed 12–058 committal proceedings for indictable offences, from 2001. Narey found that indictable cases wasted much of their time in the magistrates' court. Since 2001 there is a simple preliminary hearing in the magistrates' court, before two or three justices. Its purpose is to decide the defendant's remand status and deal with legal representation. Magistrates will usually hear a full bail application at such a hearing and may adjourn the hearing if there is insufficient information before them. Committals in either way cases were abolished by the CJA 2003 which extended s.51 of the 1998 Act, below, though this was not implemented.

Crown Court: plea and case management hearing

For all defendants at the Crown Court (except in cases of fraud 12–059 which have a special procedure under the Criminal Procedure Rules, Pt 15) they have been required, since the mid 1990s, to appear at a proceeding designed to prepare for trial and fix the date. In all class one or serious or complex cases, the prosecution provides a summary, identifying issues of law and fact and estimating trial length. The arraignment takes place at the hearing: the defendant enters a plea of guilty or not guilty to each of the charges. Following a not guilty plea, the parties are expected to inform the court of such matters as: witnesses, defence witnesses whose written statements are accepted, admitted facts, any alibi, points of law and special requirements for the trial (for example, live video links for child witnesses) and these requirements are now embodied in the case management and progression rules of the Criminal Procedure Rules, Pt 3.

If the plea is "guilty", the judge should, if possible, proceed to sentence the defendant, after hearing his plea in mitigation. This is a plea for leniency, allowing the defendant to argue any partial excuses or explanation for his admitted offences. If the judge or recorder is considering imposing a custodial sentence or non-custodial alternative, she may require a pre-sentence report to be prepared, or, where appropriate, a medical or psychiatric report. Since 1999–2000, various Crown Court centres have abandoned oral PCMHs in small class four cases and the issues are dealt with in writing. Virtual plea and directions hearings, via a secure internal website are an alternative.

Auld L.J. recommended a move away from pre-trial hearings towards standard timetables and co-operation between the parties. The Criminal Procedure Rules and the Effective Trial Management Programme now dispose of the need for PCMHs in many cases because it is up to the court's Case Progression Officer to monitor trial preparation in most cases, keeping the court abreast of timetable developments. It is up to the lawyers to certify trial readiness.

Fitness to plead

12–060   Where there is doubt as to the accused's mental capacity to understand and participate effectively in the trial, the issue of fitness to plead is now determined by the court, sitting without a jury, since the Domestic Violence, Crime and Victims Act 2004, ss.22–25, amended the Criminal Procedure (Insanity) Act 1964.

Trial on indictment at the Crown Court

Judges terminating trials; appeals against judges' terminating rulings

12–061   One of the big advantages to the defendant of a trial in the Crown Court is that the pre-trial legal argument stage provides a realistic opportunity for the case to be dismissed on the order of the trial judge, in an ordered or directed acquittal. Indeed, in 2009, 60 per cent of those pleading not guilty were discharged by the judge and a further nine per cent were acquitted on the direction of the judge: *Judicial and Court Statistics*. This is one of the elements which contribute to the acquittal rate in the Crown Court being significantly higher than that in the magistrates' court. When the prosecution appear at court and offer no evidence, the judge *orders* an acquittal and one of the biggest factors causing this is the non-appearance of a crucial witness, or their retraction of evidence. Baldwin found that this was foreseeable in many such collapsed cases and the prosecution could have been withdrawn at an earlier stage. It was doubtless research such as this which prompted the new special measures for vulnerable witnesses, described above.

A judge may *direct* an acquittal during the trial. Mostly, this happens at the close of the prosecution case when the defence have successfully invited the judge to find that there is not a sufficient case to convict the defendant, in a submission of "no case to answer". This may be decided on a point of law, or an assessment of the sufficiency of the evidence. Also, legal argument may take place at any time in the trial, where the judge is asked to rule on a point of law or evidence in the absence of the jury, in a "voir dire" hearing (a trial within a trial). When the prosecution depends on poor quality, unsupported identification evidence, the judge must direct an acquittal. Otherwise, the judge's task is to consider, without usurping the jury's function, whether there is evidence upon which a reasonable jury could convict. Directed acquittals are caused mainly by inadequate or untrustworthy witnesses but also by legal problems and evidential insufficiency (Baldwin). In *R. v Brown* [2001] EWCA Crim 961, the CA held that the judge is under a duty to keep under review whether to direct an acquittal, such power to be sparingly exercised, and should do so if satisfied that no jury on the evidence could safely convict. He may not prevent the prosecution bringing their case because he thinks the defence is likely to be believed: *Att Gen's Ref No.2 of 2000* [2001] Cr. App. R. 36.

If the judge upholds the defence submission and directs an acquittal, the prosecution did not, in the past, have the power to appeal. Pattenden powerfully argued that this meant that any wrongfully directed acquittal by the judge had to go unchallenged, which was unfair for the victim, witnesses and public. Prosecutors had much more extensive rights of appeal in some common law and European civil law jurisdictions. The Law Commission's Report, *Double Jeopardy and Prosecution Appeals* (No.267, 2001) recommended that where the judge acquitted on a point of law, the prosecution ought to have a right of appeal against an acquittal. This was accepted by the Government. Consequently the CJA 2003, Pt 9, introduced a prosecution right of appeal, in certain offences, against a judge's evidentiary ruling which has terminated the trial before a jury has been convened or during the prosecution case, or as a result of a defence submission of "no case to answer". The Act also introduced a prosecution right to appeal against a judge's ruling which has been made at any time before the close of the prosecution case. The CA may affirm the ruling and acquit the defendant, remit the case to the trial court, or order a retrial, where they think it is in the interests of justice to do so. The grounds for overturning a trial judge's ruling are if it was wrong in law, involved an error of law or principle, or was unreasonable. See now Pattenden 2009. See also Ormerod et al., 2010. They examined prosecution appeals on rulings made in Crown Court trials. They found that, although this created an unintentionally wide route of appeal, there was little danger of this exacerbating the CACD's "already unhealthy workload". (The CACD Annual Report 2009–10, December 2010, is on the Judiciary website and reports a five per cent increase in workload.)

12–062   A judge may stop a trial at any time, if he thinks adverse publicity may endanger the impartiality of the jury. This happened very controversially in 2001, to the trial of Leeds United footballers Lee Bowyer and Jonathan Woodgate, accused of beating an Asian student unconscious. The jury had already deliberated for 21 hours at the end of a nine week trial, costing £8 million, when the *Sunday Mirror* published an interview with the victim's father, alleging that it was a racist attack. The judge reported the newspaper to the Attorney General, who alone has the power to prosecute them for contempt of court.

Jury trial

12–063   If the plea is "not guilty" the court swears in 12 jurors, who will be responsible at the end of the trial for deciding whether the accused is guilty or not guilty. Once the jury is sworn in, the prosecution will open the case by outlining the facts and then calling the prosecution witnesses to give evidence to prove those facts. The defence can cross-examine all such witnesses. Undisputed evidence can be admitted by written statement. At the close of the prosecution case the defence counsel has the right, as described above, to submit "no case to answer", i.e. to argue that there is insufficient evidence upon which the jury can convict. Only the judge can invite the jury to acquit at this point: *R. v Speechley* [2004] EWCA Crim 307.

Unless such a submission is successful, the defence advocate presents the defence case and calls witnesses for the defence, possibly including the defendant. These witnesses too can be cross-examined on their evidence. The accused is not required to give evidence. This rule is called the right to silence and is discussed above.

The judge, of course, has a duty to ensure that the trial is conducted fairly and that inadmissible or irrelevant evidence is excluded. The CA has held that the judge had a duty to impose time-limits where counsel indulged in prolix or repetitious questioning on matters which were not really in issue: *R. v B* [2005] EWCA 54. In 2005, one judge provided a training exercise in how not to conduct a trial fairly, through three highly publicised CA decisions. In one case he demonstrated his preference for the prosecution case by rolling his eyes, throwing down his pen during the defence and treating prosecution witnesses much more politely: *R. v Patrick Bryant* [2005] EWCA Crim 2079; in another case he told the defence counsel that she was being silly, in front of the jury, and he showed personal animosity towards her and questioned her integrity: *R. v Lashley* [2005] EWCA Crim 2016. In the third, he told defence counsel, in front of the defendant and before hearing from the prosecution, that he had "never heard of such rubbish" as the defence version of events: *R. v. Dickens* [2005] EWCA Crim 2017. Later, *R. v Cordingley* [2007] EWCA Crim 2174 and [2008] Crim. L.R. 299 was a horrendous case of judicial bad behaviour, in which the CA said the judge "should be ashamed" of his rudeness and discourtesy. Pre-trial, he queried several times why a trial estimate of three days was necessary and warned he would require an explanation for the waste of court time at the end of the trial. Counsel was refused 10 minutes to marshal his papers after transfer from another courtroom. Although D was of previous good character and had been on bail, bail was withdrawn. The judge refused to direct that D should be given the clean clothes that had been brought for him. The defendant consequently remained in the same clothes until the afternoon of the third day and broke down in tears in the witness box because he had not been allowed to shower or change. He was convicted. The CA quashed the conviction, saying the safety of the conviction did not depend just upon the safety of the evidence but on the observance of due process.

When the final speeches by the prosecution and defence advocate **12–064** have been made, the judge "sums up" the evidence for the benefit of the jury. This summing-up and the judge's direction on law is the last speech which the jury hear before they retire to consider their verdict. In it, the judge has to balance the arguments of the prosecution and the defence, but leave the jury to decide on the issue of guilt, beyond reasonable doubt, of the accused. In complex cases and in many murder cases, the judge will give the jury written directions, approved by the advocates.

Juries must be left to deliberate in secret. They may not discuss the trial with outsiders at any time, nor may they bring in extraneous material. If jurors disobey these instructions or if a juror alleges during or after the trial that another juror has acted wrongly, the CA may "go behind" the verdict to examine the allegation of impropriety, as discussed in Ch.16 on the jury, but no juror may be questioned without leave of the CA. It is a contempt of court to question jurors, under the Contempt of Court Act 1981, s.8.

As a result of the abolition of the requirement for a unanimous verdict, by the Criminal Justice Act 1967, it is possible for the judge to accept a majority verdict of the jury, provided that there are not more than two in the minority. If there are three or more in the minority this is known as a "hung jury" and the trial is abandoned. It is then up to the prosecution whether to request a retrial. The judge will only stop this if he considers it an abuse of process. Normally prosecutions are abandoned after two juries have hung but there is nothing in law stopping a retrial.

If the jury has dropped to 11 or 10 in number, there can be a majority verdict if there is not more than one dissenter. Every effort is made, however, to obtain a unanimous verdict and the jury must have been out for at least two hours before the judge is able to accept a majority verdict. If the verdict is "not guilty" the accused is immediately discharged; if the verdict is "guilty", then after a plea in mitigation by his counsel, and, usually, pre-sentence reports, he will be sentenced by the judge. A sentencing hearing may be conducted by video link from prison.

Trial by judge alone

12–065 Following recommendations by Auld L.J., the Criminal Justice Bill 2003 aimed to introduce a procedure for trial by judge alone, in certain circumstances. Prior to the Bill, now the 2003 Act, all Crown Court trials had to be conducted by a judge and jury. The Bill would have permitted the defendant to apply to be tried by judge alone but this clause was highly controversial and not enacted.

Under s.43 of the CJA 2003, the judge could grant a prosecution application for trial by judge alone, in serious and complex frauds. This section has never been brought into force. In March 2005, the two year £60 million Jubilee Line Extension corruption trial collapsed at the Old Bailey. This was the type of trial Auld L.J. undoubtedly had in mind when he suggested the option of judge-only trials in serious and complex cases. As a consequence of this collapse and the collapse of two other long trials, in June 2005, the AG proposed to activate s.43 by delegated legislation but failed, because the measure was deeply unpopular. He again failed to persuade Parliament via the Fraud (Trials Without a Jury) Bill, 2006–07. This attempt was deeply controversial, such is the attachment to jury trial, as explained in Ch.16 on juries.

Section 44 of the 2003 Act allows the judge to direct a judge-only trial where there is a danger of jury tampering. The judge must be satisfied that there is a "real and present danger that jury tampering would take place". The second condition is that, notwithstanding any steps that could be taken, such as police protection, the likelihood of tampering is so great as to make it necessary in the interests of justice for the trial to be conducted without a jury. The section gives examples of cases where there is a real and present danger of jury tampering: where the trial is a retrial because of a previous case involving jury tampering; where the defendant or defendants have previously been involved in a case where there has been jury tampering, or where there has been intimidation or attempted intimidation of witnesses. In 2009, the CA ruled that the requirements of the section were satisfied in the case of four defendants for a 2004 bungled armed robbery at Heathrow: *R. v T* [2010] EWCA Crim 1035. The robbery had already resulted in three trials costing £22 million. At the first trial, Twomey suffered a heart attack in prison and was severed from the indictment. At the second trial the jury were reduced to nine and failed to reach a verdict. The third collapsed after a "serious attempt at jury tampering", according to the trial judge, Calvert-Smith J. The prosecution had applied under s.44 but the judge was satisfied that the jury trial could go ahead, spending up to £6 million and using 82 police officers on jury protection, then the CA reversed the decision in 2009 and ordered a non-jury trial under s.44. The CA gave guidance on such cases, including that, when a judge dismissed a jury on a tampering allegation, he should normally order that he should conduct the trial alone, even if he had considered "public interest immunity" protected material. They held that dispensing with a jury did not offend against D's fair trial rights. See case and comment at [2010] Crim. L.R. 82. The commentator suggests that jury sequestration could have been used as an alternative—on a four month trial. Marcel Berlins, in the *Guardian* criticised the fact that the cost of an alternative jury trial was taken into account. Twomey was on trial in the Royal Courts of Justice and told the *Guardian* he felt the police had born a grudge against him after he gave evidence in a 1982 police anti-corruption inquiry. See Gibb, 2009 and 2011. In *R. v KS* [2009] EWCA Crim 2377 (comment at [2010] Crim. L.R. 643), the CA quashed a judge's decision to proceed to trial without a jury. He had sentenced co-conspirators in previous trials and some of the judge's observations in sentencing the others were specific to and critical of the appellant.

In 2002, the Law Commission suggested a two stage procedure **12–066** to prosecute multiple offences. Sample counts would be used to prosecute an offender before a judge and jury and, if convicted, the defendant would be tried by judge alone for linked offences. The Commission's work on fraud highlighted the difficulty of prosecuting multiple fraud offences. This suggestion resulted in s.13 of The Domestic Violence, Crime and Victims Act 2004. This permits the prosecution to apply for trial by jury of sample counts on an indictment where there are so many counts that trial by jury of all of them would be impracticable. If the jury convicts on a sample count, the other counts may be tried by judge alone. Again, this measure is controversial, in eroding jury trial, but commentators appeared to fail to notice its passage through Parliament.

Trial of young defendants in the Crown Court

12–067 In *T and V v UK* [2000] 2 All E.R. 1024, the ECtHR agreed that the formality and ritual of the Crown Court trial must have been intimidating and incomprehensible to 11-year-old children in their murder trial and so their Art.6 rights had been violated. Consequently, in 2000, the Lord Chief Justice issued a Practice Direction requiring that youth trials should take account of the age, maturity and development of the defendant. For instance, robes, wigs and police uniform should not normally be worn; participants should be on the same level; the young defendant should be able to sit near their family or guardians and they should be given regular breaks. The court is not open to members of the public. The victim may wish to attend. See further *SC v UK* (C-60958/00) (2005) E.H.R.R. 10, where an 11-year-old child with learning difficulties had had little understanding of the trial. The same publicity restrictions apply as described above in the youth court. The Children and Young Persons Act 1933, as amended, provides that nothing may be published which is likely to lead members of the public to identify a person (victim/witness/defendant) under 18. This may require preventing the naming of adults involved.

Appeals and judicial review from the magistrates' court

12–068 The whole appeal structure in criminal proceedings is a completely confusing mess. Spencer (2006), argued that the present appeal system is illogical and contained in 10 different statutes. In 2007, the Law Commission published a consultation paper, *The High Court's Jurisdiction in Relation to Criminal Proceedings* (Law Com. CP 184). See editorial comment at [2008] Crim. L.R. 175. Nothing came of it. The editor of the Crim. L.R. reported, in September 2010, that the Law Commission said it would not proceed with its proposals on sorting out rights of appeal to the HC because of opposition but, he commented, there was a strong case for rethinking and review of the appeal system, though it is unlikely to happen at the moment unless cost savings are guaranteed. This was apparent from Auld L.J.'s thorough examination of appeals in his 2001 Review.

The convicted defendant has an unqualified right to appeal to the Crown Court on fact and/or sentence. The appeal will be heard by a circuit judge or a recorder accompanied by two lay magistrates who must accept the judge's rulings on law. They conduct a complete rehearing of the case. The witnesses give their evidence again.

The Crown Court has a duty to give reasons: *R. v Kingston Crown Court Ex p. Bell* (2000) 164 J.P. 633. If a point of law has been argued before the court, they may agree to state a case for the consideration of the Queen's Bench Divisional Court.

Alternatively, either side (prosecution following an acquittal or the defendant following a conviction) may appeal to the Divisional Court of the Queen's Bench Division by way of "case stated". This means asking the magistrates to state a case for the consideration of the High Court. This case is then prepared in writing by the magistrates' legal adviser setting out the point of law which was raised, the decision of the magistrates and the reason why they decided it as they did. If the Divisional Court decides that the magistrates were wrong, it has three options: (i) it may reverse, affirm or amend the magistrates' decision; (ii) it may remit the case to the magistrates requiring them either to continue hearing the case, or to discharge or convict the accused, as appropriate; (iii) it may make such order as it thinks fit. If the prosecution succeed in such an appeal, the case may be sent back for the magistrates with a direction to convict.

The Queen's Bench Divisional Court also exercises the High Court's supervisory jurisdiction over the functioning of magistrates' court and the Crown Court when dealing with summary cases. The proceedings may be reviewed for procedural impropriety, unfairness or bias. The QBD has stated that it would prefer that convictions were challenged by way of case stated than by judicial review: *R. v Gloucester Crown Court Ex p. Chester* [1998] C.O.D. 365. A further appeal, subject to leave being obtained, is possible to the UKSC. Such cases are rare. One example is *Sheldrake*, discussed above, on reverse burdens of proof.

Post Appeal
The Criminal Appeal Act 1995 gives the Criminal Cases Review **12–069** Commission (described below) an unconditional power to refer a conviction or sentence imposed by magistrates to the Crown Court, to be treated as an appeal.

More appeals from the Crown Court
Prosecution appeals from terminating rulings are discussed **12–070** above.

Appeals by the convicted defendant
A convicted person may appeal from the Crown Court to the CA **12–071** (Criminal Division) with leave of the CA, or if the trial judge grants a certificate that the case is fit for appeal: Criminal Appeal Act 1968, s.1 as simplified by the Criminal Appeal Act 1995, s.1. He may appeal against sentence, with leave of the CA: ss.9–11. Applications

for leave to the CA are considered on paper, by a High Court judge. If the judge refuses leave, the application may be re-heard by the CA in open court. An appeal by way of case stated on a point of law may be made to Divisional Court. An application for judicial review is precluded "in matters relating to trial on indictment" but not in relation to other matters: Supreme Court Act 1981 (renamed Senior Courts Act), s.29(3).

Prosecution Applications for retrial following acquittal

12–072   The CJA 2003, Pt 10 made a controversial exception to the double jeopardy rule, which protects a person from being tried twice for the same offence. With the DPP's consent, a prosecutor may apply to the CA to quash an acquittal and order a retrial. This can be done following trial on indictment or a successful appeal. If the CA is satisfied that there is "new and compelling evidence" ("reliable" and "substantial") against the person, in relation to the offence and that it is in the interests of justice to do so, the Court must quash the acquittal and order a retrial. In determining the interests of justice, the CA must take into account, among other things, whether a fair retrial is likely and the length of time since the alleged offence was committed. The provision applies only to serious offences such as kidnapping, terrorist offences, rape, armed robbery, certain Class A drugs offences and murder and manslaughter. This enactment follows a recommendation of Auld L.J. (Review, Ch.12). He was influenced by this suggestion in the Macpherson Report on the Stephen Lawrence Inquiry, a recommendation of the House of Commons Home Affairs Select Committee and the Law Commission Report, *Double Jeopardy and Prosecution Appeals*. *R. v Dunlop* [2006] EWCA Crim 1354 was the first time the CA exercised this new power, quashing Dunlop's 1991 acquittal for the murder of Julie Hogg. He confessed to the murder in 1999. This case was well known and highly publicised at the time that Auld L.J. made his recommendation (p.67). Dunlop pleaded guilty at his retrial in 2006. In 2011, it was announced that one of the defendants acquitted of Stephen Lawrence's murder may now be retried, using this provision.

Powers of the CA in appeals against conviction by the Crown Court

Grounds

12–073   Section 2(1) of the Criminal Appeal Act 1995 amends the Criminal Appeal Act 1968 to set out simplified grounds upon which the CA may allow a criminal appeal. "The Court of Appeal: (a) shall allow an appeal against conviction if they think that the conviction is unsafe; and (b) shall dismiss such an appeal in any other case".

The 1995 amendments resulted from the recommendations of the Runciman Commission 1993, Ch.10. These were a culmination of years of criticism from JUSTICE (1989), the House of Commons Select Committee on Home Affairs (1981), academics, MPs and many others. It was repeatedly said that the grounds of appeal in the 1968 Act were narrow and ambiguous, that the CA interpreted their powers too narrowly, that they were too ready to uphold a conviction, even where they accepted there had been an irregularity at trial, and that they were too reluctant to admit fresh evidence. The Act was designed to simplify the grounds of appeal so, for instance, it was decided in s.2 to make the ground for quashing an appeal simply a determination that it was "unsafe", as it was thought that "unsafe" was a comprehensive enough term to cover all types of miscarriage of justice which should be quashed. It was left undefined, to the regret of Sir John Smith (1995). The CA very infrequently quashes a conviction on the rather vague common law ground that they have a "lurking doubt" about its safety. Leigh examines these cases. See also in-depth analysis by Pattenden (2009).

Quashing a conviction on a technicality

Where the bill of indictment was not signed, the proceedings **12–074** were invalid: *R. v Clarke* [2008] UKHL 8. It was lamentable if defendants whose guilt there was no reason to doubt escaped their just desert but the duty of the court was to apply the law and if a state exercised its coercive power to put a citizen on trial for a serious offence, a degree of formality was not out of place. It was inescapable that Parliament had intended that a bill should not become an indictment unless it was signed. P.J.T. Fields has written an excellent critique of *Clarke* and the trend it reversed—of substance over legalism. He quoted Lord Steyn in *Att Gen's reference (No.3 of 1999)* [2001] A.C. 91 that there must be fairness on all sides in a criminal case, requiring the court to consider a "triangulation of interests. . .the accused, the victim. . .and the public." He pointed out that Parliament had progressively required co-operation from the accused over 40 years:

- Alibi notice under the Criminal Justice Act 1967.
- Providing samples in drink-driving cases, under the Road Safety Act 1967.
- Amending the right of silence under the Criminal Justice and Public Order Act 1994.
- The requirement to serve a defence statement under the CPI Act 1996.
- This trend culminated in the Criminal Procedure Rules. There is a duty to co-operate. The court's job is to actively

manage cases and identify issues early. Prior to this, the Defendant could sit back and state glibly that everything was in dispute and it was up to the Crown to prove its case.

Fields then reviewed the pre-*Clarke* case law which made points such as "The days of ambushing and taking last minute technical points are gone" and "Criminal trials are no longer to be treated as a game"—cases emphasising the overriding objective of the Criminal Procedure Rules. He suggests that the 2005 Rules were, then, part of a continuing trend, not a "sea change", as they have often been called. The Auld Review 2001 said a criminal trial was not a game, under which a guilty defendant should be provided with a sporting chance. Commenting on *Clarke*, the law lords applied a literal interpretation to the statutory requirement for a signed indictment but the trend in previous cases shows that courts have not felt slaves to precedent or the value of words. The absence of a signature made not the slightest difference to the conduct of the trial. In reality, anyway, the indictment is signed by unqualified administrative staff. The decision therefore ignored Lord Steyn's "triangulation of interests".

Receiving fresh evidence

12–075   The CA may "receive any evidence which was not adduced in the proceedings from which the appeal lies" where it is necessary or expedient in the interests of justice to do so. The Court must, in considering whether to receive any evidence, have regard in particular to:

1. whether the evidence appears to the Court to be capable of belief;
2. whether it appears to the Court that the evidence may afford any ground for allowing the appeal;
3. whether the evidence would have been admissible at the trial; and
4. whether there is a reasonable explanation for the failure to adduce the evidence at trial.(Criminal Appeal Act 1968, s. 23(2), as amended by s. 4 of the 1995 Act, paraphrased).

The Court is free to admit evidence irrespective of these criteria, however: *R. v Bowler* [1997] EWCA Crim 1957. In *Craven* [2001] Crim. L.R. 464 the CA held that, empowered as it was to receive fresh evidence and taking account of all the evidence before it, including evidence to which the jury might not have had access, they should uphold a conviction if they considered it safe. Thus a defect at trial, rendering it unfair, could be cured by a fair and proper consideration of the evidence on appeal. They applied the ECtHR case of *Edwards v UK* (A/247B) (1993) 15 E.H.R.R. 417. The same principle was applied in *Hanratty* [2002] EWCA Crim 1141 where the CA heard an appeal that put an end to one of the longest "miscarriage of justice" sagas in English legal history. Hanratty had been hanged for the "A6 murders" in the 1960s. Generations had grown up assuming him to be innocent. They took it for granted that once the CA admitted DNA evidence from Hanratty's exhumed body this would prove his innocence. To his supporters' horror, the DNA results confirmed his guilt. The CA held that the overriding consideration for the Court in deciding whether fresh evidence should be admitted was whether the evidence would assist the court to achieve justice. Justice could equally be achieved by upholding a conviction if it was safe or setting it aside if it was unsafe. Accordingly, fresh evidence could be admitted when tendered by the prosecution, even where it was not relevant to a specific ground of appeal, but rather to the guilt or innocence of the appellant at large.

As Duff (below) points out, a common reason for non-referral by the CCRC of a case to the CA is that, although fresh evidence has come to light, there is no reasonable explanation why it was not adduced at trial See CCRC Annual Report 1999–2000. The prosecution are entitled to take account of new evidence at trial and can change their allegations: *Mercer* [2001] EWCA Crim 63. In *Pendleton* [2001] UKHL 66, the leading case in this context, the House of Lords confirmed that the correct test for the CA to apply in determining an appeal related to the effect of the fresh evidence on the minds of the members of the court, not the effect it would have had on a jury. The question was whether the conviction was unsafe, not whether the accused was guilty. The CA should remind itself:

> "It is not and never should become the primary decision-maker. . .The Court of Appeal can make its assessment of the evidence it has heard, but save in a clear case it is at a disadvantage in seeking to relate that evidence to the rest of the evidence which the jury heard. For these reasons it will usually be wise for the Court of Appeal, in a case of any difficulty, to test their own provisional view by asking whether the evidence, if given at trial, might reasonably have affected the decision of the trial jury to convict. If it might, the conviction must be thought to be unsafe."

Where an appellant seeks to rely on a new witness not called by D's lawyer at trial, the CA will not admit the new evidence unless there is a lurking doubt that injustice was caused by flagrantly incompetent advocacy: *R. v Gautier* [2007] All E.R. (D) 137.

Referral to the CCRC

12–076 Section 5 of the 1995 Act gives the CA a power to direct the Criminal Cases Review Commission to investigate and report on any specified matter relevant to the determination of an appeal against conviction, where such an investigation is likely to result in the Court being able to resolve the appeal and where the matter cannot be resolved by the Court without such a reference.

The nature of an appeal to the Court of Appeal

12–077 It is important to understand that the CA does not provide a rehearing in criminal cases, unlike an appeal from a magistrates' court to the Crown Court. The limited powers of the CA were spelt out in the successful appeal of the Birmingham Six in 1991, *R. v McIlkenny* [1992] 2 All E.R. 417, in a judgment read out by the judges in turn:

> "Nothing in section 2 of the Act, or anywhere else obliges or entitles us to say whether we think that the appellant is innocent. This is a point of great constitutional importance. The task of deciding whether a man is innocent or guilty falls on the jury. We are concerned solely with the question whether the verdict of the jury can stand. The Criminal Division [of the CA] is perhaps more accurately described as a court of review."

Further, the CA may substitute a conviction for an alternative offence, or order a retrial, where it feels this is required by the interests of justice.

Retrials

12–078 There are arguments for and against retrials. A retrial is preferable for the accused over an outright dismissal of his appeal. At least he gets another chance. On the other hand it is said retrials may be tainted by publicity, as the jury may have developed their own opinions about the first trial or appeal in a high profile case. (This was unsuccessfully argued as inherently unsafe, in *Stone* [2001] EWCA Crim 297. The CA held that the question as to whether a retrial should be ordered where there had been extensive publicity had to be decided on a balance of probabilities: whether he would suffer serious prejudice to the extent that no fair trial could be held.) Also, the witnesses' memories will have faded and the element of surprise in cross-examination will be lost, as all witnesses will have become familiar with all the evidence. A retrial gives both prosecution and defence the opportunity to strengthen their case.

Attorney General's References

The AG may refer a point of law to the CA, on behalf of the **12–079** prosecution, following an acquittal: Criminal Justice Act 1972. The CA simply clarifies the law for the future, leaving the acquittal verdict untouched. The point may then be referred to the House of Lords.

Appeals on sentence

The defendant may appeal against the sentence to the CA who **12–080** may substitute any other sentence or order within the powers of the Crown Court, provided it is not more severe than originally. The Criminal Justice Act 1988, s.36 gives the AG a prosecutorial power to refer any "unduly lenient" Crown Court sentence to the CA, who then have the power to quash it and substitute any sentence within the Crown Court's powers. This applies to indictable and some either-way offences. The Attorney may then refer any such decision of the CA up to the House of Lords.

CA's workload

The Court regularly complains of being swamped with material, **12–081** as its workload is extremely high and advocates do not make life easy for the judges. In *R. v Erskine; R. v Williams* [2009] EWCA Crim 1425, Lord Judge cited Viscount Falkland in 1641: if it was not necessary to refer to a previous decision, it was necessary not to refer to it. Advocates should expect to be required to justify every citation. Anyway, appeals on fresh evidence all turned on their own facts. See case and comment at [2010] Crim. L.R. 48. The CA also had strong words in *R. v Fortean* [2009] EWCA Crim 798 about meritless applications. In this case, F had been refused leave by a single judge, on paper, giving a careful, reasoned decision. F renewed his application. The court said it was "coping" with 6,000 applications a year and applications "without any vestige of merit" hampered its work, which was why the application form contained a warning in bold letters that the court could, under the 1968 Act, order that time spent in custody as an appellant should not count towards sentence.

Appeals to the UKSC

A further appeal to the UKSC is possible by the prosecution or **12–082** the defence but only if the CA certifies that the case reveals a point of law of general public importance and either that court or the UKSC grants leave (permission).

Post-appeal: resolving miscarriages of justice

The work of the Criminal Cases Review Commission

12–083   Until 1996, the Home Secretary had power to refer cases to the CA but would only do this where all avenues of appeal had been exhausted and there was fresh evidence upon which the CA might decide that the conviction was unsafe and unsatisfactory. Following widespread criticism of this restrictive approach and the fact that a convict had to petition a member of the executive who was always reluctant to overturn a judicial decision, the Runciman Commission 1993 recommended the creation of an independent Criminal Cases Review Commission (CCRC). Consisting mainly of non-lawyers, it was created by the Criminal Appeal Act 1995, ss.8–25.

They have a very broad power to refer to the CA any conviction or sentence at any time after an unsuccessful appeal or a refusal of leave, where they "consider there is a real possibility that the conviction, verdict, finding or sentence would not be upheld" because of an argument or evidence not raised in the convicting court or an argument, point of law or information not raised prior to sentence: s.9. Section 13(2) provides an even wider power to refer any other case, in exceptional circumstances. They have a duty to take account of representations made to them and they have wide investigatory powers. They may seek the CA's opinion, direct an investigation by the police or any other relevant public body, require the production of documents, reports or opinions or undertake any inquiry they consider appropriate. The Administrative Court gave guidance on the CCRC's exercise of its powers, in *R. v CCRC Ex p. Pearson* [1999] 3 All E.R. 498. They emphasised the uniqueness of the CCRC's predictive function and stressed the broad discretion accorded to it by Parliament. They considered that, in new evidence cases, the CCRC was correct to try and predict whether the CA would be likely to exercise its powers to admit fresh evidence. In *R. v Cottrell; R.v Fletcher* [2007] EWCA Crim 2016, the CA held that the CCRC should not normally refer a conviction back to the CA just because the criminal law has changed and this is now a statutory restriction, under the Criminal Justice and Immigration Act 2008, s.42.

The 1995 Act preserves the Home Secretary's prerogative power to *pardon* a convicted individual. Jack Straw did this in 2000, where a prisoner in transit saved a life in a road accident. This power has existed since the seventh century. *R. (on the Application of Shields) v SS for Justice* [2008] EWHC confirms that the power still exists and is vested in the SS for Justice. See Quirk (2009). Section 16 gives him the power to refer any case to the Commission.

Critiques of the CCRC

Concern was at first expressed that the CCRC uses police to **12–084** investigate miscarriages of justice, some of which would have been caused by police malpractice but there is no evidence that this has caused a problem. There has always been a backlog of pending cases. The Commission has to consider about 900 cases a year and only refers about 34 back to the CA: see website. Nobles and Schiff analysed the CCRC's performance in 2005. They and others make some of the criticisms in the numbered list below.

A common critique of its powers is that it is limited to referring cases where there is a "real possibility" the CA will find the conviction unsafe. This seems to place the Commission in "an essentially dependent position" (Duff, 2001) and to require them to apply "a parasitic standard" (Nobles/Schiff, 2005). This is demonstrated in *R. v Criminal Cases Review Commission Ex p. Porter* [1999] Crim. L.R. 732. The applicant sought judicial review of a determination by the CCRC not to refer her case to the CA because they considered it unlikely the Court would admit fresh evidence or quash her murder conviction. She argued that the Commission had sought to usurp the CA's functions. The Divisional Court refused her application, because applications to call fresh evidence depended on their peculiar facts and the CCRC had given detailed reasons for its view. Duff said this case showed the Commission was diverted from its principal task of investigating alleged miscarriages of justice into detailed analysis of the jurisprudence of the CA to second guess its likely determination of a case. Duff, a member of the Scottish CCRC, using hypotheses, demonstrated just how difficult it could be for the Commission to decide on a reference. He was concerned at the over-legalistic approach of the English Commission. He suggested, for example, that where there is convincing *inadmissible* evidence of a miscarriage of justice, the CCRC should readily refer a case to the Home Secretary in the hope that he will apply the prerogative of mercy.

The CCRC's interaction with the CA is usefully examined by Nobles and Schiff, in 2005. Some of the points they make are summarised below. Critics such as the Miscarriages of Justice organisation consider that the CCRC fails to refer sufficient numbers of cases to the CA. The chairman of the CCRC, then Graham Zellick, defended them, saying they had to take account of the CA's approach. To refer too many cases would raise expectations and cause confusion and would not serve the public interest: interview with Gibb, 2004. He said the CA quashed 70 per cent of CCRC referrals, which he considered about right. Nobles and Schiff also made the following points.

1. The task of second guessing what the CA might do with a case is made more difficult by the need for both bodies to take account of exceptional circumstances.
2. The CCRC's caseload represents a potential threat to the workload of the CA so the CA has expressed some concerns over the approach of the CCRC.
3. The CA has suggested the CCRC should not re-interview witnesses in some cases. Nobles and Schiff are concerned that this may cause injustice.
4. The CA has criticised the CCRC for referring cases out of time where there has been no appeal and the Court has used the difficulties in assessing the safety of old convictions as a reason for declining to examine them.

Zellick replied in 2005. Richard Foster (2009), the new chair of the Criminal Cases Review Commission, said that before he took over, the referral rate to the CA had fallen to an all-time low and he was encouraging staff to be much more bold in referring to the CA, in an interview on Radio 4's *Today* programme, January 5, 2009.

12–085   Simon Cooper revisited the relationship between the CA and the CCRC. He pointed out that the new s.16C of the Criminal Appeal Act 1995, inserted by the Criminal Justice and Immigration Act 2008, explained above, was aimed at referrals by the CCRC to the CA based on a change in the law and aims to stop these where the CA itself would not have granted a time-extension for such an appeal. Cooper says the mischief that this Act was aimed at was "more imagined than real". He says it is not surprising that if someone was convicted on an interpretation of the law that has now been declared incorrect, they wish to appeal. They would feel just as much injustice as someone in a case where new evidence establishes they did not commit a crime. The CA, said Cooper, had always been fearful of "floodgates" but, for example, there had not been even a single appeal from someone convicted under the *Caldwell* interpretation of recklessness, since G [2003] UKHL 50 said it was wrong. Anyway, the CA has never granted appeals just because the law has changed. They always require evidence of a "substantial injustice". Also on this subject, Taylor, commenting on the case of *Stock* [2008] EWCA Crim 1862, felt that the CA had interpreted "exceptional circumstances" justifying a referral, too narrowly.

"If the CCRC is to seek to mirror the approach of the Court of Appeal and therefore only refer those cases in which there is a genuine 'real possibility' of the conviction being overturned based on the Court of Appeal's self-imposed restrictions, then the meaning of 'lurking doubt' will be virtually empty. This was not the intention behind the 1995 legislation": [2009] Crim. L.R. 188, at 190.

Compensating miscarriages of justice

Since 2006, the only means of securing compensation is through **12–086** the statutory scheme, under s.133 of the Criminal Justice Act 1988. Restrictions were made in the Criminal Justice and Immigration Act 2008, s.61. Alarmed at the cost of compensation (£38 million per year), the Government abolished an old ex gratia scheme in 2006 and developed a policy of restricting claimants to the statutory right to compensation. The assessor will make bigger discounts in awards based on his view of the applicant's conduct leading to the conviction. Similar detailed restrictions have been made by the 2008 Act. The law lords approved deducting cost of living expenses from compensation awards: *R. (O'Brien) v Independent Assessor* [2007] UKHL 10. The 2008 Act restricts the amount to a total of £5 million, or £1 million for those who have been wrongly detained for 10 years. The appellant has to prove a new or newly discovered fact. Incompetence of counsel in deploying the facts at trial was not sufficient to constitute a "miscarriage of justice": *Adams v SS for Justice* [2011] UKSC 18, upholding the CA. The UKSC defined a miscarriage of justice under s.133: "A new or newly discovered fact will show conclusively that a miscarriage of justice has occurred when it so undermines the evidence against the defendant that no conviction could possibly be based upon it".

John Spencer's articles are always informative and powerfully argued. In 2010, he addressed the question of when compensation ought (morally) to be paid and concluded that the English rules, compared with the French and German rules, are "harsh and arbitrary. . .devoid of intelligent justification". He pointed out that the House of Lords failed to agree a definition of "miscarriage of justice" in *Mullen* [2004] UKHL 18. He listed a number of "demonstrably innocent" applicants, such as victims of mistaken identity, who would now not be compensated, such as Colin Stagg, the Cardiff Three and so on. He advocated copying the moral basis of French and German law: if blameless people are forced to suffer for the public good, they should be compensated.

Note that when people like those described below were released following appeal, they were given none of the help or rehabilitation of other released prisoners. Nicholls was freed with £85 in cash and a holdall of personal possessions. He was not allowed to take with him the medication he needed as a stroke victim, nor his squeeze ball which aided recuperation. This was prison property. He was put alone in a taxi and left to catch the Isle of Wight ferry for the mainland. When Paddy Hill met him there, he was shaking, confused and blue around the lips. When Robert Brown was freed, he was given £40, a train ticket to his native Glasgow and a box of legal documents marked HMP (Her Majesty's Prisons). Both were eligible for compensation but this takes some time to secure and is not available to everyone who has been wrongfully convicted, as explained below. By the time of Sean Hodgson's successful appeal, in 2009, he was able to rely on the CA's miscarriage of justice unit, which provided healthcare, managed his medication and made sure that he was suitably housed. Nevertheless, victims of decades of wrongful imprisonment seldom recover. Six months after his successful appeal, *The Times* reported that "Mr Hodgson has struggled with everyday life, spending periods in homeless hostels and wandering the streets of London. . .In poor mental and physical health, he needs regular medication and psychiatric care." Sally Clark never recovered from her ordeal, described below. In 2007 she died, aged 42.

Identifying the causes of miscarriages of justice; the work of the CCRC

Historic cases

12–087   Given the enormous backlog, it has always concerned some of us that precious resources have been prioritised towards clearing up wrongful hangings of those long dead, such as Derek Bentley, hanged in 1952, while possible innocents still live in prison for years. In some capital cases where convictions were upheld by the CA, the Court doubted the value of the CCRC's efforts: *R. v Ellis* [2003] EWCA Crim 3556, the case involving the last woman to be hanged in Britain, in 1955, and *Knighton* [2002] EWCA Crim 2227. In its annual reports, the CCRC has defended this practice. Three cases from the 1950s where the convicted person had been hanged were quashed by the CA: *Mattan* March 5, 1998, and *Kelly* [2003] EWCA Crim 1752, both on new evidence and non-disclosure, and *Bentley* [2001] 1 Cr. App. R. 21, on the grounds of an unfair trial. In 2004, the CCRC decided not to refer the case of Timothy Evans, wrongly hanged in 1950 for murdering his baby daughter. John Christie later confessed to this and other murders and was hanged. The case, like Bentley's, had been one of the most notorious miscarriages of justice in English legal history. It had been the subject of a book, *Ten Rillington Place*, by Ludovik Kennedy and a film starring Richard Attenborough. The CCRC declined to refer the case to the CA as Evans had been given a posthumous royal pardon in 1966, on the recommendation of the Home Secretary. In judicial review proceedings, the High Court upheld the CCRC's refusal but publicly declared Evans to be innocent. One notorious case referred by the Board was that of the A6 murderer James *Hanratty* [2002] EWCA Crim 1141, mentioned above. He was hanged in 1962, and his body was exhumed in 2000 for DNA tests.

Some other references by the CCRC have involved very old convictions, which took place before the Police and Criminal Evidence Act 1984 offered protection to the accused and rendered confessions obtained in oppressive circumstances inadmissible. One such case was that of Stephen *Downing* [2002] EWCA Crim 263. In this group of cases, defects identified by the CCRC include oppressive questioning, failure to protect mentally vulnerable suspects, like Downing, failure to caution, or "verballing", meaning the police attribution of false statements to the accused.

Also in this group are cases involving police malpractice, reminiscent of the famous miscarriages of justice, such as the Birmingham Six and Guildford Four, the first of which prompted the establishment of the Royal Commission on Criminal Justice, whose recommendations led to the establishment of the CCRC. One such case was that of Robert Brown, freed on appeal in 2002, after serving 25 years in prison, the longest wrongful imprisonment served by any miscarriage of justice victim. On his arrest in 1977, Brown was a 19 year old, with one conviction for stealing a pair of shoes from a shop he broke into, who was arrested for non-payment of his fine. He was questioned over the death of a woman near his home, despite eyewitness evidence of a suspect in his thirties. In the police station, he was interrogated by two police officers, Butler and Bethell. Neither took notes. Butler punched him. They took his clothes and, while he was naked, they made him do step-ups and assaulted him. After two days' humiliation and abuse, he signed a confession. He refused to plead guilty, despite the offer of a plea bargain for a guilty plea to manslaughter. Two appeals failed before the CCRC examined the case and reported to the CA that Bethell had rewritten forensic evidence that might have established Brown's innocence. What makes this story all the more cruel, is that because Brown was an unco-operative prisoner, who went on hunger strikes and refused to work, he was ineligible for parole and so, like Stephen Downing, he spent many extra years in prison (see the account by Petty). People who do not acknowledge their guilt have often found themselves denied parole and/or remission and have spent many extra years in prison, as a result. Sean Hodgson, below, falls into this category.

Non-disclosure

Yet another man who was refused parole for protesting his **12–088** innocence was the second longest-serving victim of wrongful imprisonment in Britain, Patrick Nicholls, freed with an apology by the CA in 1998, 23 years after being wrongfully convicted of the murder of a woman who almost certainly died of natural causes. Nicholls had found the body of the 74 year old, Gladys Heath, at the bottom of her stairs and was convicted on flawed pathology evidence. The CA found that medical and police notes that raised the possibility that no murder had taken place were not passed to counsel for the Crown or to Nicholls.

Elks usefully commented that, although it was widely predicted that there would be a flood of applications to the CCRC resulting from the disclosure regime in the CPIA 1996, described above, this did not occur. Critics of the Act feared that prosecutors would wrongly withhold significant material, causing miscarriages of justice. This supports Corker's comment, above, on disclosure under the 1996 Act, that prosecutors did not have the time or resources to sift evidence into that required for primary and secondary disclosure so they gave *everything* to the defence, rather than too little. Note, incidentally, that Sally Clark's second and successful appeal rested on non-disclosure by a prosecution witness, her babies' pathologist, as explained below, but this was not a failure to disclose on the part of the CPS under the 1996 Act.

Expert evidence

12–089   Nicholls' case, above, is also an example of a conviction obtained by expert evidence which was later proven to be flawed. Two pathologists, both dead by the time of his appeal, had concluded that Mrs Heath had been suffocated and beaten about the face. The CA heard new evidence from an Irish state pathologist that her facial injuries were trivial and probably caused by a fall. In prison, Nicholls taught himself law, to advise others who protested their innocence. He befriended Paddy Hill, of the Birmingham Six, who campaigned for Nicholls after his own release.

Another person who was wrongly convicted of murder, on flawed expert evidence was Mark Dallagher, freed in 2004, pending a retrial ordered by the CA (not on a CCRC reference). He was convicted on erroneous earprint evidence. His trial had included evidence from a Dutch police inspector, supposedly an expert, who had examined an earprint at the crime scene and claimed it was an exact match to Dallagher's. In 2002, the CA found that this type of evidence was unreliable and ordered a retrial but in the meantime the police began an investigation and found that a DNA sample from the earprint proved that it could not have been Dallagher's.

The most famous contemporary case of a wrongful conviction involving a litany of flawed expert evidence was that of solicitor

Sally Clark, who was convicted and given two life sentences, in 1999, for murdering her sons, who she claimed were victims of cot deaths. She lost her first appeal but her husband, Stephen, and others waged a high-publicity campaign, supported by the Law Society. An eminent professor, Sir Roy Meadow, had given evidence to her trial jury that there was a one in 73 million chance of both of her sons dying in cot deaths. At that time, he was famous for "Meadow's law", that "one cot death is a tragedy, two is suspicious and three is murder". He reiterated this to Sally Clark's jury and to the jury at Angela Cannings' trial, below. By the time of Sally Clark's second appeal, in 2003, his theory was discredited, with other experts asserting that the chances of two cot deaths were more like one in sixty, and Sir Roy had admitted his statistics were mistaken.

The success of Sally Clark's second appeal however, rested on **12–090** the discovery of misconduct by yet another expert at her trial, the pathologist of her two dead babies, Alan Williams. In 1998, he received evidence of a potentially fatal infection in the second baby, Harry's spinal fluid but had failed to disclose it. It was found by the vigilance of Sally Clark's husband, hidden in the file on the other baby. Dr Williams had initially concluded Harry had died from being shaken, then changed his mind to claim smothering. Two years earlier, a manslaughter trial (quite unconnected) had ended when Williams admitted making an error. By 2005, Dr Williams was appearing before a General Medical Council disciplinary panel, on a charge of serious professional misconduct. Despite criticism by the CA in the Sally Clark case, and widespread attacks in the media, Williams won his appeal against removal from the Home Office register of forensic pathologists.

As if two unreliable experts were not enough, it almost defies belief that a third decided to involve himself in falsely accusing Stephen Clark of being the real murderer. Professor David Southall, then regarded as one of the country's foremost paediatricians, made the accusation after watching a TV programme showing Stephen Clark describing the baby's illness. Without having even examined the medical files on the babies, he contacted the police and told them Stephen Clark should be investigated for murder. He said their third and remaining child should be taken into care and, given Professor Southall's eminence, the local authority seriously considered doing this. He was later found guilty of serious professional misconduct by the GMC who recommended striking him off the medical register in December 2007, but this was overturned on appeal.

Following Sally Clark's successful appeal, in January 2003 [2003] EWCA Crim 1020, the evidence of Professor Sir Roy Meadow became suspicious. He had been one of the first UK experts to write about Munchausen's syndrome by proxy, wherein parents injure their children in order to draw attention to themselves. Parents have been filmed doing this but Sir Roy was too ready to offer this explanation in cases of multiple infant deaths, thus effectively reversing the burden of proof, obliging the parents to find an innocent explanation for their children's deaths.

12–091   In this context, it became predictable that the CA would overturn the conviction of Angela Cannings, on January 19, 2004 [2004] EWCA Crim 01, as she had also been convicted on his evidence, and his "Meadows' Law", of murdering her two sons, in 2002. Note that the 2004 appeal was Cannings' first appeal, not a reference from the CCRC so does not meet most definitions of "miscarriage of justice". The CA took the opportunity to lay down guidelines in such cases: where there were two or more unexplained infant deaths in a family, no cogent evidence and serious disagreement between expert witnesses, then the parents should not be prosecuted for murder. They said experts should be more open-minded, less dogmatic and where there is disagreement among reputable experts, prosecutors should be cautious. The CA added, in *R. v Kai-Whitewind* [2005] EWCA Crim 1092 that this did not automatically mean a prosecution should not be brought. It was for the jury to decide in a dispute between experts. There was ample evidence here to justify the guilty verdict. In *R.v Bowman* [2006] EWCA Crim 417 the CA gave further guidance.

Of course medical experts are also used in civil cases of alleged child abuse, where a local authority applies to the family courts to take a child or children into care, for their own protection. Sir Roy Meadow and those who followed his theories had given evidence at hundreds of such hearings, which were held in private.

After *Clark*, the AG announced a review of 258 convictions in the previous 10 years, priority being given to 50 cases where the parent was still in prison. As a result of this, 28 people had their convictions referred to the CCRC and six of these asked for their convictions to be referred back to the CA. Care cases were also reviewed, since there were many where Professor Meadows had given evidence, after which a child was taken into local authority care. Only one care order was changed on review, however. Also as a result of the widespread concern prompted by these cases, a group of agencies involved in sudden infant deaths established a working group, chaired by Baroness Kennedy. Its recommendations will have a wider impact than on infant deaths alone.

  1. Prosecution medical experts must disclose scientific data favourable to the defence.

2. They have a duty to ensure their evidence is sound and based on peer reviewed research. Medical experts should not use the courtroom to "fly their personal kites".
3. They must ensure they are independent and doctors should not give expert evidence on their own patients.
4. Doctors should be trained in the principles applied by the courts and the difference between civil and criminal courts.
5. Care should be taken in selecting the correct expert.
6. Doctors should be willing to say "I don't know".
7. Judges have a proactive duty to ensure these high standards are followed.
8. There should be a pre-trial meeting of experts.

For further detail, see the Royal College of Pathologists report, *Sudden Unexpected Death in Infancy: A Multi-Agency Protocol for Care and Investigation* and the article by Rowe.

Naturally, the public were scandalised by the fact that these convictions rested on the dogmatic and sometimes controversial beliefs of experts who were regarded as eminent in their field and who were later exposed as over-zealously applying their own over-generalised theories. Uncontrolled use of expert evidence had resulted in restrictions on its use in civil cases, as we have seen, by the Woolf reforms. Auld L.J., in the 2001 *Review of the Criminal Courts* was also critical of experts. He had expressed concern that there was no single system of accreditation of expert witnesses and no requirement for them to have any qualifications. He thought there should be a single body with the following attributes: independence; verifiable standards of current competence; a code of conduct; and disciplinary powers of removal. Keogh commented that, by 2004, the Council for the Registration of Forensic Practitioners seemed to be satisfying these needs. See also, the Law Commission consultation paper 192 and their draft Criminal Evidence (Experts) Bill, and Andrew Roberts 2009. The House of Commons Science & Technology Committee attributed Angela Cannings' wrongful conviction to systemic failures and recommended that judges should have a gate-keeping role, ensuring that evidence presented to juries is sufficiently reliable, as in the US Federal Rules of Evidence and US Supreme Court case law. Roberts says that the principal weakness concerning the reception of expert evidence is that its development has been based on pragmatism rather than principle. He calls for a judicial statement of principle, which may depend on acknowledging that we have to use fundamentally different procedures from those used for normal testimony. See also Leveson L.J.'s November 2010 speech.

False confessions

12–092   In addition to the many old pre-PACE miscarriages of justice caused by false confession, such as Downing, above, there have been successful appeals of post-PACE convictions, where confessions have been obtained from unprotected vulnerable suspects. In 2009, Sean Hodgson was freed after 27 years of false imprisonment. While in prison for theft, he falsely confessed to the 1979 murder of Teresa de Simone. He retracted this confession. At his 1982 trial, his defence that he was a compulsive liar was not believed by the jury, though he had confessed to two nonexistent murders and other fictitious crimes. His 1983 application for leave to appeal was refused. Many confessions have been exposed as false by Professor Gisli Gudjonsson, the world expert in the phenomenon of false confessions: see his 2003 *Handbook*.

New techniques

12–093   Thankfully, the Forensic Science Service usually keeps the exhibits from old trials. Retesting them with new DNA techniques has provided exculpatory evidence in a number of cases, such as that of Dallagher, above—not forgetting that in Hanratty's case it confirmed his *guilt*, of course. In November 2007, Ronald Castree was convicted of the 1975 murder of 11-year-old Lesley Molseed, after a DNA sample taken in connection with an unrelated offence was matched with a sperm sample on Lesley's underwear. Stephan Kisko had served 16 years of wrongful imprisonment for the murder, to which he falsely confessed in 1976, after two days of questioning without a solicitor. Kisko had the mental and emotional age of a 12 year old. In prison, he was beaten up and kept in solitary confinement for his own protection. His conviction was quashed on evidence that he was infertile. He died in 1993, one year after returning home. Though Lesley's clothes were destroyed in 1985, the Forensic Science Service preserved sperm samples on adhesive tape. In 1994, two police officers were summoned on charges relating to non-disclosure of evidence but were not brought to trial. Sean Hodgson, above, was exculpated by DNA testing in 2008 that showed he could not be linked to 20 exhibits preserved from the 1979 crime scene. After his successful appeal, in 2009, an inquiry was launched. The DNA proved to be that of David Lace, who killed himself in 1988. His body was exhumed. He had also confessed to the 1979 murder but was not believed because he was one of seven men who confessed to it.

Matches with old evidence obtained from new samples in the national DNA database are solving many such cold cases but civil libertarians object to its expansion. It now contains 3.6 million profiles: see Sanderson. Retaining samples from the unconvicted has been declared by the ECtHR to be a breach of the Convention on Human Rights, as we saw in Ch.4 on human rights. In addition to the many old pre-PACE miscarriages of justice caused by false confession, such as Downing, above, there have been successful appeals of post-PACE convictions, where confessions have been obtained from unprotected vulnerable suspects.

Laurence Elks, in his overview of the first ten years of the CCRC, commented that some causes of wrongful convictions have faded away, such as oppressive interviews, some persist, such as late-returned briefs, where barristers receive too little notice of the case and provide an ineffective defence. There are new factors, such as rapid developments in expert evidence: see the review of his book, published by JUSTICE, *Righting Miscarriages of Justice? Ten Years of the Criminal Cases Review Commission*, at [2009] Crim. L.R. 52.

BIBLIOGRAPHY

Archbold, published by Sweet and Maxwell, annually. This is prob- **12–094** ably the most comprehensive practitioner's manual on criminal procedure. See also *Archbold's Magistrates' Courts Criminal Practice*, annually.

Archbold News, also on *Westlaw*.

A.J. Ashworth, comments on *Rowe and Davis v UK* and *Jasper v UK; Fitt v UK* [2000] Crim. L.R. 584; comment on *R. v Davis, Johnson and Rowe* [2000] Crim. L.R. 1012; comment on *SC v UK* [2004] Crim. L.R. 130; comments on *Condron v UK* [2000] Crim. L.R. 679 and *Averill v UK* [2000] Crim. L.R. 682.

A.J. Ashworth and M. Blake, "The Presumption of Innocence in English Criminal Law" [1996] Crim. L.R. 306.

A. Ashworth and M. Redmayne, *The Criminal Process* (4th edn, 2010).

Auld L.J., *Review of the Criminal Courts of England and Wales* (2001), website.

J. Baldwin, "Understanding Judge Ordered and Judge Directed Acquittals" [1997] Crim. L.R. 536.

C. Ball, K. McCormac and N. Stone, *Young Offenders: Law Policy and Practice* (2nd edn, 2001).

C. Ball, "Youth Justice? Half a Century of Responses to Youth Offending" [2004] Crim. L.R. 167.

J. Baker, *An Introduction to English Legal History* (2002).

Lord Bingham C.J., "A Criminal Code: Must We Wait Forever?" [1998] Crim. L.R. 694; *The Rule of Law* (2010).

D. Birch, "Suffering in Silence: A Cost–Benefit Analysis of s.34 of the Criminal Justice and Public Order Act 1994" [1999] Crim. L.R. 769.

W. Blackstone, *Commentaries on the Laws of England*, Vol.IV, *Of Public Wrongs*, originally 1796, facsimile edition (1979).

B. Bowling and J. Ross, "The Serious Organised Crime Agency: Should We Be Afraid?" [2006] Crim. L.R. 1019.

M. Burton, "Reviewing Crown Prosecution Service decisions not to prosecute" [2001] Crim. L.R. 374.

M. Burton, R. Evans and A. Sanders, "Implementing Special Measures for Vulnerable and Intimidated Witnesses: the Problem of Identification" [2006] Crim. L.R. 229; "Vulnerable and Intimidated Witnesses and the Adversarial Process", 11 (1) *International Journal of Evidence and Proof*, (2007), pp.1–16 in the electronic version.

S. Camiss, "'I will in a Moment Give You the Full History': Mode of Trial, Prosecutorial Control and Partial Accounts" [2006] Crim. L.R. 38.

S. Cooper, "Appeals, Referrals and Substantial Injustice" [2009] Crim. L.R. 152.

D. Corker, "A step too far", on the 2004 Home Office White Paper, *One Step Ahead* and SOCA, (2004) 154 N.L.J. 896; "Disclosure Stripped Bare", *Archbold News*, Issue 9, November 11, 2004, p.6.

D. Corker, G. Tombs and T. Chisholm. "Sections 71 and 72 of the Serious Organised Crime and Police Act 2005: Whither the Common Law?" [2009] Crim. L.R. 261.

P. Darbyshire, "An Essay on the Importance and Neglect of the Magistracy" [1997] Crim. L.R. 627; "The Mischief of Plea Bargaining and Sentencing Rewards" [2000] Crim. L.R. 895; *Sitting in Judgment* (2011).

J. de Grazia and K. Hyland, "Mainstreaming the Use of Assisting Offenders: How to make SOCPA 2005 section 23 and section 24 work" [2011] Crim. L.R. 357.

I. Dennis, "Reverse Onuses and the Presumption of Innocence: In Search of Principle" [2005] Crim. L.R. 901; "The Right to Confront Witnesses: Meanings, Myths and Human Rights" [2010] Crim. L.R. 255.

R.L. Denyer QC, "Non-Compliance with Case Management Orders and Directions" [2008] Crim. L.R. 784.

P. Duff, "Criminal Cases Review Commissions and Deference to the Courts: The Evaluation of the Evidence and Evidentiary Rules" [2001] Crim. L.R. 341, examining the arguments of Nobles and Schiff at (1995) 58 M.L.R. 299.

L. Elks, "The Criminal Cases Review Commission—Lessons from Experience" *Archbold News*, March 8, 2004; book review of M. Naughton (ed.) *The Criminal Cases Review Commission: hope for the innocent?* (2010) *Archbold News* (1), pp.5–6, *Westlaw*.

L. Ellison and J. Wheatcroft, "'Could You Ask Me That in a Different Way Please?' Exploring the Impact of Courtroom Questioning and Witness Familiarisation on Adult Witness Accuracy"[2010] Crim. L.R. 823.

R. Evans and K. Puech, "Reprimands and Warnings: Populist Punitiveness or Restorative Justice" [2001] Crim. L.R. 794.

P. Ferguson, "Compensating miscarriages of justice" (2004) 154 N.L.J. 842; "Retrials and tribulations" (2006) 156 N.L.J. 1582.

F. Gibb, "Justice's quality controller" on the CCRC, *The Times*, November 23, 2004; "Macdonald's mission to supercharge the CPS", *The Times*, July 13, 2004; "We are determined to do more ourselves", *The Times*, April 8, 2008; "Chief prosecutor demands curb on police cautions", *The Times*, November 8, 2009; "First trial without a jury for 400 years" *The Times*, June 19, 2009 and "First criminal trial without a jury for 400 years starts", *The Times*, January 13, 2010; "Shortfalls in CPS leads to hundreds of defendants avoiding trial", *The Times* March 16, 2010.

G. Gudjonsson, *The Psychology of Interrogations & Confessions: A Handbook* (2002).

M. Hall, "The Relationship between Victims and Prosecutors: Defending Victims' Rights?" [2010] Crim. L.R. 31.

D. Hamer, "The Expectation of Innocent Acquittals and the 'New and Compelling Evidence' Exception to Double Jeopardy" [2009] Crim. L.R. 63.

Herbert's research on the increase in magistrates' sentencing powers: see synopsis by Zander at (2003) 153 N.L.J. 689 and full report by A. Herbert, "Mode of Trial and Magistrates' Sentencing Powers" [2003] Crim. L.R. 314.

Home Office, *Review of Delay in the Criminal Justice System*, 1997 (The Narey Report).

L.C. Hoyano, "Special Measures Directions Take Two: Entrenching Unequal Access to Justice?" [2010] Crim. L.R. 345.

P. Hungerford-Welch, "Prosecution Interviews of Defence Witnesses" [2010] Crim. L.R. 690.

A. James, N. Taylor and C. Walker, "The Criminal Cases Review Commission: Economy, Effectiveness and Justice" [2000] Crim. L.R. 140.

A. Jennings, A. Ashworth and B. Emmerson, "Silence and Safety: The Impact of Human Rights Law" [2000] Crim. L.R. 879.

D. Jones and J. Brown, "The Relationship between Victims and Prosecutors: Defending Victims' Rights? A CPS Response" [2010] Crim. L.R. 212.

Lord Judge C.J., "The Criminal Justice system in England and Wales—Time for Change?" speech, November 5, 2008. This speech is a really interesting insight from someone who experienced the system over decades in practice and as a judge and Lord Chief Justice; Reviews of the Administration of the Courts 2010 and 2011.

R.F. Julian, "Judicial Perspectives in Serious Fraud Cases. . ." [2008] Crim. L.R. 764.

JUSTICE, *Miscarriages of Justice* (1989).

Justice for All, White Paper, Cm.5563 (2002).

A. Keogh, "Experts in the dock" (2004) 154 N.L.J. 1762; "Police state or proportionate response" (2006) 156 N.L.J. 81; "Witness anonymity—balancing rights" (2006) 156 N.L.J. 1337; "Lights, camera, action!" (2009) 159 N.L.J. 9.

M. Lake, "Retreat from due process" (2006) 156 N.L.J. 86; "The supergrass system—a metamorphosis" (2006) 156 N.L.J. 908.

G. Langdon-Down, "A voice for the weak in court trials", *The Times*, July 16, 2002.

L. Leigh, "Lurking Doubt and the Safety of Convictions" [2006] Crim. L.R. 809.

Leveson L.J., "New Developments in Criminal Justice: The Approach to Summary Justice both in and out of Court" speech, December 12, 2007; "The Roscoe Lecture, Criminal justice in the 21st century" November 29, 2010; Speech on expert evidence, November 18, 2010.

K. Macdonald QC, "The new Code for Crown Prosecutors", (2005) 155 N.L.J. 12.

Sir William Macpherson of Cluny, *The Stephen Lawrence Inquiry* (Cm.4262-1) (1999), known as *The Macpherson Report*.

M. McConville and L. Bridges (eds), *Criminal Justice in Crisis* (1994): the fullest and best collection of critiques of the Royal Commission on Criminal Justice.

M. McConville and G. Wilson (eds), *The Handbook of the Criminal Justice Process* (2002).

H.H. Nic Madge, "Summing up—a Judge's Perspective" [2006] Crim. L.R. 817.

M. Narey, *Review of Delay in the Criminal Justice System, a Report*, Home Office (1997), referred to as The Narey Report, on the National Archives website.

R. Nobles and D. Schiff, "The Criminal Cases Review Commission: Reporting Success?" (2001) 64 M.L.R. 280; "The Right to Appeal and Workable Systems of Justice" (2002) 65 M.L.R. 676; "The Criminal Cases Review Commission: Establishing a Workable Relationship with the Court of Appeal" [2005] Crim. L.R. 173.

D. Ormerod, A Waterman and R. Forston, "Prosecution Appeals— Too Much of a Good Thing?" [2010] Crim. L.R. 169.

D. Ormerod, A.L.-T. Choo and R.L. Easter, "The "Witness Anonymity" and "Investigation Anonymity" provisions" [2010] Crim. L.R. 368.

R. Pattenden, "Prosecution Appeals Against Judges' Rulings" [2000] Crim. L.R. 971, discussing Law Commission Consultation Paper No.158 (2000); "Pre-verdict judicial fact-finding in criminal trials with juries" (2009) 29(1) O.J.L.S. 1–24; "The Standards of Review for Mistake of Fact in the Court of Appeal, Criminal Division" [2009] Crim. L.R. 15.

P. Plowden, "Make do and mend or a cultural revolution" (2005) 155 N.L.J. 328 and "Case Management and the Criminal Procedure Rules" (2005) 155 N.L.J. 416.

P. Plowden and K. Kerrigan, (2001) 151 N.L.J. 735, on disclosure.

H. Quirk, "The significance of culture in criminal procedure reform: Why the revised disclosure scheme cannot work" (2006) 10 *International Journal of Evidence and Proof* 42; "Identifying Miscarriages of Justice: Why Innocence in the UK is Not the Answer" (2007) 70(5) M.L.R. 759; "Prisoners, Pardons and Politics" [2009] Crim. L.R. 648.

R. v Criminal Cases Review Commission Ex p. Pearson [1999] Crim. L.R. 732, including comment by Sir John Smith.

M. Redmayne, "Criminal Justice Act 2003 (1) Disclosure and its Discontents" [2004] Crim. L.R. 441.

P. Roberts and C. Saunders, "Introducing Pre-Trial Witness Interviews—A Flexible Tool in the Crown Prosecutor's Toolkit" [2008] Crim. L.R. 831.

A. Roberts, "Rejecting General Acceptance, Confounding the Gatekeeper: the Law Commission and Expert Evidence" [2009] Crim. L.R. 551.

J. Robins, "Cannings case shows need for a fair system of redress", *The Times*, January 25, 2005.

J. Rowe, "Expert Evidence and sudden infant deaths: where next?" (2004) 154 N.L.J. 1757.

The Royal Commission on Criminal Justice Report, Cm.2263 (1993).

A. Sanders, R. Young and M. Burton, *Criminal Justice*, 4th edn (2010).

B. Shapiro, *Beyond Reasonable Doubt and Probable Cause* (1991).

Lord Shawcross's statement is taken from *Hansard* and quoted in the *Code for Crown Prosecutors*.

G. Slapper, "You may not be prejudiced, my Lord, but you look it", *The Times*, April 25, 2007 (on the Attorney General) and see discussion in other newspapers around that date. The HL Constitutional Affairs Select Committee examination of the role of the AG is on the Parliament website, as are the other parliamentary reports on the AG.

J.C. Smith, "The Criminal Appeal Act 1995: (1) Appeals Against Conviction" [1995] Crim. L.R. 920; comment on *Rajcoomar* [1999] Crim. L.R. 728; comments on *Chalkley* (1999) and *Mullen* (1999).

J.R. Spencer QC, "The Case for a Code of Criminal Procedure" [2000] Crim. L.R. 519, which also gives a great potted history of trial procedure and references to excellent historical sources; "Does Our Present Criminal Appeal System Make Sense?" [2006] Crim. L.R. 677; "Quashing Convictions for Procedural Irregularities" [2007] Crim. L.R. 835; "Compensation for Wrongful Imprisonment" [2010] Crim. L.R. 803.

S. Tendler, "FBI-style gangbusters will stop criminals living off hidden loot" (on SOCA, the Serious and Organized Crime Agency) *The Times*, November 25, 2004.

D.A. Thomas, comment on *R. (on the application of H, A and O) v Southampton Youth Court* [2005] Crim. L.R. 398.

N. Vamos, "Please Don't Call it 'Plea Bargaining'" [2009] Crim. L.R. 617.

N. Walker, "What does fairness mean in a criminal trial?" (2001) 151 N.L.J. 1240.

D. Watson, "The Attorney General's Guidelines on plea bargaining in serious fraud: obtaining guilty pleas fairly?" (2010) 71(1) Jo. Crim. L. 77–90.

G. Williams, *The Proof of Guilt* (1955).

M. Zander, "Silence in Northern Ireland" (2001) 151 N.L.J. 138, on Jackson's research; *The Police and Criminal Evidence Act 1984*, latest edition.

G. Zellick, "The Criminal Cases Review Commission and the Court of Appeal: The Commission's Perspective" [2005] Crim. L.R. 937.

FURTHER READING AND SOURCES FOR UPDATING THIS CHAPTER

12–095 Updates for this book on the Sweet & Maxwell website from spring 2012 and 2013.

Attorney General: *www.attorneygeneral.gov.uk*.

Audit Commission *www.audit-commission.gov.uk* though it may have ceased to exist by the time you read this.

British and Irish Legal Information Institute.

Criminal Procedure Rules.

Consolidated Criminal Practice Direction.

Crown Prosecution Service.

HM Courts and Tribunals Service.

Home Office.

Home Office Research and Statistics Directorate *http://homeoffice. gov.uk/science-research/research-statistics/*.

Judges' speeches, Judiciary website.

Judicial College, Judiciary website.

Law Commission.

Ministry of Justice.

Sentencing Council: *http://sentencingcouncil.judiciary.gov.uk/*.
Serious Organised Crime Agency *www.soca.gov.uk*.
Victim Support *www.victimsupport.org.uk*.
Youth Justice Board: see Ministry of Justice website. (The YJB may be abolished in 2011).

FURTHER MATERIAL ON MISCARRIAGES OF JUSTICE

On individuals: **12–096**
(1994) 144 N.L.J. 634; (1996) 146 N.L.J. 1552; (1999) 149 N.L.J. 1017; (1998) 148 N.L.J. 667; (1998) 148 N.L.J. 1028; Woffinden, *The Times*, June 2, 1998; D. Jessel, *Guardian*, November 19, 1996.
On Derek Bentley: D. Pannick, *The Times*, February 11, 1997.
On the Birmingham Six: *Counsel*, April 1991, p.8; (1990) 140 N.L.J. 160; L. Blom-Cooper, *The Birmingham Six and Other Cases* (1997, resulting in libel actions by the Birmingham Six).
The Bridgewater Three: *The Times*, February 22, 1997 and other newspapers; *R. v Home Secretary Ex p. Hickey* (1997).
On Robert Brown: M. Petty, "They Took my Life . . . Now I Long for Peace", *The Times*, July 22, 2004.
On Angela Cannings' conviction: J. Bale, "Mother who killed sons jailed for life", *The Times*, April 17, 2002 and other newspapers on that date.
On Sally Clark, newspaper reports of January 30, 2003; J. Batt, *Stolen Innocence: The Sally Clark Story—A Mother's Fight for Justice* (2004).
On Mark Dallagher, "Court frees man jailed for murder by 'ear-print'", *The Times*, January 23, 2004.
On Stephen Downing, (2000) 164 *Justice of the Peace* 909 and newspaper reports in 2000; on Ronald Castree, the real killer of Lesley Moleseed, R. Jenkins, "Justice at last as DNA traps girl's murderer 32 years on", *The Times*, November 13, 2007.
Guildford Four: *Legal Action*, December 1989, p.7; (1989) 139 N.L.J. 1441; (1989) 139 N.L.J. 1449.
On Hanratty: Law Report, as above; *HANRATTY—The Whole Truth*, Channel 4, May 2, 2002; newspaper reports of week beginning April 15, 2002.
On Sean Hodgson: S. O'Neill, "'I've had a dream for 27 years. That's a long time but it's finally come true'" and other items in *The Times*, March 19, 2009. On Teresa de Simone's real killer, David Lace, see S. O'Neill, "Barmaid's killer is confirmed by DNA test after innocent man spends 27 years in jail", *The Times*, September 18, 2009.
The Maguires: *The Times*, July 17, 1990 and other press coverage.
Stephan Kisko: *The Times*, February 18, 1992; D. Sanderson, "Man arrested over 1975 murder", *The Times*, November 6, 2006.

On Patrick Nicholls: D. Kennedy, "Court clears man of murder after 23 years in jail", *The Times*, June 13, 1998.

The Winchester Three: (1990) 140 N.L.J. 164.

On miscarriages of justice generally

12–097 The best contemporary source is the Criminal Cases Review Commission: *www.ccrc.gov.uk*.

INNOCENT: *www.innocent.org.uk*.

R. Buxton, "Miscarriages of Justice and the Court of Appeal" (1993) 109 L.Q.R. 66.

J.J. Eddleston, *Blind Justice* (2000) (written by an excellent story teller, with pictures).

B. Forst, *Errors of Justice* (2004).

D. Jessel, *Trial and Error* (1994).

JUSTICE, *Miscarriages of Justice* (1989); *Remedying Miscarriages of Justice*.

R. Kee, *Trial and Error: The Maguires, the Guildford Pub Bombings and British Justice* (1989).

J. Kirkby, "Miscarriages of Justice—Our Lamentable Failure?" (1991, Child and Co lecture, Inns of Court School of Law).

R. Nobles and D. Schiff, *Understanding Miscarriages of Justice* (2001).

B. Woffinden, *Miscarriages of Justice* (1989).

Part IV: Professionals in the Law

13. Lawyers

"I do not believe that many of the restrictive practices under which lawyers work can still be justified in the public interest" (Sir David Clementi, *Review of the Regulatory Framework for Legal Services in England and Wales*, December 2004).

"The quality of solicitors and counsel varies as does the quality of wine from 'unfit to drink' to vintage. Vintage tends to be very expensive beyond the means of the ordinary litigant. Most must be satisfied with 'plonk'." (Lightman J., "The Civil Justice System and Legal Profession—The Challenges Ahead" (2003) 22 C.J.Q. 235.)

"We are fortunate in the UK to have such a strong legal system, judges of the highest probity and a profession of exceptional quality. The UK's legal profession is one of the finest in the world. The expertise, the professionalism, the dedication to delivering justice is unrivalled. That is well recognised across the world. The legal sector makes a great contribution to the British economy. In the last financial year the sector's turnover was £23.3 billion—more than double what it was in 1997. And we are the second biggest exporter of legal services in the world—our exports of legal services grew to £2.6 billion in 2006." (Lord Chancellor and Justice Secretary Jack Straw MP, speech, March 6, 2008.)

"I was called to the Bar in 1963. . .It was a privilege to have been a barrister. In 25 years in practice in what is a very competitive profession only one dirty trick was played on me by another advocate. But. . .some of those who started with me made careers as advocates in criminal courts, but a large number who wanted to, did not. It was then, as it is now, a cruel profession." (Lord Judge C.J., Kalisher lecture, "Developments in Crown Court Advocacy", October 12, 2009.)

1. Barristers and solicitors

13–001   The odd characteristic of the English legal profession is that it is divided into two main branches, barristers and solicitors. This makes it very unusual but not unique, in world-wide terms. For centuries, each side has enjoyed certain protected monopolies and restrictive practices but, since 1985, most of these have been abolished by degrees. This and the aim of the Legal Services Act 2007 to liberate lawyers' business structures, have the potential to blur the division. Much of this chapter tells the story of how those monopolies and differences have been whittled away. At the end of the chapter, we turn to examine the arguments for and against fusing our divided profession.

The barrister is usually thought of as an advocate. Until 1990, barristers had virtually exclusive rights of audience before all the senior courts. They are known as "counsel" (singular and plural, like sheep). In 2010 there were 12,420 self-employed barristers, four fifths of the Bar. As the next chapter shows, senior judges are, with very few exceptions, drawn exclusively from the ranks of experienced counsel, indeed the elite of barristers, known as Queen's Counsel.

The solicitor has a right to appear as an advocate in the magistrates' court and county court and may, since the Courts and Legal Services Act 1990 (CLSA), qualify for rights of audience at all levels, but she is traditionally more familiar to the public in her role as a general legal adviser. In 2010, there were over 150,128 solicitors, of whom around 117,862 held practising certificates (*Trends in the Solicitors' Profession Annual Statistical Report 2010*, Law Society website), and 86,748 (73.6 per cent) worked in private practice. Members of the public are able to call at a solicitor's office and seek advice, whereas a barrister could, until 2004, only be consulted indirectly through a solicitor, except by specified clients, and most clients still access a barrister via a solicitor. The solicitor is sometimes likened to a general practitioner doctor and the barrister to a consultant. The analogy must not be taken too far, since the legal knowledge of the newly qualified barrister will not equal that of the senior partners of a firm of solicitors. Often, the solicitor is more of a specialist than the barrister.

Apart from the independent barristers and solicitors in private practice, a large number of other lawyers are employed in solicitors' firms (LLPs): legal executives and paralegals. Like solicitors, some barristers are also employed by LLPs and in central and local government, in the CPS, and in commerce, banking, industry and education. As the practising rules have been progressively relaxed, so more barristers do not work in the independent Bar. For instance, in 2010, there were 2,967 employed barristers (one fifth of the practising Bar). From 2011, when the Legal Services Act permits alternative business structures, there will be more firms with all types of lawyer in partnership together, or employed by, or in partnership with other professionals.

2. Training, entry and diversity

Barristers

A would-be barrister must register as a student member of one **13–002** of the Inns of Court, Gray's Inn, Lincoln's Inn, Inner Temple and Middle Temple, who have the exclusive power to call a person to the Bar. Detailed regulations govern entry to the profession. Students normally obtain a *qualifying* law degree (meaning one acceptable to the professional bodies) and then complete the one-year Bar Professional Training Course (BPTC) or complete it over two years, part-time. They are then called to the Bar. Non-law graduates have to pass a one-year course, the Common Professional Examination or Graduate Diploma in Law, before proceeding to the BPTC. Curiously, students are required to attend their Inn of Court to dine. This is a relic of the Inns' collegiate function, described below. However brilliant the student, she cannot be called to the Bar unless she has eaten all of her 12 dinners, within two years, or completed the alternative, such as residential weekends. These are now called "Qualifying Sessions", provided by the Inn or the BPTC provider, and include events such as mooting, debating, advocacy training, lectures and so on. Details and calendars are on the websites of the four Inns. After call, the student has to undergo an apprenticeship known as pupillage. This involves understudying a barrister in day-to-day practice for 12 months. Pupils may practise and appear as an advocate in the second six months. Students entering employment may undergo pupillage as an employee. A pupillage review was recently carried out by Derek Wood, at the request of the Bar Standards Board. He recommended no change. Details of the regulations for pupillage, such as fair and open recruitment, supervision and feedback are explained by Stein in *Counsel* magazine, June 2011. All barristers are required to undertake continuing professional development, which is being reformed at the time of writing, 2011.

Solicitors

The usual method of entry is a qualifying law degree and then a **13–003** one-year Legal Practice Course (LPC), or by taking a special four-year law degree. The LPC is more flexible from 2009. It is split into two parts and may be taken in stages, with different providers. Evaluation of achievement is by a statement of outcomes. Students can tailor their course to suit their needs. Non-law graduates complete a one-year conversion course (CPE or GDL, as above) before the LPC. In 2004, approval was given to the first courses geared to the needs of individual big firms, such as Linklaters and Clifford Chance. The student must serve as a trainee in a firm of solicitors, or alternative organisation, for two years full-time or four years part-time. The new SRA proposes an "outcomes-based" training so there will be an alternative route for those who do not have training contracts. They will be able to plan a portfolio of work-based learning. Their work will be supervised and assessed by the SRA. When the student has completed the training contract, or alternative, she may be "admitted" to the roll of solicitors. The solicitor may not practise without an annual practising certificate individually issued by the Solicitors Regulation Authority (SRA). All solicitors must undergo regular "continuing professional development" by attending non-examined training. This is under review in 2011 by the SRA, Bar Standards Board and Institute of Legal Executives and is the subject of research by Professor Andy Boon at Westminster.

Entering the legal profession and career progress: numbers, diversity and cost

13–004   Entry to the profession is expensive and, historically, has been difficult for disadvantaged groups. The 2010 Bar Council and Law Society statistics are more encouraging. By the twenty-first century, non-whites represented over 10 per cent of solicitors and barristers, a greater proportion than in the general population of England and Wales. Women represented about a third of practising barristers and almost half of practising solicitors. The same cannot be said for judges, in the next chapter.

Numbers

13–005   Numbers of lawyers escalated from about 1960. Since 1980, the number of solicitors with practising certificates has grown by 211.5 per cent. In the 1990s, the growth in law graduates outstripped the growth in the profession. In 2009, 13,433 people graduated in law, 8,200 of whom were women. Women were more likely than men to graduate with a first class or upper second class degree. In 2009–10, 8,098 would-be solicitors enrolled with the SRA, of whom 61.8 per cent were women and 31 per cent were BME. 8,480 new solicitors were admitted to the roll, of whom almost 59.1 per cent were women and 22.1 per cent were minority. In 2010, of those who sat the LPC examinations, 89.7 per cent passed. In 2009–10, there were 11,370 fulltime and 3,140 part-time LPC places. In 2009–10,

4,874 new solicitor traineeships were registered, 62.7 per cent being women and 19.9 per cent BME. This means that there were far fewer training contracts available than those who passed the LPC so those who could not get training contracts could not qualify and had wasted the enormous cost of the obtaining the LPC. This reflects the economic climate. Every time there is a recession, some solicitors are made redundant and the number of training contracts available shrinks, not surprisingly.

The fact that almost 20 per cent of trainee solicitors are BME compares very favourably with statistics from the 1990s. Research conducted by the Policy Studies Institute for the Law Society, tracking the progress of 4,000 law degree and CPE graduates from 1993, showed that, by 1997, 25 per cent of LPC graduates still did not have training contracts. They found a bias against women, ethnic minority applicants, those from new universities and from less privileged backgrounds, irrespective of academic performance. City recruits were 16 times more likely to have graduated from Oxbridge than a new university (*The Law Student Cohort Study*, Law Society's Strategic Research Unit). Non-whites had to make more applications than their white counterparts. Attitudes of the profession were attacked as favouring white males, by Cherie Booth QC and by senior BME solicitors, in 2000, and exposed by Thomas in *Discriminating Lawyers*. In 2002, the Law Society launched an Equality and Diversity Framework for Action, then in 2003, a Diversity Access Scheme, to provide scholarships to law students from disadvantaged backgrounds. The Society encouraged solicitors to provide work placements and mentoring schemes. By 2010, 11.1 per cent of solicitors with practising certificates were BME, compared with 5.5 per cent in 1999 and 3.1 per cent in 1993.

A 2005 Law Society Research Report, *Equality, Diversity and the Legal Practice Course*, compared success rates of whites and minorities on the LPC. There was a significant difference in performance between whites and non-whites but when other factors were controlled for, such as A-level points, class of degree and whether a training contract had been obtained, there was no difference. In 2008, Lord Bach announced a project called *Barriers leading into law*, where 32 aspiring students were given sponsors or "life coaches": MoJ, October 23, 2008.

The Law Society conducted three surveys in 2010, on issues and **13–006** barriers faced by minorities. They concluded there was a need for more role models and mentors. A disproportionate number of referrals to the SRA involve BME solicitors. The SRA says it is because they are more likely to be in smaller firms. The Black Lawyers Directory promotes BME lawyers and serves clients who desire to use the services of firms with sound diversity strategies.

BME groups are still disadvantaged in progressing within the profession, according to *Ethnic diversity in law firms: Understanding the barriers* (Law Society, 2010). A 2008 salary survey found a pay disparity between BME and white solicitors. Focus groups showed BME solicitors felt they had been ill-informed when embarking on their career and therefore felt they had made the wrong choices and missed career opportunities. It is very sad to read that "for many, finding a training contract involved several years and hundreds of applications" because this reflects the experiences of my 1980s students. The focus groups said firms apparently selected applicants according to academic achievements and the institution attended, "good, able solicitors are being passed over because of their social background". BMEs felt they had been channelled towards immigration, family, legally aided and personal injury work, which were less lucrative than company and commercial work. Some felt that City and corporate firms should be required to fulfil recruitment quotas of BME trainees. Others considered this would undermine BME solicitors. They felt they did not progress satisfactorily to partnerships within firms and that fact explained why disproportionate numbers of BMEs set up their own firms. BME partners were not considered to be better employers than white partners. *The Law Society Group Equality and Diversity Framework* reflects a Law Society commitment to "best practice" in equality, diversity and inclusion. Firms can sign up to their Diversity and Inclusion Charter.

Women as a percentage of solicitors increase year on year and by 2010 they accounted for 45.8 per cent of solicitors with practising certificates, compared with 27.6 per cent in 1993. Since 2000, the number of women with practising certificates has increased by 80 per cent. The Law Society was, nevertheless, concerned to find out why so many women left the profession after 10 years in practice. Their 2004 research demonstrated that the women who had left felt very strongly that the profession was losing valuable talent due to rigid work practices, such as long hours, perceived lack of career progression for women and little value being attributed to women solicitors. In February 2010, *The Times* reported that women comprised less than 20 per cent of partners in Britain's 30 biggest law firms. In magic circle firms, the average is 15 per cent. Women comprised 60 per cent of the graduate intake of many firms. See Spence, citing a study in *Legal Week*. Allen & Overy announced in January 2010 that it would allow partners to work part-time. Its new hires were 62 per cent women but only 15 per cent of partners were. Women left work on the verge of partnership at twice the rate of men. Some young women solicitors now seem to me to be in a worse position than women now in their fifties, who battled in the 1980s to work part-time. Half of 800 women solicitors surveyed by The Law Society and Association of Women Solicitors in 2010 feared their career prospects would suffer if they made use of family friendly policies: *Obstacles and Barriers to the career development of women solicitors*. The summary says:

"The survey. . .revealed that organisational culture, outdated perceptions of women, resistance to contemporary management practices such as flexible working, and perceptions of client expectations meant the legal sector was still very male dominated causing real issues for the retention and advancement of top female talent. Crucially, respondents felt that female solicitors achieving partner status had often sacrificed personal and family relationships and this was not considered to be a positive, beneficial or attractive aspect of career development for women in city firms. It resulted in women pursuing in-house or public sector positions in a bid to maintain a reasonable work-life balance."

More optimistically, McConnell demonstrated how the regulatory objectives of the Legal Services 2007 Act, discussed below, may be used to benefit women and minority solicitors. She quoted the 2009–10 business plan of the Legal Services Board to "promote equality". She cited examples of powerful clients successfully demanding that their legal providers have a certain percentage of women partners. Under the 2007 Act, performance targets may be set and, theoretically, these could include the promotion of flexible working: (2009) 159 N.L.J. 863. The Solicitors Regulation Authority has published a report on its progress towards equality and diversity: N.L.J. news, March 18, 2011.

Entry to the Bar is more difficult. It is overcrowded, with many **13–007** forced out of practice. The workload of the criminal Bar (half the Bar) declined in the 1990s and the Bar feared a reduction in civil work because of the Access to Justice Act 1999. In 2010, there were 460 pupillage places, representing a reduction in pupillages available since 1990. Since about 1,500 successfully complete the BPTC each year, this means some people will apply for pupillage and be disappointed. In 2008–09 54 per cent of pupils were men and 13 per cent minority. Of successful pupils, most nowadays will secure a tenancy. In 2009–10 there were 467 new private practice tenancies (permanent places) and 171 newly employed barristers. In the 1980s, there were far more pupillages available but only 10 per cent secured a tenancy in a set of barristers' chambers.

Seven per cent of the self-employed Bar in 2010 and 12 per cent of the employed Bar were known to be non-white. Women as a percentage of practising barristers have increased throughout the last five decades. In 2010, 32 per cent of the self-employed Bar were women, and 46 per cent of the employed Bar, compared with 25 per cent in 1997. At a 2002 meeting of the Council of the Inns of Court, the Inns agreed to a package of measures to try to eliminate sex and race discrimination. The Inns' benchers were overwhelmingly white and male. There was a systematic bias in favour of whites in the award of scholarships and bursaries by the Inns. As with solicitors, there is a large attrition rate of women from practice and the Bar Council in 2005 surveyed those who had left in the previous three years. In 2004, the Bar Council approved a revised Equality and Diversity Code. It emphasised the importance of giving pupils and junior tenants (new barristers) access to good quality work. Each set of chambers must have an equality policy, and diversity training is included in barristers' continuing education.

Cost and educational background

13–008   In 2011, the fee for the professional courses in London was around £14,000. Many lawyers carry large debts by the time they qualify. Ironically, the 2000 report of the PSI Cohort study found that professional sponsorship was most likely to go to those from well-off families, with 74 per cent of Oxbridge graduates receiving LPC funding, compared with three per cent from new universities. Of trainees, 60 per cent were paid below the Law Society minimum, with the disabled, non-Oxbridge graduates and those from state schools paid the least. In November 2004, a Department of Constitutional Affairs (DCA) minister urged city law firms to stop discriminating in favour of Oxbridge law graduates, saying they were 16 times more likely to find jobs in the city than those from new universities. Graduates from new universities include more ethnic minorities and those from disadvantaged backgrounds.

At the Bar, things are worse. Local authority discretionary grants, which used to fund many through the Bar exams (80 per cent of students in 1987) ceased years ago. One 1970s grant recipient from a poor background was Cherie Booth QC who said the expense of going to the Bar discriminated against the poor (1997 Bar Conference). In 2003, the Bar Council established a task force on funding entry to the Bar. Many new barristers cannot survive, because their earnings are less than their chambers rent. Hence, many drop out of the Bar within the first five years, with large debts. In 2001, the Bar Council voted to introduce compulsory financial awards to pupils and in 2011 these are £12,000 p.a. For all new lawyers, work can be hard. The PSI Cohort study showed a third of trainee solicitors regularly worked over 50 hours a week.

In June 2005, the Sutton Trust published a survey of senior judges, barristers at top chambers and partners in leading law firms. While seven per cent of schoolchildren in England and Wales attend private schools, two thirds of barristers sampled, three quarters of judges and half the solicitors had attended independent schools. Responding to such concerns, "Diversity in the Legal Services", published in 2005 by the DCA (now Ministry of Justice), encouraged leading firms and chambers to monitor diversity and to publish the details and urged them to look for recruits from a wider range of universities. The College of Law and the Sutton Trust funded a five-year *Pathways to Law* project to fund children from state schools whose parents were not professionals. In 2007, the Bar Council published a report by Lord Neuberger, then a law lord, *Entry to the Bar Working Party Final Report.* He considered too many of the wrong people were attracted to the Bar and the image of the Bar put off the right people. He wanted to attract able people from state schools who did not think of the Bar as a career and did not meet professional people. His report made a number of recommendations, including a professional training loan scheme and training in selection procedures for all those selecting pupils and tenants. The Bar then announced a new package, including a placement programme to enable state school gifted children to learn about the Bar and courts. Obviously, disadvantaged groups progress poorly in other professions too. In 2009, the Labour Cabinet Office published *Unleashing Aspiration*, which disclosed that half of professional occupations are dominated by those from independent schools, who represent only seven per cent of the population. There is less social mobility now than post-war. The new Coalition Cabinet published a report in 2010 on social exclusion by Iain Duncan-Smith, making the same point.

Are we over-lawyered?

Since 1980, the number of solicitors with practising certificates **13–009** has risen by 210 per cent. Professor Mayson of the Legal Services Institute said in 2010 that we are overlawyered, with 17,000 law graduates per year for 50 million people, compared with 12,000 in Germany for 80 million people. There had been a 70 per cent rise in numbers in the previous decade, yet only a 20 per cent increase in the number of training contracts. Rose, in 2010, pointed out that the SRA had no plans to intervene but is piloting "work-based learning" as an alternative to the training contract. The Bar Standards Board are piloting an aptitude test for entry to the Bar Professional Training Course (BPTC), testing analytical and critical reasoning and fluency in English. This raises the question of whether the SRA should do the same. The Office of Fair Trading said the Bar's test was anti-competitive. It said the test should be voluntary. The College of Law thinks the LPC should be the solicitor qualification, with further training for those who wish to practice. See also Robins

2011. In December 2010, the SRA, BSB and ILEX announced a joint review of legal education. In 2009, 1,330 students completed the BPTC, which costs £14,000 in London but only 342 completed the first six months of pupillage. In 2011, the Bar Council's pupillage sub-committee said that every year there were about 5,000 applicants competing for 500 pupillages. There is nothing new in wastage rates at the Bar but the Bar conference 2010 debated it, because there is a perpetual issue of whether it is morally acceptable to let thousands of people take the expensive professional exams when they cannot find places in either side of the legal profession. Derek Wood started reviewing Bar education in 2008 and concluded that pupillage was the best way to train for the Bar. In addition to the thousands of home-grown lawyers in England and Wales, in 2008–09, no fewer than an astonishing 26 per cent of admissions to the roll of solicitors came through the Qualified Lawyers Transfer Scheme, especially because of City firms attracting talent from overseas. Applicants, other than those applying under the EU, need to satisfy language proficiency. All need to satisfy standards of knowledge, skills, ability and character.

There is a strong counter-argument that we are not over-lawyered. In a 2010 College of Law Podcast, the chief executive of Freshfields Bruckhaus Deringer said demand for UK qualified lawyers would not dissipate, because English law, along with NY law, remained the law of choice for most global transactions. Many are made in London and lawyers can move around the world and practise English law. Nigel Savage, Chief Executive of the College of Law, predicted that in 2013–14, training contract places may exceed LPC graduate applicants.

3. Organisation and regulation

13–010   The organisation of the two main branches of the legal profession is the responsibility of two separate sets of governing bodies. Since 2010, they are overseen by a new regulator, the Legal Services Board, created by the Legal Services Act 2007, explained below.

Barristers

The Inns of Court

13–011   The Inns are administered by their senior members, Benchers. They are close to the Royal Courts of Justice. The Inns, to one of which every barrister must belong, originated around the fourteenth century as residential colleges teaching the common law to advocates, when the universities of Oxford and Cambridge only taught Roman law. They own and administer valuable property in the Temple area from which most of London's practising barristers rent their chambers.

The Bar Standards Board

This is the independent regulatory board of the Bar Council, cre- **13–012** ated in 2006, following the Clementi recommendations, discussed below. It sets training and entry standards and prescribes and enforces the Bar Code of Conduct. In 2009, it appointed a consumer panel to help it shape the new regulatory framework for lawyers, as required by the Legal Services Act 2007.

The General Council of the Bar (known as "the Bar Council")

This is the trade union of the Bar. Among its objectives are to **13–013** develop and promote the work of the Bar, to combat discrimination and disadvantage at the Bar, to promote the Bar's interests with Government, the EU, international Bars and so on, and to provide services for barristers, such as publications and conferences and practice guidance. In addition, the six court circuits have their own Bar Associations, as do specialist barristers.

Junior Counsel and Queen's Counsel ("Silks")

All practising barristers, however old, are called junior counsel **13–014** unless they have been designated Queen's Counsel (QC). In 2010, there were 1,397 QCs in independent practice; 11 per cent were women and 4.3 per cent were BME.

Treasury Counsel

An elite group of barristers, known as Treasury Counsel, are **13–015** briefed to appear for the Government in public law cases and for the prosecution in top criminal cases. In recent years this system has suffered two accusations. The first was a complaint that the selection system was secretive and discriminatory, favouring white males from a limited background, and the second was that Treasury Counsel were overpaid. A former circuit judge, in a report to the Attorney General in 2000, said they were often paid twice as much as the judges before whom they appeared and there was a second independent inquiry, in 2006. The second was established by the AG and is on the CPS website.

The barrister's clerk

It is normal for a "set" of independent barristers in chambers to **13–016** share a clerk as a business manager and it is said that the clerk, or practice manager, can make or break the barrister. The barrister's clerk arranges work and negotiates the fee unless it is a publicly funded (legally aided) case. An Institute of Barristers' Clerks represents clerks' interests. In October 2000, the *Independent* reported that some clerks earned up to £350,000, far more than most barristers. For further detail on their work, see their website and Trevelyan.

Solicitors

The Solicitors Regulation Authority
13–017   This was created in 2007, following the Clementi recommendations. It says its purpose is to protect the public by ensuring that solicitors meet high standards. They draft the entry standards and rules of professional conduct.

The Law Society
13–018   This used to be the statutory regulator and disciplinary body for solicitors but, thanks to the 2007 Act, its only remaining function is as the solicitors' trade union, promoting their interests.

Legal executives and paralegals
13–019   The routine work of a solicitor's office is largely carried out by 22,000 trainee and practising legal executives plus hundreds of paralegals and they are significant fee earners in many practices. When most people go to a solicitor's office, they may think they see a solicitor but many are interviewed by a legal executive. Their regulatory and examining body is the Institute of Legal Executives. For detail, see their informative website. In the meantime, some have drawn attention to the rise of the paralegal. The Institute of Paralegals estimates that there are 250,000 employed in the UK. Robins (2010) says the chief executive predicts that by 2020, most fee earners in law firms will be paralegals and about 6,000 paralegal law firms were created since 1998. The National Association of Licensed Paralegals thinks there are 180,000. The Law Society is currently, in 2011, studying their qualifications.

Increasing control over lawyers: the Legal Services Act 2007 and the complaints system
13–020   The Law Society's hopeless struggle to regulate solicitors and respond to consumer complaints satisfactorily is almost too painful to describe and is the reason why the 2007 Act was passed to restructure the regulation of all lawyers. Since the 1979 Royal Commission on Legal Services (RCLS) Report, there was growing governmental concern. Independent surveys exposed poor quality work. A 1995 Consumers' Association survey tested the quality of advice given to researchers posing as clients. In a variety of problems, only a small minority of solicitors gave the correct advice.

A 2000 survey found many vulnerable people felt they received a second class service and again in 2001, the Association criticised solicitors' services. In 2004, they reported on shoddy service yet again. Solicitors had not improved. Excessive delay was the commonest complaint, followed by negligence, failure to respond to letters or telephone calls and lack of respect.

The Society was failing to cope with a mounting backlog of complaints. In 1996, it replaced the discredited Solicitors' Complaints Bureau with the Office for the Supervision of Solicitors but this had no effect. It in turn was replaced, to no avail. The Practice Rules required solicitors' firms to provide an in-house complaints procedure. Research by Bristol University in 1998 found 80 per cent of clients sampled had not been told of such a procedure and it was seldom, if ever, used and the operation of the process was criticised by other researchers in 2000. Another academic, Avrom Sherr, produced a damning report on the solicitors' complaints procedures in 1999 (*Willing Blindness?—Complaints Handling Procedures*). In 1998, a Channel 4 *Dispatches* programme uncovered various dishonest solicitors who had been found guilty by the Solicitors' Disciplinary Tribunal of fraud or mishandling clients' money and who continued to practice. In 1999, the Legal Services Ombudsman, appointed under the Courts and Legal Services Act 1990 to oversee the complaints process, described it as "spiralling out of control". In 1998, Irvine L.C. warned the Society that he would ask Parliament for statutory power to take over regulation from the Society and this was granted in the Access to Justice Act 1999. In a 1999 speech to the Society, he described their complaints handling as "lamentable". In 2001, Minister David Lock gave a final written warning to the Society that it would lose its "privilege" of self-regulation if it did not radically improve matters but by July, the Legal Services Ombudsman repeated this warning. She was satisfied with complaints handling in only 57 per cent of cases. In 2003, she again reported that the situation was "unacceptable". In 2004, Falconer L.C. gave her the additional job of Legal Services Complaints Commissioner and the power to fine the Law Society £1 million if it failed to deal adequately with complaints. In 2005 Zahida Mansoor published two annual reports, in her two roles as Legal Services Complaints Commissioner and Legal Services Ombudsman. Yet again, she found that while the Bar Council provided a high level of complaints handling service, the Law Society "appears to struggle to maintain the basic quality standards that it should". The Society would be fined unless it drastically improved complaints handling. Two hundred cases were unresolved after two years and 40 per cent of complainants were dissatisfied. Despite the development of an independent regulatory section of the Law Society, in her 2007 annual report, Mansoor said that complaints had still not been handled in accordance with her instructions. She said the Service and the SRA had missed five of the 13 targets she had set for them. In December 2007, an SRA survey found consumers considered solicitors to be under-regulated. The main complaints were communication, cost and delay. The SRA decided to publicise on its website details of solicitors found guilty of misconduct. Under the 2007 Act, the compensation limit went up to £30,000. Depressingly, the 2004 CA survey, quoted above, reported that more than 40 per cent of their survey respondents who received poor service failed to complain, thinking there was no point. Of those who did complain, almost all were dissatisfied with complaints handling. One person described the Law Society as "a body drinking at the same waterhole as the legal hyenas it purports to be checking up on".

Clementi on complaints and regulation

13–021   Through exasperation with solicitors' inability to regulate themselves, but also because of the attacks on the profession by the Office of Fair Trading, Falconer L.C. established The Review of the Regulatory Framework for Legal Services in England and Wales, carried out in 2003–04 by David Clementi. He was appointed to examine what form of regulation would be best to promote competition and innovation, serve consumer interests and make lawyers more accountable. In his 2004 Review, he remarked that existing arrangements did not prioritise the public interest. He complained of the "absolute cat's cradle" of 22 existing regulatory bodies for lawyers. Unsurprisingly, he suggested abolishing lawyers' right to self-regulation. There should be a new regulator, a Legal Services Board, chaired by a non-lawyer and accountable to Parliament. Its statutory objectives would include upholding the rule of law, promoting access to justice, protecting consumer interests and promoting competition. It would have the power to exercise all regulatory functions but would normally delegate these to the professional bodies. It would assess their rules, in consultation with the Office of Fair Trading. The Bar and Law Society would have to separate their regulatory functions from their trade union functions. (The Society had already resolved to do that, in anticipation of his report and by March 2005 the Bar had proposed a Bar Standards Board which would include laypeople.) All complaints would be made to an independent Office for Legal Complaints, to provide "quick and fair redress to consumers". It would have the power to investigate complaints, mediate between client and lawyers and make binding orders for redress. It would not get involved with discipline, as executed by the Solicitors' Disciplinary Tribunal. The Government accepted

Clementi's recommendations, in their 2005 White Paper, *The Future of Legal Services: Putting Consumers First*. They promised legislation and this was enacted in the Legal Services Act 2007, as described below. Following Clementi's recommendation, the Law Society quickly established an independent Legal Complaints Service and separated off their regulatory functions to the SRA, as described above. The Bar Standards Board was also introduced, as described above, to oversee the Bar Council's former regulatory functions. Under the Legal Services Act 2007, Pts 6 and 7, the Office for Legal Complaints came into operation in late 2010. It covers all parts of the profession authorised under the 2007 Act (*www.legalcomplaints. org.uk*). A new Ombudsman scheme investigates and resolves complaints about legal services. The MoJ published a *Baseline survey to assess the impact of legal services reform* (research Series 3/10, March 2010). The research found:

"Thirty-four per cent of people in England and Wales aged 16+ were found to have used legal services in the last three years. Legal service users were generally content with their legal service providers and the services they provided. For example, 91% of users felt that they received a good service, 92% felt that their provider acted in their best interests and 92% were satisfied with the outcome of their matter".

About a quarter felt the work had taken too long and a quarter thought it was too expensive. The most commonly used services in the last three years were conveyancing (50 per cent), will writing (27 per cent), probate (17 per cent), family matters (15 per cent) and accident or injury claims (11 per cent). Eighty-one per cent thought a solicitor or trainee solicitor handled their affairs. Depressingly, a 2011 survey by the Legal Services Board found that half of the dissatisfied clients surveyed had not been told about their service provider's complaints system, as they should have been, and a number had even been charged for their complaints.

The Legal Ombudsman's office opened in 2010, not to be confused with Zahida Mansoor, the former Legal Services Ombudsman. He is Adam Sampson, a former director of Shelter (Gibb, 2010). It is a lay organisation, unlike predecessor complaints handlers, with 350 staff, and replaces eight former bodies. Lawyers will have eight weeks to resolve a complaint. The Ombudsman may order fees to be repaid, work to be re-done or compensation of up to £30,000 paid. Rose (2011) examined lawyers' ethics. The Law Society has suggested lawyers' ethics should be one of the "foundations of legal knowledge", in the academic stage of legal education and the SRA think it should be part of post-qualification training. Rose said people may be surprised they are not already. In the argument about the arrival of alternative business structures, from 2011, below, people assume non-lawyers will be tempted to act unethically but he remembered that lawyers do not have the moral high ground, citing the miners' compensation scandal. We return to the Clementi Review below, on business structures.

4. Work of barristers and solicitors

Barristers

13–022   Most barristers are independent specialist advocates, capable of objectively prosecuting in a criminal case one day and defending the next; or working for a civil claimant one day and a defendant the next. Trial advocacy requires much office research and preparation of documents and skeleton arguments. Additionally, barristers are routinely asked to give a solicitor's client a written opinion. Some who specialise in planning, tax or employment may do most of their work from their offices (chambers), or home, almost never appearing in court. Over half of practising barristers work in London. The remainder operate from around 60 provincial centres.

Until 2008, barristers were not allowed to form partnerships, other than overseas. Those in independent practice normally shared (and still share) a set of chambers and normally share the clerk and team. When court hearings overlap, another barrister usually in the same chambers has to take the case at short notice. This is called a "late brief". From a low point of 1,919 barristers in 1960, the Bar has increased annually and has not lost business to solicitor advocates, because so few solicitors have chosen to qualify. Barristers' work has diversified in parallel with solicitors' work. The Access to Justice Act 1999, while seen as threatening some publicly funded work, has permitted quality civil rights chambers to gain legal aid contracts for the first time, in the same way as firms of solicitors. Like solicitors, the Bar have developed their own pro bono scheme, some of which is directed to working with volunteers on welfare law advice. In 2000, the Bar launched BarMark, its own quality assurance standard, granted by the Bar Council and certified by the British Standards Institution.

Solicitors

13–023   The trend of the 1980s and 1990s was towards having multiple solicitors in partnership or incorporated companies, and towards larger firms or consortia and this trend increased, because of legal aid contracts, which do not favour small firms. This forced solicitors to specialise. In some of the larger London firms there are more than 100 partners who are highly specialised.

Commercial work

City solicitors advise on company formation and organisation, **13–024** taxation, insolvency, intellectual property, pensions, insurance and financial regulation. Most large London firms are now multi-national. Many serve exclusively foreign clients, contributing millions to the UK's invisible earnings. In 2008–09, the top 100 firms made £4.03 billion in profits, according to *Legal Business*, which conducts an annual survey. Nevertheless, big city commercial firms are sensitive to economic growth and recession. In the 2009 "credit crunch", Linklaters, the second biggest law firm in the world, with 500 partners and 3,000 fee earners, made 120 junior lawyers redundant in London. Other law firms paid new recruits to go on sabbatical.

Domestic conveyancing

This means transferring the legal title to real property. The 1979 **13–025** Royal Commission on Legal Services found this to be the "bread and butter" fee earner of many firms, especially as solicitors enjoyed a monopoly, at that time.

Family law

The divorce rate and growth in legal aid caused an expansion of **13–026** this work since 1980, which exploded when the Children Act 1989 permitted children to be legally aided and separately represented.

Probate

Solicitors' monopoly over probate work was abolished by the **13–027** Courts and Legal Services Act 1990 but rules to fully open the market to non-lawyers were only implemented in 2004.

Employment

This was a growth area in the 1990s. **13–028**

Social welfare

Pre-1979, solicitors were notoriously poor in providing advice **13–029** on welfare law, such as housing and state benefits. Now, firms who seek a legal aid contract must show they can provide advice in benefits.

Criminal law

This was another big growth area in legally aided work since 1980, **13–030** with the expansion of the duty solicitor schemes into magistrates' courts and police stations. The stated official aim of the criminal legal aid scheme over the last few years is to concentrate publicly funded representation into fewer larger firms of solicitors and exclude the "dabblers".

Accidents and personal injury

13–031   Specialist litigators developed since 1980, sometimes involving multi-party actions, caused by industrial disasters or the negligent release of new drugs.

Consumer protection

13–032   Although the small claims civil track is designed to be used by the litigant in person, many parties choose to be privately represented.

Individual financial advice

13–033   This relates to investments, insurance and pensions. Many firms are registered under the Financial Services Act.

Pro bono work

13–034   This means providing legal services free of charge. The Solicitors Pro Bono Group was formed in 1997, with funds donated by big city law firms, several of whom have established pro bono units. Pro bono work is examined in Ch.17.

International practice

13–035   English firms have offices in around 40 foreign countries. The Rights of Establishment Directive 98/5/EC (implemented in 2000 and explained on the SRA website) makes it easy for lawyers to open up offices in other EU states. Also, in 2011, in judgments against Belgium, Luxembourg, France, Germany, Greece and Austria, the Court of Justice of the EU reaffirmed that it is illegal for a member state to prohibit non-nationals from becoming notaries.

Advocacy

13–036   Solicitors all have rights of audience before magistrates' courts and county courts. Additionally, since 1994 they may qualify for an advocacy certificate in the higher courts.

5. Professional etiquette

13–037   It is well worth reading Hazell's 1978 book, *The Bar on Trial*, to understand the fusty profession that the pupil barrister entered in the 1970s and 1980s. This explains everything about the Dickensian culture and career background of any lawyer or judge who graduated and practised in that era. It also explains a great deal about the entrenched quality of the divide in the legal profession. The judiciary and the legal profession is organised in a hierarchy, symbolised in the layout of the courtroom and historically supported by the professions' monopolies and rules of etiquette and dress. Apart from county court district judges, the judge, usually an ex-barrister, sits on a raised dais. In old courtrooms such as Chester, this is many feet above the Bar. Until 2008, High Court judges had five different sets of gowns and two types of wig, for ceremony, different types of case and red letter days (saints' days). Even in the 1980s, advocates addressed them in grovelling language and some still do "May it please your lordship . . . ". In 2011, a court observer will still spot some grovellers. Queen's Counsel sit nearest to the judge, on the front row. They wear a special wig, a long court coat and a silk gown. Lesser barristers, most of them, known as junior barristers, sit behind them, wearing a different horsehair wig and stuff gown. On the back of their gown is a pocket, where, historically, the barrister's fee, a gift for services rendered, would be inserted by a grateful client, as this "gentlemen's profession" could not be seen to soil their hands with money. If a solicitor qualified to sit in these rows, as he could from 2004, as a solicitor-advocate, he was not permitted to wear a wig, until 2007, and this was a great source of annoyance. Behind the barristers sit the solicitors or representatives, traditionally called "outdoor clerks". It used to be the case that barristers would address one another in court as "my learned friend" and solicitors as "my friend". An outsider could be still forgiven for thinking that barristers are the superior profession, more learned, people who have passed more difficult exams and that QCs are the very crème of the intellectual crème of the law.

Barristers and solicitors are closely restricted in their professional conduct by their practice rules. Generally, except under the BarDIRECT scheme, a client must see a solicitor with their legal problem; they cannot normally go direct to a barrister. Historically, a barrister only met the lay client when the solicitor, or solicitor's representative, was present, so building up the isolation, as well as the objectivity, of the barrister. In order to prevent barristers gaining unfair advantage by cultivating the friendship of solicitors, there used to be a rule which prevented a solicitor and barrister in a case from having lunch together. Separate dining rooms were created even in the court buildings of the 1980s.

In a 2000 vote, most barristers chose to retain wigs, as enhancing the dignity and solemnity of court proceedings and a formal sign of the advocate's status and importance in the courtroom. This is despite the fact that Lord Woolf C.J. thought they were outmoded, Irvine L.C. expressed his distaste for wigs in civil disputes and Lord

Phillips C.J. abolished judges' wigs in civil cases and dispensed with most HC gowns from 2008. Solicitors, of course, regard all this as so much snobbery. They expressed disappointment at Lord Falconer's 2004 decision not to abolish QCs. Even employed barristers complained to Sir David Clementi that they felt like second class citizens compared with the independent Bar.

13–038   There used to be a rule, articulated in the 1969 case of *Rondel v Worsley* [1969] A.C. 191 that barristers could not be sued for negligent work in court, or in preparation of court work. In *Arthur JS Hall & Co v Simons* [2002] 1 A.C. 615, the House of Lords abolished this protection as no longer in accord with public policy and being out of line with the liability of other professions, such as doctors, and with lawyers in other EU states. A corollary of this immunity was the rule that barristers did not sue for their fees. Historically, barristers were not contractually bound to solicitors but were paid an honorarium, or gift for services rendered. The Courts and Legal Services Act 1990, s.61, permitted barristers to enter into binding contracts. Nevertheless, the slowness of solicitors in paying fees still puts new barristers under a severe financial strain. Finally, one result of the division of the legal profession is that no-one can practise as both a barrister and a solicitor at the same time although it is now possible to be doubly qualified. Since the Access to Justice Act 1999, however, it has become progressively easier to transfer.

6. The abolition of the professions' monopolies and restrictive practices: Bar wars

13–039   Since the mid-1970s, people questioned the desirability of allowing the legal profession to preserve its ancient monopolies. In the eyes of outsiders, they are restrictive practices, limiting competition and consumer choice and allowing lawyers to overcharge. Margaret Thatcher assumed all monopolies and restrictive practices to be anti-competitive. Her Scottish Lord Chancellor, Mackay, worshipped no sacred cows in the English legal system but if lawyers imagined that New Labour would be any more supportive, they were mistaken. In 2003, European Commissioner Mario Monti warned professions to stop acting in an anti-competitive manner and urged them to modernise practice rules. He warned that the European Commission would take a member state to the European Court of Justice if it permitted unjustified restraints on competition or protected them by law. Notice, from the following tale, what a slow struggle it has been to dismantle lawyers' restrictive practices and how both sides of the profession have passionately defended them on the ground that they best serve the public interest.

The abolition of the solicitors' conveyancing monopoly

The statutory conveyancing monopoly was one of the reasons **13–040** for the establishment of the Royal Commission on Legal Services, 1976–79. The RCLS found most solicitors' practices derived 40 to 60 per cent of their gross fee income from it. Critics complained that it allowed solicitors to overcharge. They operated a scale of fees which meant that, for conveying an expensive property, however simple the work, they charged a large amount. Solicitors defended their monopoly by claiming that their training, professional ethics and compulsory indemnity insurance all protected the public.

The Commission disappointed critics by recommending the preservation of the monopoly but the Consumers' Association persuaded the Thatcher government to promise legislation. The Farrand Committee, established by Thatcher, recommended a system of licensed conveyancers and this was enacted in the Administration of Justice Act 1985. Solicitors perceived a much greater threat from conveyancing by banks and building societies. The Building Societies Act 1986 gave the Lord Chancellor the power to permit this but it remained unimplemented throughout the 1980s. The Law Society complained that such a practice would create conflicts of interest. Lord Mackay addressed this question in a 1989 Green Paper, *Conveyancing by Authorised Practitioners*. It proposed a simplified framework. Solicitors continued to argue that the public would suffer from conflicts of interest, being persuaded to have their conveyancing done by their mortgage lender, who probably also sold them their house. They claimed that "unfair competition" from banks and building societies would extinguish most high street solicitors, thus denying the public easy access to legal services. The Government, nevertheless, promoted the Courts and Legal Services Act 1990, ss.34–53, which permits a system of licensed conveyancers. Most importantly, s.17(1) articulates the Conservative philosophy, the statutory objective of the Act.

> "The development of legal services in England and Wales (and in particular the development of advocacy, litigation, conveyancing and probate services) by making provision for new or better ways of providing such services and a wider choice of persons providing them, while maintaining the proper and efficient administration of justice."

In 2011, the SRA published a draft supervision and enforcement strategy for firms undertaking conveyancing, because conveyancing is the subject of a lot of complaints and compensation claims.

Consequences of the abolition

13–041   Solicitors relaxed their advertising ban. Conveyancing costs fell dramatically. Solicitors began selling houses. The Law Society started identifying and promoting new areas of work for solicitors. The profession has expanded each year, contrary to the Society's prediction. Most significantly, solicitors retaliated by attacking the Bar's monopoly over rights of audience in the higher courts.

Abolition of the probate and litigation monopolies: direct access to barristers

13–042   Solicitors' statutory monopolies over probate and litigation work (negotiation and case management prior to trial) were abolished by the 1990 Act, which permitted institutions and legal executives to offer probate services. As for litigation, solicitors did not fuss about this. The Bar had been contemplating for decades whether ordinary clients should be permitted to access a barrister directly, for litigation services. Since direct access was permitted in 1994, barristers of three years' call who have undertaken a special course have been able to deal with the public direct, without the need to take instructions from a solicitor. They have very slowly permitted direct access to certain groups of clients. This scheme is now called BarDIRECT and only in 2004 was it radically extended to all cases except criminal, family and immigration work. A rule of non-discrimination applies and barristers must be trained. Barristers are still not allowed to conduct litigation, however. The Access to Justice Act 1999 permitted the Bar Council to authorise litigation so the only barrier to barristers conducting litigation is now the Bar Standards Board. Because barristers historically did not and generally still do not litigate, the client must carry out certain tasks for herself, such as writing to the other side, making an offer of settlement and serving a claim form on the opposition. The barrister can draft them for her. The BSB now authorises barristers to litigate provided they satisfy training and other requirements. Heppinstall (2005) commented that it suited corporate clients very well that they could now pay for a barrister's specialist opinion without having to pay a solicitor to ask for it. Westminster Law School carried out research published as *Straight There, No Detours: Direct Access to Barristers*, in 2008. It discovered that 90 per cent of users found that instructing a barrister direct provided better value for money but direct access was criticised by the President of the London Solicitors Litigation Association. He said that the Bar was not geared up to do the administration that goes with litigation. Barristers were not used to seeing clients and their advocacy skills were likely to be dissolved if they started having to deal with administration: (2008) 158 N.L.J. 1693.

Abolishing the bar's monopoly over higher court rights of audience (advocacy)

Since county courts were created by the County Courts Act 1846, **13–043** solicitors have had rights of audience before them. In magistrates' courts, the vast majority of advocates are solicitors. Solicitors may also appear in tribunals, as may laypeople. Others who have rights of audience include employees of central and local government and other public bodies. Individuals have a right to represent themselves. Solicitors, then, are by far the most prolific of advocates but the public's image of the typical advocate has always been the robed and bewigged barrister because, until 1990 and, in practice until 1994, they had a legally protected monopoly over rights of audience in the Crown Court and all senior courts, with certain exceptions. The cases dealt with in the senior courts are, generally, more complex, time consuming and, importantly, lucrative. As they had this monopoly and they always claimed to be superior advocates, one would expect that barristers would be trained in advocacy but this is not the case, until surprisingly recently. When I remarked on poor standards of advocacy, in the UKSC, in 2010, a Supreme Court Justice who is very active in advocacy training agreed with me and he said he could tell which of the advocates appearing before him had been trained. My 2011 book on judges' work, *Sitting in Judgment*, tells some stories of poor advocacy and anyone can test this for themselves by observing courts. One can start with the UKSC and count how many times QCs pointlessly recite legislation which every judge has in front of them, in print. Advocacy training is now well-established and an Advocacy Training Council was established in 2004. There is a useful description by Haddon-Cave, in the April 2011 *Counsel* magazine.

The Royal Commission on Legal Services (1976–79)

Solicitors asked the RCLS to extend their rights of audience to the **13–044** Crown Court (at the very least). To the Bar's relief, the Commission concluded that an extension would be against the public interest. Their reasons are worth studying because they are still argued nowadays, in defence of a separate Bar:

- It would destroy the livelihood of the junior Bar (90 per cent of the Bar), who derived 30–50 per cent of their income from criminal work. Even if solicitors were only given the right to appear in guilty pleas in the Crown Court, this could still threaten the livelihood of the young criminal Bar. Also, the "offender requires the highest possible standard of representation which can only be provided by a specialist advocate".

- If it resulted in the development of substantial solicitors' advocacy practices, prosecuting or defending, this would lead to the loss of independence.
- If solicitors were given general rights of audience, it might lead to the development of large, specialist firms, which would be against the public interest.
- County court trials, which solicitors were used to conducting, could not be compared with jury trials, which required the skills of public speaking, a detailed knowledge of the law of evidence and the ability to cross-examine.
- Most solicitors' practices were not geared to providing advocacy services. Most solicitors could not absent themselves from their offices for most of the working day, sometimes for days on end.
- Such a change would be a step nearer to a fused legal profession, which the Commission did not favour.

In the very week that the Government announced a review of solicitors' conveyancing monopoly, their trade union, the Law Society retaliated by launching an attack on the Bar. To the scandalised amusement of the media, the two sides of the profession waged a bitter public debate, in the 1980s.

The Marre Report

13–045 To take the heat out of the atmosphere, the two sides established the *Committee on the Future of the Legal Profession*, (the Marre Committee) in 1986. They recommended extending solicitors' rights of audience to the Crown Court, organised by a licensing system.

Lord Mackay Again

13–046 The next significant watershed was Thatcher's Lord Chancellor's second 1989 Green Paper, *The Work and Organisation of the Legal Profession*. It acknowledged the Bar's case for restricting rights of audience:

- Judges work without legal assistance, therefore rely on the strength and adequacy of advocacy.
- Judges need to trust advocates not to mislead the court.

- Judgments create precedents. Judges look to advocates to cite all relevant authorities. "The presentation of cogent legal argument is a highly skilled task requiring not only a knowledge of the law but also constant practice in advocacy."

It concluded that this implied that rights of audience should be restricted to those who are properly trained, suitably experienced and subject to codes of conduct which maintain standards. Then Lord Mackay dropped his bombshell, making himself the instant enemy of judges and the Bar:

"The basic premise is that the satisfaction of such requirements should, for the future, alone be the test for granting rights of audience; and not whether an advocate happened by initial qualification to be a lawyer, whether a barrister or a solicitor, and whether in private practice or employed." (para.5.8)

A system of advocacy certificates, general and limited would be established, with professional bodies determining whether candidates had satisfied the relevant requirements, such as passing exams. The Lord Chancellor, after consulting the judges, would determine which professional bodies would have the power to grant audience rights.

Judicial hysteria

The judiciary, almost all ex-barristers, were deeply affronted, **13–047** considering it was their exclusive prerogative to decide who could appear before them. They launched verbal open warfare on Lord Mackay. The Bar Chairman said "the proposals will remove the control of justice from the judges and entrust it to civil servants". This would give rise to "grave constitutional dangers". Predictably, he argued "the general public will be the loser and so will justice." Judges warned of an imminent constitutional collapse. Lord Lane C.J. called the Green Paper "one of the most sinister documents ever to emanate from government". He warned, famously, "Oppression does not stand on the doorstep with a toothbrush moustache and a swastika armband". Lord Donaldson M.R. added, in similar vein, "Get your tanks off my lawn!" Judges threatened a one-day strike if Lord Mackay would not allow them extra time to respond. The long-term effect might be to "impair the competence, integrity and trustworthiness of advocates and, as a result, significantly damage the quality of justice in this country." Solicitors retorted that judges were using a double standard, forgetting that solicitors were already advocates in the lower courts.

The Courts and Legal Services Act 1990

13–048   A watered-down version of the Lord Chancellor's proposals was enacted in the 1990 Act, which established a new system for granting audience rights. He had been forced to capitulate to the judges' demands. (This, according to Irvine L.C., in 1998, proved to be the scheme's downfall.) While s.27 provided that "appropriate authorised bodies" could grant rights of audience, s.29 required them to be subjected to such a cumbersome machinery for approval, as to be almost unworkable. Further, they had to gain approval for the tiniest alterations to their codes of conduct, if these affected rights of audience. The Lord Chancellor was statutorily compelled to seek the advice of the Lord Chancellor's Advisory Committee on Legal Education and Conduct and of the Director General of Fair Trading, before taking a decision jointly with the four "designated judges". Each of the judges could veto a proposed rule change.

Effects of the 1990 Act: solicitor-advocates

13–049   By 1994, only 15 solicitors had applied for qualification. By 1998, there were only 624 solicitor-advocates, out of 70,000 solicitors. This could be because of the cost and palaver of taking the course and exams. Some solicitors, with many years' advocacy experience in the magistrates' court, could see little point in making this effort which would place them in no better position than a newly qualified barrister. Research by Davis, in 1997 found:

- Most solicitors with higher court rights qualified through being former barristers.
  Few solicitor-advocates had appeared in the senior courts.
- Several factors inhibited solicitors' Crown Court advocacy: lack of certainty over trial dates, the low volume of work, length of trials and remuneration.
- Small firms could not afford to develop in-house criminal advocacy practices.
- Civil litigation solicitors did not believe in-house advocacy would improve client service.
- Solicitors regularly exercised their county court rights, where the limit was £50,000 so extended rights were irrelevant.
- Family lawyers conducted their own advocacy as a matter of routine. High Court appearances in family cases were extremely rare.
- Solicitors did not like being stigmatised as abnormal advocates, by not being allowed to wear wigs.

In the meantime, by 1993, work for the youngest barristers was dropping, because of a reduction in case load of the criminal courts and competition in the magistrates' courts from freelance solicitors who acted as agents for other solicitors. Solicitors preferred to use them because, unlike the Bar, they were prepared to guarantee an appearance and would not return a brief at the last moment. Experienced solicitors were more skilful than new barristers and solicitors understood legal aid forms. Rather surprisingly, given the judicial backlash above, not much fuss was made when the Crime and Disorder Act 1998 granted audience rights to non-lawyers employed by the Crown Prosecution Service (CPS) in the magistrates' court.

The "sorry saga" of employed lawyers—"a mouse of reform"

The 1990s saw the Law Society and the Crown Prosecution Service **13–050** in a frustrating struggle to gain higher rights for employed solicitors and for barristers employed by the CPS. To cut a six-year long story short, proponents argued that it was bizarre to deny audience rights to someone like the Director of Public Prosecutions, who had formerly been an eminent QC. CPS employees and employed solicitors were acceptable advocates in the lower courts so why not allow them higher court rights? The Bar argued that it was against the public interest to allow prosecutions to be undertaken by state prosecutors, the CPS. The interest of justice benefited from the use of private practice solicitors and counsel, hired ad hoc by the CPS, because they took independent decisions, unconstrained by CPS instructions. CPS in-house lawyers would be determined to enhance their conviction rates.

Labour's disgust

If lawyers thought they were safe when Labour replaced the **13–051** Conservatives in 1997, they were in for a shock. In June 1998, the new Lord Chancellor, Lord Irvine produced a consultation paper, *Rights of Audience and Rights to Conduct Litigation in England and Wales*. If his predecessor's 1989 Green Papers were a bombshell, then this and its accompanying package of reforms were a rocket, designed to propel the legal profession into the modern era. The language of his foreword betrays exasperation over the failure of the 1990 Act to achieve Lord Mackay's objective of opening up rights of audience:

"there remain features of the way the [legal] profession is organised which. . .stifle innovation and maintain rigid structures, limiting consumer choice and increasing the expense of going to law. . .members of the public often complain that they are required to hire two lawyers, where one would do. . .The 1990 Act was intended to allow solicitors to obtain the right to appear in any court, thus increasing the public's choice of advocate; it was also intended to allow employed lawyers, such as Crown

Prosecutors, to appear in the higher courts. However, there has been continuing opposition to these changes. . .with the result that the Act has achieved virtually nothing. Eight years on, nearly all advocates in the higher courts are barristers in private practice.

The failure of the Act's good intentions and the inadequacy of the mechanisms it put in place to extend rights of audience are best illustrated by the sorry saga of the Law Society's attempt to obtain rights of audience in the higher courts for employed solicitors. . .After a prolonged gestation of six years to-ing and fro-ing. . .a Byzantine procedure produced a mouse of reform: employed solicitors were allowed to appear in substantive proceedings in the higher courts, provided they were led by a lawyer in private practice. The Government is not satisfied that the present state of affairs is in the public interest . . . Our view is that all qualified barristers and qualified solicitors should in principle have the right to appear in any court."

Additional arguments in the paper were:

- Audience rights needed to be restricted because the consequence of using an untrained advocate might adversely affect the client, any other party and the tax payer.
- It was irrational that barristers lost audience rights on becoming employed and regained them when they returned to private practice.
- As for their argument that barristers provided high quality advocacy, there were concerns about standards. The Public Accounts Committee showed that, at some Crown Court Centres, 75 per cent of CPS instructions had been returned. In a third of these cases, there was concern about the experience level of the new barrister who handled the case.
- The argument that junior barristers must be allowed to cut their teeth prosecuting in the Crown Court was inconsistent with arguments that the independent Bar provided uniformly high quality advocacy.
- Barristers should be employed because of their merits, not because they had a monopoly.
- Audience rights should be portable. Once a person had qualified, she should carry that qualification to any other branch of the profession.

The Lord Chancellor crystallised his plans in his 1998 White Paper, *Modernising Justice*, which accompanied the Access to Justice Bill (now the 1999 Act) and explained its background. The Bar and judges reacted with the same arguments as above: allowing a minister to decide audience rights breached the separation of powers and this was a judicial prerogative dating back to 1280. David Pannick QC dismissed this:

> "[P]arliament can and does intervene to regulate the administration of justice in all other respects. It does so because the public interest is most effectively, and democratically assessed by those we elect rather than by barristers who have been appointed to the bench . . . judges have no right to decide, and no expertise that qualifies them to decide, what the public interest requires in a policy context where there are competing considerations. . . . The special pleading of judges and barristers has had no persuasive effect on laypeople, save to reinforce their low opinion of the legal profession." (*The Times*, 1998.)

The Access to Justice Act 1999

Unmoved by protestations and backed by the Office of Fair Trading, Lord Irvine promoted the 1999 Act. Part III of the Act grants audience rights to every barrister and solicitor in all proceedings, subject only to the qualification regulations and rules of conduct imposed by their professional bodies and prohibits any restriction on the audience rights of all employed advocates. It makes advocacy rights portable. **13–052**

Progress since the 1999 Act

The Law Society and the Bar Council were forced to change their rules by July 2000 to comply with the Act and permit higher court audience rights to employed barristers. The Law Society produced a new scheme designed to make it much easier for solicitors to train for higher court audience rights. Nevertheless, by 2011, there were only 1,200 members of the Solicitors Association of Higher Court Advocates. From 2008, the Bar started attacking solicitor-advocates' quality of advocacy and some judges joined in. At the Bar Conference 2008, the chairman of the Criminal Bar Association said there had been a "huge rise" in the number of solicitors with higher court advocacy certificates and some were "truly appalling". Also, some CPS advocates who were leading murder prosecutions were barristers who left the Bar because they could not make more than a modest living. He said it was "upsetting" to watch "the destruction of the system" by "cheap and inadequate labour". Attacks on solicitor-advocates continued. In 2010, an independent review commissioned by the Law Society said that solicitor advocates' training was "not fit for purpose". A new accreditation scheme is under development. In 2011, an advisory group was established, under Thomas L.J., to advise on what has become the Quality Assurance **13–053**

Scheme for Advocates (QASA), which requires *all* advocates, including QCs, to undergo compulsory re-accreditation every five years. See research into QASA by Cardiff Law School, published in 2010 by the Legal Services Commission. Also, thanks to widespread concern about the quality of advocacy in general, another new layer of quality control has just been added. From October 2011, the CPS will only brief advocates (barristers or solicitor-advocates) who have satisfied its own quality assurance scheme and been admitted to its Advocates Panel. Their in-house employed advocates have also been quality assessed. For a truly fascinating examination of how a barrister's working life has changed and a description of the then current *six* competency frameworks for advocates, see Lord Judge's 2009 Kalisher lecture, cited at the top of this chapter.

Queen's counsel "silks"

13–054 | "[I]n the public perception the grant of silk is a licence to print money. . .informed advisers wisely recommend prospective litigants. . .to sue on the Continent. . .In those countries at least equal justice is obtainable at a fraction of the cost." (Lightman J., "The Civil Justice System and Legal Profession—The Challenges Ahead" (2003) 22 C.J.Q. 235.)

The status, first recognised in the sixteenth century, was not created by statute. It is bestowed by the Queen, exercising her prerogative power on the advice of the Lord Chancellor (LC). Until 2003, the LC held an annual competition. The change of status is, financially, something of a speculation. Once appointed, the QC is expected to appear only in the most complex and/or important cases. She is known as a "leader" because she is often accompanied by one, and sometimes two, junior counsel. There used to be a rule called the Two Counsel Rule whereby a QC had to pay a junior to appear as an assistant in court. This was abolished in 1977, following criticism by the Monopolies and Mergers Commission but it is still widely followed in practice. This has been subjected to repeated scrutiny. Regulations on public funding (legal aid) have made inroads into it. Becoming a QC is called "taking silk", since the status entitles the barrister to wear a silk gown, rather than a junior's "stuff" gown. QCs enjoy other privileges. Apart from being paid significantly higher fees, even in publicly funded (legally aided) cases, they are entitled to sit in the front row of the courtroom. Indeed, in the old courtrooms in the Royal Courts of Justice, a gate separates that row from those behind. Apart from sitting closest to the judge, they also have the formal right to address her before any other advocate.

The appointment system for silks was again under scrutiny by Falconer L.C. in 2003–04. The old criteria required candidates to have practised for 10 years, with at least five years' advocacy experience in the higher courts. This meant that solicitor-advocates (still only a handful) were not considered suitable until about 1999. The LC's criteria included outstanding ability as an advocate; high professional standing and respect; a high quality practice based on demanding cases, and demonstrably high earnings. The LC made "consultations" with the judiciary and the profession, in the selection process. Statistics revealed that very few women and ethnic minorities applied. In 2000, of 506 applicants, only 53 were women and 24 ethnic minority.

The Adam Smith Institute published a strong attack on the silk system, in Reeves' 1998 report, *Silk Cut*. They recommended abolition, for these reasons:

- The term "junior" for other barristers was misleading. The annual "silk round" occupied seven civil servants.
- Barristers employed in local authorities, the CPS and industry were not eligible.
- Very competent barristers might seldom appear before the consultant judges.
- Silks were (and are) about 10 per cent of the Bar. This keeps able juniors out.
- Clients were lured into extra expense because they thought that employing a silk would enhance their chances of success.
- Ireland was the only other EU Member State with a silk system.
- Judges have criticised the waste of public money in using silks.
- Despite the abolition of the Two Counsel Rule, silks rarely appeared alone.
- Although silks were meant to be selected for their outstanding competence as advocates, the European Court of Justice had criticised the written submissions of British lawyers as unduly long and repetitive.
- Without silk, a free market in advocacy would prevail, with reputations dependent on competence.
- An archaic and misleading title was bestowed upon relatively few practitioners, which did nothing to enhance legal services.

In 1999, over 100 MPs, led by Andrew Dismore, started cam- **13–055** paigning for abolition. At the 1999 silk ceremony, Lord Irvine defended the award of silk as "the kite-mark of quality", enabling lawyers and clients to identify the leading members of the profession and to identify likely candidates for the Bench. In 2000, when no solicitor-advocate of the six who applied was granted silk, the Law Society President, representing solicitors, condemned the rank as a perk for barristers. Since 1996, when they could first apply, only eight solicitor-advocates had been awarded the rank. In his speech at the 2001 silk ceremony, Lord Irvine insisted the appointment process was fair and open but, unexpectedly, in the Bar's 2000 annual conference, they voted overwhelmingly to reform it.

Since 1995, there has been increasing concern expressed in the press over the earnings of silks, especially legally aided for criminal defence, as related in Ch.17 on legal services—"fat cats". Judges joined in. In 1998, Lightman J. said:

> "it must be a matter of grave concern if leaders of the first rank charge fees beyond the range reasonably affordable by ordinary litigants but fees which their wealthy and powerful opponents can afford. There is then no equality before the law."

In 2001, *The Lawyer* published a survey showing silks lost as many cases as they won and in 2005, another, estimating that 30 silks earned over £1 million the previous year and 10 earned over £2 million.

Bearing in mind that the mischief of the 1990 Act and 1999 Act was to demolish the profession's restrictive practices, it is remarkable how swiftly the whole issue was reopened by the Office of Fair Trading in 2001. In 2002, the Lord Chancellor's Department (now Ministry of Justice) published a consultation paper, *In the public interest?* This was provoked by a 2001 OFT report, *Competition in the Professions*, which questioned the competitiveness of the silk system. In its response, the OFT insisted that the QC system was anti-competitive, lacked quality control and was of little use to customers. The appointments system hindered competition because the earning power and competitive position of barristers was enhanced but little extra value was offered to clients. It lacked quality control because the title QC was not removed from a barrister if standards dropped. The Bar Council rejected this, arguing that the appointments system had been modernised and was "much fairer and more transparent" and there was no barrier to competition, but the Law Society considered it inappropriate for the Queen to confer on members of a single private profession a public honour and rank which accorded them precedence. There was no logical reason why outstanding doctors or dentists should not be so honoured. Solicitors did not find the QC rank of use in selecting an advocate of guaranteed quality. They objected to the rank's being a reward for advocacy, when in litigation nowadays there was an emphasis on seeking an early settlement, usually engineered by solicitors. They also objected to the selection process, based on consultations with judges and lawyers, rather than evidence. The judiciary considered that the QC rank was helpful in identifying candidates for judicial appointments but the Bar considered this inappropriate.

In 2003, Lord Falconer (himself a QC, married to a QC) pub- **13–056** lished yet another consultation, *Constitutional reform: the future of Queen's Counsel*, which most commentators assumed signalled New Labour's intention to abolish the rank. Two thirds of respondents were barristers or judges. Most thought if the rank were to be discontinued then the Government should not be involved in a replacement quality mark. They considered that the public benefited from the rank of QC and that the mark should be confined to advocates. One group of proponents of retention were black lawyers who argued that, just as they were poised to enter the rank, the opportunity might be snatched away from them.

Lord Falconer announced his decision in 2004. He did not abolish the system but withdrew from ministerial involvement in selection. Instead, he asked the Bar and Law Society to develop new schemes for accrediting advocates. Kitemarking must serve consumers' interests by identifying excellence. He would retain responsibility for making recommendations to the Queen. He proposed (yet another) wider review. The Law Society expressed solicitors' disappointment but by November 2004, they and the Bar had agreed on a new scheme, designed to improve fairness and transparency. The current system was established in 2006 and details are on its dedicated website. "Secret soundings" with judges were replaced by a system with structured references from judges, practitioners and clients. The self-funding system is based on self-assessment of required competencies. The applicant undergoes an interview with a human resources professional, to test personal skills and understanding of diversity issues. Selection is made by a panel of judges, lawyers and lay people. Poorly performing silks may have their title revoked.

The controversy over the QC system continues. In a 2008 survey by the Law Society over half considered that the QC rank "should become a broader mark of excellence among lawyers" and over half felt that the Law Society should withdraw its support if the rank was not open to a wider range of lawyers. The survey said "few have a good word to say for the new system" and only one regarded it as an improvement on the old system. The rank is restricted to advocates so solicitors have always felt niggled that it does not serve to promote them in any way. They feel it is yet another way in which the Bar asserts claims to be the superior profession. The research showed that a lot of people were put off applying by the cost. A commissioned report by Sir Duncan Nicol, in 2009, advised against reforming the QC system yet again, saying the 2006 system was too new to judge. In the 2010 silk round, nearly 50 per cent of applicants were successful but only one solicitor-advocate was appointed (MoJ press release February 26, 2010). The Law Society Chief Executive expressed disappointment, criticising the criteria for emphasising oral advocacy in the higher courts. One hundred and twenty new silks were appointed in March 2011: 12 were non-white; two disabled; four were over 55; two of the five solicitor-advocates were successful; 48 per cent of applicants succeeded but two thirds of women did: 93 of 210 men, 27 of 41 women and 12 of 20 minority applicants. Nevertheless, veteran solicitor Sir Geoffrey Bindman QC attacked the silk system yet again in 2011. He thinks it glorifies advocacy which is "paradoxical when lawyers are urged to avoid going to court whenever possible by embracing conciliation and mediation". "Solicitor silks, like solicitor advocates generally, are still seen by the Bar as an aberration" and "the link to the Queen is a sham".

Background to the Legal Services Act 2007 on lawyers' regulatory structures, or "Tesco Law"—the Clementi Report again

13–057   From 2004, Lord Falconer allowed banks, building societies and insurance companies to handle probate. He suggested supermarkets and other retailers should be able to provide legal services and appointed Sir David Clementi to conduct his review. Commentators branded this as "Tesco law". In 2004, Clementi produced his report: *Review of the Regulatory Framework for Legal Services in England and Wales*. It was obvious that Sir David was not contemplating recommending anything as radical as many lawyers feared—such as fusion of the professions. "The review", he said, "favours a regulatory framework which permits a high degree of choice: choice both for the consumer, in where he goes for legal services, and for the lawyer, in the type of economic unit he works for." This is what he recommended:

1. Lawyers of any kind should be allowed to practice together in Legal Disciplinary Practices (LDPs). Managers could include non-lawyers. There would be a Head of Legal Practice and a Head of Finance and Administration. Non-lawyers would have to sign up to a code of practice prioritising clients. There should be a majority of lawyers in the management group but these could include any lawyers, including legal executives and licensed conveyancers.

2. Investment in LDPs could come from outside owners (e.g. Tesco/RAC) but they would need to be "fit to own" and there should be no conflict of interest. An insurance company could not own, say, a personal injury firm. The benefit of such investors would include fresh ideas, better attention to customer service than lawyers gave and competition, thus lower prices.
3. Multi Disciplinary Partnerships might be considered, once LDPs had been tested.

Reactions to Clementi

Consumer Bodies like the OFT were enthusiastic. The **13–058** Department of Constitutional Affairs indicated strong support, promising legislation. The Law Society welcomed the proposals, especially for LDPs. They said they had recommended these back in 1989. Tesco law was not a threat. Statistics showed that many solicitors already found private practice a decreasingly attractive option. For most consumers, supermarkets were a good thing. The Bar welcomed competition but said they were concerned about the ethics of non-lawyers running a legal practice. Tesco law could encourage a compensation culture. They were very hostile to MDPs, fearing conflicts of interest. They said lawyers belonged to a profession but Clementi talked of "the legal service *industry*". There was a danger of over-commercialising the law. A lawyer owed a duty not simply to his client but to the court. The Bar were not Luddites but no country in the world favoured MDPs. The Legal Action Group of lawyers said Sir David had addressed many of their concerns on regulating LDPs. The Legal Services Commission (legal aid regulator and funder) welcomed the proposals, saying a single independent regulator would better serve the needs of the vulnerable and socially excluded. It considered the Law Society and Bar Council did not meet the best interests of consumers. Tesco, in the meantime had started offering DIY kits on some areas of the law. . .

A survey of 50 of the UK's top 100 commercial law firms found that one in five expected to take advantage of the multi-disciplinary partnership model and seek outside investment. One in 10 said they were likely to be floated on the stock exchange. In its 2005 White Paper, the Government broadly accepted Clementi's proposals: *The Future of Legal Services—Putting Consumers First.*

The Legal Services Act 2007 and its results

The resultant Legal Services Bill 2006–07 was published in draft, **13–059** to maximise consultation. The Law Society President said that the Government had listened to interested parties and improved the

Bill. The Society consistently supported it. The National Consumers Council lobbied parliamentarians to try to ensure that it was not watered down. Concern was expressed by some critics that the new setup would threaten the independence of the legal profession. The Legal Aid Practitioners Group argued the very important point that the proposed Legal Services Board's powers to direct the Law Society to take certain steps breached the UN Basic Principles of the Role of Lawyers, which stated:

> "Lawyers shall be entitled to form and join self-governing professional associations to represent their interests, promote their continuing education and training and protect their professional integrity. The executive body of the professional association shall be elected by its members and shall exercise its functions without external interference."

They also quoted The Council of Bars and Law Societies in Europe which said there were "overriding reasons for not permitting forms of integrated cooperation between lawyers and non-lawyers with relevantly different professional duties" (meaning MDPs): see Miller. The complex and troubled Legal Services Bill was carried over to 2007–08. Scrutiny of the draft bill by a joint committee of the Lords and Commons ensured that the Bill was substantially amended. Clementi wanted the reforms to be in the pubic interest, not just the consumer's interest. The committee re-introduced public interest. Also, the committee felt Falconer sought to "nationalise" the legal profession by controlling appointments to the LS Board and thus shaping its politics: see Fennell.

There was intensive lobbying by the Bar and Law Society during the passage of the Bill and by 2008, critics seemed content that their concerns and foreign Bar concerns over independence of the legal profession have been addressed in the 2007 Act: see Young (2008) and Ludlow (2007). Here are the concessions and main points:

- The LC can only make appointments to the Legal Services Board after consulting the Lord Chief Justice.
- The LSB chair must be a lay person.
- The independence of the profession is an objective of the Act: s.1(1)(f).
- An LDP must have 75 per cent legally qualified managers.
- 75 per cent of shares must be held by lawyers.
- Other managers must be approved by the Law Society.
- Alternative Business Structures will be available from 2011. In licensing them, account must be taken of the regulatory

objective of improving access to justice. It is possible to limit percentage ownership by non-lawyers so there will be no 100 per cent Tesco Law.

Under the 2007 Act, "alternative business structures" are permitted from October 2011. This means any business performing "reserved legal services" (RLS), unless all interests are held by lawyers and all managers are lawyers. RLS means rights of audience, litigation, reserved instrument activities, probate, notarial activities and the administration of oaths. The Solicitors Regulation Authority is currently (2011) restructuring, ready for the introduction of "outcomes focused regulation". There will be a new Code of Conduct. Law firms and ABSs will have to appoint a compliance officer. Fines for ABSs could be set at £150 million. There is a rash of articles discussing the implications. According to *Legal Risk*, only five per cent of the *top* 100 law firms believe the Act will have "a significant" impact on them. McConnell, 2009, considered that firms that practice internationally are not likely to transform into ABSs or accept outside ownership because both are banned by the American Bar Association and there are similar problems in Europe, for instance in Germany. As for High Street firms, they will be affected because Tesco etc. will sell commoditised, standardised legal products. The Legal Services Policy Institute considers that smaller firms will lose out. This may be the case but Clementi may have envisaged this. The Law Society said, in 2009, that over-regulation might discourage barristers and solicitors from forming partnerships. In 2010, Professor Stephen Mayson found that about 80 per cent of what most law firms do is unreserved, such as legal advice, tribunal work, making wills and pre-litigation negotiation. RLS were criticised in 2010 by the Legal Services Institute, related to the College of Law. They were explored by Robins, in 2010. He remarked that they were haphazard and historic. The chair of the SRA considered them a "nonsense" and suggested that consumer protection should be extended to all solicitor activities. The Legal Services Consumer Panel is considering whether will-writing should be regulated. In 2009, Lord Hunt produced a report for the Law Society (see Gibb, 2009). He said that the public would be taken aback to learn that anyone could set themselves up as a will-writer. In 2011, Robins argued that solicitors' firms were reacting too late, and are only now joining into branded groups, like *QualitySolicitors* (100 new branches opened one week in March 2011) and *Face 2 Face* solicitors. He contemplates whether lawyers could copy *Specsavers* in a franchising scheme.

K. Underwood, solicitor, argued that firms like his might become **13–060** tempted to deregulate and spare themselves the cost of indemnity insurance and practising certificate fees and all the straightjacket of regulation. He said lawyers could be competing with a tranche of unqualified entrants to the market, in ABSs, probably 5,000 organisations, such as claims management companies, universities and so on. In January 2011, the Legal Services Consumer Panel (an independent section of the LSB) said ABSs ought not to be able to avoid regulation by setting up separate businesses to do unreserved work but they will. "The government has learned nothing from pension and endowment mis-selling, let alone from Claims Direct and the Accident Group in the legal sector."

In 2009, the BSB approved of barristers joining LDPs. It had no choice, because of the 2007 Act. They will be permitted to practise as both LDP managers and independent practitioners. They will be permitted to form barrister-only partnerships, for the time being. In 2011, the BSB confirmed that it will regulate advocacy-focussed ABSs, Legal Disciplinary Practices (LDPs) and barrister-only entities, but not MDPs. The entities it regulates may *not* be externally owned (so no Tesco law) and, unlike solicitors, may not hold client money but *may* apply to conduct litigation. A majority of owners must be barristers or advocates with higher court audience rights. Barristers will be free to manage or work for ABSs, under other regulators. For barristers to be able to form partnerships, own and manage law firms and conduct litigation is revolutionary.

As for the market, there are a number of market research studies predicting the effects on legal services from October 2011. Robins produced *Shopping Around: What consumers want from the new legal services market* (2010). Consumers were asked if they would purchase legal advice from household named companies. The most popular brand was Marks & Spencer but, importantly, 54 per cent were not impressed by household names. In 2011, he reported that research by *YouGov* found 60 per cent of adults were interested in receiving legal advice from well-known brands. The most popular was Barclays. The Co-op aimed to create one of the first ABSs, in October 2011. By June 2011, it was offering legal services through three branches of its high street banks. Co-op Legal Services offers help and advice on personal injury, wills, probate, conveyancing and employment law. The old notion of loyalty to the family solicitor had disappeared. Robins noted that it was really difficult for law firms to demonstrate quality in legal services or for consumers to assess it so a brand name would become a proxy for quality. Lawyers' kitemarks, such as Lexcel or Legal Services Commission quality marks "have close to zero recognition": "March of the big brand".

7. Fusion: do we need two professions?

Because the monopolies and restrictive practices of the two sides **13–061** of the profession have been torn down since 1985, as described above, this raises the question of whether the two sides of the profession will eventually merge and, if so whether a fused profession would better serve the public interest. Barristers have always argued that giving rights of audience to solicitors will sound the death knell to the Bar but numbers of independently practising barristers have increased every year since the Courts and Legal Services Act 1990, as they did every year since the 1960s. The Royal Commission on Legal Services 1976–79 (RCLS) and many other individuals discussed the feasibility and desirability of a fused profession. Here are the pros and cons but these points are obviously supplemented by the facts and arguments examined throughout this chapter so the reader will recognise some of the points below.

Arguments against a divided profession

Expense to the client
Why should the client pay for one or two barristers to argue his **13–062** case in court, accompanied by a solicitor's representative? Why not just let the client hire one lawyer to do everything, instead of paying for three "taxi meters" clocking up a huge bill, hour by hour? Zander provoked the establishment of the RCLS in 1976 by famously making this argument, fully explored in his book, *Lawyers and the Public Interest* (1968). Things have changed in the county court, though. As District Judge Monty Trent said, in 2010, "judges are expected to condemn as disproportionate anybody who sits in the second row, scribbling in their notebooks".

Inefficiency, failures in communication
Some witnesses suggested to the RCLS that the present structure **13–063** caused this because of the distance between barristers and solicitors. Written instructions sent to counsel were often inadequate.

Returned briefs
Very frequently, a solicitor sends a brief to chambers marked for **13–064** a named barrister. At the last minute, the brief is returned because the barrister is otherwise occupied. The solicitor then has to find another barrister or permit the brief to be passed on to another barrister in the same chambers who may be a stranger to him or the client. This causes frustration to the solicitor, denied the choice of original barrister, and may destroy the client's confidence (see Mackenzie at (1990) 150 N.L.J. 512). The solicitor may have

reassured the client of the best of service from the named barrister yet the client is faced with a stranger at the doors of the court. Many defendants complained of the shoddy service they received after meeting their barrister on the morning of trial, in Bottoms and McClean's *Defendants in the Criminal Process* (1976) and *Standing Accused* (1994) by McConville et al.

Zander and Henderson's Crown Court Study for the Royal Commission on Criminal Justice (RCCJ) 1993 provided statistics which illustrated how bad the problem was. In 66 per cent of contested cases, the CPS said the barrister who appeared at trial was not the barrister originally instructed by the prosecution. In most cases, the CPS learned of the change of barrister at the last minute. In eight per cent of cases where there was a change of barrister it was said to cause a problem. As for defence barristers, in 48 per cent of cases, the barrister at trial was not the one originally instructed and in the majority of such cases, the solicitor was informed on the day before, or on the day of hearing. In 60 per cent of cases, the defendant either saw no barrister or a different one before trial. In 17 per cent of cases, the solicitor said the original barrister would have been better than the substitute.

In 1997, research by the National Audit Office showed that CPS briefs had been returned in 75 per cent of the cases sampled and new counsel was judged to be inappropriate in almost a third of these. In 1998, the CPS inspectorate published a report on child witnesses, heavily critical that briefs were returned in half of all child abuse cases. The Legal Action Group, in evidence to the RCCJ 1993, argued that the "detachment" which the Bar claims to be an advantage is seen by the client as ignorance of his case and circumstances. Public confidence in the legal system suffers.

Arguments against fusion

Free from interruptions by clients
13–065 Barristers can concentrate on the specialist matters, benefiting from the fact that another lawyer has already identified the issues and sifted out the relevant facts.

Advocacy
13–066 In a fused system, there would be a drop in quality of advocacy, which would damage not just the interests of the client but the administration of justice. Standards would decline because the specialist knowledge of the Bar would be diluted. Specialisms need regular practice. The Bar can fairly claim to be specialist advocates.

Jury advocacy

This is a specialist type of advocacy, requiring special skills akin **13–067** to those involved in public speaking. These skills require regular practice. There may be grave consequences to the client. Emotions run high. The barrister is accustomed to this environment and can provide the necessary detachment.

Loss of choice

If the profession were fused, leading barristers would join **13–068** large firms of solicitors and so the ability to brief them would be lost to all other solicitors. Under the present system, clients in the remotest areas or with the most complex problems still have access to the best barristers. Solicitors under a fused profession would not readily refer a client to another firm. Access to advocates would be reduced. Most firms of solicitors have few partners. They could not absent themselves from the office for days on end appearing in court. It is therefore important that solicitors have access to barristers to provide services which they could not.

Cost effectiveness

The present system is more cost effective. Under a fused system, **13–069** it would be more expensive to have a solicitor to represent the client as solicitors' overheads are larger.

Orality

English practice rests on the principle of oral hearing, which **13–070** demands well prepared, experienced practitioners. (This point, like those below, was made by Mann.) It is no longer as valid as it then was. Now, skeleton arguments must be prepared in all civil cases and most appeals.

Procedure

English procedure requires a single and continuous hearing, **13–071** which requires time and undivided attention that few solicitors could afford.

Judicial unpreparedness

In England and Wales the principle of *curia novit legem* applies. **13–072** This means that counsel submits the law to the court, which is assumed to know nothing. Counsel has a duty not to mislead the court. Such a system requires specialist knowledge and experience, intensive preparation and much training. If we required judges to research and prepare the law in each case, we would need many more judges.

Comment

13–073   These are good points in relation to advocacy in the higher courts but firstly, they ignore the fact that most lower court advocates are solicitors and, since Mann wrote, the county court deals with some very important civil cases, where solicitors have rights of audience. Really Mann's arguments support the existence of specialist advocates, not a divided profession, bolstered by all the monopolies and restrictive practices lawyers enjoyed in his day. Further, the notion that solicitors generally choose the best advocate for the job, from amongst the pool of barristers, sounds great in theory but, as we have seen, in the routine of the Crown Court, in very serious criminal cases, both prosecution and defence briefs end up, more often than not, with a barrister who was not the one originally selected. Sir Geoffrey Bindman QC, a distinguished veteran solicitor and writer, produced compelling articles in 2010 calling for the unification of solicitors and barristers. He said there was no obvious rationale for the division. Like many solicitors, he had "sometimes felt aggrieved at being cast in the role of second-class citizen". There used to be a general perception that the Bar was the glamorous choice of career, "Solicitors were the pettifogging ranks who did the boring legwork". He felt that now that all the restrictive practices had largely been dismantled, "the survival of the Bar. . .depends on a mixture of mythology and practical convenience". Bindman's comments should be set in the context of the statistical trend demonstrated in *Bar Barometer Trends in the Profile of the Bar* (2011) which drew attention to a decline in the growth rate of the Bar. While Bar numbers have grown every year since the 1960s, the rate of growth has slowed in the last few years and the slowest growth rate was in 2009–10.

A report published by Jomati Consultants LLP in September 2010 said that the golden age of the Bar was over. They will dwindle in numbers and many will earn less, because public and corporate bodies are reducing their advocacy spending, solicitor advocates are increasing and larger firms may seek to do more in-house. The number of referring law firms in family and crime will decline and Bar tenancies will decrease. The Bar Council and BSB have responded by permitting new business structures such as ProcureCo, allowing barristers to obtain work directly from clients and join with solicitors to bid for work: see Bar Council website. Baroness Deech, head of the BSB, says the independent Bar must be kept going, to defend the rule of law and human rights and stand up to government (Gibb, 2011). See further, Flood (2009).

BIBLIOGRAPHY

C. Baski "Solicitor-advocate training 'not fit for purpose'", Law **13–074** Society *Gazette*, December 16, 2010.

G. Bindman QC, "All Bar none", (2010) 160 N.L.J. 711; "End of an era?" (2010) 160 N.L.J. 1428; "Wig not included" (2011) 161 N.L.J. 611.

A.E. Bottoms and J.D. McClean, *Defendants in the Criminal Process* (1976).

D. Carman, "The long arm of the law—City firms with a global reach", *The Times*, July 25, 2006.

Sir David Clementi, Review of the Regulatory Framework for Legal Services in England and Wales, December 2004: *www.legal-services-review.org.uk*.

Articles on Clementi: M. Zander (2005) 155 N.L.J. 41; S. Young (2005) 155 N.L.J. 45; E. Nally (2004) 154 N.L.J. 1461.

Department of Constitutional Affairs, *Constitutional reform: the future of Queen's Counsel*, 2003.

G. Davis, etc., (1998) 148 N.L.J. 832, on solicitors' in-house complaints procedures and on the research on solicitor-advocates, (1997) 147 N.L.J. 212.

L. Duff and L. Webley, *Equality and Diversity, Women Solicitors*, Law Society Research Study 48, Vol.II, 2004.

E. Fennell, "Protecting the country's silver", *The Times*, November 20, 2007.

J. Flood and A. Whyte, "Straight there, no detours: direct access to barristers" (2009) 16 (2–3) *International Journal of the Legal Profession* 131.

F. Gibb, "This is a profession, not an industry" (interview with the Bar Council Chairman on Clementi), *The Times*, December 14, 2004; "Too many legal 'experts' putting consumers at risk", *The Times*, October 5, 2009. "Tackling complaints: will the new Ombudsman do the trick?" *The Times*, November 11, 2010; "It is the independent Bar who will stand up for the rule of law", *The Times*, February 17, 2011.

R. Hazell, *The Bar on Trial* (1978).

A. Heppinstall "Public access to the Bar is good for all" (2005) 155 N.L.J. 1360.

Judge L.J., The Kalisher Lecture 2009, "Developments in Crown Court advocacy", October 12, 2009, judiciary website, "speeches". This is a really interesting account of life at the Bar in the twentieth century, and discussion of advocacy.

Law Society, *Ethnic diversity in law firms: Understanding the barriers* (2010).

J. Ludlow, "A Class Act" (on the Legal Services Act 2007) (2007) 157 N.L.J. 1553.

F.A. Mann on fusion (1977) 98 L.Q.R. 367.

M. McConville et al., *Standing Accused* (1994).

C. McConnell, "A profession in transition" (2009) 159 N.L.J. 1069.

R. Miller, "Cross-purpose competition" (2006) 156 N.L.J. 1113.

Lord Neuberger M.R. "The tyranny of the consumer or the rule of law", speech, November 6, 2010.

D. Pannick, "Will lawyers become reformed characters?" *The Times*, November 3, 1998, p.41.

P. Reeves, *Silk Cut* (1998) criticising the system of Queen's Counsel.

J. Robins in "An unfair divide?" (2010) 160 N.L.J. 1662; "An Unfair Divide? Part 2" (2011) 161 N.L.J. 7; "Too little too late" (2011) 160 N.L.J. 339; "March of the Big Brand?"(2011) 161 N.L.J. 523 and 648.

N. Rose, "Legal training system failing law students" *Guardian*, July 10, 2010 and "New plans to test would-be lawyers", *Guardian*, September 14, 2010; "Changing commercial climate puts lawyers' ethics under microscope", *Guardian*, February 9, 2011.

A. Sherr, *Willing Blindness?—Complaints Handling Procedures* (1999).

U. Schultz and G. Shaw, *Women in the World's Legal Professions* (2003).

A. Spence "You are a lawyer, a woman and have a family—and the big firms cannot tempt you with a partnership", *The Times*, February 8, 2010

P. Thomas, *Discriminating Lawyers* (2000).

District Judge M. Trent, "The old days" (2010) 160 N.L.J. 476.

L. Trevelyan, "The Clerk Enigma" (2007) 157 N.L.J. 1025.

K. Underwood, "Alternative business structures mean consumers will lose out", *Guardian*, January 26, 2011

T. Williams and T. Goriely, "Recruitment and Retention of Solicitors in Small Firms", Law Society Research Study 44, 2003.

N. Woodcock, "Top employers hire fewer women graduates" *The Times*, January 31, 2008.

S. Young, "A class Act" (on the Legal Services Act 2007) (2008) 158 N.L.J. 10.

M. Zander and P. Henderson, *Crown Court Study* (1993).

FURTHER READING AND SOURCES FOR UPDATING THIS CHAPTER

13–075 Updates for this book on the Sweet & Maxwell website from spring 2012 and 2013.

The Bar Council website.

Counsel, the Bar's in-house magazine.

The Institute of Legal Executives: *www.ilex.org.uk*.

The Law Society (especially the Annual Statistical Report).

The Law Society's Strategic Research Unit: *www.research.lawsociety. org.uk.*
The Law Society's *Gazette.*
Legal Action.
Ministry of Justice.
The Lawyer http://www.thelawyer.com/.
The New Law Journal on *Lexis.*

14. Judges

PD "Are you at the Bar, then?
LH "No, I'm a Law Lord"
PD "Ooh, sorry!"
LH "That's OK. I'm one of the old, white, male geezers".
(The author bumps into Lennie Hoffman at a party, 1996.)

"The system demonstrably ensured that those who were appointed were good; it did not, however, demonstrably ensure that those who were good were appointed. It was criticised as being a system under which white Oxbridge males selected white Oxbridge males." (Lord Phillips C.J., referring to the previous system of appointing judges. Judicial Studies Board annual lecture, March 2007).

This chapter starts by telling the story of the new constitutional **14–001** setup under the Constitutional Reform Act 2005, under which the Lord Chancellor's complex role was dismantled, because he was too powerful in all three organs of government, breaching the separation of powers. The Lord Chief Justice became top judge for England and Wales and he and his Court of Appeal colleagues now manage the rest of the judiciary but the Lord Chancellor, now also the Minister of Justice, remains the minister in charge of the judges, lawyers, legal aid and courts so he still has a number of judiciary-related functions, described here. After examining the constitutional concept of judicial independence, most of the chapter is spent on the highly controversial subject of the past and present recruitment systems and consequent lack of diversity in the judiciary—who can apply to be a judge; how the process of appointment now works, since the 2005 Act; an in-depth critique of what was wrong with the old system and an assessment of whether the new system is working to diversify the bench. Training and appraisal are briefly examined towards the end of the chapter.

1. The Constitutional Reform Act 2005—a new constitutional framework

14–002 | "It is a sad comment on our democracy that there has been little argument in the press, or on television about these issues, even in the broadsheet press or the serious political programmes. They are self-evidently, one would have thought, fundamental issues, the resolution of which is likely to affect our public life for decades and possibly centuries to come." (Keene L.J., 2004, speaking about the Constitutional Reform Bill.)

The Lord Chancellor

14–003   The background to the LC's current role is explained in Ch.4 on human rights. The 2005 Act resulted from the Government announcement in 2003 that it was determined to reform the constitution, by dismantling much of the role of the Lord Chancellor (LC), reforming judicial appointments and transforming the law lords into a Supreme Court. Their aim was, according to Falconer L.C., to "put the relationship between Parliament, the Government and judges on a modern footing. We will have a proper separation of powers and we will further strengthen the independence of the judiciary". As explained in some depth in Ch.4, it became apparent that the LC's tripartite role, as a member of all three organs of government: legislature (as speaker in the House of Lords), executive government (as a minister) and head of judiciary, was unacceptable under Art.6 of the Convention. This is the fair trial provision, which requires that a judge must be independent of the government. The Council of Europe (the organ enforcing the HR Convention, *not* an institution of the EU) also made it clear to the Government that the law lords' position breached the separation of powers, because, as judges, they were also peers in Parliament, entitled to speak in debate and sit on committees. Accordingly, under the 2005 Act, the LC ceased to be head of the judiciary. The Lord Chief Justice of England and Wales (LCJ) is now head. It created a new Judicial Appointments Commission (JAC) and a UK Supreme Court. It divided judiciary related functions between the LCJ and the reformed LC, the Justice Minister.

The Act places great emphasis on judicial independence. It requires the LC to be qualified by experience. He is not required to be a judge or a member of the House of Lords. Indeed, the present Coalition Government LC and Minister of Justice is Ken Clarke MP, a member of the House of Commons. The LC and *all* other ministers are now under a statutory duty to uphold judicial independence. They must not seek to influence judicial decisions, through any "special access". The LC must "have regard to" the support judges need to carry out their functions and to the need for the public interest to be represented in matters relating to the judiciary or administration of justice. This (s.3) should be read in conjunction with the Courts Act 2003, which sets out the duty of the LC to ensure that there is an efficient and effective system to support court business.

The Act provided for the LC's judicial appointment functions to be transferred to the monarch and for many others to be disposed of. These remain the responsibility of the LC:

- The framework of the courts, including jurisdictional and geographical boundaries, and allocating business between them.
- Providing and allocating money and resources for the administration of justice.
- Judges' pay, terms, conditions and training resources.
- Determining the number of judges.

> "I do swear that in the office of Lord High Chancellor of Great Britain I will respect the rule of law, defend the independence of the judiciary and discharge my duty to ensure the provision of resources for the efficient and effective support of the courts for which I am responsible. So help me God". (The 2005 Act requires a new Lord Chancellor to swear this oath.)

Lord Chief Justice

The Act declares that the LCJ holds office as President of the **14–004** Courts and Head of the Judiciary for England and Wales. He is given the responsibility of representing judges' views to Parliament and government; for judicial welfare, training and guidance and for deployment of the judiciary and allocation of work within the courts. He is entitled to lay before Parliament a written representation on any matter of importance to the judiciary or administration of justice. The following responsibilities have been transferred from the LC to the LCJ:

- Jobs for individual judges and authorisation to do particular work (known as "ticketing").
- Making rules for deploying magistrates.
- Allocating work within courts of one level.
- Appointing judges to specific posts, committees and boards. (Non-judges are appointed by the LC).

Accordingly, when he took over as head of the judiciary in 2006, 60 civil servants were installed in the Royal Courts of Justice, to run the Judicial Office for England and Wales and the Judicial Communications Office. He runs the judiciary with the help of the Heads of Division, who now comprise a Judicial Executive Board. The Judges' Council represents all judges and helps the LCJ develop policy and react to outside events such as government policy and Parliamentary activity. (See Lord Phillips' speech of March 2007 and the Judiciary website.)

The LCJ became Head of Criminal Justice and may appoint a Deputy. The Act created a Head of Family Justice, a post to be held by the President of the Family Division, who may have a deputy. These mirror the statutory posts of Head and Deputy Head of Civil Justice, established by the Courts Act 2003. The LCJ may delegate to them power to make practice directions. The Vice-Chancellor of the Chancery Division became the "Chancellor of the High Court". A post of President of the Queen's Bench Division was created. The House of Commons Justice Committee launched an inquiry into the work of the LCJ in 2011. See Parliament website.

The background to this part of the Act—the unacceptable role of the Lord Chancellor in all three organs of government

14–005   The UK has never had a real separation of powers but the LC's role constituted the most spectacular breach, as he was a key member of all three organs of government. He was not just a judge but the head of the judiciary. He was not just a minister but a most important Cabinet minister, on nine crucial Cabinet committees and chairing four of them. (The incumbent in 1997–2003, Lord Irvine, likened himself to Tony Blair's "Cardinal Wolsey".) He was not just a member of the legislature but the speaker of the House of Lords and, unlike the Commons speaker, free to participate in political debate.

In Ch.4 on human rights I explained why, by 2003, the Government were embarrassed by the criticisms of the ECtHR and the Council of Europe into dismantling the LC's role and removing the law lords from Parliament. I explained that the government's decision was preceded by attacks on the status quo by two law lords, Bingham and Steyn. I quoted Steyn's 2002 speech and revisited it in the Supreme Court section of Ch.6. Most of his speech was, however, reserved for a strident attack on the office of LC. He listed all the ways in which it breached the separation of powers and he demolished, one by one, the arguments raised in its defence, especially by Irvine L.C. To explain the problem, I can do no better than quote him at length:

"nowhere outside Britain is the independence of the judiciary potentially compromised in the eyes of citizens by permitting a serving politician to sit as a judge at any level, let alone in the highest court which fulfils constitutional functions. . .The major obstacle to creating a Supreme Court is the privilege of the Lord Chancellor of sitting in the Appellate Committee of the House of Lords. I will argue that the Lord Chancellor's participation in judicial business in the highest court no longer serves a useful purpose and is contrary to the public interest. . .The fog surrounding the figure of the Lord Chancellor, so vividly described in 1853 by Dickens in *Bleak House*, has not entirely lifted. . .By convention the Lord Chancellor is a Cabinet Minister, and he is in charge of a large spending government department. For a long time the Lord Chancellor's predominantly political role has raised questions about the propriety of his subsidiary judicial role. In her important book *The Office of the Lord Chancellor* (2001) Professor Woodhouse has shown why these questions became more acute during the Lord Chancellorship of Lord Mackay of Clashfern (1989–1996) and even more so during the period in office of Lord Irvine of Lairg (1997 to date). She attributes this to the increasing politicisation of the office. She has described in detail the vast increase in the nature and extent of the present Lord Chancellor's executive responsibilities. He is responsible for formulating and implementing policies affecting the administration of justice, which are often a matter of party political debate. In addition he chairs Cabinet committees over a large range of policy issues beyond his departmental responsibility. He is at the centre of political power in a party political sense. In all these respects he is bound by the doctrine of collective responsibility. In his legislative role he assumes some of the functions of the Speaker in the House of Commons; he takes part in debates; he speaks for the Government; and he votes. . .[U]nder the Appellate Jurisdiction Act 1876 he may and does sit in the Appellate Committee of the House of Lords, and in the Privy Council. When he sits the Lord Chancellor automatically presides, with the attendant influence of doing so. He swears an oath to act impartially when he sits judicially. In England he is the head of the judiciary. His task is to protect the independence of the judiciary. . .It is.. an astonishing proposition that a member of the executive claims to this day to have the right to decide who among the Law Lords should sit on a particular case. It is, however, by no means a theoretical point. If the Lord Chancellor has the legal power to dictate in a given case the composition of the highest court in the land, he will be entitled to exercise it and nobody will in practice know when the power has been exercised directly or indirectly. Not much legal certainty and transparency there"

Lord Irvine had sat in eight appeals with the law lords, two of which were important and involved the relationship between the executive government and citizens. His role in them was criticised in the House of Lords chamber. There was another case from which he was asked to stand down, involving a death in custody. It would be unthinkable for him to sit in any of the major cases coming before the law lords on constitutional law, devolution, or human rights. Secondly, said Lord Steyn, he did not make a significant contribution to the law lords' work. "There will not be a ripple in the pond if he ceases to sit". He concluded:

> "The practice of the Lord Chancellor and his predecessors of sitting in the Appellate Committee is not consistent with even the weakest principle of separation of powers or the most tolerant interpretation of the constitutional principles of judicial independence or rule of law."

Lord Steyn then went on to challenge Lord Irvine's defence of his tripartite role as useful because he could represent the judiciary when he sat in Cabinet and the Cabinet had a representative in the judiciary. Lord Steyn questioned whether this could be effective when he sat as a judge so little and, anyway, it was a vice, not a virtue, to assume that it was proper to inform the judiciary of the Government's wishes.

> "In no other constitutional democracy does the judiciary have a 'representative' in cabinet. . .By gracefully accepting the inevitable, the Lord Chancellor, a principle architect of the Human Rights Act 1998, will render another great service to our law".

Unfortunately, Irvine L.C. chose not to "accept the inevitable" so the following year, 2003, his close friend, Prime Minister Blair, removed him, replaced him with another friend, Lord Falconer, and announced on the same day that his government would be dismantling the 1,400 year old office of Lord Chancellor, replacing the law lords with a Supreme Court and reforming the system of judicial appointments. All this came as a big shock to some judges, most of the law lords and the media but, as I explained in Ch.4 on human rights, for those of us who had understood the implications of Art.6 of the Convention and had noticed that a key member of the Council of Europe had visited Parliament to tell us how embarrassing it was trying to explain the British constitutional setup to the emergent democracies of eastern Europe, we knew the writing was on the wall for the Lord Chancellor and the law lords. Ironically, Lord Irvine had been hoist by his own petard (blown up by his own bomb), the Human Rights Act 1998.

Attacks on the role of LC were not new. The lawyers' pressure group, JUSTICE, had called for reform for more than 20 years. Academics had frequently drawn attention to the anomalous role. Real pressure was ultimately placed directly on the Government in May 2001, when the Parliamentary Assembly of the Council of Europe called on the British Government to review the office of LC. Even Lord Irvine had conceded that he would not prescribe the office of LC to emergent democracies but he famously defended it and the lack of separation of powers, "We have never been a nation of purists but pragmatists". As for Lord Steyn, Lord Irvine dismissed him as being in a minority of one.

Nevertheless, there was a furore when the Government made its dramatic announcements in June 2003. Given the extent of the constitutional reforms and the fact that they were announced as a decision, not a proposal, commentators criticised the Government's failure to inform the Queen, and some members of the judiciary were aggrieved that they had not been consulted. Most importantly, Lord Woolf C.J. voiced his disquiet at the determination to abolish the LC. On the day Charlie Falconer replaced Lord Irvine, the day the reforms were announced, he was introduced as "the last" Lord Chancellor (though the government did not succeed in abolishing the LC, as can be seen above). He was also appointed Secretary of State for Constitutional Affairs and the Lord Chancellor's Department was renamed the Department for Constitutional Affairs (DCA). In 2007, it became the Ministry of Justice. He announced that he would not be sitting as a judge.

The anxious Lord Woolf C.J. postponed his retirement to fight for **14–006** judicial independence because of the loss of the LC, who he saw as the defender of the judiciary in the Cabinet. Indeed, he voiced his concerns so frequently, in and out of Parliament, that he could only be appeased by a January 2004 "Concordat", an agreement between him and the Government, guaranteeing judicial independence, making the Lord Chief Justice the Head of the Judiciary, guaranteeing that judicial appointments would be free from political interference and detailing how responsibilities for judicial appointments and the administration of justice were to be shared between the LCJ and government ministers. This Concordat was published on the DCA website and, as we have seen above, the guarantees secured by the LCJ were all spelled out in the Constitutional Reform Act. In the meantime, in July 2003, the Government published several consultation papers: on judicial and silk appointments, the Supreme Court and the LC's non-judicial functions. They were consulting, of course, not on *whether* these massive constitutional reforms were to take place but *how*. Another consultation paper was published, very belatedly, in 2004, on the judiciary-related functions of the LC, curiously absent from the earlier set.

Many others shared the LCJ's concern. "If the Lord Chancellor goes, who will fight the Treasury for legal aid, which carries few votes? Who will have ultimate authority over the legal profession?" asked the eminent lawyer, Lord Alexander. Lord Mackay, the last Conservative LC, agreed. The law lords had responded to the consultation papers by emphasising the LC's importance in safeguarding the rule of law and the independence of the judiciary. In response, Lord Falconer said that he was not just there to represent the views of the judiciary. "Like all Cabinet ministers I am there to ensure the public interest is served." This remark is very telling, as it illustrates starkly the problem of the LC's dual role. Radical QC Baroness Helena Kennedy was not the only person to point out that Lord Irvine had clung onto office not out of stubbornness but out of a genuine anxiety to defend the rule of law and judicial independence against the increasingly unrestrained attacks of his Cabinet colleague, Home Secretary Blunkett. I return to this point below, under judicial independence.

The Concordat pacified Lord Woolf C.J. but it did not satisfy other peers. In March 2004, the Government gave in to a demand that the Bill be referred to a select committee. It made no fewer than 400 amendments and voted to retain the title of Lord Chancellor. Parliamentary debate was reopened in October, with ex law lords even more vociferous. "What is the greatest legal office in the world?. . .the Lord Chancellor", said Lord Cooke of Thorndon, ex law lord. Lord Lloyd, another former law lord, said that the proposed new alternative of putting all ministers under a duty to uphold judicial independence was "nothing but a form of words". The Government was getting desperate to salvage the Bill. They reluctantly amended it to preserve the title Lord Chancellor. Lord Falconer grumbled that he could not see why such a post had to be held by a lawyer but he conceded this point too and that requirement appears in the Act. This followed widespread and vociferous protests that a non-lawyer could not defend the judiciary.

In all the heated debate on constitutional reform in 2003–05, it was left to the eminent academic Robert Stevens to quietly remind us that the LC had only become the champion of judicial independence in 1880 and in any event, the separation of powers and independence of the judiciary were, in the UK context, considerably flaky concepts. (See now Bingham, 2006.)

2. What is meant by the independence of the judiciary?

> "With the Executive sitting in the legislature, English discussions of the separation of powers and judicial independence have a slightly unreal quality." (Robert Stevens, 2004.)

14–007

The independence of the judiciary and the separation of powers

It is appropriate at this point to examine these uncertain concepts. Constitutional theorists, notably the Englishman Locke in the seventeenth century and the Frenchman Montesquieu in the eighteenth, praised the separation of powers as a guarantee of democracy. The concentration of governmental power of more than one type—legislative, executive and judicial—in the hands of one person or body is considered dangerous. It is notable that when a dictator or an extreme regime takes power, they dismiss judges who will not do their bidding. This happened in 2003 in Malaysia and in Pakistan in 2007. Some written constitutions try to guard against this. In the British constitution there is no point in looking for a separation of powers. All we can hope for in the UK is a system of checks and balances that allows one organ of government to be kept in check by the others.

14–008

Stevens, in *The Independence of the Judiciary* (1993) attributed to Blackstone (*Commentaries*, 1765) the concept of the judiciary as one of the three organs of government which needed independence from the other elements, though he reminded us that from 1701 to 1832, the judges were an integral part of the ruling oligarchy. "Nothing underlines the atheoretical nature of the British Constitution more than the casualness with which it approaches the separation of powers" (1993). It is a constitutional myth, Stevens has often said, that there is independence of the judiciary in England (1994). All the Act of Settlement 1701 provided for was independence for individual judges, not for the independence of the judiciary as a whole, as a co-equal branch of government, in Montesquieu's sense, as the judiciary is meant to be in the USA. Our judges simply moved from being "lions under the throne" to lions under the Parliamentary mace.

By this he means, as Dicey pointed out in the nineteenth century, the rule of law was dependent on the supremacy of Parliament so the task of judges was and is to carry out the will of Parliament. Our judges do not have the power to judicially review primary legislation and declare it to be unconstitutional, as does the US

Supreme Court. The only exceptions have come in the European Communities Act 1972, which gave the judges power to declare a UK Act to be incompatible with EU law (see Ch.3) and the Human Rights Act 1998 (see Ch.4), permitting them to reinterpret primary legislation, where possible.

14–009   Nor did our judges have control over an independent budget and court service. As Professor Scott pointed out, since the Beeching reforms in the Courts Act 1971, until 2006, judicial administration in England was not "judiciary-based" but "executive-based", unlike the US and the Australian Federal courts. (I might comment at this point that Scott and other constitutional lawyers forgot the one exception—magistrates. They controlled their own budget until 2005, as explained in Ch.15 on magistrates.) During the Beeching reforms, the judges argued that their collective independence required them to be in control of the courts but they lost the argument. Increasingly, governments have sought to increase executive control over court management and expenditure. Judges objected to this, often in hysterical terms, throughout the late 1980s and 1990s. They were fond of quoting early US constitutionalist, Alexander Hamilton, writing in *The Federalist* (No.78), who described the judiciary as the weakest and least dangerous department of government. Sir Francis Purchas (1993; 1994) even likened 1980s developments to the Nazi regime. Lords Lane and then Taylor C.JJ. publicly attacked Mackay L.C. in 1991 and 1992. In 2003, lay justices were similarly alarmed at the Courts Bill's threat to dismantle magistrates' courts committees. Professor Scott argued that there was the opportunity for strengthening the separation of powers by making the senior courts "judiciary-based". The 2005 Act does that in part. It allows judges much more autonomy to manage the courts and much of the time of CA judges is spent on managing the judiciary. Judges do not have control over the courts or judiciary budget, or real control over how to spend it, though.

Lord Phillips, President of the UKSC, gave a speech in February 2011, concerned about the means of funding the UKSC and the danger to independence. In planning the Court, Lord Falconer had assured Parliament that it would be paid for direct by the Treasury. "That ring-fences the Supreme Court budget and ensures that it cannot be touched by Ministers". The 2005 Act did not provide for that but for the cost to be spread through the civil courts of the three jurisdictions. This did not work out. There was no money from England and Wales so the LC made up the difference. Thus, the UKSC was not independent. The budget was cut. They had managed with 11 judges for years and Lord Phillips said they would not mind a change of law to allow for a reduction but there were serious ramifications in the lack of independence of the UKSC. Half its cases are public law. Human rights cases like the 2004 Belmarsh case irritate governments and render the Court vulnerable. I return to this point, below.

Although judges think it is constitutionally desirable to have judges running the courts, for the sake of separation of powers, it cannot be assumed they will always make a better job of it than an executive agency, however. Prior to the Courts Act 1971, when the county court judges (around 90) managed their own affairs, with the help of a registrar, they claimed the system had worked well but at assize level, judicial-centred case management was archaic and produced lengthy delays. Until 1972, we had the bizarre set-up of each assize judge being followed around his circuit by all relevant paperwork, clerks and other functionaries, from one assize town to another. A day was set aside for travelling (a relic of horse drawn transport) and a day each for packing and unpacking. During this period the court was incommunicado to all users.

Similarly, the power of magistrates to run their own courts until 2005 had many negative consequences. The abolition of magistrates' courts committees by the Courts Act 2003 resulted from a recommendation of Auld L.J.'s *Review of the Criminal Courts*. I for one urged him to get rid of them. Researching in the 1970s, I found that magistrates' training varied radically, depending on the views of the local MCC, as did the quality and qualifications of the clerks (legal advisers) they hired. Throughout the 1980s, many magistrates' courts were closed (see Ch.6), destroying local justice, and such closures were often the decisions of MCCs. By 1998, they had all acquired different computer hardware and software systems which could not communicate with one another or with other criminal justice agencies. Attempting to co-ordinate all these systems then replace them was an enormous waste of public money.

In its case law activity, if not in its management, our judiciary **14–010** has grown in review power and independence since 1960 and this has re-adjusted the balance of power between the three organs of government. Stevens pointed out that judicial review of executive (government) action had grown out of all recognition. This, I would add, was escalated by introducing a much easier judicial review procedure in 1981 and has been developed on the judges' own initiative, in very significantly broadening the concept of what is "unreasonable", when striking down subordinate legislation and governmental decisions. Then the Human Rights Act 1998 has added new grounds to their tool kit of review. As Stevens said, it is exactly the sort of *droit administratif* that Dicey denied we had. Whenever a Government has tried to oust the power of the courts to review executive action, the courts have circumvented it. In 2004, Labour introduced a Bill which would have abolished judicial review of decisions over asylum seekers and Lord Woolf C.J. criticised it, in a public lecture. In another speech, Lord Steyn attacked the Bill as "contrary to the rule of law" and to the principle of "open justice for all".

An extreme example of the struggle between the judiciary and government over what judges saw as an authoritarian piece of primary legislation was the law lords' declaration of human rights incompatibility of anti-terrorism legislation in December 2004 in *A (FC) v SS for the Home Dept* [2004] UKHL, the Belmarsh case, which is what Lord Phillips was referring to above, in 2011. It is discussed in Ch.4. The judges, in cases like this, see themselves as upholding the rule of law and civil liberties established centuries ago in the ancient unwritten British constitution, and as giving force to the will of Parliament. Helena Kennedy, below, was writing in February 2004 but her words could have been about the Belmarsh case, 10 months later.

"Populist governments can get all manner of laws through Parliament; the whole purpose of human rights principles is that in their application they provide standards against which all law must be measured. . .A common mistake is that MPs come to equate a party political majority with 'Parliament'. . .They seem to think that, as long as a Commons majority approves of what a minister does, nothing more need be said about the legality of his or her behaviour. . .The judges are in fact asserting the supremacy of parliament rather than their own. . .If they fulfil their function properly, judges will at times upset public opinion and governments because they will protect the interests of unpopular minorities—those accused of crime, asylum-seekers, paedophiles, prisoners and probably fox-hunters". (Baroness Helena Kennedy QC, 2004.)

Cases like this have frustrated ministers and prompted them to complain, publicly. In 2004, Stevens said that history had just repeated itself. Judges were nervous at the threatened abolition of the LC because they feared a non-lawyer replacement could not protect them from the increasingly bitter and personal attacks of a powerful minister like Home Secretary David Blunkett. This struggle between judges and government rumbles on, as described below, in 6. Governments see themselves as having a democratic mandate that the "irresponsible" judges lack. Michael Howard recently said,

"The power of the judges, as opposed to the power of elected politicians, has increased, is increasing and ought to be diminished. More and more decisions are being made by unelected, unaccountable judges, instead of accountable, elected Members of Parliament who have to answer to the electorate for what has happened" (Quoted by Lord Phillips, 2011).

This type of concern, over judges' growing review powers, led to calls for candidates to the UKSC be publicly examined, a point addressed below. One judge has also expressed concern over the potential of the UKSC to develop its reviewing power. Lord Neuberger M.R. was a law lord who did not want to join the UKSC. At the time of writing, he is happily back in the CA, as Master of the Rolls. On "Top Dogs", a 2009 BBC Radio 4 programme about the UKSC, he said that transforming the law lords into this court could cause it to become more powerful, to try and assert itself, especially as the European Convention on HR permitted them to reinterpret legislation. "I think we have to be very careful before we find ourselves giving the judges more power". Lord Phillips, the UKSC President, and Lord Bingham, outgoing senior law lord, were swift to deny this.

The surprise creation of a Ministry of Justice

The idea of a ministry of justice was mooted in the nineteenth **14–011** century and it was judicial panic about that prospect which led to the LC becoming head of the judiciary in cabinet. This idea was Labour party policy when they were in opposition, until 1997. Some believed that such a ministry, headed by a Cabinet minister from the House of Commons, would provide a counterweight to the power of the Home Office. Many other countries have such a ministry. Its creation in May 2007 made judges think that the government had not understood their duty to protect judicial independence, under the 2005 Act, because they did not even tell the judges, let alone consult them. The LC and the LCJ both learned about it in a Sunday newspaper. Senior judges were very concerned to ensure that judicial independence was maintained and that HM Courts Service did not suffer cuts resulting from sharing a budget with the over-stretched prison service. They expressed strong views on the lack of consultation and the dangers of the change when they appeared before the House of Lords Constitutional Affairs Committee (HLCC). The HLCC and the House of Commons Constitutional Affairs Committee criticised the Government for failing to realise the constitutional implications. The HLCC wanted greater protection for judicial independence. Note the strongly worded castigation in 2006–07 in their

Report on *Relations between the executive, the judiciary and Parliament*, July 2007.

"We are disappointed that the Government seem to have learnt little or nothing from the debacle surrounding the constitutional reforms initiated in 2003. The creation of the Ministry of Justice clearly has important implications for the judiciary. The new dispensation created by the Constitutional Reform Act and the Concordat requires the Government to treat the judiciary as partners, not merely as subjects of change." (para.175.)

Individual judicial independence

14–012   While we do not have an independent judiciary with a power equal to that of Parliament (the "lions" are *under* the "mace"), we do protect the independence of individual judges. In modern times, independence and impartiality is a fundamental principle of the United Nations Basic Principles on the Independence of the Judiciary, General Assembly Resolution 40/31 and 40/149 and the European Convention on HR, Art.6, as enacted into UK law in The Human Rights Act 1998. Judicial independence seems to contain these elements:

1. Security of tenure

14–013   Making them easily removable would subject them to political interference. Senior judges enjoy a formidable security of tenure. Under the Act of Settlement 1701, they may only be removed following a motion by both Houses of Parliament. No English judge has been removed in this way. Until 2005, removing and disciplining the lower judiciary (that means circuit judge and below) was the LC's job. In the 2005 Act, power of discipline is transferred to the LCJ. With the agreement of the LC, he may advise, warn or reprimand any judge. Under the Courts Act 1971, the LC can remove a circuit judge from office on the ground of incapacity or misbehaviour. Under the 2005 Act this can only be done with the LCJ's consent. The Office for Judicial Complaints is discussed below.

Concern arose that short term judicial appointments, which the English legal system relies on, breached Art.6 of the Convention. This arose from the Scottish case of *Starrs v Ruxton* [2000] J.C. 208. It was held that a temporary sheriff in Scotland was insufficiently secure in his judicial role to satisfy Art.6. Immediately, the LC abolished the post of assistant recorder. He announced that all part-time appointments would be for a period of at least five years.

2. High salaries

These are fixed by a non-governmental body, the Senior Salaries **14–014** Review Body. A high salary was meant to protect them from corruption. Relative to 1825, when judicial salaries were fixed at £5,500, and relative to modern barristers' earnings, judges are not very highly paid, now. Most senior judges and many circuit judges are appointed from the ranks of Queen's Counsel, whose average earnings are over £250,000 per year. Several earn millions. Judges' salaries are currently frozen, from 2009. A High Court judge is paid £172,000 and a circuit judge £128,000 which is less than the highest earning primary head teacher, at £231,000 (*Daily Mail*, May 10, 2011). Lord Woolf C.J. warned, in 2005, that unless HC salaries were kept at a level that did not undermine the status of the job, there was a risk that senior barristers would turn down the offer of a judicial post.

3. Judges cannot be MPs and should not engage in politics

It was very common in the early twentieth century for judges **14–015** to have been MPs and a political career was seen as a good background for life on the bench. This died out in the latter half of the century. Lawyers were heavily represented in Parliament, throughout history. Indeed, Parliament's hours were organised around court sittings so a lawyer could appear in court in the morning and in the House in the afternoon. Stevens (2004) observed that even in 1960, a third of judges had been MPs or Parliamentary candidates.

It is important to acknowledge, though, that a few members of the lower judiciary have been local councillors, some senior judges have been high profile "political animals" and no attempt has ever been made to separate lay magistrates from politics. Many of them are local councillors. In the 1970s, in some towns, most councillors were also magistrates. By convention (political tradition), the law lords were meant to refrain from taking part in political debates in the House of Lords, confining themselves to debates on law reform Bills, but much recent law reform has been very politically charged, notably the debates on the Criminal Justice Bill 2003, when the LCJ attacked the Home Secretary's plans to set jail terms for murderers. Masterman gave examples of cases in which individual law lords could not sit in judgments involving legislation upon which they had expressed a view in Parliament.

Out of court, judges are meant to refrain from controversial and outspoken speeches but the rule has frequently been broken, said Stevens (1993), giving the example of Lord Goddard C.J.'s enthusiasm for hanging and flogging, in the 1950s. Lord Denning frequently courted controversy in the 1970s and 1980s. He gave speeches in law schools, even during an election campaign, attacking secondary picketing. A reprimand was famously delivered by the LC to Melford Stevenson J. for describing the Sexual Offences Act 1967, legalising private homosexual acts, as "a buggers' charter".

14–016 In 1988, Mackay L.C. suspended the Kilmuir Rules, which had prevented judges speaking out in public. This was taken advantage of by Judge James Pickles, who invited media attention at every opportunity, culminating in the development of his own chat show. One day, in 1990, he went too far. He called a press conference in a Wakefield pub, in which he discussed a Court of Appeal case which had criticised him and called the Lord Chief Justice "an aged dinosaur". This was too much for the tolerant and mild mannered Mackay L.C. He released his letter of "serious rebuke" to the press, in which he sought loyalty to the CA and instructed the judge to stop taking substantial fees for his media appearances. After his retirement, in 1991, Pickles became the *Sun's* star columnist, styling himself "Judge Pickles", a title he was no longer permitted to use. James Pickles' books tell the story of his cat and mouse games with two Lord Chancellors in entertaining detail.

In his campaign for the Chancellorship of Oxford in 2003, Lord Bingham "call me Tom" of Cornhill, then senior law lord, was very outspoken and set up his own website. He called for the legalisation of cannabis, stating it "is stupid to have a law which is not doing what it is there for". He wanted all wigs and gowns banned and better pay for judges.

One controversial practice that critics say forced judges into the political arena in an undesirable manner was the use of judges to chair public inquiries. This was an enormous waste of judicial time. Masterman (2004) gave the example of Lord Saville who had been hearing the Bloody Sunday inquiry since 1999. This deprived us of one of twelve Law Lords for almost ten years. See Beatson's extensive examination of this topic but the practice has now stopped.

Like many law students, I read J.A.G. Griffiths' *The Politics of the Judiciary*, which taught us how Labour governments were suspicious of judges, because of their reputation for conservatism and for undermining Labour legislation. I never thought I would see judges opposing governments from the *left* but from 1996 to 2010, the two main political parties tried to outdo one another on being tough on crime and terrorism and asylum seekers. Judges are consistently the voice of the liberal left, of human rights and the rule of law. The litmus test for this is that attacks on judges now come from the right wing press.

---

4. Judges cannot be sued for remarks in court

5. Parliamentarians do not criticise judicial decisions

Stevens pointed out that this convention is set down in *Erskine* **14–017**
May, Parliamentary Practice but remarked that, while the rule about
not commenting on cases sub judice seemed to have remained
intact, criticism of judges has been more acceptable in recent decades. In evidence to the House of Lords Constitutional Affairs
Committee in 2007, the judiciary argued that individual judges
should not be asked to explain their decisions because they were
accountable via the media and they are "institutionally accountable". Judges are sometimes criticised in Parliament, as they were
in 2011, for granting of super-injunctions to protect public figures,
like footballers but Lord Judge C.J. said judges were only trying to
enforce the Human Rights Act that Parliament itself had passed.

6. Politicians should refrain from criticising judges out of court

Thanks to Home Secretary David Blunkett, this rule seemed to **14–018**
have flown out of the window in 2000–05. In *R. (Q) v SS for the
Home Dept* [2003] EWHC 195 (Admin), Andrew Collins J. ruled that
the Government's policy of requiring asylum seekers to register on
arrival in the UK was unfair. Blunkett launched into a vendetta,
supported by the *Daily Mail*, which showed no appreciation of the
separation of powers. He complained of being "frankly fed up"
with judges overturning measures Parliament had debated. The
LCJ and other judges defended Collins J. as upholding the will of
Parliament. Irvine L.C. was scathing about his Cabinet colleague,
"Maturity requires that, when you get a decision that favours you,
you do not clap. And when you get one that goes against you, you
don't boo." This illustrated the argument of those who supported
the continued presence of the Lord Chancellor in the Cabinet.
Things went from bad to worse in 2003. A retired judge, Sir Oliver
Popplewell accused Blunkett of being a "whiner" and Blunkett
said judges were out of touch with public views on sentencing, in
a speech to the police. "I just want judges that live in the same real
world as the rest of us. I just like judges who help us and help you to
do the job". In the same week, he said the chairman of the Bar, had
"lost the plot", in criticising his plans on criminal justice. Blunkett
grumbled when the courts took away his power to determine life
prisoners' release dates, because of the Human Rights Act (see
Ch.4).

As it turned out, judges were right to be anxious in the 2003
debate to ensure that the Constitutional Reform Act should require
that ministers should respect their independence. The very next
year, when Lord Bingham refused to "discuss" the Belmarsh case

with him, Home Secretary Charles Clarke complained "The judiciary bears not the slightest responsibility for protecting the public and sometimes seems utterly unaware of the implications of their decisions for our society"(quoted by Lord Phillips, 2011). Stevens considered the guarantee of judicial independence in the 2005 Act to be meaningless and as far as some ministers are concerned, it has proven to be ineffective. Prime Minister Blair showed a lack of appreciation of independence, as guaranteed by his own Constitutional Reform Act, in July 2005, when he expressed the hope that judges would now change their hostility toward terrorist legislation after the suicide bombings of July 7 (7/7). Retired judges, Lords Ackner and Donaldson defended the judiciary. Blair was also irritated by the Belmarsh case. His wife, Cherie Booth QC, was swift to defend the judges' human rights record. JUSTICE launched a *Manifesto for the Rule of Law*. In it, they asked governments to refrain from criticising judges in a way that would diminish public confidence.

In summer 2006, Vera Baird, junior minister for the Department of Constitutional Affairs, joined in the *Sun's* campaign against judges, described below, making mistakes of fact, and forgetting the Lord Chancellor's (her senior minister's) and her own statutory duty to defend the independence of the judiciary. She had to apologise. The main target of the attack was a judge who had announced to a paedophile (Sweeney) that he would be eligible for parole after five years of his sentence. Critics did not understand that he was obliged to read this out, and that the law and government ministers prescribed the parole regime. The House of Lords Constitutional Affairs Committee were severely critical, in their 2007 report, mentioned above,

> "The Sweeney case was the first big test of whether the new relationship between the Lord Chancellor and the judiciary was working properly, and it is clear that there was a systemic failure. Ensuring that ministers do not impugn individual judges, and restraining and reprimanding those who do, is one of the most important duties of the Lord Chancellor. In this case, Lord Falconer did not fulfil this duty in a satisfactory manner."

7. The media should refrain from criticising judges

14–019　Looking at newspaper reporting over the centuries, I doubt that this was ever a convention. Stevens reports that the idea that criticising a judge was a contempt of court was invented by the CA in 1900 to protect Darling J. It is clear that by now, judge-bashing is a hobby of the *Daily Mail* and a fairly frequent indulgence of other "red top" newspapers. When Lord Woolf spoke up for asylum seekers and the rule of law, he was met with "loutish pummelling" by certain papers, as *The Times* columnist Anthony Howard put it. Lord Woolf C.J. made speeches deprecating this behaviour but it never had any impact. At long last the LCJ established a press office in 2005, to defend the judiciary. In June 2006 the *Sun* started a "name and shame" campaign against judges it considered to be over-lenient and Lord Phillips C.J. publicly defended them.

8. Freedom from interference with decision making

14–020 It is a hallmark of undemocratic regimes that the government tells the judges how to judge. Judicial freedom in this sense includes the discretion to conduct procedures as they see fit. A lengthy spat went on in 2003–04 between Lord Woolf and David Blunkett, over sentencing and whether the judiciary or the executive should decide the minimum sentence for murder, for example, and who should decide when to release prisoners. The Home Secretary suffered a series of defeats before the European Court of Human Rights and the House of Lords, under Art.6 of the Convention, which prescribes that judges, not government ministers, should exercise judicial powers. The UK was the only country in the Council of Europe that permitted executive control over sentencing, something that Blunkett could never understand was unacceptable under Art.6. Blunkett retaliated by amending the Criminal Justice Bill 2003 to introduce statutory minimum sentences. Lord Woolf was very outspoken in criticising this. Lord Donaldson, a former Master of the Rolls, said the Bill's provisions on sentencing revealed the Home Secretary's total misunderstanding of the judiciary in the British unwritten constitution. He explained this element of individual judicial independence, as he saw it.

> "Parliament can limit the powers of judges, can indicate its view of what should be the appropriate sentences for the normal sort of offence. What it cannot do, either directly or through guideline-making bodies, is to dictate what should be the proper sentence in individual cases, the circumstances of which are infinitely variable." (House of Lords chamber, June 17, 2003.)

9. The rule against bias

14–021 Individual judges are meant to conduct proceedings in a fair and unbiased manner, without interfering in the presentation of the case. If they "step down into the arena" of the court (metaphorically) the result may be appealed or judicially reviewed. Similarly, judges must recuse themselves (stand down) if they have a connection with any of the parties or the issues. In *Pinochet Ugarte (No.2), Re* [2000] 1 A.C. 61, the House of Lords extended the rule that a judge was automatically disqualified from a hearing in which he had a pecuniary interest to cases where the judge was involved personally, or as a director of a company, in promoting some cause. In this case, the law lords had to re-hear a case in which Lord Hoffman had failed to declare his connections with Amnesty International. In June 2000, following *Locabail* [2000] Q.B. 451, the Lord Chancellor published guidance to judges on outside interests, on his website. The bias test is now set out in *Medicaments and Related Classes of Goods (No.2), Re* [2001] 1 W.L.R. 700, by Lord Phillips M.R. (as paraphrased in *The Times* law report, February 2, 2001):

> "The Court first had to ascertain all the circumstances which had a bearing on the suggestion that the judge was biased. It then had to ask whether those circumstances would lead a fair-minded and informed observer to conclude that there was a real possibility, or a real danger, the two being the same, that the tribunal was biased. The material circumstances would include any explanation given by the judge under review as to his knowledge or appreciation of those circumstances."

Helow v SS for the Home Dept [2008] UKHL 62 added that the question is one of law, to be answered in the light of the relevant facts. This may include a statement from the judge as to what he knew at the time but there was no question of cross-examining the judge.

In 2004, the Judges' Council produced a *Guide to Judicial Conduct*, now on the judiciary website, explaining to judges the practical implications of the requirement for independence, impartiality, propriety, equality of treatment, competence and diligence. These requirements were laid down in the Bangalore Principles of Judicial Conduct, initiated by the United Nations in 2001. All judges receive equal treatment training and a substantial handbook. If judges behave discourteously or partially in court, they will rapidly find they may be the subject of complaint or an appeal. Examples are given in Ch.12 on criminal procedure.

In *Howell v Lees Millais* [2007] EWCA 720 the CA heavily criticised Peter Smith J. The judge was negotiating with a firm of solicitors for a consultancy, if he were to retire from the bench. It ended with an acrimonious email from the judge. Shortly after this, a hotly contested trust case came before him, involving a partner in the same firm. The QC asked the judge, by letter, to recuse himself and he refused to do so. This application was renewed in court, with a partner from the firm appearing as a witness. There was then an astonishing exchange between the judge and the QC. The judge remarked that the QC's application was nonsense, that he ought to grow up and that he lived on another planet. He threatened the QC with "professional consequences". The judge still refused to stand down so the claimants applied to the CA and the hearing occurred three days later. The Master of the Rolls, leading the court, said the transcript "did not make happy reading". The judge was referred to the Office for Judicial Complaints for his failure to recuse himself and was reprimanded. This is a sad case. The judge was the darling of the press a few months earlier, portrayed in a very favourable light, when he wrote his own code within his judgment in the case on the book *The Da Vinci Code*. Just as cringe worthy was the story behind *El Farargy v El Farargy* [2007] EWCA Civ 1149. In a preliminary hearing, the HC judge commented on the unco-operative behaviour of H, an Egyptian Muslim, and asked "What good would that do if he chose to depart on his flying carpet?" He asked counsel if H's evidence was "a bit gelatinous. . .like Turkish delight?" He suggested that maybe he should not take the case then, remarkably, refused to recuse himself. The CA called his remarks "regrettable and unacceptable".

10. A politically independent appointments system

For many decades, the system was in the hands of one person, **14–022** the LC, a politician, and was criticised as an affront to judicial independence and open to political abuse. Stevens' 1993 book gives ample examples of political appointments. Most notably in modern times, Lord Donaldson was appointed Master of the Rolls by Margaret Thatcher after many controversial years chairing the National Industrial Relations Court, the scourge of trade unions. He languished unpromoted during the interim Labour governments. It does not follow, however, that Prime Ministers will always select judges according to party political bias. Famously, Conservative John Major appointed Sedley J., a sometime member of the Communist Party, and some of his other senior appointments were of fairly outspoken radicals. The danger of allowing politicians to appoint judges is illustrated by a story told in 2004 by Keene L.J.:

> "When Margaret Thatcher was Prime Minister, she had a conversation with one of her back benchers, who told her that the then Lord Chief Justice, Geoffrey Lane, had said something critical of government policy. Her response, as I have been told by the backbencher in question was 'What, my Lord Chief Justice?' That is emphatically not how the system should be."

11. Impartiality

This is a close relation of independence. Individual judges are **14–023** meant to be impartial, hence the rule against bias, but from the

1970s critics have attacked the appointment system and rules of eligibility for the judiciary on the grounds that it produces a judiciary of "old, white, male geezers" as Lord Hoffman called himself, in the quotation heading this chapter. Judges such as Baroness Brenda Hale and Laura Cox J. have long argued that judges who are so demographically imbalanced cannot possibly be impartial in their judgments over a diverse population. This brings us neatly to the appointments system.

3. Who can apply to be a judge?

14–024 Qualifications for being a judge are all set out in statute. Historically, most judicial appointments were restricted to barristers, the exception being registrars in the county court. Since solicitors have always had rights of audience in county courts, they have always been eligible for appointment as county court registrars, now called district judges. The Courts and Legal Services Act 1990 based eligibility on rights of audience. As part of the Government's attempt to diversify the judiciary, described below, the Tribunals, Courts and Enforcement Act 2007 amends this. Part 2 changes the minimum eligibility requirements to stipulate that an applicant must satisfy the "judicial-appointment eligibility condition". In almost all instances, this means the applicant must be a barrister or solicitor and must have had relevant experience in law for the qualifying period, meaning if a person was a legal adviser, or law lecturer, say, for five years, whilst qualified as a solicitor or barrister, they would satisfy the five year judicial appointment eligibility condition. Section 52 specifies what is meant by gaining experience in law to satisfy the eligibility condition. It includes working as a paralegal, teaching and researching law, acting as an arbitrator and so on. Section 50 permits the LC to extend qualification to legal executives and members of other designated bodies and by 2010, this had been done. In respect of many judicial offices, the number of years for which a person must have held qualification before they become eligible for judicial office is also reduced. Below, all those who now have to be qualified for five years previously had to have been qualified for seven years.

Justices of the Supreme Court
14–025 When the Supreme Court replaced the House of Lords Appellate Committee in 2009, (see Ch.6), the first Justices were the existing law lords and their qualification was the same, as prescribed by the Constitutional Reform Act 2005. They were

appointed by the Queen by letters patent. They must satisfy the judicial-appointment eligibility condition on a 15 year basis, or have been a qualifying practitioner for 15 years. The PM still recommends appointments but under the 2005 Act, he has no discretion. He must pass on the recommendation made to him by the LC. The new selection system is described below. The Act creates posts of President and Deputy President. The first President was selected in 2008, Lord Phillips of Worth Matravers, who was LCJ at that time. New Justices are now given the courtesy title "My Lord" or "My Lady". Note the alleged scandal of judges forcing Jonathan Sumption QC out of the recruitment race in summer 2009, before the new appointment system came into force: F. Gibb (2010). He had the last laugh when he was appointed direct to the UKSC from the Bar in 2011. This is unusual but not unique. Though almost all members of the top court (former law lords and now UKSC) are former CA judges, at least two law lords were recruited direct from the Bar. Lord Slynn was a judge in the European Court of Justice. As with the law lords, there is always one Justice from Northern Ireland and two from Scotland.

The Heads of Division: Master of the Rolls, Lord Chief Justice, Chancellor (of the Chancery Division), and Presidents of the Family Division and Q.B.D., e.g. The Right Honourable Lord Neuberger of Abbotsbury M.R.

These are appointed by the Monarch on the advice of the **14–026** Prime Minister. The Queen takes no part in the choice and the PM is advised by the Lord Chancellor. Recruits must be Lords Justices of Appeal (and most are) or qualified as such. The Judicial Appointments Commission (JAC) selects just one candidate and that person's name must be passed onto the PM from the LC. They have lost the discretion in the selection process that they had before the 2005 Act was passed. The LC may only reject a candidate or ask the selection panel to reconsider if he considers the selected candidate unsuitable.

Lords Justices of Appeal, e.g. The Right Honourable Sir Stephen Price Richards, Lord Justice Richards, or Richards L.J.

These judges sit in the CA. They are appointed by the Monarch **14–027** on the advice of the PM, who receives a recommendation from the LC who, in turn, will be given just one name by the JAC. They must satisfy a seven-year "judicial appointment eligibility condition" or be judges of the HC, which is the normal route.

High Court judges, e.g. The Honourable Sir Peter Coulson, or Coulson J., or Mr Justice Coulson

14–028   These are appointed by the Queen on the advice of the LC. They need to satisfy a seven-year "judicial-appointment eligibility condition", or to have been a circuit judge for at least two years. A few appointments are made from circuit judges and the rest are mainly barristers who have practised for 20 to 30 years and are QCs. The Courts and Legal Services Act 1990 made solicitor-advocates eligible for appointment.

Deputy High Court judges

14–029   These are appointed by the Lord Chancellor, under the Supreme Court Act (renamed Senior Courts Act) 1981, s.9 (4). There is a policy of testing out potential HC judges by appointing them to sit part-time, as deputies.

Retired judges

14–030   The LC has power to authorise retired senior judges to sit part-time until their 75th birthday.

Circuit judges, e.g. Her Honour Judge Barnes

14–031   These are appointed by the Queen on the recommendation of the LC, under the Courts Act 1971. From 2006, they have been selected by the JAC. They must satisfy the judicial appointment eligibility condition on a seven year basis, meaning solicitor with a Crown Court advocacy certificate, or barrister, or be a recorder or have been in fulltime office in another judicial capacity, such as a district judge. The LC will normally consider only applicants who have sat as recorders for at least two years, or 30 sitting days. Once appointed, circuit judges may sit at the Crown Court or county court, or both. Some sit in the specialised jurisdictions, such as chancery or mercantile cases. Experienced circuit judges may be authorised to hear HC cases. Some senior circuit judges sit occasionally in the Criminal Division of the CA.

Deputy circuit judges

14–032   These are appointed by the LC from among retired judges.

Recorders, e.g. Cherie Booth QC

14–033   These are part-timers appointed by the Queen, on the recommendation of the LC for a renewable period of five years. From 2006, they have been selected by the Judicial Appointments Commission. Appointees must satisfy the judicial-appointment eligibility condition on a seven year basis. In other words, they must be a barrister or solicitor. They sit in the Crown Court and/or the county court, handling less serious matters than a circuit judge. They are required to sit for at least 15–30 days per year, of which at least 10 days should be in one continuous period.

District judges, e.g. District Judge Gold

These are appointed by the Queen, under the 2005 Act. They sit **14–034** full-time in the county courts, disposing of over 80 per cent of all contested civil litigation. The statutory qualification is to satisfy the judicial-appointment eligibility condition on a five year basis. The LC normally only considers applicants who have been serving deputy district judges for two years. From 2006, they are selected by the JAC. They are appointed on the recommendation of the LC.

Deputy district judges

They sit part-time for 20–50 days per year. Their performance **14–035** is appraised and helps inform the selection process of those who apply for fulltime posts.

Registrars and masters of the High Court

These mainly deal with interlocutory (pre-trial) HC work, as trial **14–036** managers. Taxing masters tax costs. They are normally appointed aged 40–60, from the ranks of deputy masters. They must satisfy the judicial-appointment eligibility condition on a five year basis. From 2006, they are appointed by the Queen, on the recommendation of the LC but selected by the JAC.

District judges (magistrates' courts)

They are described in depth in the chapter on magistrates. They **14–037** sit full-time in the magistrates' court and must normally have served as a deputy. They must satisfy the judicial-appointment eligibility condition on a five year basis.

Tribunal judges

They are described on the Judiciary website. **14–038**

4. The judicial appointments system from 2006

This section examines the new system and the consultation that **14–039** preceded it before analysing in greater detail the arguments that provoked this reform.

The Constitutional Reform Act 2005

14–040   The Act radically altered the system of appointments to meet mounting criticism of the old system, whereby most appointments were effectively in the gift of the Lord Chancellor, who consulted with the judiciary. In this section, I examine the new statutory framework and below, the background consultation and arguments. The wording of these sections and schedules of the Act is complex so I have relied heavily on the explanatory memorandum accompanying the Act.

Selecting and appointing UK Supreme Court (UKSC) Justices

14–041   When a Justice is needed, a special Selection Commission is appointed, in accordance with the 2005 Act. It consists of the President of the UKSC, the Deputy and one member from each of three Judicial Appointments Commissions, Scotland, Northern Ireland and England and Wales. At least one must be a non-lawyer. Once the LC has accepted the selection made, the Commission is dissolved. Selection must be on merit. The Commission must consult senior judges and ministers from each jurisdiction. Once a selection has been made, the LC can accept it or ask the Commission to reconsider, or reject their selection but the Act severely curtails his discretion in doing this and limits the acceptable grounds for rejection. When the creation of the UKSC was announced in 2003, law lord, Lord Steyn commented that a small appointing commission, like this, would be appropriate,

> "the new system will have to be more open and transparent than has so far been the case. . . it should be a neutral and impartial body. It must therefore be in no way identified with the government or civil service. On the other hand it should not be entirely dominated by judges." (2003.)

The Act provides for "acting judges" to be used to supplement the permanent SC Justices, where the president or deputy requests it. They must be drawn from the Supplementary Panel or Courts of Appeal of the three jurisdictions of the UK. The Panel consists of retired UKSC Justices, in the same way that retired Lords of Appeal in Ordinary could supplement the fulltime law lords. The background discussion to all of this is contained in the 2003 consultation paper, *Constitutional Reform: a Supreme Court for the United Kingdom*, which is archived on the Department of Constitutional Affairs website, along with a summary of responses. The Supreme Court was also the subject of law lords' speeches and many academic articles, which are discussed and listed in Ch.6 and above.

Judges growth in judicial reviewing power, referred to above, is what that prompted Stevens (back in 1994) and others to argue that the views of the judges are a matter of public interest so maybe candidates for the top courts should be carefully publicly examined before appointment, as they are in the USA and South Africa, since judges' decisions frequently have political repercussions. Furthermore, in enforcing the HR Convention, the courts have effectively become constitutional watchdogs and the extreme argument is that the UKSC Justices now effectively constitute a constitutional court. For this reason, John Patten, a former Conservative Home Office Minister, argued in favour of public hearings before the appointment of a law lord, similar to those when a new US Supreme Court Justice is appointed (*The Times*, March 16, 1999). Dawn Oliver examined these oft-repeated arguments in 2003 but emphasised the problems. She questioned what criteria such a confirmation hearing would apply. A Parliamentary Committee would be less qualified than an appointments commission to make a decision on a candidate's suitability. A hearing was likely to be concerned with a judge's beliefs and politics, which ought not to be relevant in the UK. Ultimately it could lead to a reduction in security of tenure. Our system assumed judges were open minded and would not let their own prejudices influence them and this had generally worked. The idea was revived in Gordon Brown's Cabinet's consultation paper, *The Governance of Britain: Appointing Judges.* Zander called it "A waste of space". Coming just a year after the establishment of the JAC, it was "ridiculous". He attacked the implicit suggestion that the judiciary should change to reflect "the communities of Britain", as judges do not serve communities. They serve the law, the administration of justice and, in a vague sense, the community and "The very idea that Parliament should exercise a role in the making of judicial appointments sends shivers down the spine of lawyers". The politicised selection system for USSC Justices is well publicised in England and lawyers and judges do tend to find it repugnant, because of the undignified spectacle of US candidates making all manner of meaningless assertions to try to get elected. Sonya Sotomayer had to retract five speeches containing the assertion that "a wise Latina woman with the richness of her experiences would, more often than not, reach a better conclusion", once adding ". . .than a white male who hasn't lived that life". She also asserted, like some of her predecessors, that a judge's job was to apply law, not make it (see Smith, 2009). This is a farcical notion in a common law country and all the more so in the USSC.

Other judges—The Judicial Appointments Commission

14–042   The Act created a new independent Judicial Appointments Commission (JAC), which, in 2006, assumed responsibility for the judicial appointment selection process in England and Wales and for appointments to UK-wide tribunals made by the LC. The JAC selects one candidate for each vacancy, or several candidates where multiple vacancies arise, and reports that selection to the LC. The Commission makes selections for appointment of the Lord Chief Justice, Heads of Division, Lords Justices of Appeal and HC judges, and Sch.12 of the Act lists the offices below the HC for which the Commission will make selections (with tribunal members being the largest group of appointments). In other words, selection of the lower judiciary (circuit judges and below) is purely a matter for the Commission.

The LC appoints or recommends for appointment the selected candidate, or rejects a candidate, once, or asks the Commission to reconsider, once. Having exhausted these options of rejection and reconsideration, the LC *must* appoint or recommend for appointment whichever candidate is selected. The Act makes special provision for the appointment of the LCJ and Heads of Division and of Lords Justices of Appeal; in these cases the Commission will establish a selection panel of four members, consisting of two senior judges (normally including the LCJ) and two lay members of the Commission. The appointments of Lords Justices and above continue to be made by The Queen formally on the advice of the Prime Minister after the Commission has made a recommendation to the LC.

The Act requires the Commission to encourage diversity and specifies that "selection must be solely on merit" and that appointees must be of good character. This is the first time that this has been a statutory requirement. Under the pre-2006 system, the LC's informal criteria specified that appointments must be made solely on merit. The LC is able to issue guidance to the Commission, to which they must have regard, but it is for them to determine the detailed appointments procedures they follow. Guidance can only be issued after consultation with the LCJ and after being approved in draft by both Houses of Parliament. The Commission must report on its selections and methods to the LC and he can, in consultation with the LCJ, require them to make specific reports.

14–043   Schedule 12 sets out the membership of the JAC and its powers and responsibilities, which reflect its status as an executive non-departmental public body. There is a lay chairman with five other lay members, five judicial members, two legal professionals, the holder of an office listed in Sch.12 and a Justice of the Peace. Commissioners are appointed for five years and can hold appointment for a maximum of 10. Chris Stephens was appointed to chair it, part-time, for three years, from February 2011. He was chairman of Traidcraft and of a development charity. The other commissioners work for three days per month. The details of the way the JAC operates are on its website, as are its frequent reports on its progress in diversifying the judiciary. It advertises each new competition. As well as requiring a written self-assessment application form and references, it administers assessment days or selection days and, for some posts, written qualifying tests which are designed to assess legal reasoning, forensic judgment and ability to explain decisions. Aspiring judges can subject themselves to practice tests. Selection exercises are tailored to the posts for which the JAC is recruiting. The written tests were discussed by J. Sumption QC, a JAC Commissioner, now appointed direct from the Bar to the UKSC, in *Counsel* magazine, in April 2011 and, as an example, Toulson L.J. explains senior circuit judge selection in the November 2010 edition of *Counsel*.

Removal of judges, discipline and complaints

The LC has statutory powers to remove judicial office holders **14–044** below the HC (including tribunal members and lay magistrates) for incapacity or misbehaviour. These powers can be exercised only with the agreement of the LCJ. The LC previously exercised an informal, non-statutory power to discipline judges, considering complaints about judicial conduct and, where necessary, writing warning or admonitory letters, as can be seen above. Part 4 of the Act makes statutory provision for a disciplinary system in relation to judges, in cases falling short of removal, in which the Lord Chief Justice is given power to advise, warn or reprimand, following disciplinary proceedings, with the agreement of the LC. This does not affect the LCJ's general ability to speak informally to any judge on any matter which concerns him, without having to inform or obtain the agreement of the LC. The LCJ may suspend judges from sitting, with the agreement of the LC. The LCJ has the power to make regulations and rules governing disciplinary cases, with the agreement of the LC. The Judicial Appointments and Conduct Ombudsman, who must be a lawyer, is able to consider complaints about the handling of disciplinary cases. The Ombudsman must report annually to the Lord Chancellor.

Under previous legislation, a Liverpool county court judge, William Ramshay, was removed, following endless complaints and an unseemly battle with the press. Judge Keith Bruce Campbell was removed, in 1983, following his conviction for smuggling 125 litres of whisky and 9,000 cigarettes. Judges often resign before they can be removed. Circuit Judge Angus MacArthur resigned from the Bench in 1997, shortly before being convicted for his third drink-driving offence and jailed for 28 days. In 1998, commentators were critical when Butler-Sloss L.J. was offered retraining instead of prosecution for careless driving after a crash which left a passenger with facial injuries. The problem with cases where judges receive lenient treatment is that the public may perceive them to be above the law.

There is no statutory definition of "misbehaviour" so it was up to the interpretation of the LC of the time, although this has become much clearer, now the Judges' Council has published a *Guide to Judicial Conduct* on the Judiciary website. Appended to it is guidance to the judiciary on reporting their minor offences, agreed by the LC and LCJ. Using his powers under the Constitutional Reform Act, the LCJ has passed the Judicial Discipline (Prescribed Procedures) Regulations 2006. These are on the website of the Office for Judicial Complaints, created by the 2005 Act. Its latest *Annual Report* gives general details of complaints about judges, and outcomes. 1,571 complaints were made in 2009–10. One in four complained about behaviour or inappropriate comments. Of 28 office holders removed from office, 25 were magistrates: five were involved in court proceedings or had criminal convictions and three were accused of professional misconduct. There were 18 resignations during the conduct of investigations.

Judges who leave office

14–045   In 2005, Laddie J. announced that he was leaving the HC out of boredom and because he would prefer teamwork in a solicitor's firm to the isolation of his judicial role. Michael Cook, a former circuit judge, also announced that he was to join a firm of solicitors. In 2007, following consultation, the Government concluded that the convention that former judges should not return to practice should remain in place. It had been suggested that permitting judges to return to practice might encourage more applicants but there was insufficient evidence that lifting it would increase diversity. It is not strictly true that there is a ban on judges resigning and returning to practice, as has sometimes been said. In 1970, Sir Henry Fisher left the HC after two years, to work in the City. Like Laddie J., he found the job boring. He also despised the snobbery of some other HC judges.

Immediate background to the new appointments scheme: the 2003 consultation paper *Constitutional Reform: a new way of appointing judges* and responses

Since the 1970s, criticism had mounted that the appointments system was unfair and drew from too narrow a pool of potential candidates and this is explored in depth, below, in s.5. Most judges were chosen by just one man, the LC, a politician. He appointed (and still appoints) all lay justices, on the recommendation of local advisory committees. He selected all of the lower

> "We are fortunate to have a judiciary that is politically neutral, **14–046**
> uncorrupt, and of the highest calibre, with an international
> standing second to none. However we intend that a Judicial
> Appointments Commission will insulate more the appoint-
> ment of judges from politicians. It will also promote opening
> up appointments to some of those groups of lawyers which are
> under-represented in the judiciary at the moment, including
> women, ethnic minorities and, at the higher levels, solicitors."
> (Falconer L.C., announcing the consultation papers on constitu-
> tional reform, July 2003, DCA Press Release 296/03.)

judiciary (circuit judges and below) and he put forward names
for the senior judiciary, to be considered by the PM. He consulted
widely among the existing judiciary, seeking their opinions on
candidates for the judiciary. Lord Chancellors made progres-
sive reforms, from 1994, but these did not satisfy the critics. The
Bench was said to be too narrow, in terms of class, education, age,
gender and ethnic background. The old scheme was repeatedly
criticised by academics, politicians, the pressure group JUSTICE,
the Law Society and women and minority lawyers' groups. The
most thorough exposure of these views was collected in the
House of Commons Home Affairs Committee, third report for
the session 1995–96, *Judicial Appointments Procedures Volume II,
Minutes of Evidence and Appendices* (1996), abbreviated here to
"JAP" and examined in s.5.

As part of the package of constitutional reforms announced in
2003, the Government proposed to reform judicial appointments
and its proposals were set out in the consultation paper named
above. They sought views on their declared intent to create a new,
independent commission for selecting judges in England and
Wales, to replace the Lord Chancellor because:

"In a modern democratic society it is no longer acceptable for
judicial appointments to be entirely in the hands of a Government
Minister. . .the appointments system must be. . .transpar-
ent. . .accountable. . .inspire public confidence. . .the current judiciary is overwhelmingly white, male and from a narrow social
and educational background. . .the Government is committed to
opening up the system of appointments. . .from a wider range
of social backgrounds and from a wider range of legal practice."
(Foreword by Falconer L.C.)

The LC went on to point out that Scotland and Northern Ireland
already had independent commissions. The Government did not
believe in a continental style career judiciary "but they do believe

that new career paths should be looked at to promote other opportunities and diversity in appointments."

The paper described three possible models: an appointing Commission; a Commission which would make recommendations to a Minister or a hybrid Commission which made junior appointments and recommended senior appointments. The Government favoured a recommending commission, with appointments made by a Minister, with 15 members being appointed by competition: judges, lawyers and non-lawyers. A judicial ombudsman would deal with complaints about appointments.

14–047   The Commission for Judicial Appointments, the former watchdog, had a critical influence. It considered that the majority of the proposed Commission (JAC) should be lay persons, applying best practice on human resources. The Law Society favoured the hybrid model, with the Commission making a single recommendation for a senior vacancy and very narrow ministerial discretion. Appointment to the senior judiciary must be by open competition only. "The absence of any appearance of cronyism is vital to establishing a positive public perception". Tackling the discriminatory aspects of the current process, such as automatic consultation of a homogeneous pool of senior judges, should be a priority. Processes should be speeded up. The Bar Council thought the Minister should have a statutory duty to protect judicial independence. Criteria should be set out in statute, and detailed by the Commission. They referred to their own Glidewell Report 2003 on ways to encourage diversity. The Judges' Council wanted the LCJ to head the judiciary.

On January 26, 2004, Lord Falconer L.C. and Lord Woolf C.J. made speeches in the House of Lords announcing the details of the proposed new statutory framework for constitutional reform. These principles became known as The Concordat. To the undoubted relief of the Government, the LCJ was now in support, having warned in 2003 that the proposed changes posed the biggest threat to judicial independence for centuries. The judges were clearly annoyed that the reforms had been announced without informing them. There had then been extensive negotiations between the judiciary and the LC. Crucially, Lord Falconer QC understood the importance of judicial independence:

"The reforms seek to clarify and embed in statute the principle of judicial independence. Judges must enforce, impartially, the law made by Parliament. The executive must continue to guarantee security of judicial tenure and remuneration, and ensure that the judiciary is supported by an efficient and effective system of court administration. . .there should be a general statutory duty [to uphold]. . . judicial independence. . .there should be a separate specific duty falling on the Secretary of State for Constitutional Affairs to defend and uphold the continuing independence of the judiciary." (*Hansard*, Column 13.)

As can be seen from the contents of the Act, above, the Government changed plans to embody many of the above comments in the Bill. Seventy-six per cent of respondents emphasised the importance of judicial independence. The JAC's responsibilities now extend to tribunal members and were meant to extend to lay justices, as desired by the Law Society and the Bar. In 2011, though, local advisory committees still recommend candidates for magistrate appointments, an old established system.

For judicial appointments up to and including the HC, the JAC advertises vacancies and selects candidates and, after consulting the LCJ, *recommends* a single candidate to the LC, giving reasons. Notice that the Secretary of State's discretion is severely curtailed, as this was favoured by 75 per cent of respondents to the consultation. Notice this new JAC is a recommending commission, despite the fact that the majority of respondents favoured an appointing commission, to guarantee judicial independence, or a hybrid commission. The 24 per cent favouring a *recommending* commission did so because it provides ministerial responsibility to Parliament and it is closest to the old appointment system. Almost all judges are now appointed following open competition and this even applies to specific jobs, such as resident judge in the Crown Court and judges who undertake training. As for heads of division appointments, notice the involvement of the most senior judges, since many respondents felt their views were especially valuable. Also, any appointee would have to command the respect of those colleagues.

5. Deeper background: problems with the old system of appointing judges

The roles of the Lord Chancellor and Prime Minister

As Griffith said, in successive editions of *The Politics of the* **14–048** *Judiciary*, "The most remarkable fact about the appointment of judges is that it is wholly in the hands of politicians". He traced the history of patronage—judicial appointments as a reward for political services. Some bodies had expressed concern about this long ago, such as a JUSTICE sub-committee in 1972 and the Bar in 1989. This point has been discussed under the heading of "Judicial

Independence", above. Nevertheless, as Drewry pointed out, by 1998,

> "even the sternest critics of the present arrangements would surely have to concede that any vestige of the old party political 'spoils' system that prevailed until the early part of this century has been eradicated. Above all the neutrality of judges is underpinned by the strong commitment to the constitutional principle of judicial independence, which is regularly reaffirmed by politicians of all political parties as an essential pillar of the rule of law."

Anyway, he continued, the debate about the political background of judges,

> "has been overtaken in the last couple of decades by the transformation of party political ideology and the social class structure. Even if one accepts that judicial ideology may over the years have displayed some sympathetic resonance with traditional Conservative values, many of those values were displaced or distorted in the 1980s or 1990s by New Right free market radicalism, and Margaret Thatcher's and John Major's ministers were often given a very hard time by the courts." (1998).

Critics remained concerned about the potential for political appointments, as can be seen from Keene L.J.'s comment on Margaret Thatcher, above. Griffith said whether the PM merely accepts the LC's advice on senior appointments or interferes will depend on the personalities of the two but Rozenberg insisted that Thatcher vetoed some of Lord Mackay's suggestions (JAP, p.273). Rodney Brazier, in evidence to the same 1995 Select Committee, voiced the concerns of many:

- The concentration of power in the hands of one person, without the benefit of a structured system of advice, was unsatisfactory. The system lacked openness, relied on unstructured questions to advisers of unknown identity. There was no accountability to Parliament.
- The increased size of both branches of the profession meant the Lord Chancellor could not have adequate knowledge of all potential candidates. (The 1992 JUSTICE report said that, some 50 years earlier, with a Bar of 1,500 and under 100 judges, the Lord Chancellor was personally involved in choosing judges.)

Some modern commentators still advocate removing the role of the Prime Minister. One was Sir Thomas Legg, who had helped Lord Chancellors to select judges for many decades. Another was Sir Iain Glidewell, in his 2003 report for the Bar Council. He considered the system to be constitutionally unacceptably.

In 2005, the PM's role in judicial appointments was the subject of a different type of criticism. Tony Blair was attacked for "cronyism", not for the first time. He selected Potter L.J. to be the new President of the Family Division, with little experience of the family courts. Potter had been the Bar pupil-master of Charlie Falconer, Blair's flatmate. This followed a pattern: Blair had appointed Falconer to replace Lord Irvine, who happened to be Blair's pupil-master and who introduced Blair to his wife, Cherie Booth. Frances Gibb, Legal Editor of *The Times* commented that "The appointment caused disbelief among senior judges, who had tipped Lord Justice Thorpe". Thorpe L.J. had dedicated his judicial life and much of his spare time to promoting the reform and development of family law and procedure on an international scale. He was the Deputy President of the Family Division. Professor Cretney, the leading academic family lawyer, remarked on the irony that this appointment was made at the very time when the Constitutional Reform Bill was before Parliament, designed to replace cronyism with an appointment system that was fair, open and transparent.

In March 2008, Jack Straw, Minister of Justice and the next LC, introduced the Draft Constitutional Renewal Bill and White Paper, saying "The Bill proposes to remove the Prime Minister entirely from the making of judicial appointments, and the Lord Chancellor from making appointments below the High Court." The Bill was dropped, however.

The call for sweeping reform—a Judicial Appointments Commission

The suggestion for an advisory or appointing commission had **14–049** been made many times, for instance, by a JUSTICE sub-committee in 1972 and reiterated in 1992. Visible and real independence from the executive and judiciary would be crucial. The proposal was designed to secure a more diverse bench. The Law Society said, in evidence to the Home Affairs Committee, in 1996, that its advantages would be removing ministerial control, formalising selection procedures and criteria to reflect good recruitment practice, and achieving public confidence in the objectivity and even-handedness of the selection process (JAP, 237). In 1996, the Judges' Council disagreed. The Liberal Democrats and Labour supported a Commission. Labour set out its plans in several policy documents, when in opposition, in 1995-97, although the proposal did not appear in the party's 1997 election manifesto. Supporters were disappointed when, in October 1997, Irvine L.J. of the newly elected Labour Government announced that he had decided not to establish a Commission. Instead, he announced some reforms of the system and promised to consider establishing an ombudsman, for those aggrieved by the appointments process, and a system of performance appraisal. He appointed Sir Leonard Peach to examine the appointments system and Peach reported in 1999.

In the meantime, two papers, by Thomas and Malleson, had been commissioned by the Lord Chancellor's Department, under the joint title, *Judicial Appointments Commissions—The European and North American Experience and the possible implications for the United Kingdom* (1997). Malleson reviewed US and Canadian models and found there was no strong evidence to suggest that the use of commissions as opposed to other appointment methods had any significant effect on the make-up of the judiciary in terms of competence or representativeness. A more important variable might be their approach to the appointment process. The experience in Ontario suggested that active attempts to recruit under-represented groups could have a significant effect on the type of judges appointed. She found that public confidence in the use of commissions was generally very high. Examining continental European appointment systems, Thomas drew attention to differences in the appointment processes that explained differences in judicial composition. Women made up a significant proportion of the judiciary in most of the countries examined and at least half of incoming judges in France, the Netherlands, Germany and Italy. She explained that, as recruitment was through public examination based on university-level knowledge of the law, women normally fared better than men. She concluded:

> "Recruitment of judges later in their professional career, as occurs in common law countries, tends to bring into play social forces which reduce women's chances: family commitments and professional discrimination. Civil law, bureaucratic-style judiciaries have favourable employment conditions for women (maternity leave, flexible working hours, etc.,) and the judiciary is seen as a positive career choice for women law graduates." (LCD Research Series 6/97, p.21.)

She suggested that the continental practice of involving lower ranking judges in judicial appointments commissions might also encourage an increase in the appointment of women judges, minorities and other less traditional types. It shifted the criteria for appointment and lessened the influence of legal elites who tended to favour the status quo.

In Peach's 1999 report, he recommended a Commission for Judicial Appointments and this was done in 2001. This was *not* the model suggested by JUSTICE. It simply kept the appointments process under constant review and published an annual report. Critics still called for an appointing commission. In July 2000, Lord Steyn became the first law lord to call for a commission. The Law Society pointed to Genn's study, *Paths to Justice*, 1999, which found that the public thought that judges were old and out of touch.

The head of this new CJA was Sir Colin Campbell, a non-lawyer. **14–050** He and the other commissioners had broad recruitment experience in commerce and industry. Sir Colin's views themselves became a catalyst for reform. From their standpoint of outsiders, the commissioners clearly found some aspects of the old appointment system shocking and indefensible and their annual reports carried highly publicised and trenchant criticisms which doubtless embarrassed the Government, as can be seen from some quotations from their reports. The Annual Report for 2003 commented that the system of appointing judges and Queen's Counsel was rife with wide "systemic bias" against minorities, women and solicitors that infected the way the legal profession and judiciary operated. See more below. The only real objection to selecting judges by means of an appointing commission was "the danger of leading to a bland, antiseptic bench, technically competent but 'safe'." (Stevens, 2004.)

The old system of "secret soundings"—"comment collection"

Prior to the 1990s, aspirants did not apply for a job as a judge. **14–051** They were invited to join the bench by the metaphorical "tap on the shoulder" by the LC, whose civil servants gathered files of fact and opinion on potential judges and kept candidates under constant review. Until 1960, the Bar was around 1,000, so the LC was presumed to know all the candidates personally. By 1990, this could not work, as the Bar was so much bigger. Many candidates for recorderships and the circuit judiciary applied for the job and some were still invited but there was no standard application form, other than for district judges. In empirical research on the judiciary reported in *Sitting in Judgment: The Working Lives of Judges* (2011), I interviewed judges who claimed that there was a system of seniority in certain chambers in their circuits. When each barrister achieved sufficient seniority in chambers, the LC would ask if they were interested in becoming a QC or, for those less talented, a circuit judge, so they knew to expect that their "turn" would come.

In many Crown Courts and county courts in the provinces, most people had been barristers in the same local chambers.

Hailsham L.C. published his selection criteria in the 1980s. Mackay L.C. made countless speeches urging more women and ethnic minorities to put themselves forward. In 1994–95 he at last opened up the recruitment and selection system by advertising lower judicial posts (circuit judge and below) on the internet, with detailed job specifications, and introducing interview panels. The problem was that, despite many reforms made by Lords Mackay and Irvine, the LC was still heavily reliant on "consultations" with existing judges. They were referred to by critics as "secret soundings", to the irritation of Irvine, who valued them. The Judges' Council, in their 1996 evidence to the Home Affairs Committee defended the system:

> "judges see and hear most of the potential candidates before them, day in, day out, from a position in which they are uniquely well placed to assess their professional competence and personal qualities, and to compare them with competitors in the field." (JAP, p.219).

The Equal Opportunities Commission, in their evidence, expressed "a major concern":

> "Selection for appointment should depend on an objective assessment of the applicant's skills and abilities. Given the predominance of men in the senior ranks of the judiciary, the bar and the solicitor's profession, there is an increased risk of stereotypical assumptions being made with regard to 'female' as opposed to 'male' qualities and aptitudes. It is therefore the Commission's view that the practice of canvassing opinion is certain to risk introducing impressionistic and subjective factors into the recruitment process." (JAP, p.211).

If consultations were to continue, then those consulted should at least receive training, they argued. Most critics made the simple point that any system which relied on the say-so of a limited group was inevitably vulnerable to members of that group selecting people like themselves. As Chris Mullin MP retorted:

> ". . . it appears to be self-perpetuating does it not? They all know each other, many of them went to school together, most of them were at university together and they have no doubt known each other all the time dining in their various Inns of Court. They are

males aged between 55 and 66 on average. . .and they appear to move in very limited circles." (JAP, p.5).

The Law Centres Federation called the Bar and the judiciary "in effect a self-perpetuating oligarchy or clique" (JAP, p.227). The Association of Women Barristers urged that the soundings system should be abolished (JAP, p.193). The Law Society, representing solicitors, said the system disadvantaged those who were not from the standard background for judges and perpetuated the weight given to advocacy skills. They wanted "soundings" replaced with a system of objective tests and interviews, such as is used in civil service recruitment (JAP, p.229). The Bar Association for Commerce, Finance and Industry (employed barristers) called the system "wholly indefensible in the 1990s" (JAP, p.204). The Association of Women Solicitors opposed the system because it disadvantaged women and solicitors who were unlikely to appear before serving members of the judiciary and it placed undue emphasis on advocacy skills. The African, Caribbean and Asian Lawyers' Association said that the composition of the judiciary reflected neither the British population nor the legal profession.

The accusation that the system perpetuated a clique was strikingly **14–052** illustrated by research undertaken on behalf of the Association of Women Barristers. Examining 104 High Court appointments made during 1986–96, 70 (67.3 per cent) came from a set of chambers of which at least one ex-member was a judge during the consultation period. Only 58 of 227 sets of London chambers produced judges, of which seven sets produced an astonishing 30 appointees. Of the 131 sets outside London, they produced only seven judges. The 104 appointees, from a pool of 8,800 barristers, replaced over two thirds of the judges, yet came from roughly the same chambers as those they replaced (Hayes, 1997).

Peach (1999) suggested that each candidate should nominate three referees and this change was made. The problem was, however, that this extensive "soundings" system went on alongside the use of referees, until 2005. Many judges were sent the list of candidates applying for various judicial posts and each judge chose upon whom to comment (I observed this in my research). Otherwise, Peach expressed his confidence in the system. This disappointed all critics, especially the Law Society, who repeated their condemnation of the "secret soundings" system, as they insisted on calling it, as an "old boys' network". Peach did, however, recommend that the consultations system be supplemented with alternative methods of evaluating an applicant's suitability, such as one-day assessment centres and psychometric and competence testing (Malleson, 2000). In June 2000, Malleson and Banda reported to the LC on *Factors affecting the decision to apply for silk and judicial office.* They exposed widespread dissatisfaction, the same disgruntled groups repeating the complaints made to Parliament in 1995. Many repeated the call for a judicial appointments commission.

Assessment Centres were piloted in 2002 for deputy district judges and HC masters. They were used instead of traditional interviews, to identify whether the approach encouraged more applications from under-represented groups. Candidates had to show political correctness, awareness of other cultures, proficiency in relating to people from a diverse society and "empathy and sensitivity" in the building of positive relationships with litigants, witnesses, advocates and colleagues. The assessments included practical exercises and role-play, an interview and written examination. In 2003, they were reported to be a success and eventually extended to recorder selection. As mentioned below, judges caused the first selection process used by the JAC to be re-run, because it did not take account of their views and Malleson argued that judges' opinions are indeed a useful resource.

"The creation of a system of open selection is not, however, inherently incompatible with the consultations process which still has strong defenders. In common with all peer-based appointments, promotions, or performance review systems, it allows decisions to be based on the knowledge and views of those who best know the work and characteristics of the candidates" (2009).

The Commission for Judicial Appointments savages the old boys' network

14–053   In the meantime, the "consultations" system continued, for most judicial posts and in the selection of QCs. Here, I examine the comments of the CJA because they demonstrate how recruiters and employers from the real world were horrified at what they found and because some of their sensible prescriptions for reform are still not in place, as far as I can see, in 2011. Their 2003 report was highly condemnatory. They uncovered some vague and markedly subjective comments about applicants, by judges and lawyers, which bore little relation to the professed selection criteria, such as

- "She's too primly spinsterish".
- "She's off-puttingly headmistressy".
- "She does not always dress appropriately".
- "Smug and self-satisfied and pompous".
- "Down and out scruffy".

The commissioners, all non-lawyers, with wide experience in commerce and industry, had not come across comments like them, in 20 years of experience, said Sir Colin Campbell, their outspoken chair. He complained that there was an over-emphasis on the views of the senior judiciary. Such comments were symptomatic of a "wider systemic bias in the way that the judiciary and the legal profession operate, that affects the position of women, ethnic minority candidates and solicitors in relation to silk and judicial appointments". There was a strong case for abandoning the consultation process. He also felt that HC appointments, which were still mainly made by the "tap on the shoulder" method, should all be filled by application and interview.

In their next annual report, 2004, their recommendations were even more forceful. There was a need to improve fairness and transparency. Great weight was given to the views of the senior judiciary and this factor skewed the recruitment process towards those who were visible to them, to the detriment of solicitors. Consultations should be replaced with a more structured and accountable method of collecting views on candidates' suitability. "We call for much fuller audit trails of how selection decisions have been reached." Much of their evidence was gleaned from applicants who had been turned down. Having examined 18 complaints, they even recommended an apology from the DCA in nine cases.

They were very prescriptive about what needed to be done. All candidates must have an equal opportunity to demonstrate their suitability. All relevant evidence must be evaluated against known competencies and appropriate criteria. Judicial opinions could be taken account of but gleaned in a much more organised and restricted manner, concentrating on objectivity and relevance. They welcomed the extension of appraisal of part-time office holders, as that could provide useful information in selecting for full-time posts. They noted that the 2005 Act would require appointment on merit. That could not be assessed from the candidates' personal profile without examining their capacity to do the job.

They added that the appointment process did not recognise skills **14–054** demonstrated by other judicial office holders, such as tribunal chairs, who dealt with cases at least as demanding as those heard by circuit judges. This disproportionately affected women, since they accounted for 24 per cent of tribunal chairs. The system was also institutionally biased against full-time judicial office holders, who were not visible to the consultees.

They were especially critical of the High Court competition. The system whereby senior judges could nominate people for consideration for the HC was unfair because this meant different information was available for nominees and applicants. This led to "serious inequalities" in their treatment. There was no information on how the Heads of Division arrived at their shortlist. Candidates were not considered according to appointment criteria but by undisclosed criteria. Under a reformed system, head hunting would be acceptable but all candidates should apply through the same route. A new working group headed by Thomas L.J. was swift to take this point on board. In 2005, all those who were to be considered for the HC had to apply in writing and include a 1,500 word self-assessment. The 2004 report is well worth reading in full as it exposes in some detail the shortcomings of the former appointment process and gives practical examples of how this prejudiced the chances of some applicants. It made frustrating reading for those of us who were writing student essays containing identical criticisms back in the 1970s. In *Sitting in Judgment* (2011), I explore in depth judges' stories of how they were recruited to the bench through the evolving process, from the 1970s to 2003.

Restricting appointments to those with rights of audience: the emphasis on advocacy

14–055   The gist of the above criticism, that those who do not appear before the right judges will not be selected, was compounded by the law itself, the Courts and Legal Services Act 1990, which based all judicial appointments on audience rights and it should be noted that this problem was *not* cured by the Constitutional Reform Act 2005. The system still excludes most solicitors (and there are 10 times as many of them as barristers) from appointment directly to the High Court and all those with purely academic qualifications from all judicial appointments. The Judges' Council defended this restriction, in 1996:

> "Successful advocates must develop and exhibit the ability, founded upon sound judgment, to evaluate the strengths and weaknesses of their opponent's case as thoroughly as their own. . .In addition, the administration of justice in England and Wales depends upon lawyers who appear before the court owing their paramount duty to the interest of justice, and not advancing arguments or evidence which are improper, mendacious or corrupt." (JAP, p.219.)

Groups like JUSTICE have long argued that prowess as an advocate, standing in court arguing one side of a case, does not demonstrate the skills needed of a judge, to sit quiet and give an impartial hearing to both sides and exercise fair judgment.

"The best drama producers may not be the best critics; the best players do not necessarily become the best referees. In particular the strong combative or competitive streak present in many successful advocates is out of place on the bench." (JUSTICE, *The Judiciary in England and Wales*, 1992.)

The Law Society argued that the emphasis on advocacy "actually impairs the selection of the best candidates". Fulltime advocates suffered the disadvantage of a lack of experience of dealing with clients directly, or of conducting litigation, which could lead to "a rather unworldly approach" (JAP, pp.234–235). Other jurisdictions do not limit the judiciary to practising advocates and use is made of academics as judges in the highest courts. Thinking of the qualities needed of judges in the CA and the UKSC, they spend most of their time considering and developing points of law. Academic lawyers devote their whole careers to developing expertise in specialist areas of the law.

Lord Irvine accepted some of these criticisms. As a result of the Peach Report and Banda and Malleson's research, he re-wrote the appointment criteria to emphasise that he did not regard advocacy experience as an essential requirement for appointment to judicial office, from 1999. The Constitutional Reform Act 2005 did not alter the legal requirement that candidates have rights of audience as a barrister or solicitor. Most respondents to the 2003 consultation paper favoured perpetuating the restriction. This is hardly a surprise, since most respondents were barristers, solicitors, judges or their representative organisations. Nevertheless, the Tribunals, Courts and Enforcement Act 2007 made enormous inroads into the restrictiveness of the law, as explained above, in s.4. This was an overt attempt to widen the recruitment pool.

6. The remaining problem in 2011—lack of diversity

So the old system was blamed for producing the current lack of **14–056** diversity but the problem lies deeper than this, in the law itself, and in the legal professions, themselves unrepresentative, as seen in Ch.13. In 2004, Falconer L.C. published a consultation paper, *Increasing Diversity in the Judiciary*. It is the job of the new Judicial Appointments Commission to devise methods of securing greater diversity but Lord Falconer did not wait around until 2006. Thanks to the efforts of Mackay and Irvine L.CC., since 1994, the lower sections of the judiciary have become more diverse but this was not enough for Lord Falconer.

Composition in 2011—does this really demonstrate a lack of diversity?

14-057   Statistics are regularly updated on the judiciary website. At the time of writing they were as follows.

- All judges are barristers or solicitors, except one, who is a legal executive. The majority of circuit judges and above are barristers but civil district judges are predominantly solicitors.
- In 2011, there are 12 white UKSC Justices, one of whom is a woman, Baroness Hale of Richmond, the first woman to be appointed as a law lord, in October 2003. Only one was a solicitor.
- Of the 37 all-white judges in the CA, *none* was a solicitor. Three were women.
- Of the 108 High Court judges, *one* was a solicitor and 16 were women, three were non-white.
- Of the 680 circuit judges, 101 were women and 80 were solicitors; 16 were ethnic minority.
- Of the 448 county court district judges, 401 were solicitors and 110 were women; 26 were minority.
- Of the 143 District Judges (Magistrates' Courts), 37 were women and 94 were solicitors. Only four were minority.

The 2004 consultation paper assumed such (similar) statistics demonstrated a lack of diversity but Jack (2004) challenged this. Judges, he pointed out, were older than the population at large. Of 45–64 year olds in the population, only 5.1 per cent were ethnic minority and the Bar of that age had a similar ethnic profile. If all judicial posts were counted, including lay and lawyer tribunal members, as the consultation paper acknowledged, 24.9 per cent of all judicial posts were held by women. This *over*represented eligible women, he said, as 20 per cent of barristers and 23 per cent of solicitors in that age group were women. He concluded that the current appointment system was already producing greater diversity and the consultation paper smacked of "false political correctness". Nevertheless, Arden L.J. drew attention to the absence of women in HC appointments in 2005–08, in a very powerful and informative speech.

"The value of women has been accepted in many other walks of life. For instance, 17% of ambassadors, 19% of Members of Parliament, 23% of permanent secretaries and 61% of the Government Legal Service are women. . .women judges account for 17% of the judges of the European Court of Justice; 18% of the judges of the High Court of New Delhi, India; 19% of the judges of the Federal Constitutional Court of Germany; 27% of the judges of the Constitutional Court of South Africa, 29% of the judges of the High Court of Australia; 30% of the judges of the Court of Appeal of New South Wales; 31% of the judges of the European Court of Human Rights; 44% of the judges of the Supreme Court of Canada and so on." (AWB, June 2008.)

Lack of social diversity

The 2004 consultation paper barely mentioned the lack of social **14–058** and educational diversity but this has been criticised for decades. It was famously attacked by Griffith in *The Politics of the Judiciary*. The *senior* judiciary (HC, CA and UKSC) is dominated by Oxbridge graduates, educated at the top public schools (fifth edn, 1997, p.18). The Labour Research Department published regular surveys of the judiciary and in December 2002, they reported that new Labour had failed to make the judiciary any more diverse in this respect, since they came to power in 1997. The survey found that 67 per cent went to public school and 60 per cent attended Oxford or Cambridge universities. Under New Labour, those in the senior courts were *more* likely to have been public school educated; the average age of the judges was over 60.

It goes without saying that judges will always be middle class, by definition, because they are recruited from lawyers, but judges' lack of educational diversity is extreme. I have argued that the criticism of *senior* judges for being predominantly Oxbridge educated is misplaced, however. Judges in the senior courts need to be exceptionally clever and highly educated. Top judges in other jurisdictions are graduates of elite universities. Oxbridge graduates are predominant in other power elites in the UK, such as politics and commerce. Criticism should be directed at the historic class divisiveness of entry to Oxford and Cambridge, which favoured applicants from independent schools, who still form a disproportionately high proportion of entrants. (See Darbyshire, 2007, for unique interview material from 77 judges, describing their backgrounds, now updated in *Sitting in Judgment*, 2011.)

Why is lack of diversity a problem?

Lord Mackay did not think it was, "It is not the function of the **14–059** judiciary to reflect particular sections of the community, as it is of the democratically elected legislature" (JAP, p.130). He expected composition would broaden over time. Griffith attacked this sentiment as "weasel words" (JAP, p.261). Lord Irvine appeared to take a different view from his Conservative predecessor: "I believe that the judiciary should be a microcosm of the community that it serves." (Interview on the *Today* programme, March 21, 1999) and clearly Lord Falconer considered it to be an urgent problem, in 2004.

Many have argued that an imbalance in the judiciary warps the administration of justice itself. For instance, Pannick argued "the quality of judicial performance would be improved if more of the bench enjoyed the experience peculiar to more than half the members of our society" (*The Times*, July 30, 1996). Hewson (1996;1997), of the Association of Women Barristers, listed examples of gender bias in judicial and tribunal decisions and advocated the research and educational work of gender bias task forces, such as existed in the US, where the National Judicial Education Program identified three types of gender bias: stereotypical thinking about the nature and roles of men and women, how society values women and men, and myths about the social and economic realities of women's lives.

On her appointment as the first female law lord, Baroness Hale spelled out why the judiciary needed more women. Quoting Canadian Chief Justice Beverley McLachlin, she argued it would promote public confidence; be symbolic, as the judiciary are required to promote equality and fairness; be a sound use of human resources, tapping the intellectual qualities of the missing half of the population and bring a different perspective to judgments.

14–060 She acknowledged that the last point was controversial and that most of her judgments could have been written by a man. Nevertheless she agreed with McLachlin that jurists were informed by their background and experience. For cultural, biological, social and historic reasons, women's experience was different. She concluded: "The present judiciary is disadvantaged but means well. Few if any are actively misogynist or racist but they have a lamentable lack of experience of having female or ethnic minority colleagues of equal status." (Hale, 2003). Hunter, McGlynn and Rackley would agree with academic colleagues, Feenan and Moran that some judgments would be different if they were not written by white, heterosexual males. The authors of the collection *Feminist Judgments* (2010) demonstrate the potential difference by writing "missing" judgments in key cases in the ELS. Professor Hunter argues that we need affirmative action to broaden our judiciary, like some Australian states. See further, Malleson (2006), who challenged the traditional UK hostility to affirmative action in judicial selection. She thought it was not incompatible with the merit principle.

USSC Justice Sandra Day O'Connor used to say the question of whether more women judges would make a difference was "dangerous and unanswerable". It is dangerous to assert, without research evidence, that changing the composition of the judiciary will automatically change the nature of decision-making. That it would do so seemed to be the tacit assumption of Vera Baird QC, speaking for the Fawcett Society in 2005. She thought that introducing more women into the judiciary would result in more rape convictions, perhaps not realising that there is very strong evidence that female *jurors* and female dominated juries are more likely to acquit. Letters to *The Times* in reply made some wise comments, on October 11, 2005. Sonia Sotomayer used to make speeches claiming that a wise Latina woman (like her) with a richness of experience would "reach a better conclusion" but she had to retract that sentiment in order to get appointed onto the US Supreme Court, as explained here. In November 2005, the LC started a recruitment drive, saying ". . .over time, if the group of people who are judges are 50 per cent men, 50 per cent women, that will have a significant effect on the sort of discretionary decisions judges make all the time". Malleson (2004) has warned, however, that "The idea that a judge can represent the interests of a group from which he or she is drawn is clearly incompatible with the notion of impartial justice." There was no empirical evidence that women more effectively represented the views of women. American research disclosed little difference between male and female judicial decision-making (reiterated by Genn, 2009, at p.153). Malleson said that one might hope that diversifying the judiciary would increase their range of skills and experience which would enhance decision-making in general but the real reason for including under-represented groups was that "the corrosive impact of their absence on the legitimacy of the judiciary is now too great to ignore." The 2004 DCA consultation paper said:

> "Society must have confidence in that the judiciary has a real understanding of the problems facing people from all sectors of society with whom they come into contact. . .We must ensure that our judicial system benefits from the talents of the widest possible range of individuals in fairness to all potential applicants and to ensure that talent, wherever it is, is able to be appointed." (*Increasing Diversity in the Judiciary.*)

It said the media portrayed judges as elderly, male and of a narrow social class and they and the public concluded that judges were out of touch (see further *Sitting in Judgment*, 2011, Ch.2).

I cannot say whether diversifying the judiciary would make a difference to their decisions. Indeed, I saw nothing to indicate that it would, throughout my research years, sitting next to judges, though that was not the topic of my inquiry. I did point out, however, that previous researchers and writers had shown that the composition of the *top* court, in terms of personalities, does determine the outcome of cases. I found that UKSC Justices acknowledge this fact and are keen to sit in bigger benches more often, to eliminate the lottery effect. I argued that since this is a law-making court, confining itself to points of law of general public importance, it is essentially a political court, especially now it is fuelled by the Human Rights Act. It is not party political but clearly its composition matters, practically and symbolically.

14–061 My own view on this issue is that, regardless of whether bench composition affects decision-making, the visible lack of diversity in our judiciary is, quite simply, an international embarrassment. It is one of the pernicious outcomes of our divided and divisive legal profession, described in the last chapter, where the rank of QC and jobs as judges have been perceived as a perk of the Bar. Few critics make the most obvious point that solicitors constitute 90 per cent of the legal profession, yet they are concentrated at the bottom of the judiciary. I describe in some detail in *Sitting in Judgment*, how the judicial hierarchy reflects the hierarchy of the legal profession, with most senior judges drawn from the QC rank, most circuit judges recruited from the Bar and most district judges being solicitors. The book is laced with stories from solicitor judges of how they suffered from the snobbery of barristers and of how they were steered down to the district bench when they applied to be a judge. Nevertheless, while it is said that lack of diversity in our legal profession has *caused* lack of diversity in our judiciary, this cannot fully explain the narrow makeup of our top courts compared with other countries. As Malleson has pointed out, the argument that underrepresented groups will eventually "trickle up" to our top courts, notably the UKSC, is "weakened by the fact that many other top courts in common law countries around the world had succeeded in diversifying their membership despite being similarly drawn from those who have first had a career of some kind in legal practice". She pointed to the number of women in the Canadian and Israeli Supreme Courts and the South African Constitutional Court, "the rainbow court". She said most other top courts draw from a wider range of career backgrounds. For instance, the year after Malleson wrote this, Elena Kagan, who had never served as a judge, was appointed to the US Supreme Court.

Why specific groups are underrepresented or overrepresented

The exclusion of solicitors

They were the most persistent critics of the old system. As the **14–062** 1990 Act confined judicial posts to those with rights of audience, this excluded them from much of the bench. Their route onto it was to become a recorder or district judge and seek promotion, or gain rights of audience as a solicitor-advocate, in the Crown Court or above, which very few solicitors have done. Prior to the 1990 Act, solicitors could not be promoted above circuit level. This provoked the criticisms that the system was unfair and produced too narrow a pool of candidates. In 2011, there are still only two solicitors in the entire senior judiciary.

Solicitors complained that the published criteria, pre-2006, still placed too much emphasis on career success and income. The requirement for part-time sitting, prior to fulltime appointment, was too lengthy. Short blocks of sitting were disruptive of solicitors' practices. Other minor judicial appointments, such as tribunal chairman did not seem to be a stepping stone to the circuit bench, since few were promoted. Lords Mackay and Irvine remained unmoved by these criticisms. By 1999, solicitors had become exasperated in the lack of reform and the Law Society announced they were boycotting the "consultations" system. In other words, if solicitors were consulted on potential candidates, they would not offer an opinion. Lord Irvine condemned the action as a "disservice to its members". There has not been an enormous amount of progress here, a point which I address below.

The emphasis on silk

Most HC judges now in office were recruited from QCs, as **14–063** were many circuit judges. Solicitors, women and ethnic minorities alleged that this was unfair, because the selection system for silks disadvantaged them, because of the emphasis on advocacy and because the method of recruitment pre-2006, was via the same "consultations" system as was used to select judges. Baroness Hale keeps pointing out that only 10 per cent of silks are women.

Race—was the old appointments system discriminatory?

In a provocative 1991 article, Bindman suggested that the old **14–064** system was indirectly discriminatory and thus illegal. He cited the Commission for Racial Equality's code of practice for employers, which discouraged recruitment through the recommendations of the existing workforce where the workforce was predominantly from one ethnic group and the labour market multi-racial.

Recruitment by word of mouth was a common cause of discrimination. Lord Mackay refuted this criticism. He said he could only reach his objective of increasing the number of women and minorities on the Bench if he could find a sufficient proportion of them in the practising profession of the appropriate age and standing.

His successor, Lord Irvine, appeared equally frustrated at the low numbers of minorities applying. At the Minority Lawyers' Association Conference in November 1997, he reiterated Tony Blair's embarrassment that there were no black senior judges and only one per cent of circuit judges were BME. He explained that only about one per cent of barristers of 15 years' call, the group eligible for HC appointments, were minority. The root cause was long-term discrimination in the legal profession: "I cannot solve all the problems by myself. The professions need to ensure their houses are in order." Black lawyers remained cynical. The 2004 appointment of Linda Dobbs J. was welcomed but Lord Falconer's launch of the 2004 Judicial Appointments Annual Report was very misleading. A press release entitled "Continued Increase in Minority Ethnic Judicial Appointments" boasted that 14.8 per cent of judicial appointments had gone to minorities but this included *lay* members of tribunals. The 2011 statistics, above, speak for themselves.

The exclusion of women

14–065   The statistics are quoted above. As for the circuit bench, recruitment was examined by Hughes in 1991, in *The Circuit Bench—A Woman's Place?* She challenged the 1990s excuse made by Lord Mackay that the numbers of women on the Bench would naturally increase as the number in practice increased. Examining two cohorts of barristers, she found that women took longer than men to be appointed to the Bench and were recruited from a much narrower age range. Their late appointments could not be accounted for by maternity leave. Of the 173 circuit judges appointed during 1986–90, only 4.6 per cent were women. The majority of women judges surveyed thought that, although some had suffered discrimination early in their legal careers, the judicial appointments system did not discriminate against women. Nevertheless, many women had had low career expectations and one third had been invited to apply to the bench, without having put themselves forward. This was consistent, said Hughes, with employment research which showed that women were less likely to apply for promotion and more inclined to accept initial rejection than men. Thus she concluded that to restrict appointments to applicants rather than head-hunting, would damage the recruitment of women.

The Association of Women Solicitors complained that the requirement to sit part-time for several years was a double bind for women solicitors. They might annoy their business partners by disrupting their practice and reducing their earning capacity shortly after taking a career break or maternity leave. The judicial atmosphere was unwelcoming to women. Women were disadvantaged by the existence of male clubs, where judges and barristers lunched. The Inns of Court and freemasonry provided opportunities for male barristers to fraternise with judges.

Some of their recommendations, and those of other parties have since been followed, such as open advertising and reformed selection criteria (partly satisfied in 1995) and the removal of obstacles to employed barristers (in the Access to Justice Act 1999). Malleson and Banda (2000) found that white female barristers felt the demands of practice put them off applying for judicial office, as did a lack of confidence in being taken seriously. Although some cited family responsibilities as a reason for not applying, an equal number considered the compatibility of judicial work with family responsibilities was a reason for applying. The quotation below, from the UK Association of Women Judges, spells out the problem.

Gays and lesbians

Martin Bowley, then President of the Bar Lesbian and Gay **14–066** Group, had a sorry personal tale of prejudice to tell the Home Affairs Committee, in 1995. He had been informed that he was not appointed to the Bench because this was against the Lord Mackay's policy "since [homosexuals] were particularly vulnerable to public and private pressures". This rule was dropped in 1994. The Lord Chancellor's Department judicial appointments group staged the first special recruitment event at the Lesbian and Gay Law Conference in 2000.

Freemasons

Where a judge is suspected of being a freemason, it is sometimes **14–067** alleged that he has favoured "brothers" appearing before him, as barrister, solicitor, Crown Prosecutor, police witness or one of the parties. The problem of alleged bias is exacerbated by the fact that, unlike common membership of a golf club, membership of the freemasons is much more difficult to discover. Furthermore, they have secret signals with which to greet one another. In the context of judicial appointments, there was a further concern that aspirant barristers who were freemasons (all male) had a special relationship with recommending judges who were also masons. The House of Commons Home Affairs Committee reported on its investigation into *Freemasonry in the Police and the Judiciary* (Third Report, 1997).

In evidence, the United Grand Lodge of England refuted all allegations of bias or corruption, especially the frequent allegation that masons owed an allegiance to their fraternal oath which overrode their professional duties or ethics and the judicial oath. The Judges' Council and Lord Mackay could see no cause for concern. It was disclosed that 32 senior freemasons were judges, in 1997, plus an unknown number of more junior freemasons. The Law Society and the Association of Women Barristers argued that judges and senior police officers should not be freemasons. In its evidence, Liberty detailed one case alleging corrupt masonic connections. They said they knew of many such instances. The Association of Women Barristers listed "a significant number" of legal masonic Lodges. As a result of all this, Lord Irvine required all incoming judges to publicly disclose membership of the freemasons.

What was the government response to such criticisms, in 1994–2004?

14–068   As described above, various reforms took place from 1994. A working party on equal opportunities in judicial appointments and silk was set up in 1997, consisting of representatives of the Bar Council, Law Society, and minority lawyers' groups. It reported to the LC in 1999, making 42 recommendations aimed at increasing numbers of women and ethnic minorities applying for silk and judicial appointment. Many were implemented immediately, or following the 1999 Peach report. A work-shadowing scheme was established, to allow lawyers to sit with judges in court. All the 1990s reforms resulted in some success and the number of applicants increased, not just because of reforms but because of the perceived downturn in some areas of lawyers' work.

Attempts to increase diversity from 2005—can they ever work?

14–069   Falconer L.C.'s 2004 paper examined what other tactics might be used to enhance recruitment, in addition to 2005 Act. The annexes are very informative, as they contain comparative information on diversity of judges in other jurisdictions and diversity in other professions. While acknowledging that the shortcomings in the old process had been a major factor, the consultation paper rightly said that there were other problems. There was a lack of diversity in the legal profession. Statistics showed that "trickle-up" was working, since the numbers of women and minorities entering the profession was now much greater, but was very slow. There was indeed a "trickle out" rate, with women dropping out. Applicants delayed applying, which made the problem worse. People were applying many years after becoming eligible. The paper explored how to improve communication on what judicial appointment offered as a career option; the requirements for judicial office; the working practices of the judiciary and opportunities for progression, and what more might be done by the legal profession to diversify the applicant pool.

Communication

Eligible lawyers felt there was still not enough information **14–070** available in an accessible format and there was an unawareness of appointment competitions.

Requirements for appointment

The consultation paper sought opinions on the statutory quali- **14–071** fications, based on audience rights. It noted that academics and researchers were experts on the law but were excluded, unless they were also barristers or solicitors. Similarly, the requirement for several years of post-qualification experience (seven for a district judge or ten for a recorder) conflicted with an appointments process that claimed to be merit-based. (The CJA annual report 2004 had complained that requiring a HC judge to have 20 years experience was indirectly discriminatory, as only 14 per cent of practitioners with that length of experience were women).

The paper sought opinions on whether the policy requirement for people to sit as a part-timer before being considered for a fulltime appointment deterred certain people and asked whether it should be relaxed, amended or abandoned. The paper articulated the rationale behind requiring people to sit part-time before appointing them full-time:

1. Full-time judicial office was unique, in being a job for life. It was essential to appoint people who were capable and would continue to be capable of doing a good job. Part-time service allowed them to demonstrate that.
2. It allowed part-timers to see if they wanted to become a judge.
3. It allowed them to build their skills and experience. This was essential for non-practitioners like academics.
4. It afforded an opportunity to appraise them.
5. It was a way of ensuring a high and consistent standard of fulltime appointments.

On the other hand it posed a problem for people with caring responsibilities and for solicitors whose firms banned them from part-time judicial office or who were hostile to it. In 2005, the LC announced that he would introduce legislation to make a wider range of lawyers eligible for judicial appointments. Legal executives and patent agents are now eligible. Selection under the 2007 Act and delegated legislation is based on post qualification experience not just rights of audience. Barristers and solicitors who are also lay justices are able to count those sittings when applying for salaried judicial posts.

The appointment process

14–072   The 2004 paper acknowledged the 1990s reforms. It pointed out that policy had already been amended to remove the upper and lower age limits on appointment; that it had been made clear that advocacy experience was not essential and that interview panel members had been retrained and now included lay people with human resources experience.

Judicial working practices

14–073   The 2004 paper pointed out that *salaried* part-time judicial work had been introduced in 2001 for those who could not do a full-time job. This is different from a fee-paid deputy or recorder appointment. It is a salaried fractional appointment as a professional judge. By 2004, 40 judges worked like this, on a flexible basis. Some judges job-share (Bertodono, 2009). The paper suggested it should be better publicised to existing judges that they could apply for promotion.

The legal profession

14–074   The paper dealt in some detail with the attrition rate of women from the legal profession. Crucially, women tended to leave before the point at which they might be expected to apply to be a judge. Another problem was the lack of support given by the profession to those who sought judicial appointment. This was especially acute for solicitors, some of whom were forced to choose between partnership and applying to be a deputy district judge or recorder. The paper complained of the cost of entering the profession, the cost of university tuition fees and a sense of bias against degrees from certain universities. In their response to the 2004 paper, The UK Association of Women Judges spelled out the problem for women:

> "The vast majority of successful candidates to the High Court Bench are drawn from the most successful members of the Bar. The majority of candidates to the Circuit Bench are drawn from practising members of the Bar. Yet the Bar is a profession in which is difficult for women to excel, and extremely difficult to excel if there are home commitments such as having and raising children or looking after elderly relatives, or supporting a partner. A

successful practice at the Bar, particularly in London, is not a job, it is a way of life. It involves being available, often at short notice, to take on an urgent matter, perhaps with travel away from home, working late in the evenings and at weekends. It involves uncertainty over which days are going to be committed, and holidays being forfeit for the sake of work. There is the uncertainty of being self-employed, with the consequential lack of employment rights. There are no regular hours, or days, or places of work. It is a job which is very self-reliant (rather than being team related) and involves selfless and selfish dedication. Any woman who is trying also to run a home and family will find this daunting, however much outside assistance she can use. Many talented women give up the Bar and many allow themselves to be 'sidetracked' in chambers. This does not apply to all, of course, but the women who do manage to keep a high profile practice and run a home and family are exceptional, and they are few. Many women feel that the price paid is too high".

Even if women did manage to keep a busy practice afloat they could not afford the time for "networking" at evenings and weekends. They suggested that one solution was that all women lawyers should be trawled for judicial appointments, including employed lawyers and academics.

Progress from 2006 seems very slow indeed, the main hurdle being the failure to attract applicants from underrepresented groups. In a March 2007 speech, Mrs Justice Dobbs, the first black HC judge, pointed out that she was 0.06 per cent of the senior judiciary and no women had been appointed since 2005. A judicial diversification strategy was launched in 2007. Its aims were to widen the range of people eligible to apply but also to "ensure that the culture and working environment for judicial office-holders encourages and supports a diverse judiciary and increases understanding of the communities served". A five-point plan to encourage more solicitors to apply for judicial office was launched by the minister for judicial diversity, in 2007, including publicising the benefits to the individual and their firm.

The new JAC did not make an auspicious start in 2006. It chose to re-run its first circuit judge competition when the senior judiciary complained that candidates' applications were rejected without their references having been read (obviously, judges did not want to let go of their opportunity to be consulted). Two hundred rejected candidates were reconsidered. This provoked criticism from district judges applying for CJ posts, of favouritism towards barristers who could get references from judges. Keith Vaz MP, said he was "appalled" and called on the Judicial Ombudsman to inquire. Then the LC had to reappoint 21 immigration judges after they threatened him with judicial review for not renewing their five-year contracts (Gibb, 2007). JAC chair Baroness Prashar said that for the judiciary to diversify, it was necessary for the legal profession to make itself diverse. She defended the JAC against judicial accusations that they were responsible for the shortage of judges. The delay in its first selection of 102 circuit judges was caused by "human error" (interview by Gibb, *The Times* law supplement, September 11, 2007). In 2008, the JAC was criticised by academics for not using affirmative action, as other judiciaries have done. (Malleson and Russell made an international collection of critical perspectives, 2006).

14–075　　In October 2008, the Judiciary commissioned independent research to find out what attracts people to or puts them off applying to the senior judiciary. Professor Dame Hazel Genn interviewed recent HC appointees and 29 highly qualified barristers and solicitors and she cited some of the (hilarious) responses in her Hamlyn lectures on civil justice in December 2008. The review report is on the Judiciary website and is referred to in news release 01/09, January 7, 2009. The full report is worth reading.

> "It's a very jolly life not being a judge. Getting loads of money, making jokes and doing really interesting work. You do really unusual, fascinating things working with people you like. There is lots of flexibility, long holidays, no bureaucracy. Why would you stop?" [Female silk]

> "I have no interest in full-time appointment. . .Five-fold reduction in income. Less control over professional life and I would feel bound to go on Circuit. . .I have young children. . .I like to have dinner with my husband and friends rather than talk to a load of High Court judges. . .The hours of service. . .60–70 hours. . . judges have a huge workload and other activities. I can take a week off if I want to. The loss of autonomy and flexibility is an issue. . .The idea of spending the next 15 years of my life being a High Court judge doing rubbish work is frankly too depressing to contemplate. . ."

As the JAC has a statutory duty to promote diversity under the 2005 Act, it has a Diversity Forum, whose work is explained in the JAC Annual Report. The 2008–09 research reports indicate that the following factors discourage potential applicants and these are outside the control of the JAC:

- The policy of requiring applicants to have served part-time (in fee paid work);

- lack of availability of salaried part-time working (this means the lack of full-time appointments on a fractional basis;
- a lack of diversity among lawyers; and
- working conditions within the judiciary (2008–09 *Annual Report*).

Research published by the JAC in June 2009 showed that "unfounded myths" were deterring solicitors from applying for judicial appointments. The press release on *Barriers to Application* summarises the findings:
   "For example:

- One third. . .believe that they cannot apply unless they know a High Court judge who will act as a referee.
- It is still widely believed that to become a judge one needs to be a barrister, have the right kind of education, be part of the right social network and know the top judges.
- It is believed that being under 40 or working class is a disadvantage.
- Many still do not see the appointments process as based solely on merit. For example, women think men have an advantage and men think women are favoured." (JAC website.)

Nevertheless, over half said they would consider applying if they could work part time. The Law Society President remarked that permitting CPS lawyers to apply was a Law Society success. It might diversify applicants because, of the 3,155 CPS lawyers, 54.5 per cent are women and 15.1 per cent BME: (2009) 159 N.L.J. 837. Baroness Neuberger headed a committee which reported in *The Report of the Advisory Panel on Judicial Diversity* 2010, MoJ press release February 24. The main points were:

- In a democratic society, the judiciary should reflect the diversity of society and the legal profession. This would enhance public confidence.
- There is no quick fix.
- We lack a coherent, comprehensive strategy.
- We need to address everything, from the legal career to appointments at the top level, also addressing retention and promotion. They list what is needed. For example, the JAC should revise its merit assessment criteria, to clarify its commitment to diversity.
- Achievements so far include the development of the Solicitors in Judicial Office Working Group, joint action by the MoJ,

JAC and Directorate of Judicial Offices and "real momentum" on the need for appraisals.
- Heads of the legal profession need to be included in the effort.
- We need a "mythbusting" campaign.

By 2011, it is still an uphill battle to recruit solicitors, as Lord Mackay found in the 1980s. In March 2011, the JAC advertised for 98 recorders, yet in the previous recruitment drive in 2008, solicitors represented only 20 per cent of applicants. In January 2011 they published a *Statistical digest of judicial appointments of Solicitors in England and Wales from 1998–99 to 2008–09*, containing some depressing statistics. No practising solicitors were appointed to the High Court in 1999–2009. The number of solicitors applying to the circuit bench remained constant at 12 per cent but appointees declined from ten to six per cent, since the creation of the JAC. On three circuits, while the number of recorder applicants had increased to 20 per cent, only nine per cent of appointees were solicitors. The proportion of solicitor DJ appointees *declined* from 89 per cent to 68 per cent in the post-2006 period. Their 2009 report *Barriers to Application for Judicial Appointment Research*, found that for barristers and solicitors there was a massive aspiration gap in terms of how likely they were to apply in the future. Whereas half of the barristers surveyed (49 per cent) expected to apply for judicial office (20 per cent were "very likely"), this fell to only one in five solicitors (22 per cent) with only six per cent "very" likely (p.1). The Law Society has set up a mentoring group to encourage more solicitors to apply and the work-shadowing scheme was re-launched in 2007 and the JAC and Law Society launched a joint plan to support solicitor applicants, in January 2011. The proportion of solicitor recorders in three circuits rose from five per cent to nine per cent and this was claimed to be a success. This is depressing, though. Recorder is the route in to the circuit bench and, as I keep emphasising, there are about 10 times as many solicitors as barristers. As we saw in the last chapter, many of the fee earners in solicitors' offices are legal executives. In 2010, for the first time, fellows of the Institute of Legal Executives were able to apply for part-time employment as immigration and asylum judges and the first one to be a DJ was appointed. In 2010, senior paralegals were invited to apply to become judges in the first tier tribunals.

The JAC claimed success in diversifying the High Court, with BME and women lawyers performing well in the 2010 HC selection. In May 2011, the first progress report of the Judicial Diversity Taskforce claimed that work had been done on achieving the

Neuberger Report's 53 goals. It comprises the Bar chairman, President of ILEX, President of the Law Society, Chairman of the JAC, the LCJ, the Senior President of Tribunals and Justice Minister Lord McNally. They claimed a considerable amount had been achieved in outreaching to schools and universities, by "diversity and community relations judges". For instance, some DCR judges are mentoring students from low income backgrounds.

As for diversity in sexuality, the JAC refuses to gather informa- **14–076** tion on sexuality from judges which was deprecated by Leslie Moran in his Stonewall lecture of June 2010. He thinks data should be collected and the JAC should make a positive commitment to sexual diversity and the Judges' Council should establish a standing committee or working party on equality and diversity with lesbian and gay judicial representation. The leading writer on the judiciary is Professor Kate Malleson. In a pessimistic 2011 article co-authored with Barmes, they comment:

[T]his brief critical interrogation of how judicial recruitment pools are constructed shows that access to the judiciary cannot be fairly opened to all until group segmentation and stratification in the legal profession is broken down and/or the appointments system becomes significantly less deferential to the legal professions' (skewed) internal hierarchies and ascriptions of value. In current conditions it is clear that however neutral and meritocratic the judicial appointments process, diversity will remain elusive while the demonstrably false premise obtains that appointments are from an equally neutral, meritocratic legal profession."

In other words, the post-2006 recruitment and selection process has not changed and cannot change the fact that judges are still recruited from the same types of lawyer as always, because of systematic group-based inequality in the legal profession and in professional and public life. Public bodies like the JAC have a statutory duty to pursue equality and diversity aims which they have a limited capacity to bring about. At my time of writing, 2010–11, we seem to be in an almost obsessional phase of asking whether the JAC is doing enough to diversify the judiciary. As if the plethora of evaluations by the JAC, the Ministry of Justice (Neuberger report) and the judiciary (Genn) were not enough, in May 2011, the House of Lords Constitution Committee launched yet another inquiry into the judicial appointments process. The Parliament website says:

"The Committee will ask whether the appointments system is fair, independent, transparent and open. It will examine a range of questions including the following.

- Does the judicial appointments process secure an independent judiciary?
- Should Parliament scrutinise judicial appointments?
- How can public understanding of the appointments process be improved?
- Is the system based on merit?
- Do we have a sufficiently diverse judiciary?"

A more radical suggestion—a career judiciary

14–077   Most continental countries have developed a career judiciary. Descriptions are given in Thomas's discussion paper (see further Bell, 2006). Most judges are recruited soon after graduating in law. They are selected like civil servants, by competitive examinations, which sometimes include psychological and fitness testing, as well as legal knowledge, which results in women being the majority of recruits. The new recruit must attend courses at judicial college and then starts off at the bottom of the ladder and may, if successful, be promoted through the ranks to the senior judiciary. It is common to require continuing education and further examinations. Few judges are selected from amongst practising lawyers. A portrait of judges in France was drawn in an article by Sage (1998), who claimed that judges were young, radical and middle-class.

From time to time, it has been fashionable to suggest a career judiciary in England and Wales. Most witnesses giving evidence to the 1995 Home Affairs Committee did not mention such a radical plan. The Judges' Council rejected the suggestion on the basis of profound differences between common law systems and the legal systems of continental Europe. The Home Affairs Committee agreed with Brazier's opinion that the judiciary was already a career, in the sense that a career path of a judge may involve sitting in courts of a progressively higher rank. Nevertheless, the Committee firmly rejected any move to a career judiciary in this country. Dawn Oliver, in 2003, examined arguments in favour of a career judiciary but pointed out that it is not on the active agenda in the UK at present, or that of any common law jurisdiction. The habit of recruiting judges from practice was "deeply embedded". The high status that our judges enjoyed and respect for the rule of law in the UK relied to an extent on the seniority and successful prior careers of those appointed.

Proponents of a career judiciary generally point out that this would significantly lower the age of the judiciary and inevitably make it much more diverse. Not everyone considers the youth-fulness of European career judges to be an asset. Stephen Jakobi, Director of *Fair Trials Abroad* had more experience than any lawyer in the comparative merits and shortcomings of the lower judiciary around Europe:

"Countries that seek to attract young people to the bench at an early age but also insist on prolonged professional training and the existence of either experienced colleagues sitting with them or lay assessors until they reach maturity (e.g. Germany and the Netherlands) seem to deliver a quality of justice commensurate with international standards. Those where judges start young but where one or more of these other factors are missing (e.g. Spain and France) do badly." (2003).

He thought the British system worked well. Malleson argued ((1997) 60 M.L.R. 655) that, since 1970, the judiciary had undergone a process of formalisation which had resulted in the creation of a *form* of career judiciary for the following reasons: the judiciary had expanded massively; the majority of work in the criminal courts (she meant the Crown Court) was carried out by part-time recorders, many of whom were seeking promotion. This must have strongly influenced their behaviour. Significantly, performance appraisal had only been introduced to monitor the suitability of part-time judges for promotion.

7. Training and appraisal

We lack the systematic form of judicial training and examina- **14–078** tions which are a universal requirement for continental judges. It has been said that our system of recruitment direct from practising professional advocates is the antithesis of training.

The fear of undermining judicial independence
For centuries, judges resisted the suggestion that they undergo **14–079** training, on the ground that it might undermine their independ-ence. One of the most famous books written by a judge about judg-ing is Lord Devlin's *The Judge* (1978). In it, he delivered a 20-page tirade against a 1976 Home Office Consultative Working Paper suggesting the introduction of training. Here are some extracts:

"when in 1948 I was appointed to the High Court. . .I had never exercised any criminal jurisdiction and not since my early days at the Bar had I appeared in a criminal court. I had never been inside a prison except once in an interviewing room. Two days after I had been sworn in, I was trying crime at Newcastle Assizes. . .for centuries judicial appointments have been made on the basis that experience at the Bar is what gives a man the necessary judicial equipment. . .where the independence of the judges may be touched or appear to be touched, it is a good thing to have a protocol. Protocol should, I think, decree that in the acquisition of background information a judge should be left to his own devices" (pp.34–35).

The sentiments were typical of judges of that era. He thought training belonged on the continent. Nevertheless, the Judicial Studies Board was established in 1979.

Malleson challenged the claim that judicial training and performance appraisal posed a threat to independence ((1997) 60 M.L.R. 655). She commented that judges used the objection of threat to their independence as a sort of trump card to play when opposing any innovation in the judiciary but they failed to explain what they meant by independence. Certainly, in opposing the establishment of the Board, judges insisted on freedom from control by the executive, or interference by any outsider, such as an academic director of studies. For this reason, the Board (now College) is still run by judges. Its independence is now guaranteed because the 2005 Act passed responsibility for training to the LCJ and he exercises this via an Executive Board and an Advisory Council.

Malleson pointed out, however, that judges perform a dual function: a constitutional role as one branch of the State counterbalancing the interest of the executive and Parliament and a distinct social service role carried out in their day-to-day work in the courts. Training and performance appraisal were not matters which affected the constitutional position of the judges, "they are concerned with the way in which legal services are provided to the public" (p.660) and are much more likely to bring pressure to bear on the decision of a judge in a particular case but, as JUSTICE had said in their 1992 report,

"Judicial independence has never justified substandard justice. . .Judicial independence is constrained by the principle of good administration, for which someone or some body must be accountable to Parliament" (p.4).

Training and performance appraisal, she concluded, did not pose any threat, if they were confined to updating the law and questions of how judges handled cases before them (such as fair dealing between the parties and handling delicate issues sensitively). The Judges' Council set up a working party on appraisal in summer 2007.

The current training regime

New recorder recruits attend a frightening skills-based residential course, with a mock jury before they sit. Judges I interviewed considered it to be a brilliant but gruelling baptism of fire. Deputy DJs must attend civil training before sitting. Following a training review by Professor Dame Hazel Genn, in 2011 the JSB became a virtual Judicial College. Its current strategy and training details are in its annual report and, from 2009, in an annual prospectus, on the Judiciary website. It acknowledges the difficulty of evaluating the success of training. The first prospectus, 2010–11, aimed to offer judges a choice of continuation seminars, instead of standardised ones, and to move away from black letter law to the acquisition of judicial skills. Nevertheless, as can be seen from the stories about training in *Sitting in Judgment*, the new recorders' mock trial was ahead of its time as a challenging, skills-based session. Delivery of law updates is shifting to e-learning. Circuit and district judges are required to attend one national residential seminar a year, plus usually one day on circuit. They have piloted a much-trumpeted generic skills seminar on "The Craft of Judging", including peer review, but it is not mandatory. According to the 2011–12 prospectus, it includes:

> "Assessing credibility, making a decision and giving a well-structured oral judgment; dealing appropriately with unexpected and high conflict situations in court; managing a case and giving a well-reasoned oral ruling; dealing with ethical and other problems that confront judges inside and outside court."

For circuit judges who hear criminal, civil and family cases, their four days per year may be used up on one of those jurisdictions every three years so if they were to attend the judgecraft course, they would have to sacrifice one of those. Training for handling litigants in person is embedded in a variety of training exercises. In 2008, the JSB published "a single consolidated *Framework of Judicial Abilities and Qualities for the High Court and the Circuit and District Benches* to replace the previous framework which was for the Circuit and District Benches only". It is meant to be a self-help guide. It emphasises fair treatment in every aspect of judging and

14–080

491

explains how this is to be integrated into training. The judges' version is available on the website, with a shorter public version. They were developed after discussions with 500 judges and with practitioners. Until very recently, there was a gap in judicial training as new HC judges had none. In 2009, the JSB's senior judiciary committee proposed that new HC judges have five days' training in their first year and two days thereafter and that was agreed. It piloted a three-day serious crime seminar for them in 2010, and the 2011–12 prospectus also contains HC seminars in civil and family cases. There is at last a HC Director of Training. Deputy DJs have had the benefit of mentoring and appraisal since 2002, as have lay magistrates before them. A mentoring scheme was introduced for recorders in 2009 and another has been developed for HC judges. They are given an information pack. New HC judges are *offered* a flexible programme of sitting-in and visits, devised with their Head of Division and they may, as before, attend continuation seminars geared for circuit judges and evening seminars in the Royal Courts of Justice, and they have access to e-learning and written material. The seminars are normally chaired by a CA judge and are attended by CA and HC judges. They cover topical issues, for example, on the Mental Capacity Act and the new tribunal system.

The call for judicial performance appraisal

14–081   Critics have called for some form of performance appraisal for full-timers, possibly linked with training. For instance, the Royal Commission on Criminal Justice, 1993, said: "We are, however, less satisfied that adequate monitoring arrangements are in place and find it surprising that full-time judges seldom if ever observe trials conducted by their colleagues" (para.98).

One outspoken proponent was Judge Holden. He was persuaded in favour of such a scheme when he was President of the Independent Tribunal Service. The seven regional chairmen were responsible for monitoring the 1,000 legally qualified tribunal chairmen. The results, argued Holden, were useful in a monitoring system, providing an important basis for promotion or the renewal of an appointment. Such a monitoring system could become part of a training exercise (*The Times*, November 9, 1993).

Judicial performance appraisal was part of Labour policy prior to their election to power in 1997. Since then, it has been extended from tribunals to the lay magistracy, since 1998, then extended to deputy district judges and, following the Peach recommendations, it was extended to all part-time appointments. Peach also advocated self-appraisal. Some judges and commentators argue that it should be extended to all full-time judges. For an interesting article, see Susskind (2003). Auld L.J. (2001) was in favour. Most solicitors were well used to appraisal systems. "A trial judge's job is a solitary one", he observed. "The only judge he sees in action is himself". He acknowledged that some judges considered it a threat to independence but magistrates had coped. Appraisal could be conducted by a team of three, not all of whom need be judges or retired judges (*Review of the Criminal Court of England and Wales*, Ch.6).

8. Research

Except for the law lords, about whom there was nothing we did **14–082** not know, thanks to a string of books, there is very little research on judges in England and Wales, as explained in *Sitting in Judgment* (2011). This is partly caused by historic judicial hostility and partly by academic laziness or lack of interest. In her 2008 Hamlyn lectures (2009) Professor Dame Hazel Genn D.B.E. rightly said that there is an "information black hole":

"There is virtually nothing to be read on styles of judging, court behaviour, influences on decision making, managing the routine, managing the complex, the realities of life in court in the post-Woolf era, what approaches are effective for fact gathering, how credibility is assessed, what styles of communication work best with unrepresented parties" (p.131).

The UCL Judicial Studies Institute was launched in November 2010, directed by Professor Genn and Professor Cheryl Thomas. It says it is "the country's first and only centre of excellence in research, teaching, policy engagement and scholarship on the judiciary". This signifies the shrinking of the distance between researchers and the judiciary.

In my research, I work-shadowed a very broad sample of 40 judges and interviewed 77, at every level of the ELS, in all six circuits, with a view to finding out what judges did and what they were like. I enjoyed unprecedented help from the judiciary, thanks to the support of Igor Judge, who is currently, in 2011, the Lord Chief Justice of England and Wales. I was even permitted to observe and report on the deliberations of the CA. My main findings were that the public image of judges as out of touch is grossly unfair, given that the most disturbing and disturbed of people fill their courts; a surprising number of judges are from humble origins; most are not self-important; some, especially family and senior judges, work ridiculously hard, over long hours, on cases that are require the analysis of a mass of documentation, which is often highly technical. Their working conditions are often appalling, with courts that are badly designed or in need of repair, staff that are an underpaid, poorly trained, scarce resource and scandalously poor IT. They are hard pressed to progress the cases through their lists because the agencies that appear before them are all underfunded so cases are not properly prepared. Nevertheless, all but three of the 77 sampled loved their job. They saw themselves as giving something back to society. In 2009, Genn referred to them as "heroic". An example of recent empirical research is part of this encouraging new trend because it uses interview material is Fielding's 2011 article, in which he compares the attitudes of English and American judges to selection, training and sentencing.

BIBLIOGRAPHY

14–083 Arden L.J, D.B.E., address to the Association of Women Barristers AGM, June 3, 2008, on her disappointment at the lack of women HC judges. Includes interesting statistical comparisons.

Auld L.J., *Review of the Criminal Courts in England and Wales* (2001) Ch.6.

V. Baird QC, "Judges are chosen from too small a gene pool", *The Times*, September 20, 2005.

BBC Radio 4, "Top Dogs", September 8, 2009.

J. Beatson, "Should Judges Conduct Public Inquiries?" (2005) 121 L.Q.R. 221–252.

J. Bell, *Judiciaries Within Europe: A Comparative Review* (2006).

G. Bindman, "Is the system of judicial appointments illegal?" Law Society's *Gazette*, February 27, 1991, p.24.

T. Bingham, "The Old Order Changeth" (2006) 122 L.Q.R. 211–223.

N. Browne-Wilkinson, "The Independence of the Judiciary in the 1980s" [1988] P.L. 44.

Lord Clarke of Stone-cum-Ebony M.R., "Selecting Judges: Merit, Moral Courage, Judgment & Diversity", speech, September 30, 2009.

Commission for Judicial Appointments, website archived in 2007: *http://www.webarchive.org.uk/pan/15580/20070220/www.cja.gov.uk/index.html*.

The Concordat between the Lord Chancellor and Lord Chief Justice, January 2004, is properly known as "Constitutional Reform—The Lord Chancellor's judiciary-related functions: Proposals", on the archived Department for Constitutional Affairs website *http://webarchive.nationalarchives.gov.uk/20100512160448/http://www.dca.gov.uk/index.htm*.

The Constitutional Reform Act 2005 and explanatory notes.

S. Cretney, "He may be an eminent man, but is he right for the job?" *The Times*, February 21, 2005.

Daily Mail Reporter, "Teachers' Pay as much as Cameron: Pay limits for heads will soar as much as 25% to £140,000", *Mail Online*, May 10, 2011.

P. Darbyshire, "Where do English and Welsh Judges Come From?" (2007) 66 *Cambridge Law Journal* 365–388; *Sitting in Judgment: the working lives of judges* (2011).

S. de Bertodano, "I hope my new role will encourage others", *The Times*, June 4, 2009.

DCA, *Increasing Diversity in the Judiciary*, 2004, CP 25/04: (DCA archived website, in the consultation papers).

G. Drewry, Comment [1998] P.L. 1.

Etherton L.J., speech on judicial diversity, July 9, 2009, reproduced at [2010] P.L. 727; also interviews at [2010] P.L. 655–662 and 662–671.

D. Feenan, "Women judges: gendering judging, justifying diversity", (2008) (35) (4) J.L.S.

N.G. Fielding, "Judges and their work" (2011) 20(1) *Social and Legal Studies* 97–115.

J. Flood and A. Whyte, "Straight there, no detours: direct access to barristers" (2009) (16) 2 *International Journal of the Legal Profession* 131–152.

Professor Dame Hazel Genn, *The attractiveness of senior judicial appointment to highly qualified practitioners* (Directorate of Judicial Offices for England and Wales, 2008, Judiciary website); *Judging Civil Justice* The Hamlyn Lectures 2008 (2009).

F. Gibb, "Crony taunts return with job for friend of Falconer" *The Times*, January 13, 2005; "Convictions are quashed following trial judge's bad temper" *The Times*, July 22, 2005; "Why diversity is still proving difficult" *The Times*, March 13, 2007; "Is this an unseemly rush to change?" *The Times*, May 1, 2007 (on the Ministry of Justice); Supreme ambition, jealously and outrage", *The Times*, February 4, 2010.

House of Commons Home Affairs Committee, Third Report, Session 1995–1996, *Judicial Appointments Procedures Vol.II* (HMSO, 1996) (abbreviated in the text to JAP).

J.A.G. Griffith, *The Politics of the Judiciary* (5th edn, 1997).

Dame Brenda Hale, "Equality and the Judiciary: why should we want more women judges?" [2001] P.L. 489.

B. Hale, "Welcome to the white men's club" *The Guardian*, October 30, 2003.

J. Hayes, "Appointment by invitation" (1997) 147 N.L.J. 520.

B. Hewson, on gender bias in judicial decisions, *The Times*, September 17, 1996 and (1997) 147 N.L.J. 537 and see C. McGlynn at (1998) 148 N.L.J. 813.

A. Howard, "Lord Woolf v The Home Secretary" *The Times*, March 9, 2004.

R. Hunter, C. McGlynn and E, Rackley (eds), *Feminist Judgments: From Theory to Practice* (2010).

A. Jack, "Number-crunching for diversity" (2004) 154 N.L.J. 1664.

S. Jakobi, "Younger judges", letter, *The Times*, July 10, 2003.

Sir Igor Judge, "Heroes and Villains", speech, October 13, 2003, Judiciary website.

Lord Judge C.J., speech, "Judicial Independence and Responsibilities", May 5, 2009.

Judicial Appointments—Balancing Independence, Accountability and Legitimacy (2010), a collection of essays published jointly by ILEX, The Bar Council, The Law Society and the JAC.

Keene L.J., "Changing the Constitution: the Executive, the Judiciary and the John Adams Problem", the 80 Club Lecture, Liberal Democrat Lawyers Association, June 23, 2004, reproduced in *The Legal Democrat* 2004.

Baroness Helena Kennedy, "A good brand: is that all the Lord Chancellor is?" *The Times*, February 24, 2004.

Sir Sidney Kentridge, "The Highest Court: Selecting the Judges" (2003) 62(1) *Cambridge Law Journal* 55.

C. Kinch QC, "Judicial Maladies" (on recent examples of "cantankerous and difficult" judicial behaviour), *Counsel*, November 2010, p.20.

Labour Research Department Press Release, December 2002 and later material *www.lrd.org.uk*.

Legal Studies (special issue on the constitutional reforms, especially judicial appointments) Vol.24, Issues 1 and 2, March 2004.

Sir Thomas Legg, "Brave New World—The New Supreme Court and judicial appointments" (2004) 24 *Legal Studies* (special issue) p.45.

Lord Lloyd of Berwick, "Constitutional reform or vandalism?" *The Times*, September 14, 2004.

Lord Mackay of Clashfern, "Is there to be a Lord Chancellor no more?" *The Times*, July 13, 2004.

K. Malleson, *The New Judiciary* (1999); "Judicial Training and Performance Appraisal: the problem of judicial independence" (1997) 60 M.L.R. 655; "The Peach Report on Silk and Judicial Appointments" (2000) 150 N.L.J. 8; "Creating a Judicial Appointments Commission: Which Model Works Best?" [2004] P.L. 102; "Rethinking the merit principle in judicial selection" (2006) 33(1) JLS 126–140; "Appointments to the House of Lords: Who Goes Upstairs", in L. Blom-Cooper, B. Dickson and G. Drewry, *The Judicial House of Lords 1876–2009* (2009).

K. Malleson and F. Banda, *Factors affecting the decision to apply for silk and judicial office* LCD Research Report No.2/2000 (2000), DCA archived website.

K. Malleson and P.H. Russell (eds), *Appointing Judges in an Age of Judicial Power*, 2006.

R. Masterman, "A Supreme Court for the United Kingdom: two steps forward but one step back on judicial independence" [2004] *Public Law* 48.

Lord Neuberger M.R., "Who are the masters now?" (on judicial supremacy v parliamentary sovereignty), speech, April 6, 2011, judiciary website.

D. Oliver, *Constitutional Reform in the UK* (2003), Ch.18.

D. Pannick, "Preventing the Ministry of Justice causing injustice" *The Times*, May 8, 2007.

L. Peach, *An Independent Scrutiny of the Appointment Process of Judges and Queen's Counsel in England and Wales: A Report by Sir Leonard Peach* (1999).

Sir Francis Purchas wrote several items in the 1993–94 *New Law Journal* and see Judge Harold Wilson at (1994) 144 N.L.J. 1453. They argued against executive control of the courts and judiciary.

The Report of the Advisory Panel on Judicial Diversity (Ministry of Justice, 2010) and *Improving Judicial Diversity—Progress towards delivery of the "Report of the Advisory Panel on Judicial Diversity 2010"*, May 2011.

A. Sage, on French judges, *The Times*, December 1, 1998.

I.R. Scott, "A Supreme Court for the United Kingdom" (2003) 22 C.J.Q. 318.

R. Smith, "Judging the Judges" (2009) 159 N.L.J. 1154.

R. Stevens, *The Independence of the Judiciary* (1993); "On being nicer to James and the children" (on independence, countering attacks on Mackay L.C.) (1994) 144 N.L.J. 1620; "Reform in haste and repent at leisure: Iolanthe, the Lord High Executioner and Brave New World" (2004) 24 *Legal Studies* 1.

(Lord) J. Steyn, "The Case for a Supreme Court" (2002) 118 L.Q.R. 392; "Creating a Supreme Court", *Counsel*, October 2003, p.14.

J. Sumption QC, "Making the Grade", *Counsel,* April 2011, p.18.

R. Susskind, "In this modern world, should the judges themselves be judged?", *The Times* July 22, 2003.

The Governance of Britain—Judicial Appointments, Cm.7210 (2007).

C. Thomas and K. Malleson, "Judicial Appointments Commissions: The European and North American Experience and the possible implications for the United Kingdom" (1997) L.C.D. Discussion Paper 6/97, summarised on the DCA archived website.

Toulson L.J., "Stepping up to the Bench", *Counsel*, November 2010, p.27.

The United Nations website.

D. Woodhouse, *The Office of Lord Chancellor* (2001).

497

Lord Woolf C.J., Squire Centenary Lecture, "The Rule of Law and a Change in the Consitution", Cambridge, March 3, 2004, Judiciary website.

M. Zander, "A waste of space", (2007) 157 N.L.J. 1649.

Newspaper articles from 2003–04 describing the spat between the Government and the judges over sentencing, the Asylum and Immigration (Treatment of Claimants etc.) Bill 2004 and constitutional reform, especially May 15, 2003, June 17, 2003, March 9, 2004, May 10, 2004.

FURTHER READING AND SOURCES FOR UPDATING THIS CHAPTER

14–084　Updates for this book from spring 2012 and 2013 on the Sweet and Maxwell website.

Judiciary of England and Wales website, including judges' speeches.

The Judicial College is on the Judiciary website.

The Judicial Appointments Commission website, especially general information on the appointments process and "research", under "publications".

The Office for Judicial Complaints.

The Ministry of Justice.

Parliament, especially the Constitution Committee and the Justice Committee.

The Department of Constitutional Affairs archived website, as the DCA was replaced by the Ministry of Justice in 2007.

UCL Judicial Studies Institute *www.ucl.ac.uk/laws/judicial-institute*.

Counsel.

International Journal of the Legal Profession.

The New Law Journal.

Part V: Laypeople in the Law

15. Magistrates

Of the minority of cases where a trial does take place, its usual forum is the unromantic and unseen magistrates' court, where McBarnet's 'ideology of triviality' is daily acted out and upon which the majority of defendants must rely for the benefit of 'participatory democracy' and the safeguarding of their civil liberties."
(Darbyshire, 1991.)

1. Laypeople in the legal system

The English legal system is unique, in worldwide terms, in **15–001** making such extensive use of laypeople as decision-makers, as magistrates, jurors and tribunal members. This is partly the product of history but is now justified as keeping the law in touch with the public affected by it. In 2011, magistrates celebrated their 650 year history. They were recognised by statute in 1361. There are almost 30,000 lay magistrates and they are by far the most important judges in the English and Welsh legal system because, along with professional magistrates called district judges (magistrates' courts) (DJMCs), they deal with over 95 per cent of defendants to criminal charges, from start to finish, and over 90 per cent of all sentencing. They hear almost all prosecutions of young offenders, in the unseen youth court. Furthermore, they have a very significant civil workload, including family cases. Their jurisdiction in children's family cases is as powerful as that of the county court and the High Court. Magistrates also sit in the Crown Court, alongside a circuit judge, hearing criminal appeals from the magistrates' court. For most people, an appearance in court constitutes an appearance before the magistrates. Research demonstrates that the public are remarkably ignorant about magistrates. The MORI poll cited below found a third of the public did not know that the majority of magistrates were laypeople and hugely underestimated the proportion of cases heard by magistrates. Most law books give the impression that magistrates' jurisdiction is trivial. Criminal procedure and the law of criminal evidence have been developed around judges' and Parliament's false assumption that most criminal cases are dealt with by judge and jury. This is a big mistake, as I have pointed out (Darbyshire, "Neglect", 1997). I examine the pros and cons of lay versus professional magistrates below.

2. Appointment and removal

15–002   Both lay justices and DJMCs are Justices of the Peace. Lay justices are appointed by the Crown on the advice of the Lord Chancellor. His department, the Ministry of Justice (MoJ), is responsible for recruitment policy. The Lord Chancellor's powers of appointment and removal are now set out in ss.9 and 10 of the Courts Act 2003. Magistrates are recruited locally and were required to live near their bench. The Courts Act 2003 abolished this rule but local recruitment and selection continue. Section 7 of the Courts Act replaces local commissions with one national Commission of the Peace for England and Wales. The Lord Chancellor receives recommendations for appointment from 100 local advisory committees. The Judicial Appointments Commission was meant to be taking over responsibility for selecting magistrates, which it was given in the Constitutional Reform Act 2005. This plan seems to have been scrapped. In February 2010, the MoJ launched a consultation on advisory committees, *Reorganisation and Change of Name for the Lord Chancellor's Advisory Committees on Justices of the Peace* CP 03/10. The Ministry wanted to reduce them, to save money, and change their name. Advisory Committees are non-statutory and directed by the Lord Chancellor; 43 per cent are chaired by the Lord Lieutenant. The Government have decided to cut the number to 49, from 2012, based around justices' clerkships. They are composed mainly of magistrates but the Lord Chancellor requires that a third are non-magistrates. Since 1999, committee members have received standard training.

Any adult aged 18–70 can apply to be a magistrate, though appointments are seldom made over 65. British nationality is not a condition, under the Act of Settlement 1701 and this was reaffirmed recently. Qualities required by the Lord Chancellor are good character, ability to understand documents and communicate, obedience to the law, social awareness, maturity, understanding of people, a sense of fairness, logical thinking, reliability and commitment to serve the community. Some people's jobs preclude them from consideration, such as police officers, MPs, and MEPs.

Some criminal offences, bankruptcy and recent bans from driving *may* be a barrier to recruitment (from "Can you be a magistrate?" Directgov website). All candidates undergo a two-stage interviewing process, meant to ascertain if they possess these qualities and judicial aptitude. Lay justices are unpaid volunteers. They are entitled to travelling expenses, subsistence payments and a loss of earnings allowance but it by no means compensates those who operate small businesses. Few justices claim their allowances (Morgan and Russell, 2000).

Criticism of the appointment system

The persistent problem with the magistracy was its lack of diver- **15–003** sity. Some said that this was partly caused by the fact that magistrates select new magistrates. Even the Magistrates' Association called this system a "self-perpetuating oligarchy", in evidence to the House of Commons Home Affairs Select Committee in its report on Judicial Appointments Procedures, (1995), although the 2000 report of the Lord Chancellor's Equality Working Group refuted this. Advisory Committees were given no advertising budget. They advertise locally and contact local community groups for help in recruitment (Darbyshire, "Concern", 1997). The Lord Chancellor ran the first national recruitment campaign for a month in 1999. It aimed to destroy the stereotype that magistrates were white and middle class. Magistrates' courts organise open days to publicise their work and the Magistrates' Association runs a "Magistrates in the Community" campaign, addressing schools, employers and local groups and they have run a national mock trial competition, in an endeavour to demystify the magistracy and attract applicants.

The problem of achieving a balanced bench

Successive Lord Chancellors have boasted that the magistracy **15–004** represents the community. This is not the case. Like many before me, I argued, using the support of statistics and research, that it was predominantly Conservative, white and middle class (see "Concern", 1997). Here, we shall examine whether these concerns have been met. Unlike others, I was and still am also concerned that magistrates are too *old*. Since I made that argument in 1997, their age profile has become significantly older. At long last, Lord Chancellors appear to be trying to address all these problems on a national level. Lord Falconer launched a National Strategy for the Recruitment of Magistrates in October 2003, which is still effective. It responded to complaints of lack of diversity and recommendations made by Auld L.J., in his 2001 *Review of the Criminal Courts*. About 2,000 new justices are appointed annually (statistics, Judiciary website). Recruiting more young magistrates is a key diversity objective of the Ministry of Justice. The 2010 consultation paper said:

"The Advisory Committees have provided positive progress on recruitment and diversity recruiting a greater proportion from BME backgrounds (10.1% compared to 7.3% for Magistrates overall) and younger magistrates (44% under 50 years compared 20% for Magistrates overall)" (para.7).

Age

15–005 **"The Lord Chief Justice has expressed the need for magistrates of fatherly rather than grandfatherly age"** (R.M. Jackson, in *The Machinery of Justice* (1st edn, 1940).)

"In theory, you can become a magistrate at 21. In practice nobody is ever appointed before 27" (Rosemary Thomson, then chairman of the Magistrates' Association in evidence to the House of Commons Home Affairs Committee, 1995). In 1997 ("Concern"), I complained that, since the peak age of offending is around 18 for males and 15 for females, magistrates' age profile makes a double generational difference between the bench and the accused. Lord Chancellor Irvine made it clear that this did not bother him. Indeed, he raised the maximum age for new magistrates from 60 to 65, in the hope of achieving a more socially balanced bench. I complained in 1997 that only 22 per cent of lay justices were under 40. By 2011, the situation is very much worse. The 2011 statistics disclose that fewer than four per cent of lay justices are under 40, and 82.3 per cent of magistrates are over 50. Following the 2003 launch of the Recruitment Strategy, the youngest ever magistrate was appointed in North Sussex, in 2005, a 21-year-old Asian. Some Sunday newspapers criticised his appointment. This made for great publicity but, as is apparent from the statistics, such appointments are very rare.

Social class and politics

15–006 Successive studies, cited in my 1997 article, demonstrated over-representation of the middle classes and certain occupational groups and this was confirmed by Morgan and Russell (2000), who found the magistracy to be "overwhelmingly drawn from managerial and professional ranks". Curiously, the 2003 Recruitment Strategy complained of "[T]he general but erroneous view" that magistrates were middle aged and middle class. This was contradictory, since the department's own figures confirmed that this was the case. Indeed, that was the very reason for launching the Strategy. It then went on to say, correctly, "There is a general difficulty in attracting applications from the working public". Various reasons have been identified for this, since the mid-twentieth century. People who travel in their jobs may be unavailable. People who run small businesses may find the loss of earnings allowance inadequate. Insufficient blue collar workers are attracted to apply (see evidence of the Magistrates' Association and others to the Home Affairs Committee, in 1995). Despite the fact that their jobs are protected by the Employment Rights Act 1996, it may be that people fear they will be sacked for taking time off to be a magistrate, or will irritate work colleagues, or hamper their chances of promotion. A story was told by one magistrate of how he had resigned from his job because his employer denied him the seven days' leave he needed to train as a new magistrate and expected him to fulfil many of his bench sittings from his annual leave (*The Magistrate*, February 2001). The 2003 Strategy acknowledged that employers needed the message that magistrates acquire marketable transferable skills. These are now listed on the magistrates' recruitment website and applicants are given a DVD to explain to their employers the benefit of employing a magistrate. The Recruitment Strategy added that some single parents could not spare the time to undertake voluntary work and many people cannot afford to undertake voluntary unpaid work. There are no publicly available statistics on magistrates' occupational backgrounds, in 2011.

In November 2003, Falconer L.C. announced that voting patterns would no longer be used as a means of determining how far the local bench represented the community. They have been replaced by indicators using a mix of occupational, industrial and social groupings, matched against the 2001 census data. This development follows the same trend in the full-time professional judiciary, of distancing the bench further and further from party politics because, for most of the twentieth century, party politics had been a big issue on the bench. As explained in the section on judicial independence, in the previous chapter on judges, it was impossible to keep party politics off the magistrates bench and in the 1970s, in some towns most of the magistrates were local councillors. Indeed, going further back in time, magistrates *were* the local government until councils were created by the Local Government Act 1888. The 2010 consultation paper on advisory committees reminds us that they were indeed established in 1911, following complaints of political selection:

"The position of Magistrates was seen as a reward for political services. This was highlighted by the large variation in Magistrates appointed under different Governments either side of the 1906 elections" (para.2).

Clearly we have shifted from a position in the twentieth century where party political allegiance was overt and Lord Chancellors always instructed advisory committees to select politically balanced bench, to a position where, by the twenty-first century, the bench is supposedly so independent of party politics that it is taboo even to ask a candidate what party they support. This directly mirrors the mainstream judiciary, as we saw in Ch.14.

Race

15–007 Historically, the lay magistracy has under-recruited minorities. It used to be difficult to attract applications. The contrast is visible in court, where non-whites are over-represented among defendants and victims. This was especially acute in areas of minority population concentration ("Concern", 1997). Recognising this, Lord Chancellors Mackay (Conservative), then Irvine, then Falconer (Labour), tried to compensate by appointing more non-whites than there are in the population at large. Recruitment of non-whites has been above eight per cent every year since 1999. This doubtless reflects the success of various recruitment drives, including the Operation Black Vote shadowing scheme, described below. At last, according to the 2011 statistics, eight per cent of lay justices are non-white, slightly above the 7.9 per cent non-white of the population of England and Wales, according to the 2001 census. In 1997, I commented that the worst visible differences, though, were in areas of large non-white populations. As can be seen from the 2011 statistics, however, a great effort has been made to recruit non-whites in areas of high minority populations. For instance, of the 3,292 magistrates in London, there are 667 non-white magistrates and in Birmingham, 137 of the 882 magistrates are non-white. Of course, there is still a visible difference between predominantly white benches and the population appearing before them in court so it is to be hoped that the advisory committees will sustain their effort to recruit more non-whites in these areas.

In 2004, the Department of Constitutional Affairs (now MoJ) published research by Vennard and others, "Ethnic minority magistrates' experience of the role and of the court environment". It aimed to explore whether minority magistrates had experienced racism and whether they complained of this; what was the impact of perceived discrimination and racism upon their satisfaction with the role and what levels of responsibility minority magistrates achieved. There were 128 magistrates from 14 benches interviewed. The findings were as follows:

1. Most respondents considered racism endemic in this country.

2. Respondents were motivated to become magistrates from a sense of civic responsibility and a desire to put something back into the community. Others derived personal satisfaction and some aspired to make a positive contribution in cases involving minority defendants.
3. 70 per cent had wholly favourable initial impressions of their bench and were as fully integrated as they wished to be. 30 per cent initially felt uneasy or marginalised. A few continued to feel outsiders.
4. 72 per cent had not encountered racist attitudes or behaviour in their fellow magistrates. Of the other 28 per cent, they typically felt they had been excluded or marginalised by a white chairman but, as only a minority of chairmen acted in this way, they nevertheless enjoyed a good relationship with most white colleagues.
5. Four believed they had been subjected to unequal treatment.
6. Most praised their justices' clerk and her team. Eight per cent found staff had displayed racist attitudes towards others. 13 per cent recalled racist behaviour by lawyers; nine per cent by the police and 12 per cent by defendants.
7. Most were impressed by the efforts made by their court to be fair but 21 per cent had observed magistrates displaying racist attitudes towards defendants.
8. Magistrates identified a number of obstacles to recruiting minorities: financial disincentives; employers' reluctance to allow time off; the white, middle class image of the magistracy and the misperception that only educated, professional people could be magistrates.
9. 20 per cent fewer minority magistrates had become bench chairmen. There was an underrepresentation of minorities in the family court.

Disability

The Equality Working Group (below) reported a shortage of **15–008** applications from disabled people so the recruitment website now encourages applications.

Gender

Many commentators complained in the past that the magis- **15–009** tracy was overwhelmingly male. This was patently not true, as I pointed out in 1997, nor is it true now. It was caused by an assumption and by their failure to examine the readily available annual statistics. The 2011 statistics show that 51.1 per cent are women. This roughly 50:50 proportion has remained constant since the 1970s.

Current attempts to enhance diversity: background to the National Recruitment Strategy

15–010   In response to the report of the Stephen Lawrence Inquiry (1999), the Lord Chancellor's Department (now MoJ) set up an audit of its procedures to assess whether they provided equality of opportunity and supported diversity. An Equality Working Group was established to seek ways of encouraging applications from all sections of society, eliminating discrimination and producing a diverse bench. In a 2000 report, they praised the efforts of Irvine L.C. to foster a nationally co-ordinated approach to recruiting a diverse bench in a fair way but made various recommendations, including that the department should do the following:

- Attract media attention to raise the magistracy's profile among underrepresented groups.
- Train advisory committees to distinguish between positive action and positive discrimination.
- Communicate zero tolerance of discrimination.
  Copy the Territorial Army model of presenting awards to local employers who allowed staff time off to be magistrates.
- Consider how to change people's attitudes to colleagues who take time off to serve.
- Develop an integrated national strategy to replace the present piecemeal one.
- Make court buildings more accessible for disabled magistrates.
- Find out why justices resign. It seemed to be because they could not fulfil the sittings required.
- Ensure dress codes were not culturally biased.

Auld L.J. emphasised the value of the lay magistracy in his 2001 *Review of the Criminal Courts* but commented that there was "scope for improvement, particularly in the manner of their recruitment, so as to achieve a better reflection, nationally and locally, of the community" (p.98). He recommended:

- Reviewing community relations and educational initiatives of benches to inform the public better and attract more suitable candidates.
- Supporting local advisory committees with a National Recruitment Strategy (now done).
- Equipping advisory committees with local and national demographic data.
- Reviewing ways to make service as a magistrate more attractive to a wider range of the community.

- Finding a substitute for measuring diversity by political affiliation (now done in 2003, as seen above).

In 2001, the Lord Chancellor's Department and Operation Black Vote launched the magistrates' shadowing scheme, in seven regions, encouraging members of minority ethnic communities to sit with lay justices, in the hope of recruiting some of them to the Bench. The evaluation report *Judiciary for All*, was published in 2003. Lord Irvine said the scheme had been successful in challenging participants' views of magistrates and allowing magistrates to gain an understanding of minority communities. The scheme was launched nationwide in 2004. In October 2003, Falconer L.C. launched the National Strategy for the Recruitment of Lay Magistrates. The Strategy repeated some of the concerns which I had expressed in 1997.

The Government said it wanted to increase recruitment and retention of a diverse spectrum of the population; raise the profile of the magistracy and dispel misconceptions; encourage younger people; target ethnic minorities and the disabled and make sitting days more flexible. Recruitment campaigns are now targeted at underrepresented groups, as demonstrated by local demographic data. Some plans were simple (and overdue), such as developing a recruitment leaflet, and others more complex, such as educating employers that magistrates can import transferable skills useful in their jobs. They promised an extensive advertising campaign using a variety of channels. Since then, advertisements have occasionally been placed on buses but there is no significant advertising budget.

Removal

The Lord Chancellor can remove the name of any magistrate **15–011** from the Commission, under the Courts Act 2003. This is rarely done but is usually because a magistrate refuses to enforce a particular law, or for personal indiscretion, such as conducting an obvious extra-marital affair with another magistrate. Under the Constitutional Reform Act 2005, complaints are now the responsibility of the Office for Judicial Complaints. Their *Annual Report 2009–10* discloses that 28 judicial office holders, including tribunal judges, were removed from office last year, 25 of whom were magistrates, as follows:

"Removal from office occurred on 28 occasions. 12 of these were where (*sic*) for not fulfilling judicial duty and 5 as a result of civil proceedings, criminal or road traffic convictions, 6 as a result of inappropriate behaviour or comments, 3 for professional misconduct and 1 each for motoring offences and conflict of interest. If a judicial office holder resigns during a complaint investigation this is recorded, but the investigation ceases. There were 18 resignations during conduct investigations" (p.20).

3. Training

15–012   Lay justices are non-lawyers. They need to understand basic procedure, the rules of evidence, in outline, the elements of the law they commonly apply and how to behave appropriately in court. Until 2005, training was the responsibility of local Magistrates' Courts Committees (MCCs) and justices' clerks. Consequently, its quality differed from court to court, dependent on local attitudes and how much the Committee was prepared to spend, as described in *The Magistrates' Clerk* (1984).

The Courts Act 2003, s.19 provided for rules to be made about lay justices' training and appraisal. MCCs were abolished in 2005 and replaced by local courts boards. Responsibility for training passed to the Lord Chancellor. Following the recommendation of Auld L.J., the Government promised, in its 2002 White Paper, *Justice for All*, that "the JSB [now Judicial College] will have a much stronger role in magistrates' training, to ensure more consistency in standards across the country". It is responsible for advising on, developing and monitoring the training of lay magistrates, which is still delivered locally, in practice by magistrates' clerks. It also organises the training of bench chairmen and training for district judges (magistrates' courts). The training regime is summarised on the Magistrates Association website. New magistrates are trained to achieve four basic competences: applied understanding of the framework within which magistrates operate and the abilities to follow basic law and procedure, think and act judicially and work effectively as a team member. They are assisted by a mentor and appraised. The Judicial College has been applying more uniformity. As magistrates are all now part of a unified national bench, training needs to allow them to move easily from one bench to another if, say, they move house. Training is provided according to their appraised individual needs. After around 18 hours' initial induction, usually a weekend course, and a few hours of observing court proceedings, if necessary, the justice may commence sitting, as a "winger". The new justice will undertake about six mentored sittings within 12–18 months, and may receive consolidation training. The justice will be appraised after 12–18 months and every three years thereafter. After four or five years, she may undertake chairmanship training. Justices also appointed to the specialist courts, the youth courts and family proceedings courts, must undertake specialist additional training. All are offered regular continuation training and ad hoc training as the need arises.

4. Organisation

Until 2005, magistrates' courts were administered by local magis- **15–013** trates' courts committees (MCCs), consisting of magistrates. MCCs spent their allocated budget on staff, administration, recruitment and training for magistrates and clerks. Since magistrates' courts have historically been locally organised, one of their hallmarks was their idiosyncratic differences in practice, procedure and inter-pretation of the law. In 2001 Auld L.J. recommended that MCCs be replaced by local courts boards and a central executive agency, administering all courts. This was done from 2005, under the Courts Act 2003. There are 21 boards. Magistrates were opposed to the abolition of MCCs. Boards must contain at least one judge, two lay justices, two people with knowledge or experience of the courts and two local people. From 2005, all courts are administered by Her Majesty's Courts Service, renamed in 2011 HM Courts & Tribunals Service. An Inspectorate was established in 1994, to identify and disseminate good practice. It was closed in 2010 by Ken Clarke, Minister of Justice. Nationally, the Magistrates' Association speaks for the magistrates as a collective body.

Lay justices sit in pairs or groups of three (legal maximum). District judges (magistrates' courts) normally sit alone. In the Youth Court, three justices of mixed gender sit, or one district judge, or a mixed bench. Collectively, magistrates are known as "the Bench" and they are addressed as "Your Worships". The Chairman of the Bench is annually elected.

5. District judges (magistrates' courts), formerly known as stipendiary magistrates

DJMCs are full-time professionals. Under the Tribunals, Courts **15–014** and Enforcement Act 2007, applicants must satisfy the judicial appointment eligibility condition on a five-year basis. Rules may be made reducing the qualification-time and opening up eligibility to other groups of lawyers and so legal executives are now eligi-ble, since 2010–11. Applicants will normally have sat as deputies, part-time, for at least two years, or have served for 30 court-sitting days. There were, in 2010, 143 DJMCs in England and Wales and 151 deputies. DJMCs are normally appointed in their early forties so are younger, on average, than lay justices. Deputies are normally barristers, solicitors or justices' clerks, aged 35–55. Historically, although most cases in Outer London and the provinces are heard by lay justices, most cases in Inner London have, for the last three centuries, been dealt with by these professionals, stipendiary magistrates or "stipes" as they used to be known. Later, professionals were appointed in some provincial cities, to meet increased caseloads, because they deal with cases more speedily than justices. The Royal Commission on Criminal Justice, 1993, recommended that there should be a more systematic approach to the role of stipendiaries so a unified stipendiary bench was created by the Access to Justice Act 1999 when they were renamed district judges.

6. Magistrates' clerks

15–015   "In many ways the most important person in the whole set-up of the administration of justice" (Lord Parker C.J., in the House of Lords debate on the Justices of the Peace Bill 1968).

The importance of magistrates' clerks, legal advisers, should not be underestimated. Lay justices and DJMCs are arbiters of both fact and law so, in criminal cases, they perform the functions of both judge and jury in the Crown Court. Both lay justices and DJMCs are advised by magistrates' clerks and since the lay justices are appointed because they are not, generally, lawyers, they are wholly dependent on their clerks for advice on law and practice. Remember that this is in the context of magistrates handling over 95 per cent of criminal business and a substantial amount of family business. Section 28 of the Courts Act 2003 states:

> "(4) The functions of a justices' clerk include giving advice to any or all of the justices of the peace to whom he is clerk about matters of law (including procedure and practice) on questions arising in connection with the discharge of their functions, including questions arising when the clerk is not personally attending on them.
> (5) The powers of a justices' clerk include, at any time when he thinks he should do so, bringing to the attention of any or all of the justices of the peace to whom he is clerk any point of law (including procedure and practice) that is or may be involved in any question so arising."

and s.29 emphasises the independence of the clerks in their advisory functions. In 1955, Glanville Williams said that, "If legal argument takes place in court, the argument is addressed to the justices, who may hardly follow a word of it; in reality, however, it is intended for the ears of the clerk". This is still the case. Indeed, the High Court warned magistrates that they should follow their clerk's advice, in *Jones v Nicks* [1977] Crim. L.R. 365. Williams said that the danger arising from this was that clerks could be tempted to interfere in proceedings in a way that is "theoretically unwarrantable." The only significant piece of empirical research on magistrates' clerks was my own, conducted in the 1970s and reported in *The Magistrates' Clerk* and thus too old to be of any practical application. I found examples of clerks effectively taking decision-making out of the justices' hands, especially in relation to the admissibility of evidence, and I found examples of clerks who were prepared to admit to very significant influence over lay justices, especially over sentencing. I also found significant differences in approach, from clerk to clerk and court to court. Since the 1970s, magistrates and legal advisors are much better trained and most legal advisors are now professionally qualified. I would hope and expect that, if this research were to be replicated, I would find far fewer inconsistencies in practice and that both clerks and justices would have a better sense of their proper role. I would hope not to find any of the displays of unfairness or prejudice that I reported in *The Magistrates' Clerk*. Having said all this, research by McLaughlin in 1990 found that clerks *did* still influence magistrates' decision making.

As Glanville Williams pointed out in 1955, if clerks or legal advisers retire (behind the courtroom, with the justices) to give advice to the justices, as they often do, it may give the impression that the clerk could exercise undue domination over the justices. He suggested that clerks give their advice in open court. In 2000, when I was asked to advise Auld L.J. on the implications of the Human Rights Act 1998 in magistrates' courts, I expressed the same opinion, drawing attention to Art.6 of the Convention, on fair trial. Since the 1990s, all clerks and legal advisers have been trained to give their advice in open court, where possible, and that, where they give advice in the retiring room, that this should be repeated in open court. This has now been spelled out in The Criminal Procedure Rules 2010 Pt 37.14 (Pilkington, 2010), which clarifies the legal adviser's role and specifies that an adviser is not necessary where the court includes a DJ, as follows.

"Duty of justices' legal adviser

(1) A justices' legal adviser must attend, unless the court—

   (a) includes a District Judge (Magistrates' Courts); and
   (b) otherwise directs.

(2) A justices' legal adviser must—

    (a) give the court legal advice; and

    (b) if necessary, attend the members of the court outside the courtroom to give such advice; but

    (c) inform the parties of any such advice given outside the courtroom.

(3) A justices' legal adviser must—

    (a) assist an unrepresented defendant;

    (b) assist the court by—

        (i) making a note of the substance of any oral evidence or representations, to help the court recall that information,

        (ii) if the court rules inadmissible part of a written statement introduced in evidence, marking that statement in such a way as to make that clear,

        (iii) ensuring that an adequate record is kept of the court's decisions and the reasons for them, and

        (iv) making any announcement, other than of the verdict or sentence."

The chief clerk at each court is called the justices' clerk. A justices' clerk may be in charge of more than one Bench and the nationwide trend of the last three decades has been to amalgamate several Benches under one clerkship. In the 1970s, there were over 400 justices' clerks. Until very recently, there were around 70 and in 2007 the Government was considering reducing their numbers to 43. The Justices' Clerks' Society's response to this consultation was understandably hostile. They pointed out that this would not work. If the JC were in charge of too many justices he would lose his effective pastoral and personal working relationship with them. For instance, if there were to be a single justices' clerk for the East Midlands, they would serve 2,318 magistrates with a population of 4,222,865 and have a weighted caseload of 929,464. They seem to have lost the argument because, after consultation, the Government reduced their numbers and there are now 49, assisted by 1,800 legal advisers. Of course, since many justices' clerks are in charge of more than one court and since most courts have more than one courtroom in session at a time, the justices' clerk necessarily delegates advisory functions to her assistants. Some justices' clerks are in charge of whole counties.

These assistant clerks are called court clerks, or more usually, legal advisors. Since 2010, they must be professionally legally qualified, thanks to legislation introduced in 1999. Delegated legislation in 1980 required that, if not professionally qualified, court clerks should be law graduates or equivalent, or possess a special clerks' Home Office diploma in magisterial law, or be qualified by five years' experience before 1980. This led to the curious situation where, in some provincial courtrooms, the court clerk advising the lay justices is not professionally qualified. More anomalous is the fact that in Inner London, where most cases are heard by DJMCs, they are often advised by professionally qualified clerks, barristers or solicitors. The nationwide situation remains patchy. Disappointingly, the over 40s were exempted from the 1999 Rules, because some areas were so dependent on unqualified clerks that they would not all be able to qualify in time. More disappointingly, those who were in post in 1998 were also exempted from qualification. The Ministry apparently does not keep statistics on legal advisers' qualifications.

The clerks' staff, like the justices' clerks, used to be recruited and paid by local magistrates' courts committees. Justices' clerks and other legal advisers were very anxious when it became clear that they were to become part of Her Majesty's Courts Service in 2005. Since the justices' clerk may exercise judicial functions and these are routinely delegated to other legal advisers, they pointed out that it was anomalous and a breach of the separation of powers for them to become civil servants like the clerks of other courts (for instance, the Crown Court), who do not give legal advice or exercise judicial functions. The Justices' Clerks' Society submitted a paper to Falconer L.C. suggesting that justices' clerks should be judicial officers appointed by the Judicial Appointments Commission and accountable for the quality of justice in local magistrates' courts. The Lord Chancellor could see no problem with justices' clerks being civil servants. Justices' clerks and their staff are now appointed by the Lord Chancellor under s.27 of the Courts Act 2003.

Concern over clerks' powers

In 1999, I raised the following concerns. Under the Crime and **15–016** Disorder Act 1998, extensive pre-trial judicial powers may be delegated to a single justice or justices' clerk, exercisable in an early administrative hearing or pre-trial review, as suggested by the Narey Report, *Review of Delay in the Criminal Justice System* (1997). In reality this is delegated to court clerks (legal advisers). In the Lords' debate on the Bill, Lord Bingham C.J. expressed the same concern: pre-trial management powers are judicial and clerks are not judges. Magistrates should be doing the judging. As a result of Lord Bingham's intervention, fewer management powers were given to clerks than they wanted. Case management powers are now set out in general terms in the Criminal Procedure Rules

2010 but these cross-refer to the existing legislation. Justices' clerks and legal advisers are, of course, listed as potential case managers.

7. History

15–017   Most people consider that a royal proclamation in 1195, which set up keepers of the peace to assist the sheriff in the maintenance of law and order, was the origin of the justice of the peace. Clearer evidence comes from statutes in 1327 and 1361 under which "good and lawful men" were to be "assigned to keep the peace", holding administrative rather than judicial authority and, like the present-day justice, not legally qualified and acting part-time. The title Justice of the Peace was first used in the 1361 statute. In 1363, a statute required four quarter sessions to be held annually, and gradually the power to deal with criminal cases was added to the administrative work. From 1496, justices were permitted to try the minor (summary) criminal cases locally at petty sessions, instead of at quarter sessions, so giving rise to magistrates' courts as courts of summary jurisdiction, as they now are. When quarter sessions were replaced by the Crown Court in 1972, magistrates retained their role, hearing appeals alongside a circuit judge. Magistrates were the local government until elected authorities were created under the Local Government Acts of 1888 and 1894.

8. Should lay justices be replaced by professionals?

Lay justices' conspiracy theory

15–018   Despite repeated assurances to the contrary by successive Lord Chancellors and then by Auld L.J., some lay justices have a theory that there is a conspiracy to replace them with professionals, whose numbers have steadily grown over the 1990s. This is typified by Robson's article. In 2002, she warned that this could be the point "where the lay magistracy may be launched on a long farewell". In his speech to the Magistrates' Association, The Lord Chancellor hoped the white paper *Justice for All* (2002) "banishes the myths of a few years ago" that "the lay magistracy was an endangered species". Magistrates, he said, would become part of a unified national bench, giving them greater flexibility to be shifted to different courts. Nevertheless the Lord Chancellor assured them of the "primacy of local justice and individual availability".

Some lay justices' anxiety has not abated, despite the fact that the Criminal Justice Act 2003 potentially doubled their sentencing powers (never brought into force) and Lord Chancellor Falconer expressed an intention to double recruitment of lay justices in 2004–07. For instance, in 2011, Robson repeated the same allegation that there was a plot to professionalise the magistracy, despite the fact that lay justice numbers have increased even since 2010. I have found examples of the theory dating back to the 1970s and earlier. The problem arises because modern magistrates are ignorant of their own history. I tried to explain what the true position was in a 2002 essay. While they are correct to point out that stipendiaries (DJMCs) have increased in numbers since 1950, they have neglected to notice that lay justices have increased in numbers too. Lay justices also sit far more often than they did previously. In the year 1948, over 65 per cent of justices sat less than 26 times and 10 per cent did not sit at all. Nowadays, lay justices are required to sit on 26 occasions per year but they sit, on average, over 41 times a year (Morgan and Russell, below). Most importantly, as I was at pains to point out in 1997, "Neglect", magistrates' jurisdiction has increased out of all recognition in over the last few centuries, as more and more criminal business has shifted down from the assizes, now Crown Court, onto the shoulders of the magistracy. Offences are regularly reclassified downwards, from indictable to either-way, or from either-way to summary only. When new offences are created they are usually summary only or either-way, thus guaranteeing that they will all or mostly be tried by magistrates.

The curious position of London

In Inner London, for the best part of three centuries, most cases **15–019** in the magistrates' courts have been heard by stipendiaries, now DJMCs, whereas in outer London and the provinces, most cases were and are heard by lay justices. The position is rendered odder by the fact that Inner London was the first to professionalise its clerks so by the 1970s we had the anomalous position where cases in Inner London were routinely tried by a professional magistrate, advised by a lawyer, whereas elsewhere most cases were decided by lay justices, advised by court clerks who were not lawyers. There is no logic to this difference. It arises from history. Professional magistrates were appointed from the eighteenth century in London in response to concern about corruption among local lay justices.

When stipendiary numbers increased in the provinces, they were installed at the request of the local benches, usually to help out with a large workload. Since 1999, when the stipendiary bench was organised on a national basis, the Lord Chancellor can appoint a district judge anywhere and shift her around, as the need arises.

This means that there are many DJMCs who sit in different courts on a rota basis or are brought in to handle long and/or complex trials.

The lack of logic in our current distribution of criminal cases

15–020   As I pointed out in "Neglect" (1997), there is no logic in the way in which we currently allocate criminal cases. This is still the case. While DJMCs may do more of the serious work of the magistrates' courts, they are not confined to that. In the courts where they sit alongside lay justices, parties may not be able to predict in advance whether they will be heard by a lay bench or a DJMC, because if one court finishes early, the clerk is sent to fetch work to relieve the list of a busier bench. In the magistrates' court, a defendant may find himself tried by a judge alone, a DJMC, but he has no choice. If he is tried in the Crown Court, having pleaded not guilty, again he has no choice. He must be tried by judge and jury. Yet in most other common law jurisdictions he could choose a non-jury trial before a single judge, called a "bench trial".

The value of lay justices

15–021   The last body to consider this, prior to Auld in 2001, was the 1948 Royal Commission on Justices of the Peace. This passage illustrates comprehensively the principled reasons for keeping lay justices.

> "(L)ike that of trial by jury, it gives the citizen a part to play in the administration of the law. It emphasizes the fact that the principles of the common law, and even the language of statutes, ought to be. . .comprehensible by any intelligent person without specialized training. Its continuance prevents the growth of a suspicion in the ordinary man's mind that the law is a mystery which must be left to a professional caste and has little in common with justice as the layman understands it. Further, the cases in which decisions on questions of fact in criminal cases are left to one man ought to be, as they now are, exceptional." (p.7.)

Doran and Glenn (2000), commissioned to examine *Lay Involvement in Adjudication* for the review of the criminal justice system in Northern Ireland, provided a very useful survey of issues raised in debate between supporters and detractors of the principle of lay participation, as below.

The right of participation in the adjudicative process

15–022   Every person has an equal right to participate in matters of general concern. Lay participants are more representative of the local community and establish a link between the courts and local affairs. On the other hand, in reality, some members of the community are excluded from participation and lay adjudicators are a social elite.

The personality of the participants

Lay participants possess an informal and experiential body of **15–023** knowledge gleaned from the local environs, whereas professionals possess formal technical knowledge. The problems with this are whether participants are truly local, whether "local knowledge" sits happily with the concept of acting as a neutral arbiter and whether participants will encounter defendants outside the court-room in an embarrassing or dangerous context. The argument that the professionals' training makes them superior can be countered by training lay participants but that might destroy the "layness" for which they are valued.

The process of participation

It is said to be safe to entrust minor matters to lay participants **15–024** because they are legally advised and because the guilty plea rate is high. The problem with this argument, however, is that it trivi-alises the work of the lower courts and, as I have pointed out above, English and Welsh magistrates are not confined to trivia, as are lay magistrates in other jurisdictions. It is also argued that lay involve-ment injects realism and popular values into decision-making so that law and legal procedure become less mysterious. Further, lay people are said to be cheaper, more flexible and less case-hardened and their reasoning based on reasonableness, equity and fairness. There are problems with these arguments. There is no evidence that the law is kept less complex by the presence of lay persons on the bench. Those who sit regularly may become just as case-hardened as professionals. The vague form of reasoning of laypeople pro-duces inconsistent decisions and regional disparities that are less susceptible to review, create uncertainty and diminish public con-fidence. Professionals are said to be more consistent and procedur-ally correct. On the other hand, some say that professionals can be inflexible, legalistic, detached from the community and less sym-pathetic with arguments raised before them. Bearing in mind that magistrates are volunteers, giving up lots of spare time for training and making life harder for themselves if they have a full-time job, their morale can be adversely affected and feel undervalued when courts are closed, as they are being in 2011. Thornhill (2010) regret-ted the closure of magistrates' courts and their replacement in some instances, with neighbourhood and community justice panels.

Several pieces of research allowed us to reach a better informed opinion on the practical differences between lay and professional magistrates, to test the assumptions underlying the arguments of principle above. In 1990, Shari Diamond's research affirmed lawyers' long held anecdotal assumption that professional magistrates are harsher in sentencing than lay justices. In research reported in *The Role and Appointment of Stipendiary Magistrates* (1995) Seago, Walker and Wall aimed to examine the function of stipendiaries. They found that:

- Very few courts had rules for allocating work to stipendiaries.
- There was a striking difference between the work of stipendiaries and acting (deputy) stipendiaries, who were kept away from more legally and evidentially complex cases.
- Metropolitan stipendiaries appeared to be almost twice as quick to hear contested cases as provincial stipendiaries.
- Most of their judicial work was general list cases but they also heard long trials (especially those lasting more than a day) or complex or highly publicised trials and they had a heavier caseload than lay justices.
- Stipendiaries dealt with all types of work more speedily than lay justices. One provincial stipendiary could replace 32 justices and one metropolitan stipendiary could replace 24 justices.

In discussing the future role of stipendiaries, the authors suggested that pressure on the Crown Court could be relieved. "Consideration could be given to an enhanced jurisdiction (up to two to three years' imprisonment) for a trial tribunal consisting of a stipendiary and two lay magistrates". In 2000, a major research project was undertaken for the Home Office and Lord Chancellor's Department. It is reported in *The Judiciary in Magistrates' Courts* by Morgan and Russell. Its aims were to investigate the balance of lay and professional magistrates and the arguments in favour of that balance. Apart from the findings on composition, above, they concluded:

- Lay justices sat on 41.4 occasions per year, on average. Additionally, they spent a working week on training and other duties. They sat in threes, in 84 per cent of cases.
- All professionals sat in court around four days a week, rarely with lay justices.
- Their finding on stipendiaries' work allocation was the same as Seago, Walker and Wall. Stipendiaries' time was concentrated on either-way rather than summary cases.
- Stipendiaries heard 22 per cent more appearances than lay justices. If their caseloads were identical, they could deal with 30 per cent more appearances.

- Stipendiary hearings generally involved more questioning and challenging.
- Stipendiaries showed more command over proceedings and would challenge parties responsible for delay. People applied for fewer adjournments and were less likely to be granted them.
- Lay justices were less likely to refuse bail or use immediate custody as a sentence.
- Court users had more confidence in stipendiaries. They were seen as more efficient, consistent in decisions, questioning appropriately and as giving clear reasons. Lawyers admitted to preparing better for stipendiaries.
- Court users considered lay justices better at showing courtesy, using simple language and showing concern to distressed victims.
- Few members of the public had heard there were different types of magistrate. Most thought lay justices would be better at representing the views of the community and sympathising with the defendants' circumstances but that stipendiaries would be better at making decisions on guilt and innocence.
- One stipendiary could replace 30 lay justices. Doubling stipendiary numbers would cut down court appearances but increase the prison population. The net cost would be about £23 million per year.

The Institute for Public Policy Research commissioned a MORI public opinion poll on the magistracy and then asked Sanders to compare the skills and experience which lay and professional magistrates brought to the bench. His 2001 paper, *Community Justice—Modernising the Magistracy in England and Wales* reports the following. The MORI poll found a third of the public polled did not know that the majority of magistrates were laypeople and hugely underestimated the proportion of cases heard by magistrates. Only 29 per cent thought magistrates did a good job and 61 per cent thought they were out of touch; 49 per cent were unhappy that magistrates were legally untrained; and 42 per cent would be more confident in a mixed panel.

Mixed benches

In 1948, the Bar recommended that peripatetic stipendiaries be **15–025** created, to travel around and sit with local lay justices and that was done in some areas. I briefly discussed mixed benches in 1997, as did Seago, Walker and Wall in 1995. I mentioned that this pattern was common in Eastern Europe. As I pointed out in 1997, the obvious danger here is that the professional will dominate the lay participants and some of the research on the Eastern European models verifies this, as Vogler was swift to point out in 2001. Sanders, above, concluded that the skills of both professional and lay magistrates, sitting as a mixed bench, are needed in deciding complex cases: legal skills to apply the relevant law to the facts; social skills to assess character and judge honesty and managerial and administrative skills. Panel decision-making was preferable to sole decision-making. Justice should be transparent and account-able. This was promoted by lay participation. Public confidence needed to be safeguarded and increased.

The Civil Liberties Trust, in its 2002 report, "Magistrates' Courts and Public Confidence—a proposal for fair and effective reform of the magistracy", called for reform of the magistracy to inspire public confidence. They recommended mixed tribunals, with the lay justices and professionals separately responsible for the fact-finding and the law. Magistrates should be drawn randomly from the population and required to sit for a specified period of time. Alternatively, the current lay magistracy should be expanded.

My response to Vogler was to argue, in 2002, that he was not comparing like with like. In all the European examples he gave, the lay participants were and are more like jurors. Our lay justices are appointed to sit frequently for many decades and are trained and experienced in fact finding and sentencing. Further, as I had already pointed out in 1997, this danger could be averted by train-ing the professionals not to dominate the lay justices and training the lay justices not to defer to the professional. Besides, as I have also pointed out before, we have over 100 examples of mixed tribu-nals in England and Wales, dealing with civil cases, as described in Ch.11 on alternatives to the civil courts, above. The mixing of lay and professionals there does not seem to have caused problems.

15–026   Auld (2001) considered all these arguments of principle and the research above and made some controversial recommenda-tions, which I will not deal with in great depth, because they were rejected by the government. In brief, he recommended the creation of a middle tier of his proposed unified criminal court, called the "district court", with lay justices sitting together with one DJMC. The lay justices would participate in fact finding but the DJMC would do the sentencing. Many commentators were opposed to this. The Law Society thought the cost of running a middle tier would outweigh the benefit. I criticised the proposed mixed bench because the lay justices would be relegated to the position of jurors; the DJMC would do the sentencing alone. I can see no logic to this suggestion, given that justices are experienced sentencers and given that the justices are there to represent the community including, presumably, local attitudes to the relative gravity of local crimes. Morgan and Sanders, in 2002, criticised Auld's suggestions in relation to magistrates. Both felt he had disregarded their findings and conclusions. Other responses to the Auld Review, in relation to magistrates and all other recommendations, are to be found on the Criminal Courts Review website.

Having rejected Auld's proposal for a middle tier criminal court, the government opted instead to double magistrates' sentencing powers. This was done in the Criminal Justice Act 2003, s.154. This is unlikely to come into force, because it has not been activated by 2011. If it ever does, the potential effect will be to significantly increase the criminal case load of the magistrates' courts, which simply continues the trend of the last two centuries of shifting work down onto the shoulders of the magistracy. Magistrates who were the subject of doctoral research by Herbert were opposed to this change. Many felt they were already being asked to handle cases at the extreme of their ability.

BIBLIOGRAPHY

Auld L.J., *Review of the Criminal Courts of England and Wales* (2001), **15–027** otherwise known as the Criminal Courts Review.

C. Barnett J.P., Speech at the Magistrates' Association A.G.M., November 19, 2008.

The Civil Liberties Trust is part of the pressure group, Liberty: *www. liberty-human-rights.org.uk.*

P. Darbyshire, *The Magistrates' Clerk* (1984); "The Lamp That Shows That Freedom Lives—is it worth the candle?" [1991] Crim. L.R. 740; "An Essay on the Importance and Neglect of the Magistracy" [1997] Crim. L.R. 627; "For the New Lord Chancellor—Some Causes of Concern About Magistrates" [1997] Crim. L.R. 861; "A Comment on the Powers of Magistrates' Clerks" [1999] Crim. L.R. 377; "Magistrates", in *The Handbook of the Criminal Justice Process* (McConville and Wilson eds, 2002).

S. Doran and R. Glenn, *Lay Involvement in Adjudication*, Criminal Justice Review Group (2000).

Department of Constitutional Affairs, *National Strategy for the Recruitment of Magistrates*, October 2003, DCA archived website.

S. Diamond, "Revising Images of Public Punitiveness: Sentencing by Lay and Professional English Magistrates" (1990) *Law and Social Inquiry* 191.

A. Herbert, "Mode of Trial and Magistrates' Sentencing Powers" [2003] Crim. L.R. 314; synopsis by M. Zander at (2003) 153 N.L.J. 689.

The Home Office, *Review of Delay in the Criminal Justice System*, 1997 (The Narey Report).

House of Commons Home Affairs Committee, Third Report, Session 1995–1996, *Judicial Appointments Procedures, Vol.II* (HMSO, 1996).

Justice for All, White Paper, 2002 *http://www.archive2.official-documents.co.uk/document/cm55/5563/5563.pdf*.

Lord Chancellor and Secretary of State's Directions for Advisory Committees on Justices of the Peace, Ministry of Justice (2008).

H. McLaughlin, "Court Clerks: Advisers or Decision-Makers?" (1990) 30 *British Journal of Criminology* 358.

R. Morgan and N. Russell, *The Judiciary in the Magistrates' Courts* (2000), Home Office.

R. Morgan, "Magistrates: The Future According to Auld" (2002) 29 *Journal of Law and Society* 308.

G. Robson, "The Lay Magistracy: No Time for Complacency" (2002) 166 *Justice of the Peace* 624; "A clouded future?" (2011) 175(20) *Criminal Law & Justice Weekly* 288.

St. J. Pilkington, "The legal adviser in the retiring room" (2010) 66(4) *Magistrate* 27.

A. Sanders, *Community Justice* (2000) IPPR; "Core Values, the Magistracy and the Auld Report" (2002) 29 *Journal of Law and Society* 324.

P. Seago, C. Walker and D. Wall, *The Role and Appointment of Stipendiary Magistrates* (1995).

Seago et al., "The Development of the Professional Magistracy in England and Wales" [2000] Crim. L.R. 631.

J. Thornhill, "Making the most of the magistracy" (2010) 66 (5) *Magistrate* 23.

J. Vennard, G. Davies, J. Baldwin and J. Pearce, "Ethnic minority magistrates' experience of the role and of the court environment", DCA Research Report 3/2004, in the research section of the archived DCA website.

G. Williams, *The Proof of Guilt* (1955).

R. Vogler, "Mixed Messages on the Mixed Bench", *Legal Action*, May 2001, p.8.

FURTHER READING AND SOURCES FOR UPDATING THIS CHAPTER

15–028 Updates for this book from spring 2012 and 2013 on the Sweet & Maxwell website.

Criminal Law and Justice Weekly, on *Lexis*.

Directgov website for details on recruitment, training and other basic information: *www.direct.gov.uk*.

The Justices' Clerks' Society: *www.jc-society.co.uk*.

The Magistrate magazine on *Westlaw*.

The Magistrates' Association: *www.magistrates-association.org.uk*.
Office for Judicial Complaints *http://judicialcomplaints.judiciary.gov. uk*.
Annual statistics on magistrates in office, including gender and ethnicity, are on the Judiciary website.

16. The Jury

"Each jury is a little parliament . . . The first object of any tyrant in Whitehall would be to make Parliament utterly subservient to his will; and the next to overthrow or diminish trial by jury, for no tyrant could afford to leave a subject's freedom in the hands of twelve of his countrymen. So that trial by jury is more than an instrument of justice and more than one wheel of the constitution: it is the lamp that shows that freedom lives." (Sir Patrick Devlin, *Trial by Jury*, 1956.)

"(T)he liberties of England cannot but subsist so long as this palladium remains sacred and inviolate" (Sir William Blackstone, *Commentaries on the Laws of England* Vol.IV, 1769).

"The collective experience of this constitution. . .both when we were in practice at the Bar and judicially, has demonstrated to us time and time again, that juries up and down the country have a passionate and profound belief in, and a commitment to, the right of a defendant to be given a fair trial. They know that it is integral to their responsibility. It is, when all is said and done, their birthright; it is shared by each one of them with the defendant. They guard it faithfully. The integrity of the jury is an essential feature of our trial process. Juries follow the directions which the judge will give them to focus exclusively on the evidence and to ignore anything they may have heard or read out of court." (per Judge J., *In the matter of B* [2006] EWCA Crim 2692, para.31.)

"Out of all the citizens (possibly some three million) who, in the course of any year, find themselves in difficulty with the law, only a small portion (32,000 in 1984) will be tried by a jury. The underlying logic of this situation we find puzzling in the extreme. If society believes that trial by jury is the fairest form of trial, is it too costly and troublesome to be universally applied? . . . But if jury trial is not inherently more fair, given its extra cost and trouble, what are the merits which justify its retention? Society appears to have an attachment to jury trial which is emotional or sentimental rather than logical." (The Roskill Committee on Fraud Trials, 1986, para.8.21.)

"The symbolic function of the jury far outweighs its practical significance . . . this sentimental attachment to the symbol of the jury is dangerous. Adulation of the jury is based on no justification or spurious justification. It has fed public complacency with the English legal system and distracted attention from its evils . . . The truth is that for most people who pass through the criminal justice system this palladium is simply not available and for those who can and do submit themselves to its verdict, it will not necessarily safeguard their civil liberties." (Darbyshire, 1991.)

1. "The lamp that shows that freedom lives"

16–001   As illustrated by the adulation above, this ancient institution arouses strong emotions in the hearts of the English and Welsh, as it does with Americans and others living in the common law daughter-countries of the English legal system. This is because, for centuries, jury trial was central to our legal systems. The use of ordinary people as fact finders in civil and criminal cases was and is perceived by some as the *only* democratic way of organising a legal system. The opinion surveys cited in the previous chapter show that most people have no idea that over 95 per cent of defendants to criminal charges are dealt with by magistrates. Of the remainder who appear before the Crown Court, most plead guilty, so, only around one per cent of defendants receive a jury trial (see detail in Ch.12 on criminal procedure and the latest *Judicial and Court Statistics*). As for civil cases, the jury had almost died out by the beginning of the twentieth century. By now, there are very few civil jury trials per year. Nevertheless, there is still enormous faith in juries.

2. Selection of jurors

Widening jury participation from 2004

16–002   Jurors are drawn from the electoral roll at random. Randomness is not prescribed by the Juries Act but is a matter of practice. Prior to 2004, as I pointed out in 1991, statutory excusals and avoidance of jury service destroyed randomness.

Selection from the electoral roll

The Juries Act 1974, as amended, specifies that every adult, aged **16–003** 18–70, who is on the annual electoral roll and who has lived in this country for at least five years is qualified to serve as a juror. In our research for Auld L.J., for the Criminal Courts Review 2001 (CCR), we (Darbyshire, Maughan and Stewart, 2001) examined jury research worldwide. We argued that selection from the electoral roll is a flawed system. Research as long ago as the 1960s, in the US, demonstrated that electoral lists are not representative of communities and this has been confirmed in Australia and New Zealand. This is caused by such factors as population mobility and residential status, which are linked to class and income levels. We pointed out that census data in England and Wales showed non-registration to be high among ethnic minorities, the 20–24 age group and renters, and it was known that some people do not register to vote in order to avoid council tax. As long ago as 1968, Federal US legislation required that in summoning jury pools, the voters' list should be supplemented with other source lists, such as drivers' licence lists and utility lists and we recommended that the Juries Act should be amended to copy this method. Auld L.J. accepted our recommendation and repeated it in Ch.5 of his *Review*. He considered that jury eligibility should be based on *eligibility* to vote not on inclusion on the roll. The Government rejected this in their response. In their 2002 White Paper, *Justice for All*, they said that instead, they would continue the work of the Electoral Commission to improve the quality of the electoral roll and ensure in particular that minority ethnic communities register themselves. My objections to this refusal are threefold: it does not respond to our findings on population mobility or wilful refusal to register; no good reason was given for not adopting our recommendation; and thirdly, if the census is to be used as a test of the representativeness of the roll, then that too is defective, as there are gaps in the census. The same groups who did not register to vote also failed to complete the census, such as young men. Governments claim that very few households do not complete the ten year census but that by no means guarantees inclusiveness.

Problems caused by statutory excusals, ineligibility and disqualification

16–004   "I am summon'd to appear upon a Jury, and was just going to try if I could get off" (Hawles' *The Englishman's Right: A Dialogue between a Barrister and a Jury-Man*, (1680)).

Until 2003, the Juries Act disqualified some people from service and contained long lists of people who were ineligible or excusable as of right, according to their occupation or status. For example, members of the legal profession, judges, magistrates, members of the prison and probation services and the clergy were ineligible. The 1965 Morris Report (*The Report of The Departmental Committee on Jury Service*, Cmnd.2627) considered that those with special knowledge or prestige attached to their occupations would be unduly influential over their fellow jurors. The Royal Commission on Criminal Justice 1993 (RCCJ) upheld this view but Auld L.J., in the CCR 2001, did not agree.

Members of the armed forces, medical practitioners, chemists, vets, peers and MPs and those aged 65–70 had a right to be excused, as did members of religious organisations, whose tenets or beliefs were incompatible with jury service and those who had done jury service in the previous two years. In 1991, I complained that exempting long lists of people from jury service was the "very antithesis" of randomness. The problems caused by the Act and the excusal rate were affirmed in 1999 by Home Office research conducted by Airs and Shaw. They found that a quarter of a million people were summoned for jury service every year. In a sample of 50,000 people summoned in June and July 1999, only one third were available for service, about half of whom were allowed to defer their service to a later date. Of the remaining two thirds: 13 per cent were ineligible under the Juries Act, or disqualified or excusable as of right; 15 per cent failed to attend on the day, or their summonses were returned as "undelivered"; and 38 per cent were excused. As a result of their findings, a Jury Central Summoning Bureau (JCSB) was created, in Blackfriars, taking over the summoning of jurors from individual Crown Court centres. The excusal rate was high and inconsistent between Crown Court Centres so this was an attempt to regularise the position and tighten up on excusals.

The JCSB reported to us that, because of the rate of non-attendance and excusals, it was still necessary to summon four times as many jurors as were needed, around England and Wales, and six times as many as were needed in London (see, though, Thomas, 2007). We also found that if people simply did not respond to a jury summons, then they might not be pursued. It was left to each individual Crown Court to chase those who did not attend and in London there was no budget allocated for this. In our paper, we recommended repeal of the categories of excusable as of right and ineligible in the Juries Act. Auld L.J. received a number of arguments to the same effect. He examined the regime in New York, where the law and procedure had been tightened up to prevent people avoiding and evading jury service. The presumption in NY was that everyone should do jury service, with very limited grounds for excusal.

The solution—repealing ineligibility

Auld L.J. considered the reasons for making groups such as **16–005** lawyers ineligible for jury service but did not agree, "People no longer defer to professionals or those holding particular office in the way they used to do" (2001, Ch.5). He also considered the objection that if people connected with the criminal justice system did jury service, they would lack openness of mind but he could not see why they should be any more prejudiced than shopkeepers or house owners who had been burglary victims, or people who held strong views over such issues as euthanasia or drugs. Nor did he accept the objection that professionals would infer and transmit to fellow jurors the fact that if the accused did not mention his previous good character, that was because he had previous convictions. Like the Morris Committee, he considered that such a possibility was widely known among the public and would be known by anyone who had already done jury service. He acknowledged the objections to having judges serving on juries but "I consider that it would be good for them and the system of jury trial if they could experience at first hand what jurors have to put up with." He was also heartened by the fact that a number of US judges had had to do jury service and spoke warmly of it. He considered the objection that judge-jurors might know the judge or lawyers in the trial and, depending on seniority or personality, this might inhibit the judge or advocates in their conduct of the case. This problem, he responded, could be dealt with by discretionary excusal on a case by case basis. There was no need for the current blanket ban. He noted that the Morris Committee had decided to preserve the ineligibility of the clergy on the grounds of possible embarrassment caused by their pastoral role and compassionate instincts but observed that there were many others in the community with similar roles and instincts. Auld L.J. accordingly recommended that everyone should be eligible for jury service, save for the mentally ill.

The solution—abolishing the right to excusals

16–006   Scrutinising the list of excusable people, he noted that the Morris Committee had reasoned that this was in the public interest because such groups owed special and personal duties to the state or were responsible for the relief of pain and suffering. Again, his Lordship felt any problems could be dealt with by way of discretionary excusal. As for the 65–70 age group, he could see no reason for excusal unless they could show they were mentally or physically unfit. As for those who had recently done jury service, he observed that if all these statutory exclusions were done away with, being summoned twice for jury service would occur less frequently. He thought the JCSB could consider, on the basis of their statistical observations, excusing people for longer periods.

The disqualified

16–007   Auld L.J. recommended that the category of the disqualified should not change and this was accepted by the Government. Consequently, the Criminal Justice Act 2003 preserves the disqualification of those who have ever been sentenced to custody or its alternatives for five years or more or who, in the last ten years, have been sentenced to custody or an alternative for three months. Those on bail are also disqualified. The 2003 Act, Sch.33, continues the ban on mentally disordered persons. In 2004, the Social Exclusion Unit published a report, "Mental Health and Social Exclusion" suggesting that the categories of mental disorder excluding a person from jury service were too many. The ban failed to distinguish between someone being treated by a doctor for mild depression and someone who had been sectioned under the Mental Health Act 1983. In 2005, the Department of Constitutional Affairs and Home Office issued a joint consultation paper. Those who cannot participate effectively as a juror because of physical incapacity may have their summons discharged by the judge. This is discussed below.

Discretionary excusal

16–008   In our review of research, we found that people try to get out of jury service all over the world and the commonest excuses are childcare, family commitments, employment problems and loss of wages. Excusals were examined by Airs and Shaw. Auld L.J. noted the high excusal rate, 38 per cent, and recommended that where an excuse appears to be well-founded, JCSB officers should aim to deal with it by way of deferral instead of excusal.

The Government's response—*Justice for All* and the Criminal Justice Act 2003

The Government agreed with Auld's recommendations. Their **16–009** 2002 White Paper, *Justice for All*, contained their responses and plans. In a chapter entitled "Enhancing the Public's Engagement", they said "We believe that members of the community have the responsibility and a duty to carry out jury service if they possibly can". The Criminal Justice Act 2003 enacted their proposals. It amended the Juries Act, s.1 to provide that virtually everyone should be qualified for jury service provided they are not mentally disordered or disqualified. Summoning officers are obliged to excuse serving members of the armed forces if their commanding officer certifies that their absence would be prejudicial to the efficiency of the armed service. The 2003 Act amended s.9 of the Juries Act to place a duty on the Lord Chancellor to issue guidance to the JCSB on how its discretion should be exercised in granting deferrals and excusals.

In *Justice for All*, the Government promised to improve jury service. Jurors had a right to be treated with respect and to expect minimal disruption to their personal lives. They agreed with our finding that too many jurors were kept hanging around. Jurors should be supported with more information and advice. They claimed that the JCSB had shifted the balance from excusal to deferral and that this had increased the pool of potential jurors. The 2003 Act came into force on April 2, 2004 and the Government claimed that this would significantly increase the pool of potential jurors. They promised that only those who proved they could not defer service to another period within 12 months would be excused, and then only in exceptional circumstances. Their press release said that compelling reasons for deferral included death or illness of a close relative; health reasons; pre-booked holiday; being a serving member of the armed forces where absence would be detrimental; and religious festivals. Compelling reasons why eligible people could be excused included insufficient understanding of English, certain care responsibilities and being a member of a religious order or society whose beliefs are incompatible with jury service. This summarises the jury summoning guidance issued in December 2003 and now on HM Courts & Tribunals website, *Guidance for summoning officers when considering deferral and excusal applications*, discussed below. In response to concern that some of those summoned for jury service feared for their employment, the Employment Relations Act 2004, s.40 protects jurors from employment detriment or dismissal.

Public reaction to widening jury participation

When Auld L.J. published his proposals and during the passage of **16–010** the 2003 Act through Parliament, there were predictable objections.

Newspapers came out in a rash of letters from doctors and nurses claiming that the National Health Service would collapse in their absence. My response to this is to repeat a calculation I made in 1997 that we cited in our paper for Auld L.J. Of all adults aged 18–70 in England and Wales, each only had a one in six chance of being summoned for jury service during their eligible lifetime. Thanks to the changes made by the 2003 Act, a person's chances of ever doing jury service are now reduced. If doctors and nurses, like everyone else, now have a one in 12 chance of doing a fortnight's jury service once in their lifetimes, this is hardly going to cause the collapse of the NHS as we know it. Furthermore, many health care professionals are not UK citizens and so will not be called for jury service.

Another battery of objections came from judges and lawyers, claiming that lawyer-jurors might have undue influence over other jurors. One would surely hope, however, that lawyers and judges would have the integrity not to try to influence fellow jurors. By analogy, the old pre-2004 law did not exclude legal academics, or non-practising solicitors. I sat on two juries in 1990 and did not disclose that I taught law; nor did I try to sway my fellow jurors (Darbyshire, 1990). Well aware of these objections, in 2003 the Government issued a consultation on "Jury Summoning Guidance", on deferral and excusals, in 2003. They reiterated Auld L.J.'s reasoning:

"Concerns have been raised about the possible effect on the fairness of the trial of allowing lawyers and others involved in the administration of justice to sit on juries. The fear is that they might exercise undue influence over their fellow jurors by virtue of their specialist knowledge of the justice system. However, the Government is satisfied that these concerns are unfounded. The American experience, where, in a number of states, judges, lawyers and others holding positions in the criminal justice system have sat as jurors for some time, is that their fellow jurors have not allowed them to dominate their deliberations. In England and Wales, a large number of people with extensive knowledge of the criminal justice system—legal academics, law students and civil servants working in criminal justice—currently do jury service. There is no evidence to suggest that the involvement of any of these groups in jury service has been a problem. More generally, the diluting effect of the process of random selection, and the group dynamic of the jury, serve to protect the integrity of the deliberative process".

Dyson L.J., then a Court of Appeal judge and now a UKSC Justice, was the first judge to be called for jury service. He told me in 2005 that he was disturbed that one circuit judge had rejected him from a jury on the grounds that he knew him. Considering this to be an unacceptable reason, Dyson L.J. wrote to the Lord Chief Justice to object. In the meantime, he did serve on another jury. At the same time, a number of lawyers were attempting to avoid jury service, especially in the Old Bailey, by asking judges to be excused in trials where they knew the advocates. Some excusals were granted until the Recorder of London, the resident judge at the Old Bailey, issued a local Practice Direction that this was unacceptable. Both Auld L.J. and the Government in its consultation paper had recognised that lawyers and judges might need to be excused if they knew trial participants. This problem has now been resolved by requiring judges or recorders to do jury service in an area in which they do not sit as a judge. Of course famous judges, such as Dyson L.J. are known to all judges and lawyers—but then so was Elizabeth Hurley when she did jury service in the Old Bailey. The Bar Council issued guidance, in 2004, to barristers summoned for jury service. It warned them that it was neither necessary nor appropriate to conceal their profession, nor was it necessary to volunteer such information. They should remember they were sitting as one equal member of a tribunal of fact and not in their capacity as barristers. They should not offer advice or an opinion as to the law and they should not contradict the judge's direction on law.

The jury summoning guidance reflects the criteria listed above. **16–011** Additionally, it says that if people find it difficult to get to court they can be offered another court. MPs can be allowed to sit outside their constituencies. Shift workers can ask for deferral. Those with physical disabilities should be treated sympathetically and so on. In its conclusions, the government clarified the position of those working for the Crown Prosecution Service (CPS). They should not sit on any case where the CPS is prosecutor, that is, most criminal cases. It was accepted that it would be appropriate to extend excusal on the grounds of previous jury service to five years but that would require legislation. They agreed that "extreme circumstance" needed defining.

Test cases on the 2003 Act reforms have been heard by the House of Lords. Three appellants complained that they had had people in their juries who would have prejudiced a fair trial: police officers and a CPS lawyer: *R. v Abdroikov* [2007] UKHL 37. The law lords upheld the claims of bias. Justice had not been seen to be done. Dissenting, Lord Rodger said that the judgment drove a coach and horses through the 2003 Act. Zander called this precedent "a troublesome decision". He was disappointed that the majority three were not persuaded by the powerful argument in the dissent that there are *twelve* jurors. It was applied by the CA in *Khan*

[2008] EWCA Crim 531. A police officer who had been involved in a number of drugs operations sat on a jury on a drugs trial. The LCJ dismissed the appeal:

> "Where an impartial juror is shown to have had reason to favour a particular witness, this will not necessarily result in the quashing of a conviction. It will only do so if this has rendered the trial unfair, or given it an appearance of unfairness. To decide this it is necessary to consider two questions:
>
> i) Would the fair minded observer consider that partiality of the juror to the witness may have caused the jury to accept the evidence of that witness? If so
>
> ii) Would the fair minded observer consider that this may have affected the outcome of the trial? (para. 10). . .We do not consider that familiarity with the particular offence charged against an offender would lead the objective observer to suspect a police juror of bias." (para.48.)

Randomness

16–012   The legal and philosophical sources of the notions of randomness and representativeness are difficult to discover. They do not appear in the Juries Act 1974, which, as we have just seen, significantly disrupted randomness until 2004, but there are statements elsewhere. The Morris Committee Report (1965) said "a jury should represent a cross-section drawn at random from the community" and a 1973 Practice Note by the Lord Chief Justice stated "a jury consists of twelve individuals chosen at random from the appropriate panel". The obiter statement of Lord Denning in the *Brownlow* case [1980] Q.B. 530 reviewed the two "rival philosophies" as he called them, of our random jury and the highly selected US jury. He said:

> "Our philosophy is that the jury should be selected at random from a panel of persons who are nominated at random. We believe that twelve persons selected at random are likely to be a cross-section of the people and thus represent the views of the common man. Some may be moral. Others not. Some may be honest. Others not . . . The parties must take them as they come."

Lord Denning's reference to the philosophy behind US jury composition acknowledges that while we believe in random selection, they believe that impartiality can only be guaranteed by a very elaborate selection system, by means of a voir dire. This means the completion of questionnaires by potential jurors, who are then questioned in open court, plus a generous allocation of peremptory challenges exercisable by each party, to exclude those considered undesirable. In high profile US trials, such as the Rodney King Beatings trials 1992–93, the 1995 O.J. Simpson trial and the 2005 Michael Jackson trial, jury construction may take weeks or months and wealthy defendants like Simpson and Jackson spend thousands hiring expensive "jury consultants" to help them. Selection from the electoral roll in England and Wales is now done randomly by computer, by the JCSB, since late 2000. Before the 1980s, Crown Court jury summoning officers were given the freedom to select jurors from the roll, as they chose, and this led to some selecting alphabetically whilst others selected street by street.

Race

In 2007, Thomas published the results of empirical research, **16–013** discussed below, that suggested that BME groups are not under-represented now on juries in England and Wales. In the 1980s, however, there were complaints from black defendants that jurors were summoned from white areas. In one trial the judge ordered an adjournment and, in another, ordered a jury to be summoned from a different district, in the hope of producing a mixed jury. The CA has ruled, however, that a jury may not be racially constructed. In *R. v Smith (Lance Percival)* [2003] EWCA Crim 283, they affirmed this rule, laid down in *R. v Ford* [1989] Q.B. 868. The US Supreme Court has ruled likewise.

The RCCJ 1993 recommended that the prosecution or defence should be able to apply to the judge, pre-trial, for the selection of a jury containing up to three people from minority communities, in cases with a racial dimension where the defendant or alleged victim was non-white. We reiterated this recommendation in our paper for Auld L.J. and he adopted it, relying on our research. We concluded, on examining worldwide research on juries that, while the findings on gender and verdict and age and verdict are equivocal, there appeared to be a clear relationship between racial composition of juries and verdicts. Research demonstrated that three jurors was the crucial number to have any impact on the verdict. We also pointed out that specially constructed juries are not unprecedented in English law. For over five centuries until 1870, foreigners had the right to be tried by a jury half composed of foreigners, *de medietate linguae*. The Law Society, Race Relations Committee of the Bar Council and the Commission for Racial Equality and others also supported this recommendation.

Auld L.J. pointed out, as we had done, that minorities are under-represented on juries because many do not register to vote, as disclosed by Airs and Shaw's 1999 research: 24 per cent of black citizens, 15 per cent Asian and 24 per cent other ethnic minority citizens did not register to vote. He commented that a limited sample for the Review in three centres in 2000 "showed a noticeable lack of ethnic mix in jury trials at all three centres". Other solutions to the problem, contemplated by the RCCJ 1993 and by Auld L.J. would be to allow the judge to transfer a trial to an area with a better ethnic mix or amalgamate the jury panel with another jury panel from a mixed race area. He rejected these suggestions because it smacked of forum shopping and could cause upset where a defendant and an alleged victim disagreed.

16–014   The first obvious objection to our recommendation, which we acknowledged, is that the type of racial construction we proposed destroys randomness. Auld L.J. considered this and weighed it against the problem that an estimated 400,000 crimes a year were racially motivated and this had recently been recognised by statute and the philosophy of Art.6 of the European Convention which requires objective impartiality. He concluded that randomness was not an end in itself. We recognised another objection to our suggestion for racial construction—a "thin end of the wedge" argument. If it were permitted in a racially charged case, why not allow parties to demand a jury of mixed sexuality in a "queer-bashing" case? Auld L.J.'s response to this was that, while all jurors may bring their own prejudices, that is invisible compared with colour and will be overcome by the differing views of other jury members. Our research had indicated that white juries were or were perceived to be less fair to black than to white people. He thought the problems of racially constructing a jury were not insurmountable. The Summoning Bureau could ask people to disclose their ethnicity on receiving a summons. Initially attracted to Auld L.J.'s recommendation, the Government eventually rejected it, in *Justice for All* (2002), para.7.29 because it would:

- undermine the fundamental principle of randomness;
- assume bias on the part of the excluded jurors;
- place the minority jurors in a difficult position;
- generate tensions in the jury room;
- place undue weight on the views of the minority jurors; and
- place a new burden on the court to determine which cases should receive special treatment and provide a ground for unmeritorious appeals.

Research by Thomas on *Diversity and Fairness in the Jury System* was published by the Ministry of Justice in 2007.

"[T]he…summoning process does not discriminate…against BME groups: a representative section of the local BME community are summoned and serve as jurors in virtually all Crown Courts. [The research] also exposed a number of widespread myths. . .There is no mass avoidance of jury service among the British public. . . This was the reality of jury service in England and Wales even before the introduction of new juror eligibility rules in 2004, which have nonetheless increased participation in the jury system. . .the case simulation research with real jurors showed that racially mixed juries in highly diverse communities did not discriminate against defendants based on the race of the defendant. This was despite the fact that race did influence the decisions of some individual jurors who sat on these juries in cases where race was not presented as an explicit element in the case. What remains to be answered is whether all-white juries, which decide cases in most Crown Courts, also do not discriminate against defendants based on race." (Summary.)

As can be seen, Thomas challenges some of the assertions above, especially on the issue of avoidance of jury service. We return to Thomas below, to examine her 2010 findings on the effect of race on jury decision-making.

Welsh language

Some Welsh judges argued to Auld L.J. that, in a case where a witness gives evidence in Welsh (as is her right), and it has to be translated into English, that witness is at a disadvantage. They suggested that it ought to be possible to select a bilingual jury in such cases. The lack of facility to do so infringed the principle that English and Welsh were to be treated as equal by the courts and caused potential for injustice. Auld L.J. examined other judges' arguments that selecting a bilingual jury would exclude 90 per cent of the defendant's peers, who spoke only English. He declined to resolve the issue but suggested it was worthy of further consideration by someone else. Parry argued in favour, though Thomas's 2007 research indicated that there appeared to be such a low level of Welsh fluency among serving jurors in Wales that it would be difficult to arrange jury trials on a regular basis with full bilingual juries (p.112). **16–015**

Vetting

The group summoned to attend at a particular Crown Court location is called "the panel", from which juries are selected for trials over a certain period (usually two weeks) and the prosecution at this stage may exercise a problematic form of scrutiny known as "vetting" and then the prosecution and defence may exercise rights to challenge. It must be understood, however, that vetting and all types of challenge are extremely rare, since the late **16–016**

1980s. Controversy arose during the highly publicised Official Secrets Act trial in 1978, known as the "ABC Trial" (because of the three defendants' surnames: Aubrey, Berry and Campbell). *The Times* exposed the fact that successive Attorneys General, using prerogative power, had been secretly vetting the backgrounds of potential jurors in this and other politically sensitive trials and trials involving professional gangs. The AG was forced to reveal his guidelines on vetting. In 1980 the two divisions of the Court of Appeal gave rather conflicting rulings on the legality of jury vetting. In *R. v Sheffield Crown Court Ex p. Brownlow* [1980] Q.B. 530, the Civil Division, led by Lord Denning, unanimously ruled jury vetting by the police to be illegal but the case was closely followed, in the Criminal Division, by *R. v Mason (Vincent)* [1981] Q.B. 881, in which police vetting had taken place, as part of the routine in Northamptonshire. The Court held that this was supportable as common sense. In response, the Attorney amended his guidelines, enhancing controls over vetting and distinguishing between: (a) vetting carried out by the police; and (b) "authorised checks", requiring his personal consent:

1. Police may check criminal records, to establish that jurors are not disqualified.
2. "Authorised checks" may be done with the Attorney's permission, following a recommendation by the DPP. The DPP decides what part of the information disclosed should be forwarded to the prosecution (note: not the defence). Such checks will not be carried out in politically motivated cases, except in terrorism cases. In, for example, official secrets trials, vetting will only be permitted where national security is involved and the hearing is likely to be in camera.
3. The Attorney will consider and, in other cases, the Chief Constable may consider, defence requests for information revealed on jurors.

The RCCJ 1993 recommended routine screening for criminal convictions. In 1997, I asked the Conservative Attorney General, Sir Nicholas Lyell, how often he authorised vetting. He had never heard of vetting, which suggests that the practice was, by then, very rare. By 2011, the issue is never heard of and there appears to be no publicly available information on whether vetting takes place by the AG or the police.

Challenges to the Array

16–017   All parties have a common law right, preserved by s.12(6) of the Juries Act 1974, to challenge the whole panel, on the grounds that the summoning officer is biased or has acted improperly. For example this was attempted in *Danvers* [1982] Crim. L.R. 680, by a black defendant, on the grounds that the all-white jury did not reflect the ethnic composition of the community.

Challenges by the Prosecution

The prosecution may exclude any panel member from a particular jury by asking them to "stand by for the Crown" without reasons, until the whole panel, except for the last 12, is exhausted. Reasons, "cause", must be given for any further challenges but, with panels often consisting of 100 or more, the prosecution rarely needs to explain its challenges. The Roskill Committee (1986) recommended the abolition of this right but the Government declined to include it in the Criminal Justice Bill 1986. The Attorney General announced, in 1988, that the prosecution's right to stand a juror by without giving reasons would now be limited to two instances: to remove a "manifestly unsuitable" juror or to remove a juror after authorised vetting. This goes some way towards responding to complaints over the imbalance between prosecution and defence rights of challenge. **16–018**

Challenges by the Defence

Once the jury are assembled in court, the judge invites the juror to step down if she knows anyone involved in the case. The defence may then challenge any number of potential jurors for cause, (i.e. good reason acceptable to the judge) but what is an acceptable "cause" was qualified by a 1973 Practice Note issued by the Lord Chief Justice, who stated that it was contrary to established practice for jurors to be excused on grounds such as race, religion, political beliefs or occupation. This followed a trial of alleged anarchists called "The Angry Brigade", where the defence had requested the judge to ask people to exclude themselves if, for example, they were members of the Conservative Party or if they had relatives in the police force or serving in the forces in Northern Ireland. **16–019**

It is also clear that the reasons must be those known to the defence and should not normally be ascertained by examining the potential juror in court. In other words, no practice exists such as the "voir dire" system in the US, where potential jurors are examined by the judge or lawyers, psychologists and other professionals to discover any prejudices. There have been occasional, well-publicised exceptions, in the 1980s, where the judge has permitted examination of jurors on their affiliations or beliefs, notably in cases involving black defendants. In the 1995–96 Maxwell brothers' fraud trial, potential jurors were questioned on their views of the evidence because of prejudicial pre-trial publicity.

Until 1989, the defence could make a certain number of peremptory challenges, that is, challenges without reasons. This right was progressively reduced then abolished by the Criminal Justice Act 1988. This resulted from the Conservative Government's belief that the right to peremptory challenge was being abused and from the recommendation of the Roskill Committee that it be abolished. This leaves a gross imbalance between prosecution and defence rights of challenge. The abolition of peremptory challenge is in sharp contrast to the US where, dependent on state law, each party usually has a generous number of "peremptories", as explained above, to help them try to exclude unsympathetic jurors. Auld L.J. received very few suggestions that challenges be reintroduced in English law and made no recommendations.

Excusal by the Judge

16–020   Under the Juries Act, the judge may discharge from service any juror about whom there is doubt as to "his capacity to act effectively as a juror" because of physical disability or insufficient understanding of English. Additionally, judges have a common law discretion to discharge jurors and they occasionally interpret this quite broadly. Following the widening of jury participation aspired to by the Criminal Justice Act 2003, a sub-group of judges considered how judges should now exercise their right of excusal. This is set out in the Consolidated Criminal Practice Direction 2007, Pt IV.42. This is in addition to the system of excusals and deferrals operated by the Jury Central Summoning Bureau, described below. Each resident judge considers a weekly pile of letters seeking excusal and jurors make verbal requests to judges, in the courtroom. In addition, jurors are summoned for a two week period so, in trials lasting more than two weeks, all potential jurors are given the chance to opt out. Sean O'Neill, crime and security editor of *The Times* said, in 2008,

> "I have reported on dozens of important criminal cases in the British courts, including every high-profile terrorist trial since 2003. . .Most big cases start with a parade of potential jurors queuing up to tell the judge why they should be excused because of holiday, work, illness or some other reason, the remnants—usually those not bright enough to come up with a half- decent excuse—are left to try some of the most complicated cases."

This standard practice before long trials, plus the judge's discretion to effectively entertain an appeal from the Summoning Bureau's decision, must be taken account of when reading Thomas's findings, above.

Deaf jurors

Under s.9 of the Juries Act 1974, where there is doubt as to a **16–021** person's ability to act effectively as a juror, the summoning officer is obliged to bring that person before a judge. The judge must discharge the summons where she is of the opinion that the person will not be capable of acting effectively as a juror, on account of his disability. The exclusion of deaf jurors, by prohibiting their sign interpreters from the jury room, is considered by Majid (2004).

3. Function of the jury

The purpose of having the jury is to enable the decision on fact to **16–022** be taken by a small group from the community, rather than for it to be left entirely in the hands of the lawyers.

After hearing the judge's "summing up" of the evidence and directions on the law, the jury retire and consider their verdict in private. In a civil case, they normally answer a series of questions set for them by the judge and advocates, which determines liability. The jury may set the level of damages awarded. In a criminal case, on the pronouncement of the verdict by the foreman of the jury, the accused is found either "guilty" or "not guilty". If "not guilty" the defendant is acquitted and is free to leave the court; if "guilty" he is convicted, and the judge sentences him. The jury has no part to play in the decision as to sentence. Equally the jury has no part in decisions on law or legal procedure. A judge will often have to ask the jury to retire, so that she can hear arguments on and decide on a point of law. The judge often has to determine points of law, procedure and admissibility of evidence before the jury are empanelled. Such rulings are discussed in Ch.12 on criminal procedure.

The decline of the jury in civil cases

The civil jury declined in the twentieth century. Although a **16–023** jury of eight may be called in the county court or Queen's Bench Division at the discretion of the judge, this is rare, except in the one growth area for jury trials since 1990, tort actions against the police. Civil jury trials only amount to a few hundred per year. In the following tort actions, s.69 of the Supreme Court Act (now known as the Senior Courts Act) 1981 grants a right to jury trial: libel, slander, malicious prosecution, false imprisonment and fraud but it can be refused if prolonged examination of documents, or accounts, or other complex material is involved. In all other cases, the judge has a discretion to allow a jury trial. The trend away from jury trial in civil cases has been comparatively rapid. In 1933, 50 per cent of civil cases involved a jury. In *Ward v James (No.2)* [1966] 1 Q.B. 273

a five-judge Court of Appeal (CA) decided that trial by judge alone should be the usual mode of civil trial.

The most important reasons for the disuse of the civil jury are inconsistent and exorbitant damages awards. Examples of this include the £600,000 libel damages awarded to Sonia Sutcliffe, ex-wife of the "Yorkshire Ripper", against the publishers of *Private Eye*, which led Ian Hislop to comment: "If this is justice, I'm a banana". This was later reduced to £60,000. The Courts and Legal Services Act 1990, s.8 provided for rules to empower the CA to substitute its own award of damages. It has obviously been easier to achieve consistency in damages awards for personal injuries because they are now left to the judges. Throughout the 1990s, juries continued to make outlandishly high awards in defamation actions of the rich and famous, much to the exasperation of the judiciary. Notice the disgust of Sir Thomas Bingham M.R., in *John v MGN* [1995] EWCA Civ 23, an appeal in which the *Mirror* group succeeded in getting the CA to reduce to £75,000 the jury's award of £350,000 to Elton John, for alleging that he displayed symptoms of an eating disorder at a Hollywood party:

"It is in our view offensive to public opinion, and rightly so, that a defamation plaintiff should recover damages for injury to reputation greater, perhaps by a significant factor, than if that same plaintiff had been rendered a helpless cripple or an insensate vegetable. The time has in our view come when judges, and counsel, should be free to draw the attention of juries to these comparisons."

Also in 1995, a jury award of £750,000 damages made to footballer Graeme Souness, against his ex-wife for calling him a "dirty rat" in the *People*, was settled, pending appeal, for £100,000. In 1996, four large awards of damages against the Metropolitan Police in jury trials for actions such as false imprisonment provoked the Metropolitan Police Commissioner to call for judicial guidelines to be set down for juries in these cases, similar to those in defamation cases. The Faulks Committee (1974) recommended that juries should no longer be available as of right in defamation actions for these reasons, which give us some insight into why the civil jury declined generally.

- Judges were not as remote from real life as popularly supposed.
- Judges gave reasons, whereas juries did not.
- Juries found complex cases difficult.
- Juries were unpredictable.

- Juries were expensive (jury trial is more time-consuming, as explanations have to be geared for them, not a judge).

Coroners' juries

The coroner, whose task it is to inquire into sudden death, can **16–024** and in some circumstances must, call a jury for the inquest. The coroner's jury, after hearing the evidence, returns a verdict as to the cause of death and the coroner must record this verdict. The issue of coroners' juries giving reasons in certain cases is discussed Ch.4 on human rights. Famously, a jury determined the 2008 verdict at the inquest into the deaths of Princess Diana and Dodi Al Fayed.

4. Majority verdicts

For centuries, the English legal system required that the verdict **16–025** of the jury in both civil and criminal trials should be unanimous. If unanimity could not be achieved then a retrial was necessary. In the 1960s there was increasing criticism of this requirement, particularly on the part of the police who pointed out that one member of the jury, if "nobbled" by the defendant or his supporters, could cause a retrial by simply refusing to agree with the other 11 in a criminal case. The Criminal Justice Act 1967 permitted a majority verdict of 10:2 to be accepted by the judge, or 10:1, or 9:1 if one or two jury members had been discharged. The jury must spend at least two hours seeking to achieve unanimity. If the verdict is "guilty" the fact that it is a majority verdict must be disclosed. Majority verdicts were permitted in civil cases from 1972 and the law is now consolidated in the Juries Act 1974, as amended. Auld L.J. received few comments that the system should be changed.

5. Jury secrecy

The secrecy of jury deliberations is protected. They deliberate **16–026** alone in the jury room and disclosure of deliberations is a crime under the Contempt of Court Act 1981, s.8. The section is so broad as to preclude bona fide research into jury decision-making. The RCCJ 1993 recommended its amendment, as did the Law Commission, in their 1995 annual report but Auld L.J. disagreed, in his 2001 Review. He contemplated the view of Lord Hewart C.J., expressed in 1922, that the value of the jury's verdict lies only in its anonymity and the view of Glanville Williams, in *The Proof of Guilt*, 1955, that "the real reason for keeping the jury's deliberations secret is to preserve confidence in a system which more intimate knowledge might destroy." (p.205.) Auld L.J. asked:

> "Should section 8 of the 1981 Act be amended to permit legitimate research (and, while we are about it, to enable the Court of Appeal, Criminal Division, to examine conduct in the jury room the subject of appeal)? Or is public confidence in juries' oracular verdicts so precious to our legal system that we should not put it at risk? Many fear that the very undertaking of intrusive research—that is, into how individual juries reach their decisions—could damage public confidence by sewing doubts as to the integrity of verdicts . . . On the other hand, such research might show that all is not well and that changes are needed." (p.166.)

He considered our (2001) argument that there is a wealth of jury research, worldwide, from which lessons could be learned and most of it is of a non-intrusive nature. He cited the 1994 New York Jury Project and the 2001 New Zealand criminal trial jury study and concluded that ample lessons could be learned from non-intrusive research of this kind. He recommended no amendment to s.8. There should, instead, be careful consideration of all available existing research material throughout the common law world (summarised in our paper), with a view to identifying and responding appropriately to all available information about how juries arrived at their verdicts. If and to the extent to which such information was insufficient, jury research should be considered that did not violate the 1981 Act.

In 2005, the DCA published a consultation paper "Jury Research and Impropriety", again raising the question of whether the s.8 protection of jury secrecy should be amended. The paper states that jury secrecy "has long been regarded as a cornerstone of the legal system" but in recent years, after the incorporation of the European Convention on Human Rights into English law:

> "there has been increasing debate on whether the current law has got it right. Is there a risk that the necessary confidentiality of the jury process could lead to potential miscarriages of justice and, if so, is there a way of reducing this risk without fundamentally undermining the jury process?" (p.5.)

The paper canvassed views on whether:

- any or all aspects of the way in which juries deliberate should be subject to research;

- there are circumstances in which a jury's deliberations should be subject to external investigation; and
- any aspect of the common law rule rendering inadmissible any evidence from jury deliberations should be clarified or amended.

The paper set out the Government's provisional views, proposing that any research into deliberations should only be allowed if permitted by the minister and undertaken in accordance with conditions agreed by him and the Lord Chief Justice. A code of conduct should guarantee confidentiality.

As for impropriety, the paper set out the current law as stated in recent appeals where there had been allegations of impropriety, notably *R. v Mirza* [2004] UKHL 4, below, and recommended that the law should be left as it is. Such allegations should be dealt with on a case by case basis. The paper explained the background to s.8: it had not been government intention in 1981 to prohibit bona fide research but, after lengthy deliberation on its dangers, the House of Lords made last minute amendments which precluded research. The potential benefits of research might include:

- Understanding the factors jurors consider important when determining guilt/innocence.
- Improving information, guidance and directions.
- Discovering what jurors think of the trial process.
- Examining whether all jurors are able to participate.
- Determining whether there is any evidence of gender/racial or other bias.
- Suggesting any other factors which would allow jurors to do their job better.

The risks included:

- Inhibiting the frankness of jury discussions.
- Undermining the finality of verdicts.
- Damaging public confidence in the jury system.
- Where the research is not bona fide or is slanted, exposing jurors to harassment.

They concluded that any change in the law must be designed to improve support for jurors. In 2008, some people raised concerns about jurors telling stories of their experiences to the newspapers. See, for instance, Bawdon. She reported on a rash of cases in which jurors had told the media that conviction verdicts in which they participated were wrong.

6. Allegations of impropriety or bias

16–027   Occasionally, a defendant or a court hears allegations from a juror that there was something unsatisfactory about the deliberations or the way in which the jury arrived at their verdict and the trial court or the CA has to decide how far they can breach jury room secrecy to investigate. The consultation paper set out the common law rule, articulated in *R. v Mirza*, by Lord Hope, "the court will not investigate, or receive evidence about, anything said in the course of the jury's deliberations while they are considering their verdict in the retiring room." The consultation paper examined cases in which the court had departed from this rule:

- *Ellis v Deheer* [1922] 2 K.B. 113: some of the jurors could not hear the verdict announced and disagreed with it. The CA declined to hear evidence of jury deliberations.
- *Hood* [1968] 1 W.L.R. 773: a juror was a relative of the defendant's wife and may have known of the defendant's record. The CA admitted an affidavit from the juror that he did recognise the accused, because this did not deal with what took place in the jury room.
- *Brandon* (1969) 53 Cr. App. R. 466: the jury bailiff made remarks to the jury which might have indicated that the accused had a record. The court admitted evidence of what the bailiff said.
- *Young* [1995] Q.B. 324: while staying overnight in a hotel, four jury members tried to contact the deceased via a ouija board. He allegedly told them the defendant had murdered him. The CA held that it could inquire into what took place in the hotel but not in the jury room.
- *McCluskey* (1994) 98 Cr. App. R. 216: one of the jurors used a mobile phone to make a business call, during deliberations. The CA admitted evidence from him that he did have his phone.

Article 6 of the European Convention on Human Rights, as described in Ch.4 on human rights and Ch.12 on criminal procedure, requires a fair trial. In *Remli v France* (1996) 22 E.H.R.R. 253 the ECtHR made it clear that the Convention imposes an obligation on the national court to check whether a tribunal was impartial. In *R. v Mirza*, the House of Lords (HL) held that the s.8 prohibition on the admission of jury deliberations did not breach Art.6. The case law of the ECtHR has not undermined the principle of secrecy of jury deliberations. In *Gregory v UK* (1998) 25 E.H.R.R. 577, the ECtHR stressed that the tribunal, including the jury, must be impartial from a subjective as well as an objective point of view. In that case, one juror had passed a note to the judge during deliberations which read "Jury showing racial overtones. One member to be excused". The judge had warned the jury to decide according to the evidence and they returned a majority guilty verdict. The ECtHR acknowledged that jury room secrecy was fundamental and made no attempt to overturn the principle.

In *Sander v UK* (2001) 31 E.H.R.R. 44 a juror complained to the trial judge that jurors had been making racist jokes. The judge read out the complaint and adjourned the case overnight, asking the jurors to consider whether they could try this case solely on the evidence. The next morning the jury refuted the allegations and said they could decide according to the evidence. One juror apologised and said he thought he could be the cause of it. He claimed he was unbiased and outlined his connections with minority people. The ECtHR found a breach of Art.6, because one juror had admitted racist jokes and that could not be reconciled with refutation of racism by the majority.

In *R. v Mirza*, the HL affirmed a line of cases on the common law prohibition against receiving evidence of deliberations. The rule only protected the secrecy of deliberations, not extraneous evidence of jury bias so was not disproportionate and therefore not in breach of Art.6. The House recognised that there could be cases where evidence should be admitted that the jury had completely failed to discharge its duty, such as by using a ouija board. Lord Hope said it was the collective decision-making, free from outside interference, that gave jury trial its strength. The tribunal was presumed to be impartial until the contrary was proven. Attempts to soften the rule in the public interest should be resisted if jurors were to continue to perform their vital function of safeguarding individual liberty. The jury's introductory video should be amended to warn jurors to raise concerns before the verdict, when they could be investigated and dealt with by the trial judge. (Here, a juror had written after the trial, alleging prejudice by other jurors, and in the case joined to *Mirza*, called *Connor and Rollock* [2004] UKHL 2, a juror alleged that her jury were prepared to find the accused both guilty just for the sake of reaching a quick verdict.) The House dismissed suggestions that if a court examined jurors it would be in breach of s.8 of the Contempt of Court Act 1981. This was incorrect because the court could not be in contempt of itself. Better information could be given to appeal courts so they could scrutinise allegations to the high degree required by Art.6. The CA could call for a report from the trial judge. A Practice Direction was swiftly issued in 2004. Jurors should be notified of the importance of bringing to the attention of the judge any concerns about fellow jurors while there was still time to put things right but it was undesirable to encourage inappropriate criticism. This is now contained in the Consolidated Criminal Practice Direction, Pt IV.42.

16–028   After 2005, allegations of impropriety have continued, sometimes with extremely expansive results. *R. v Mirza* was applied in another HL decision, *R. v Smith, R. v Mercieca* [2005] UKHL 12. Here, a juror had written to the judge alleging coercion by some jurors of others and that deals were being done in order to reach a swift decision. The House upheld the trial judge's decision not to question the jurors about their deliberations. The judge had been correct to give the jury further directions and warn them not to be bullied but he was insufficiently comprehensive and emphatic. He should have given them a stern warning to follow his directions on law and to decide on their verdicts without pressure or bargaining.

In *Karakaya* [2005] EWCA Crim 346, a juror downloaded information from the internet, for use in jury deliberations. The CA quashed the defendant's convictions on the ground that this offended against the principle of open justice. The public and the defendant should know the material considered by the decision making body. The prosecution and defence were entitled to a fair opportunity to address all the material considered by the jury. No evidence must be introduced after the jury retired. Jurors should not conduct their own private research. See now *R v Marshall and Crump* [2007] EWCA Crim 35. In *A.G. v Scotcher* [2005] UKHL 36 the HL upheld the contempt conviction of a juror who had written to the defendant's mother expressing concern at the jury's deliberations. His desire to expose a miscarriage of justice was no defence.

In *R v Cornwall* [2009] EWCA Crim 2458 (and see commentary at [2010] Crim. L.R. 504), an outspoken *Sun* columnist, S, was the jury foreman with well-publicised views on knife-crime, drugs, immigration and sentencing but this was held not to be grounds for quashing the conviction. The difference between him and another juror was that he had expressed his views publicly. There was nothing to suggest that S was not faithful to his juror's oath. If a writer had expressed strong views about the *law*, he would be well-advised to draw this to the judge's attention. *Gough* (1993) and *Abdroikov* (2007) were considered: would a fair-minded and reasonable observer conclude that there was a real possibility or danger of bias? By 2011, the frequency of allegations of jury nobbling, by defendants, as in the *Twomey* case, and misconduct by jurors seems to have increased in recent decades and some judges fear that it is almost impossible to stop jurors researching the background to their cases on the internet. The first Facebook-related conviction for contempt of court took place in June 2011. Joanna Fraill, a juror, and

Jamie Sewart, an acquitted defendant, were convicted and jailed in the High Court after communicating on Facebook about the jury's deliberations during a multimillion pound drug trial in 2010, causing it to collapse (Halliday, 2011). See Lord Judge C.J.'s speech on juries and the internet, 2010.

7. "Jury equity" and the unreasoned verdict

Jurors do not give reasons for their decisions. An interesting **16–029** historical survival is the rule that jurors cannot be punished if they bring in a perverse acquittal contrary to the direction of the judge. This was laid down in *Bushell's Case* in 1670 where two Quakers were charged with tumultuous assembly. The jury were ordered to convict, but instead returned a verdict of "not guilty". The judge sent the jury to prison until they paid a fine by way of punishment. On appeal, it was held that the fine and imprisonment could not be allowed to stand. In *R. v Wang* [2005] UKHL 9, the HL affirmed that there were no circumstances in which a judge could direct a jury to convict, even in cases where the burden of raising a defence rested on the defendant and he had failed to discharge it. The jury were free to deliver an acquittal that the trial judge considered to be perverse. The Ponting trial of 1985 saw a jury bring in a verdict of "not guilty" in an Official Secrets Act case where a conviction had been expected. This freedom to ignore the law and resort to their consciences, is called "jury equity" in the UK and "nullification" in the US. There are many more modern day examples. For instance, there have been several acquittals of defendants who have used cannabis to relieve the pain of such illnesses as multiple sclerosis. An example of jury equity that met approval with the news media, as it seemed to reflect popular sentiment, occurred in March, 2009. Kenneth Batchelor was acquitted of murdering a would-be burglar. The circumstances were very similar to the Tony Martin case ten years earlier. Burgess (2009) reported that:

> "[He] fired a shotgun at 'very close quarters' at 42-year-old Matthew Clements, who had climbed the scaffolding of his home to try to force open an upstairs window. Mr Batchelor had received a barrage of threatening phone calls from Mr Clements, a 20-stone nightclub bouncer, who was demanding maintenance money from the Batchelor family following a former relationship between his girlfriend and Mr Batchelor's brother Gary, which produced three children. The jury at Maidstone Crown Court took just one hour unanimously to acquit Mr Batchelor of the murder of Mr Clements who, the court heard, had an 'explosive

temper' and had become 'fixated' with demanding money from the Batchelor family."

In our 2001 paper for Auld L.J., we concluded that jurors could be asked to give reasons for their decisions.

"They could be given a series of questions, agreed between counsel and judge, as they are in civil trials. [See] Thaman's account of how the procedure works in Spain. (The New Zealand Law Commission recommended a series of sequential questions or a flow chart in complex trials, para.318). If jurors are to be asked for reasons, then they must surely be told of their power to acquit in the face of condemnatory evidence, as an exercise of jury equity."

Auld L.J. pointed out that the ECtHR had ruled that the unreasoned verdict of a Danish jury was not a breach of the Convention. The problem with an unreasoned verdict is that it can make appeal difficult and it is an anomaly compared with other criminal tribunals. The magistrates and the district judge (magistrates' court) are both required by Art.6 of the Convention to give reasoned decisions. Auld L.J. said:

"A reasoned judgment tells the parties why they have won or lost; it is more likely to be soundly based on the evidence than an unreasoned one; and, by its openness is more likely to engender public confidence in the decision-making system." (p.169.)

He agreed with our suggestion of giving the jury a series of questions but reached the opposite conclusion on jury equity. He regarded the jury's ability to acquit or convict in the face of the law as "a blatant affront to the legal process and the main purpose of the criminal justice system—the control of crime". He surprised commentators by recommending that the law should be changed to declare that juries had no right to acquit in defiance of the law or disregard of the evidence (p.176). This recommendation outraged critics of the Auld Review and, unfortunately, destroyed much of its credibility. In 1991, I had attacked the unfairness and irrationality of jury equity, using the same reasoning as Auld L.J. did 10 years later but it seems to me that suggesting it should be banned is pointless. The very reason why the British and Americans heap praise on the jury system is its ability to defy the law. It is argued that the jury acts as a check on officialdom, on the judge's power, and a protector against unjust or oppressive prosecution, injecting jury "equity" by deciding guilt or innocence according to a feeling of justice rather than by applying known law to facts proven beyond reasonable doubt: for example Kalven and Zeisel said, in *The American Jury* (1966),

"It represents also an impressive way of building discretion, equity and flexibility into a legal system. Not least of the advantages is that the jury, relieved of the burdens of creating precedent, can bend the law without breaking it."

Unsurprisingly, in the furore on this point that followed publication of the *Review*, the Government did not follow this recommendation.

Taxquet v Belgium ECtHR (926/05), November 16, 2010 is quite a worrying case for the English legal system because it implied that some of our criminal offences, notably the vague way in which we label principal offenders and accomplices as being guilty of the same crime, might have to be reviewed. T applied to Strasbourg on the ground that there was a breach of Art.6, because the jury had not given reasons for their decision. They were simply asked by the court's president to answer whether T was guilty of murder as perpetrator or through assistance or incitement; whether it was premeditated; whether he was guilty of attempted murder, as perpetrator or through assistance or incitement, and whether that was premeditated. The Court unanimously held that, though there was no Convention requirement for jurors to give reasons, the accused and the public must be able to understand the jury's verdict. There must be sufficient safeguards in place, such as directions from the presiding judge and precise unequivocal questions, forming a framework on which the verdict is based. A. Ashworth's comment at [2010] Crim. L.R. is very useful. He points out that 24 contracting states, signatories to the European Convention on HR, have collaborative judge and jury systems, 10 have a traditional jury system and 14 have no jury trial. The UK, France and Ireland made submissions to the Grand Chamber, as interveners. The UK and Ireland argued that the judge's directions provided a sufficient safeguard. He commented that the judgment left its application to the law of complicity unresolved and a procedural challenge could now be mounted.

8. History

During its long history, the jury has completely changed its role. **16–030** Generally, jurors should have no prior knowledge of the case, and will be able to reach their verdict entirely on the evidence presented at the trial. Originally, however, the jury's role was a combination of local police and prosecutor. Centuries before a paid police force was created, the responsibility for law and order lay with the community. This meant the local "jury" arresting suspected offenders, and then bringing them before the visiting judge and swearing, like prosecution witnesses, to the guilt of the accused. There was nothing unusual in this use of representatives in the early community. It can be seen also in the local inquiries which led to the creation of the Domesday Book, and the system of inquisitions post mortem, the inquiry held on a death as to the ownership of the lands and goods of the deceased. Throughout the Middle Ages juries were used in the settlement of civil disputes concerning the ownership and tenancy of land and the right to an advowson (the right to present to the living of a church).

It was only with the passage of centuries that the use of the jury as uninvolved judges of fact developed. Even then the original concept survived, leading to the distinction between the grand jury and the petty jury. The grand jury of 24 members met only at the start of assizes or quarter sessions in order to find a true bill of indictment against the accused. Since the accused had previously undergone the preliminary inquiry by magistrates, who had heard the prosecution case and had decided to commit the accused for trial, the decision of the grand jury became a complete formality. It was abolished by the Criminal Justice Act 1948. US jurisdictions retain the grand jury to indict the accused in certain cases. The petty (trial) jury of 12 emerged in the thirteenth century to replace trial by ordeal, condemned by the ecclesiastical authorities. It became increasingly distinct in its functions from the grand jury, although it long maintained its composition from witnesses of fact deciding matters from their local knowledge. In the fifteenth century the petty jury assumed its modern role in criminal trials as the adjudicator of fact.

In civil cases the jury appears to have had its origin in the Assizes of Clarendon in 1166, and the Assizes of Northampton in 1176, establishing the grand and petty assizes. Again the jury was at first called to decide a case from its local knowledge, but over time it became an impartial judge of the facts. The system allowed for trial to be in two parts. The local jury would hear and deal with the case, then send their findings to the judges at Westminster where the judgment would be given.

9. Inroads and attempted inroads into the criminal trial jury

Failed attempts to withdraw the right to elect jury trial

16–031 As explained in Ch.12 on criminal procedure, in cases of medium seriousness, called "triable either way", where the magistrates express no preference as to mode of trial, the defendant has the right to elect trial by magistrates in their court or judge and jury in the Crown Court. Governments have been thinking of removing the right to elect jury trial long before the RCCJ recommended they do so in 1993. Drawing conclusions from Home Office and other research, they concluded that the system was not being used as intended. They found that, while defendants often opted for Crown Court trial in the belief that their chances of acquittal were greater, many nevertheless changed their plea to guilty at the Crown Court; defendants often opted for Crown Court trial in the mistaken belief that, if convicted, the Crown Court judge would impose a lighter sentence than magistrates. Magistrates sent a number of cases to the Crown Court where the defendant ultimately received a sentence within the magistrates' own sentencing powers. Governments perceive this as an enormous waste of money because proceedings in the magistrates' court are far cheaper than those in the Crown Court and this applies to sentencing proceedings, last minute guilty pleas and contested cases, trials. For instance, in 2010, Ken Clarke, Minister of Justice, said a last-minute guilty plea in the Crown Court cost just over £3,200, compared with under £300 in the magistrates' court.

The RCCJ recommended that the defendant should no longer have the right to insist on jury trial. Where prosecution and defence could not agree on mode of trial, the decision should be referred to the magistrates. The Commission was subject to academic criticism, especially by Professors McConville and Bridges, alleging that it had misinterpreted the Home Office research. Nevertheless, the (Conservative) Home Office published a consultation document, *Mode of Trial*, in 1995. In it, they outlined three options designed to shift more cases from the Crown Court to the magistrates' courts:

1. The reclassification of more offences as triable only summarily, i.e. only in the magistrates' court.
2. The withdrawal of the defendant's option to insist on jury trial in the Crown Court.
3. A requirement that the defendant enter the plea before the trial/hearing venue is chosen.

The Government chose to enact the third and least draconian of these options. Given the sentimental attachment to jury trial in criminal cases, it would be politically inexpedient to remove the defendant's right to opt for jury trial in all either-way cases. Instead, s.49 of the Criminal Procedure and Investigations Act 1996 (now amended) was passed. This requires magistrates, before determining mode of trial, to ascertain the accused's plea, in the hope of persuading the magistrates to keep more cases in the magistrates' court. This and successive legislation is explained in Ch.12 on criminal procedure. Before this plan could take effect, however, The Narey Report was published in 1997 and reiterated the recommendation that the defendant's right to elect jury trial be removed. In 1998, the newly elected Labour Home Secretary published *Determining Mode of Trial in Either Way Cases—A Consultation Paper*. It set out the familiar arguments on abolishing the defendant's right to elect jury trial, as follows.

For abolition

16–032
- The right was not ancient. It dated from 1855 and had nothing to do with Magna Carta.
- 22,000 defendants elected for Crown Court trial in 1997 but most changed their plea to guilty, after significant inconvenience and worry to victims and witnesses, and considerable extra cost.
- By definition, elected cases were those which magistrates had determined were suitable for themselves. The mode of trial decision should be based on objective assessment by the court of the gravity of the case, not the defendant's perception of what was advantageous to him, such as a greater prospect of acquittal.
- It was questionable whether defendants opted for jury trial to defend their reputation, because nine tenths of those electing already had previous convictions.
- Most defendants chose jury trial because they wanted to delay proceedings, to apply pressure to the Crown to accept a guilty plea to a lesser offence, or to deter witnesses, or to put off the evil day.
- Few other jurisdictions allowed the defendant such an element of choice. In Scotland, the sheriff's court decides on the trial venue.

Arguments in favour of the status quo

16–033
- The right helped to promote confidence in the criminal justice system.
- Whereas magistrates were broadly concerned with the seriousness of the offence, it was the defendant's reputation which the public saw as a justification for continuing to allow the right to elect.
- When people who had never been accused of a crime defended the right, it was usually on the basis that they

would want such a right if they were charged with something of which they were innocent.

- It was assumed that Crown Court trial was fairer. Defendants who chose it rightly believed they had a higher chance of acquittal.
- Some arguments went to the merits of trial by jury, for example, the jury's capacity to acquit contrary to legal proof of guilt.

One proposal in the paper was to take away the right of those defendants who had previous convictions and who had, therefore, already lost their reputations. Consequently, Home Secretary Jack Straw introduced the Criminal Justice (Mode of Trial) Bill in 1999. This would have abolished the defendant's right to elect, placing the mode of trial decision in the magistrates' hands. The Bill attracted enormous opposition, notably from the Bar, the Law Society, the Society of Black Lawyers and from lawyers' groups such as the Legal Action Group (LAG). LAG argued the following (*Legal Action*, September 1998):

- The main reason defendants opted for jury trial was that they rightly saw their chances of obtaining justice in the Crown Court as significantly higher, as the acquittal rate was higher and many cases were dismissed by the judge. (For modern statistics, see the annual *Judicial and Court Statistics*.)
- Electing jury trial brought into play a range of other safeguards, such as greater disclosure of the prosecution case. (This point was also made by many other commentators.)
- Removing the right to elect would significantly disadvantage black defendants. Courtney Griffiths QC (*Counsel*, April 1999) added that research by the Runnymede Trust, in 1990, showed that, whereas under one third of white defendants, given the option, elected for jury trial, 45 per cent of black defendants elected. This was an intelligent choice. Only two per cent of magistrates were then non-white. Home Office research at Leicester magistrates' court showed white defendants had a substantially better chance of being granted bail. They were less likely to receive immediate custodial sentences than blacks.
- The suggestion that defendants elected jury trial to put off the evil day was not borne out by research.
- Delays would increase, caused by mini-trials about venue.
- When he was in opposition, Jack Straw had called the proposal "short-sighted".

Wolchover and Heaton-Armstong added:

- A defendant who delayed a guilty plea to obtain some advantage could not expect the same sentence discount as one who pleaded earlier and, since 1986, advocates had had a duty to warn defendants of this.
- Tactical elections for jury trial would continue to decline because of the introduction of the "plea before venue" procedure and because of s.48 of the Criminal Justice and Public Order Act 1994, which allowed the sentencing court to take account of the timing of the guilty plea.
- As experienced defence counsel, they denied that defendants caused delay to "put off the evil day". On the contrary, the most frequent and obvious cause of a last minute plea was the defendant's loss of courage.
- The argument was about the loss of a traditional common law right.
- Loss of liberty was no less serious for an habitual thief than loss of good name for someone with no previous convictions.

Both the Bar and Law Society opposed the plan to abolish the right to elect. A number of other commentators emphasised that jury trial was (and still is, incidentally) inherently superior to summary trial, especially as listing a case for a Crown Court trial triggered a much more careful review of the case by the prosecution, which would often result in dropping the case or reducing the charges. This also implied that, if magistrates were to decide on mode of trial, they would be doing so on inadequate information.

16–034 Further, at the Crown Court, a professional judge reviewed the strength and admissibility of the evidence, whereas magistrates were both fact-finders and arbiters of the law. Nigel Ley added that criminal defence solicitors in magistrates' courts were often ignorant of the law, as were magistrates' clerks. Some critics said that magistrates' courts were seen as police courts; magistrates were seen as part of the establishment and magistrates were not as socially and ethnically diverse as the jury. A *New Law Journal* editorial ((1999) 149 N.L.J. 549) argued that there were other ways of cutting down the cost and length of jury trials, such as reducing jurors to six, or having them sit in the magistrates' court with lay justices doing the sentencing, or cutting out the opening statement and permitting the judge to sum up only on law.

This first Bill was heavily defeated in the House of Lords, in 2000. Home Secretary Jack Straw replaced it with the Criminal Justice (Mode of Trial) No.2 Bill, which was again defeated in the Lords in 2000. Prior to the 2001 election, he threatened to use the Parliament

Acts to push though a third Bill. He did not do this because Auld L.J. was part way through his comprehensive Review. In 2001, Auld reiterated the recommendation that the right to elect jury trial should be removed. After consulting on this, the Government received predictable responses from all the groups cited above, raising the same objections that they had already argued many times before. The Government therefore dropped plans to remove the right to elect. Instead, they passed the Criminal Justice Act 2003, enabling them to double magistrates' sentencing powers, as an alternative means of keeping more cases down in the magistrates' court but, as described in the previous chapter, this has never been implemented. As I write, in 2011, history is repeating itself, as the Coalition government has again raised the very same issue of how to save the waste of money and resources (as they see it) caused by trivial cases going to the Crown Court. In his 2010 consultation paper on legal aid, the Minister of Justice, Ken Clarke, said

> "Too many criminal cases that could adequately be dealt with in the magistrates' court are going to the Crown Court. Increasing numbers of those cases go on to plead guilty, often at a late stage in the proceedings. This is inefficient and ineffective for the criminal justice system as a whole and does not represent best value in legal aid expenditure".

The remainder of the quotation is in Ch.12 on criminal procedure, under the heading "Offences triable either way—Mode of trial, 'Case allocation'".

Should we permit the defendant to elect trial by judge alone?

Auld L.J. thought that defendants in the Crown Court should **16–035** be entitled to opt out of jury trial by choosing trial by judge alone. We discussed this in our 2001 paper for him. I have long argued (1991 and 1997) that it is inappropriate to speak of the "right" to jury trial in indictable cases which must go to the Crown Court, because the defendant has no choice. In these cases and cases where the defendant has opted for a Crown Court trial, if he pleads not guilty, then he will be tried by judge and jury. He cannot opt for trial by judge alone, or a "bench trial" as it is called in the US. The English legal system is odd among common law systems, because the accused does have this choice in the US, Canada, New Zealand and a number of Australian states. Doran and Jackson have examined judge alone trials not only in Northern Ireland, in the Diplock Courts, but in bench trials in other jurisdictions. Auld L.J. was persuaded to investigate this procedure in some depth. He found that in some Canadian provinces, up to 90 per cent of defendants opted for a bench trial. In the US, judge alone trial tends to be chosen where prosecution and defence cannot agree to a plea bargain but Auld L.J. found there were other defendants who preferred a judge alone trial, too:

- Those who believed themselves innocent in a factually or legally complex case who were anxious for the tribunal to understand their case.
- Defendants with technical defences who wanted fully reasoned decisions which would ease an appeal.
- Defendants charged with offences which attracted public opprobrium, such as sex or violent offences.
- Minorities who considered a judge to be more objective than a jury.
- Where there has been adverse publicity.
- Defendants in cases turning on alleged confessions or identification.
- Where local lower tier judges were well known to and trusted by the legal profession to conduct fair trials.

He recommended that defendants should, with the consent of the court, be able to opt for judge alone trial in cases tried on indictment. The Government accepted his recommendation, in *Justice for All* (2002), para.4.2. The Criminal Justice Bill 2003 aimed to introduce a procedure for trial by judge alone, where the accused requested it. This clause met opposition from the Conservatives and Liberal Democrats and did not survive into the Act. This was intensely frustrating to those of us who had campaigned for this change in the law. For my part, I cannot see a single logical reason why the accused should not be given the right to opt out of jury trial and be tried by judge alone. As I explained in the previous chapter, I drew attention to the illogicality of our present system, in 1997: in the magistrates' court, the defendant may be tried by three lay justices or a single judge—he cannot choose between them; in a Crown Court trial he must be tried by jury.

The judge's right to order trial by judge alone

Jury tampering

16–036   Section 44 of the Criminal Justice Act 2003 allows an application for a judge alone trial where there is a "real and present danger" of jury tampering, and other conditions are satisfied, as explained in Ch.12 on criminal procedure. The inclusion of this clause in the Bill resulted from lobbying by the police. As explained in Ch.12, after an unsuccessful appeal, the first defendants to be tried under this section, Twomey and others, were tried for a £1.7 million armed robbery at Heathrow, by Treacy J., sitting alone, in 2010. (The trial started at the Royal Courts of Justice but was moved to the Old Bailey after one defendant absconded.) At least two more trials were conducted by judge alone, in 2010, acting under the same section. This has been condemned by the Criminal Bar Association as the thin end of the wedge in reducing trial by jury. See Fresco and Gibb, and Gibb, 2009 and 2010. As explained in Ch.12, the CA had ruled in *R. v T* [2010] EWCA Crim 1035 against a jury trial which would have cost £1.5 million to £6 million for various levels of protection for the jury. Critical lawyers argued that the 800 year old right to jury trial was beyond price. Judges, all ex-lawyers themselves, are generally strongly in favour of jury trial and Lord Judge C.J. was very sensitive to criticism of his Court of Appeal ruling in the Twomey case and the "thin end of the wedge" argument. He insisted "We believe in the jury system—every judge I know", when interviewed in *Law in Action*, BBC Radio 4, October 27, 2009.

Long and complex frauds

There has also been a long-standing concern by some that jury **16–037** trial is inappropriate in long and complex frauds. Jurors' difficulty in understanding evidence is most acute in fraud trials and was considered by the Roskill Committee on Fraud Trials in 1986. Fraud trials are notoriously long (sometimes over 100 days), expensive and highly complicated. The Committee said:

"The background against which the frauds are alleged to have been committed—the sophisticated world of high finance and international trading—is probably a mystery to most or all of the jurors, its customs and practices a closed book. Even the language in which the allegedly fraudulent transactions have been conducted will be unfamiliar. A knowledge of accountancy or bookkeeping may be essential to an understanding of the case. If any juror has such knowledge, it is by chance" (para.8.27).

The Committee recommended that the jury be abolished in complex criminal fraud cases and be replaced by a Fraud Trials Tribunal of a judge and two lay members. This debate was revived in 1992, following the Guinness trial and the Blue Arrow fraud trial, lasting over a year, and again in 1996, following the acquittals after the Maxwell trial. The suggestion was revived by Labour Home Secretary, Jack Straw, in 1998, in "Juries in Serious Fraud Trials", a Home Office consultation paper. In his Review, Auld L.J. considered fraud and other complex cases at length. He said the problem was compounded by the unrepresentative nature of juries, particularly in fraud and other complex cases. Even the Bar Council had acknowledged that it was difficult to find representative juries for long trials. The Serious Fraud Office had commented to him that these trials were often too much for jurors and ill health or claimed ill health was a cause of delay or severance. Auld L.J. listed the arguments for and against juries in cases of serious and complex fraud:

- Jury trial was a hallowed democratic institution and the defendant's right in serious cases;
- random selection ensured fairness and independence;
- the question was usually one of dishonesty, essentially a matter for the jury, who because of their number and mix were better equipped than a smaller tribunal of professionals;
- there was no research evidence that they could not cope with long and complex cases or that their decisions were contrary to the evidence;
- there was openness and impartiality in the parties having to explain the case to the jury in simple and digestible form and there was scope for improvement there.

On the other hand:

- if juries were the defendant's peers, they ought to be experienced in the professional or commercial context of the alleged offence;
- the volume and complexity of evidence might make dishonesty difficult to determine;
- the length of such trials was an unreasonable intrusion into jurors' personal and working lives;
- juries in these trials were unrepresentative;
- such long trials were a strain on the defendant, victim and witnesses;
- judges, with legal and forensic expertise, and/or specialist assessors would be better equipped to deal with such cases fairly and expeditiously;
- there would be the benefit of openness, since there would be a publicly reasoned and appealable decision;
- the length of these trials was very costly to the public and unduly delayed the efficient disposal of other cases.

He contemplated the alternatives: special juries; judge alone; a panel of judges or a judge and lay members. He recommended that, as an alternative to jury trial in long and complex frauds, the nominated trial judge should be able to direct trial by himself, sitting with lay members or, where the defendant had opted for trial by judge alone, by himself. The Government responded to his recommendation in *Justice for All*. They rejected the idea of recruiting people experienced in complex financial issues because of the difficulty of recruitment so they proposed that such cases be tried by judge alone. They estimated this would not affect more than 15–20 trials a year. Accordingly, the Criminal Justice Act 2003, s.43, had it ever been implemented, would have allowed the prosecution to apply for a judge alone trial in a long and complex fraud case *but* the Government promised the Opposition that they would not activate this section without further research and consideration and it has never been implemented.

In March 2005, the Jubilee Line Extension corruption trial collapsed in the Old Bailey, after taking almost two years and wasting £60 million of public money. The trial had suffered massive delays and interruptions. One juror had already been removed, as he was suspected of benefit fraud. The trial finally collapsed when another juror said he could not afford to go on and a third said he was going on a six week holiday. The Attorney General ordered an immediate inquiry and Lord Woolf C.J., who was not in favour of judge alone trials, said trials should be organised so they took no longer than three months or, exceptionally, six months. The Bar, who also opposed removal of jury trial in such cases, supported his remarks. Naturally the case fuelled the revival of arguments in favour of ordering judge alone trials in such cases. The Director of the Serious Fraud Office called for juries in serious fraud trials to be replaced. He thought a judge sitting alone or with assessors would provide the advantage of a reasoned decision. Some cases, he claimed, could not be tried in the suggested six months. The SFO's conviction rate fell from 70 per cent to 64 percent in 2004–05. The AG put forward a draft statutory instrument to implement s.43. It was opposed by the Law Society, the Bar and JUSTICE. The Bar argued that trials collapse through a lack of preparation not through the fault of jury trial. The Government established a review team on how to prosecute fraud, the progress of which is reported on the AG's website and in the meantime, the AG requested urgent roundtable discussion with opposing peers but this failed. The Government introduced a single issue bill, the Fraud (Trials without a Jury) Bill. It was predictably defeated by the Lords. In order to avoid lengthy jury trials, the AG then decided to consult on whether to offer plea bargains in serious fraud cases. Plea bargaining is discussed in Ch.12 on criminal procedure. After consultation in 2008, in 2009, she published the *Attorney General's Guidelines on Plea Discussions in Cases of Serious or Complex Fraud*. As the guidelines are still on the

563

AG's website, in 2011, it appears that they were adopted by her successor, Dominic Grieve QC MP. See news media, legal news media and law journals for this debate in 2008–09. Research by Julian shows strong support for retaining the jury from judges who tried serious frauds.

10. Research

Helping the jury to do their job

16–038   In our 2001 paper for Auld L.J., we made a number of recommendations to help the jury perform their function of finding the facts and applying them to the law as directed by the judge, based on our analysis of all the relevant jury research, including the following (Auld L.J.'s responses in the Criminal Courts Review are bracketed).

1. If English judges are to continue to sum up the evidence, they should be told not to recite their notes but to draw attention to the main points, to areas of conflict and to how the law applies to the issues of evidence. (Auld made similar recommendations in Ch.1, p.537.) In my later research on judges, reported in *Sitting in Judgment* (2011), no judge that I observed simply repeated their notes. Indeed, I found that judges took great care to craft jury directions and sum up the evidence.
2. Juries in criminal trials should be given a series of questions to answer, as they are in civil trials (adopted by Auld L.J.). In my research on judges, I found that some judges did this, to try to help the jury structure their thoughts.
3. Juries have a great deal of difficulty in understanding and applying judicial instructions. They should be rewritten by psycholinguists, taking account of the large body of research from the US. (Auld L.J. went further than this, recommending that the judge should not direct the jury on law save by implication in the series of factual questions he puts to them.) In 2008, a judicial working party was considering how to simplify jury instructions. They have moved away from specifying that the judge must use a particular form of words but the reader can judge for herself whether they are comprehensible to jurors. I am not confident that they are. Sean O'Neill, crime correspondent of *The Times* remarked on "barely literate" jurors (2008) and Liz Campbell wrote, from her experience as a juror, in the *Evening Standard* (2009) "It was alarming how many people struggled to read the oath".

In Thomas's in-depth empirical research (2010), she found that only 31 per cent of experimental jurors actually understood the directions fully in legal terms used by the judge and that written instructions increased juror comprehension. Perry, a former barrister and expert in plain English examined the 2010 Crown Court Benchbook (on jury directions) and suggested "One might start by editing out the hard words and elegant expressions from the Benchbook".

4. Jurors should be given written instructions on the law and pre-trial instructions, where possible, as it is illogical and difficult for jurors to receive instructions on what evidence is important after they have heard it, as they now are. (Adopted by Auld L.J. at p.522–3. He also recommended that judges should use visual aids where possible and be provided with PowerPoint and presentational software accordingly.) Judges do not generally use PowerPoint but prosecutors commonly use it in complex cases. In my research on judges, I found that each judge in the sample had used written jury instructions on at least one occasion and some used them quite often. At least one judge said he had increased his use of written instructions since he read the article by Madge (2006), wherein Judge Madge said he did it in all cases. See also, a speech by Moses L.J. in November 2010. He reiterated Auld L.J.'s suggestion that a list of questions should be given to the jury. He also said juries should be told of the defence before the trial starts.

5. Certain basic instructions, such as those on the burden and quantum of proof, could be pinned on the jury room wall. (Not discussed and not acted upon.)

6. Juries have immense difficulty in understanding the quantum of proof "beyond reasonable doubt". When judges explain it to mean "sure", many jurors look for absolute proof of guilt, which is impossible. The word "sure" should be eliminated from the judges' explanation of BRD. (Not discussed.)

7. Juries should be instructed to discuss the evidence before voting as this makes them deliberate more thoroughly. (Not discussed.)

8. Real jurors in England and Wales experience a great inhibition against asking questions, often to the detriment of their deliberation. Encouraging jurors to ask questions, take notes occasionally and discuss the evidence at an interim stage may all help to keep them awake and alert and to make sense of the trial, to help them remember the evidence more accurately, to understand the case and make their deliberation more focussed. (Not discussed.)

We also made some recommendations to make life more comfortable for jurors, again resulting from our examination of jury research and personal accounts of jurors:

1. Many people resent giving up time for jury service and the abiding memory of most jurors is boredom, waiting for a trial or for legal argument to take place in their absence. In long trials, the jury trial should proceed in the mornings, while jurors are more alert, and legal argument in the afternoons. In my later research on judges, I found that some of them did this, as a matter of common sense.
2. Heat, cold, boredom and their passive role may reduce jurors' arousal levels. Court managers should check courtroom temperatures and jurors should have breaks. This recommendation was ignored. In my research on judges, I reported on many courtrooms that were far too cold, including one that was extremely cold, thanks to the judge. I reported the consequent and sometimes farcical effects this had on jurors.
3. Small discomforts all irritate jurors. Court personnel should be more responsive and polite to them.
4. Jury service can be emotionally and physically stressful.
5. In long trials, we should copy the US system of sitting two or more "alternates" alongside the real jury, in case of illness or indisposition.
6. Auld L.J. adopted this last recommendation but the Government rejected it, to my frustration. As is obvious from the story told above, the Jubilee Line fraud trial would have been spared from collapse, at enormous cost, had this cheap and simple expedient been adopted.

Auld L.J. summarised our findings and made a number of suggestions for keeping the jury better informed and for providing them with better facilities, including working facilities, so they could carry on their business while waiting around. In *Justice for All* the Government responded very briefly. They promised to continue their reforms of jury service to keep jurors better informed and ensure their time was not wasted. In 2004, the Home Office published findings on "Jurors' perceptions, understanding, confidence and satisfaction in the jury system: a study in six courts", by Matthews, Hancock and Briggs. The key findings were:

1. Most respondents gained a more positive view of jury trial.
2. Confidence in the jury system was closely associated with perceived fairness of the process and ability to consider evidence from different perspectives.

3. A jury's representation of a broad spectrum of views was a key factor in jurors' confidence in the Crown Court trial.
4. Jurors were very impressed with the professionalism and helpfulness of court personnel, especially the performance, commitment and competence of judges.
5. The main impediment to understanding was legal terminology. Jurors felt evidence could sometimes be presented more clearly.
6. Over half said they would be happy to do service again, reporting a greater understanding of Crown Court trial and a feeling of having performed an important civic duty.

As part of the inquiry into the collapse of the Jubilee Line fraud trial, above, Lloyd-Bostock and Thomas questioned jurors about their experience and how well they managed to cope with the evidence. The trial caused most of the jurors serious ongoing problems with employment, afterwards:

"Return to work for seven of the 11 interviewed presented continuing problems nearly five months on. These include one who has been made redundant, one in an employment dispute, one required to undertake extensive re-training who has missed a definite and much desired promotion, and one signed off by his doctor as suffering from stress as a result of the work situation. A further three are back with their employers but report experiencing serious set backs in their positions because of their prolonged absence." (Lloyd-Bostock, 2005.)

Jury decision-making
Most research into jury deliberation and decision making is **16–039** conducted by constructing shadow juries or mock juries. They may be asked to sit in on a real trial, or, more usually, to watch an edited audio or videotape of a real trial. The drawbacks of this type of research are well known. The mock jurors often do not reflect composition of a real jury, as they are paid students. They are volunteers not conscripts, like real jurors. They usually sit through a three hour video rather than a two day trial. Most importantly, they are not under the same pressure as real jurors, since their verdict will not affect a real victim and the liberty and reputation of a real defendant. Nevertheless, this is all that researchers can hope for, since they are banned from sitting in on jury deliberations in virtually all jury systems. Apart from this, a researcher's presence is bound to affect deliberations. In some US jurisdictions, researchers have been allowed to listen to audiotaped deliberations.

The 2005 DCA consultation paper, "Jury Research and Impropriety", discussed above, asked whether researchers should be allowed into the jury room. This question is rather pointless, I suggest, as virtually no respondent is likely to favour that and Parliament is highly unlikely to permit it. The paper also asks whether research should be permitted into jury deliberations. This could be conducted by asking jurors questions after they have served. Again, questioning jurors is not permitted in most jurisdictions, although many academics have for years advocated the amendment of s.8 of the Contempt Act to permit this, as explained above. In our paper, we examined all English language jury research, worldwide, up to 2001; we also examined juror's personal accounts of jury service to test the cross-cultural applicability of foreign research, most of which is American. Among our findings, summarising this vast body of research were:

1. The most popular theory on how jurors individually consider the trial and verdict is the cognitive story model. The juror reorganises information into a narrative story by using the trial evidence, prior knowledge (which, as real jurors' accounts show, may be wrong) and what makes a complete story. Accounts of real English and Welsh jurors strongly support the story model and the research finding that the adversarial trial process presents evidence in a way which hampers the juror's construction of a story.
2. It is questionable how effective the average juror is at judging the truthfulness of a witness based on demeanour but real jurors' accounts show that many of them are influenced by whether they approve or disapprove of witnesses.
3. Although *Turnbull* allows a warning that even truthful and impressive witnesses can be in error, some American jurisdictions allow a much greater input from experts on the reliability of eyewitness evidence and other expert evaluation of different types of evidence.
4. The accounts of real jurors show they are frustrated by the fact that pieces of evidence have been excluded from the story and they speculate on what this evidence might be. They sometimes refer to jury trial as a game.
5. Jurors may be disproportionately influenced by evidence they are told to ignore and are influenced by previous convictions.
6. Joining defendants and multiple charges can confuse juries.
7. Juries are much better at remembering evidence than individual jurors but real juries sometimes argue in the jury room over the contents of the evidence.

8. Since juries consider the evidence more thoroughly when they are not "verdict driven", it maybe thought desirable to encourage them to discuss the evidence thoroughly before taking a vote on verdict. (The same point made by New Zealand Law Commission.)

2010 saw the publication of an extremely important piece of research by Thomas. It was large scale, using 68 simulated juries at Nottingham and Winchester, 668 post-verdict juror surveys and measuring average outcomes in 68,000 verdicts, nationwide, in 2006–08. The main points (paraphrased) are as follows:

- Verdicts of all-white juries did not discriminate against BME defendants.
- White juries in Winchester (a white area) had almost identical verdicts for white, black and Asian defendants but white juries at Nottingham (racially diverse, where almost all jurors are white) "had particular difficulty reaching a verdict involving a BME defendant or a BME victim". They were significantly more likely to convict a white D accused of assaulting a BME person than a white person.
- The only personal characteristic that appeared to affect juror decision-making was gender. Female jurors were more likely to be persuaded to change their vote than men, who rarely changed their minds.
- Examining 551,669 verdicts in 2006–08, the study examined whether offence type and severity, court, or number of charges had any correlation to verdicts.
- The study *confirmed* BME defendants were consistently more likely than whites to plead not guilty.
- BME defendants were three and a half times more likely to face a jury verdict relative to their representation in the population.
- There was a 63 per cent jury conviction rate for white and Asian defendants and a 67 per cent conviction rate for blacks.
- This strongly suggests that racially balanced juries are unnecessary for fairness BUT there are concerns about the *appearance* of fairness with all-white juries, especially at courts where mainly all-white juries try substantial numbers of BME defendants.
- At all Crown Courts, the proportion of BME defendants was greater than in the local population or BME jurors.
- HMCS should, therefore, ensure that court users understand how representative juries are, locally.

- Only 12 per cent of all Crown Court charges are decided by jury deliberation; 59 per cent of all charges result in a guilty plea. Only 0.6 per cent of all verdicts are hung juries (juries which cannot reach a verdict).
- Juries convict on 64 per cent of all charges, with the highest conviction rates in direct-evidence cases and the lowest where jurors must be sure of the state of mind of D or V.
- Conviction rates rose with the number of charges: 40 per cent on one charge, 80 per cent where there were five charges.
- Contrary to popular belief and previous government reports, juries convict in rape cases more often than not: 55 per cent (of 4,310 verdicts).
- Conviction rates in busy courts range from 69 per cent to 53 per cent. There were no courts with a higher acquittal than conviction rate.
- Most jurors at Blackfriars and Winchester *felt* they were able to understand directions but most at Nottingham felt they were difficult to understand.
- BUT Only 31 per cent *actually understood* the directions fully in legal terms used by the judge.
- Written instructions increased juror comprehension. (As we said in 2001, in our paper for Auld L.J. . . .)
- Most jurors recalled media coverage of their trial only during the trial but in high-profile cases, 35 per cent remembered pre-trial coverage and 20 per cent of these said it was difficult putting this out of their minds.
- Some jurors looked for information on their trial on the internet.
- More should be done to instruct and continually remind jurors of the rules on impropriety.

For another welcome example of contemporary research, see Ellison and Munro. In 2010, Coen and Heffernan pointed out that we have not discussed juror comprehension of expert evidence much, in contrast with the US. I would add that that indeed applies to all aspects of jury selection and functioning. In the meantime, a great deal could have been learned from our survey of the existing mass of research and from such projects as the New Zealand Law Commission's research which questioned real jurors. There is much that could be done without the need even to question real jurors.

Public attitudes

16–040   Conversations with non-lawyers in England and Wales, like those in the US, show they are firm supporters of the jury system, which is why Jack Straw's repeated attempts to remove the defendant's choice in either-way cases met with such strong opposition among lawyers and politicians. We finish this chapter on the same subject with which we commenced: attitudes towards the jury. In 2009, the Ministry of Justice published research by Roberts and Hough, who concluded:

"It is striking that despite differences in the nature of the jury—as well as differences in the wording of specific survey questions—the positive reaction to the jury in England and Wales also emerges from surveys conducted in other common law countries. . .In addition, there is clear opposition in this country to proposals to restrict the right to trial by jury."

BIBLIOGRAPHY

J. Airs and A. Shaw, "Jury Excusal and Deferral", Home Office **16–041** Research and Statistics Directorate Research Study No.102, 1999, National Archives *www.nationalarchives.gov.uk*.

Auld L.J., *Review of the Criminal Courts of England and Wales* (2001) (The Criminal Courts Review), Ch.5.

F. Bowden, "Silence was golden: why juries just can't keep quiet", *The Times*, March 18, 2008.

K. Burgess, "Homeowner Kenneth Batchelor cleared of murder after shooting dead intruder", *The Times*, March 11, 2009.

L. Campbell, "We should be proud to do a day in court", *The Evening Standard*, June 4, 2009 (on her experiences as a juror). See newspaper databases, such as UK Newsstand.

M. Coen and L. Heffernan, "Juror Comprehension of Expert Evidence: A Reform Agenda" [2010] Crim. L.R. 195.

The Criminal Justice Act 2003.

P. Darbyshire, "Notes of a Lawyer Juror" (1990) 140 N.L.J. 1264 (same issue also contains other accounts of jury service); "The Lamp That Shows That Freedom Lives—is it worth the candle?" [1991] Crim. L.R. 740; Letter to the editor [2008] Crim. L.R. 888.

P. Darbyshire, A. Maughan and A. Stewart, "What Can the English Legal System Learn from Jury Research Published up to 2001?" available on the Kingston University website, research repository. It is summarised in P. Darbyshire "What Can We Learn from Published Jury Research? Findings for the Criminal Courts Review 2001" [2001] Crim. L.R. 970.

Department for Constitutional Affairs, "Jury Research and Impropriety", Consultation Paper CP/04/05, on the DCA archived website, National Archives.

P. Devlin, *Trial by Jury* (1956).

S. Doran and J. Jackson, "The Case for Jury Waiver" [1997] Crim. L.R. 155 (on judge alone trials).

L. Ellison and V. Munro "Getting to (not) guilty: examining jurors' deliberative processes in, and beyond, the context of a mock rape trial" (2010) 30 (1) *Legal Studies* 74–97.

Home Office, *Determining Mode of Trial in Either Way Cases—A Consultation Paper*, 1998.

A. Fresco and F. Gibb, "lawyers fear more trials without jury after guilty verdict in £1.7m robbery", *The Times*, April 1, 2010 and also on the same date, on judge alone trials, see F. Gibb, "High cost of protection is eroding legal bastion".

F. Gibb, "First trial without a jury for 400 years" *The Times*, June 19, 2009.

J. Halliday, "Facebook juror and defendant guilty of contempt", *guardian.co.uk*, June 14, 2011.

J. Jackson and S. Doran, *Judge Without Jury: Diplock Trials in the Adversary System* (1995).

Lord Judge C.J., "Jury trials", speech, on the problem of jurors deriving information from the internet, November 16, 2010, judiciary website.

"Jury Summoning Guidance", December 2003, a consultation paper on the DCA archived website.

R. F. Julian, "Judicial Perspectives on the Conduct of Serious Fraud Trials" [2007] Crim. L.R. 751–768.

Justice for All (2002), White Paper. This set out the Government's responses to the Criminal Courts Review (2001) and explained Government plans to enact the Criminal Justice Act 2003 and to develop criminal justice policy: *http://www.archive2.official-documents.co.uk/document/cm55/5563/5563.pdf*.

Law in Action, BBC Radio 4, March 1, 2011, "As trials become more complicated, Joshua Rozenberg asks what is the future for juries?" BBC iPlayer.

N. Ley, on the superiority of Crown Court trial: (1999) 149 N.L.J. 1316.

S. Lloyd-Bostock, *Report on Interviews with Jurors in the Jubilee Line Case*, HM Crown Prosecution Service Inspectorate, October 2005, *http://www.hmcpsi.gov.uk/documents/services/reports/THM/JLJuryIntsRep.pdf*.

Lord Chancellor's Department, *Report of the Committee on Fraud Trials* (1986) LCO 36/95, "The Roskill Report".

H.H. Judge Nic Madge, "Summing up—a Judge's Perspective" [2006] Crim. L.R. 817.

A. Majid, "Jury Still Out on Deaf Jurors" (2004) 154 N.L.J. 278.

R. Matthews, L. Hancock and D. Briggs, "Jurors' perceptions, understanding, confidence and satisfaction in the jury system: a study in six courts", Home Office Research, Development and Statistics Directorate Findings 227 (2004).

M. Narey, *Review of Delay in the Criminal Justice System*, Home Office, 1997 "The Narey Report" *www.nationalarchives.gov.uk*.

New Zealand Law Commission Report 69, *Juries in Criminal Trials*, 2001: *www.lawcom.govt.nz*.

S. O'Neill, "Trial by jury no longer guarantees justice", *The Times*, September 15, 2008.

R.G. Parry, "'An important obligation of citizenship': language, citizenship and jury service" (2007) 27(2) L.S. 188–215.

D. Perry, "direction", on jury directions, *Counsel*, March 2011.

Report of the Departmental Committee on Jury Service (The Morris Report) Cmnd.2627 (1965).

J.V. Roberts and M. Hough, *Public opinion and the jury; an international literature review*, Ministry of Justice Research Series 1/09 (2009).

Speeches by Moses L.J., November 2, 2010 and Lord Judge, November 18, 2010.

C. Thomas, *Diversity and Fairness in the Jury System*, Ministry of Justice Research Report 02/07 (2007) (see, however, P. Darbyshire, letter to the editor, June 30, 2008 [2008] Crim. L.R. 888); *Are Juries Fair?* Ministry of Justice Research Series 1/10, MoJ website.

Wolchover and Heaton-Armstrong's arguments are at (1998) 148 N.L.J. 1614, and see 150 N.L.J. 158.

N. Woolcock, "Fights, friendships sickies. . .life as a juror on the 13-month terrorism trial" *The Times*, May 3, 2007.

M. Zander, "A touch of bias?" (2007) 157 N.L.J. 1530.

Other material as referred to in the text.

The attempts to suppress Baldwin's findings on the CPS are discussed by Ashworth in the editorial of the *Criminal Law Review* for August 1997.

SOURCES FOR UPDATING THIS CHAPTER

Updates for this book from spring 2012 and 2013 on the Sweet & **16–042** Maxwell website.

The New Law Journal (on *Lexis*).

The Legal Journals Index on *Westlaw*. Search case law and journals on *Westlaw* and *Lexis*.

The National Archives contains old material from the Home Office and The Department for Constitutional Affairs websites.

Home Office Research and Statistics Directorate: *www.homeoffice.gov.uk/rds*.

Ministry of Justice website.

Newspapers from databases and archived articles on individual newspaper websites.

Note that most jury research is published in social science journals and social science databases.

17. Legal Services

"The real difficulty in getting an adequate system of legal assistance is that some influential people do not consider that it is desirable. There is an idea that litigation is not a thing to be 'encouraged'. . .It is noticeable that these same people do not suggest that wealthy persons or corporations should be discouraged from litigating. . .This attitude may be seen in the *Final Report of the Committee on Legal Aid for the Poor*. . .proposals to help poor people by a scheme similar to the National Health Insurance Acts were rejected on the ground that 'It is manifestly in the interests of the State that its citizens should be healthy, not that they should be litigious'. This attitude is a compound of ignorance and stupidity. . .the ignorance being that of the upper classes" (R.M. Jackson, *The Machinery of Justice in England*, 1940, the first edition of the first ELS textbook, commenting on this crucial recommendation in 1928 that a National Legal Service should *not* be established).

"The effective replacement in civil litigation of public funding by the conditional fee agreement is in direct contradiction of the message we received when the Human Rights Act was introduced, namely that rights were coming home. If Human Rights have come home, they are largely unemployed. There is all too often no wherewithal to protect or enforce them. The conditional fee provides at best a fig leaf to cover the nakedness of the legal system in protecting those in need of protection." (Lightman J., of the High Court, Chancery Division, in the Edward Bramley Memorial Lecture University of Sheffield, April 4, 2003.)

"It must surely be a short sighted economy for us to withdraw the availability of public funding from the under-privileged. It promotes the sense that the protection of the law is for the 'haves' and not the 'have-nots'. The price to be paid for this in

terms of respect for the law and social cohesion should not be underestimated."
(Lightman J., "Access to Justice", speech to the Law Society, December 5, 2007.)

"He has spent the last six months in Guatemala providing a safe passage to local human rights lawyers. He does not carry a gun. His T-shirt symbolises the message: 'The world is watching, and there will be a hullabaloo if we come to any harm'".
(Sir Henry Brooke, describing the pro bono work of a young solicitor, winner of a pro bono award, in a November 2007 speech to the Law Society.)

17–001 If the rule of law states that everyone should be equal before the law then, surely, this implies that everyone should have equal access to the law, the courts and legal services. Furthermore, the law presumes that we all know the law. Ignorance of the law is no defence to a civil or criminal action. I suggest, then, that one of the requirements of a civilised modern democracy must be the promotion of and access to information on our legal rights and duties. The first principle was broadly accepted in the English legal system from the middle of the twentieth century. It is supported by the European Convention on Human Rights. Article 6 requires fair trials and lays down the principles for the requirement of legal services in civil and criminal cases. It is set out fully in Ch.12. The section relevant to legal representation is as follows:

"In the determination of his civil rights and obligations or of any criminal charge against him, everyone is entitled to a fair and public hearing . . . Everyone charged with a criminal offence has the following minimum rights . . .b. to have adequate time and facilities for the preparation of his defence; c. to defend himself in person or through legal assistance of his own choosing or, if he has not sufficient means to pay for legal assistance, to be given it free when the interests of justice so require . . ."

As can be seen, Art.6 requires representation in criminal cases where "the interests of justice" require it. This phrase is identical to the test for granting criminal legal aid (LA) in England and Wales under the Poor Prisoners Defence Act 1903 and was doubtless copied from it by the UK lawyers who drafted the Convention. The Convention also requires legal help or representation in civil cases, according to what the litigant needs to ensure "equality of arms" with the opposition. This must be determined on a case by case basis, as is illustrated in Ch.4 on human rights. The Lord Chancellor and his Ministry of Justice are responsible for legal services. He and his junior ministers are answerable in Parliament.

As we shall see, there was much use of the phrase "access to justice" in the 1990s. This means, broadly: being able to make full use of legal rights, through adequate legal services, i.e. advice, assistance and representation, regardless of means. It also means the ability to make full use of the court structure and rights of appeal. Legal services are dealt with here and access to justice via the civil courts is dealt with in Ch.10 on civil procedure. The Royal Commission on Legal Services 1979 defined legal services as "services which should be available to any person or organisation requiring advice or assistance of a legal character, whether payment for the service is made from public or private funds".

Before the mid twentieth century, there was no systematic, statutory, widespread provision of LA. In civil cases, poor people with less than £5 in capital could be represented in Royal courts (High Court) cases under the *in forma pauperis* procedure, placed on a statutory basis in 1494. Since poor people were rarely involved in proceedings in the Royal courts, this was not much use. By 1875, free representation in criminal cases was limited to the dock brief system. A prisoner could obtain the services of a barrister for one guinea plus a clerk's fee. The barrister could not refuse. Legal advice schemes were virtually unknown in the nineteenth century. Abel Smith and Stevens describe the very stilted development of LA and advice in the first half of the twentieth century. The Law Society, the solicitors' trade union, made sure that solicitors gained control over statutory schemes. The demand for accessible advice and civil representation became urgent in clearing a backlog of divorce cases, rendered more acute by the Second World War. Services were provided for the armed forces. In 1944–45, the Rushcliffe Committee considered how best to provide legal services for those who could not afford them. The LA scheme established after this by the Legal Aid and Advice Act 1949 was to provide for services through the private practice lawyer who claimed a fee from the State. This model of delivery of publicly funded legal services is sometimes referred to as the judicare model. Their second recommendation, for a network of legal advice centres staffed by fulltime state salaried lawyers was never implemented. This would have been comparable with state-funded doctors' surgeries in the National Health Service.

The Committee considered whether a state department or the **17–002** local authorities should administer the system but, concerned that both of these had an interest in so many cases, chose to leave administration in the hands of the Law Society. Leaving lawyers holding the purse strings was a curious policy, given that lawyers were the financial beneficiaries of the LA Fund and this is probably one of the reasons that by the 1980s at least half of all private practice solicitors earned some or most of their income from LA. The 1949 Act was slow in being implemented because of lack of funds. Criminal LA arrived later, also delivered through private practice lawyers but dispensed via the court. Legal advice was provided under a third scheme and dispensed to individual clients by their solicitors. By the 1970s, when all three schemes were fully established, around 70 per cent of the population qualified for some kind of help. Sir Henry Brooke said, in a 2007 speech, that the LA scheme used to be the envy of the world and most lawyers, as he then was, undertook legally aided work. By 1988, the three schemes were put on a systematic basis in one statute, the Legal Aid Act 1988. At the same time, lawyers' fingers were at last taken off the purse strings. The Legal Aid Board was created to fund and manage the civil LA scheme and legal advice. Criminal LA, as before, was dispensed by the criminal courts, normally the court clerks in magistrates' courts. All types of aid were available only to those who passed a means test, with those who could afford to contribute being required to do so. The three types of aid had different means tests. Civil and criminal LA were subject to merits tests.

Despite all of this provision, it proved to be inadequate. Sociologists and lawyers in the 1960s and 1970s exposed the continuing phenomenon of "unmet legal need", which occurs when someone has a legal problem which goes unsolved. The causes were identified (see below) and alternative legal services developed in the voluntary sector, outside the LA scheme, in an attempt to fulfil some of those needs. By the 1980s and 1990s, the LA budget was increasing out of control but, ironically, a diminishing percentage of the population was eligible for it and fewer cases were aided. It was clear that, whichever political party was elected in 1997, it would have to curb the LA budget and target it better to provide the right type of help to the right people. When New Labour were elected, they devised this new scheme, explained here, which is currently, in 2011, about to be replaced by the Coalition Justice Minister and Lord Chancellor, Ken Clarke, although his Legal Aid, Sentencing and Punishment of Offenders Bill will have a rough ride through Parliament.

1. The Access to Justice Act 1999 and the 2011 Bill

17–003   Civil LA and advice was replaced by the scheme of publicly funded legal services provided for in the Access to Justice Act 1999, administered by the Legal Services Commission and the Community Legal Service. Criminal LA and advice was replaced by the Criminal Defence Service, in April 2001. This replaced the total framework for LA consolidated in the Legal Aid Act 1988. The Labour Lord Chancellor explained the Act's aims in a White Paper, *Modernising Justice.*

The Legal Services Commission

This was a non-departmental public body established by the 1999 **17–004** Act to dispense LA. The *Modernising Justice* paper said it would develop local, regional and national plans to match provision to needs, taking account of local views. It would develop quality criteria and enter contracts with lawyers and non-lawyers (alternative providers) for the provision of legal services. It is abolished by the 2011 Bill.

The Community Legal Service

Under the 1999 Act, a Community Legal Service (CLS) man- **17–005** aged civil LA and advice until 2011. It was empowered to set and monitor standards and provide accreditation schemes for service providers (this means lawyers and others providing legal services). The Lord Chancellor provided the budget for the LSC to maintain a Community Legal Service Fund. It worked with Community Legal Service Partnerships, bringing together funders such as local authorities and charities with legal service providers, such as solicitors and volunteer advisers. The CLS website was launched in 2000. In 2011, its successor was shut down. People can now use the DirectGov website and Ministry of Justice websites to check their eligibility and get the directory of providers. The sites have pages on specific problems such as debt. Citizens' Advice provides some advice online. In 2004, the Government launched a self-help website, on debt and tax credits. Information points were made available in libraries and law school advice clinics, providing information leaflets. Advice lines were established, giving a full casework service.

The funding code for civil cases

Under the 1999 Act, the LSC prepared a Funding Code, subject to **17–006** the Lord Chancellor's approval. Under the Coalition government proposals, this will now be prescribed by the Lord Chancellor. Eight categories of service were excluded, so people had to pay for them privately, for instance, by persuading a lawyer to act under a conditional fee agreement, or get help from a charity, or a Citizens' Advice Bureau (CAB), or from a lawyer acting pro bono, or they were be left to represent themselves:

1. personal injury, apart from clinical negligence, death or damage to property;

2. conveyancing;
3. boundary disputes;
4. wills;
5. trust law;
6. defamation;
7. company or partnership law;
8. other business matters.

Apart from the first, these categories were *always* excluded from LA, since it was invented. Then Lord Irvine announced in 1998 that personal injuries would be excluded. In his 2010 consultation paper, Ken Clarke, the Coalition LC, said the present system was unsustainable. Tough decisions would have to be taken.

"In reaching our view about which types of issue and proceeding should continue to justify legal aid, we have taken into account the importance of the issue, the litigant's ability to present their own case (including the venue before which the case is heard, the likely vulnerability of the litigant and the complexity of the law), the availability of alternative sources of funding and the availability of alternative routes to resolving the issue. We have also taken into account our domestic, European and international legal obligations. Each of these factors is explained in more detail below." (para.4.12.)

He said his plans would prioritise cases where the individual faced homelessness, judicial review cases challenging government action, money claims with a special element, "which arises out of the abuse of a child or vulnerable adult, or out of serious abuse of state power", and other issues as listed in the last section of this chapter. The consultation paper explained:

"The existing legal aid scheme is very broad and allows public funds to be expended on any issue not explicitly excluded. In order to target legal aid resources in a more focused way on specific issues, we propose to specify the types of issue and levels of service which are available under the revised scheme in legislation, when the Parliamentary timetable allows. Civil legal aid will not routinely be available for any other issue." (para.4.32.)

Financial eligibility limits

17–007 These are updated by regulations, every April. Only clients with very low incomes and capital are entitled to fully funded legal services. Those whose income or capital fall above certain limits have to pay a contribution towards certain (but not all) legal services, assessed according to means. This is the same as the old pre-1999 LA scheme. The Access to Justice Act 1999 preserved the statutory charge. This means that the legal aid fund may place a first "charge" on any real property, such as a house, recovered or preserved in funded proceedings. The logic behind this is to ensure people pay towards the cost of their cases if they are able; it encourages people to act reasonably and not to incur excessive legal costs and it puts them in a similar position to a privately paying client.

Contracting

The introduction of general civil contracting brought a massive **17–008** shift in funding of legal services. Whereas, under the old pre-1999 LA scheme, any solicitor could provide legally aided services, providers of legal help (solicitors and advice agencies) were then limited to those who had a contract to deal with a specified number of cases. To get this, an advice agency or firm of solicitors had to demonstrate that they satisfied the quality criteria evaluated by peer review. Ken Clarke said there had been complaints that auditing of lawyers' case files was too onerous so this would be reconsidered. In his 2010 paper, the Coalition said in the short term they would be looking for efficiency savings and in the long term, civil and family work would be remunerated on the basis of competitive price tendering, a device that the Labour administrations had tried introducing many times, like the Conservatives before them. It was bitterly opposed by lawyers.

Criminal Defence

Under s.12 of the 1999 Act, the LSC were obliged to establish **17–009** the Criminal Defence Service (CDS) and this replaced criminal LA. The Coalition proposes abolishing the CDS and returning to criminal LA, controlled directly by the Ministry of Justice. Section 15 of the Access to Justice Act 1999 provided that the represented individual may select any representative to act for him and it may be from a prescribed group but the applicant may not be restricted to a person employed by the LSC. It is a requirement of Art.6 of the ECHR that the applicant's choice is not limited. In 2000–01, the Government announced proposals to develop a system of public defenders directly employed by the LSC. The first four such offices were introduced in 2001 and there were eight by 2004. From 2001, all solicitors' firms undertaking publicly funded criminal defence had to have a contract. Only solicitors working to quality standards were eligible for a contract. Defendants are allowed to make a reasonable change at any time. The decision remains in the hands of the court because the judge or magistrates are free from any accusation of economic interest. At a Crown Court, each resident judge usually has a pile of such applications to determine, weekly.

Means and merits test

17–010   The merits test for a criminal representation order is the "interests of justice test", copied from the Poor Persons Defence Act and Art.6 of the ECHR. The criteria applied are set out in the 2011 Bill. They repeat the "Widgery criteria" developed in the 1960s and include likelihood of loss of liberty, livelihood, reputation, or that the case involves a substantial question of law, or the need to trace witnesses, or expert cross-examination, or that the accused may not be able to understand the proceedings, or present his own case, and so on. Tony Blair's government originally scrapped the means test for representation in magistrates' courts. This had to be reinstated, by the Criminal Defence Services Act 2006 because the plan turned out to be too expensive.

2. Background to the 1999 Act

Alternative legal services

17–011   Alternatives grew out of the inadequacies of the original pre-1970 LA scheme but they have continued to flourish. Unmet legal need occurs where someone has a legal problem but it goes unsolved through lack of access to legal services. Despite LA schemes being in place by 1972, unmet need was identified by social research and social welfare lawyers in the 1960s and 1970s. It was (and is) caused by:

- the high cost of legal fees;
- fear of lawyers, fear of cost;
- lawyers' lack of training and unwillingness to serve poor clients' needs for advice in welfare law;
- the inaccessibility of lawyers' offices to poor or rural clients;
- the creation of new legal rights without the funding to enforce them;
- people's ignorance that the law could solve their problem;
- the fact that the LA scheme omitted certain services, such as representation at tribunals.

As a result, alternatives to private practice lawyers had been developed by radical lawyers, charities and others to try and fulfil these needs. Many can no longer be seen as alternatives because they have now been absorbed into the mainstream, by the 1999 Act, where they have succeeded in securing a contract as a service provider. Indeed, in the 2010 consultation paper, the Coalition government has said they will take account of whether an alternative source of help exists, before granting aid.

Law Centres

From 1970 law centres, copied from US Neighbourhood Law **17–012** Centres, were very gradually established in poor areas, with a shop front image, where employed lawyers and paralegals will provide advice and representation on such matters as welfare law and immigration. They have always suffered from vulnerable funding. Those financed by local authorities found they were biting the hand that fed them, when they acted for groups suffering bad public housing. Law centre funding was sporadic and sometimes they would have to close temporarily. By 2011 there were 55 law centres, plus affiliates and associated members. For information, see the Law Centres Federation website.

Citizens' Advice Bureaux

The Second World War exacerbated the need for advice and a **17–013** thousand bureaux were established throughout the country by the end of the war. The Rushcliffe Committee 1944 recommended that they should be preserved. Expanding these was a policy of the Thatcher government from 1979. In 2011, their website said they provided advice at over 3,500 locations, with the aid of 21,000 volunteers, helping 2.1 million clients with 7.1 million problems in 2009–10.

Advice centres

In the twentieth century, hundreds of independent advice centres **17–014** grew up, some providing general legal advice, some more specialised. In the first half of the twentieth century, generalist advice centres were known as the Poor Man's Lawyer, with lawyers providing free advice, usually in the evenings. Such centres need to make a referral if substantive legal help is needed, beyond advice. During the war, regional advice centres, staffed by solicitors and organised by the Law Society, supplemented the CABx. Nowadays advice centres are sometimes called law clinics and many are attached to university law schools. Organisations and interest groups sometimes provide free specialist legal services, including representation, and sometimes make referrals. Examples are charities such as the Child Poverty Action Group, Shelter, Youth Access, The Money Advice Trust, Dial UK (disability advice), Mind, the Refugee Legal Centre, and so on.

Pro bono lawyers

17–015   During the 1990s, both the Law Society and the Bar Council established pro bono groups to try to persuade professionals to give some of their services free. The Free Representation Unit, a group of Bar students, was established in a pub in Chancery Lane in 1972. They practice advocacy by representing tribunal applicants. Another example is the CAB in the Royal Courts of Justice providing help for litigants in person. As explained in Ch.10 on civil procedure, in addition to its full-time employed solicitors, hundreds of lawyers work pro bono. Inspiring examples of wide ranging pro bono work in this legal system and by human rights lawyers abroad were given by Sir Henry Brooke, retired Lord Justice of Appeal, in a November 2007 speech. In April 2011, a LawWorks survey found that 65 per cent of law schools were engaged in pro bono activity. The first national pro bono centre was launched in October 2010. The Legal Services Act 2007 permits costs to be ordered to a winning lawyer, acting pro bono, and paid to the Access to Justice Foundation, which funds support networks for more pro bono work.

1990s attempts to enhance access to justice

17–016   The Conservative administrations of the 1990s devised various ways of enhancing access to justice, which were expanded under Labour from 1999. They permitted conditional fees in two types of legal work. They attempted to draft laws in plain English and to make court procedures simpler and cheaper, providing advice leaflets in multiple languages. Mackay L.C. was given the crystal award by the Plain English Campaign for simplifying court leaflets. (Incidentally, judges are keen on this too. Lord Woolf C.J. made it his personal mission to eliminate legal Latin. It was he who was asked to simplify civil procedure. The "Woolf reforms" are described in Ch.10.) Governments encouraged the use of alternative dispute resolution (ADR), as explained in Ch.11. People were encouraged to take out private legal expenses insurance. Duty solicitor schemes, funded under the LA scheme, provided emergency help and representation in police stations and the magistrates' courts.

Background to the Access to Justice Act 1999—uncontrolled cost and inefficiency

17–017   Throughout the late 1980s then the 1990s, both the Conservative Government then their Labour successors were determined to do something radical to reform the provision of legal services, for the following reasons:

- The cost was "spiralling out of control", according to the Conservative Lord Chancellor, Lord Mackay. LA was the only demand-led draw on the Treasury. Some years in the 1990s, the cost rose by around 20 per cent, despite the fact that fewer people were being legally aided. Separate representation for children, provided by the Children Act 1989, and the development of duty solicitor schemes in police stations and the magistrates' courts were just two items which accelerated the cost increase. The media were swift to point out that some people who were apparently very wealthy got LA. One example was the Maxwells, sons of Robert Maxwell, whose LA bill for defence in their fraud trial was over £14.5 million.
- Funders were unco-ordinated. LA was designed to deliver legal services through the medium of private practice barristers and solicitors so "alternative" legal services received very little of the huge LA budget and they were dependent on a precarious mix of sources, such as charities, local authorities and other government departments.
- Criminal LA was administered unevenly. Research showed that the merits test was applied inconsistently by different magistrates' courts. The Audit Commission criticised them eight years running for failure to apply the means test properly.
- "Fat cat lawyers", as Irvine L.C. called them, were charging the LA Board exorbitant fees.
- In 1999, Hazel Genn published a survey of how people solved their legal problems: *Paths to Justice*. She found that people were generally disturbingly ignorant about their legal rights and obligations.

The 1999 Act scheme was quite visionary and radical. In 1995, Labour had had the simple idea of finding out how much money was spent on LA (by the State) plus the great variety of alternative legal services in England and Wales (by charities, local authorities and other government departments) and working out what people's legal needs were and how they could best be fulfilled, within this overall budget, whether through private practice lawyers or alternatives. Thus they disposed of the assumption underlying the pre-1999 scheme that legal services should be delivered through the medium of the private practice lawyer. Lawyers and "alternative" providers were to be funded from the same legal services budget. Like most modern statutes, though, the Act was just a framework. In a 1998 consultation paper on the Community Legal Service, the government said that people needed basic information and advice on rights and responsibilities, not necessarily to go to court. Six thousand professionals (lawyers) and thirty thousand volunteers at Law Centres and other advice centres, such as Citizens' Advice Bureaux, etc. provided this for £250 million pounds per year. This was sufficient but service was fragmented and unco-ordinated. The idea of the scheme was simply to assess need locally and match provision to need.

Conditional fee (no win no fee) agreements partly replaced LA

17–018   Private conditional fee agreements (CFAs) are defined, in s.58(2) of the 1999 Act as "an agreement with a person providing advocacy or litigation services which provides for his fee and expenses, or any part of them, to be payable only in specified circumstances". This generally means an agreement that a fee will be paid only if the lawyer wins the client's case. CFAs are prohibited in criminal and virtually all family proceedings.

Speculative litigation was illegal under the common law offences of champerty and maintenance, abolished in 1967, and unenforceable in English law from the Statute of Westminster 1275, until the Courts and Legal Services Act 1990 permitted CFAs. In Scotland, it has long been permissible for a lawyer and client to conduct litigation on a speculative basis. In the US, a variety of contingency fees is permissible, the most common being that the lawyer takes a percentage of the sum recovered in litigation. By contrast, the English distaste for such deals was expressed by Blackstone in his *Commentaries on the Law of England* (1765): "This is an offence against public justice, as it keeps alive strife and contention, and perverts the remedial process of law into an engine of oppression" (quoted in Lord Mackay's Green Paper, below).

The Royal Commission on Legal Services 1979 agreed but in 1989, Mackay L.C. published a green paper, *Contingency Fees*, setting out the options. It provoked a very hostile reaction from the judiciary. The subsequent (Conservative) Courts and Legal Services Act 1990 did not permit contingency fees but "no win no fee" contracts, with the lawyer permitted to take a percentage uplift of 100 per cent above her normal fee if she won the case. CFAs were permitted in personal injury, insolvency and human rights cases. Labour, having condemned this, in 1995, as "little more than a gimmick designed to mask the chaotic state of the LA scheme", adopted CFAs as one of the main elements of their legal services policy, two years later. Labour Lord Chancellor, Lord Irvine proposed abolishing most of civil LA and said litigants would instead be able to enter into private CFA contracts.

"[A]ccess to the civil courts is open only to the very poor and the very rich. . .By extending no-win, no-fee arrangements justice becomes available to all. Legal help will become affordable...Civil legal aid has tripled in cost in six years...The income received by lawyers has risen on average by 20 per cent a year over the same period...The number of cases supported has fallen...There is no extra money...For too long, legal aid has been abused. Too many weak cases...have been taken on...Conditional fees will make lawyers look harder at the cases which are brought to them." (Speech, Law Society conference, 1997.)

This provoked an explosion of attacks from lawyers. Irvine was taken aback by these "savage and grave allegations" (see *Gazette*, December 1997). The Law Society launched an expensive and graphic press campaign portraying the death of LA, in spring 1999. They used full page newspaper advertisements depicting a crying child suffering from bad housing, a beaten woman and a black man who had been falsely imprisoned and discriminated against. Irvine L.C. retaliated with a furious press release, denying all these allegations. He was forced to make concessions. The Bar and the Law Society advocated a Contingency LA Fund, to which successful litigants would contribute, which would pay the costs of unsuccessful litigants. Research by the Policy Studies Institute on 197 CFA cases concluded they were not working well. If litigants were allowed to recover their success fees from the defendants they defeated, this would significantly reduce the risk to plaintiff and lawyer so LA blackmail could be replaced by CFA blackmail. Insurance companies warned of extra expense to them, as defendants, causing insurance premium inflation. The Forum of Insurance Lawyers complained that a windfall of extra fees would be paid to successful solicitors in uplifted fees for no good reason. By 2010–11, these warnings turned out to be prophetic, as we shall see below, not to mention the "compensation culture" and uncontrollable civil costs, discussed in Ch.10. The current intention of the Coalition Government, in 2011, is to go one step further and introduce contingency fees, following a recommendation of Jackson L.J.'s review of civil costs, as explained briefly below and further in Ch.10.

3. Evaluation of Labour's 1999 Act—did it provide access to justice and value for taxpayers' money?

When reading evaluations of any legal aid or legal services **17–019** scheme, I would invite the reader to bear in mind the following. The Law Society, representing solicitors, and Bar Council, representing barristers, are very powerful trade unions. Their effective publicity machinery promotes lawyers' financial interests. The press is flooded with comments from the profession when any change is proposed which affects them. They oppose most changes. They always argue that what they want is in the public interest. Their professional monopolies have maintained a stranglehold over legal services throughout the twentieth century and they normally defend the interests of private practice lawyers. All of this is graphically illustrated by what Irvine L.C. called the "sorry saga" of their behaviour over rights of audience since the ineffective Courts and Legal Services Act 1990, a story told in Ch.13, on lawyers.

Living with CFAs

17–020   In *Nothing to Lose?* researchers Yarrow and Abrams (1999) reported that clients found CFAs confusing. They did not understand success fees. Sometimes they did not understand that the solicitor would get nothing if the case was lost. The solicitor would not let them drop the case, because the insurance policy would not pay out the solicitor's fees if they did. In 2001, Moorhead and Scherr raised ethical questions over the lack of understanding of the client of the risk they were taking. Both the Master of the Rolls, Lord Phillips, and the Law Society were worried about costs and disputes about who should fund CFAs. Research by Yarrow, *Just Rewards?* revealed that solicitors were using CFAs to overcharge.

In a very important interpretive case, *Callery v Gray* [2001] EWCA Civ 1117, Lord Woolf C.J., who designed the Civil Procedure Rules, Lord Phillips M.R. and Brooke L.J. tried to make some sense of the mess of litigation over who paid for success fees and insurance premiums in small claims resulting from traffic accidents. They gave a highly purposive interpretation to the new regime: it was to achieve access to justice for people who could not afford it so it was an inevitable consequence of government policy that defendants should be subjected to additional costs. Defendants, with the help of the court, should be able to limit success fees and insurance premiums to a reasonable amount. Their Lordships thought that a reasonable success fee in cases like this which had a 98 per cent success rate was 20 per cent, a far cry from the crippling 100 per cent success fees that Jackson found had made much civil litigation ridiculously expensive, discussed in Ch.10.

Research in 2001 by accountants Stoy Hayward suggested that law firms "cherry picked" winnable cases for CFAs. In 2004, Citizens' Advice published a damning report, *No Win, No Fee, No Chance,* based on 385 evidence reports, confirming this. People with meritorious but low value cases were left without a remedy. There was no regulation of the quality or cost of advice. Consumers, such as accident victims in hospital, were often subjected to high-pressure sales tactics. They were not clear of the risk. People often thought the contracts were genuinely "no win no fee" and failed to appreciate that they might have to pay the premium to insure against losing. One woman was left with only £15 from £2,150 in compensatory damages. Prof Richard Moorhead found that 12 per cent of employment cases were backed by contingency fees. Only one third of lawyers were prepared to act on a "no win no fee" basis because of the 25–30 per cent chance of losing and the fact that the cap for unfair dismissal compensation was £63,000 and the average award was £3–4,000 (Robins, 2009). A *Times* leading article "Sickness in Health", December 21, 2009 said that the Government's "noble goal", to make justice available to all, had become a "costly nightmare", as hospital payouts for clinical negligence had gone from nothing, two decades earlier, to £769 million per year, with much of the money going to lawyers. The NHS litigation authority complained to Jackson L.J. that the costs sought by claimant's lawyers were disproportionately high and were "indefensibly expensive". "Claimants, who were once the David in cases of medical negligence, with the odds of success stacked against them, have become the Goliaths".

On the other hand, others argued that CFAs opened up access to **17–021** justice. Solicitor Adam Tudor wrote to *The Times* (February 8, 2005) saying that since 1998, his firm alone had successfully represented over 100 libel claimants from all walks of life (LA was always unavailable for defamation). Wade (2009) argued that CFAs had helped credit crunch victims who would otherwise be unable to act against banks and so on who had given them negligent financial advice. For further discussion of the "costs war" provoked by the introduction of CFAs and allegations that they have facilitated a "compensation culture" and inflated civil costs, see Ch.10. As discussed in that chapter, Jackson L.J., in his review of civil costs, recommended that we take a more radical step now to permit contingency fees, where the lawyer takes a percentage of damages won. This was welcomed by Ken Clarke, Minister of Justice, in 2010–11 any they are permitted by the 2011 Bill Act.

Unmet need persists

The Law Society and Legal Action Group expressed serious con- **17–022** cern that, by 2003, so many solicitors' firms had withdrawn from the legal services scheme that there were "advice deserts", such as Kent, where there were no solicitors doing publicly funded housing law. In *Geography of Advice* (2004), Citizens' Advice reported a "postcode lottery": 40 per cent of Bureaux considered they operated in an "advice desert"; 60–68 per cent reported difficulties finding a publicly funded immigration lawyer, or family or housing lawyer. Clients had to travel over 50 miles to get help.

In a 2003–04 study for the Legal Services Research Centre of the Legal Services Commission, *Causes of Action: Civil Law & Social Justice*, Pleasance et al. surveyed over 5,000 adults. Their findings were as follows:

1. One third of adults had experienced at least one civil law problem over 3.5 years.
2. One fifth took no action.
3. About one million problems a year were left unsolved, as people did not understand basic rights.
4. Of those who took action, 37 per cent chose to handle their problems alone. Of the 63 per cent who successfully sought advice, almost as many approached an advice centre as a solicitor.
5. Socially excluded groups were especially vulnerable to civil justice problems. Legal problems were experienced by 80 per cent of people in temporary accommodation, two thirds of lone parents and over half of the unemployed.
6. Half the adults surveyed reported multiple problems. They occurred in clusters, such as personal injury leading to loss of home or income. Relationship or marital breakdown could cause multiple problems. This confirmed Genn's finding in *Paths to Justice* (1999).
7. 15 per cent who sought advice did not obtain any, especially with problems of homelessness, rented housing, anti-social neighbours or benefits.
8. People were least likely to take action on mental illness, clinical negligence, unfair police treatment, personal injury or domestic violence.
9. People would often first discuss a problem with a doctor or social worker.
10. The report identified "referral fatigue". The more advisers a person was referred onto, the less likely they were to follow up all those referrals.

An editorial in *Legal Action*, June 2003, added that there was evidence from youth work agencies that young people were reluctant to engage in the legal system. Innovative youth projects had demonstrated that advice services which were integrated into trusted venues achieved a high level of success. Another, in April 2004, remarked on the disturbing level of public ignorance revealed by surveys and called for a strategic approach to public legal education.

The LSC responded by launching "Jobcentre Plus", training staff to "signpost" the unemployed and others to advice and information, because they often suffered clusters of problems, launched a telephone helpline, to offer advice on debt, welfare benefits and education, and helplines in courts, put information on their website in 10 languages, funded video-conferencing facilities in isolated regions, established outreach clinics in town halls, community centres and GP's surgeries, created a one-stop shop for domestic violence victims and piloted a duty solicitor scheme at county courts, to give emergency advice to those facing eviction. They acknowledged a "troubling lack of awareness in basic civil rights".

In March 2009, LAG published *The Justice Gap*, to coincide with **17–023** the 60th anniversary of legal aid. They argue that LA had fallen short of its original aims and there was "a marked difference between the numbers of cases pursued to enforce rights and the many potential cases that people never take up as they are either not aware of their rights or they decide it is not worth the trouble to take it further—this is 'the justice gap'". For example, in the February 2009 edition of *Legal Action*, Jon Robins reported that their research for the book began in Dover Magistrates' Court, watching 35 housing repossession cases, where "traumatised" people were subject to proceedings from their mortgage lenders and making last-minute negotiations. The provision of legal advice was arbitrary and the beleaguered CAB adviser running the help desk said "Homeowners arrive unsure of what is going on, totally ill-informed and prepared to lose their home because they think there is no alternative." He also wrote an article in the 2009 *New Law Journal*, complaining of the lack of legal aid in tribunals. He said only seven per cent of families of personnel killed in Afghanistan or Iraq received legal aid for representation at the inquests. Inquests for deaths in custody *are* within the scope of legal aid, following the McPherson Report: *R. (Main) v Minister for Legal Aid, The Times*, December 18, 2007. LAG were concerned by February 2009 (see *Legal Action*), at the decline in the not-for-profit sector of legal service providers.

Research such as that of Genn (1999) and Moorhead (2006), discussed in this chapter, has repeatedly indicated that problems occur in clusters. Under the post-1999 legal services scheme, legal advice has become fragmented. Service providers are normally limited as to what they may provide advice. Very few can satisfy all a client's needs so the client has to approach different advisers. Research has also shown that providers are not always good at signposting clients to other advice services and clients, naturally, suffer from referral fatigue and cannot be bothered to access multiple advisers. Fox, Moorhead, Sefton and Wong researched the capacity of community legal advice centres and networks to offer integrated advice in family and social welfare law. They made the point that if effective advice is accessed early it can stop "triggers" that create more problems.

Criminal Defence

17–024   An illustration of the wastefulness of post-1999 system of free LA arose when footballer El-Hadji Diouf was granted free representation. Despite earning £40,000 a week, he qualified because his native language was French and he thus satisfied the interests of justice test. Then the reintroduction of means testing in magistrates' courts caused chaos, as cases were adjourned awaiting defendants to produce the necessary evidence of their income and outgoings and their spouse's signature. About 90 per cent of professionals surveyed said it was not running well. See (2006) 156 N.L.J. 1779.

Public defenders

17–025   English and Welsh lawyers have traditionally visualised the US public defender as providing a second class service to criminal clients and this coloured many of the responses to the LCD consultation in 2000. The Bar Council, defending the independent Bar, naturally opposed salaried defenders. By 2004, public defenders had been piloted for over three years in Scotland. Goriely et al. compared case outcomes and client satisfaction between public and private solicitors: the public defender (PD) was more likely to resolve the case at a pleading or intermediate stage. Cases were more likely to end in a conviction. PD cases were more likely to plead guilty. There were similar levels of satisfaction but clients tended to complain the PD was too "businesslike". A 2002 LSC report on the PD system pilot schemes in six places in England and Wales found them to be a "considerable success". The 2004 annual report of the PDS claimed high levels of client satisfaction. The LA Practitioners' Group criticised the PDS as a white elephant, representing poor value for money for taxpayers. Research was published in 2007 by Bridges, Cape, Moorhead and Scherr evaluating PDs over a six year period. It showed that PDs operated at a high level of quality with, for instance, high levels of peer-review assessment in their court work, but their officers were more expensive to run than private practices. By 2008, four of the eight offices were closed, as they were not cost-effective.

Law centres—still vulnerable

17–026   After 1999 the number of law centres increased to 65, including some mobile services for rural areas, but they remain vulnerable to withdrawal of funding and they have decreased to 55 in 2011. For instance, in Leicester, the Council merged the law centre with the CAB and then announced a £100,000 reduction in funding, which, observed the Law Centres Federation Director, exemplified an emerging trend to "advice only" services (Annual Report 2003–04).

Contracting, fixed fees and competitive tendering—unpopular ways of paying lawyers

Under the pre-1999 LA scheme, any barrister or solicitor could **17–027** do legally aided work, with little accountability and no check on the quality of their work. The idea of limiting LA suppliers to contracted lawyers was first mooted in the Conservative Government's *Legal Aid Efficiency Scrutiny* (1986), and met fierce opposition. The Legal Aid Act 1988 permitted contracting. Franchises were offered to solicitors' firms who chose to participate. They had to satisfy certain conditions and were subjected to strict audits. The Law Society remained hostile. Labour's 1999 contracting scheme went much further than this, by requiring *all* providers to have contracts. Firms were given just a few months to apply. Lawyers said contracting would exclude many firms, such as small ethnic minority practices, depriving the public of access to justice. The compliance deadline had to be put back. The same shambles was repeated over criminal contracts. Eventually, the Law Society withdrew its opposition and encouraged solicitors to enter contracts. There were widespread complaints of excessive bureaucracy.

The quality requirement under the new contracts exposed deficiencies, which showed Labour's plan was working as intended. Research on legal advice was published after a two-year study by the Institute of Advanced Legal Studies in 2001. It examined 80,000 cases in 100 solicitors' offices and 43 not-for-profit agencies and found:

- the quality of advice depended on the time spent and adviser's experience;
- there needed to be further improvements;
- organisations in the not-for-profit sector took longer to carry out their work than solicitors but gave higher quality advice;
- referral levels were poor and referrals were consistently late.

Richard Collins, head of the Criminal Defence Service, defended criminal contracting and reminded readers why legal advice at police stations was now limited to accredited representatives:

"It should be recalled that it was often criminal defence solicitors who believed themselves to have an excellent reputation, and considered supervision to be unnecessary, who were deploying unqualified representatives in the police station whose poor standards led to the need for the accreditation scheme." (*Focus* magazine, LSC.)

This quotation understates the mischief that had had to be remedied by 1999. As Bridges and many others pointed out, the uncontrolled growth of LA since 1960 was linked to the massive increase in lawyers, who were not accountable for the quality of services they provided. The rest of us who are funded by the public sector expect quality control and accountability. Research such as that reported in the book *Standing Accused* (1994), exposed the appalling state of criminal defence, under the pre-1999 LA scheme, by some solicitors and barristers. Barristers would appear in court having done no case preparation and not knowing the client from Adam. Some solicitors would send the office cleaner to sit behind counsel in court. Mostly, when someone asked to see a duty solicitor in a police station they would not get a solicitor but just anyone the duty solicitor chose to send. This book, plus many police investigations, uncovered widespread fraud by some solicitors who thought nothing of sending a secretary to sit behind counsel in court and charging the LA Board for a trainee solicitor. The Royal Commission on Criminal Justice 1993 found that most defence barristers did not meet their client until the morning of trial.

By 2003, once compulsory contracting was established, there were concerns that many firms were abandoning contracted LA work. A Law Society survey in 2003 found that 90 per cent of respondent practitioners were dissatisfied with the system, citing poor pay and excessive bureaucracy; 78 per cent threatened to drop or reduce publicly funded work (*Gazette*, January 2003). In 2004, the Society President warned that the LA system would collapse and large sections of the population would be left without access to justice. The Birmingham Law Society President said underfunding had led to the "cancer" of solicitors poaching one another's clients. In 2002–03, the LA Practitioners Group and the Law Society complained of a recruitment crisis. Trainee solicitors were not attracted to a career in LA work. In response, it was decided to fund trainee solicitors in LA firms. To address complaints of bureaucracy, they announced, in 2003, that they were establishing a "preferred supplier" pilot. Strong performers would be rewarded with new contracting and payment arrangements, guaranteed work and other incentives. The LSC clearly did not feel threatened by the loss of criminal defence solicitors. On the contrary, by 2004, they planned a significant cut in the number of contracts. The Chief Executive said that they planned to award contracts by a system of competitive tendering. Contracts in London could be cut from 488 to 150, where there was an oversupply. They hoped lawyers who "dabbled" in criminal defence would drop out. Winners would be rewarded with "light touch auditing".

The legal profession would not co-operate. The LSC conceded **17–028** that it would not be able to achieve its aims, by 2005, and published a consultation paper on tendering in London. Competitive tendering would initially be aimed at lower court work, with firms bidding for a share of police station and court duty work. In 2005, the *New Law Journal* reported a "furious" reaction from solicitors but solicitor Andrew Keogh cynically opposed the rhetoric of his profession's leaders. Contrasting the pre-1999 LA system with the post-1999, he said:

> "Solicitors controlled the market; the state wrote the cheque. Many. . .long for the days of unquestioning respect for solicitors and a deep pocket. . .Only a fool could seriously believe the government will raise general remuneration rates given a total legal aid spend of £1.1 bn on criminal defence services. . .Those who speak of a collapse in provision do so in the face of evidence to the contrary and a healthy supplier base in crime. . .some are beginning to believe their own rhetoric. There was no collapse in 1994 when franchising arrived, none in 2001, at the start of contracting, and none in 2004, when the second round of contracts were offered. Supply deserts are few."

When fixed fees for some work were introduced, lawyers complained bitterly. In 1993, Mackay L.C. introduced them in magistrates' courts. Solicitors sought a judicial review by the High Court and have done this repeatedly whenever a Lord Chancellor has tried to curb their fees. Solicitors maintained, and still do, that the amount they are paid does not allow them to provide an adequate service. Using statistical analysis, Bridges showed that their argument lacked evidence and historical context. The growth in LA, especially in magistrates' courts, was linked to the rapid growth of the profession, in the 1970s and 1980s. Bridges thought lack of quality had more to do with solicitors' inability to keep abreast with legal developments through having small case loads. Lawyers managed to resist for more than a decade all attempts to force them to compete in a tendering system so one wonders how Ken Clarke's current (2010–11) identical proposal will fare. Articles in *Counsel* contain reminders that the Bar has always resisted any "one case, one fee" system but they acknowledge that unless they concede to this, they will not be able to compete in tendering against other suppliers and will thus lose work.

The cost continued to rise

17–029   The cost of LA was still rising by 20 per cent a year and by 2004, it was costing £2 billion per year. The average cost per case was still rising. By 2005, we had the largest LA budget in the developed world. Nevertheless, the Legal Action Group argued that this only represented 0.4 per cent of public spending, compared with £135 billion on welfare benefits and £73 billion on the NHS. By 2004, family cases absorbed 80 per cent of the civil budget but most of the cost increase was caused by the rising cost of criminal defence. The causes of this were the abolition of the means test in magistrates' courts, the number of increasingly complex prosecutions brought by bodies such as the Serious Fraud Office and the creation of 360 new offences, in 1997–2004. In the LAG's view, it was a "scandal" that the Treasury failed to compensate the LA budget to cover the increased cost of all its new crime initiatives (*Legal Action* editorial, December 2004). Criminal defence overspent, reducing the budget available for the civil and family cases. Critics argued it should be ring fenced. The Criminal Defence Services Act 2006 reintroduced means testing for criminal defence, claimed to save £35 million per year. In October 2009, Bowles and Perry for the Ministry of Justice compared spending in three common law countries and four European jurisdictions with spending in England and Wales. They found that spending here was unusually high. This appeared to be caused by a higher case load and higher average cost per case.

"Fat cats" and very high cost cases

17–030   The pre-1999 scheme was criticised because budget was eaten up by very high cost cases. The media were scandalised about the high earnings of some barristers. In 1995, Lord Woolf M.R. called for a move to more fixed fees and a stop to wasteful practices: unnecessary separate representation, use of two advocates, use of solicitors to sit behind counsel and undue prolixity. The Lord Chancellor's Department (LCD) (now Ministry of Justice) warned the Bar of the intention to fix fees for civil work. The Bar was hostile. Lord Irvine, then shadow Lord Chancellor, said in 1996 and at the 1999 Bar conference that one per cent of cases "swallowed up" 40 per cent of the criminal LA budget. In 1997, the LCD issued league tables of the highest paid barristers. A number earned over £400,000 for Crown Court work. Irvine attacked the price of lawyers. He famously told the House of Lords, "there are a significant number of QCs who earn a million pounds per annum. . .Fat cat lawyers railing at the inequity of court fees do not attract the sympathy of the public." (*The Times*, July 15, 1997). In 1999, the Law Society joined in. The Bar objected that there was a big gap in earnings between QCs and other barristers. In 1997, solicitor Arnold Rosen put forward a powerful argument on this area of "exquisite privilege", "As if by magic potion, the day after a barrister places the letters QC after his or her name, the fees rise. Can such higher fees be justified when paid for by the tax-payer—not the client?" In 1999, the Lord Chancellor tightened regulations on the assignment of QCs in publicly funded cases. Orders may now only be made for two advocates or a QC if the defence case involves substantial novel or complex issues of law or fact which could not be adequately presented without a QC and either the prosecution has senior counsel or the defence case is exceptional. In 2000, a 10 per cent cut in fees for publicly defended criminal work was announced, to reduce disparity between prosecution and defence fees, amid protests by the Bar. In 2001, the graduated fees scheme was introduced, including an integrated payment scheme for prosecution and defence lawyers. In 2005, the problem of fat cats and high cost cases persisted. Around one per cent of cases were absorbing 49 per cent of the criminal defence budget. A March 2004 editorial in *Legal Action* commented: "We suggest that keeping silks in the manner to which they are accustomed should not be given a higher priority than, for example, preserving the commendable fairness and simplicity of the police station duty solicitor scheme". In a 2010 press release, Jack Straw L.C. reported, "in 2008/09. . .there were 874 barristers who earned between £100k and £299k and a further 75 barristers who received more than £300k" (from the LA fund). This is not to say that all legally aided lawyers are fat cats. Legally aided solicitors were among the worst paid public sector workers according to a *Guardian* survey in 2009, with an average salary below £25,000, less than prison officers and sewage plant workers: (2009) 159 N.L.J. 1641.

4. "The legal aid crisis"—calls for a fundamental restructuring in 2004

Ken Clarke was not exaggerating in 2010 when he complained **17–031** there had been over 30 reviews of LA in recent years. All of the above concerns prompted a battery of reviews in 2004, by the Law Society, the Constitutional Affairs Select Committee (an all-party Parliamentary committee), the Advice Services Alliance and one for the Department of Constitutional Affairs, by Matrix Research and Sheffield University. They are examined in the 2008 edition of this book. As well as repeating the well-known criticisms above, between them, they made many points, including

1. The civil LA budget should be separated, as a matter of urgency, from the rest.
2. The government should develop a programme of public legal education.
3. Government departments should recognise their role in creating demands on the LA budget.
4. ADR and consumer redress schemes should be promoted.
5. Salaried services (like law centres) might tackle unmet need.
6. Peripatetic advisers should be used.
7. There could be more use of private legal expenses insurance and CFAs.
8. Over-specialisation could prevent a holistic approach by solicitors. There should be consortia to provide a one-stop shop for early advice and prevention.
9. LA was restricted to those who had nothing. It excluded people of modest means and thus denied them access to justice.
10. The aims and functions of the CLS should be more transparent, clarifying its role in tackling social exclusion.
11. Community Legal Service Partnerships were not working as intended. People had dropped out.
12. The telephone advice line, launched in 2004, was not working as intended. Only 23 per cent of users were from target groups. There was a similar problem with the Money Advice Debtline.

In response, the LSC published its own consultation, proposing to re-focus the LA scheme, in both family and civil cases, away from litigation and into early effective dispute resolution. This partly resulted from pressure from the CA. Lord Woolf in *Anufrijeva v London Borough of Southwark* [2003] EWCA Civ 1406 had criticised the disproportionate and "truly horrendous" cost of appeals under the Human Rights Act in maladministration cases. He said the Administrative Court would only grant permission to apply for judicial review where it could be explained that complaining to the Ombudsman or another complaints procedure was not more appropriate. From 2003, the LSC started shifting its much-criticised audit system of lawyers over to peer review and refocused audits according to risk. They introduced salaried solicitors and case workers for legal advice on asylum and immigration and limited the suppliers, in response to criticism, including by the courts, that there were too many providers touting for business amongst asylum seekers and bringing hopeless cases.

In 2005, the DCA announced cuts in funding civil cases to promote early settlement, cutting eligibility for representation and increasing eligibility for help (advice and so on). Controls would be exercised over multiple and repeat applications in private law family cases. JUSTICE complained that this would encourage early but ineffective dispute resolution. Poor people would give up even if they had a good case. In 2005, the Government published another consultation paper, *Making Legal Rights a Reality*. The LSC proposed establishing 75 Community Legal Advice Centres in deprived areas. Alarmingly, this scheme failed to acknowledge existing law centres. The Legal Services Research Centre published research by Professors Cape and Moorhead, *Demand Induced Supply? Identifying Cost Drivers in Criminal Defence Work*. They found the cost of LA on Crown Court cases had "risen dramatically" over the previous 10 years. Government and prosecution policies had increased the number and seriousness of criminal cases and the amount of work that had to be done: increased police investigative power, greater use of technology in investigations (DNA testing, CCTV and so on). There were also procedural changes requiring defence lawyers to do more work. While crime had decreased, more of those arrested were prosecuted, with an increase in seriousness of cases. There had been an increase in imprisonment rates, requiring more LA. In 2005, the Lord Chancellor published *A Fairer Deal for Legal Aid*, announcing reform of the management of large, complex cases and reducing the amount spent defending the highest cost criminal cases. Analysis had shown that half of all LA in the Crown Court went on one per cent of cases. In 2006, the Labour Government asked Lord Carter of Coles to report on how to improve the purchasing of publicly funded legal services. Falconer L.C. accepted the proposals set out in his report, *Legal Aid: a Market-Based Approach to Reform* and issued a consultation paper, "Legal Aid: a sustainable future". It proposed best value tendering for LA contracts; new responsibilities for Law Society and Bar Council to enhance quality of suppliers; fixed fees for solicitors in police stations to encourage more efficient practices, including cutting costs related to waiting and travelling times; revised graduated fees for Crown Court advocates and a new graduated fee scheme for Crown Court litigators to reward earlier preparation and resolution of cases (fees would be severely cut for the top-earning barristers, to allow those at the lower end to be paid more); increased controls and audit capacity to give greater control over hours worked and quality checks; standard fees for civil and family work and new graduated fees for solicitors in private law family and child care proceedings.

Willman, like other lawyers, was critical. She said the most "gall- **17–032** ing aspect" of government plans was that "efficiency is equated with seeing large numbers of clients dealt with as cheaply as possible, regardless of the type of case or outcome". "Legal help" work was already unprofitable at £50–60 per hour in London and less outside. The DCA and LSC published yet another consultation paper. Law Society research suggested that 800 solicitors' firms would cease to deliver criminal defence services. Critics again feared BME solicitors would be squeezed out, because many were sole practitioners or in small forms (see Ch.13). The DCA published yet another paper in November 2006, including its scheme of fixed fees. Twenty-eight solicitors' firms published an open letter to the Lord Chancellor, opposing the plans.

One lawyer was prepared to defend the Carter reforms, Andrew Keogh. He said research for Carter showed that the UK spent 10 times more on LA than its nearest rival. He saw no harm in the closure of more law firms. Lawyers demonstrated in Parliament Square in March 2007. In February 2007, they sought judicial review of government plans on the Very High Cost Case Panel. The Government seemed determined to introduce fixed fees for civil cases despite a ruling by Beatson J. that the unified contract breached EU law. The Carter plans were very heavily criticised by the House of Commons Constitutional Affairs Committee in a June 2007 report but the government responded that it was going ahead. The committee drew attention to a 32 per cent reduction in family providers. The government said that the number of contracted providers was adequate as there had been an increase in acts of advice. The committee said that it was not fair to include travel costs and waiting time in fixed fees. The government responded that these were included, calculated according to historic costs. By spring 2008, all bodies representing defence lawyers urged them not to sign the new contracts. Barristers boycotted a VHCC panel set up in January 2008 so the LSC decided to create a panel of litigators and a list of accredited advocates for VHCCs. Litigators would be able to negotiate their fees and advocates, contracted for individual cases, would be paid graduated fees for core advocacy tasks and negotiated rates for case specific tasks. In May 2008, a convicted drug offender avoided a confiscation order of up to £4.5 million, because 30 barristers refused to act for the fixed fee of £175 per day and the defendant could not pay for his own advocate because his assets were frozen. The judge accepted D could not have a fair trial on the point. See Gibb (2008). The LSC announced cuts in family graduated fees, in February 2009. That, and proposed further cuts would result in a 55 per cent cut in payments, said the Bar Council. Lord Bach, LA minister, said average fees for contact and residence disputes had risen from £800 to £1,450 in five years, "unsustainable". He said child protection work would receive an extra £4.4 million. Nevertheless, in October 2009, Government announced that they were going ahead. Family lawyers said more firms would close.

The number of family LA practices dropped from 4,500 in 2000 to 2,800 since 2006 (Gibb, 2009). The Law Society applied for judicial review and won in the High Court: *R. (Law Society) v Legal Services Commission* [2010] EWHC 2550. I have recounted the tale above in tedious and repetitive detail because it is a *repetitive* cat and mouse game between governments and lawyers and illustrates the points I make in the next section.

5. Ken Clarke's plans for legal aid 2010–11

In 2010, the Coalition government replaced Labour. Ken Clarke **17–033** became Minister of Justice and Lord Chancellor, with a remit to cut the justice budget drastically. His 2011 Bill and policies propose a wholly new regime, replacing Labour's 1999 setup. I have included a fairly detailed account of the latter, though, because Ken Clarke is making some identical proposals to those made years earlier and they may come unstuck for the same reasons. We have seen repeating themes in this chapter, as follows.

1. In the early twentieth century, we opted for the judicare model of provision of legal services in England and Wales, paying taxpayers' money in the form of fees to private practice lawyers rather and setting up a National Legal Service of salaried lawyers, like the NHS. This helped to encourage the enormous growth of lawyers, described in Ch.13, especially when we invented new resource intensive legal services, such as independent representation for children and, duty solicitor schemes.
2. Lawyers' capacity to protect their work and resist change should not be underestimated. The judicare model has suited them very well. The story in this chapter is testament to their tenacity. Competitive tendering was mooted in 1986. They have resisted countless attempts to introduce it but Ken Clarke is proposing it yet again.
3. We are said to have the world's most expensive LA system. Ken Clarke is in the identical position to his predecessors, Labour Lord Irvine, in 1998, and Conservative Lord Mackay, in 1990, in insisting that this cannot go on.
4. When any Lord Chancellor tries to introduce a change in lawyers' remuneration, they bitterly oppose it and readily take the LC to the High Court in judicial review proceedings. I have lost count of these cases. If the LC tries to implement changes without adequate consultation, this is grounds for review, hence the silly number of consultations. Judges are

lawyers. The lawyers win most challenges. Lawyers think they also have the whip-hand because they can simply refuse to enter contracts for government funded work. Lord Chancellors panic, postpone their plans and issue yet another consultation. Lord Chancellors are lawyers too, incidentally.

5. If the number of LA practices is cut, this will not automatically deny citizens access to justice, *provided* there are suitable alternatives. Most people want advice and this can be provided by phone, internet and bodies like Citizens Advice.

6. Government must provide adequate alternatives, or risk breaching Art.6 of the European Convention on Human Rights.

7. Bureaucracy is a necessary corollary of quality control but lawyers ought to be accountable if they benefit from public funding, like anyone else. When they were unregulated, boasting that they were the world's best lawyers, they got away with scandalous behaviour and defrauding the old LA scheme, as exposed by the fascinating research reported in *Standing Accused*. They only have themselves to thank for further regulation.

In *Legal Aid: Reforming Advocates' Graduated Fees* (2010), the Government consulted on aligning defence fees with (lower) prosecution fees. It was proposed to reduce fees over three years and devise a new scheme for handling very high cost cases. This problem of the imbalance between prosecution and defence fees, making lawyering in Crown Court cases imbalanced, was identified about 20 years ago and, as described above, lawyers have resisted repeated attempts to deal with it.

In November 2010, Ken Clarke published a consultation paper (CP12/10) called *Proposals for the Reform of Legal Aid in England and Wales* Cm.7967. He said the legal aid system was one of the most expensive in the world and bore little resemblance to the scheme introduced in 1949. It covered a very wide range of issues, including some that should not require any legal expertise. There had been 30 consultations since 2006. Lawyers could not organise their practices against constant change. It was unsustainable. "I want to discourage people from resorting to lawyers whenever they face a problem, and instead encourage them, wherever it is sensible to do so, to consider alternative methods of dispute resolution which may be more effective and suitable." He said he was consulting on the Jackson recommendations on civil procedure, explained in Ch.10 of this book, and sentencing, asking David Norgrove to reform family procedure and he would reform civil procedure to make greater use of mediation "In the meantime, I have been working with the Home Secretary and the Attorney General on ways in which we can transform procedures in the criminal justice system" (Foreword). Here, I summarise the main points, with comments, but do bear in mind that these are *proposals*. They have as much chance of becoming law and working as intended as the litany of "reforms" listed above.

- The Ministry of Justice needs to reduce its budget by 23 per **17–034** cent, £2 billion. These proposals would cut legal aid costs by £350 million.

   "These proposals complement the wider programme of reform to move towards a simpler justice system: one which is more responsive to public needs, which allows people to resolve their issues out of court without recourse to public funds, using simpler, more informal, remedies where they are appropriate, and which encourages more efficient resolution of contested cases where necessary. . .It is an approach which demands that we make tough choices to ensure access to public funding in those cases that really require it, the protection of the most vulnerable in our society. . ." (Foreword).

- Chapter 2: The key to efficient use of resources was reform of the criminal justice system: cutting bureaucracy, improving communication between agencies and case management. On sentencing: they would deliver a "rehab revolution", with sentence discounts to encourage the earliest possible guilty pleas. Restructured lawyers' fees would encourage this. (This plan was deeply unpopular with the public and withdrawn by June 2011.) In civil cases, the Jackson review of costs recommended more proportionality, and making success fees and "after the event" insurance irrecoverable.
- Chapter 3: history.
- Chapter 4: no change in criminal legal aid eligibility.
- Chapter 5: sets out proposals for eligibility changes in civil and family legal aid, including taking account of property equity. Contributions from clients' income should increase. Everyone with £8,000 disposable capital should contribute, including those on benefits. Everyone with £1,000 should pay a lump sum of £100, in addition to contributions from income, because they will then have a financial interest in the outcome. This will be collected by the LA provider. Capital disregards should be abolished. Currently, 2011, pensioners on low incomes get LA if they have £100,000 cash or a home worth £300,000. Capital will mean actual property equity so

people with high mortgages will become eligible so there will be a £200,000 capital disregard, with £300,000 for pensioners, in most cases. They planned to increase contributions from 20–30 per cent of disposable income, to increase their financial interest in the outcome of the case.

- Remuneration for lawyers and other providers: competitive pricing should be introduced in crime (from police station to Crown Court), then family and civil. In the meantime, the structure of criminal fees should be altered, "to encourage. . .quicker and more efficient justice". This means he wants to encourage earlier plea bargaining, as explained in Ch.12 of this book.
- Chapter 7: sets out proposals to reduce all civil and family fees "across the board" by 10 per cent. Barristers and solicitors are paid different civil fees. Risk rates should be extended to very high cost civil cases because they increase the chances of success. The use of QCs in family cases should be controlled. They are used in care cases and paid up to £100,000.
- Chapter 8: experts' fees ought to be reduced by 10 per cent and move towards fixed or graduated fees with hourly rates for limited hours. In civil cases, there are no standard hourly expert rates.
- Chapter 9: proposes alternative sources of funding, including using the interest from solicitors' client accounts (they are currently not obliged to pay all the interest), as in Australia, NZ, US, S. Africa, Zimbabwe and France; taking a proportion of legally aided claimants' damages towards a Supplementary Legal Aid Scheme; and encouraging legal protection insurance, as recommended by Jackson L.J. Unfortunately, private legal expenses insurance has been suggested by Lord Chancellors since the 1970s or earlier and all research shows that the British have little appetite for it (Robins, 2010). While people are happy to insure pets for £12 a month only one in seven of 2,000 consumers were prepared to pay £75 per year for legal expenses insurance.
- Chapter 10: proposes bringing LA within an executive agency of the MoJ, abolishing the Legal Services Commission as a non-departmental body; reducing bureaucracy. This followed a recommendation of Sir Ian Magee, who had been commissioned by the previous Labour government to review the delivery of LA: *Review of Legal Aid Delivery and Governance*, March 3, 2010. The writing had already been on the wall for the LSC. The Labour government proposed to abolish it after the Parliamentary Public Accounts Committee reported in February 2010 that the LCS's "lax financial controls" caused

it to overpay solicitors £25 million in 2008–09. The National Audit Office made the same point in December 2009.

- Chapter 4: sets out proposals to limit the scope of LA but the power will be retained to grant aid to some cases that fall outside scope.
- Target resourcing: the grant of LA depends on the capacity of a person to represent themselves, the type of proceedings, adversarial or inquisitorial, the complexity of law and evidence. Legal aid should be the "funder of last resort", the conditional fee agreement (no win no fee) being the first resort. The Ministry have taken account of other sources of advice. Other organisations, e.g. voluntary sector, can provide advice on welfare and housing. The Government have taken account of other means of dispute resolution, e.g. ombudsmen, complaints procedures.

> "[We] propose a revised civil legal aid scheme which focuses resources on those cases where the litigant is at risk of very serious consequences. Examples include facing the removal of their children, physical harm, or homelessness, or where legal aid is justified to ensure a fair society through empowering citizens to hold the state to account or to meet our legal obligations, for example, in relation to reciprocal arrangements on international child abduction."

- The civil LA merits test will be retained.
- There is a massive annexe listing what was currently "in scope", in 2010–11, what would be retained and what would be removed.
- "In scope" would in future include: children's care cases; judicial review, except business cases, as at present; matters covered by European or international agreements providing reciprocal access to legal assistance; cases where litigants are incapable of representing themselves, e.g. physically or emotionally vulnerable, elderly, frail, disabled, asylum-seekers; immigration detention; international child abduction and family maintenance; claims against public authorities for abuse of power, breach of human rights and negligence; allegations of abuse and sexual violence; community care; debt where the client's home is at immediate risk; domestic violence; mediation in private family cases; housing; mental health; registration and enforcement of EU legislation judgments; children in private law children cases; help at inquests, harassment, care standards, gang violence injunctions; currently-funded discrimination; environmental matters; EU cross-border litigation; appeals only on matters that fall "within scope".

- "Out of scope": the existing exclusions; money claims, such as consumer credit and contracts, except e.g. damages for child abuse or serious abuse of state power; cases resulting from the litigant's own decision, e.g. immigration; representation in inquests and tribunals, generally; ancillary relief (family property), without violence (currently in scope and costing £319 million, though in 2008, 73 per cent were not contested).

  "We propose to make changes to the courts' powers to enable the Court to redress the balance in cases where one party may be materially disadvantaged, by giving the judge the power to make interim lump sum orders against a party who has the means to fund the costs of representation for the other party. In doing so, the Court would also incentivise the contributing party to negotiate a settlement. The materially disadvantaged party could apply for an order at any stage of the proceedings, where they could demonstrate that they could not reasonably procure legal advice by any other means (as is currently permissible under maintenance pending suit provisions)."

- "Out of scope" would be clinical negligence; criminal injuries; education, employment; housing, e.g. right to buy; welfare benefits; tort and other general claims.
- "Out of scope" would be private law children and family cases. "Legal aid is encouraging long, drawn-out and acrimonious cases which can have a significant impact on the long-term well-being of any children involved".
- Cases in the public interest are currently funded but this criterion should not necessarily bring a case back in scope, in future.
- There should be a funding scheme for excluded cases, to meet our obligations under the European Convention on Human Rights. The proposed criteria would be: significant wider public interest, overwhelming importance to the client, or complexity.
- The paper emphasised telephone advice "we will provide a simple, straightforward telephone service. . .the single gateway to civil legal aid services", expanding the CLA helpline to include paid-for advice services. Specialist advisers could offer a referral fee (meaning they would pay a fee to have queries forwarded to them).
- They acknowledged the increase in numbers of litigants in person. Many cases could be resolved out of court. Many such cases will be in user-friendly courts or alternative fora.

There was no evidence on the impact of a litigant in person on the outcome of proceedings, according to research published by the Department of Constitutional Affairs, in 2005. The author of this research, Professor Moorhead, claimed that the Ministry was misrepresenting his research, in the consultation paper, and we saw in Ch.10 that the legal aid proposals disturbed judges, in 2011 at the thought of having to cope with many more litigants in person.

- Lawyers were paid more for guilty pleas in the Crown Court, plus a committal fee.
- The fees should be made more even, in triable-either-way (TEW) cases, and the committal fee should be abolished.
- Currently, advocates and litigators are paid more for a cracked trial than an early guilty plea, sometimes double, regardless of whether extra work has been done. The paper proposed to harmonise guilty plea fees in indictable and serious TEW offences. They would increase guilty plea fees by 25 per cent, to encourage early guilty pleas. They would stop paying the extra 25–40 per cent fees in murder cases, aligning them with rape. (In October 2010, Lord Judge C.J. told the Justice Select Committee, in Parliament, that the LA system in crime and family work did not incentivise efficiency.)
- Litigators and advocates were paid according to the number of pages of prosecution evidence. This should be replaced with a better indicator of complexity.
- Three sets of fees applied in magistrates' courts: rural, urban and London. The London differential was not justified, given the supply of London solicitors.
- Some CPS rates were significantly lower than defence rates, e.g. sentencing hearings were half.
- Fees in very high cost cases should relate to outputs not hours of input.
- In 2008–09, legal aid payments to QCs and leading juniors cost £52 *million*. The average number of prosecution pages has increased by 65 per cent since 2004–05. This reflects the use of mobile phone records.

The Law Society proposed an alternative set of savings at *www.soundoffforjustice.org*. The Family Law Bar Association said there would be a dangerous inequality of arms in domestic violence cases. The alleged victim would be legally aided; the alleged perpetrator would not. The very obvious flaw in the proposals is that in family cases, people will make false allegations of domestic violence in order to get legal aid. R. Smith pointed out in 2009 that even at that time when the MoJ was claiming that we spend much more per capita on LA than other countries that it was exaggerating. They ignored the research paper by Bowles and Perry examining what the true figures were. In the meantime, the Bar Chairman acknowledged at their 2010 conference that they would need to diversify away from LA work. They are (yet again) exploring the viability of a Contingency Legal Aid Fund. This idea goes back at least as far as the 1980s. The fund would be used for deserving cases that would not otherwise be brought, because of lack of money. Some of the winnings would then be back into the fund. Bar chairman Peter Lodder QC, summarising the Bar's response said the proposed legal aid cuts "will cause irreparable damage" but there was also a danger of creating greater costs to society, especially with the increased burden of litigants in person: *Counsel,* April 2011.

BIBLIOGRAPHY

17–035   The Access to Justice Act 1999.

F. Bawdon, on Yarrow and Abrams' research, "Nothing to lose?" (1999) 149 N.L.J. 1890.

Sir Henry Brooke, Second Annual Nottingham Pro Bono Lecture, November 15, 2007, Judiciary website.

R. Bowles and A. Perry, *An International Comparison of Publicly Funded Legal Services and Justice Systems*, MoJ research series 14/09 (2009).

R. Collins, defending CDS contracting, "Reports of death greatly exaggerated" (2000) 150 N.L.J. 1520.

Department of Constitutional Affairs, *Modernising Justice* (1998), White Paper.

C. Fox, R. Moorhead, M. Sefton and K. Wong, "Community legal advice centres and networks: a process evaluation" (2011) 30 (2) C.J.Q. 204–222.

H. Genn, *Paths to Justice—What People Do and Think About Going to Law* (1999).

Citizens' Advice, *Geography of Advice*.

F. Gibb, "Drugs offender keeps £4.5m after 30 barristers refuse to take his case", *The Times*, May 6, 2008: "Vulnerable youngsters put at risk by plans to slash legal aid" *The Times*, October 26, 2009.

T. Goriely et al., "Does Mode of Delivery Make a Difference to Criminal Case Outcomes and Clients' Satisfaction? The Public Defence Solicitor Experiment" [2004] Crim. L.R. 120.

A. Keogh, "Value for money or a leap into the unknown" (2005) 155 N.L.J. 157; "Carter—the crunch" (2006) 156 N.L.J. 1149.

Lightman J., "The Civil Justice System and Legal Profession—The Challenges Ahead" (2003) C.J.Q. 235.

Matrix Research and Consultancy, "Estimating the size and nature of the civil legal advice sector in England and Wales" DCA research report 4/2006 (2006).

M. McConville, L. Bridges, J. Hodgson and A. Pavlovic, *Standing Accused* (1994).

R. Moorhead and A. Scherr on CFAs, "Midnight in the garden of the CFA people" (2001) 151 N.L.J. 274.

R. Moorhead and M. Robinson, "A Trouble Shared—legal problems clusters in solicitors and advice agencies" DCA research report 8/2006 (2006).

P. Pleasence et al., *Causes of Action: civil law and social justice*, 2004, Legal Services Research Centre, as summarised in *Legal Action*, March 2004, at p.9. LSC's reply is set out in *Legal Action*, April 2004, at p.10.

P. Pleasence, V. Kemp, and N.J. Balmer, "The Justice Lottery? Police Station Advice 25 Years on from PACE" [2011] Crim. L.R. 3.

J. Robins, "The Justice Gap" (2009) 159 N.L.J. 131.

A. Rosen, "An artificial market?" (1997) 147 N.L.J. 630.

Stoy Hayward's research on conditional fees (2001) 151 N.L.J. 1078.

L. Skinns, "The Right to Legal Advice in the Police Station: Past, Present and Future" [2011] Crim. L.R. 19.

R. Smith, "Reviewers, lies and statistics" 159 (2009) N.L.J. 1527.

A. Wade, "Credit-crunch victims turn to no-win, no-fee for help", *The Times*, May 7, 2009.

S. Willman "Access to justice or Tesco law?" (2006) 156 N.L.J. 1537.

Yarrow, *Just Rewards?* summarised at (2001) 151 N.L.J. 750.

M. Zander, "Full speed ahead?" (2007) 157 N.L.J. 992 and 912.

FURTHER READING AND SOURCES FOR UPDATING THIS CHAPTER

Updates from spring 2012 and 2013 on the Sweet & Maxwell **17–036** website.

Citizens' Advice: *www.citizensadvice.org.uk*.

Counsel.

Law Centres Federation: *www.lawcentres.org.uk.*

The Law Society.

The Law Society's *Gazette*.

Legal Action.

Ministry of Justice.

The New Law Journal, available on *Lexis*.

Index